HENNING, Charles N. International financial management, by Charles N. Henning, William Pigott and Robert Haney Scott. McGraw-Hill, 1978. 576p ill (McGraw-Hill series in finance) index 77-24757. 16.50 ISBN 0-07-028175-0. C.I.P.

CHOICE   NOV. '78

Business, Management,

& Labor

The only comprehensive international financial management text covering both the macro and micro aspects of the subject in depth. Other texts, such as David A. Rick's *International dimensions of corporate finance* (1978) and Rita Rodriguez and Eugene Carter's *International financial management* (1976), cover only one aspect. J. Fred Weston and Bart W. Sorge's *Guide to international financial management* (1977) covers both aspects but not in depth. The text is well written and uses the institutional/historical approach rather than the theoretical. Emphasis is on practicality. Chapters 16 and 17 are excellent in their treatment of the differences in accounting systems and practices and the variations in tax systems. Each chapter contains selected references for further study. A unique feature is the 200-word glossary of terms used in international finance as well as common abbreviations. Subject and name indexes; appendixes. Recommended for college libraries.

About the authors

CHARLES N. HENNING is currently Professor of Finance and Business Economics at the University of Washington's Graduate School of Business. Highly regarded as an expert in finance and economics, he has served as an economic analyst for the U.S. Department of Commerce, educational advisor for the Pacific Coast Banking School, and consultant for The Boeing Company, the Washington Bankers Association, and the Operations Research Office (affiliated with Johns Hopkins University). He is also author or coauthor of several books: *International Finance; Money, Financial Institutions and the Economy;* and *Financial Markets and the Economy.*

WILLIAM PIGOTT, Associate Professor of Finance at the University of Washington, is coauthor with Charles Henning of *Financial Markets and the Economy.*

ROBERT HANEY SCOTT, Professor of Business Economics at the University of Washington, has written extensively in the field of finance. He has contributed to such publications as the *Journal of Finance, The Banker,* the *Quarterly Journal of Economics,* and the *Journal of Financial and Quantitative Analysis.* Professor Scott is coauthor with Charles Henning of *Financial Markets and the Economy,* author of *The Pricing System,* and coauthor of *National Income Analysis and Forecasting.*

McGRAW-HILL SERIES IN FINANCE

Professor Charles A. D'Ambrosio
University of Washington
Consulting Editor

INTERNATIONAL FINANCIAL MANAGEMENT

1 2 3 4 5 6 7 8 9 0 F G F G 7 8 3 2 1 0 9 8 7

This book was set in Times Roman by Black Dot, Inc.
The editors were J. S. Dietrich and Barbara Brooks;
the cover was designed by Albert M. Cetta;
the production supervisor was Dennis J. Conroy.
The drawings were done by ANCO/Boston.
Fairfield Graphics was printer and binder.

Library of Congress Cataloging in Publication Data

Henning, Charles N
    International financial management.

    (McGraw-Hill series in finance)
    Includes index.
    1. International finance. 2. International business enterprises—Finance. I. Pigott, William, date joint author. II. Scott, Robert Haney, joint author. III. Title.
HG3881.H427   658.1'5   77-24757
ISBN 0-07-028175-0

Charles N. Henning
William Pigott
Robert Haney Scott

Professors of Finance, University of Washington

Inter-national Financial Management

McGRAW-HILL BOOK COMPANY

New York   St. Louis   San Francisco   Auckland   Bogotá   Düsseldorf   Johannesburg   London   Madrid
Mexico   Montreal   New Delhi   Panama   Paris   São Paulo   Singapore   Sydney   Tokyo   Toronto

Contents

Foreword

The lives of most people engaged directly or indirectly in foreign exchange
markets have been nothing if not eventful over the past few years, and usually
far too exciting for comfort. Statement No. 8 of the Financial Accounting
Standards Board has brought the impact of exchange rate fluctuations immediately to bear on the profit and loss accounts of all U.S. corporations with
overseas operations. As a consequence, the complexities of the world of
international finance have increasingly become a matter for concern among a
much wider range of individuals than ever in the recent past.

This particular book fills a yawning gap in the literature on international
finance by embracing both the macro and micro elements of the subject.
Commercial bankers or corporate treasurers have to understand the factors
determining exchange rates as well as how exchange rate variations directly
affect their own balance sheets and operations. The Eurodollar and Eurobond
markets have become major alternative sources of borrowing to the traditional
domestic outlets. In fact, there is a growing practice among bankers to offer
potential borrowers the alternative of tapping either market for funds.

The need for understanding flows equally in the other direction. No central
banker or government official with responsibilities for international monetary
policy can function effectively without a working knowledge of the day-to-day

operations of the foreign exchange and the Eurodollar markets. The break-down of the old Bretton Woods regime of fixed parities in early 1973 was, in part, caused by enormous short-term capital flows emanating from the Euro-markets. The authors manage to knit these different aspects of international finance into a comprehensible and comprehensive structure, and they are to be commended highly for their success.

They suggest that the system of more or less freely floating exchange rates may continue. I would argue, in addition, that not only has there been no alternative to floating since 1973, but the system has become progressively more efficient. To virtually everyone but the day-to-day operators in the market, the main feature of the floating system would probably be the great and unpredictable swings in exchange rates. This would apply to the amplitude of exchange rate movements over periods of weeks or months and for periods as short as one day. In 1973, exchange rate fluctuations were truly dramatic and unprecedented in the lifetimes of most foreign exchange rate dealers. For example, in the five months after February, the dollar fell nearly 40 percent against the Deutsche mark and Swiss franc before rising by more than 20 percent against both currencies before the end of the year. Similarly, 1974 saw a number of substantial swings in exchange values.

Yet, with a number of exceptions, the degree of exchange rate volatility of the dollar against the main traded currencies has diminished considerably and steadily since 1974. The exceptions have centered on problems associated with the running of the European "Snake," which is, in effect, a mini–Bretton Woods, or with weak currencies such as the pound or the lira. However, once domestic action was taken in the United Kingdom and Italy in 1976 to tackle chronic inflation problems, those currencies stabilized.

By the same token, the floating system was able to cope with the trauma of the massive increase in oil prices late in 1973. The attendant shift in financial resources to OPEC from the oil-consuming nations is almost universally expected to exert an unbearable strain on the international financial system. The most serious current problem is that of ensuring a combined flow of financial resources to developing and less developed countries to cover their balance of payments requirements, but this issue is only partly related to the increase in oil prices. The international banking system was able to absorb the billions of OPEC funds with relative ease while fears of currency instability caused by switches of funds by OPEC from one currency to another proved groundless. OPEC recycling turned out to be more of a problem in prospect than in retrospect. This, in turn, was a reflection of the flexibility of the international banking system and of the floating exchange regime itself.

The combination of a major change in the mechanics of the international financial system and a recognition of the need to have a better understanding of the actions of banks and corporations has resulted in more attention being paid in official and academic circles to the micro aspect of international finance. Led by the United States, there has been a discernible trend toward the dismantling of restrictions on capital flows. This means that the money and capital markets of the world have become much more closely integrated. Recently, attention has been focused on the possibility of cofinancing operations between international institutions such as the International Monetary Fund and the World Bank and commercial banks.

It is against this background that the student of international finance has to approach the subject. This book gives the reader a framework for real understanding of the processes involved and injects a flavor of the fascination and excitement of the field.

Geoffrey Bell
Director, Schroder International Limited

Preface

Our purpose in writing this book is to fill a major gap in available textbooks in international finance. Some texts focus on multinational business finance and give only brief consideration to topics such as the international monetary system, balance of payments problems, effects of different inflation and interest rates, and so on. Books at the other end of the spectrum usually do not adequately consider such factors as accounting and tax influences on international financial decisions, capital budgeting and working capital management for international firms, and foreign exchange operations of such firms. Yet in the field of international finance, macrofinancial and microfinancial considerations are interrelated. Foreign exchange operations of business firms, for example, are based on analyses of varying rates of inflation in different countries, interest rates in various world money and capital markets, and the mutual interaction of current exchange rates and expected future rates. At the same time, accounting and tax systems differ in various countries, and these differences also affect financial decisions. The understanding of international finance is incomplete unless both aspects are properly considered.

This book is therefore designed to cover both macro and micro aspects of international finance. Balances of payments, the international monetary system, international banking, exchange rates, and international money and capital markets are analyzed as the milieu within which financial managers in international and multinational firms operate.

This book is primarily a text for schools of business at the undergraduate or graduate (primarily M.B.A.) level. It may also be useful in courses in economics departments and for those currently engaged in international finance, either in business firms, financial institutions concerned with international banking and/or international investment, or government agencies.

The chapters have been used in both undergraduate and graduate classes in the School and Graduate School of Business Administration, University of Washington, for a number of quarters. In graduate courses some additional reading assignments from the suggested references at the ends of chapters or in other sources are desirable.

In most universities only one semester or one quarter is devoted to international finance. We have tried to provide a book suitable for this use. In some cases, if time is short, instructors may wish to omit certain chapters— such as Chapters 4 or 13. Appendixes may be omitted if desired. Chapter 2 is in large part review for students who have had courses in international business or international economics, and may be covered rather quickly in such cases.

In a few universities, a second course or quarter (or semester) is available for international finance. For this it would be possible to use a casebook or individually selected cases in international finance as an aid in developing analytical ability. Alternatively, with some use of such cases or of outside readings as supplements, this book could be used for a two-quarter or two-semester sequence.

It is presumed that students in courses in which this book is used will have had a course in elementary economics, including some discussion of international trade theory and perhaps the theory of economic development. Some students may have had a course or courses in the field of international business, giving them more background in institutional, cultural, and managerial factors.

Parts One and Two (Chapters 1–6) cover balance of payments theory and the development and reform of the international monetary system. This forms a major part of the foundation for analysis of actions by firms in the light of changes in the international economic environment. Parts Three and Four (Chapters 7–13) include discussions on international banking and investment and the international money and capital markets in which many firms must obtain funds. Part Five (Chapters 14–19) focuses on international financial management—analyzing the international financial environment, the need for and means of protecting against international financial risks, accounting and tax factors which affect international financial operations, international capital budgeting decisions, and the day-to-day finance function in international and multinational firms. Finally, Part Six (Chapter 20) covers some financial problems related to economic development, which is of growing importance for international banking, international investment, and activities of multinational business firms.

The authors wish to acknowledge the extremely helpful aid and comments of many persons. First, Professor Desmond McComb of the University of Southampton, England, read and commented on the manuscript and wrote drafts of some sections for Chapters 16 and 17. His aid was invaluable and his perceptivity and judgment were especially beneficial. Professor Gerhard G. Mueller read and commented on Chapter 16 and merits thanks for many helpful suggestions. Professor Dudley W. Johnson read and commented on some chapters, and we appreciate his review. Finally, several reviewers selected by the publishing company read and commented on the entire manuscript. Among these, special thanks are given to Professors Gunter Dufey of the University of Michigan and Ian H. Giddy of Columbia University for their painstaking efforts and numerous valuable suggestions. They went far beyond the call of duty in efforts to be helpful, and their comments resulted in many changes which the authors believe were significant improvements. As always, errors which remain are the responsibility of the authors.

Finally, Miss Joanne Beaurain typed the final manuscript, and we appreciate her careful work.

Charles N. Henning
William Pigott
Robert Haney Scott

Part One

Introduction: International Social Accounting and Balance of Payments Adjustment Processes

A quarter of Coca-Cola's worldwide earnings is reportedly generated in its Tokyo subsidiary. Citibank, second largest bank in the United States, obtains about three-fifths of its income from international operations. The world's largest private bank, Bank of America, in 1975 held international earning assets of $27 billion, more than half of its total earning assets of $49 billion. U.S. imports, for many years about 3 to 4 percent of gross national product (GNP), are now over 7 percent of GNP, with a rising trend. One estimate indicated that in the early 1970s approximately 500 multinational corporations (MNCs) had total assets of over $500 billion and may have accounted for about one-fifth of world GNP. Newspapers are full of discussions of the Organization of Petroleum Exporting Countries (OPEC), "petrodollars," recycling of funds, international monetary reform, and related topics.

Even small architectural firms find that they can design buildings for Tokyo or Teheran as well as for Chicago. Banks in large financial centers are beginning to assign titles such as World Banking Division to their international operations; banks in inland states are establishing international banking departments. We ought to know why international business and financial activity is becoming so much more important, how business firms manage international financial operations, how financial institutions operate in international financial markets, and how the international economic environment affects business and bank management.

Perhaps no other area seems so filled with mystery and glamour as that of international finance. The terminology is technical and unfamiliar to most. Experts often seem to disagree. Yet an understanding of international finance is essential not only for those whose jobs send them overseas but for those employed in firms in any way involved in international transactions.

The aim of this book is to provide a clear introduction to all aspects of international finance: (1) the social accounting and economics involved; (2) the operation of the international monetary system; (3) the activities involved in international banking, foreign exchange rates, and international money markets; (4) the causes and effects of long-term lending and investing in international capital markets; (5) the considerations faced by business management in financing international operations; and (6) the tremendous international problem of financing economic development.

Some basic economic, political, and financial concepts are introduced in Chapter 1; these are fundamental to analyses contained in the rest of the book.

Chapter 2 explains balances of payments (BOPs). These social accounting statements serve the same functions internationally that national income accounting and flow of funds accounts serve domestically. They provide a classified system for statistical data. Just as private firms' financial statements can be used to evaluate their financial positions, BOPs can be used to evaluate international financial positions of countries, and hence for evaluating a major aspect of the financial risk in dealing with firms in foreign countries.

In Chapter 3, various processes of adjustment in BOPs are discussed. As a simple example, an increase in exports, like an increase in any type of final sales, leads to higher national income or GNP. But higher national income leads to more imports, since imports are part of consumption and consumption rises with income. Whether the increase in imports is likely to balance the increase in exports is analyzed in Chapter 3, but clearly at least a partial adjustment occurs. Related changes may involve prices, interest rates, government controls, and exchange rates (prices of foreign currencies). Analysis of these changes helps us understand reasons for government international financial policies and their impact on business firms, the likelihood of changes in exchange rates which affect income and costs, and reasons why international firms may borrow in certain countries and maintain large cash balances in others.

Chapter 1

Some Basic Concepts

Examples of remarkable growth in international trade and investment are easy to find. Brazil's exports increased by 55 percent in one 5-year period (1969 to 1974), and its holdings of gold and foreign currency reserves by 62 percent. Iran bought more tanks from Britain within a short period than the British army had for its own use, and bought a 25 percent interest in the steelmaking subsidiary of West Germany's Krupp firm.

Some international investment occurs in rather unlikely places: PepsiCo has a bottling plant in the Soviet Union. Foreign operations are often quite profitable: as one example, Brunswick Corporation obtained nearly 25 percent of its total net profit from a joint venture selling bowling equipment in Japan.[1]

International banking is also growing as it serves international trade and investment. Citibank, mentioned in the introduction, has more than 250 branches overseas, plus affiliates and subsidiaries.[2] It now operates in more than 100 countries. Some banks, however, enter international banking without overseas offices; they use correspondent banks for overseas activities.

[1]Louis Kraar, "Japan Is Opening Up for *Gaijin* Who Know How," *Fortune*, March 1974, pp. 146–157.

[2]Sanford Rose, "Why They Call It 'Fat City,'" *Fortune*, March 1975, pp. 106–110, 164–167.

As international trade, investment, and banking have grown, dramatic changes have occurred in the international financial environment. The lira lost one-fourth of its value from 1972 to 1974, and Italy's trade deficit in 1974 exceeded its monetary reserves at their nominal value.[3] Italy owes a large international debt, as does Britain, but does not have the potential income from North Sea oil that Britain has. How does one analyze Italy's financial position? What does it mean if Italy has a $5 billion BOP deficit in a year?

Business firms operating internationally face important financial questions: is it possible or likely that a country such as Italy might impose restrictions to prevent remittance of funds back to the United States? How does a firm properly consolidate its financial statements when some are in lira, some in francs, and so on, and when exchange rates between these currencies are "floating" (moving up and down relatively freely)? Does it make a difference that a company operates in some countries with inflation of 5 percent a year and in some with inflation of 60 percent a year? Can firms forecast changes in exchange rates, which indicate relationships among values of different currencies? Where should they borrow money? Even the architectural firm mentioned as designing buildings for Tokyo and Teheran as well as for Chicago should know something about international finance when it provides services internationally.

Finally, although about three-fourths of the world in terms of income is now outside the United States, part of the world—comprising billions of people—is desperately poor. The industrialized "first world" and the Communist "second world" must consider economic and financial problems of the "third world." In fact, the third world is now divided. One group of countries now obtains greatly increased revenues from its oil resources. Some other less developed countries (LDCs) are increasing their output quite rapidly. Others, the "fourth world," face even more serious financial problems than before 1973 because they must import oil at higher cost and seem unable to increase exports significantly.

Clearly, international finance is increasingly important for business executives, bankers, investors, and the public generally. At the outset we need to understand some fundamental concepts which underlie international finance.

International finance arises from international production and trade just as domestic finance arises from domestic production and trade. Production and trade are possible without finance, but they become awkward and in a modern economy almost impossible. The needed "double coincidence" of barter—I must have in exchangeable quantities what you want and you must have in exchangeable quantities what I want—is not necessarily present. In a modern economy, financial assets can be obtained and held without being consumed, and can be used as a claim on future goods and services. Of course, people could paper their walls with stocks and bonds which have become worthless, but normally financial assets are not consumed. They facilitate (1) resource

[3]Robert Ball, "Bankruptcy, Italian Style," *Fortune*, February 1975, pp. 89–92, 146–152.

transfers from those who do not wish to consume them now to those who do and (2) the holding of claims on resources, to be exercised in the future—and in the meantime the resources can be used to produce more goods and services.

Although international finance is thus very important, we begin with the basic activity, international trade. What does it consist of, what characteristics does it have, what is its basis? We do not necessarily need to study all details of its conduct, although much of that process is discussed in connection with international banking and the financing of trade, in later chapters.

THE BASIS OF INTERNATIONAL TRADE—THE PRINCIPLE OF COMPARATIVE ADVANTAGE

The basis of international trade was explained by the founders of economics—Adam Smith and David Ricardo, among others—when they formulated the principle of *comparative advantage*. The presumption is that some individuals and some countries can, for various reasons, produce some types of goods and services more efficiently than other individuals and other countries can. It might even be possible that some country could produce every product more efficiently than could other countries. (Some thought that the United States had nearly reached that situation for many products in the early 1950s.) But even if this were true, it would be to the advantage of that country and of other countries to trade, unless one country had the *same degree* of advantage in producing every product. This is very unlikely. As long as a country has a *greater* advantage (a *comparative* advantage) in some lines, it benefits by specializing in those lines, exporting those goods and services and importing other goods and services from other countries. A country gains by specializing in products in which it has the greatest comparative advantage because any shift of resources to other products reduces output. Of course a country must produce enough of the goods and services in which it has a comparative advantage not only to meet its own needs but to export in exchange for imports of goods and services needed to meet demand.

We recognize that national defense needs and the possibility of foreign embargoes on sales of certain products may cause a country to seek self-sufficiency in some commodities. The United States may wish to be more nearly self-sufficient in petroleum. Political and military questions intrude constantly in international trade and finance, as indeed they do to some extent in domestic business, although sometimes the domestic intrusion is less obvious.

INTERNATIONAL FINANCE

Unless it is strictly barter, international trade must be financed. Sellers of goods and services must accept some types of financial assets that they are willing to hold, able to use to buy imports, or able to sell to others. Among some countries in the 1930s and for a time in the 1940s, world trade was largely on a barter basis or a government-to-government basis. In fact, in dealing with Communist countries, international finance is still of minor importance. But for most international transactions, barter is as awkward as it would be domestically. Exporters, importers, tourists, transportation companies, insurance companies, and others are involved in international finance. Multinational companies, operating in many different countries, confront international financial questions in decisions on foreign investment, management of assets and liabilities, and remittance of funds.

By Alfred Marshall's definition of economics as the "study of mankind in the ordinary business of life," international finance is certainly a part of economics. Even by a type of definition more commonly used today, specifying economics as the study of the optimal selection of scarce means for alternative ends or uses, international finance is part of economics. Alternative means of financing must be selected to attain the greatest gain or the least loss.

Finance has been more precisely defined as that part of economics related to *claims* rather than to consumable goods and services, under conditions involving uncertainty. Financial assets—money, savings accounts, insurance policy cash values, stocks, bonds, and mortgages—are *claims* on resources. They are held for future use, although sometimes not for long. Hence one must always look at their potential *future* value, and the future is always *uncertain*. In international finance even greater uncertainty is encountered than in most areas of finance, although perhaps not more than in investment in stocks. Indeed, the foreign exchange market may be compared in many ways to the stock market, as we shall find later. A bank holding large amounts of pounds sterling may lose 30 percent or more of the value of its holdings if the pound is devalued or depreciates in value.

FINANCIAL ASSETS AND THEIR PRICES

Financial assets—claims on wealth—may be held for long or short periods of time. Bonds and stocks may be held for a lifetime. Money can be spent for consumption immediately, and in fact one definition classifies as money only those assets generally used to make payments, or more precisely for final settlement of debt. (In a sense I can buy goods with a credit card, but for final settlement I must send currency or a check.) Internationally, gold was for a long time a major asset for final settlement of debt. For a time, gold and dollars were widely used for this purpose. Recently, gold has been very little used, but some is still held by central banks and governments for potential use.

Financial assets, like other assets, have prices. The price of money is the reciprocal of the price level—that is, if the price level rises in inflation, the value of money falls concomitantly. Money may or may not earn interest. Other financial assets, including some which are sometimes counted as money, such as time deposits in commercial banks, do earn a return. In many countries interest is paid on demand deposits, and in 1975 there was a proposal in Congress to permit such payment in the United States. Since financial assets are normally held for some period of time (long or short), their prices depend on the interest expected. On some assets dividends are paid instead of interest. Dividends usually fluctuate more (are more uncertain) than interest. The value of any financial asset which provides for future return in the form of interest or dividends depends on expected future amounts of such returns. But it also depends on the current return on *comparable* assets, because an investor dissatisfied with the return on one asset may shift to another asset if its return is higher. The price of a financial asset is the expected return discounted for some future time period at the rate of return earned on comparable assets.

In international finance there are some special uses of terms related to financial assets and their prices. Understanding these terms is essential for later discussions. Let us consider four terms: currency, currencies, foreign exchange, and foreign exchange rates (or simply exchange rates).

Currency

Domestically, currency means coins and paper money. This distinguishes currency from what is now in developed countries the major form of money—bank demand deposits. In international finance, coins and paper money are seldom used except by tourists and others who usually make small payments. Hence currency, in this meaning, is not a very important concept in international finance.

Currencies

The term *currencies* and its singular form *currency* are used in international finance, however, to mean financial assets denominated in the monetary unit of one country (a currency) or in the monetary units of various countries (currencies). Thus dollar bills are a form of a currency; so are deposits in U.S. banks. Some people go so far as to include bonds denominated in U.S. dollars as U.S. currency in this sense. A person trading currencies is generally buying or selling title to deposits in foreign banks. If it is said that the dollar is a strong currency, it means that the value of title to deposits in U.S. banks is high or rising. It may, of course, also mean that title to other financial assets denominated in dollars is high or rising.

Whereas any given country usually has only one currency, one unit of account in which records are kept, and one means of payment (for example, dollars), in international finance there are many currencies. During the U.S. Civil War, in the North gold and greenbacks were both money, and they fluctuated in value both in purchasing power and in relation to each other. Such situations are unusual within countries, however. Usually Gresham's law holds—if two types of currency have the same *nominal* value, the one which has less *market* value will drive the other out of circulation for monetary use.

An important development, largely in the twentieth century, has been the establishment in almost every country of a central bank, the major function of which is to control growth of the money supply in that country. Hong Kong is one exception; few others come readily to mind. Central banks and their role in controlling the creation of money (currencies) are very significant.[4] With the widespread use of central bank notes as paper money and of demand deposits in banks as checkbook money, governments and central banks are in a position to control rates of growth of money supplies at very little cost and independent of the availability of any commodity such as gold. Thus central banks may be able to control the domestic value of money and to affect its foreign value.

Foreign Exchange

The term *foreign exchange* can have two meanings. It can mean the whole process of making international payments, or it can mean financial assets used to make such payments. The latter meaning is far more common.

Holding foreign exchange usually means holding title to deposits in foreign currency in foreign banks. Most payments are made by transfer of such titles. In buying foreign exchange, I may buy paper money or coins, but usually I buy a check or draft drawn on a deposit in a foreign bank, or I simply acquire title to such a deposit. Foreign exchange may be purchased by teletype, telephone, or cable, without any use of paper instruments, although written confirmation is usually later involved. As electronic funds transfer systems improve, it may be possible to transfer funds from a deposit account in Tokyo to one in London as easily as it is now possible to call one's bank to have funds transferred from one's savings account to one's checking account. When that is widely possible, banks all over the world will necessarily compete with each other. The possible impact, especially on banks holding accounts of companies and individuals knowledgeable in international finance, should be obvious.

Foreign exchange payments normally involve, then, changes in ownership of deposits in foreign banks. Such transfers are called short-term capital movements. When I buy German marks, I usually obtain title to deposits in German banks, and this means that, if I bought the marks from Germans, some deposits are now owed to me (a foreigner) instead of to Germans.[5] There has been a flow of *short-term capital* from Germans to foreigners. There is nothing mysterious about this, and use of such terms as short-term capital should never cause confusion. Short-term capital is simply short-term financial assets— money, savings deposits available on short notice, or short-term securities.

Since most international payments are made by transfers of title to bank deposits, it is helpful to think immediately of U.S. imports and other purchases from foreigners, such as those by American tourists abroad, as adding to U.S. bank deposits held by foreigners, if payments are in dollars or through use of dollar traveler's checks. If payments are in foreign currencies, it is helpful to

---

[4]The role of finance in an economy is discussed in many texts on money and banking or financial markets. One such recent text is Charles N. Henning, William Pigott, and Robert Haney Scott, *Financial Markets and the Economy* (Englewood Cliffs, N.J.: Prentice-Hall, 1975). See Chap. 1 for a brief review of the role of finance, financial institutions, and financial markets, and Chaps. 4 and 16 for an analysis of the creation and control of the money supply.

[5]Especially since the advent of Eurodollars, deposits in banks in a country are not always denominated in that country's currency. Eurodollars are deposits denominated in one currency (chiefly U.S. dollars) but held in banks in another country. Thus to U.S. residents they are not foreign exchange although they are foreign assets.

think of the payments as being made through reductions in U.S. bank deposits held abroad in foreign banks. A bank draft in sterling is usually a draft by a U.S. bank on a British bank, often one in which the U.S. bank holds a deposit. If such a draft is sent by an American importer to a British exporter in payment for goods, the deposit held by the American bank in the British bank is reduced.

Foreign Exchange Rates

Domestically, money has no quoted price. *Changes* in the price or value of money are measured by changes in the reciprocal of some index of the price level. One should never make the mistake of confusing interest rates with the price of money. Interest rates are prices for the *use* of money for a time. An increase in the money supply is likely to cause the price or value of money to fall, other things being equal. A continuing fall in the value of money is termed inflation. The effect of a change in the money supply on interest rates requires careful analysis. In the short run, an increased money supply may cause interest rates to fall, as the additional money available leads people to shift to some extent from holding money to holding other (chiefly financial) assets, thus causing prices of the latter to rise and interest rates to fall. A $100 bond bought at $120 yields a lower *rate* of return (interest) than the same bond bought at par. However, if the money supply continues to increase, the supply of other financial assets (promissory notes, bonds, etc.) may also increase as business firms and individuals seek to borrow at the lower interest rate. As this occurs the interest rate begins to rise. If the process continues long enough, the interest rate rises above its original level. This is especially likely if spending increases sufficiently to cause inflation. With inflation, savers want higher interest rates because they recognize that the *real* interest rate obtained is falling, and borrowers feel that they can pay higher rates because they can charge higher prices for goods they sell, using part of this margin to pay the interest. These relationships of prices and interest rates are fundamental to an understanding of the role of price levels and interest rates in international finance.

Internationally, there is usually a price for any monetary unit. This price is the rate of exchange; exchange rates are prices for currencies. Thus money has an *explicit* international value.

Like other prices, exchange rates are determined by private supply and demand unless subject to government controls. Parts of the supply and demand arise from payments necessary for goods and services purchased in international trade. Parts arise from speculation, which means simply purchase or sale of foreign currencies in the hope of gain or to avoid loss because of expected changes in the prices of such currencies. If the financial assets (currencies) bought or sold earn interest, interest rate changes may be a factor affecting the demand for them and the supply of them. Even from this brief introductory analysis, we can see that two other factors are important determinants of the demand for and the supply of foreign currencies, and hence of exchange rates: (1) the possibility of inflation or deflation, and (2) changes in relative efficiency in production in different countries, which cause changes in real purchasing power of currencies for goods and services.

In discussing prices of international financial assets, special attention must be given to social, cultural, and political, as well as economic, factors. Societies differ in their attitudes toward risk taking, and these differences affect asset preferences. People in some countries have strong preferences for specific assets (witness France's attempt to increase its gold holdings, especially during the de Gaulle era, 1958–1968). Some other governments and central banks have almost no gold, but hold large deposits in banks in foreign countries. Policies of central banks in controlling rates of growth of money supplies also differ and significantly affect rates of inflation. Thus these policies are important factors affecting foreign exchange rates. Interest rates also vary, reflecting differences in plentifulness of capital, differences in monetary policies, and differences in rates of growth in real and nominal income and saving.

SOME INTERNATIONAL POLITICAL CONCEPTS

These considerations lead us to turn our attention to some fundamental international political concepts. Two political concepts are particularly important for international finance—the concept of the state or the nation-state and the concept of sovereignty. The existence of states and their sovereignty sometimes means that economic deduction alone is insufficient to predict what will happen. Finally, the concept of sovereignty has very important implications for the status of international law.

The State

The term *state* is used in political science to refer to a nation, and the gradual development of the Western state system has emphasized the significance of national boundaries and the power of a nation or a state to determine its own policies within its borders.[6]

The state in this sense, which had been important in Roman times, ceased to be of importance in the Middle Ages. In the feudalism of the Middle Ages, people were immediately dependent on their overlords, whose power was based on land tenure. But as the Middle Ages came to a close, nationalism began to develop in various countries. If any one date must be selected to mark the beginning of the importance of the nation-state, it might be the Peace of Westphalia in 1648, ending the Thirty Years' War. The treaties of Osnabrück and Münster, which together constituted the Peace of Westphalia, recognized the independence of all the leading Christian states of Europe and the principle of territorial sovereignty in both political and religious matters.[7]

---

[6]The *Western state system* means the system of sovereign national governments which emerged first in Europe and gradually spread throughout the world. It may be contrasted with the "city-state" systems of ancient Greece or with Oriental central-country patterns and with the feudalism of the Middle Ages.

[7]Russia was not at that time recognized as a European power, and Turkey, a non-Christian country, was outside the scope of the treaties.

No new central authority replaced the power of the Holy Roman Empire, and the Pope's authority was henceforth severely limited. In the absence of a central organization competent to maintain international law and order, security for individual states was generally obtained by forming alliances—the balance of power principle.

As the Western state system developed, and in fact expanded to Asia, and central banks came into existence almost everywhere, governments began more active intervention in controlling monetary policy and thus affecting both inflation and real economic growth. Desire for *independence* in monetary policy, conflicting with the *need for coordination* of monetary policies to avoid undesirable effects of one country's policy on other countries, created tension. We shall find that this tension had great impact on the international monetary system.

Sovereignty

Nations face a fundamental dilemma because international law may conflict with the principle of sovereignty. The principle of sovereignty was at first a means of bringing feudal lords under the authority of kings and emperors. In its extreme form, sovereignty means the right of any nation (state) to do as it wishes within its boundaries—the freedom of the state from control by any higher power.

Although the doctrine of sovereignty as the absolute power of states to act as they wish within their own boundaries has been modified over time, the concept is still important.[8] Article 2 of the Charter of the United Nations recognized that "The Organization is based on the principle of the sovereign equality of all its Members" and that "nothing contained in the present Charter shall authorize the United Nations to intervene in matters which are essentially within the domestic jurisdiction of any state or shall require the Members to submit such matters for settlement under the present Charter."

Modifications of the principle of sovereignty may be made through international agreements, implicit or explicit. The principle has thus gradually been limited to some extent. Since international authority is weak, agreements must be maintained by the willingness of the signatory governments to abide by them. It is therefore important in most international agreements that each signatory party believe there is some benefit for it. As one example, if an international currency is created, it must have characteristics which make it desired by all or most parties. Otherwise they are likely to avoid its use and to continue to demand gold or certain national currencies for settlement of debts.

Most countries are unwilling to relinquish sovereign powers such as that of creating money. The importance of that power is illustrated by the fact that the U.S. Constitution states in Article I, Section 8, that "Congress shall have power to coin money" and "regulate the value thereof," and the same article, Section

---

[8]Many books [e.g., Clyde Eagleton, *International Government*, 3d ed. (New York: Ronald, 1957)] point out limitations on the principle of sovereignty. At one extreme it is asserted that the state is sovereign and that naked power politics and war are the only final authorities. At the other extreme it is sometimes assumed that nations can always be subjected to international law.

10, provides that "no State shall . . . coin money . . ." It has been difficult to obtain agreement on the power of an international institution to create money.

States, Sovereignty, and Economic Deduction

The operation of the principle of sovereignty and the different attitudes and interests of different countries sometimes produce unexpected results. For example, one might think on the basis of economic deduction that when the world supply of wheat increased, as it did in the late nineteenth century with the opening of lands in the Western United States, the price of wheat would have fallen generally. One might also think that other countries would have imported more wheat from the United States, on the basis of the principle of comparative advantage. The importance of different reactions in different countries is illustrated by differing responses to the falling price of wheat. England imported more wheat and reduced its own grain acreage, as might have been expected. But countries such as Germany, France, and Italy imposed tariffs on grain imports. Denmark imported more wheat and at the same time increased rather than diminished its grain acreage, because it expanded its livestock industry.[9]

International Law

The simplistic view is sometimes held that international law is nonexistent or unimportant because from time to time countries resort to war to settle disputes. If we acted upon the belief that there is no international law, we could never hope for binding international agreements. But international law has long been recognized as a body of principles that most nations respect. When Germany violated the treaty of 1839 by which it had guaranteed Belgium's neutrality, and invaded Belgium in 1914, the action was widely regarded as reprehensible. Such violations of international law clearly occur, but this does not mean that international law does not exist. Many principles of international law are accepted for long periods of time. There *is* a body of international law, however deficient enforcement powers may at times seem to be. The establishment of the League of Nations and later of the United Nations created additional mechanisms for discussion of international problems and for making some types of international agreements.

Domestic law as well as international law can be swept away, at least temporarily, in revolutions and wars. But this does not mean that laws do not exist. A country may be neutral for many years, its neutrality may be respected by many nations, and it may obtain substantial benefits. These are not totally offset by acts such as Germany's invasion of Belgium in 1914.

The establishment of an International Military Tribunal at Nuremberg and the resulting trial, execution, imprisonment, and acquittal of various defendants accused of war crimes was another landmark in the development of

---

[9]Charles P. Kindleberger, "Group Behavior and International Trade," *Journal of Political Economy*, February 1951, pp. 30–46.

international law. It is noteworthy that the SA (Sturmabteilungen), the Reich Cabinet, and the General Staff and High Command were judged not to be criminals as organizations, whereas the Nazi Party, the SS (Schutzstaffeln), the SD (Sicherdienst), and the Gestapo (Geheime Staatspolizei, or Secret Police) were so classified. Serious issues were raised concerning the punishment of crimes not covered by preexisting written international law and the plea that some defendants acted under orders of superiors. These issues are likely to be debated by jurists for a long time. The point is simply that international law does exist, it is being developed, and the fact that it is violated at times does not mean that it is insignificant.[10]

POLITICAL FRAGMENTATION AND ECONOMIC INTEGRATION

In the past century, the world has generally been moving toward political fragmentation. Evidence may be found in the breakup of colonial empires, the formation of new nation-states—sometimes of minuscule size but claiming sovereignty—and the imposition of barriers on emigration and immigration, on foreign investment, and even on foreign trade. Of course, the trend has not been consistently in this direction, and various efforts have caused some reversals. The efforts led by the United States to reduce trade barriers after World War II are one example. The successful effort to create the European Common Market and plans for further economic and political integration within that unit are other examples. Tariff barriers were indeed reduced after World War II, although it is debatable to what extent *nontariff* barriers have been reduced. The effort to form an organization to establish exchange rates by agreement is another example—but the effort to establish stable but adjustable exchange rates broke down, at least temporarily, in 1973.

Meanwhile, economic factors have resulted in expanding international trade and investment and in the growth of multinational firms operating in many countries. Such firms are not necessarily concerned about, or necessarily most active in, the countries in which they have their nominal headquarters. Large projects are increasingly needed in economic development, sometimes so large that their financing is beyond the means of individual countries. Financing may also be beyond the means of individual financial institutions, and require joint ventures.

Throughout this book we shall find that the conflict between political separatism and economic integration is creating problems for the international monetary system, for international banking, for business firms operating internationally, and for the financing of economic development. Worldwide inflation and worldwide recession in the period 1972–1975 emphasize the need

---

[10]A very useful review is provided by such a book as Charles G. Fenwick, *International Law*, 4th ed. (New York: Appleton-Century-Crofts, 1965). See also Richard A. Falk, *The Status of Law in International Society* (Princeton, N.J.: Princeton, 1970) and Adda B. Bozeman, *The Future of Law in a Multicultural World* (Princeton, N.J.: Princeton, 1971).

for international cooperation and agreement—yet the desire for independent monetary policies has led to failure in some cases to agree on joint action. The seriousness of the problem, which pervades all phases of international finance, has been evident but solutions have not been forthcoming.

Economic integration requires some degree of cooperation concerning currencies, exchange rates, barriers to trade and payments, and barriers to movements of factors of production. Yet political fragmentation has created obstacles to such cooperation.

SCOPE OF INTERNATIONAL FINANCE

This book is an introduction to the entire field of international finance. Just as domestic finance may be divided into major areas such as financial markets, banking, investments, corporate finance, and others, international finance has similar divisions dealt with in consecutive parts of this book. In general, international finance is more complex because a single constant national environment cannot be assumed; many environments and many currencies are involved.

Part One deals with the social accounting framework for international transactions—BOPs and data on the international investment positions of countries. BOPs serve the same purposes as private accounting statements such as income and flow of funds statements, national income accounts, and national flow of funds accounts. BOPs are properly classified as a form of flow of funds statement because they show sources of funds (exports, investment income, receipt of gifts and grants, borrowing, and so on) and uses of funds (imports, transfer payments abroad, loans and investments abroad, and acquisition of international reserve assets). Data on international investment positions are less accurate and until recently have been given less attention; the same is true for comparable national balance sheet data.

Central banking is discussed in Part Two, devoted to the international monetary system. Central banks such as the Federal Reserve System attempt to control growth of the money supply within their territories. Although there is no full-fledged world central bank, the International Monetary Fund (IMF) performs many of the tasks of a central bank, and in recent years created money in the form of special drawing rights (SDRs, termed by some "paper gold"). This money creation was unusual and has not continued, and the SDRs can be used only for specified purposes.

Part Three is devoted to international commercial banking, foreign exchange rates, and money markets. Emergence of the Eurodollar market for deposits and loans denominated in U.S. dollars but handled by banks outside the United States has resulted in a truly international money market having significant effects.

Long-term capital flows (investments and long-term lending) are discussed in Part Four, which focuses on causes of such flows, on institutions and markets such as the Eurobond market developed to facilitate such flows, and on the effects of such flows on BOPs and income.

Corporate finance or financial management is a major area in domestic finance, and students frequently take courses in this area. Discussion of this aspect of international finance in Part Five generally presumes some elementary knowledge in this area and focuses on matters of chief concern in international operations. These include such problems as forecasting the international environment, especially inflation, interest rates, and exchange rates; protecting against exchange risks and political risks; accounting problems arising because accounting systems vary and because accounting values and economic values are not always the same; problems arising from differences in tax systems; problems in evaluating foreign investment decisions; and the finance function of managing assets, liabilities, equity, and remittances when funds may be obtained in various financial markets and invested in different countries.

Finally, in Part Six a relatively brief treatment of some issues involved in financing economic development indicates the relationship between domestic and international means of financing development, the impact of financial markets and institutions on economic development, and the significance of economic development for international and multinational business firms.

The book concludes with a short epilog containing a glance at the future of international finance. The period 1971–1973 probably represented a watershed in this field. Although the future is uncertain, some likely trends are discernible.

QUESTIONS FOR DISCUSSION

1 How does the existence of the Western state system affect the prospects for such changes as the proposed development of a single European currency?

2 How does the difficulty of enforcing international agreements affect the development of an international currency? Does this mean that only something such as gold, which has long been recognized as having special value in international settlements, must be the basis of an international currency?

3 Clarify what is meant by the statement that a balance of payments is similar to a source and use of funds statement, rather than to either a balance sheet or an income (profit and loss) statement.

4 Is it correct to assume that, if economic changes occur in one country to a greater extent than in another country, there *must* be changes in either prices and wages, real income, interest rates, or exchange rates of one country relative to those of the other?

5 What is meant by an "international monetary system"? What characteristics constitute a "system"? What is meant by a "breakdown" of the system?

6 Domestically, banks hold deposits, make loans and investments, and operate the payments system. Incidentally they may do many other things. Is this also true in international finance? Are there major differences?

7 Business forecasting in international finance involves one special aspect not involved in domestic business forecasting—the forecasting of exchange rates. What methods do you think might be used for such forecasting, and why?

8 In what sense is the Eurodollar market an international money market, whereas the New York money market is not, although many foreign institutions are active in the New York money market, either directly or indirectly?

9 Why do long-term capital flows *clearly* affect other international payment items?
10 Make a list of special factors that you think may be important in international managerial financial decisions.

SUGGESTED REFERENCES

Many international economics texts are available and most of them discuss some of the international financial topics treated in this book, but usually quite briefly. Leland B. Yeager, *International Monetary Relations*, 2d ed. (New York: Harper & Row, 1976) provides thorough coverage of the macrofinancial or monetary relations aspects of international finance. Robert Z. Aliber, *The International Money Game*, 2d ed. (New York: Basic Books, 1976) is a very interesting and witty book which is perceptive and thought-provoking.

The field of international *managerial* finance has been covered by several recent texts: David B. Zenoff and Jack Zwick, *International Financial Management* (Englewood Cliffs, N.J.: Prentice-Hall, 1969); J. Fred Weston and Bart W. Sorge, *International Managerial Finance* (Homewood, Ill.: Irwin, 1972); and David K. Eiteman and Arthur I. Stonehill, *Multinational Business Finance* (Reading, Mass.: Addison-Wesley, 1973). Also useful in this field are Gunter Dufey, *Financial Management in the International Corporation: An Annotated Bibliography* (Ann Arbor, Mich.: Graduate School of Business Administration, University of Michigan, 1971), and Lee C. Nehrt, (ed.), *International Finance for Multinational Business* 2d ed. (Scranton, Pa.: International Textbook, 1972), a book of readings. A highly analytical treatment of much of this field is provided by Robert Z. Aliber, "The Short Guide to Corporate International Finances," Chicago, 1975. (Mimeographed.) For reference and for self-study, J. Fred Weston and Bart W. Sorge, *Guide to International Financial Management* (New York: McGraw-Hill, 1977) is useful; it also contains problems which could be assigned to supplement this text.

Current information may be found in such magazines as *The Economist* (London) and *Euromoney*, and in such newspapers as the *Wall Street Journal*. Useful for facts, but not including much interpretation of data, is the *International Monetary Fund Survey*, published twice a month. In the same category, an *International Letter* is issued weekly by the Federal Reserve Bank of Chicago, and articles have frequently appeared in the *Monthly Review* of the Federal Reserve Bank of New York. More interpretative comments can be found in some issues of the *Review*, published monthly by the Federal Reserve Bank of St. Louis, and in some issues of the *New England Economic Review*, published by the Federal Reserve Bank of Boston. Recently some very valuable articles have appeared in certain issues of the *Economic Review*, published by the Federal Reserve Bank of San Francisco—for example, articles on world inflation and on international banking. (This publication was formerly the *Business Review* and before that the *Monthly Review*.) In 1977, the *Monthly Review* of the Federal Reserve Bank of New York was changed to a *Quarterly Review;* semiannual reports on Treasury and Federal Reserve foreign exchange operations continued to be published in certain issues.

Especially on the macrofinancial side, one cannot afford to overlook the excellent pamphlet series published by Princeton University, especially the *Essays in International Finance* and the *Princeton Studies in International Finance*. For example, essay No. 115 contained views on the 1976 agreement on monetary reform and study No. 36 was concerned with the formation of international financial centers.

Bank publications are useful for information concerning current developments in international finance. For example, *International Financial Markets*, published monthly by Morgan Guaranty Trust Company, contains useful discussions of market developments, while *International Finance*, published by Chase Manhattan Bank, contains comments on various events.

In the area of international managerial finance, journals in which significant articles have appeared in recent years include the *Journal of Finance*, the *American Economic Review*, the *Journal of International Business Studies*, the *Journal of Financial and Quantitative Analysis*, the *Columbia Journal of World Business*, the *Harvard Business Review*, *Financial Management*, the *Financial Analysts Journal*, *Fortune*, and the *Journal of Commercial Bank Lending*.

Finally, mention must be made of the very scholarly articles in the IMF *Staff Papers* and the informative articles in *Finance and Development*, published jointly each quarter by the IMF and the World Bank.

In a fast-moving field such as international finance, there is no substitute for reading from the current literature, even though some is difficult, there is some repetition, and the selection of important developments requires perceptive judgment.

Chapter 2

International Social Accounting—Balances of Payments and the International Investment Position

Understanding the social accounting statement most widely used in international finance, the balance of payments, is essential for the analysis of the international payments process, international lending and investing, the foreign exchange market, and interrelationships among various transactions. BOP data are now collected and published by almost all governments. In the United States, publication of BOP data antedated publication of GNP data, largely because of government concern with international transactions and the collection of import duties.

Much less attention has been given to the international investments of a country *at* given dates than to its international transactions *during* periods of time. This was in part because of government concern with such things as import duties and in part because of the difficulty of obtaining reasonable estimates of the values of international investments after they were made. With the increasing importance of international investment since World War II, more attention has been given recently to international investments. Assets held abroad and liabilities to foreigners are discussed in the last section of this chapter.

NATURE OF BALANCES OF PAYMENTS

BOPs show the international transactions of a country for periods of time, usually years or quarters. Although "partial" BOP statements, showing transactions with one foreign country or area, are sometimes compiled, the usual BOP covers all foreign transactions, whether with governments, individuals, or firms which are "residents" of (governing, living in, or incorporated in) foreign countries.

An attempt is made to include all international transactions, whether they involve payments or not. In general, barter transactions and gifts are included when data can be obtained. The BOP might more accurately be called a "balance of international transactions" statement, and in fact this term was used by the U.S. government report for 1940–1945. However, most international transactions involve payments, and hence BOP, the original term, continues to be used.

"Residence" is often difficult to determine. Governments and their agencies are residents of the countries they govern. Corporations are residents of the countries in which they are incorporated or do most of their business; thus foreign subsidiaries of U.S. firms are "residents" of foreign countries. Branches are residents of the countries in which they are located. Tourists, diplomats, and military personnel are residents of the countries from which they come, the presumption being that they are *temporarily* abroad. Workers abroad may be counted either way.[1]

Double-Entry Accounting

The BOP uses double-entry accounting. In effect, each transaction is recorded as both a debit and a credit. The usual accounting rule may be used: Increases in assets and decreases in liabilities or net worth are debits, while increases in liabilities or net worth and decreases in assets are credits.[2] For example, an export of wheat reduces assets and is a credit. An import of foreign automobiles increases assets and is a debit. For the wheat export, the debit entry is usually a reduction in the foreign purchaser's (or his bank's) demand deposit in a U.S. bank (a U.S. liability). If payment is made in foreign currency, the debit

[1]Italy, for example, has counted Italian workers temporarily abroad as residents of Italy, but as residents of foreign countries if considered to be working permanently outside Italy. If temporarily abroad, their work counts as exports of services and their spending as imports of goods and services, while their remittances do not appear at all in the BOP. If permanently abroad, only their remittances appear. To analyze the foreign exchange market, remittance data are useful and should be recorded, but from the standpoint of national income accounting it is logical that only earnings of "permanent" workers be counted as part of the income of countries where they work. For more discussion of this, see Charles P. Kindleberger, *International Economics*, 5th ed. (Homewood, Ill.: Irwin, 1973), p. 304. For details on U.S. practices, see *The Balance of Payments Statistics of the United States* (Washington, D.C.: Government Printing Office, 1965).

[2]The appropriateness of standard accounting rules was stressed by Robert L. Sammons, "Some Balance of Payments Pitfalls: Comment," *American Economic Review*, December 1951, pp. 938–939.

is usually to bank balances in foreign currency held abroad by U.S. banks (assets).[3]

Readers familiar with "source and use of funds" or "flow of funds" statements may recognize that the BOP is neither a balance sheet nor an income statement. It is a form of flow of funds statement showing *changes* in assets, liabilities, and net worth over time. Within this framework, exports, investment income from abroad, gifts received from abroad, borrowing from abroad, and other credits are sources of funds. Imports, investment income paid abroad, gifts sent abroad, lending and investing abroad, and acquisition of international reserve assets (assets acceptable for final settlement of international debt) are uses of funds.[4]

Examples of Recording of Transactions

Some illustrations of selected transactions may be helpful. Transaction 1 is an export of goods and the payment for them, recorded as follows:[5]

Debit	**Credit**
Short-term liquid liabilities $10,000	Exports $10,000

The debit is a decrease in bank deposits of foreigners, because they usually pay for U.S. exports in dollars, reducing their U.S. bank deposits.[6]

Transaction 2 is spending by U.S. tourists abroad. If they cash U.S. dollar traveler's checks at hotels in Europe, the hotels deposit the checks in banks and the banks send them for deposit credit in the United States. The resulting increases in deposits of European banks in U.S. banks show as additions to U.S. short-term liquid liabilities:

---

[3]Credits are often misleadingly termed receipts and debits payments, but exports (credits) are *not* receipts—they *give rise* to receipts. Also, exports and other credits are often shown as pluses or with no sign, and debit items as minuses. No problem arises for exports or imports, but this can be confusing for some items. Gold shown with a plus might be interpreted as an addition to gold held by a country, whereas it actually means an export. Even the terms export and import may be misleading. Capital *exports* are *debit* items: a country which exports capital is acquiring financial assets—promissory notes, bonds, stocks, or evidences of direct investments.

[4]This is the best and simplest way to view the BOP: Sources of funds are exports of goods and services, investment income, transfer payments received from abroad, and long-term and short-term borrowing; uses of funds are imports of goods and services, payment of income on investments of foreigners, transfer payments abroad, long-term and short-term lending and investing, and increases in reserve assets (the international equivalent of cash). Negative uses of funds, such as reductions in holdings of reserve assets, may be shown with minus signs, with a word such as decrease, or by putting the figures on the credit side.

[5]In practice, compilers of BOP data obtain all export documents for a period and record a single figure for exports, rather than attempt to record individual transactions. Data on payments come chiefly from banks. That data come from different sources is one reason for errors.

[6]Although it would be possible to record a debit for accounts receivable as a temporary offset to export credits, this is not done. Data on exports can be obtained from customs houses and data on payments from banks, but data on accounts receivable would be harder to obtain. When exports are increasing or decreasing, figures overstate or understate current demand for dollars to pay for exports because payments are usually made after some allowed time. This should be kept in mind in using BOP data to analyze the foreign exchange market.

Debit	Credit
Tourist expenditures $1,000	Short-term liquid liabilities $1,000

Transaction 3 is the receipt of investment income by a U.S. firm from its foreign investments. A subsidiary abroad may send a dollar draft to the U.S. parent firm. When this draft is cleared, foreigners' deposits in U.S. banks decrease:[7]

Debit	Credit
Short-term liquid liabilities $100,000	Income from investments abroad $100,000

Transaction 4 is a gift by a U.S. resident to a family abroad, of a bank draft or other form of remittance. Usually the draft goes to a foreign bank, which pays the family in local currency and obtains an increased deposit balance in a U.S. bank:

Debit	Credit
Private remittance $500	Short-term liquid liabilities $500

Transaction 5 is a loan by a U.S. bank to a foreign firm. Since loans are not normally resold, this is termed a *nonliquid* capital flow. In making the loan, the bank creates or increases a deposit balance for the foreign firm.

Debit	Credit
Nonliquid capital $1,000,000	Short-term liquid liabilities $1,000,000

Transaction 6 is an allocation of special drawing rights (SDRs) by the International Monetary Fund (IMF) to the United States. SDRs are discussed in more detail in Part Two, but they may be termed "paper gold"—international money created by the IMF to supplement gold. The entry is:

Debit	Credit
Reserve assets: SDRs $10,000,000	Allocation of SDRs $10,000,000

The debit shows an addition to U.S. reserve assets; the credit indicates its source.

Transaction 7 is the use of some of the SDRs to obtain foreign currency needed to make payments. Assume that a foreign government or central bank wants payment in a currency that the United States does not hold. Title to some SDRs can be transferred to a foreign government or central bank in exchange for the desired currency, and that currency used for payment.[8] The transaction

---

[7]Demand deposits held by U.S. firms increase correspondingly but this does not appear in the BOP, which records only changes in liabilities owed to foreigners.

[8]It would of course be possible to buy the foreign currency in the foreign exchange market, but that action might drive up the foreign exchange rate (the value of the foreign currency), making the purchase more costly. Values of SDRs were originally guaranteed in gold or dollars, and are still more stable than the values of most single currencies.

involves two steps, as shown below, because SDRs are used to acquire foreign currencies and the currencies used to make payments:

	Debits			**Credits**	
Reserve assets:			Reserve assets:		
foreign currency	$2,000,000		SDRs	$2,000,000	
Short-term liquid			Reserve assets:		
liabilities	$2,000,000		foreign currency	$2,000,000	

Short-term liquid liabilities decrease because it is assumed that the payment reduces debt to the foreign government. SDRs are a means of payment only among governments or central banks.

Figure 2-1 shows all seven selected transactions in approximately the positions in which they might appear in the U.S. BOP, and corresponding entries in foreign BOPs. For transaction 6, the foreign entry is made by the IMF, not by a foreign country. For this purpose, an international institution like the IMF is treated as if it were a foreign country. The IMF records the U.S. holdings of SDRs as a liability (of the IMF) and makes a debit entry for the allocation. SDRs are liabilities of the IMF in the same way that Federal Reserve notes and deposits are liabilities of Federal Reserve Banks. In both cases money is created, although SDRs are a special kind of money, with limited use for payments among central banks.

Note that often one entry for a transaction is either a credit or a debit to Short-Term Liquid Liabilities, because in U.S. transactions most payments are made by increasing or reducing foreigners' deposits in U.S. banks. It is possible to have entries for Short-Term Liquid Assets, as illustrated by the entries in the lower part of Figure 2-1. When dollar traveler's checks are spent in England, for example, British banks increase their dollar deposits in U.S. banks. This increase is a debit to Short-Term Liquid Assets in the British BOP.

A Balance of Payments Statement

A more complete BOP statement for the United States for 1973 is shown in Table 2-1. Data for 1973 are used purposely because relationships for several years thereafter were distorted by the huge rise in oil prices. This statement differs slightly in form from the partial statement in Figure 2-1. Readers should become accustomed to the considerable variety of forms BOP statements take in current literature and statistics.

Because each transaction is recorded, in effect, as both a debit and a credit, total debits must equal total credits. Deficits or surpluses in a BOP are measured by selecting certain items and comparing total debits and credits for them only. The deficit or surplus must be matched by an equal balance with opposite sign for the remaining items. Items are said to be "above the line" or "below the line" in the BOP. In Table 2-1, dotted lines separate seven different balances within the statement (items A–G). These are discussed later in this chapter. Within certain divisions, especially the bottom three, items below the

U.S. Balance of Payments

	Uses of Funds		Sources of Funds	
(2)	Tourist expenditures	$ 1,000		
(4)	Private remittances	$ 500		
(5)	Nonliquid capital outflow	$ 1,000,000		
			Exports $ 10,000	(1)
			Income from investments abroad $ 100,000	(3)
(6)	Reserve assets: SDRs	$10,000,000	Allocation of SDRs $10,000,000	(6)
(7a)	Reserve assets: SDRs	− 2,000,000	Short-term liquid liabilities (foreigners' bank deposits) decrease $ 10,000	(1)
			increase 1,000	(7)
(7a)	Reserve assets: foreign currencies	2,000,000	decrease 100,000	(3)
			increase 500	(4)
(7b)	Reserve assets: foreign currencies	− 2,000,000	increase 1,000,000	(6)
			decrease 2,000,000	(7b)

Foreign Balance of Payments*

	Uses of Funds		Sources of Funds	
(1)	Imports	$ 10,000		
(3)	Income paid on foreign investments	$ 100,000	Tourist receipts $ 1,000	(2)
			Remittances from abroad $ 500	(4)
(6)	Allocation of SDRs	$10,000,000	Nonliquid capital flow (borrowing) $ 1,000,000	(5)
(1)	Short-term liquid assets (bank deposits in U.S. banks) decrease	$ 10,000		
(2)	increase	1,000		
(3)	decrease	100,000		
(4)	increase	500		
(5)	increase	1,000,000		
(7b)	decrease	2,000,000		
(7b)	Reserve assets: SDRs	$ 2,000,000	SDRs $10,000,000	(6)
(7a)	Reserve assets: currencies	− 2,000,000		
(7b)	Reserve assets: currencies	2,000,000		

*This represents the combined BOP statement of all foreign countries, including international financial institutions such as the IMF.

Figure 2-1

Table 2–1   United States Balance of Payments, 1973

(In Billions of Dollars)

	Debit	Credit	Balance Debit	Balance Credit
Current account:				
Merchandise exports		70.3		
Merchandise imports	69.6			
A *Trade balance*				0.7
Military receipts		2.4		
Military payments	4.5			
Income on U.S. investments abroad		18.6		
Payments of income on foreign investments in the U.S.	8.8			
Receipts from travel and transportation		8.7		
Payments for travel and transportation	11.0			
Other services (net)		1.0		
Balance on services				6.2
B *Balance on goods and services*				6.9
Transfer payments (gifts and grants):				
Private	1.2			
Government	2.6		3.9	
C *Balance on current account*				3.0
Capital account:				
Long-term capital:				
Direct investment in U.S.		2.1		
Direct investment abroad	4.9			
Portfolio investment in U.S.		4.1		
Portfolio investment abroad	0.8			
Government loans abroad (net)	1.5			
Other long-term (net)	0.9			
Balance on long-term capital			1.8	
D *"Basic" balance*				1.2
Nonliquid short-term liabilities		0.5		
Nonliquid short-term claims	4.7			
Allocation of special drawing rights (SDRs)*				
Errors and omissions	4.8			
E *Net liquidity balance*			7.8	
Liquid liabilities to private foreigners		4.4		
Liquid claims on private foreigners	1.9			
F *Official settlements balance*				5.3
U.S. liabilities to foreign official holders		5.1		
G *Money account balance*			0.2	
U.S. reserve assets		0.2		
Totals†	117.2	117.4		

*No allocation of SDRs was made in 1973.

†Totals do not coincide precisely, because of rounding.

Source: Modified from statement shown in *U.S. Balance of Payments Trends,* Federal Reserve Bank of St. Louis, quarterly.

line are regarded as "settlement" items (means of financing the deficit or surplus in the items above the lines).

The two major divisions of the statement are the current account and the capital account. The current account includes income and expenditure items, and thus shows the flow of *income* into and out of the country during the period.[9] Entries in the current account are "current" in that they do not give rise to future claims, while capital account entries indicate changes in future claims. Loans should be repaid, gold is a claim on goods and services, and so on.

The capital account includes loans, investments, and other transfers of capital assets, and the creation of liabilities. Capital assets are assets (houses, factories, stocks, bonds, and so on) which yield a return over the period during which they are held. While classification of current account items is fairly well standardized, various classifications are used in the capital account, that in Table 2-1 being one of several common forms. With effort, some comparability with other U.S. statement forms and with foreign statements can be obtained.

Relationship of Current Account to National Income

The balance of goods and services items in the current account corresponds to the net exports item (NE) in GNP. That is, NE constitutes that part of GNP purchased by foreigners net of domestic purchases from abroad. Net imports of goods and services are subtracted from total domestic spending to obtain a figure for GNP, because net imports are consumed but not *produced* domestically. GNP is intended to measure the amount of goods and services *produced* for final consumption during a period of time by residents of a country, including corporations.

Clearly, NE understates the role of foreign trade in GNP. It would be more appropriate to deduct imports from consumer, business (investment), and government spending, and then record total exports as that part of GNP purchased by foreigners. But the present practice is followed because of statistical difficulties in determining the amount of imports in each category.

Figure 2-2 shows two ways of viewing a country's output.[10] The left side (2-2a) shows the three major categories of spending for the purchase of output—consumer, business (investment), and government expenditures—plus a figure for net exports as the *net* amount purchased by foreigners. Alternatively, the amount of goods and services produced and consumed domestically might be estimated and total exports shown as a separate item in GNP, as in

---

[9]It may be useful to remind readers that income transactions involve purchases of currently-produced goods and services or transfers of income into or out of an area or country, while financial transactions involve transfers of financial assets—loans, purchases of bonds, money transfers, etc.

[10]A defect of Fig. 2-2 is that it cannot be drawn properly for a country with an excess of imports over exports. Net imports reduce GNP, since they are output *not* produced within the country. Fig. 2-2 is a useful diagram, nevertheless.

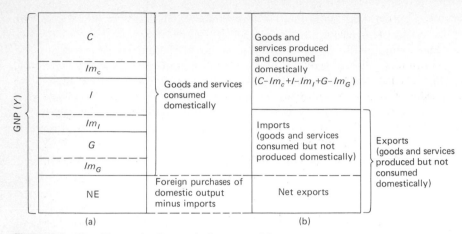

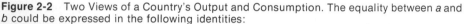

Figure 2-2 Two Views of a Country's Output and Consumption. The equality between *a* and *b* could be expressed in the following identities:

$$Y \equiv C + I + G + NE \equiv (C - Im_C) + (I - Im_I) + (G - Im_G) + X$$

in which Im_C, Im_I, and Im_G designate imports for consumption, investment, and government, respectively.

The $C + I + G + NE$ classification is that normally used. The right-hand equivalent expression shows similiar fractions of GNP purchased by consumers, business, and government, and a larger fraction exported.

Figure 2-2*b*. Viewing the situation this way gives quite a different picture. The relationship of exports to the amount of goods produced *and* consumed domestically differs from that of net exports to total domestic spending. Net exports may seem minuscule in a country like the United States, but exports are a sizable proportion of total goods and services produced. GNP figures may lead to the failure to appreciate the importance of export industries in total production and thus to the failure to recognize reasons for government and other actions to aid exports.

In national income accounting, some countries often use a figure termed gross domestic product (GDP) instead of GNP. Such a figure does not include income derived from abroad. It is useful in measuring fluctuations in *domestic* output and income. In the United States, income derived from abroad has usually been small enough to matter little whether GDP or GNP is used. But in the second quarter of 1974, because of local takeover of part of the equity of an oil company in the Middle East owned in large part by American firms, and a subsequent decline in their investment income from abroad, GNP showed a decline while GDP did not. Some economists saw this as evidence that the decline in GNP in early 1974 was caused mainly by international factors, with no domestically initiated recession. A domestically generated recession came later, as sales and inventories declined sharply in the last quarter of 1974. The recession of 1973–1975 may thus be regarded as a two-stage recession.

The current account is not likely at any time to be exactly in balance. A surplus or deficit in it is offset by a deficit or surplus somewhere in the capital account. The capital account is complex because it includes many types of transfers of capital assets, both long-term and short-term and both real and financial.

An attempt is usually made to separate these two subcategories: (1) loans and investments made in the hope of gain or to avoid loss, often termed *autonomous* flows, and (2) financial asset transfers made simply to settle debt, often termed *settlement* items, *compensatory* items, or *accommodating* flows. The aim has been to isolate the latter items, and their net value is often referred to as *the* surplus or deficit in the BOP. Several measures of "the" surplus or deficit are discussed later in this chapter.

SIGNIFICANT RELATIONSHIPS IN THE BOP

In BOP statements as in other financial statements, certain relationships are especially significant in measuring changes in financial position. Of course we noted that total debits equal total credits, but within the statement every group of items usually shows either a debit or a credit balance. The most significant relationships are discussed in the following paragraphs.

Trade Balance (A)[11]

In Table 2-1, the trade balance (the difference between merchandise exports and imports) was only $0.7 billion, much less than the balance on services. But for countries in which service transactions are of little importance the trade balance may be a good measure of income and outgo.

As noted in Chapter 1, it is presumed that in the absence of restrictions trade takes place on the basis of comparative advantage.[12] Countries differ in efficiency in various lines of production because of natural resource endowment, plentifulness or scarcity of capital, and education and training of labor. Changes in the trade balance may result from changes in efficiency. Such changes occur slowly in most cases, although the rapid development of the economies of Japan and West Germany after World War II shows that under certain conditions changes can occur quickly.

Changes in prices and exchange rates can also cause changes in the trade balance. Any change such as the sharp increase in oil prices in 1973–1974 means a change in the *terms of trade*, the volume of exports traded for a volume of imports with the same value. In cases like this the terms of trade are worsened—more goods are exported in exchange for the quantity of goods imported for the same amount of dollars, and a trade deficit may occur for oil-importing countries unless exports increase rapidly.

Devaluations and downward floating of the exchange value of a country's

---

[11]Letters in parentheses refer to letter designations of items in Table 2-1.

[12]The principle of comparative advantage must not be overlooked when attempting to analyze and forecast exchange rates. Although price changes are important, it is clear that changes in relative efficiencies among countries must be counted as possible causes of shifts in demand.

currency have this same effect on the terms of trade. Devaluations may be necessary at times, but as Hjalmar Schacht told Hitler, you get more goods and services in real terms if your country has a relatively high value for its currency. (Schacht was Hitler's economic adviser.)

Even if devaluation eventually results in increased exports and reduced imports, initially the trade balance and the terms of trade may worsen in the "J-curve" effect. The initial impact of devaluation is adverse since local currency import prices rise relatively quickly, while the *volume* of exports rises slowly because it takes time to market additional goods. The volume of imports may also drop slowly, as importers continue hoping to sell the same volume of goods at higher prices. It is generally believed that volume effects eventually dominate, as they did for the United States after the devaluations of 1971 and 1973. The enormous rise in the cost of oil imports in 1974 and succeeding years partly offset the volume effects, however.

It may be useful in computing a balance of trade to eliminate such special disturbances by excluding petroleum imports and exports. Agricultural exports may also be excluded, because they too have been affected by special conditions.[13]

As noted above, a sudden change such as the rise in OPEC oil prices does create problems. It is in effect a tax subtracted from the incomes of oil-importing countries, reducing income available for domestic spending. A slowdown in economic growth or a recession in oil-importing countries was thus to be expected, although it might have been offset by prompt investment of OPEC funds in these countries.

One reason for particular attention to the trade balance is that figures are available with little delay. They are published monthly, within about a month of the end of the period covered. Such figures are slightly different from the final BOP trade figures because they do not include certain adjustments for imports into the Virgin Islands from foreign countries, imports or exports of ships, nonmonetary gold, gift parcels sent through the mails, and some other minor items. Since trade balance figures measure actual shipment, not payments, they may be misleading for the analysis of the foreign exchange market unless data are also available on the financing of trade. No implication of "good" or "bad" should be attached to any trade balance without analysis of its causes.

Balance on Goods and Services (B)

For most industrialized countries, the balance on goods and services—$6.9 billion in Table 2-1—indicates a more important relationship than does the trade balance; that is, the current income position of a country vis-à-vis foreign countries, excluding gifts and grants, which may fluctuate from year to year. A deficit in this balance means that the country is spending more for purchases of goods and services from foreign countries than it is obtaining in income from

---

[13]Patricia H. Kuwayama, "Measuring the United States Balance of Payments," *Federal Reserve Bank of New York, Monthly Review*, August 1974, p. 185.

sales of goods and services to foreign countries. If the current income position shows a deficit, it is important to analyze the means of financing it and the probability of reducing it. It does not necessarily indicate financial difficulty, but it warrants careful examination of the international transactions and economic trends in the country. The United States had such deficits in the late nineteenth century, when the western railroads were being built and wheat and other crop lands brought into production. Britain and Italy have had such deficits in recent years, with less indication of potential ability to eliminate them in the future.

Although the balance on goods and services corresponds to the net exports item in GNP, net export figures in GNP may differ from those in BOP statistics because of procedures used for approximating items on which information is not complete and because of differences in timing and revision of the two sets of data. Some items in the balance are subject to substantial error even for the United States. An example is foreign earnings of U.S. oil companies for the period 1966–1973.[14]

Net exports of goods and services are financed by transfer payments to foreign countries plus net foreign investment.

Current Account Balance (C)

The current account balance ($3.0 billion in Table 2-1) differs from the balance on goods and services only in including transfer payments (gifts and grants). These comprise remittances (which may be quite regular in amount) to charities and relatives abroad, and also special gifts and grants, including foreign aid. Although foreign aid is now generally rather small in amount, sometimes special government transfers temporarily distort the current account balance. The question may be raised whether governmental loans should also be included, since many are similar in purpose to grants. Thus although the current account balance is a widely used figure, it should be analyzed carefully.

The current account balance is financed by net foreign investment. In reviewing capital account items, however, we find them so diverse and the motives for capital flows so varied, that net foreign investment is not a very meaningful concept.

Both the balance on goods and services and the current account balance are defined in the same way for the United States and for foreign countries in general. In principle, these balances for all countries taken together should total zero.

"Basic Balance" (D)

Deriving a "basic balance" figure is an attempt to include insofar as possible all items fluctuating around basic long-run trends, which therefore can be forecast with more accuracy than other items. A "basic balance" figure is the current

---

[14]See *Survey of Current Business*, June 1974, for revisions of the figures, based on results of a special survey.

account balance plus long-term capital items. But there is question about both the holding period for some loans and investments and the relative stability of some items (for example, direct investment) usually included in the basic balance. And direct investment, in the BOP, includes flows of funds between parent companies and overseas affiliates, which may be affected by interest rate considerations, tax factors, and accounting practices of multinational firms.

In interpreting BOPs, the basic balance may be a focal point. But although widely used, the concept of basic balance is difficult to define and measure. Although the distinction between autonomous and accommodating transactions is theoretically useful, its empirical application is difficult.

Even if the basic balance can be correctly measured, there is some question whether it should be interpreted in the same manner for a country which is "banker to the world" and a major trading nation as it is for other countries. A bank typically has assets (loans and investments) which are longer-term than its liabilities. Most liabilities of a bank are short-term, consisting mainly of more or less volatile deposits. Thus a deficit in the basic balance for a country which is banker to the world may be acceptable up to some limit. Of course, a bank (or a country) eventually may incur risks of being unable to redeem its liabilities in generally accepted assets. But this point is difficult to define and forecast.

Liquidity Balance (E)

The liquidity balance is the basic balance plus flows of nonliquid short-term capital (chiefly bank loans), allocations of SDRs, and errors and omissions. This balance is equal to, or may be said to be financed by, changes in liquid liabilities to foreigners and in reserve asset holdings. Traditionally the most significant figure in the BOP, the liquidity balance was viewed as an indication of a change in the ability of a country to "defend its currency"—that is, to defend the exchange rate. For a reserve currency country such as the United States this was very important, because the major reason foreign countries hold dollars was the belief that the dollar was stable in value. A deficit on the liquidity balance indicated an increase in liquid liabilities or a decline in reserve asset holdings available to meet such liabilities, or both.[15]

Thus a liquidity balance of −$7.8 billion, as shown in Table 2-1, would in the past have been regarded as a serious adverse balance. But its meaning in the era of floating exchange rates after early 1973 is not clear. Even when exchange rates were fixed, the meaning was not as clear as might have been desired. The line between liquid and nonliquid items is not easy to draw, and the question of the appropriate place for inclusion of the errors and omissions item is debatable.

---

[15]A leading proponent of the liquidity measure of deficits was Walther Lederer. See his *The Balance on Foreign Transactions: Problems of Definition and Measurement*, Special Papers in International Economics, No. 5 (Princeton, N.J.: Princeton, 1963).

Official Settlements Balance (F)

As it became evident in the 1960s that reserve assets, especially gold, would not be surrendered by the United States to meet liabilities to *private* foreigners, another measure of the deficit or surplus came into use.[16] This was termed the official settlements balance—$5.3 billion in Table 2-1. This balance is the liquidity balance less the increase (or plus the decrease) in liquid liabilities to private foreigners. Some minor adjustments were made for semiliquid liabilities to foreign governments and central banks which were treated as liquid liabilities in the official settlements measure.

When U.S. banks borrowed abroad, the liquidity balance deficit increased but the official settlements deficit did not. When such borrowings were repaid, the liquidity deficit was reduced, but the official settlements deficit increased if foreign banks held more dollars than they wished to hold and sold them to their central banks. Central banks were often involuntary purchasers of such foreign exchange as they tried to hold exchange rates at fixed levels. Unless central banks bought the dollars, their sale would tend to reduce the exchange value of the dollar and cause the values of other currencies to rise. The presumption in focusing attention on the official settlements balance was that, although the United States would not release gold to private foreigners, it would settle balances due foreign governments in gold. After 1971, when the U.S. government announced that it would no longer release gold for either purpose, the significance of the official settlements balance was diminished.

Some argued that in these circumstances it might be best to count only decreases in reserve asset holdings as deficits.[17] It had already been noted that neither the liquidity balance nor the official settlements balance was a perfect measure of *unwanted* additions to foreign holdings of dollars, because with increased trade and the use of dollars for many payments, some additional dollars were *needed* each year for payment. Clearly, the target was *not* a zero deficit by either measure.

Fluctuations in the official settlements balance, the liquidity balance, and the balance on goods and services differed in the period after 1965. The balance on goods and services gradually approached a deficit position, which it reached in 1971. Productive efficiency in foreign countries was increasing and the *relative* degree of inflation was diminishing vis-à-vis the United States. The

---

[16]Norman S. Fieleke, "Accounting for the Balance of Payments," Federal Reserve Bank of Boston, *New England Economic Review*, May/June 1971, pp. 2–15. As Fieleke admits, there is asymmetry in counting only losses of reserve assets as a deficit. As long as the U.S. dollar is a reserve asset, increases in dollars held abroad tend to cause inflation in foreign countries unless offset. However, since there is no U.S. deficit (by this measure) if foreigners simply increase their dollar holdings, there is no corresponding impetus toward deflation in the United States.

[17]Some reasons for attaching less significance to both the official settlements and the liquidity balance in a period of floating exchange rates are indicated in the *Economic Report of the President*, 1975, p. 212, where it is noted that "reliance on these balances could lead to serious analytical misjudgments. The question of how the organization of our balance of payments data can be made more useful is currently under review."

liquidity balance deficit in 1969 increased greatly as U.S. banks borrowed abroad. Finally, the balance on goods and services did not become positive immediately following the devaluation of the dollar in 1971, but by 1973 it was positive. Presumably the shift in trend was largely the result of devaluation.

U.S. liabilities to monetary authorities of OPEC countries have increased tremendously in recent years. These are counted as deficit items in the official settlements balance, but should they be? Are they accommodating (passive accumulations) or autonomous (investments motivated by the usual economic considerations)? Some analysts now wish to exclude liabilities to OPEC countries from the official settlements balance because of such doubts. And if OPEC countries put some funds into Eurodollar deposits (dollar deposits in Europe), as they have done, this shows up in U.S. BOP figures as liabilities to *private* foreigners (the Eurodollar banks). Is the situation accurately reflected in this way?

BOP statements provide much useful data, but now more than ever it is misleading to focus on any *one* relationship as the indicator of external influence on an economy.

The Money Account Balance (G)[18]

In recent years a monetary approach to BOP theory has been widely discussed. Those advocating this approach view the really significant measure of BOP impacts as being the impact of international transactions on the domestic money supply. This impact is measured by the *money account balance.* For the United States, the money account balance is changes in U.S. holdings of gold and foreign exchange minus (or plus) changes in foreign deposits in Federal Reserve Banks, which may offset the changes in reserve assets. These are the international items which may affect the money supply.[19]

Changes in liabilities to foreign governments and central banks do not necessarily affect the money supply. The acquisition of dollars by foreign governments and central banks may affect money supplies in foreign countries, but if they invest their dollars in, for example, U.S. Treasury securities, purchased from private holders, there is no effect on the U.S. money supply. There is only a transfer of title to money from U.S. residents to foreign governments and back to U.S. residents.

Although the monetary approach to BOP theory has analytical value and for this reason is discussed in Chapter 3, the money account balance may not have the significance some attribute to it. The importance with which it is

---

[18]The reader should compare the very negative review of most BOP measures by Donald S. Kemp, in "Balance of Payments Concepts—What Do They Really Mean?" Federal Reserve Bank of St. Louis, *Review*, July 1975, pp. 14–23, with the more moderate evaluation by Patricia H. Kuwayama, cited in footnote 13, above.

[19]If U.S. authorities acquire gold or foreign currencies, they pay by check and the checks are deposited in banks. Clearing the checks gives the banks additional reserves, so that both deposits (money) and the potential increase in money are greater. If foreign governments or central banks receive the payments, they *may* deposit the checks in their accounts in Federal Reserve Banks, offsetting the factors tending to cause change in the money supply, at least temporarily.

viewed depends upon the emphasis on money supply changes as the most important determinant of changes in income, output, and employment, and upon the extent to which the central bank (the Federal Reserve System in the United States) is able to offset changes caused by international factors.[20]

Total Debits and Credits

All BOP statements show equal totals of debits and credits since an errors item is included to compensate for errors, and if there were no errors every transaction would have offsetting debits and credits.

DISCONTINUATION OF PUBLICATION OF CERTAIN BALANCES

Pursuant to the recommendation of an Advisory Committee on the Presentation of the Balance of Payments Statistics, publication of the official settlements balance, the net liquidity balance, and the "basic" balance was discontinued in the spring of 1976. This recommendation resulted from managed floating exchange rates, the accumulation of large amounts of dollars by the oil-exporting countries, and increasing difficulties of distinguishing between short-term and long-term, liquid and illiquid, and official and private holdings of capital assets.[21] The Advisory Committee wished to encourage a form for presenting data which would facilitate use of the data without encouraging misleading conclusions arising from focusing too much attention on certain balances.

Some analysts in private institutions, however, argued that although the balances are imprecise measures, they add to understanding and hence should be published.[22] The problem is analogous to that arising from focusing on a figure for the unemployment rate or on a figure for business firm earnings per share, without analyzing the components of such figures. As one bank publication concluded, "those who want to evaluate the U.S. international payments situation will now be forced to delve more thoroughly into the accounts. This process should lead to a better understanding of the forces at work."[23] Whether the change in data publication introduced in 1976 is likely to be permanent is a matter for speculation. Focusing on a single figure for the

[20]The process of change in money supply through the monetary base (currency and bank reserves) and the monetarist-fiscalist controversy are described in Charles N. Henning, William Pigott, and Robert Haney Scott, *Financial Markets and the Economy* (Englewood Cliffs, N.J.: Prentice-Hall, 1975), Chap. 4 and pp. 365–371. Readers whose knowledge of the money creation process is not up-to-date may wish to review these sections.

[21]The publication of detailed data is to continue, so that except for the liquidity balance, those who believe that these balances are useful can calculate them from the data. The liquidity of certain financial assets is difficult to evaluate. See *Wall Street Journal*, May 17, 1976, p. 2, and IMF *Survey*, June 7, 1976, p. 166.

[22]See, for example, Citibank, *Economic Week*, June 1, 1976, pp. 1–3, and June 28, 1976, p. 5.

[23]Chase Manhattan Bank, "U.S. Payments Position Proves Hard to Define," *International Finance*, May 31, 1976, p. 1.

"surplus" or "deficit" in a BOP clearly is apt to be misleading, and some means of encouraging analysis of the entire BOP data is surely desirable.

SURPLUSES AND DEFICITS IN THE 1970s

Until the 1970s, great concern was evidenced by governments when deficits or surpluses were large or continued. The United States restricted capital outflows and some debit items in the current account to reduce deficits. Germany acted to moderate the expansionary and inflationary internal effects of continuous surpluses.

With the general acceptance of at least an interim period of floating exchange rates beginning in 1973, and with huge BOP surpluses generated by a number of OPEC countries, attention shifted to the problem of "recycling" these funds to offset deficits. Efforts were proposed to reduce the dependence of Western countries and Japan on imported oil. The economic and military effects of future possible oil embargos were major considerations. As noted, the U.S. recession of 1973–1975 began at the time of the Arab oil embargo in late 1973. When a recession of the more usual type developed in late 1974, the whole recession had the appearance of two stages—the first caused mainly by BOP factors, the second by overaccumulation and a consequent reduction in inventories plus a decline in consumption.[24]

The foregoing comments suggest that international factors affecting the U.S. economy are even more important in the 1970s than before. Table 2-2 compares some U.S. BOP relationships in the 1970s with the same relationships in 1965. The dramatic shift from positive to negative trade balances, current account balances, and especially "basic" balances, is evident.

[24]One economist argued that two errors in government policy—a monetary policy at first too expansive and then too restrictive and safety and antipollution requirements for automobiles which caused a sharp decline in consumer demand for autos—were major causes of the severity of the 1974–1975 recession. See Paul W. McCracken, "1974's Economic Air Pocket," *Wall Street Journal*, April 25, 1974, p. 8.

Table 2–2   Selected U.S. BOP Figures, 1965 and 1970–1974
(In Billions of Dollars)

	1965	1970	1971	1972	1973	1974
Trade balance	5.0	2.2	− 2.7	− 6.9	0.7	5.5
Balance on goods and services	7.1	3.6	0.8	− 4.6	6.9	3.6
Current account balance	4.3	0.4	− 2.8	− 8.4	3.0	− 3.6
Basic balance	−1.8	−3.0	− 9.6	− 9.8	1.2	−10.9
Liquidity balance	−2.5	−3.9	−22.0	−13.9	−7.8	−19.0
Official settlements balance	−1.3	−9.8	−29.8	−10.3	−5.3	− 8.4

Source: Federal Reserve Bank of St. Louis, *U.S. Balance of Payments Trends.*

The shifts which occurred in recent years may be better appreciated from Table 2-3, showing a summary global balance of payments, with significant balances for different groups of countries. Note the huge rise in the trade balance of the major oil exporters and the sizable trade deficits of the LDCs. The recession in industrial countries and oil conservation measures in 1974–1975 reduced exports of oil-producing countries but their imports continued to rise, resulting in much smaller trade and current account balances in 1975 than in 1974.

When such dramatic shifts occur, there must be adjustments. In Chapter 3 we examine adjustment processes and show how they may restore an appropriate balance in international accounts without significant direct government intervention. We also discuss the nature of government intervention, generally regarded as a last resort but necessary if adjustments do not otherwise occur. Before leaving the subject of international accounting, however, brief attention must be given to data on the international investment position.

THE INTERNATIONAL INVESTMENT POSITION

Much more emphasis has been given to gathering and publishing data on international income and capital *flows* than to balance sheet data on *stocks* of assets and liabilities. The rapid rise in U.S. foreign investment since the late 1950s, however, and the recent trend toward direct investment in the United States by OPEC countries and others has brought attention to U.S. international assets and liabilities. The Foreign Investment Study Act of 1974 authorized the collection and analysis of data on foreign investment in the United States, although the President emphasized that this did not mean a change in U.S. policy. With some exceptions for national security and certain special industries, the United States has not imposed special restrictions on foreign investment. Treatment is in general the same for foreign and domestic investors, in most industries.

Table 2-4 shows the nature and geographic distribution of U.S. foreign assets and liabilities at the end of 1974. The values of direct investments are not accurate indications of their market values or their values as going concerns because such investments are shown at book value—the value of initial investments plus or minus annual additional investment or disinvestment. Some government loans to foreign countries may not be collectable at face value, especially when payment is to be received in foreign currencies which may be difficult to convert into dollars or other "hard" currencies.

It is interesting that although U.S. foreign asset holdings exceeded liabilities to foreigners, liabilities to Western Europe exceeded assets held there in spite of the heavy U.S. foreign investment in that area. This largely reflects the buildup of Western European holdings of U.S. government securities, purchased as Western European governments accumulated dollar deposits and

Table 2-3 Global BOP Summary
(In billions of U.S. dollars)

	Year	Trade	Balance on services and private transfers	Current account	Capital account balance*	Change in liabilities to foreign official agencies†	Balance financed by transactions in reserve assets
Total all countries‡	1973	19.6	−10.2	9.3	3.9	5.9	19.0
	1974	30.4	−16.2	14.2	10.5	20.0	44.6
	1975	23.7	−20.5	3.1	8.5	9.4	21.0
Industrial countries	1973	12.2	− 0.3	11.8	−13.2	5.8	4.3
	1974	−10.5	0.9	− 9.6	− 5.3	18.4	3.4
	1975	20.9	− 1.4	19.4	−19.6	4.2	4.1
Major oil exporters	1973	18.8	−12.6	6.2	− 1.9	...	4.3
	1974	82.3	−15.6	66.7	−23.7	0.1	43.0
	1975	50.8	−15.8	35.0	−15.0	0.1	20.0
Other primary producing countries	1973	−11.4	2.7	− 8.7	19.0	0.1	10.4
	1974	−41.4	− 1.5	−42.9	39.5	1.6	− 1.9
	1975	−48.0	− 3.3	−51.3	43.1	5.1	− 3.1
More developed areas	1973	− 4.8	6.1	1.3	1.0	− 0.1	− 2.3
	1974	−19.1	4.8	−14.3	9.5	0.4	− 4.4
	1975	−18.9	4.6	−14.3	10.3	1.7	− 2.3
Less developed areas	1973	− 6.6	− 3.5	−10.0	18.0	0.2	8.1
	1974	−22.4	− 6.3	−28.6	30.0	1.3	2.5
	1975	−29.1	− 7.9	−37.0	32.8	3.4	− 0.8
Africa	1973	0.7	− 2.3	− 1.6	2.0	0.1	0.5
	1974	0.5	− 2.9	− 2.4	2.5	0.3	0.4
	1975	− 2.4	− 2.6	− 5.0	4.0	0.5	− 0.5

Asia	1973	− 2.8	0.8	− 2.0	4.6	. . .	2.6
	1974	− 9.7	0.6	− 9.1	10.4	0.9	2.2
	1975	−10.6	1.0	− 9.5	10.1	0.7	1.3
Middle East	1973	− 4.3	2.3	− 2.0	3.2	0.1	1.1
	1974	− 5.9	1.9	− 4.0	4.0	0.1	0.1
	1975	− 7.7	1.7	− 6.0	4.4	1.5	− 0.1
Western Hemisphere	1973	− 0.2	− 4.2	− 4.4	8.3	. . .	3.8
	1974	− 7.3	− 5.8	−13.2	13.0	. . .	− 0.1
	1975	− 8.5	− 7.9	−16.5	14.4	0.6	− 1.5

*This balance is computed residually as the difference between the balance financed by transactions in reserve assets and the sum of the current account balance and the change in liabilities to foreign official agencies; it includes net errors and omissions as well as reported capital movements, government transfers, and gold monetization.

†The concept of "liabilities to foreign official agencies" used in this table encompasses use of Fund credit and short-term BOP financing transactions in which the liabilities of the borrowing country are presumably treated as reserve assets by the creditor country.

‡Global BCP aggregations inevitably contain many asymmetries arising from discrepancies of coverage or classification, timing, and valuation in the recording of individual transactions by the countries involved. A major area of asymmetrical classification during recent years concerns the recording of official claims placed in Eurocurrency markets. These transactions, although treated as changes in reserve assets by the investing countries, are recorded as capital inflows by the recipient industrial countries. Had such transactions been recorded symmetrically, the global summations would show both a larger net capital outflow and a larger aggregate change in liabilities to foreign official agencies. If identified Eurocurrency reserve placements are excluded from the recorded net capital account balances of the industrial countries, their adjusted net capital outflows amount to $21.2 billion, $23.9 billion, and $26.2 billion over the years 1973, 1974, and 1975, respectively.

Data: As reported to the Fund and Fund staff estimates

Source: IMF Survey, September 20, 1976, p. 274.

Table 2–4   U.S. Foreign Assets and Liabilities,* Year End 1974
(In Billions of U.S. Dollars)

	Canada	Western Europe	Japan	Latin America and other Western Hemisphere	Other countries	International organizations and unallocated	Total
Assets							
Private long-term	48.3	51.0	4.5	25.1	21.9	9.2	160.0
Private short-term	4.4	10.5	13.7	14.7	7.1	Negl.†	50.4
U.S. government long-term	.2	8.2	.6	8.3	17.0	2.0	36.3
U.S. monetary reserves	Negl.	Negl.	Negl.	...	...	15.9	15.9
U.S. government foreign currencies and other short-term assets	Negl.	.1	Negl.	Negl.	1.8	Negl.	2.0
Total	52.9	69.8	18.8	48.1	47.8	27.1	264.6
Liabilities							
Private long-term	7.5	40.3	1.5	3.0	3.3	1.7	57.2
Private short-term	3.4	24.0	N.A.‡	8.8	N.A.	3.0	49.6
U.S. government long-term	.1	1.7	11.4	.1	1.3	...	3.6
Foreign official agencies¶	3.7	44.2	N.A.	4.5	N.A.	...	76.6
Total	14.7	110.2	17.1	16.4	24.1	4.7	187.0

*Securities are market value and all others are book value.
†Negligible.
‡Not available.
¶U.S. government liabilities to foreign official reserve agencies are included with other U.S. liabilities to "foreign official agencies."
Source: International Economic Report of the President, 1976, p. 161.

desired to obtain better yields on such funds than the low rates of interest paid on bank deposits.

SUMMARY

BOPs are systematic records of transactions between residents of a country and those of all (or designated) foreign countries. Certain figures in BOPs have been widely interpreted as indicating a better or worse international economic position of a country, and also as measuring the strength or weakness of its currency. Yet it is increasingly evident that no single figure can be used for this purpose. There are at least six or seven currently used measures, each with some variants for special purposes.

Until recently, one major use of BOP data was to determine whether there was a "fundamental disequilibrium" in the BOP—that is, one which might have to be corrected by a change in the foreign exchange value of the country's currency. With managed floating exchange rates since 1973, the data are now useful to predict mutually determined changes in exchange rates and official reserve holdings.

The distinctions between income payments and capital flows (current account versus capital account), between volatile and relatively stable items (sometimes measured by other items versus the "basic" balance), and between official and private foreign holdings of a currency are still important. It might be thought that if foreign governments do not intervene in the foreign exchange market, the official settlements balance is insignificant. But the situation in recent years has been a *managed* float of exchange rates, and the official settlements balance is still significant. However, changes in its size and in exchange rates are *mutually* determined under a managed float.

The foregoing suggests that BOP analysis is much more complex today then formerly. BOP data are useful, but without information concerning their basic and surrounding conditions they are of limited value as guides to policy. The increase in international capital flows since the 1950s, the increasing variety of such flows, and the increasing sophistication of international financial managers make it much more difficult to determine motives. Yet without analysis of motivation, prediction is uncertain. Even when exchange rates were relatively fixed, some gain in official reserves could be attributed to a desire to accumulate such reserves, as Machlup pointed out.[25] If OPEC official oil earnings are in part invested in U.S. government securities, is this passive accumulation of dollars and hence a part of a deficit and an indication of weakness of the dollar, or is it voluntary investment and hence a sign of foreign confidence in the dollar?

Increased complexity is not a reason for abandoning the attempt to analyze the impact of foreign transactions. But we should carefully define our purposes, and then select data and relationships in the BOP that are helpful.

[25]Fritz Machlup, "Three Concepts of the Balance of Payments," in *International Payments, Debts, and Gold* (New York: Scribner, 1964).

APPENDIX: Nature of Specific Items in BOPs

CURRENT ACCOUNT ITEMS

The current account includes exports and imports of merchandise and of services like those for tourists and transportation and communications. It also includes military expenditures and receipts for sales of military equipment abroad, and investment income (interest, dividends, and profits) received and paid. Gifts and grants are usually included, although in some statements they are shown in a separate section.

Exports and Imports of Merchandise

Data on merchandise exports and imports are generally obtained from documents filed with customs houses and other government offices. There are significant valuation problems: Values may not be comparable even if honestly stated, with no attempt to avoid customs duties or, for example, to overvalue exports as a means of obtaining funds from abroad in the guise of payments for exports.[26] Military exports under government grants are not included as exports in U.S. BOP figures. Since demand for them basically comes from the U.S. government rather than from foreign sources, these exports are treated as special transfers. In the GNP accounts, their purchases are included with government purchases of goods and services rather than with net exports.

Services

Tourist expenditures are for both goods purchased abroad and services such as hotel rooms and tours. Transportation and communications services include those of shipping companies and airlines and those of telephone and telegraph companies. Other payments, sometimes classified separately, are for insurance obtained from foreign insurance firms (for example, Lloyd's of London), for royalties on books and for exhibiting movies, for engineering services, and so on.

Concern may be expressed if one particular debit item (for example, tourist expenditures) exceeds the corresponding credit item (tourist revenues). A "travel gap" may be viewed with alarm.[27] Many economists feel that such balances have limited significance, since they may well be offset by other items. Clearly, every country is likely to have an excess of debits for some items and an excess of credits for others. Kindleberger refers to a colleague's sarcastic comment on the "U.S. banana gap."[28] It seems reasonable to avoid extremes: one need not bemoan an excess of expenditure for a certain item, but it may sometimes be useful to attempt to attract more revenue.

Military spending abroad includes wage payments for services performed by civilians and the cost of materials for projects such as construction of barracks or airfields. It also includes money paid to troops stationed abroad, minus estimated amounts they send home. In wars some services may be provided free of charge by the

---

[26]For example, values may be reported f.a.s. (alongside a ship, but not including cost of loading), f.o.b. (including cost of loading), c.&f. (including cost of transportation to the foreign destination), c.i.f. (including also the cost of insurance), and in other ways. International agencies have tried to formulate rules for valuation to obtain as much uniformity as possible, but many differences exist. Of course in some countries smuggling is widespread, and import and export values must be estimated or simply understated.

[27]The "tourist gap" is discussed, for example, in "Travel and the Devalued Dollar," *Morgan Guaranty Survey*, October 1973, pp. 5–9.

[28]Charles P. Kindleberger, op. cit., p. 317.

governments of countries in which troops operate. A credit entry is necessary to offset the debit entry if, for example, civilian services are paid for in local currency supplied by the local government to the U.S. military. The credit entry may be in the current account if no reimbursement to the local government is anticipated. No claim is created; in effect, the local government is paying a share of the U.S. military expenses. The entry may be in the capital account if later reimbursement is expected, indicating liability for such reimbursement.[29]

Investment income received from abroad or paid abroad is included in the current account section because it is derived from the service of supplying capital. In the U.S. BOP, interest, dividends, and profits remitted from subsidiaries and branches abroad are included as investment income. Branch profits are included even when *not* remitted. Retained earnings of subsidiaries incorporated abroad are not included, however.[30]

For most of the foregoing items there are both debits for expenditures and credits for sales or other income. Often a single net amount is entered for the difference, especially if flow in one direction is very small; but it is usually more informative, and now more common, to show both entries. In view of the diversity in practice, however, readers must examine BOPs carefully to be sure what is included in each classification.

Transfer Payments (Gifts and Grants)

Although they are now usually included in the current account, there is some disagreement concerning proper classification of gifts and grants. For those making gifts, they are expenditures; for those receiving them, they are income—a special form of income, however, because they do not result from production of goods and services. Gifts and grants can be shown in a separate section of the BOP if desired, though it is hardly necessary because of their small size relative to other items.[31]

Note in Table 2-1 that government grants abroad in 1973 totaled only $2.6 billion. Foreign aid is not currently a major item. In fact, foreign gifts and grants by the U.S. government and residents in 1973 totaled only $3.8 billion, only about 3/10 of 1 percent of GNP. Government loans abroad totaled only about $1.5 billion, 1/10 of 1 percent of GNP. Compare these percentages with those for charitable contributions shown on your income tax return if you file one.

Since the current account shows income and expenditure, if debits exceed credits, expenditures abroad exceed income from abroad. For some developing countries

---

[29]Details concerning methods of recording particular items are discussed in a number of U.S. Department of Commerce publications. For a brief treatment of some problems of recording, see Charles N. Henning, *International Finance* (New York: Harper & Row, 1958), Chap. 2.

[30]Some time ago it was pointed out that this understates the size of U.S. investment abroad. A more accurate indication of the extent of such investment would be provided if retained earnings of U.S. subsidiaries abroad were included as investment income and at the same time as an investment outflow from the United States. Present practice began when, in the 1930s and 1940s, it seemed doubtful whether remittance of investment income of this type could be expected in any sizable amounts. For one discussion, see Emilio G. Collado, "Private U.S. Direct Investment Abroad," in *International Banking and Foreign Trade*, lectures delivered at the Ninth International Banking Summer School, Rutgers University (London, Europa, 1956).

[31]One reason for the special classification of gifts and grants is that they are a special type of income. If the area covered by a BOP were expanded to include both the country making grants and the recipient country they would be not income but transfer payments, thus illustrating the fallacy of composition: from a microeconomic viewpoint, transfers are income to those who receive them and expenditures for those making them. However, if a macroeconomic view is broad enough, they may not be income as defined in national income accounting.

borrowing for economic development the excess of debits over credits on current account may not present a problem, but often a deficit on current account is a clear sign of financial difficulty because it indicates a net outflow of income. Internally the effect is the same as that occurring in a recession. Indeed, a sharp rise in import value, resulting from a sharp increase in oil prices, was a major factor in the early part of the U.S. recession of 1973–1975.

CAPITAL ACCOUNT ITEMS

Loans, investments, and amounts transferred to settle debts are recorded in the capital account. This section of the BOP thus includes bank and other short-term loans to foreign firms and institutions, purchases of foreign stocks and bonds (generally termed *portfolio* investment), purchases of foreign business firms or establishment of branch offices or subsidiary firms abroad (*direct* investment), and transfers of financial assets to settle debt.[32] Direct investments, portfolio investments, and loans are presumed to be made to obtain returns in the form of interest, dividends, profits, or capital gains. Hence their amounts should depend on relative interest rates and relative rates of return on real capital assets (rates of profit). Transfers of financial assets for debt settlement are presumed to be made because debt must be settled in some internationally acceptable form.

Clearly, various classifications may be used for items in the capital account—direct and portfolio investment, private and government lending and investing, long-term and short-term loans and investments, and so on. Whatever categories are used, it is usual to separate long-term from short-term capital movements, because long-term capital flows are presumably motivated primarily by expected return. Short-term capital flows may occur for many reasons: (1) the need to finance trade, as in the case of an increase in accounts receivable when collections are slow; (2) the *flight of capital* motivated by fear of loss from anticipated government restrictions or confiscation; (3) *exchange rate speculation* motivated by hope of gain from differences in interest rates; (4) *interest arbitrage* motivated by hope of gain from differences in interest rates; or simply (5) a need to settle debt. Only a part—and probably quite a small part—of short-term capital flow is motivated by hope of gain from interest rate differentials.

Long-Term Capital Flows

Long-term capital flows include the purchase of foreign stocks and bonds, the purchase of foreign firms, and the establishment of branches and subsidiaries abroad. Capital movements are customarily treated as long-term if the original maturities of loans or investments are more than one year or are indeterminate. Since some line must be drawn between purchase of stock as one form of portfolio investment and purchases made as direct investment, the U.S. Department of Commerce counts ownership of 10 percent or more of the equity of a firm as direct investment.

As previously mentioned, retained earnings of foreign subsidiaries are not included in U.S. BOP figures. Therefore, the total long-term investment shown by adding the

---

[32]BOP figures are especially inadequate as measures of the direct investment that can occur without a flow of capital internationally—for example, when subsidiaries obtain funds locally or when they retain earnings (as long as the parent company retains enough ownership to justify their classification as direct investments).

figures from BOPs over a period of years is less than the total U.S. long-term capital invested abroad. Total investment is estimated from time to time in Treasury Department surveys of U.S. investment abroad. Any comparison of foreign investment amounts shown in the BOP with gross private domestic investment (GPDI) must take into account the conceptual differences involved.

The U.S. government makes relatively little direct investment abroad, but many countries which have much more government ownership of industry make such investments in sizable amounts.

Portfolio investment is presumably motivated by desire for interest or dividend return and for capital gains on stocks. Relative interest rates, with adjustment for risk differences, are a significant factor in determining the amount of portfolio investment. For statistical purposes, since foreign branches and subsidiaries abroad are treated as residents of foreign countries their loans and investments are not reported in the BOP. Loans by U.S. banks to their branches abroad, borrowings from their branches abroad, and other foreign loans and borrowings are reported, however. Of course, most such flows are short-term.

Short-Term Nonliquid Capital Flows

Short-term capital flows include bank loans and similar short-term fund movements which would be hard to liquidate quickly without loss. Such loans are normally held to maturity or longer. Like long-term capital flows, they are presumably motivated by opportunities for gain resulting from higher return, or by opportunities to make loans when domestic loan demand is relatively low.

Allocations of SDRs

In the 1960s major countries agreed that there did not appear to be enough gold for final settlement of international debt. World trade was increasing much more rapidly than was the amount of gold held by monetary authorities. It was not thought desirable to raise the price of gold, and dollar holdings were increasing rapidly. The proportion of dollars to other reserve assets was becoming unduly high. Major industrial countries therefore agreed, and members of the IMF voted by a large majority, to create special drawing rights (SDRs), mentioned earlier. SDRs were allocated to all member countries except a few which declined to participate, and allocations were recorded in BOP statements.

There has been some dispute whether allocation of SDRs should be recorded above or below the line, wherever it is drawn in the BOP. If recorded above the line, as is usually done, countries receiving allocations show increased holdings of reserve assets, and hence presumably a better financial position.[33]

Errors and Omissions

An errors and omissions item, needed because data are obtained from many different sources, could be placed almost anywhere in the BOP, since by definition it is not known where errors occurred. It is usually placed near the short-term capital item, however,

---

[33]It may be argued, however, that if a country had the same deficit in two successive years but received an allocation of SDRs the first year and none the second year, the BOP would show less increase (or no increase) in reserve assets the second year, even though the country's trade and investment picture had not changed at all. Is that analytically helpful in evaluating the country's financial situation?

because it is believed that more errors and omissions occur in that item than in others. For a number of years, the errors and omissions item in the U.S. BOP was a debit, and it was thought that this largely reflected a failure to report outflows of funds for short-term investment in foreign countries. Perhaps transfers to numbered Swiss bank accounts were part of the flow. Had errors been random it was unlikely they would consistently have been on one side of the BOP.

Settlement Items

The major problem in BOP classification and analysis is in connection with settlement items—items passively received or given up in settlement of debt.[34] Reserve assets have always been regarded as settlement items since their presumed purpose is to settle debt.[35] In addition to reserve assets, for many years only liquid liability items were classified as settlement items but recently the great difficulty of determining liquidity has been recognized. In an earlier period, liquid U.S. claims on foreigners (liquid assets) were not treated as settlement items, on the ground that the U.S. government could not under most conditions confiscate such assets and use them in settling foreign debt; but recently the absurdity of treating liquid private assets and liquid private liabilities differently was recognized. Previously, a U.S. resident who deposited funds in a bank in Canada was regarded as making an investment, but if the Canadian bank then redeposited the same amount of funds in a bank in the U.S. it was regarded as obtaining a settlement of debt!

In the 1960s, since in practice the U.S. government would not release gold to private foreign holders of claims on U.S. banks, it was questioned whether such items were settlement items. Clearly, they were not held as potential claims on the U.S. gold stock, and this raised the possibility that such claims were held by foreigners as working balances, to obtain interest, or for some other purpose. In the 1970s, when U.S. gold was no longer released at all, questions began to be raised about the significance of balances acquired and held by foreign governments and official agencies.[36] Were they desired rather than simply passively held in settlement of debt?[37] As noted in the body of the chapter, these questions led to the discontinuation of publication of the liquidity balance

[34]The distinction between liquid assets held because of a *desire* for additional liquidity and those passively accepted as settlement items was stressed by Charles P. Kindleberger, *Balance-of-Payments Deficits and the International Market for Liquidity*, Essays in International Finance, No. 46 (Princeton, N.J.: Princeton, 1965).

[35]Although reserve assets supposedly should be sufficient to meet temporary deficits, trade deficits alone have sometimes exceeded the nominal value of reserve assets held by a government. Rapid inflation, slow growth in real income, and rapidly increasing consumption expenditures may create large current account deficits. An attempt is made to borrow to meet the deficit temporarily. See, for example, Robert Ball, "Bankruptcy, Italian Style," *Fortune*, February 1975, pp. 88–92, 146–152.

[36]A review of the changing role of gold in the international monetary system may be found in a special issue of the review published by the Federal Reserve Bank of San Francisco, *Gold*, Winter 1974–1975.

[37]Among a number of attempts to develop a model of the demand for international reserve assets, see M. June Flanders, *The Demand for International Reserves*, Princeton Studies in International Finance, No. 27 (Princeton, N.J.: Princeton, 1971). She found that none of the posited independent variables produced high correlations, either singly or in multiple correlation analysis, with the ratio of reserve assets to imports. The ratio itself ranged from about 5 percent to about 180 percent. The majority of countries had ratios between 30 percent and 60 percent. The reader can benefit from a careful examination of her list of variables (op. cit., pp. 24 ff.).

and the official settlements balance, though the latter can still be calculated from published data.

Meantime, monetarist economists pointed to the importance of the money account balance's ability to affect the domestic money supply and hence affect inflation and the exchange value of the dollar.

Much of the problem arises from a penchant to regard one statistic as "the" measure of the BOP situation. A surplus or deficit, however measured, was sought as "the" indicator just as the rate of unemployment is widely regarded as "the" indicator of the unemployment situation. There certainly is justification for examining BOP and unemployment data in detail rather than relying on a deficit or unemployment-rate figure alone. And the question of what are settlement items when debt doesn't have to be settled between countries because the exchange value of currencies may be permitted to fall or rise, clearly presents an enigma.

QUESTIONS FOR DISCUSSION

1 Are exports debits or credits in the BOP? Are exports of capital debits or credits? Explain.

2 What is the difference in financial position between a country with a deficit on current account and a country with a deficit in its "basic balance," but not on current account?

3 Changes in reserve assets and in liquid liabilities to foreigners are considered to be payments or settlements items in BOPs, while changes in nonliquid short-term capital items are not. Why the difference in treatment? (Incidentally, for some time the United States also distinguished between short-term liquid liabilities and short-term liquid assets, recording the former as payments items and the latter above the "payments" line. Explain this classification also.)

4 In the first quarter of 1974, a U.S. government grant to India of $2 billion ($8 billion at an annual rate) enabled India to repay some previous loans. Explain the effect of the grant and the loan repayments on the current account balance, on the "basic" balance, and on the official settlements balance in the U.S. BOP.

5 Explain the following quotation: "An increase in liquid liabilities to foreigners no longer represents the effects of past efforts to defend the dollar nor the probability of being required to do so in the future." (*Balance of Payments Trends*, 2d quarter, 1974).

6 Should gold be considered to be a payments item (reserve asset) or a current account item (export or import)? Why?

7 Is the size of the net exports item in GNP a good indicator of the importance of international transactions to an economy? Why or why not?

8 Since retained earnings of foreign subsidiary companies do not show up in U.S. BOP figures, what can be concluded about the size of foreign investment compared to the sum of capital export figures shown in BOPs for past years?

9 CARE packages, remittances made through banks, and government foreign aid are included in the grants and remittances item in the BOP. What are the probable offsetting credit entries for each of these three items, in the U.S. BOP?

10 What has been the effect of the growth of multinational firms on the size of short-term capital flows? Explain.

SUGGESTED REFERENCES

U.S. BOP accounting before the change in the spring of 1976 is clearly explained in three articles in recent issues of the reviews of two Federal Reserve Banks: Norman S. Fieleke, "Accounting for the Balance of Payments," Federal Reserve Bank of Boston, *New England Economic Review*, May/June 1971, pp. 2–15; Christopher Bach and Anatol Balbach, "The New Look for the Balance of Payments," Federal Reserve Bank of St. Louis, *Review*, August 1971, pp. 8–11; and John Pippenger, "Balance of Payments Deficits: Measurement and Interpretation," Federal Reserve Bank of St. Louis, *Review*, November 1973, pp. 6–14. The first article is a general review, and the others add comments on recent changes and interpretations.

Convenient statistical data on important items in the U.S. BOP were until early 1976 presented in *U.S. Balance of Payments Trends*, issued quarterly by the Federal Reserve Bank of St. Louis; in early 1976 the title of the release was changed to *U.S. International Transactions and Currency Review*. The trade balance, balances on goods and services, and balance on current account can readily be calculated from figures in this release. More detailed figures are found in the *Survey of Current Business*, published by the U.S. Department of Commerce.

Sources which may be consulted concerning the interpretation of BOP data after the change in publication practices in 1976 include: Normal S. Fieleke, *What is the Balance of Payments?* (Boston: Federal Reserve Bank of Boston, 1976) and Janice M. Westerfield, "A Lower Profile for the U.S. Balance of Payments," Federal Reserve Bank of Philadelphia, *Business Review*, November/December 1976, pp. 11–17. The latter reviews the ways in which changes in the international monetary system and in the complexity of international capital movements have affected the significance of published BOP figures.

The *International Economic Report of the President*, issued annually since 1973, is useful for a review of U.S. international economic problems and policies. Readers may also benefit from the perspective provided by such articles as Hans H. Helbling, "Recent and Prospective Developments in International Trade and Finance," Federal Reserve Bank of St. Louis, *Review*, May 1974, pp. 15–22, for long-run comparisons of such indicators as relative inflation, relative labor costs, demand for petroleum and imports of petroleum, and the rise in total U.S. imports as a percent of U.S. GNP.

An overall review of U.S. BOP concepts was provided in *The Balance of Payments Statistics of the United States*, Report of the Review Committee for Balance of Payments Statistics to the Bureau of the Budget, April 1965. Minor changes in concepts in 1971 were reported in articles cited above. The review of the Advisory Committee on the Presentation of the Balance of Payments Statistics, issued in 1976, is also significant.

Discussion of events of the early 1970s and their impact on balance of payments analysis is covered in recent *Economic Reports of the President*; for this aspect, see especially the reports of 1972 and 1975.

A discussion which supplements this chapter is found in Robert M. Stern, *The Balance of Payments* (Chicago: Aldine, 1973), Chap. 1, "Balance of Payments Concepts and Measures." The interpretation of various measures of balance in the BOP was discussed in two articles published by Federal Reserve Banks in 1975: Patricia M. Kuwayama, "Measuring the United States Balance of Payments," Federal Reserve

Bank of New York, *Monthly Review*, August 1975, pp. 183–194, and Donald S. Kemp, "Balance-of-Payments Concepts—What Do They Really Mean?" Federal Reserve Bank of St. Louis, *Review*, July 1975, pp. 14–23.

Data on BOPs of most countries are published by the IMF in *International Financial Statistics*, monthly, and *Balance of Payments Yearbook*, annually. Monthly loose-leaf issues of the *Yearbook* are also available.

Chapter 3

Balance of Payments Adjustment Processes

We found in Chapter 2 that there are a number of measures of a surplus or a deficit in various subparts of the BOP. These measures are useful in analysis, but since a deficit on current account, for example, may be offset by a surplus on long-term capital account, such a deficit may not necessarily be crucial. The most significant deficits or surpluses when fixed exchange rates were common were those measured by the liquidity balance, the official settlements balance, or the money account balance. A liquidity deficit involves an increase in liquid liabilities to foreigners and/or a loss of reserve assets. An official settlements deficit is the same, but the only increases in liquid liabilities counted are those to foreign governments and central banks. A money account deficit involves a loss of international assets or other foreign account changes which may affect the money supply through its base (bank reserves and currency).

Do deficits and surpluses set in motion other changes? Do these changes tend to reduce the deficits or surpluses? Under what conditions do such changes occur and how do they operate? We try to answer these questions in this chapter.

BOP theory gives affirmative answers to the first two questions. This is not to say that every deficit eliminates itself. BOP adjustment processes may work poorly, they may be interfered with, and their effects may not be sufficient, even if they work well, to eliminate deficits completely. Before examining the processes of adjustment in BOPs balances of payments, a discussion of the concept of equilibrium in the BOP is useful.

THE CONCEPT OF EQUILIBRIUM IN THE BALANCE OF PAYMENTS

Equilibrium in the BOP may be most easily understood by considering three questions. First, what is equilibrium? Second, what is an equilibrium exchange rate? Third, what is equilibrium in the BOP? Since equilibrium in the BOP is an equilibrium of flows over time, not an equilibrium of offering prices at a given time, its definition involves some problems.

The Concept of Equilibrium

Equilibrium is an important concept in economic theory. It means a condition in which changes cease to occur in some variable because forces affecting this variable are equalized, and it has been assumed that the forces do not change. The most common reference is to price equilibrium. A price is said to be an *equilibrium price* if, under given conditions, it has no further tendency to rise or fall, because demand and supply are equal. At any higher price supply is usually greater than demand, causing the price to fall; at any lower price demand is usually greater than supply, causing the price to rise.[1]

The Equilibrium Rate of Exchange

In international finance, price equilibrium would refer to exchange rates. The equilibrium exchange rate would be that rate at which there would be no tendency, under given conditions, for it to rise or to fall, because demand and supply for foreign exchange would be equal. Because demand and supply for foreign exchange arise from debit and credit items in BOPs, equilibrium for an exchange rate also implies some form of equilibrium in the BOP.[2] That is, if the exchange rate is at an equilibrium point, the BOP items which give rise to a demand for foreign exchange must equal those which give rise to a supply of

---

[1]Although upward sloping demand curves are not likely to exist, backward sloping supply curves may cause an unstable equilibrium point in the foreign exchange market. A fall in an exchange rate from such a point, for example, may induce both more demand and more supply. See Fritz Machlup, "The Theory of Foreign Exchanges," *Economica*, Vol. VI (New Series), November 1939, pp. 357–397. See also Leland B. Yeager, *International Monetary Relations*, 2d ed. (New York: Harper & Row, 1976), Chap. 8. We develop this point more fully in Chap. 9.

[2]Barter items and gifts and grants of goods and services should be excluded, since they do not involve purchase or sale of foreign exchange. However, because these items involve equal debits (for example, gifts) and credits (for example, exports), their exclusion does not affect the relationship of demand and supply for foreign exchange.

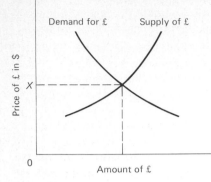

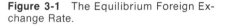

Figure 3-1 The Equilibrium Foreign Exchange Rate.

foreign exchange. Figure 3-1 shows the demand for and the supply of foreign exchange as determinants of an exchange rate or price for a foreign currency, X being the equilibrium rate.[3]

Settlement items must be excluded, because with their inclusion total demand always equals total supply. Thus what Fritz Machlup termed the *accounting* BOP is an ex post concept (based on past transactions) in which total debits, as we have seen, always equal total credits. Machlup coined another term, *market balance*, for the amounts of foreign exchange demanded and supplied by those who are not trying to influence the exchange rate—that is, excluding "compensatory" settlement items.[4] Thus in analyzing market demand for and supply of foreign exchange, only items arising from the need to pay for goods and services or the desire to gain from investments or exchange rate fluctuations should be included.

With a few exceptions such as gifts and grants, items on the debit side of the BOP are those giving rise to a demand for foreign exchange, assuming that goods and services are priced in foreign currencies. Items on the credit side give rise to a supply of foreign exchange, on the same assumption. As for the United States, many items are priced in dollars, and foreign exchange transactions occur in foreign countries. Debit items give rise to a supply of dollars in a foreign country rather than to a demand for foreign currency in the United States. For example, if U.S. importers pay for goods priced in dollars, foreign exporters normally receive the dollars and exchange them at their banks for local currency needed to replenish inventories and pay wages and other costs.

Note that a demand for foreign currency *is* a supply of dollars, in any event. This is different from commodity and services markets, in which demand and supply are expressed as amounts demanded and supplied at

---

[3]Here we ask the reader to assume that in the foreign exchange market demand and supply curves have the usual downward and upward slopes. As noted, we return in Chap. 9 to the possibility of unstable equilibria arising from different slopes.

[4]Fritz Machlup, "Three Concepts of the Balance of Payments and the So-Called Dollar Shortage," *Economic Journal*, March 1950, pp. 46 ff.

various prices in dollars. The demand curve for a foreign currency at the same time constitutes a supply of dollars. If an English suit costs £30, the cost to importers is $150 per suit if the rate for the pound is $5, $120 if it is $4, $90 if it is $3, and $60 if it is $2. If we know or can estimate the demand for English suits at these various dollar prices, we know the demand for sterling for buying suits. This demand for sterling is the number of suits that can be sold at each dollar price times the dollar price, and that is also the supply of dollars. This can be indicated as shown in Figure 3-2.

   Note that the supply curve has a range in which it is positively sloped and probably elastic, a range in which it is inelastic, and a range in which it turns backward. Expressed simply, an elastic supply curve is one in which supply increases by more than 1 percent with a 1 percent rise in price. Backward slope in supply curves is characteristic in foreign exchange markets if the entire range or at least a wide range of rates is considered. For the moment, let us assume that the pound is worth more than it is now and consider the demand and supply only between the rates of $3 and $5 per pound, which existed for many years. For many years $2 was an unrealistically low value for the pound and $\frac{1}{2}$ an unrealistically high value for the dollar. We therefore ignore the upper part of the supply curve for dollars and the lower part of the demand curve for pounds thus disregarding the backward-sloping area. (We discuss the problem of backward-sloping supply curves later, in Chapter 9.) Ignoring these ranges, the supply curve has an upward slope.

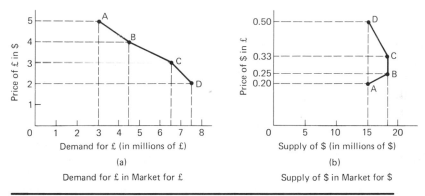

(a) Demand for £ in Market for £   (b) Supply of $ in Market for $

Exchange rate (dollars per pound)	Demand for suits (number)	Demand for pounds (millions of pounds)	Supply of dollars (millions of dollars)
5	100,000	3.0	15
4	150,000	4.5	18
3	200,000	6.0	18
2	250,000	7.5	15

Figure 3-2 Derivation of Demand and Supply Curves for Foreign Exchange. Points A, B, C, and D in a correspond to points A, B, C, and D in b.

Within the range of $5 to $4, there is a 20 percent decline in the price of sterling with a 50 percent increase in demand for it, an elasticity of 2.5. There is, however, only a 20 percent increase in the supply of dollars, or an elasticity of 1. (For every 1 percent fall in the exchange rate for sterling, there is a 1 percent rise in the supply of dollars.)[5] Between the range of $4 and $3, the supply of dollars is inelastic. (With a 1 percent fall in the exchange rate for sterling, there is no change in the supply of dollars.) Readers may compute other elasticities.

Equilibrium in the Balance of Payments

Now assume that exchange rates are fixed, or nearly so—that through some mechanism or government intervention, exchange rates hardly change. Then adjustment, if it occurs, must come in various BOP items without a change in the exchange rate. There must be changes such that surpluses or deficits are eliminated from the BOP, so that the *market* BOP is in equilibrium. If equilibrium is reached with a given exchange rate, that rate is termed an equilibrium exchange rate. Now it is evident why equilibrium in the BOP is not as simple a concept as that of an equilibrium price.

One additional consideration must be taken into account. The BOP is, as indicated in Chapter 2, a flow statement. Some of the flows are expenditures and income; others readjust stocks of financial and real assets held within and outside countries of which individuals and firms are residents. Early theory focused primarily on income and expenditure (current account) flows. Later in this chapter we give more attention to stock adjustment flows.

Income flows vary, and it is unlikely that deficits or surpluses can always be avoided. There are seasonal, cyclical, and secular trend movements in various income items. If a foreign exchange rate is an equilibrium rate, it must produce equilibrium in the BOP over some period of time. Some temporary deficits or surpluses are inevitable, and shifts in reserve assets and/or changes in liquid liabilities to foreigners are used to meet them.[6] An equilibrium rate of exchange must produce equilibrium in the BOP over some period long enough to allow for random fluctuations in various items.

A thoughtful reader may at this point raise the question: are there not mechanisms which may lead to readjustments in BOPs over periods of time, so that an equilibrium rate of exchange, if it exists, may remain unchanged? Clearly, if conditions change drastically, governments may act to affect certain items in the BOP. Their actions are discretionary adjustment mechanisms. There are also nondiscretionary adjustment mechanisms.

Three types of nondiscretionary mechanisms tend to affect, and sometimes to eliminate, deficits and surpluses. We consider them in the following order: (1) the "price-specie flow" mechanism, (2) shifts in real income, and (3) interest rate changes. We then consider: (4) discretionary government controls

---

[5] In our discussion, it is assumed that a 1 percent fall in a foreign exchange rate is the same as a 1 percent rise in the value of the local currency. This is technically not quite correct—a 50 percent fall in a foreign exchange rate would be a 100 percent rise in the value of the local currency. But for very small changes it is close to being correct, and the assumption is helpful in our examples.

[6] Keep in mind that liquid liabilities to foreigners are assets—reserve assets if they are held by governments or central banks—from the foreigners' points of view.

over BOP items and exchange rates, and (5) discretionary and nondiscretionary changes in exchange rates themselves as mechanisms affecting BOP items. Finally, we examine a recent view of the adjustment process as essentially changes in portfolio preferences, as individuals and firms adjust to changed preferences in response to an external factor like a change in the size of the money supply—a monetary theory of BOP adjustment.

THE PRICE-SPECIE FLOW MECHANISM

In the last part of the nineteenth century and the first part of the twentieth century, it was generally assumed by many economists and by most central bankers that the major tasks of a central bank were (1) to be a "lender of last resort," so that banks could borrow from the central bank when other resources were not available, and (2) to maintain the stability of the external value of a country's currency, as well as its internal value.[7] Once established, exchange rates were presumed to be fixed. The gold standard was adhered to by many major industrial countries. This meant that each country was ready to buy or sell gold freely at fixed prices. This in turn meant that a firm, bank, or individual could obtain at a fixed price sufficient gold from its government to obtain a fixed amount of another currency. The foreign currency could be obtained by shipping the gold to the foreign country and presenting it to the foreign government for conversion into that country's currency. The only cost involved was for shipping and insuring gold, plus a small fee if charged by the governments. Shipping was later largely dispensed with by asking governments or central banks to tag or "earmark" gold to indicate changes in ownership.

Most central banks had some required or desired relationship of gold holdings to liabilities—for example, the requirement that Federal Reserve Banks hold gold, gold certificates, or gold credits equal to a certain percentage of their deposit and note liabilities. Liabilities of central banks are, for the most part, currency plus deposit reserves of commercial banks. When gold flowed into a country as a result of a BOP surplus, payment by the government for the gold resulted in an increase in deposits in commercial banks, an increase in the reserves of commercial banks, an increase in liabilities of the central bank, and an increase in gold, gold certificate, or gold credit holdings of the central bank. With increased reserves available to the commercial banks, the money supply would increase unless actions were taken to counteract that result.[8] Similarly,

---

[7]The concept of a lender of last resort was extensively discussed in literature concerning policies of the Bank of England from 1797 to 1844. As a lender of last resort, the central bank has a responsibility to the financial system—although not to any particular financial institution—not to permit widespread bank failures. It was assumed that "last resort" lending would be at a penalty rate, thus discouraging such borrowing except in emergencies. Finally it was assumed that central banks should keep gold reserves above a critical minimum—the point at which public apprehension would lead to an attempt to convert paper currency into gold. For a recent discussion, see Thomas M. Humphrey, "The Classical Concept of the Lender of Last Resort," Federal Reserve Bank of Richmond, *Economic Review*, January/February 1975, pp. 2–9.

[8]In a classic study, using Canada's experience in the period 1900–1913 as an example, Viner examined the operation of the price-specie flow mechanism in practice. See Jacob Viner, *Canada's Balance of International Indebtedness, 1900–1913* (Cambridge, Mass.: Harvard, 1924).

when gold flowed out, reserves of central banks were reduced, causing a restriction of credit and of the money supply. To the extent that central banks were passive "lenders of last resort," the process worked automatically.

If the exchange rate (price) for any foreign currency rose slightly, banks and others could ship gold, obtain foreign currency, and thus avoid paying the higher rate for foreign exchange. This shift in demand for foreign exchange served to prevent a further rise in the exchange rate.

Of course such a shift would not occur unless the rate rose by an amount exceeding the cost of shipping and insuring gold. The point at which this occurred was termed the *gold export point*, and there was a similar *gold import point* on the other side of the fixed par value of any foreign currency, if it had a fixed par value. The par value was determined by the relative amounts of gold stated to be in each currency, or contained in them if gold coins were minted. Thus if the currency unit of the United States had contained 25 grains ($^{25}/_{480}$ of a troy ounce) of gold and if the British pound had contained 100 grains, the par exchange rate would have been $4 for £1. Actually the U.S. dollar was defined as 25.8 grains of gold $^9/_{10}$ fine, and the British pound as approximately 113 grains of fine (pure) gold. The gold export point in the United States would have been slightly above $4 per pound, the difference being the approximate cost of shipping and insuring gold. Banks would have found it advantageous to ship gold if the rate for sterling rose much above $4 per pound.

As noted, many economists in that period took the viewpoint that central banks should be primarily lenders of last resort, and that the exchange rate for each major currency should remain stable.[9] The idea of active management of the money supply in order to control a country's economy was not widely accepted as it now is. Far more reliance was placed on "natural" (nongovernmental) forces for slowing economic booms and for turnarounds leading to economic recoveries from recessions. There were exceptions, and evidence exists of many cases of central bank intervention.[10] Nevertheless, central banks were generally less active than now. Stability in the external value of a currency was given higher priority than stability in internal prices and incomes, though the priority was implicit. Prices, moreover, could and did fall significantly as well as rise. Even as late as 1920–1921, wholesale prices in the United States dropped by about 100 points, from an index of approximately 250 to about 150 (base, 1914 = 100), when the postwar boom collapsed and inventories were sharply reduced.

Under conditions of full employment, or almost full employment, an increased money supply will produce an almost proportionate increase in prices—inflation. In other circumstances the increase in prices may be less than

[9]Benjamin M. Anderson, *The Gold Standard Versus 'A Managed Currency'*, Chase Economic Bulletin, vol. V, no. 1, Mar. 23, 1925, presented a clear statement of this position. The central bank, in his view, was obligated to make loans to financial institutions to prevent panics; to raise short-term interest rates to check an outflow of gold; and also, if there were speculative excesses, to act to reduce speculation.

[10]Arthur I. Bloomfield, *Monetary Policy Under the International Gold Standard, 1880–1914* (New York: Federal Reserve Bank of New York, 1959) showed that central banks played a more active role than most textbooks indicated.

proportionate, since there may also be a significant increase in output and real income. The quantity theory of money, at that time embodied in the proposition that a change in the money supply would tend to lead to a nearly proportionate change in the price level, was a key element in this analysis. A decline in the belief in the "old" quantity theory of money, as its assumptions seemed invalid (neither total output in real terms nor velocity of money appeared to be constant), was one reason for more attention to other adjustment mechanisms discussed later in this chapter.

Theory of the Price-Specie Flow Mechanism

When any country experienced inflation, whether caused chiefly by internal or external forces, it was likely to find its exports reduced as the higher prices (higher in foreign currencies as well as in the domestic currency because of fixed exchange rates) made its goods harder to sell. It was also likely to find its imports increasing as higher domestic prices led to more purchases of foreign goods. As this occurred, its reserve assets would be diminished and at some point the money supply would decrease, leading to a fall in prices and wages, and this in turn to reduced imports and encouragement for exports. The deficit would begin to be reduced and balance would gradually be restored. As long as there was a deficit an outflow of reserve assets would continue and the process of readjustment would go on. Thus, automatically, any significant deficit would be reduced until a near balance was regained. The steps in the process are listed in Figure 3-3.

Similarly, any significant BOP surplus would lead to an accumulation of reserve assets, an increase in the money supply, a rise in prices, and hence to a decrease in exports and a stimulus to imports.[11] Gradually the surplus would be eliminated.

A Historical Example

Viner's study of Canada in the period 1900–1913 described a good example of the way in which the price-specie flow mechanism operated.[12] Canada was

[11]The central bank may try to prevent the increase in the money supply and the rise in prices, but then the surplus (and its pressure) continues.
[12]See Viner's study, referred to in fn. 8.

Country A (Deficit country)	Country B (Surplus country)
1 Loss of reserve assets	1 Gain in reserve assets
2 Reduction in money supply	2 Increase in money supply
3 Decline in domestic prices	3 Increase in domestic prices
4 Increase in exports and decrease in imports	4 Decrease in exports and increase in imports
5 Reduction in balance of payments deficit	5 Reduction in balance of payments surplus

Figure 3-3 The Price-Specie Flow Mechanism

engaged in long-term borrowing in England during that period, producing a surplus on capital account in Canada's BOP. English banks placed sterling balances to the credit of Canadian borrowers, and these short-term liquid asset debits in Canada's BOP temporarily offset the credits resulting from the long-term borrowing. As balances were used to buy imports, debits occurred in the current account. But much of the total was not used immediately. Canadian borrowers sold the sterling to their local banks. These banks converted the sterling balances into dollar balances by buying dollar exchange, thus transferring the balances from London to New York. Then, as Canadian banks needed increased reserves because of increased spending and borrowing in Canada in connection with economic development, Canadian banks transferred funds into Canada by the purchase of Canadian dollars and (when the exchange rate reached the gold import point) by the shipment of gold. Conditions provided an excellent test of anticipated results.

One surprising fact was that balances in New York were treated by the Canadian banks as secondary reserves—readily available and convertible into Canadian funds or gold whenever the banks desired. Thus these reserves made credit easier in Canada without the necessity of large gold shipments. Gold shipments were much smaller than anticipated. The easing of credit did provide a basis for an increase in the money supply in Canada.

Viner found that, in fact, Canadian prices did rise as credit became more easily available. Although world prices were rising, Canadian prices rose more, fulfilling the expectation that a BOP surplus would result in an increase in domestic over world prices.

Moreover, Viner found that certain prices increased more than others. The greatest increase occurred, as might have been expected, in prices of goods sold domestically in Canada. Prices of goods exported from Canada increased less, because Canadian exporters had to compete in world markets in which competition from other countries at unchanged prices was a factor restraining price increases. Prices of goods imported into Canada increased least because they were primarily determined in world markets, where expansion of money and credit in Canada had little effect.

With increased money and credit and higher prices in Canada, based in part on an inflow of gold, Canadian imports increased. The increase in imports relative to exports created an excess of merchandise debits in the BOP. This, together with the imports from England previously mentioned, offset the credits recorded as loans.

Thus the sequence of events was: loans to Canadian firms (credits in Canada's BOP), increase in balances held first in London and then in New York (short-term capital debits), some gold movements into Canada (debits), an expansion of money and credit in Canada, greater price increases in Canada than elsewhere, and an increase in imports relative to exports (debits exceeding credits). The gold standard price-specie flow mechanism had the expected results. Clearly countries were closely tied together in this situation. An independent monetary or fiscal policy would, at least in part, have offset the adjustment.

As James Ingram pointed out, instead of assuming that the inflow of borrowed capital was the initiating change, it could be assumed that change was initiated by internal economic growth, giving rise to investment opportunities for British capital.[13] Also it might have been assumed that both capital inflow and economic growth were causes. Incorporating the factor of internal economic growth and the resulting attractiveness of external investment by Britain adds to the completeness of the theory. It also explains the increase in Canadian exports which occurred, though it was less than the increase in imports. Otherwise, the increase in exports is not readily explained, since the basic theory without the factor of economic growth would lead one to expect a decline in exports.

The investment of British capital during the period 1880–1914 in the United States, Canada, and in various parts of the British empire is discussed more fully in Part Four. Here it may be noted that such capital moved freely, with little concern about confiscation, prevention of return remittance of interest payments, or other problems. Economic adjustments occurred relatively smoothly. The process of political fragmentation, significant since World War I, was not yet an important factor.

Note also that although the price-specie flow mechanism does not operate in the same way as it did early in the twentieth century, it still has an effect. Especially, an inflow of reserve assets (either gold or foreign currencies) may create a potential problem of inflation. The effect can be minimized by permitting exchange rates to float or by a central bank acting to offset the effects of a factor that may cause an increase in the money supply. However, if a central bank restricts the money supply sufficiently, interest rates, especially short-term rates, rise sharply, and this may lead to an inflow of capital and hence of gold and/or foreign exchange currencies.

An important conclusion is that under fixed exchange rates, for countries which accept them, relative rates of inflation and relative interest rates (allowing for differences in risk) remain approximately the same. Inflation is encouraged in some countries and restrained in others, unless actively combated by central banks.

THE REAL INCOME MECHANISM

Although various economists mentioned real income effects of BOP transactions, an extensive analysis of the real income mechanism came with acceptance of Keynesian theory. Keynes was concerned with analyzing the determination of the level of real income. Since national income accounting developed at approximately the same time, the two analyses fortunately combined in a theoretical framework and a number of hypotheses which could be tested empirically by using national income data.

---

[13]James C. Ingram, "Growth in Capacity and Canada's Balance of Payments," *American Economic Review*, March 1957, pp. 93–104.

Keynesian Theory

Keynes emphasized real income and was less concerned with effects of price level changes, although he discussed such changes in the latter part of his best known book, *The General Theory of Employment, Interest, and Money*. In that book he was chiefly concerned with factors determining national income or gross national product (GNP). Analysis of real income changes usually begins with the income identity:

$$C + I + G + NE = \text{GNP}$$

which can also be stated as $C + I + G + X - Im = \text{GNP}$, in which C is consumer spending, I is investment or business spending, G is government spending, NE is net exports or net spending by foreigners, X is exports, and Im is imports. All are expressed in real terms, that is, adjusted for changes in the general level of prices.

The equation is called an income identity because the sum of the items on the left, which represent spending, equals income (or output) shown on the right. Imports must be subtracted because spending for imports is not spending for output produced domestically.

Since spending by one party is income for another party, we can also use a different income-spending identity. This identity states that total spending equals consumption (C) plus saving (S) plus taxes (T) plus net transfers abroad in the form of gifts (FTr) or investment (NFI). Transfers abroad may be ignored if attention is focused on total investment, including what is usually a small amount of net foreign investment, on the left side. The full identities are:

$$C + I + G + X - Im = C + S + T + FTr + NFI$$

The Multiplier in a Closed Economy

For simplicity, we may begin with a closed economy—one without international transactions. For further simplicity, government may be ignored by assuming that its spending is in the form of either consumption or investment. Then

$$C + I = Y(\text{GNP})$$

If it is assumed that consumption is primarily a function of, or is dependent upon, income (the consumption function), a change in income would presumably be generated by a change in investment. (Failing that, fiscal policy might be used to increase income for consumers, a conclusion emphasized by some Keynesians but not necessarily flowing from Keynesian theory in all circumstances, since under many conditions investment may increase for various reasons.) How much would income increase if investment increased?

If
$$\Delta Y = \Delta C + \Delta I$$

or
$$\Delta I = \Delta Y - \Delta C$$

so that $$\frac{\Delta I}{\Delta Y} = \frac{\Delta Y}{\Delta Y} - \frac{\Delta C}{\Delta Y}$$

Taking the reciprocal,

$$\frac{\Delta Y}{\Delta I} = \frac{1}{1 - \dfrac{\Delta C}{\Delta Y}}$$

or $$Y = \frac{1}{1 - \dfrac{\Delta C}{\Delta Y}} \times \Delta I$$

Thus the increase in income would be $\dfrac{1}{1 - \dfrac{\Delta C}{\Delta Y}}$ times the increase in investment.

This expression is termed "the" multiplier (although there are many multipliers, since a multiplier is simply the increase in a larger variable generated from an increase in a smaller variable). The symbol b is often used for $\dfrac{\Delta C}{\Delta Y}$. For simplicity, assume that consumption depends on income as follows:

$$C = a + bY$$

If we are dealing only with *changes* in Y, a may be ignored, and $\Delta C = b\Delta Y$, or $b = \dfrac{\Delta C}{\Delta Y}$. The coefficient b is the marginal propensity to consume (MPC)—the ratio of a small increase in consumption to an accompanying small increase in income.

A refinement of the income identity can be used to take into account the fact that spending depends on income after taxes. Begin with the expenditure or income equation (identity). Assume that consumption is some constant plus some fraction of income after taxes, so that $C = a + b(Y - T)$. Assume that taxes are some constant, z, plus some fraction of income, so that

$$T = z + xY$$

Then $$Y = a + b(Y - z - xY) + I + G$$

$$Y = a - bx + b(1 - x)Y + I + G$$

$$Y[1 - b(1 - x)] = a - bz + I + G$$

$$Y = \frac{1}{1 - b(1 - x)} \, a - bz + I + G$$

Thus the multiplier for any change in investment or in government spending is $\dfrac{1}{1 - b(1 - x)}$, and the multiplier for a change in taxes is $\dfrac{1}{1 - b(1 - x)}$. Income (Y) will rise by $\dfrac{1}{1 - b(1 - x)}$ times any increase in investment or in government spending and by $\dfrac{1}{1 - b(1 - x)}$ times any decrease in taxes.[15] Keep in mind that b is the marginal propensity to consume (MPC), $1 - b$ is the marginal propensity to save (MPS), and $1 - b(1 - x)$ is the marginal propensity to save out of disposable income (income after taxes).

The Multiplier in an Open Economy

Beginning with the expenditure equation for a closed economy without international transactions, $Y = C + I + G$, an open economy with international transactions may be indicated by adding X and Im, so that the equation becomes $Y = C + G + I + X - Im$. Using the alternative expression for income, $Y = C + S + T$ (ignoring FTr and NFI for simplicity), it is evident that

$$C + S + T = C + I + G + X - Im$$

or $$S + T = I + G + X - Im$$

or $$S + T - I + G = X - Im$$

That is, if $S + T > I + G$, $X > Im$ and there is a credit (positive) balance in the current account.[16] Hence there must be a debit balance in the capital account—either an outflow of capital motivated by desire for gain or an inflow of reserve assets and/or a decrease in liquid liabilities to foreigners.

Notice that if exports exceed imports, domestic spending is less than output. On the other hand, if imports exceed exports, spending (sometimes called *absorption* in this context) is greater than output. If this situation seems to create a problem—for example, if the excess of imports is too large or continues too long—the obvious remedies would seem to be either to increase output (if possible) or to reduce spending. We use this in a later analysis.

---

[14]The fraction $1-b$ is the marginal propensity to save (MPS) since in this simple example income is either consumed or saved.

[15]Note that a change in government spending has a greater effect on income than has a change in taxes of the same magnitude. Since b is simply a shorthand expression for $\dfrac{\Delta c}{\Delta y}$, and since the multiplier is $1 = \dfrac{\Delta c}{\Delta y}$, $1-b$ must be the marginal propensity to invest as well as the marginal propensity to save. Ex post saving and investment are equal, since in real terms what is saved (not consumed) is by the same token invested (held in the form of assets which give service over a period of time).

[16]Saving and taxes are leakages from the income stream, while investment and government spending return funds to the income stream. If insufficient funds are returned, spending by foreigners for a country's (net) exports may return the remaining funds necessary to balance saving and taxes.

What is the multiplier for a change in investment *or* exports? That is, by how much does income rise if either investment or exports increases by a small amount? Begin with the identity

$$C + G + I + X = C + T + S + Im$$

or $$G + I + X = T + S + Im$$

If temporarily we assume a balanced budget, $G = T$, then $I + X = S + Im$ and $\Delta I + \Delta X = \Delta \Delta S + \Delta Im$, or, if very small changes are assumed, $dI + dX = dS + dIm$.

Let us define marginal propensity to import *(MPIm)* as the increase in imports with an increase in income. Then, with very small changes assumed,

$$dIm = MPIm \times dY$$

So, $$dI + dX = (MPS + MPIm)\, dY$$

and $$\frac{dY}{dI} = \frac{1}{MPS + MPIm} \qquad \text{(holding } X \text{ constant)}$$

or $$\frac{dY}{dX} = \frac{1}{MPS + MPIm} \qquad \text{(holding } I \text{ constant)}$$

In an open economy, the multiplier is the reciprocal of the sum of *MPS* plus *MPIm*. The multiplier is the same for a change in investment *or* for a change in exports.[17] Although this multiplier is often referred to as the foreign trade multiplier, it is simply "the" multiplier for an open economy.

Now suppose that exports equal imports, and then exports increase. Do imports also increase by enough to restore balance? No. For since

$$dIm = MPIm \times dY = MPIm\, \frac{1}{MPS + MPIm} \times dX = \frac{MPIm}{MPS + MPIm} \times dX$$

the change in imports cannot be as great as the change in exports because *MPS* and *MPIm* are both fractions, and usually small fractions. Only if *MPS* were zero could the increase in *Im* be as great as the increase in X, and this is very unlikely. Most countries save *something* out of added income.

---

[17]Since saving and imports are both treated as leakages from the income stream, the *MPS* and the *MPIm* must be added to obtain the total propensity *not* to spend income for consumption. Note that here consumption means consumption out of domestic output only. Reference to the two views of income and output discussed in Chap. 2, and to Fig. 2-1, may be helpful. The analysis indicated at this point and other relationships were used by one economist to estimate the size of the *MPIm* for the United States; see Robert H. Scott, "The U.S. Marginal Propensity to Import: Estimates Derived from a Hicksian Model," *Malayan Economic Review*, April 1970, pp. 120–125. From data for 1951–1967, the *MPIm* appeared to be close to 0.1.

What is the effect on the trade balance (B, or $dX - dIm$)? Well,

$$dX - dIm = dX - \frac{MPIm}{MPS + MPIm} \times dX = \left(1 - \frac{MPIm}{MPS + MPIm}\right) \times dX$$

$$= \frac{MPS}{MPS + MPIm} \times dX$$

So the trade balance improves (B increases), but by less than the change in X, unless MPS is zero. (Since we assume there are both imports and exports—$MPIm$ is not zero—we assume changes in trade with changes in income.) Since B increases, but not as much as X, the income adjustment does not *entirely* restore balance.

The analysis may be expanded to include a discussion of a change in imports. An increase in imports reduces income and consumption (domestic). Consumption falls by the amount of the increase in Im, so dIm equals $-dC$. Income falls by

$$-dY = \frac{MPIm}{MPS + MPIm} \times dC$$

With a fall in income, imports fall by

$$MPIm \times dY = \frac{MPIm}{MPIm + MPS} \times dC$$

So the *net* "worsening" of the trade balance is

$$1 - \frac{MPIm}{MPS + MPIm} \times dIm = \frac{MPS}{MPS + MPIm} \times dIm$$

Thus the trade balance is "worsened" as long as MPS is greater than zero.

Both the MPC and the $MPIm$ are fractions, and so is the MPS. If the sum of the MPS out of disposable income, $1 - b(1 - x)$, plus the $MPIm$ were 1, a change in exports would have no net multiplier effect on income. The change in X would be offset by the change in Im and in S. Clearly, it is not likely that the sum of these two marginal propensities will total 1. In most countries, both the MPS and the $MPIm$ are less than $1/2$, in fact substantially less than $1/2$. Hence the multiplier effect of an increase or of a decrease in exports is usually significant.

In countries where exports constitute large fractions of GNP (for example, the Scandinavian countries, England, Japan) the foreign trade multiplier is very important quantitatively. Shortly after World War II it was remarked that "when the United States sneezes, Europe catches pneumonia," because a relatively small decline in income and in imports into the United States was accompanied by a much larger *percentage* decline in exports and income in European countries. As domestic output increased in Europe, this situation changed somewhat, but a recession in the United States may still be quite significant for foreign countries.

Foreign Repercussions

If exports of country A rise and, because of the multiplier, imports rise (but not as much as exports), the income in foreign countries decreases, but not as much as the increase in exports of country A. The rise in imports of country A means more export sales for foreign countries, and these partly offset the decline in income caused by rising imports from country A into the foreign countries.

Thus there are foreign repercussions of an increase in exports. The extent of such repercussions could be estimated if the marginal propensities to consume, to import, and to export in various countries were known. Since they are not precisely known, and in any event change frequently, only rough estimates can be made. It should be clear, however, that foreign repercussions initially help offset the original multiplier effect of a rise in exports. The repercussion effects diminish with successive rounds because all the marginal propensities are fractions, usually small fractions.

It should also be clear that, unless actions are taken to prevent it, the effect of the foreign trade multiplier, although partly offset by foreign repercussions, is to "export" booms and recessions from a country where they originate. In recessions imports fall, along with other consumption. This reduces income in foreign countries. With less income they import less, but the repercussion effect of the fall in their imports is not enough to offset the recessionary effect of the fall in their exports.

This analysis, then, tells us that an increase in exports of country A is partly offset by an increase in imports arising from the increased income produced by a rise in exports. It is also partly offset by repercussion effects which reduce exports. Increased exports by country A mean more imports by foreign countries, hence a reduction in their income, hence less consumption and less imports after a time. Part of the original increase in exports of country A is eliminated.

It might be thought that these effects could completely offset an increase in net exports, so that any BOP surplus would be temporary. However, the offset is only partial. It could be total only if the *MPIm* and the *MPS* were very high. If so, any increase in exports and hence in income would cause a large increase in imports, and the multiplier would be low, with not much increase in income resulting from an increase in exports. A situation in which an increase in exports would be entirely offset is possible to imagine but very unlikely. Hence an increase in exports does cause some change in the balance on current account, and the adjustment mechanism does not fully eliminate this change.[18]

---

[18]This was pointed out by Lloyd Metzler, "The Theory of International Trade," in Howard S. Ellis, ed., *A Survey of Contemporary Economics*, Vol. I (Homewood, Ill.: Irwin, 1948).

In summary: with no interference, the price-specie flow mechanism continues to operate as long as there is either a deficit or a surplus, and could eventually eliminate either one. Real income shifts generate other real income shifts which partly, but only partly, offset any deficit or surplus arising in the BOP. It might be expected or hoped that the price-specie mechanism together with real income shifts would cause eventual readjustment in the BOP even if there is some interference with the price-specie flow mechanism. But in practice the adjustment mechanisms do not seem to have worked very well.[19]

A monetary mechanism of adjustment also exists, but consideration of this mechanism is deferred to the end of this chapter, following discussion of the effects of interest rate changes, government controls, and exchange rate adjustments.

Historical Examples

During the depression of the 1930s, countries often tried to restrict imports in order to switch demand from imported to domestic goods in the hope that this would maintain income. It is clear from the preceding analysis that reduction in imports also reduces exports. Thus although domestic income might rise with a switch to domestically-produced goods, it would fall as a result of the multiplier effects of reduced exports. If foreign countries retaliated, as they frequently did, no country was likely to gain very much and benefits of trade were lost. This helps to explain why international trade and investment suffered *more* than domestic income during the 1930s, although both suffered severely.

By using another pair of concepts, the *income elasticity of demand for imports* and the *income elasticity of demand for a country's exports*, and comparing these for various countries, we can predict which countries are likely to have BOP surpluses and which to have deficits. Of course, other factors may cause surpluses and deficits, so we must use our predictions cautiously. Income elasticity of demand for imports is the percent increase in imports that accompanies a 1 percent increase in income. Income elasticity of demand for a country's exports is the percent change in exports that accompanies a 1 percent change in income. Countries with high income elasticities of demand for imports are likely to have deficits, while those with high income elasticities of foreign demand for their exports are likely to have surpluses. The two factors may sometimes offset each other, as perhaps in Japan, which has had both. On the other hand, the United States and the United Kingdom, although they have had about average income elasticities of demand for imports, have had very low income elasticities of foreign demand for their exports—and therefore might be expected to have deficits on current account.[20]

---

[19]Richard E. Caves commented that "the broad impression that one gets from discussions of these mechanisms . . . is that they are either weak or get short-circuited by government action"; Richard E. Caves, "The International Adjustment Mechanism," in *The International Adjustment Mechanism* (Boston: Federal Reserve Bank of Boston, 1970), p. 10.

[20]H. S. Houthakker and Stephen P. Magee, "Income and Price Elasticities in World Trade," *Review of Economics and Statistics*, May 1969, pp. 111–125.

EFFECTS OF CHANGES IN INTEREST RATES

Rising business activity is often accompanied, after it has continued for a time, by rising interest rates. The demand for funds rises more rapidly than the supply. The rise in interest rates may attract foreign capital.

Keep in mind that, as indicated earlier, there are many motives for international capital movements: hope of profit on foreign investment, fear of loss of wealth held at home, need to make international loans or investments in order to gain trade, hope of speculative gain from exchange rate changes, and hope of gain from changes in interest rates. Only that part of international capital movements affected by changes in interest rates concerns us at this point. Although rising interest rates may attract capital from abroad, it is not possible to conclude that the magnitude of such movement is always large.[21]

With the rise in business activity in the United States in the early 1960s, there was much discussion of this point, and of a government effort termed "Operation Twist," intended to raise short-term interest rates relative to long-term rates, thus "twisting" the yield curve which shows relationships between yields and varying maturities. The success of Operation Twist was debatable, one study concluding that although short-term rates rose, this may have been largely because of the innovation of negotiable CDs, which paid sufficient interest to attract funds, thus causing other short-term rates to rise.[22] In any event, the effort did not result in much inflow of capital, and the problem of capital outflow continued.

To the extent that there is an inflow of capital with an increase in exports, the magnitude of the rise in business activity may increase. Additional foreign capital provides more funds for investment, and through the multiplier effect additional investment causes more consumption. Thus interest rate changes may increase surpluses or deficits in the BOP. If the central bank acts to raise interest rates in order to curtail the rise in business activity, the resulting attraction of some foreign capital may partly offset the bank's action and make its objective difficult to achieve.

An example of this situation was West Germany in the 1950s. Business

---

[21]See Philip W. Bell, "Private Capital Movements and the U.S. Balance-of-Payments Position," in *Factors Affecting the United States Balance of Payments*, studies compiled for the Subcommittee on International Exchange and Payments of the Joint Economic Committee (Washington, D.C.: Government Printing Office, 1962) and Peter B. Kenen, "Short-Term Capital Movements and the U.S. Balance of Payments," and Benjamin J. Cohen, "A Survey of Capital Movements and Findings Regarding their Interest Rate Sensitivity," in *The United States Balance of Payments*, Part I, "Current Problems and Policies," Hearings before the Joint Economic Committee, July 1963 (Washington, D.C.: Government Printing Office, 1963), pp. 153–191 and 192–208. Bell found very little interest rate sensitivity of capital flows, but opinions differ.

[22]One study by Franco Modigliani and Richard Sutch, "Debt Management and the Term Structure of Interest Rates: An Empirical Analysis of Recent Experience," *Journal of Political Economy*, Supplement, August 1967, pp. 546–561, was inconclusive because of inability to distinguish between effects of the development of a market for negotiable CDs and of Operation Twist. The focus of Operation Twist on trying to raise short-term interest rates may be explained thus: (1) short-term interest rates fluctuate more than long-term interest rates, and (2) many foreign investors (especially banks and governments) prefer relatively safe, short-term liquid investments.

activity was increasing and exports were rising. Both reserve assets and foreign capital flowed in, and attempts to prevent inflation by increasing interest rates and tightening the money supply led to more inflow of capital and more exports.[23]

Interest rate changes may thus be an obstacle to readjustment of BOPs, as a country tries to raise interest rates to limit a boom but finds that the rise in interest rates attracts foreign capital. A clear distinction must be made between the international effects of interest rates on capital movements and the internal effects of interest rates in reinforcing the price-specie flow mechanism. A rise in interest rates internally was considered appropriate for a country with rising income, rising prices, and a loss of reserve assets. Tightening credit would tend to cause a slower increase or perhaps a decrease in the money supply and a decrease or slower rise in nominal income and prices.[24] Thus it would help reduce a current account BOP deficit. But a rise in interest rates may attract international capital flows. An inflow of capital could cause a rise in business activity, resulting in a partial offset to the adjustment process.

We now begin to find that consideration of the capital account complicates BOP analysis. Most early theory focused attention on the current account. The growing importance of the capital account—that is, of financial assets and their international movements—forces more attention to financial changes.

Deficits on current account are called *flow* deficits because they represent an outflow greater than the inflow. As flow deficits continue, if the money supply does not increase, money in the hands of the domestic public is reduced. At some point, the public should begin to respond to the loss of nominal money by reducing expenditures. Thus these deficits can continue indefinitely only if financed by the creation of credit by the monetary authority.[25] The deficit might be reduced by slowing or stopping the growth of the money supply or by policies that divert spending from imported goods and services to nontraded goods and services. Of course, for such policies to succeed, the country must be able to increase output of the nontraded goods and services.

Deficits in the capital account are called *stock* deficits because they result from efforts to change the composition of stocks of financial and real assets held in portfolios. Foreign investments are attractive, perhaps because of a domestic increase in the money supply which results in an excess of supply over demand for money. Stock deficits are self-terminating at some point in a static economy, as portfolio adjustment is completed. Of course, if the economy grows, portfolio desires change. Stock deficits do *not* reduce domes-

---

[23]For a detailed discussion, see Leland B. Yeager, *International Monetary Relations*, 2d ed. (New York: Harper & Row, 1976), Chap. 24.

[24]Arthur I. Bloomfield, *Monetary Policy under the International Gold Standard, 1880–1914* (New York: Federal Reserve Bank of New York, 1959) showed that although central banks generally did raise discount rates when there was a loss of reserve assets, they did not often raise them enough to cause the monetary base (bank reserves and currency) to shrink.

[25]The type of analysis presented here was originated by Harry G. Johnson among others. See, for example, Harry G. Johnson, "Towards a General Theory of the Balance of Payments," in *International Trade and Economic Growth* (Cambridge, Mass.: Harvard, 1958).

tic income as current account deficits do, *nor do they reduce wealth*. Residents are simply shifting from domestic financial assets to foreign investment. There is no assurance that either the adjustment mechanisms previously discussed or exchange rate changes will eliminate such deficits. If it is desired to halt them, the appropriate policy is some form of control over the acquisition of foreign assets through foreign lending and investment. Controls might be imposed, for example, if the monetary authority lacked, or believed it lacked, the reserve assets needed to meet a deficit until it terminated. Although such a situation was not always analyzed in these terms, it suggests why controls over capital flows are more widely accepted than controls over current account payments. Let us turn, then, to the role of the government and the controls governments may use in limiting or halting deficits or surpluses.

GOVERNMENT CONTROLS

Governments have two significant reasons for establishing controls over foreign payments and receipts. First, governments may find that they have inadequate reserves to finance deficits and/or that they are increasing liquid liabilities to foreigners on a scale that threatens to create future difficulties if redemption of the liabilities is requested. Second, changes in exchange rates affect such broad segments of an economy that governments often think it necessary to support exchange rates within some range or *band*, just as they think it necessary to try to control inflation or deflation, even though they may take no action to limit fluctuations of individual commodity and service prices.

Exchange control is broader than trade controls, since it controls financial transactions. These may be current account payments and receipts or capital account transactions, while trade controls affect only current account items.

Theory of Exchange Control

Exchange control is usually resorted to because outpayments are greater than receipts. Depreciation of the value of a country's currency and a rise in values of foreign currencies would result if a free market in foreign exchange were permitted. The government must therefore force those who obtain foreign exchange through exports and other transactions to sell their foreign exchange to the government or designated banks. At the same time, it must allocate this foreign exchange to importers and other purchasers of foreign exchange. Since demand is greater than supply in these circumstances, some of those who wish to buy foreign exchange cannot be permitted to do so. The situation is shown in Figure 3-4, in which it is assumed that the German government attempts to keep the exchange value of the mark at 40 cents (equivalent to $2\frac{1}{2}$ marks per dollar). Demand and supply in a free market would result in an equilibrium rate of 25 cents (equivalent to 4 marks per dollar). The government must force the sale of the supply of foreign exchange, OA, to it or to designated banks, and must allocate that supply to those who want to buy it. The government must designate in some way those who may purchase foreign exchange or the

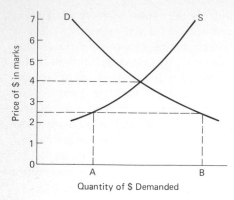

Figure 3-4 Foreign Exchange Market Under Exchange Control.

purposes for which it may be purchased. Quantity AB would be purchased but this is legally prevented. Black markets usually begin to develop in foreign exchange.

Exchange control restricts imports so that they are less than they would be under free market conditions. If a country maintaining exchange control devalues its currency, imports increase if permitted. If, in Figure 3-4, Germany devalued the mark from $2^{1}/_{2}$ marks per dollar to a level closer to 4 marks to the dollar, the supply of foreign exchange would increase and therefore the purchase of foreign exchange for imports could increase. Releasing pressure for imports, may lead to less pressure for domestic spending, and inflation may actually diminish. Since more of the demand can be satisfied, prices of goods imported and produced domestically may fall.[26]

Spread of Exchange Controls After 1931

The widespread use of exchange controls in the twentieth century, aside from some use during World War I, began with the international financial crisis of 1931. It was found that the Kredit-Anstalt, a large branch banking institution in Austria, became insolvent. Banks in New York, London, and Paris, had they acted together, perhaps could have prevented spread of panic. But Austria and Germany had just announced a customs union, eliminating customs duties between the two countries; German banks has relatively large deposits in Austria, so any aid to Austria was likely to aid Germany. French banks and the French government, especially, were unwilling to take steps which would have this effect. Panic spread from Austria to Germany, and German banks had to restrict deposit withdrawals. English banks, with large deposits in German banks, also came under pressure as German bank failures were expected. (Meanwhile, of course, thousands of banks were failing in the United States, and although these failures were not particularly related to the international

---

[26]See Edward M. Bernstein, "Strategic Factors in Balance of Payments Adjustment," IMF *Staff Papers*, August 1956, pp. 166–168, and Egon Sohmen, "The Effect of Devaluation on the Price Level," *Quarterly Journal of Economics*, May 1958, p. 97.

situation, the psychological impact throughout the world was negative.) The value of sterling fell in the foreign exchange market, there was an outflow of gold, and England was under heavy financial pressure. On Sunday, September 20, 1931—such announcements were frequently made on Sundays while financial markets are closed—England abandoned the gold standard. As various countries followed suit, exchange rates began to fluctuate, and many countries began to institute controls over foreign exchange. By the end of World War II more than a decade later, almost all countries in the world except the United States and a few small countries had established direct controls over foreign exchange transactions.

Controls established were of three main types. At first, in some major countries (notably the United States and Britain) the controls were *indirect*, consisting simply of purchase and sales of foreign exchange by the governments, acting through exchange stabilization funds. Many countries, including Britain, also established a *single official rate* of exchange, while a number of countries, especially in Europe and in Latin America, established *multiple rates*. Finally, because of the extensive holdings of sterling deposits by banks, firms, and governments in many countries, a system of exchange control was evolved in Britain to *restrict transfers of ownership of bank deposits.*[27] Transfer was quite strictly limited in some cases and quite freely permitted in others. For example, free convertibility was permitted for sterling in accounts held by Americans, since otherwise Americans were very unlikely to deposit new funds, and Britain was anxious to attract such funds in order to maintain its extensive international banking operations.

Government-to-Government Trade

World War II brought direct control over foreign trade and foreign exchange by almost all governments. Foreign lending and investment almost came to a halt, and much trade was conducted under special government programs, of which the best known was probably the lend-lease program of the United States. Between many pairs of countries, especially those which were enemies, there was no legal trade, and no exchange rate of any significance existed. The international financial system had largely disintegrated, and it seemed necessary to establish a new system, especially if international lending and investment, as well as international trade, were to be expanded.

FLUCTUATING EXCHANGE RATES

If adjustments are not made in price levels, real income, or through imposition of government controls, they must come—if deficits or surpluses persist long

---

[27]Paul Bareau pointed out that in such areas as Kuwait, which was within the sterling area, exchange controls were not likely to be as effective as in Britain; hence some funds no doubt escaped from control. See Paul Bareau, "Exchange and Payments Control and Their Influence on Foreign Trade," in *International Banking and Foreign Trade*, lectures delivered at the Eighth International Banking Summer School, Christ Church, Oxford (London: Europa, 1955), p. 42.

enough or are great enough—through changes in exchange rates.[28] Governments may try to maintain stable exchange rates, but change them at infrequent intervals by *devaluations* or *upward revaluations*. These changes imply sudden adjustments, usually by relatively large amounts. If governments do not make this attempt, exchange rates may "float"—depreciate or appreciate. Depreciation or appreciation is usually gradual, although in recent years it has sometimes been rapid. Such floating is, however, seldom permitted to respond entirely to forces of private supply and demand. In many cases governments seem to believe that it is necessary to intervene in fluctuations of exchange rates. Exchange rates are pervasive in their effects on prices of *all* exports and *all* imports of a country, and have indirect effects on prices of nontraded goods (home goods). Moreover, export sectors in most economies are relatively strongly organized, and likely to put pressure on a government to intervene if exchange rate movements affect them adversely. Even if theoretical arguments seem validly to suggest that floating exchange rates would not be harmful, many governments are reluctant to change from a system of fixed rates to one with less predictable results.

Nevertheless, in many periods exchange rates have fluctuated or floated, and when many exchange rates have been stable, some have floated as exceptions. Unfortunately, most of the experience with floating or flexible rates has been during and after World War I and during the Depression of the 1930s. Experience since early 1973 has hardly been long enough to draw conclusions, and this period also has been one of some economic disruption, because of the large BOP deficits incurred by many industrialized countries as a result of the rise in oil prices. The experience with floating rates by single industrialized countries independently is not very widespread, that of Canada being the most important.[29]

Our concern at this point is with the effects of officially imposed devaluation and with the depreciation which occurs if currencies are permitted to float. Although the discussion is couched in terms of devaluation and depreciation, with a little thought the principles may be applied to upward floats and revaluations.

Devaluation, the Terms of Trade, and the Balance of Payments

Two important questions now concern us. First, what effect does devaluation or downward floating of the exchange value of a currency have on the terms of

---

[28]This is the starting point of the argument, offered by Friedman and elaborated by Sohmen, that flexible or free market exchange rates are preferable to fixed rates. If adjustments in exchange rates are sometimes necessary because of relative changes over time in productivity and price levels in different countries, gradual fluctuation may be preferable to larger changes in exchange rates at longer intervals. We consider this and other arguments in Chap. 9. See Milton Friedman, "The Case for Flexible Exchange Rates," in *Essays in Positive Economics* (Chicago: University of Chicago Press, 1953) and Egon Sohmen, *Flexible Exchange Rates: Theory and Controversy* (Chicago: University of Chicago Press, 1961).

[29]A distinction is sometimes made between flexible exchange rates, which are permitted to fluctuate in accordance with market forces, and "floating" rates, which are permitted to fluctuate within some limits.

trade for the country? Second, is devaluation or downward floating likely to improve the BOP? Is it likely to increase exports and other credit items and/or to reduce imports and other debit items?[30]

Terms of Trade   It is frequently assumed that devaluation makes the terms of trade worse, since it means lower export and higher import prices, and thus, presumably, larger physical quantities of exports are shipped out in exchange for smaller quantities of imports. This may be true, but on careful examination we find that we must limit ourselves to that: it *may* be true.

Devaluation reduces export prices in *foreign* currency, and raises import prices in domestic currency. What we want to know, however, is the effect on both categories of prices in the *same* currency. Let us use the home currency for convenience. Devaluation raises import prices in the home currency (except where exchange control has existed, as discussed above). It also raises *export* prices in the home currency, because foreign demand increases as prices in terms of foreign currency seem cheaper. If the demand for exports is quite elastic, the impact would be significant. If the *supply* of exports were inelastic—for example, if a country were unable to significantly increase its output of export goods—the rise in price could be substantial. If at the same time import demand were elastic and the foreign supply of such goods were inelastic, import prices would rise very little. In such a situation, the terms of trade would improve.

There is no reason to believe that the foregoing situation is common, but neither is there proof that other situations are more likely. Joan Robinson thought that world demand for a country's exports is likely to be less elastic than the supply of its imports, because most countries specialize to some extent and therefore are likely to be more important factors in the world market for their exports than in the market for their imports. On these assumptions, devaluation makes the terms of trade worse, but we cannot be sure that these assumptions reflect common situations.[31]

Countries have generally resisted devaluations, perhaps because they thought their terms of trade might worsen, perhaps because devaluations signify financial weakness, perhaps because it was feared that the burden of repayment of foreign-currency-denominated debt would be increased. Actually, of course, if devaluation improves the BOP position, it may make servicing foreign debt easier.

Devaluation and the BOP: The Elasticities Approach   The first approach to the question whether devaluation would "improve" the BOP was an analysis of elasticities. At this point we assume that the foreign exchange market is like

---

[30]These questions were the subject of a lengthy debate. Machlup listed 15 articles, written between 1945 and 1955, each revising the conclusions reached by a previous writer. See Fritz Machlup, "The Terms-of-Trade Effects of Devaluation upon Real Income and the Balance of Trade," *Kyklos*, Fasc. 4, 1956, pp. 417–450.

[31]Yeager, op. cit., p. 202, discussed Joan Robinson's view and pointed out that after the French and Finnish devluations in 1957, their terms of trade seemed to improve somewhat.

other commodity and services markets, with upward-sloped supply curves and downward-sloped demand curves.[32]

Whether devaluation is likely to increase exports and restrict imports depends on the elasticities of supply and demand for goods and services. More precisely, if for simplicity we consider only two countries (A and B), it depends on four elasticities: the elasticity of the demand for exports of country A (elasticity of demand for imports in country B), the elasticity of demand for imports in country A, the elasticity of supply of goods in country A, and the elasticity of supply of goods in country B. For simplicity, some early theorists assumed that the elasticities of supply are infinite, on the assumption that there is unemployment in both countries. Then the important elasticities are the two elasticities of demand. If their sum is greater than 1, devaluation will improve the trade balance, because a 1 percent change in price (through a change in the exchange rate) will produce more than a 1 percent change in the combined increase in exports plus decrease in imports. If devaluation did not improve the trade balance, equilibrium would not be stable: devaluation would lead to further devaluation because the trade balance would become "worse," not better. The condition that the sum of the two demand elasticities must be greater than 1 for stable equilibrium to exist has been termed the Marshall-Lerner condition.[33]

A great deal of attention has been devoted to the elasticity conditions, with rather inconclusive results. The formula for determining how much, or even whether, devaluation will improve the BOP is complex, and empirical measurement of the elasticities very difficult. Considering only the current account, an equilibrium position is likely to be stable, because the Marshall-Lerner condition is likely to be met. World demand for the exports of country A is likely to be elastic because most countries have competition from exports of the same products from other countries. Demand for imports is likely to be elastic because many products are produced at home as well as imported. Buyers can shift from imported to home-produced goods of the same general nature. Many economists ridiculed the idea of an unstable equilibrium as implausible.[34] For the current account only, this seems reasonable. In Chapter 9 we consider whether the case is as clear-cut for the BOP as a whole (excluding settlement items).

If the stability condition is met, devaluation of an overvalued currency brings the rate closer to the equilibrium rate—or perhaps below it, if the

---

[32]Later in this book, this assumption is relaxed because a backward-bending supply curve is possible in foreign exchange markets in which capital movements play a large part.

[33]See the discussion of the Marshall-Lerner condition in Anne O. Krueger, "Balance-of-Payments Theory," *Journal of Economic Literature*, March 1969, pp. 1–26, esp. pp. 4–7. She derives the Marshall-Lerner condition formula, also derived in Leland B. Yeager, op. cit., Chap. 8, Appendix, and in other places. As Yeager points out, demand elasticities need not exceed 1 to insure a stable equilibrium point if supply elasticities are less than infinite, which is the more general case. This is sometimes termed the Robinson-Metzler condition.

[34]See, for example, Gottfried Haberler, "Monetary and Real Factors Affecting Economic Stability," *Banca Nazionale del Lavoro Quarterly Review*, September 1956, p. 97.

devaluation is too great. In any event, the rate will tend to move toward the equilibrium rate. If the stability condition is not met, devaluation might simply lead to the need for more devaluation, because in that case both the demand for and the supply of foreign exchange would increase with devaluation.

We would give more attention to the elasticities question if it were not for two major considerations. First, not only does the Marshall-Lerner condition seem plausible, but purchasing power parity theory, discussed in detail in Chapter 9, states that equilibrium exchange rates are those which tend to result in currencies having the same purchasing power in various countries, with allowances for transportation costs, tariffs, and so on, of course. If so, there must be stable equilibrium exchange rates. Second, the whole elasticities approach has been criticized—how can elasticities be determined empirically unless we already know how the entire economy behaves? Since this knowledge is difficult to achieve, is there not a simpler approach?[35]

Devaluation and the BOP: The Absorption Approach   With this in mind, the absorption approach was suggested as a simpler analysis. When we considered the income-expenditure identity, we noted that a deficit on current account means that expenditure (or absorption) is greater than output. In the simplest case, if $Im > X$, then $C + I + Im > C + I + X$. The country is spending more than its output. Will devaluation correct this? To do so, devaluation must increase output or reduce absorption, or both.

Is it likely that devaluation will increase output? There is no reason to think that devaluation will automatically result in employment of idle resources, nor do other possibilities seem likely. Moreover, even if output increased, there is no assurance that the increased output might not be absorbed by increased domestic consumption and investment. The conclusion is that devaluation is a very uncertain remedy for an excess of absorption over output. A more direct and more certain remedy would be to increase output and/or reduce consumption through proper use of monetary and fiscal policy.

An excess of expenditure over income (output) implies that the private economy (business and consumers) is reducing its cash balances. When deposits are transferred to foreign ownership to pay for excess imports, the money supply is not changed. But when foreigners, not needing all of such balances, sell them in the foreign exchange market where they are bought by a government or central bank if it is trying to maintain fixed exchange rates, the amount of money in the hands of the *public* is reduced. If this is to continue, the velocity of circulation of money must increase or the money supply must be increased by the central bank, or both. Since it seems probable that an increase in velocity of money has some limit, it is reasonable to conclude that BOP deficits (and surpluses) of this type are monetary phenomena. They could not

---

[35]S. S. Alexander, "Effects of a Devaluation on a Trade Balance," IMF *Staff Papers*, April 1952, pp. 263–278, and "Effects of a Devaluation: a Simplified Synthesis of Elasticities and Absorption Approaches," *American Economic Review*, March 1959, pp. 22–42.

continue indefinitely if the money supply were not being increased too rapidly.[36]

The Role of Money Introduction of the suggestion that proper use of monetary policy was necessary led to further consideration of the role of money. Flow deficits (current account deficits) can continue only if the central bank finances them through creation of money (expansion of credit), because unless that occurs, flow deficits lead to smaller and smaller holdings of money by the domestic public, and at some point money holdings become too small to meet the demand for money. (Payments abroad do not change the size of the money supply, but they do transfer title to bank deposits—money—to foreigners.)[37] Flow deficits might be eliminated by reducing expenditures or possibly by switching expenditures from imports to nontraded goods (home goods). Devaluation might aid in causing a switch of expenditures, but import surcharges and quantitative controls could also be used.

Deficits on capital account are different, as noted earlier. Since they involve no loss of wealth and no excess of expenditure over income, there may be no reason to try to eliminate them. It is not likely that devaluation would be very helpful in reducing these deficits, since it does not necessarily affect expectations of gain on holdings of foreign assets versus holdings of domestic assets or money. If a country does not have enough reserve assets to finance the shifts of investment from domestic to foreign assets, there is some reason to try to reduce them. But the best remedy would be to increase rates of return (interest and profits) on domestic financial assets. For a reserve currency country like the United States, the problem of loss of reserve assets may not arise if foreign countries can be induced to hold dollars. Thus in spite of recurrent capital account deficits in the 1960s and efforts to reduce them, it was not until the United States had a current account deficit in 1971 and a great loss of reserve assets that devaluation was eventually chosen as a policy.

The Role of Home Goods Home goods have been defined as nontraded goods—goods produced in the home country, but neither exported nor imported in significant quantities. Devaluation has no *direct* effect on their prices.[38] It does, however, lead to a reduction in prices of home goods *relative* to prices of traded goods (primarily imported goods, usually). Thus there may be a shift toward consumption of home goods and production of export goods,

[36]Harry G. Johnson, *International Trade and Economic Growth* (Cambridge, Mass.: Harvard, 1958), p. 157.

[37]More properly, this refers to transactions forming the balance on goods and services. The reader may note that up to this point, relatively little of the theory concerns capital movements. The theory of capital movements is *financial* theory, involving risk, return, and liquidity of financial assets, and their values in the light of anticipated future returns discounted at appropriate rates. This theory has been developed extensively in recent years, but its application to international assets has been limited.

[38]Ivor F. Pearce, "The Problem of the Balance of Payments," *International Economic Review*, January 1961, pp. 1–28.

and a shift away from higher-priced imported goods. The role of home goods is still being explored, and some complex models have been developed. Some possibilities may be suggested by reference to actual events.

A Recent Situation

The devaluations of the U.S. dollar in 1971 and in 1973 may have led to shifts toward consumption of home goods, and thus to increases in their prices, as the limit of productive capacity was nearly reached in some industries. The devaluations may also have resulted in shifts toward production of export goods, and to increased exports. Such shifts may have limited the increase in output of home goods. The devaluations may thus have been a significant causal factor in the very rapid inflation which followed, both by causing a rise in prices of imported goods, which spread to goods in which imported materials were used, and by causing a shift in demand toward home goods and of output toward export goods, thus increasing prices of home goods. There is still controversy concerning the situation in the world inflation of 1971–1975 and beyond, but these possibilities suggest that devaluation may not have been desirable.

THE MONETARY THEORY OF THE BALANCE OF PAYMENTS[39]

The introduction of the absorption approach and the role of money into BOP theory has led to a monetary theory of the BOP. This theory deserves further comment because it has been developed rather recently, because it is still being refined, and because it has some advantages even in its present state of development. Other approaches do not treat the current account and the capital account together. The elasticities approach is primarily concerned with the current account, and the absorption approach generally ignores the capital account. Yet capital flows have become increasingly important. Also, the elasticities and absorption approaches do not include portfolio choice theory. Modern financial theory is essentially a theory of portfolio choices based on safety, liquidity, and return for various assets.

Supply of and Demand for Money

Note that the theory emphasizes changes in the supply of and demand for money. In this view, the size of the money supply is an exogenous factor, determined basically by central banks, although both commercial banks and the

---

[39]The presentation of theory in this section draws very heavily on Donald S. Kemp, "A Monetary View of the Balance of Payments," Federal Reserve Bank of St. Louis, *Review*, April 1975, pp. 14–22. Kemp summarizes the approach and provides references to important earlier work. See especially Robert A. Mundell, *Monetary Theory: Inflation, Interest, and Growth in the World Economy* (Pacific Palisades, Calif.: Goodyear, 1971) and Harry G. Johnson, "The Monetary Approach to Balance-of-Payments Theory," in *Further Essays in Monetary Economics* (Cambridge, Mass.: Harvard, 1973), pp. 229–249.

public influence the determination. Crucial items in BOPs are those which affect the money supply, domestic or foreign. Other parts of the BOP and other balances tend to be ignored or regarded as relatively unimportant in the monetary theory of the BOP.

It is assumed that there is a relatively efficient world market economy—in the long run, if exchange rates are fixed, interest rates and other rates of return on comparable financial assets differ only because of differences in risk and maturity. Price levels in various countries must change in line with each other. If exchange rates are permitted to float freely, prices may change at different rates in different countries, being offset by opposite changes in exchange rates.

Any disparity between actual and desired money balances is self-correcting. It is recognized, however, that correction takes time, and in a short period may not be completed. It is also recognized that governments or central banks may try to neutralize the effects of changes in money supply on BOPs, but it is assumed that in the long run they cannot succeed. In the long run, surplus countries are exporting goods, services, and/or long-term capital assets for foreign currency or other reserve assets. At some point the accumulation of money (foreign currency balances) must seem excessive, even to governments.

Under fixed exchange rates, domestic monetary policy cannot entirely control the size of the domestic money supply. Too much money will lead to an outflow of funds, including international reserve assets, which will eventually slow the increase in the domestic money supply. In effect, fixed exchange rates are regarded as a check on inflation, and to some extent on deflation. We return to the arguments for fixed and for flexible or floating exchange rates in Chapter 9, but it seems to be apparent that those who believe each country should have considerable independence in monetary policy favor flexible exchange rates. (We shall find in Chapter 9 that this preference may not be justified.) Those who favor fixed rates usually believe that governments face pressures toward inflation which they find it difficult to resist, and that therefore some international restraint on inflation in the form of fixed exchange rates is helpful.

The Situation of Reserve Currency Countries

In the monetary theory of the BOP, a reserve currency country (one whose currency is held by other countries as a reserve asset) has an adjustment process different from that of other countries. An expansionary monetary policy may not affect the international reserves of a reserve currency country, whereas it does affect the reserves of other countries. A reserve currency is simply one which other governments or central banks are willing to hold in sizable amounts. Hence they are willing, up to some point, to increase their holdings of such assets. Fixed exchange rates do not present a barrier to inflation for a reserve currency country in the same way that they do for other countries.

If there were no reserve currency countries, BOP surpluses and deficits would result in the redistribution of reserve assets, but no change in the total. When reserve currency countries exist, the level of total reserve assets in the world does change as a result of BOP surpluses and deficits. Therefore, nonreserve currency countries find it hard to control the size of the money supply in their own countries. The impact of monetary policy in a reserve currency country is spread around the world. The amount of reserve assets held by a reserve currency country need not change, but other countries gain or lose reserves, and their price levels are affected to nearly the same extent as those of the reserve currency country. The monetary policy of a reserve currency country is *crucial* to the world economy. Since the United States is the chief reserve currency country, the U.S. monetary policy is particularly crucial.

Freely Floating Exchange Rates

If exchange rates are permitted to float freely, there are no gains or losses in international reserve assets. The size and rate of growth of the money supply in each country are determined by that country's monetary policy. But the demand for money may vary because, given this condition, rates of inflation may vary. The exchange value of any currency, in the long run, should be determined by the rate of growth in money supply and in real income relative to those rates in the rest of the world. Inflation is thus the major cause of depreciation of the value of a currency, since rates of growth in real income are not likely, in general, to change as rapidly as rates of inflation.

Evaluation of the Monetary Theory of the Balance of Payments

The foregoing statements represent an extreme position, because great emphasis is placed on the rate of growth of the money supply. Although the rate of growth of real income is also taken into account, it is not emphasized. Nor is the possibility that depreciation or devaluation of a currency may, under some conditions, cause inflation. We examine that question in Chapter 9.

Nevertheless, the monetary theory of the BOP is important. Clearly, changes in money supply are to some extent exogenous and significant. If changes in the size of the money supply in various countries are a major cause of BOP changes, deficits and surpluses in BOPs will tend to disappear in the long run, in the absence of government controls such as tariffs or other barriers to trade. The only effect of tariffs is to distort trade from the pattern consistent with the most efficient use of resources—that is, from trade based on comparative advantage.

The monetary theory of the BOP points up the importance of the question whether it is possible (or desirable) for one country to isolate itself from other countries and especially to control its monetary policy independently. If so, monetary cooperation among countries is not necessary. Floating exchange rates would be desirable to permit changes in relative values of currencies based on different rates of inflation and of real growth. If isolation is impossible or undesirable, some coordination of monetary policies of major industrialized countries should be sought, hence some impact of foreign economies on domestic changes is inevitable. Moreover, if fixed exchange rates are a goal, rates of inflation among major industrialized countries must be kept somewhat in line.

The problem remains that reserve currency countries like the United States are not necessarily constrained to avoid inflation even if agreement were reached to maintain relatively stable exchange rates, unless such reserve currency countries agree to redeem their currencies in some other asset, such as gold. Thus in negotiations, if fixed exchange rates are considered, the question of convertibility of reserve currencies into other assets is very likely to arise.

SUMMARY

Deficits or surpluses in settlement items may be corrected wholly or partially by one or more of the following: the price-specie flow mechanism, the real income shift mechanism, interest rate changes, government controls, or changes in exchange rates. The effects of the price-specie flow mechanism, the real income shift mechanism, and government controls are in general quite well understood. Effects of interest rate changes are less clearly defined, but probably less important. Effects of exchange rate changes are still being studied. Although devaluations are not necessarily the most effective policy actions to readjust BOPs—measures to reduce expenditures or to increase output may be more effective—it is widely accepted that under many conditions devaluation can "improve" the BOP.

Emphasis on expenditure reduction and upon the role of portfolio shifts in financial assets in affecting BOP deficits and surpluses has led to an emphasis on the role of money in BOP changes. A monetary theory of the BOP has emerged, giving great emphasis to changes in the money supply as causes of BOP changes. Such a theory is extreme, and most economists, although they accept the importance of money in determining the level of nominal and real income, do not give it as great a role as do those who emphasize the monetary theory of the BOP. This theory does, however, integrate the current account and capital account into one analysis of BOP changes. It also recognizes that both the transmission of changes in the supply of money to changes in income and shifts in portfolio balances represent a process of portfolio choice of assets and perhaps even of consumption, based on safety, liquidity, and return of various assets and services.

The monetary theory of the BOP may be used in arguing for independent monetary policies and flexible exchange rates, but it may also be used in arguing for stable but adjustable rates as a barrier to unwise spending and monetary policy.

The monetary theory of the BOP also illustrates clearly the significance of a reserve currency country—its influence on the world money supply and the fact that fixed exchange rates may not present a barrier to inflation in a reserve currency country in the same way they do in other countries.

QUESTIONS FOR DISCUSSION

1 Contrast the equilibrium concept in price theory with the concept of equilibrium in the BOP.

2 Do you think that the price-specie flow mechanism still operates to help eliminate deficits or surpluses in BOPs? Give some evidence or reasons why you do or do not think so.

3 If taxes and saving are regarded as domestic *leakages* from income available for consumption, and imports as a *foreign* leakage, what important differences can you point out?

4 Multipliers are simply derivatives of functions—that is, slopes of lines at specified points, the lines indicating relationships between a dependent variable and an independent variable. Derive the investment multiplier for a closed economy and the investment or foreign trade multiplier for an open economy. By analogy, explain what you think is meant by a money multiplier.

5 Could the effects of changes in interest rates reinforce the self-correcting influences of the price-specie flow and the real income mechanisms, instead of partly offsetting those forces? If so, how?

6 Compare flow deficits in the current account with flow-stock adjustment deficits in the capital account. In what ways do they differ?

7 Assume that the major tools of macroeconomic policy are monetary and fiscal policy. On this assumption why is the question whether or not a Phillips curve (relationship of rate of unemployment to rate of inflation) exists important for a decision on the desirability of flexibility in exchange rates?

8 Make your own evaluation of the monetary theory of the BOP. How useful is it as an approach? How valid are its conclusions?

9 Refer to the publication of the Federal Reserve Bank of Boston, *The International Adjustment Mechanism*. What is your opinion of the views presented by the two Miltons (Friedman and Gilbert) on whether the adjustment mechanisms worked satisfactorily enough?

10 Why can the real income shift mechanism probably provide only a *partial* adjustment, whereas, if it operates, the price-specie flow mechanism could provide full adjustment?

SUGGESTED REFERENCES

Everyone interested in BOP theory should read Ragnar Nurkse, *Conditions of International Monetary Equilibrium*, Essays in International Finance (Princeton: Princeton, 1945), reprinted in *Readings in the Theory of International Trade* (Philadelphia: Blakiston, 1949).

A basic treatise on the foreign trade multiplier is Fritz Machlup, *International Trade and the National Income Multiplier* (Philadelphia: Blakiston, 1943).

The theory of adjustment mechanisms through price-specie flows, real income shifts, exchange rate adjustments, and government controls is carefully reviewed in Leland B. Yeager, *International Monetary Relations* (New York: Harper & Row, 1966), Chaps. 5–7. More recent BOP theory is reviewed in Anne O. Krueger, "Balance of Payments Theory," *Journal of Economic Literature*, March 1969, pp. 1–26.

A thorough, detailed discussion of exchange control systems may be found in Raymond F. Mikesell, *Foreign Exchange in the Postwar World* (New York: Twentieth

Century Fund, 1954). The International Monetary Fund issues an *Annual Report on Exchange Restrictions* (1974 was the 25th).

A very readable presentation of the arguments, pro and con, whether the adjustment mechanisms have worked satisfactorily enough is found in *The International Adjustment Mechanism* (Boston: Federal Reserve Bank of Boston, 1970).

For a discussion of the "managed floating" of exchange rates after February 1973, see the *Economic Report of the President*, February 1975, pp. 200–203.

The close connections between the increased reliance on monetary policy in recent years as an instrument for the attainment of policy goals, and the floating of exchange rates is reviewed by Donald L. Kohn, "Interdependence, Exchange Rate Flexibility, and National Economies," Federal Reserve Bank of Kansas City, *Monthly Review*, April 1975, pp. 3–10.

For a summary of a considerable amount of research on the relationships between monetary and fiscal policy actions on the one hand and fixed and flexible exchange rates on the other hand, see Robert M. Stern, *The Balance of Payments* (Chicago: Aldine, 1973), especially Chap. 10.

For the view that devaluations do not encourage exports, see Arthur B. Laffer, "Do Devaluations Really Help Trade?" *Wall Street Journal*, February 5, 1973, p. 10. See also Arthur B. Laffer, "Balance of Payments and Exchange Rate Systems," *Financial Analysts Journal*, July-August 1974, pp. 27–30. For a study of the experience of some less developed countries, see Avinash Bhagwat and Yusuke Onitsuka, "Export-Import Responses to Devaluation: Experiences of the Nonindustrial Countries in the 1960's," IMF *Staff Papers*, July 1974, pp. 414–462.

A very clear discussion of the monetary theory of the BOP is presented by Donald S. Kemp, "A Monetary View of the Balance of Payments," Federal Reserve Bank of St. Louis, *Review*, April 1975, pp. 14–22. For more detailed discussions, see Jacob A. Frenkel and Harry G. Johnson, eds., *The Monetary Approach to the Balance of Payments* (Downsview, Ontario, Canada: University of Toronto Press, 1976). For a relatively brief analysis showing how monetarist theories of BOP adjustments grew out of the monetarist critique of basic (often termed Keynesian) analysis of the determination of income and output, see Herbert G. Grubel, *Domestic Origins of the Monetary Approach to the Balance of Payments*, Essays in International Finance, No. 117 (Princeton: Princeton, 1976).

The International Monetary System

Part Two traces the development of the international monetary system. London once financed more than 90 percent of world trade and payments, but the center of gravity shifted gradually to the United States, although London remained important. Gold was still a major international reserve asset until after World War II, but the slow growth of the world's monetary gold stock, combined with rapid growth of the supply of dollars, resulted in dollars becoming an even more important reserve asset. Finally, it appeared that a world gold standard in its original form was no longer feasible, while neither the experience with flexible exchange rates in the 1930s nor the experience with government controls in the 1930s and 1940s seemed favorable. A new institution was therefore created as the major mechanism for management of the international monetary system. The International Monetary Fund (IMF), as the new institution was named, navigated between the Scylla of fixed exchange rates and the Charybdis of freely flexible rates for a quarter of a century before an unusually severe crisis led to recognition of a need for another reform.

Chapter 4 covers the analysis of the experience before World War II, involving a number of years of an international gold standard, some experience with flexible exchange rates, a serious international financial crisis in 1931, and the gradual formation of a network of government controls which by 1945 had nearly strangled world trade, and had all but eliminated international lending and investment.

Chapter 5 discusses the experience of the IMF in the 25 years culminating in the crisis of August 1971. While the IMF cannot be given credit for all the favorable developments during that period, it contributed to relative calm until faced by an irresistible need for reform.

Chapter 6 discusses the recognition in 1971 of the need for reform and the efforts toward reform in the succeeding few years. Most of the major questions await answers: What is to be the basic international reserve asset or assets, and how are other international reserve assets to be made convertible into that asset(s)? How can adjustments in exchange rates under a stable but adjustable rate system be triggered without waiting for decades? In a world of multinational business firms, with liquid assets in countries throughout the world, how can speculative flows of liquid capital be limited without imposing restrictions which strangle trade and investment? Finally, perhaps foremost, how can exchange rates be sufficiently, but not excessively, flexible?

Chapter 4

The International Monetary System before 1945

The word *system* implies some form of organization or planned development. A system may be the result of a long period of change and of the slow growth of institutions and customs. As these become interrelated and habitual, it becomes clear that certain ways of handling activities have become accepted. As more participants become accustomed to certain procedures, and as laws and rules gain force, it may be said that a system has developed.

On the other hand, in some cases a system may be organized in a very short time, perhaps at an international conference. Such a system is usually modified over time, however, so that it eventually assumes forms somewhat different from its initial design.

Both types of development have occurred in the case of the international monetary system. In this chapter we discuss the slow evolution of the monetary system in the period before 1945. In Chapter 5 we discuss the relatively rapid development of a new international monetary system in the period 1944–1946 and its subsequent evolution to 1971 within the basic framework.

AN INTERNATIONAL MONETARY SYSTEM

A distinction must first be made between the international *financial* system and the international *monetary* system. A financial system is a collection of institutions, instruments, laws, rules, and customary procedures for handling transactions involving *claims* on goods and services. Such claims are financial assets from the viewpoint of those who hold them, and liabilities from the standpoint of those who create them. An exception is gold, which is an international financial asset but not a liability. Because of this fact it is unique, as is made clear in this chapter.

The concept of the international monetary system is narrower than that of the international financial system. The monetary system involves the institutions, instruments, laws, rules, and procedures for handling international payments, especially those in final settlement of debts. Money has sometimes been defined as whatever is used in final settlement of debt.[1] Internationally, central banks have come to be the institutions which make final settlements, and hence the assets they use have been termed international money. Because central banks hold reserves of such assets, they have also been termed *reserve assets*.

Two significant differences between a domestic monetary system and the international monetary system merit consideration.

First, the domestic monetary or payments system includes both procedures for shifts in bank balances held in central banks and for transfers of coins, paper money, and checks which constitute payments by the public.[2] Other transactions, including purchases made with charge account cards, are credit transactions; payment in currency or checks on demand deposits is usually necessary for final settlement. The same three types of transfers exist in international payments: transfers between central banks, shifts of funds through activities of commercial banks, and credit transactions similar to those which occur domestically. Internationally, however, more importance is often attached to the shifts between central banks. Transfers of title to demand deposits in commercial banks in international transactions cause such balances to increase and decrease. If banks in one country do not wish to accumulate

---

[1]An excellent book which used this definition and stressed its appropriateness is Albert G. Hart, *Money, Debt and Economic Activity* (Englewood Cliffs, N.J.: Prentice-Hall, 1948), pp. 4–5. The definition was retained in subsequent editions. There are, of course, other bases for defining money: (1) the degree of correlation of the supply of whatever assets are counted as money with some measure of business activity, perhaps GNP, favored by economists such as Milton Friedman, and (2) a definition based on the degree of substitutability of other assets for currency—those which have a high degree of substitutability in terms of shift of demand from currency to such other assets being counted as money. Difficulty has arisen in using the latter definition because different studies have found different degrees of substitutability of, for example, thrift account deposits for demand deposits and currency.

[2]In the United States at the present time a number of developments suggest that there may be a major expansion of the institutions involved in the payments system at some time in the not-too-distant future. Check transfers may be made from negotiable order of withdrawal (NOW) accounts in mutual savings banks and savings and loan associations in Massachusetts and New Hampshire. Mutual savings banks in some states are now permitted to offer checking services. And in at least one state, such institutions have installed point-of-sale terminals in retail establishments so that payments may be made instantaneously without the use of checks or currency. These developments are in addition to arrangements in such institutions in other states for making payments through non-negotiable transfers, when firms receiving payments are willing to accept such payments at the financial institution office.

larger deposit balances in banks in another country, they may sell their deposits. Central banks then buy them if they do not wish the value of such foreign balances—the exchange rate—to fall. To prevent a fall in the exchange rate (a rise in the value of the local currency), central banks usually use reserve assets to buy currency. Because it involves exchange rates, this ultimate settlement process in some respects has special importance in international finance. Of course, transfers by commercial banks also involve exchange rates, but actions by central banks are usually the ultimate determinants of whether an exchange rate changes significantly.

Second, in domestic monetary systems, what is money, in the sense of assets which may be used for final settlement of debt, was frequently affected in the past to some extent by government fiat making certain assets legal tender. Assets classified as legal tender have to be accepted by creditors in settlement of debts—if they refuse to accept them, interest can no longer be collected. Internationally, legal tender has never existed, because there has been no international government with power to designate certain assets as legal tender. Over a period of years certain assets came to be generally acceptable for final payments. In the latter part of the nineteenth century, these assets were principally gold and sterling bank deposits. By 1945, U.S. dollar bank deposits were equally as acceptable as sterling, and perhaps more so.

Domestically, most monetary systems now involve a central bank, commercial banks, the instruments (currency and checks) used to make payments, the rules and procedures for handling these, and the wire transfer of other means sometimes used for making payments. Similarly, the international monetary system comprises the various central banks, commercial banks which deal in international finance, the deposits and instruments (drafts, for example, instead of checks) generally used to transfer title to deposits, and the cable, telephone, and telex facilities for making transfers.[3]

The domestic financial system includes a wide variety of other financial institutions and instruments, and this is also true for the International financial system. There are many documents used in addition to the negotiable instruments used for payments.[4] As indicated, deposits in foreign banks as well as gold are held by central banks as reserve assets. Thus deposits in certain

---

[3]In law, a *draft* is an order drawn by one person (or firm or institution) on another person (or firm or institution) to pay a certain amount of money to a third party (in some cases the third party is the drawer of the draft). A draft thus involves three parties (drawer, drawee on whom the draft is drawn, and payee, to whom payment is made). This contrasts with promissory notes or bonds, which involve only two parties, the maker and the payee. A draft is often referred to as a bill of exchange.

[4]In law, *instruments* must involve a sum of money to be paid, while *documents* need not. Thus negotiable instruments involve money payments; examples are checks, drafts, and promissory notes. When properly drawn they are negotiable, which means that their ownership may be transferred from one party to another simply by endorsement (signing in some form). Warehouse receipts, stock certificates, and a number of other documents, including bills of lading, may be negotiable, although they need not be. If they are negotiable, they always include the wording "to the order of" or "to John Smith" or "order." (Note that this wording is also found on checks, drafts, etc.)

currencies are used both by central banks and for commercial payments; when used for commercial payments the currency is termed a *vehicle* currency, and when used or held by central banks it is termed a *reserve* currency. The U.S. dollar has served widely for both purposes.

Before World War II, there was no *international* central bank, and as is discussed later, the IMF created for the postwar era had only *some* powers of a central bank. Central banks of individual countries made most final settlements through transfer of gold or deposit balances in sterling or U.S. dollars. A transfer of gold reduced reserve assets of one country and increased those of another. On the other hand, a transfer of sterling from the United Kingdom to another country could be effected by *creation* of sterling deposit liabilities owed to the other country. The same was true for the Unites States. Hence reserve currency countries, as Britain and the United States came to be termed, had a somewhat different status from that of other countries. They, and only they, could finance purchases, loans, and investments by creating debt. They were "bankers to the world," creating international money. If other countries had deficits in their balance of payments, they had to export gold, thus reducing their holdings of an important international moetary asset.[5] But as long as foreign countries accepted dollars or sterling, the United States and the United Kingdom could settle deficits by creating additional liabilities.

THE GOLD STANDARD

The international monetary system which was generally accepted among major industrialized countries before World War I is referred to as the gold standard. In a sense, a term such as "gold-sterling" standard would have been more appropriate. Two major assets were generally accepted as international reserves: gold, and deposits in British banks (sterling)

Most major industrial countries adopted the gold standard. This meant that a unit of a country's currency was defined as a certain weight, a part of an ounce, of gold. Whether or not that currency unit was actually embodied in a coin did not make any difference. In the United States, there was no $1 gold coin, but there were $5, $10, and $20 gold coins. The ounce used in weighing precious metals has traditionally been the troy ounce, somewhat larger than the better known avoirdupois ounce, and divided into 480 grains. When a number of currency units, such as the pound sterling, the dollar, the franc, the mark, and eventually the Japanese yen, were defined in terms of a given weight of gold, it was also provided that gold could be obtained, at least for certain international payments, from the treasuries of these countries in the specified amounts.

A pound sterling could be converted into 113.0015 grains of fine gold, and a

---

[5]It should be noted that this process is essentially the same as that used when an individual buys a house with no down payment, creating a mortgage for the full purchase price. The difference is that the deposit liabilities created by Britain and the United States were international money—other nations would accept them in payments. Mortgages and other long-term debt instruments cannot normally be used for payments.

U.S. dollar into 23.22 grains. Thus the pound was defined as 113.0015/23.22 times as much gold as the dollar, or 4.8665 times as much gold. In terms of gold the pound was worth $4.8665.[6] This amount of dollars was termed the *par value* of the pound.

Since any bank could obtain pounds sterling (acquiring and shipping gold, and subsequently exchanging it for sterling) at $4.8665 per pound, there was little reason for any bank to pay more for sterling, except for handling charges, shipment costs, and insurance costs for gold acquired and exchanged for sterling. These added perhaps 0.5 percent to the cost of obtaining sterling. Roughly, then, it might be said that no bank was forced to pay more than about $4.88 per pound for sterling as long as the gold standard existed for both the United States and the United Kingdom.

Par Values and Gold Export and Import Points

The par values and the possibility of obtaining and shipping gold, together with the addition (or subtraction) of the cost of shipping and insuring gold, determined the range within which exchange rates could fluctuate. As long as banks could obtain sterling via the acquisition and shipment of gold for no more than $4.88 (approximately), there was no reason for the exchange rate to rise above that point. Similarly, there was no reason for it to fall below $4.84 (approximately). Gradually, it became unnecessary to ship gold, as procedures were developed for "ear-marking" gold to indicate its ownership, but in the period before World War I, gold shipments occurred. For this reason, at the outbreak of World War I, it was possible for the exchange rate to fluctuate beyond the gold export and import points, because insuring shipments of gold suddenly became much more costly, and shipments became too risky to undertake when U-boats began to sink many ships.

The pound sterling actually rose far above the gold export point to approximately $7 for a short time at the outbreak of World War I. The explanation of this event involves another important facet of the gold standard system at that time.

London's Dominance in International Finance

The gold standard as an international monetary system worked well in the period before World War I because of London's dominance in international finance. International reserve assets were sometimes said to have consisted of gold alone, but actually they consisted of gold and deposits in British banks (sterling). Most of world trade—the percentage has been estimated at more than 90 percent—was financed in London.[7] International capital movements were relatively small, and a substantial amount of such movements also involved sterling. In many countries, exporters would draw drafts, not on

---

[6] Small handling charges imposed by government for purchase or sale of gold are ignored in this calculation. Also it may be noted that the U.S. dollar was officially defined as 25.8 grains of gold $9/_{10}$ fine, which is 23.22 grains of fine gold.

[7] Albert C. Whitaker, *Foreign Exchange*, 2d ed. (New York: Appleton, 1933), p. 157.

importers in the countries to which they sold, but on London discount houses or acceptance houses (similar to banks). These drafts, when properly drawn and accompanied by the proper documents, were "accepted" by the London acceptance houses, assuring payment at maturity. The exporters could obtain payment at their own local banks, which then held London "acceptances." By selling these in London, deposit credits in London banks could be obtained. The foreign banks then held sterling deposits. Importers were responsible for providing funds to "honor" (pay) the drafts at maturity. For this purpose, if the importers were not British, they or their banks bought sterling. Since foreign banks were content to leave their deposits in London, there was continuous demand for sterling by importers and their banks, and under most conditions if demand was heavy and the exchange value of sterling rose, gold flowed to London. When gold shipments could not safely be made in August and the following months of 1914, the demand for sterling led to a rise in the exchange value of sterling.[8]

As long as deposits in London banks were accepted as international reserve assets and as working balances by foreign commercial banks and central banks, London owed the world but did not have to pay. On the other hand, the world owed London, and did have to pay, for imports financed through London. That is, importers in many countries had to buy sterling to provide funds to meet letter of credit agreements. So long as there was no great fear of bank failures and no great concern over Britain's ability to honor its obligations, there was little reason to withdraw deposits from London banks except as they might be needed to make payments. The keystone of the international monetary system before World War I was the confidence in the stability of the British financial system, in sterling deposits, and in gold. There was no question of comparing sterling deposits with any other reserve asset: U.S. dollars, for example, were hardly used in international finance, and few American banks even had international banking departments.

Spread of the Gold Standard

The adoption of the gold standard began with England early in the nineteenth century. Although an attempt was made as late as the 1860s by a number of European countries which formed the Latin Monetary Union to establish bimetallism for gold and silver, discoveries of new supplies of silver tended to reduce its value. Defeat of France in the Franco-Prussian war of 1870 and the establishment of the gold standard in Germany, together with less demand for silver in other areas, led to a diminished use of silver as international money. The United States was forced to abandon redemption of paper money in metal during the Civil War, but the Specie Resumption Act of 1875 provided for redemption of paper money in gold beginning in 1879. Although coins could be redeemed at the Treasury for some years in "lawful money," and lawful money in this sense included silver dollars and silver certificates, so that the United

[8]For an interesting description of London as a center of international finance before 1914, see Benjamin M. Anderson, *Economics and the Public Welfare* (Princeton, N.J.: Van Nostrand, 1949), esp. pp. 12–13.

States had a "limping" gold standard for some time, the Gold Standard Act of 1900 formally established the gold standard.

The spread of the gold standard was thus a gradual process, as various countries for various reasons defined their monetary units in gold, thus fixing the gold values of their currencies. When the dollar was defined as 25.8 grains of gold (480 grains equal one troy ounce), $9/10$ fine, or 23.22 grains of fine gold, the value of gold in terms of dollars, in government sales and purchases, was thereby fixed at $20.67 per ounce. A number of writers treat the period 1880–1914 as the period of the gold standard. Dates of adoption of the gold standard by a number of countries are shown in Table 4-1.

It has never been a presumption that, for a period to be characterized in a particular manner, all countries in the world must be in the same status. The period from World War II to 1973 has been characterized as a period of stable but adjustable exchange rates, with full recognition of the fact that many nations, especially (LDCs), did not have stable exchange rates during that time.

Precise dates for the beginning and ending of the period of the gold standard cannot be specified, but World War I had significant effects. The gold standard, although restored by many countries, was never the same after World War I.

World War I and Subsequent Return to the Gold Standard

World War I had a serious effect on the international monetary system because it reduced confidence in sterling deposits as an international reserve asset. Britain had been forced to abandon the gold standard during World War I because of the excess of payments (debits) over credits in its balance of payments, and the impossibility of providing gold to settle the total difference. The United States and to some extent France became more important in

Table 4–1   Dates of Adoption of the Gold Standard by Selected Countries

Great Britain	1816
Germany	1871
Sweden, Norway and Denmark	1873
France, Belgium, Switzerland, Italy, and Greece	1874
Holland	1875
Uruguay	1876
United States	1879
Austria	1892
Chile	1895
Japan	1897
Russia	1898
Dominican Republic	1901
Panama	1904
Mexico	1905

Source: Lester V. Chandler, *The Economics of Money and Banking* (New York: Harper & Row, 1948), p. 94.

international finance as well as in international trade. The United States experienced an export boom after World War I, as it extended credit to Britain and Europe, and as Britain extended credit to Europe. Europe needed goods and services of many kinds, and the United States was in a position to supply them. The resulting strain on the U.S. economy was reflected in a rise in the price level as the money supply was expanded to finance additional economic activity.

Many other countries had also temporarily abandoned the gold standard, but of course none of these actions had the same significance as the action of the British government. After all, Britain had financed 90 percent of world payments. The British government, recognizing the importance of sterling and of British institutions, in international finance, wished to return to the gold standard as soon as possible. Delay occurred because of the sharp recession in the United States in 1920–1921, as the post-World War I inflation ended and prices fell by over 40 percent. Recovery in the United States was quick, however, and a degree of recovery also occurred in Britain.[9] After a disastrous hyperinflation which ended with the value of the mark at 4 trillion to the dollar, Germany also experienced stabilization, and was able to return to the gold standard in 1924.

The German hyperinflation—one of the few such cases in modern history—offers an opportunity to test the validity of the general assumption that causation runs from money to prices to exchange rates. This is the heart of the purchasing power parity doctrine as well as of the quantity theory of money. But the question may be asked: is it possible that causation sometimes runs from exchange rates to prices to the money supply?

The evidence seemed to some scholars to be conclusive that the accepted theory was correct—causation ran from the money supply to prices and then to exchange rates. The fact that depreciation of the mark in the foreign exchange markets sometimes occurred before domestic price increases in Germany suggested the opposite direction of causation, but was not very meaningful. The German government printed new mark notes and sold them on the foreign exchange market to obtain foreign exchange to pay reparations. Thus an initial impact in the foreign exchange market was to be expected, but the basic cause was the printing of paper money.[10] Moreover, whenever the increase in the money supply slowed down, it became necessary for the Germans to sell foreign exchange to obtain marks—and the exchange value of the mark increased temporarily. The key to the problem seemed to be to try to hold the line against the issue of new paper money, and this the Reichsbank (Germany's central bank) did not seem able to do, except in brief periods such as November 1923.[11]

---

[9]The sharp recovery in the United States is documented in Frederick C. Mills, *Economic Tendencies in the United States* (New York: National Bureau of Economic Research, 1932).

[10]Benjamin M. Anderson, *Economics and the Public Welfare* (New York: Van Nostrand, 1949), p. 94.

[11]Costanino Bresciani-Turroni, *The Economics of Inflation* (London: Allen & Unwin, 1937), pp. 398–402.

The end of the German hyperinflation, stabilization of the new German currency, and Germany's return to the gold standard in 1924 caused Britain to take similar action in 1925. Britain, however, in view of higher costs and prices and the handicap of outmoded methods of production in many lines, could not permanently sustain the old par value to which it returned. Britain's difficulties were of key importance because of its significance in international finance, discussed at the beginning of this chapter.

The Gold Standard After World War I

The gold standard as it existed after World War I, especially in the period of the late 1920s after Germany, Britain, and other countries had returned to the gold standard, was different from the gold standard existing before World War I.

The major difference was that instead of two international reserve assets—gold and sterling—there were several. Both the United States and France had become much more important in international finance, and dollar and franc deposits were used for some financing. In general, however, countries other than Britain had small amounts of gold. The supply of gold had never been very large in relation to the volume of sterling deposits, and relative to the total of sterling, franc, and dollar deposits it was still smaller. When some countries, including France, accumulated sterling balances, they sometimes attempted to convert these into gold, drawing upon Britain's limited gold reserves. The system may be termed a *gold exchange standard*—gold could be obtained in countries other than Britain by obtaining sterling exchange (drafts on sterling bank deposits) and then converting the sterling drafts into gold in Britain. As long as sterling deposits were the only international reserve asset other than gold, and as long as there was confidence in sterling, Britain could operate with very small gold reserves. But when there were a number of countries whose bank deposits constituted international money for payments, and when confidence in different currencies varied, the system could not operate well.

A second important difference was that flexibility in costs and prices, essential to the operation of the price-specie flow mechanism, no longer existed to the same degree. This was especially important in Britain, because only with a decline in costs and prices could the former par value of the pound have been maintained in the long run. Because flexibility in costs and prices was lacking, confidence in sterling deteriorated, although the results did not become definitive until 1931.

WORLD DEPRESSION—1929

Meanwhile, in the United States, an expansion of bank credit led to a gradually more rapid rise in real estate and stock market prices. The 1920s were notable because commodity price indexes remained stable and wholesale prices even declined, as funds were invested in real estate and stocks. The imbalance in high real estate and stock market prices had inevitably to be corrected when investors examined the discounted future income to be expected from these investments. The stock market (and, in some areas of the country, real estate) crash in 1929 was followed by the Great Depression of the 1930s, which involved most of the other major industrial countries of the world as well as the United States.

It is impossible to examine fully here the controversy over the causes of the Great Depression: To what extent was the stock market crash a cause of the Depression? How did the extensive reduction in the money supply contribute to a decline in business activity? Was the decline in rates of profit, which began early in 1929, significant?

Alternative Explanations of the Depression

One explanation of the Depression is that the expansion of money and credit was greater, especially in the later 1920s, than was needed for trade and commerce; the unneeded money went into stock market and real estate speculation. Then when credit expansion ceased, the stock market declined, real estate prices fell, and the general reduction in credit caused a decline in business activity. The question to be asked is why the expansion of money and credit did not result in a greater increase in either real output or prices of commodities and services. One promising line of thought, not much expressed by experts at the time, is that wage rates did not increase much, and hence consumer income, which is the basis of consumer spending under most conditions, did not rise sufficiently to cause much rise in either real or nominal GNP.

Changes which today seem small may have had significant effects. The Federal Reserve Banks reduced discount rates in mid-1927 and expanded the money supply, although both changes were modest by recent standards. The purpose was apparently to ease the strain on Britain's gold reserves, since gold was moving to the United States—in part because funds invested in the United States could earn higher returns. When, following the sharp rise in stock market prices in 1927–1929, it seemed necessary to raise the discount rate and to slow the growth of the money supply, foreign funds were again attracted.[12]

An alternative monetary explanation of the Depression, is advanced by monetarist economists such as Milton Friedman. Friedman has argued that what began as a small recession turned into a major depression because as

---

[12]For a brief discussion of these factors, see Leland B. Yeager, *International Monetary Relations*, 2d ed. (New York: Harper & Row, 1967), pp. 332–334. For a more lengthy and vivid discussion, see Benjamin M. Anderson, *Economics and the Public Welfare* (New York: Van Nostrand, 1949), Chaps. 24–28. Of special interest is Anderson's discussion of the 1927 conference of the four major central bank governors—Strong of the Federal Reserve Bank of New York, Norman of the Bank of England, Rist (a respected economist) of the Bank of France, and Schacht of Germany. According to Anderson, Rist was much concerned about the growth of the gold-exchange standard, and the accumulation of sterling and dollar reserves (instead of gold) by the Bank of France. (Incidentally, it was sterling sales by France which triggered England's abandonment of the gold standard in 1931.)

business declined the money supply was reduced: "When the United States embarked on deflation and proceeded to reduce its monetary stock, the rest of the world was forced into a major contraction."[13] Professor Friedman demonstrated impressive evidence of a correlation of the decline in business activity with the decline in the money stock, not only during the Great Depression, but in the five other instances between 1867 and 1960 in which a major depression (a decline in real GNP of more than 10 percent) occurred. He also pointed out that in each case the decline in the money supply began before the decline in business activity.

Other economists rejected purely monetary explanations and cited such factors as lack of investment outlets during the 1930s.[14] Still others argued that overproduction of foodstuffs and raw materials in Europe, the burden of European war debts, and the financial crisis of 1931, discussed below, were causes of the Depression. No doubt these factors contributed to the severity of the Depression, but it is difficult to assign to them the prime responsibility.

Because of their relevance for possible future situations, our interest centers on international factors affecting the length and depth of the Depression, and causing it to spread nearly worldwide.

International Factors in the Depression

The precariousness of the international gold standard was recognized. The pyramiding of gold exchange standards on a relatively small base of gold holdings located in certain countries represented a broad expansion of credit on a very narrow gold base. Any serious strain on those countries without substantial gold holdings could cause difficulties for the gold exchange standard countries. More important, strains on a gold standard country resulting in a flow of gold reserves to another country could cause a financial crisis. Some economists, such as Hicks, thought the gold supply inadequate.

In addition, Britain's effort to return to the old par value for sterling was probably an error, and France's devaluation of the franc in the 1920s may have been too great. These inappropriate par values for currencies, established at a time when there was little effort toward international agreement, aggravated BOP problems.

It is also clear that the decline in imports and in foreign lending by the United States, as the Depression reduced income and spending, led to a decline in exports of other countries. The decline in U.S. imports was given impetus by a sharp increase in the U.S. Smoot-Hawley tariff of 1930, following an earlier increase in 1922. Countries heavily dependent on exports found their incomes sharply reduced, their consumption falling, and their unemployment levels rising. International lending by the United States, at a high level in the 1920s as U.S. investors bought foreign stocks and bonds as well as domestic securities,

---

[13]Milton Friedman, *The Balance of Payments: Free versus Fixed Exchange Rates* (Washington, D.C.: American Enterprise Institute for Public Policy, 1967), p. 90.

[14]Alvin H. Hansen, *Full Recovery or Stagnation?* (New York: Norton, 1938).

dropped even more sharply than general business activity during the period 1929–1932. Thus foreign countries found they could not finance essential imports through their own exports, nor could they continue to finance them through U.S. credit.[15]

In a thoughtful review, Charles P. Kindleberger concluded that ". . . the depression was so wide, so deep, and so long because the international economic system was rendered unstable by British inability and United States unwillingness to assume responsibility for stabilizing it."[16] Specifically, these two countries failed to promote relatively free trade, especially for "distress goods," hence prices and incomes fell drastically; they failed to provide contracyclical long-term lending to meet financial needs; and they failed to act as short-term lenders of last resort through discounting in a crisis, especially in 1931. There is no doubt that these factors contributed to the length and severity of the Depression. Whether international factors weighed so heavily vis-à-vis domestic factors such as prior overexpansion of credit (Anderson) or contraction of the money supply as business activity declined (Friedman) cannot be unequivocally asserted.

The International Financial Crisis of 1931

In 1931 an international financial crisis began with the insolvency of a branch banking institution in Austria, the Kredit-Anstalt. This failure of a branch banking system caused withdrawal of funds from Austria. Withdrawals were also made from German banks because they had sizable deposits in Austrian banks. Depositors wanted to withdraw their funds before banks became insolvent and funds were blocked. Perhaps British, American, and French banks, acting together, could have made loans to Austria and prevented the spread of panic, but French banks would not cooperate in aid to Austria in view of the customs union of Austria with France's former enemy, Germany. Panic spread, and "standstill" agreements were worked out to halt withdrawals of funds by providing moratoria on debt payments. Nevertheless, withdrawals from British banks began, and the pound was under heavy pressure. As the Bank of France sold sterling, Britain decided that it could no longer support the value of the pound, and abandoned the gold standard on September 20, 1931. Since the pound thereafter did not have a fixed value in relation to gold or dollars, its usefulness as an international reserve asset was diminished.

Exchange control began in Austria and spread to Germany, first as an effort to prevent withdrawals of funds held on deposit in banks[17] rather than to prevent payments for current purchases of goods and services. But as such purchases came to be used, through fictitious pricing and other devices, as

[15]The huge drop in both imports (current account) and foreign lending (capital account) of the United States led to the development of the concept of "dollar shortage." See Hal B. Lary and others, *The United States in the World Economy* Economic Series No. 23 (Washington, D.C.: U.S. Department of Commerce, 1943).

[16]Charles P. Kindleberger, *The World in Depression, 1929–1939* (London: Allen Lane, Penguin, 1973), p. 292.

[17]Howard S. Ellis, *Exchange Control in Central Europe*, Harvard Economic Studies, Vol. 69 (Cambridge, Mass.: Harvard, 1941).

means of evading exchange controls, regulations became more strict, and the network of controls which developed during the period of Hitler's power gradually prevented expansion, and indeed forced contraction, of world trade and investment.

The economic and political uncertainties following the financial crisis of 1931 led to an outflow of gold from Europe and an inflow of gold to the United States, in amounts of $1 billion in some years and much more than that in other years. This "golden avalanche," as it was termed by some economists, led to possession by the United States at one point of about 80 percent of the world's monetary gold.[18] There was a high correlation, and very likely a direct connection, between gold inflows and net inflows of capital. Owners of gold sought safety for their assets by shipping the gold to the United States and accepting dollar financial assets in return, because at that time the dollar seemed safe and firmly fixed in value in relation to gold. The dollar was devalued in 1933 by an increase in the price of gold from $20.67 to $35 an ounce, but after that devaluation there seemed little reason to fear further decline in the dollar's value. The price of $35 per ounce made gold sales in the United States more attractive. The dramatic shift of gold holdings from the rest of the world to the United States is shown in Figure 4-1. The change in price of

[18]Frank D. Graham and Charles R. Whittlesey, *Golden Avalanche* (Princeton, N.J.: Princeton, 1939).

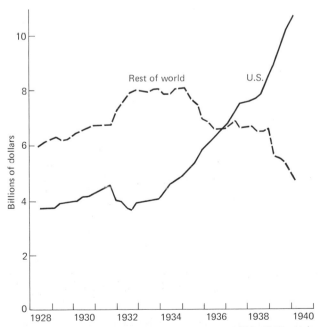

Figure 4-1 Gold Holdings of Governments, 1928–1940. *Note:* Does not adjust for change in price of official gold. (*Source:* Federal Reserve Bank of San Francisco, *Business Review,* Winter 1974–1975, p. 17.)

official gold is not taken into account in the chart. With the change in price, U.S. monetary gold holdings by the time of Pearl Harbor totaled nearly $23 billion, and although several billions in gold were spent during the war to buy strategic materials, especially in Latin America, U.S. gold holdings immediately after World War II were still over $20 billion, or about three-fourths of the world's monetary gold stock.

The gold standard of the 1880–1914 period and the gold exchange standard of the 1925–1931 period had given way to a mixture of fluctuating exchange rates for some countries and exchange controls by governments in other countries. It did not seem likely that a gold standard could be restored in the immediate future, and certainly the gold-sterling standard of 1880–1914 was gone.

A Word of Warning

People are sometimes, as in 1974, tempted to ask whether a financial crisis like that of 1931 might recur. It should be noted that the situations have both similarities and differences. Whatever the causes of the Depression of the 1930s, they were probably not the same as the causes of the postwar recessions of 1948–1949, 1953–1954, 1957–1958, 1960–1961, and 1969–1970 in the United States. To give just one example, the recession of 1969–1970 resulted at least in part from deliberate restriction of the growth of the money supply in 1969 to try to halt the inflation which had become serious by then. Moreover, these recessions differed in major ways from the recession of 1973–1975. The latter came in two stages—a decline from the autumn of 1973 to the spring of 1974 triggered by the sharp increase in the world price of oil, compounded by world food shortages and other problems; and a second decline from the autumn of 1974 to the spring of 1975, in which inventory liquidation was a major factor. Another new element in the recession of 1973–1975 was the long decline in profits as a percent of GNP from 1966 to 1970, which had not been fully offset by a rise in profits during the brief business expansion from 1971 to 1973. Profits as a percent of GNP declined generally from the mid-1960s to 1970, and had not attained their previous relationship even in early 1976. Historical analysis can be used to suggest conditions giving rise to crises, but differences as well as similarities must be kept in mind.

FLUCTUATING EXCHANGE RATES DURING AND AFTER WORLD WAR I

World War I ended the stability of exchange rates for currencies of major industrial countries, a key element in the international monetary system before the war. When World War I began, the combination of payments due London for imports under bank credits and acceptances of London houses and the continuing confidence in sterling (and hence no significant withdrawal of sterling deposits) caused the exchange rate for the pound to rise sharply. Gold shipment points became ineffective as limits on fluctuations in exchange rates, and the rate for sterling rose as high as $7. As wartime expenditures occurred and their effect on incomes in Britain began to be recognized, the exchange rate for sterling began to fall, and dropped as low as $3.18 by early 1920 in the aftermath of the war.

The Behavior of Exchange Rates

When the attempt to restore the gold standard during the 1920s ended in disaster in the Depression of 1929–1932 and the international financial crisis of 1931, the international monetary system began to disintegrate. By the end of 1932, major currencies of the world could generally be categorized as those of the "gold group," which maintained their currencies' values in terms of gold, those of Germany and some other countries which maintained their currencies' values by strict exchange controls enforced under a dictatorship, and those of other countries, which permitted their currencies to depreciate. Many currencies depreciated by as much as 35 to 50 percent. Those countries which did not permit their currencies to depreciate (chiefly the United States, France, Belgium, Switzerland, and the Netherlands) were confronted by strong deflationary pressures. The impact was especially heavy on U.S. agricultural exports and on some other natural resource exports, such as lumber. With depreciation of some currencies by as much as 50 percent, exports of those countries increased. Exchange rates fluctuated, sometimes erratically. Many countries complained that other countries purposely encouraged currency depreciation to engage in a "beggar-my-neighbor" policy. International trade was at a low level, and international capital flows had virtually stopped.

Applying the real income analysis developed in Chapter 3, it is evident that currency depreciation could encourage exports, discourage imports, and cause a shift in real income from other countries into countries which depreciated their currencies. Since the United States did not depreciate its currency after the change in the price of gold at the beginning of 1934, this may have been a factor in making the Depression in the United States longer and more serious than it might otherwise have been.[19]

The depreciation of currencies, especially that of the pound, meant a decline in the foreign exchange component of international reserves in comparison with the gold component. With limited production of gold and with the tremendous flow of gold to the United States, most countries found their gold holdings reduced. There was no substitute for the gold exchange standard which had been the replacement for the pre-1914 gold standard.

The exchange rate situation in the 1930s presented a mixture of widely fluctuating rates, which created difficulties for other countries, and rates maintained by exchange controls, which tended to reduce total trade and hinder all trade by reducing imports to the level of exports at the overvalued exchange

[19]See Lester V. Chandler, *America's Greatest Depression, 1929–1941* (New York: Harper & Row, 1970), especially p. 108, where he states that "on balance, however, the declines of foreign exchange rates—the rise of the exchange rate on the dollar—had a sharply deflationary impact on the American economy."

rates. When demand for foreign exchange arising from imports and other debit items in a country's BOP exceeded the supply of foreign exchange arising from credits, exchange controls limited demand by rationing exchange in some manner.

Nurkse's Analysis

A particularly influential analysis was that of Ragnar Nurkse, made for the League of Nations during World War II, Nurkse concluded that it was essential to reestablish a network of relatively stable exchange rates by agreement among the nations involved. His analysis led him to believe that individual setting of par values by countries themselves led to subsequent disintegration. Each country tended to establish a par value in the light of what appeared to be its own best interests.

He also argued that disruptive speculation was likely to dominat foreign exchange markets under flexible exchange rates. He argued that when a currency showed signs of depreciation, speculators hurried to sell it, thus intensifying the decline in its exchange value. The rise in import prices which accompanied depreciation of a currency might induce importers to speed up orders and thus to accentuate downward pressure on the exchange value of the local currency. Capital markets were also likely to be impeded by fluctuating exchange rates. Lending tends to push the exchange value of the local currency down, and if the rates rise before the loan is repaid, repayment is at a higher exchange rate. With fluctuating exchange rates, lenders or borrowers may thus suffer losses. The argument is familiar in a domestic setting: borrowers benefit from inflation, lenders from deflation.

Nurkse concluded that overvalued currencies of important industrial countries rather than exchange and trade controls were the basic cause of difficulty, the latter being merely symptoms. The solution he believed to be required was the establishment of a network of exchange rates "by simultaneous and coordinated international action."[20] The question remains unanswered whether nations could have decided upon and established equilibrium exchange rates at that time. It was not possible to do this even in 1946, after World War II was over. There is also the question whether, since overvaluation of some currencies means, by definition, undervaluation of others, those countries whose currencies were relatively undervalued may not have escaped some of the negative effects of disequilibrium rates. However, few developed countries escaped the disastrous effects of the Great Depression.

Perhaps after all, as Kindleberger suggested, the major problem was the failure to lend by those countries which should have stabilized the system (primarily the United States and Britain). The network of exchange and trade controls, created because countries could not borrow enough to buy more than they could sell, for a time restricted imports to levels which could be balanced

[20]Ragnar Nurkse, *International Currency Experience* (Geneva: League of Nations, 1944), p. 117.

by exports. This led to contraction of output in major countries as reduction of imports by one country led to fewer exports and therefore reduction in imports by other countries.

The importance of leadership in the stabilization of the international monetary system, and of lending by some country or countries in crises seems evident. Had an international short-term lending institution existed, it could possibly have carried out the role of lender of last resort. Dispersal of leadership among a number of countries runs the risk that no country may assume active leadership. In the world of the 1970s, it appears that leadership can most easily be assumed by the United States, in spite of the phenomenal rise in income and output in West Germany and Japan.

Clearly, some coordination of policies of major countries is desirable to maintain growth of world trade and investment. Such coordination runs counter to the desire of many countries to pursue independent monetary and fiscal policies at particular times. The outcome of this conflict of interests is most significant for all concerned with international finance.

WORLD WAR II AND THE INTERNATIONAL MONETARY SYSTEM

Any return to freer trade and investment and any effort to reestablish an international monetary system on a more orderly basis were prevented by the outbreak of World War II in late 1939. Although economic recovery in the late 1930s could have justified the removal of trade and investment restrictions, World War II led to more extensive and tighter controls on international trade and investment. Trade between enemy nations became illegal and much of the trade between friendly nations or allies consisted of munitions and supplies for wartime economies. Private markets for most currencies almost ceased to exist in many countries. Much of the trade that continued was handled under various intergovernmental agreements. There was almost no role for international finance. This meant that markets for foreign exchange, exchange rates, and other institutional mechanisms had to be reestablished when the war ended.

Intergovernmental Transactions

The increase in intergovernmental transactions meant a decline in private international trade. Most intergovernmental transactions were essentially either barter transactions or gifts (grants) made to facilitate carrying on the war. The network of trade and exchange controls meant that the usual methods of financing often could not be used. Consequently the financing of trade was not an urgent problem during the war.

The Network of Exchange and Trade Controls

The network of exchange and trade controls threatened to stifle international trade and almost did eliminate international investment, as is discussed in Part Four. Milton Friedman has argued that exchange controls with fixed exchange rate promote the waste of resources. If imports of luxury goods are prohibited and exchange permits for payments for such imports are refused, a black market tends to develop and countries which can do so are stimulated to produce luxury goods domestically. Sometimes they produce these goods much less efficiently than do other countries. Indeed, if the principle of comparative advantage has operated, this is presumably the case. If nationals go abroad and earn money, they may be discouraged by controls from importing needed articles and induced instead to spend their money in foreign countries for whatever they can consume in goods and services. Friedman has further argued that devaluation of an overvalued currency, the exchange value of which is higher than the rate which would balance purchases and sales of it in a free market, is inevitable.[21] But devaluation might not necessarily occur in wartime. In wartime, controls may be maintained by penalties, by appeals to patriotism, and by physical controls over production.

It was clearly likely that the network of exchange and trade controls would be maintained until the end of the war and by a number of countries for a period of time after the war. The reestablishment of a freer international monetary system to encourage postwar trade and investment could be planned during the war, however, and implementation as soon after the end of the war as possible would permit a new beginning under improved conditions.

THE NEED FOR CHANGE IN THE INTERNATIONAL MONETARY SYSTEM

Economists and central bankers concerned with the international monetary system almost unanimously agreed, toward the end of World War II, on the need for change and for the establishment of a new system. London's dominance of international finance, the keystone of the gold standard system before World War I, was gone. The importance of the U.S. dollar and the magnitude of physical output in the United States indicated that there would be a great demand for dollars when the war ended. Countries whose industries had been heavily destroyed would need equipment to rebuild them, and many countries would need food from the United States. It was recognized that these needs might be met on a government-to-government basis for a short time after World War II, but this could not continue indefinitely if private trade were to resume. It was clear that dollars would be scarce relative to the demand for them, and it was recognized that many countries would need funds both for imports and to replenish their reserve assets.

[21]An interesting collection of articles by Milton Friedman is gathered together in *Dollars and Deficits* (Englewood Cliffs, N.J.: Prentice-Hall, 1968). See especially his discussion of the case of India, pp. 56–59. Agreement with Friedman that fixed exchange rates may cause a misallocation of resources, and that devaluations of overvalued currencies are inevitable, does not necessarily imply agreement with his policy view that flexible exchange rates are the best system. Fixed but adjustable exchange rates established by international agreement are a possible alternative. A conclusion concerning policy is best developed after further analysis of international banking and exchange rates in Part Three.

Governments could have waited for a new international monetary system to evolve to replace the system which had worked well before 1914 but which could not work well in the circumstances existing from 1914 to 1944. This would, however, have meant a period of uncertainty when action seemed urgently needed. The action taken was the creation of a major international institution, the International Monetary Fund (IMF), discussed in the next chapter. Other complementary institutions were also created, but the IMF was clearly the most significant. The period of 1946 to 1971, at least, may be termed the era of the IMF for the international monetary system.

CONCLUSION

What may be concluded from our review of nearly three-quarters of a century of history of the international monetary system? First, the system worked quite well from 1880 to 1914 because there was only one major international financial center, London, and there was confidence in both gold and sterling. Under such conditions not much gold was needed. Moreover, no serious inflation occurred during that period and trade and investment were relatively free of controls, compared to some later periods. Any future reform of the international monetary system will probably work well only if one major financial center is dominant and if inflation is held to moderate rates in major countries.

Problems emerged after 1914 and culminated in the financial crisis of 1931. First, the gold exchange standard with several competing international financial centers (London, New York, Paris, and others) did not work well and there was not enough gold at the fixed price for such a system's needs. Second, inflation was sometimes a serious problem as was, notably, the hyperinflation in Germany in the early 1920s. Raising the price of gold would have been likely to cause more inflation. Thus it may be concluded that a gold standard would not be likely to work in the future even if nations strongly desired its reestablishment, a desire expressed by very few.

Third, the United States adopted policies detrimental to the smooth operation of an international monetary system. It made unwise foreign investments in the 1920s and almost ceased international lending and investing after 1929. It raised tariffs in 1922 and again in 1930 when world trade was declining for other reasons. The importance of a major international "lender of last resort" is clear; it could be a country such as the United States or it could be an international institution.

Serious decline in world trade and investment in the early 1930s gave rise in most countries to such actions as the competitive depreciation of currencies and exchange and trade controls. Officials concerned with international monetary problems came to believe that establishment of stable foreign exchange rates by agreement and concerted international effort to eliminate exchange and trade controls were needed. That need is quite clear, but the precise form of such international consultation and agreement may vary with conditions.

Finally, experience before 1945 suggests that stabilization of economic conditions within major countries is essential to the stabilization of international monetary conditions. Although such stabilization might occur if each major country followed rules such as those of the gold standard, this seems unlikely under modern conditions. Thus consultation on economic policies, especially those relating to inflation and international lending and investing, appears desirable.

APPENDIX: The Bank for International Settlements (BIS)

An institution which has played a rather important but little understood role in relation to the international monetary system is the Bank for International Settlements (BIS), established in 1930. German reparations payments had been reduced, and as a part of the Young Plan of 1929 for their further modification, it was arranged for Germany to obtain commercial loans abroad, pay scaled-down reparations immediately, and service the loans over a period of years. The BIS was established to facilitate these transfers. It was chartered in Switzerland, with capital provided by the central banks of Germany, Belgium, France, the United Kingdom, Italy, and Japan, and by a group of private banks in the United States. In addition to specific tasks related to reparations payments, it was provided that the BIS should promote cooperation among central banks. As a central bank institution, instead of a government institution like the IMF, it can operate without publicity and with less restraint.

BIS annual reports analyze international financial developments from a point of view not likely to be held by any one central bank or government. Additionally, the BIS has operated in the foreign exchange and Eurodollar markets. Some central banks intervene in such markets by channeling funds through the BIS. "Rescue operations" for some currencies have on occasion been negotiated through the BIS. The traditional semi-independence of central banks makes the BIS an important forum for central bank cooperation, often vital to progress. For a brief review of the BIS, see Henry H. Schloss, *The Bank for International Settlements*, New York University Bulletin, Nos. 65–66, September 1970.

QUESTIONS FOR DISCUSSION

1 Distinguish between an international financial system and an international monetary system. What is money? Why is money important?

2 What was the importance of the dominance of London, in international finance, in the international monetary system before 1914?

3 Distinguish between the gold standard of the period of, roughly, 1880–1914, and the gold exchange standard of the period from 1924 or 1925 to 1931.

4 Some have argued that major mistakes in U.S. government and central bank policy were responsible for the depression of 1929–1941 and for the disruption of the international monetary system during that period. What actions are singled out as

mistakes in this view? How did these actions adversely affect the international monetary system?

5   Is an international financial crisis like that of 1931 possible today? Why or why not?

6   Discuss Nurkse's view that cooperation and agreement in the establishment of par values for currencies were necessary. If his view was correct in 1944, is it correct today? If it was not correct then, is it still incorrect today? Why or why not?

7   Friedman has strongly argued against both price controls and exchange controls, on a similar basis. Are his arguments sound? To the extent that they are valid, is his argument against fixed but adjustable exchange rates also valid? Why or why not?

8   Why was a period of "dollar shortage" inevitable after World War II? Was this likely to be a continuing situation, or one which would disappear after a time? Why?

9   The "economic liberals" (in contrast to "political liberals") in the early part of the twentieth century advocated a gold standard and fixed exchange rates, but otherwise they advocated freedom for prices and wages to fluctuate. How do you reconcile the two views? On the other hand, current believers in "economic freedom," such as Milton Friedman, advocate both flexible exchange rates and flexibility in prices and wages. How do you explain the shift in views from the old "liberalism" to the new?

10 In the early part of the twentieth century, economists such as Benjamin M. Anderson criticized the quantity theory of money as a mechanical theory, arguing that the value of money and hence the demand for money and the velocity of money depended on social attitudes. Anderson himself doubted that confidence could be developed, on a long-term basis, in anything but gold as an international reserve asset, because governments always tend to overspend and thus depreciate the value of assets (such as paper money or bank deposits) which they create or permit banks to create. What do you think? Why?

SUGGESTED REFERENCES

A provocative examination of international finance in the period from 1914 to World War II is contained in Benjamin M. Anderson, *Economics and the Public Welfare* (Princeton, N.J.: Van Nostrand, 1949). Although Anderson's views are controversial, and other views should be read to obtain a balanced viewpoint, his analysis is thought-provoking. Anderson believed that the value of money depends on confidence in its purchasing power, and that although such confidence might be maintained for some time through social means, it was almost inevitable that any type of debt money would lose value in time because governments have a perennial tendency to overspend in relation to the possible increase in real output in their economies. For similar views by a present-day economist, see Jacques Rueff, "The West is Risking a Credit Collapse," *Fortune*, July 1961, pp. 126–127, 262, 267–268. See also Herbert G. Grubel, ed., *World Monetary Reform* (Stanford, Calif.: Stanford, 1963); in that book an article by Rueff, "Gold Exchange Standard a Danger to the West," was reprinted on pp. 320–328.

A very scholarly study is that by William Adams Brown, Jr., *The International Gold Standard Reinterpreted, 1914–1934,* 2 vols. (New York: National Bureau of Economic Research, 1940).

Anderson's views were largely superseded because of the wide acceptance of the Keynesian viewpoint. Lord Keynes, in addition to being a general economic theorist of the first order, was one of the major participants in creating the IMF, although its form was not as he desired in all respects. For Keynes' views on the international monetary system, see *Proposals for an International Clearing Union*, presented by the Chancellor of the Exchequer to Parliament by Command of His Majesty, April 1943 (London: H.M.'s Stationery Office, Cmd. 6437). It is interesting to read Anderson's critique of the Keynes plan: "I condemn the Morgenthau and Keynes plans *in toto* as putting the cart before the horse . . . let the government open trade lines, let the government cooperate with the bankers in seeing to it that reforms on the other side accompany the offer of . . . loans on this side, and we should get investors' money for the rehabilitations of Europe . . . the follies of the '20's would look microscopic if we adopted the Keynes-Morgenthau plan" (*Postwar Stabilization of Foreign Exchange, the Keynes-Morgenthau Plan Condemned, Outline of a Fundamental Solution*, Los Angeles, Capital Research Company, 1943, pp. 36–38).

Many detailed studies of exchange controls are available, but three volumes are of general value: John B. Condliffe, *The Reconstruction of World Trade* (New York: Norton, 1940); Howard S. Ellis, *Exchange Control in Central Europe*, Harvard Economic Studies, Vol. 69 (Cambridge, Mass.: Harvard, 1941); and Margaret S. Gordon, *Barriers to World Trade* (New York: Macmillan, 1941).

The concept of a dollar shortage was introduced in the report of the U.S. Department of Commerce, Hal B. Lary and others, *The United States in the World Economy*, Economic Series No. 23 (Washington, D.C.: Government Printing Office, 1943).

The period from the establishment of the gold standard by a number of countries in the 1870s to the end of World War II is reviewed in detail in Leland B. Yeager, *International Monetary Relations*, 2d ed. (New York: Harper & Row, 1976), Chaps. 15–19. Yeager's footnotes cite a large number of the most useful other sources.

For a review of central bank activity during the period of the gold standard, see Arthur I. Bloomfield, *Monetary Policy Under the International Gold Standard, 1880–1914* (New York: Federal Reserve Bank of New York, 1959). Those interested in the operation of the gold standard before 1914 should also consult Arthur I. Bloomfield, *Short-Term Capital Movement Under the Pre-1914 Gold Standard*, Princeton Studies in International Finance No. 11 (Princeton, N.J.: Princeton, 1963). Bloomfield shows that although differentials in short-term interest rates and fluctuations of exchange rates within the gold points played a major role in causing international short-term capital movements, other factors such as preferences for markets for lending or borrowing, availability of credit, debt service requirements, and changes in needs for working balances in particular centers were also significant.

As background for analysis of current efforts to reform the international monetary system, discussed in Chap. 6, Stephen V. C. Clarke, *The Reconstruction of the International Monetary System: The Attempts of 1922 and 1933*, Princeton Studies in International Finance No. 33 (Princeton, N.J.: Princeton, 1973) reviews the unsuccessful international conferences of 1922 in Genoa and of 1933 in London, which marked attempts to strengthen the international monetary system. The failure of these conferences left the international monetary system in chaos, and led to the creation of the IMF at the Bretton Woods Conference in 1944.

Chapter 5

The International Monetary System, 1946–1971

The IMF agreement, an intricate arrangement among member nations for the operation of the international monetary system, inaugurated a new era. The gold standard of 1880–1945 had required simply that each nation adopting it define its currency in terms of a weight of gold and buy and sell gold at the price corresponding to this weight.[1] As long as the U.S. government was willing to buy and sell gold at this price, it was fulfilling its commitment.[2]

Under the IMF agreement, each member country undertook numerous obligations. This provided strength because all member countries agreed to these provisions, but it also was a weakness because the complexity of the provisions led to some disputes and to unwillingness, in some cases, to abide by the agreement. Nevertheless, the IMF agreement and the activity of the IMF are the major features of the international monetary system in the period 1946–1971.

---

[1]Thus if 23.22 grains of fine gold were defined as a dollar, the dollar was worth 23.22/480 of an ounce of gold (a troy ounce contains 480 grains). The dollar was thus worth 0.048375 ounce of gold, and an ounce of gold was worth $20.67 (since an ounce is 20.67 times 0.048375 ounce).

[2]Small fees could be charged by the government for purchases and sales.

PURPOSES OF THE IMF AGREEMENT

The IMF agreement (often called the Bretton Woods agreement because it was negotiated at the Bretton Woods, New Hampshire, international finance conference in 1944) grew out of the conditions existing at the end of World War II. These conditions had produced general agreement on the following propositions: (1) The stable exchange rates existing under the gold standard were in general desirable, but under certain conditions adjustments in exchange rates are necessary. (2) Experience with fluctuating or flexible exchange rates had been unsatisfactory. The reasons for this unsatisfactory experience (whether because flexible rates had been in effect primarily in periods of world depression or war or because there were inherent defects in a system of flexible exchange rates) were not extensively debated. (3) The complex network of government controls that evolved during the period 1931–1945 was detrimental to the expansion of world trade and investment, wasteful and discriminatory, and an unwarranted interference by government with private business in the international field. On the other hand, it was recognized that some conditions require government controls over international trade and payments.

Thus the purposes of the IMF agreement were conditioned by experience with the gold standard, periods of flexible exchange rates, and the network of government controls. The purposes of the IMF agreement may be stated succinctly:[3]

1 To promote international monetary cooperation by establishing an institution (the IMF) for this purpose

2 To expand world trade and investment

3 To promote relatively stable exchange rates

4 To reduce or eliminate the network of government restrictions on international payments

5 To have a fund available for short-term or medium-term loans of currencies needed to facilitate maintenance of stable exchange rates during temporary imbalances, until it became clear that a change in an exchange rate was needed

6 To shorten and reduce the amplitude of deficits or surpluses in balances of payments

The keynote of the gold standard had been the acceptance of certain unstated but understood rules; the keynote of the IMF system was the acceptance of rules established in detail by international agreement.

The stated purposes continued to guide the IMF during the period 1946–1971 with no major changes in general aims, in spite of many changes in specific rules and procedures.

[3]*Articles of Agreement, International Monetary Fund* (Washington, D.C.: International Monetary Fund, 1944), art. 1.

ORGANIZATION OF THE IMF

General management of the IMF was vested in a Board of Governors, one governor and one alternate being appointed by each member country to meet annually and to exercise basic general powers. Other powers were vested in the Executive Directors, appointed or elected by countries, according to their size and importance in world trade (groups of countries were combined for election of directors).

Nonmembers of the IMF are chiefly the countries which have centrally planned economies and are little concerned with international finance—the Soviet Union and its satellites, mainland China, and others such as North Korea and Vietnam. Switzerland did not join because it has maintained a policy of not joining international organizations, with a few exceptions such as the Red Cross and some other nonpolitical organizations.[4]

The Executive Directors choose a Managing Director who serves as their presiding officer and who is responsible for organization and appointment of staff and for the direction of the work of the IMF.

Voting

Weighted voting, rather than one vote for each country, was specified in the IMF agreement. Originally each country had 250 votes plus one vote for each $100,000 of its quota in the IMF (described below). The purpose of weighted voting was to give greater power to lending countries, and the net effect in the original agreement was to give the United States and the United Kingdom together approximately 40 percent of the voting power. The United States retained enough votes throughout the period to veto important decisions, which required an 80 or 85 percent majority vote.

Relationship to the UN

The IMF agreement was formulated before the United Nations Conference was held, although not before the idea of a United Nations organization had been considered. Like other international organizations, the IMF was "brought into relationship," in the legal phraseology, with the United Nations by an agreement. This agreement specified independence for the IMF—justified by the need for independent control of monetary affairs. The need for independence arose from the temptation for governments to overspend and to create inflation. For the same reason central banks also often enjoy a degree of independence from the governments of the countries in which they exist.[5]

---

[4]Switzerland had belonged to the Latin Monetary Union, formed in 1865 by France, Belgium, Switzerland, and Italy, and joined by Greece in 1868. Gold and silver coins minted by each country were to circulate freely in all those countries, but the rise of the gold standard and the decline of silver as a monetary metal finally ended the significance of the Union as its member countries adopted the gold standard in the 1870s.

[5]See, for example, Leland M. Goodrich and Edvard Hambro, *Charter of the United Nations, Commentary and Documents*, rev. ed. (Boston: World Peace Foundation, 1949), p. 349.

PAR VALUES OF CURRENCIES

The IMF agreement provided that each country should, except under special dispensations, establish a par value for its currency in terms of either gold or U.S. dollars. At the same time the value of the U.S. dollar in terms of gold was not to be changed except in very special circumstances. Thus the foundation of the gold-dollar standard was laid. Dollars and gold were the keystones of the system, in relation to which other currencies were stabilized in value.

Each country agreed not to permit the rates at which current foreign exchange transactions were carried out within its territory—since it had jurisdiction only in that area—to vary by more than plus or minus 1 percent from an established par value. Permissible variation of forward or future contract exchange rates was to be determined by the IMF. Thus the variations in exchange rates were to be limited to a range about twice that under the gold standard (with gold export and import points generally about 0.5 percent above or below par). Countries occupied by enemies during World War II and certain countries with special financial problems were permitted to postpone establishment of par values.[6].

By 1970, most countries had par values for their currencies, and 35 countries had accepted obligations (under Article VIII of the IMF agreement) not to impose restrictions on payments for current account transactions. Currencies of these countries were convertible into gold. Becoming an "Article VIII" country carried some prestige, but it meant that the step was irreversible unless the country was prepared to engage in confrontation with the IMF.

Figure 5-1 shows that even in 1970 and the first half of 1971, current exchange rates did not generally fluctuate more than about 1 percent from par. The major exception was the Deutsche mark in the second quarter of 1971. By that time the flow of funds into Germany was so great that the German authorities temporarily closed the foreign exchange markets on May 5, 1971.

Fixed but Adjustable Exchange Rates

Emphasis of the IMF agreement was on stability of exchange rates. The wording of the agreement with respect to changes in par values was that "a member shall not propose a change in the par value of its currency except to correct a fundamental disequilibrium." The term *fundamental disequilibrium* was not defined, and much controversy arose concerning its interpretation.

The system was biased against upvaluations, and these were few. Since a country could propose a change in par value only to correct a fundamental disequilibrium in its BOP, the most likely reason for proposing a change was a deficit in the BOP, and the most likely change was devaluation. The only significant upvaluations were those by West Germany and the Netherlands in 1961 (only 5 percent) and by Germany in 1969 (about 9 percent). No provision was made for the United States to change the value of its currency—the value

---

[6]A considerable number of countries retained this special dispensation; by 1960, 10 member countries still had not established par values.

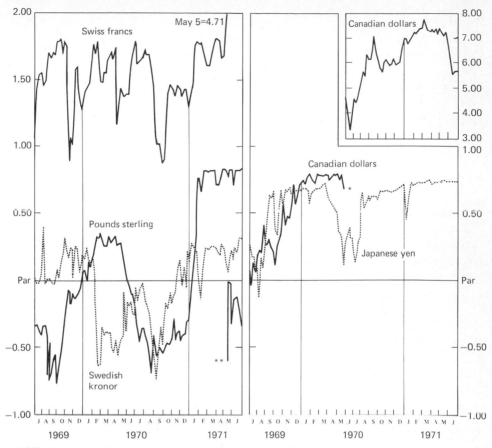

* Effective June 1, 1970 the Canadian authorities have not maintained the exchange rate for their currency
within the established margins.
** Revaluation of the Swiss franc, effective May 10, 1971.
[1] Based on Wednesday noon quotations in New York.

Figure 5-1　Spot Exchange Rates: Selected Currencies Against U.S. Dollar, July 1969–June
1971[1] (spread from par in percent). (*Source:* IMF, *Annual Report*, 1971, pp. 136–137.)

of gold at $35 per ounce and the corresponding value of the dollar as $1/35$ of an
ounce of gold were the keystones of the system.

Member countries made the decisions to devalue or upvalue, and the IMF
could not even object if the total change (including previous changes) was not
more than 10 percent. It could object to larger changes but was required to state
its position within 72 hours if a change was not more than 20 percent. It was
recognized that exchange rate changes had to be made quickly, before
speculators had a chance for large profits. Moreover, the IMF could not base an
objection on the internal (domestic) policies of a country even if its staff
believed the country could have made some other appropriate adjustment,
perhaps in prices and wages.

The IMF's major weapon was the power to declare a country ineligible to
use IMF resources. A well-known example is the introduction of multiple

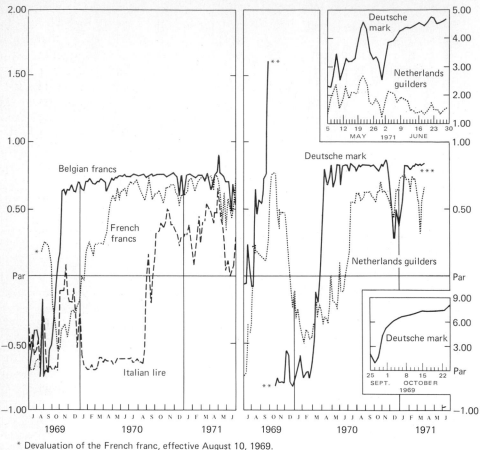

* Devaluation of the French franc, effective August 10, 1969.
** Revaluation of the deutsche mark, effective October 26, 1969.
*** Effective May 10, 1971 the German and the Netherlands authorities have not maintained the exchange
rates for their currencies within the established margins.
¹ Based on Wednesday noon quotations in New York.

Figure 5-1   *(Continued)*

exchange rates by France in 1948. Fortunately, during the period 1948–1952
France was receiving Marshall Plan aid from the United States and hence had
less need for IMF funds than it would have otherwise. By 1954 France had
made changes in its exchange rate system which caused the IMF to restore its
eligibility.

Fundamental Disequilibria in BOPs

Much discussion occurred after 1946 concerning the meaning of the term
fundamental disequilibrium.[7] It was generally agreed that a long-continued and

[7]This term was not defined in the Articles of Agreement of the IMF. There was much
discussion of its meaning by economists; see, for example, Seymour E. Harris, ed., *Foreign
Economic Policy for the United States* (Cambridge, Mass.: Harvard, 1948), especially the chapters
by Alvin H. Hansen and Gottfried Haberler.

large loss of reserve assets was evidence of such a condition. More controversial was the view that there might be a fundamental disequilibrium if a country had downward pressure on its prices and wages at the same time that it had signficant unemployment. Such a country presumably would have lost reserve assets had it sought to attain "full employment," for the adjustment process described in Chapter 3 would have caused deficits. Especially, the real income shifts created by rising expenditures, money supply, prices, and imports would have created BOP deficits or would have made them greater had they already existed.[8] Economists had different views concerning the appropriate steps to be taken: devaluation or depreciation of the currency on the one hand or an attempt to reduce prices and wages to relieve the unemployment problem on the other.

The international monetary system continued to be viable for many years without a clear-cut resolution of this controversy. Its viability during this period was an advantage for world trade and investment, as was the steady (if slow) progress toward relaxation of exchange and trade controls.

Initial Par Values

The IMF did not object to initial par values proposed in 1946 even though staff members probably thought many of them too high. *Why* it did not object is not certain, but a number of reasons can be suggested. First, countries with limited export facilities, whether because of wartime destruction of industry or for other reasons, could not increase their exports by lowering their currency par values. Second, many countries needed to import and to borrow for reconstruction; lower par values would have raised the cost of such borrowing and importing. Third, in the uncertain situation existing after World War II, calculation of appropriate par values was difficult. Some economists pointed out that relatively high par values tended to cause a shift of resources away from export industries and toward home-goods industries. They also tended to cause increased imports—sometimes resulting in deficits on current account.[9]

Devaluations

By 1949 it was clear that devaluations of a number of currencies were necessary. The major currency to be devalued was the pound sterling. Since many countries which traded heavily with Britain were members of the sterling area—that is, they accepted sterling in payment for exports and paid in sterling for many imports—it was natural that many of these countries devalued at the same time as Britain. When the United States recession of 1948–1949 reduced

---

[8]David C. Rowan, "Towards a National Exchange Policy: Some Reflections on the British Experience," Federal Reserve Bank of St. Louis, *Review*, April 1969, pp. 17–26, used a Keynesian framework and some assumptions concerning exports and long-term capital flows to show that under these conditions with full employment Britain would have had a deficit in its current account in its balance of payments every year from 1959 to 1967—and might therefore have devalued much earlier than 1967.

[9]See the discussion in Charles N. Henning, *International Finance* (New York: Harper & Row, 1958), p. 361.

U.S. imports from Europe, pressure on the pound sterling toward a lower exchange value increased.

Americans paid for some imports from the sterling area with so-called "cheap sterling"—sterling held by nonresidents of the sterling area and traded in New York for less than regular sterling. Supposedly, cheap sterling was not convertible into U.S. dollars, but switch arrangements were sometimes used to deliver to the United States goods purportedly destined for nondollar countries and paid for with sterling not convertible into dollars. Because this sterling sold outside Britain at a lower rate than convertible sterling, Britain was in effect selling some exports for fewer dollars. This tended to confirm the impression that the pound was overvalued, and rumors of devaluation spread.

As this occurred, traders sought to borrow in London, thus putting more downward pressure on the sterling exchange rate. Sterling area traders sought to buy quickly before prices rose and to delay selling until they could sell cheaper. These "commercial leads and lags" added further to the downward pressure on the sterling exchange rate.

This was the period in which Harrod (Oxford University economist and author of a biography of Keynes) referred to "low-browed international financiers"; much later the phrase used was "the Gnomes of Zurich." British annoyance at the speculative pressure is understandable.

In September 1949, after brief consultation with the IMF, Britain devalued by 30.5 percent. Approximately 30 countries, most of them members of the sterling area, followed—in a few cases with different percentages. Major currencies not devalued included the U.S. dollar, some Latin American currencies, the Swiss franc, and the Japanese yen.

This widespread devaluation did not lead to the same continuing international financial crisis as that which followed the currency depreciation of 1931. The U.S. recession in 1948–1949 was relatively brief and shallow, the period was generally one of inflation, and the Korean war broke out in June 1950, causing great demand for many products produced in sterling area territories—for example, rubber and tin in Malaya. In fact, the effects of the devaluations and of the Korean conflict are so intertwined that it is difficult to estimate the results of devaluation.

Some British economists believed that the British BOP did not improve immediately and that the rise in import prices introduced cost-push inflationary pressures into Britain. However, the British pound was not devalued again for 18 years. This period of stability has also given rise to controversy. Deficits occurred, but not annually. It is not clear that another devaluation sooner than 1967 would have significantly improved the British position, although clearly if Britain had had full employment instead of high unemployment, imports would have been greater (because imports depend on income and on consumption in general) while exports probably would not have been greater (because they depend on world markets). Thus deficits would probably have been larger and more regular.

France is an example of a country which devalued its currency on a number of occasions during the 1946–1971 period, forced to do so by a high rate of inflation resulting from government domestic expenditures and heavy spending for wars in Indochina and in Algeria.

West Germany, on the other hand, is an example of a country which struggled against "imported inflation." West Germany rebuilt its industry, stabilized prices, and imported labor; the rapid rise in output led to increased exports and a BOP surplus on current account. Germany sought, with some success, to prevent inflowing foreign currencies from causing inflation although some of the measures taken, such as raising interest rates, caused other inflows of funds in search of high yields.

Clearly, there were stresses during the period, but two things should be noted: stability of exchange rates and gradual elimination of exchange and trade controls were achieved, especially with the current account convertibility of major European currencies in 1958, and world trade and investment increased at more rapid rates than domestic output in most countries.

The Japanese yen had been given a par value of 360 to the U.S. dollar in 1949, a rate very close to purchasing power parity, that is, to its purchasing power relative to that of the U.S. dollar. This rate was maintained throughout the period. In some ways, like Germany, Japan rebuilt its industry and increased output at a rapid rate (an average increase in real output of about 11 percent a year, the highest in the world). However, because Japan lacks so many natural resources, imports increased concomitantly with exports, and it was not until toward the end of the period that Japan began to develop a BOP surplus and an inflow of reserve assets (chiefly foreign exchange—Japan has never held much gold).

Strains on the IMF par values were evident in the late 1960s, but countries were reluctant to upvalue currencies (especially West Germany, Japan, and Belgium). Clearly, a problem of the IMF system was a long delay in changing par values when it became evident that change was needed—and the resulting rather large change when it did occur.

Canada's Floating Exchange Rate

The most interesting exception to the IMF stable exchange rate system was Canada's floating exchange rate from 1950 to 1962 and again from 1970 on. Canada faced special problems in 1949–1950. In 1949, the decision was to devalue from 1 dollar to 90 cents in terms of U.S. dollars. Had Canada not devalued, its exports to Britain (which devalued by 30.5 percent) would have declined, and they were more important than its imports from Britain. However, Canada's imports from the United States were more important than its exports to the United States, and a large devaluation would have increased import costs.

In 1950, the concern was somewhat different. Canada had a surplus on long-term capital account—American investors, seeking favorable opportunities in Canada, were investing large amounts. As these funds flowed in, Canadian banks obtained more U.S. dollars than they wished to hold; as they sold U.S. dollars, the Bank of Canada (Canada's central bank) had no alternative but to buy U.S. dollars if it wished to keep the Canadian dollar at its new par value. Canada therefore decided to "float" its dollar, permitting it to rise if investors continued to make investments in Canada. The hope was that the Canadian dollar would move to an equilibrium level consistent with Canada's basic BOP balance. The IMF agreed to this floating rate for two reasons: (1) Canada did face special circumstances in having a surplus on long-term capital account and had no need to change its par value because of current account surpluses or deficits and (2) Canada was not an extremely large factor in world trade. Its floating rate did not constitute a very important exception to the IMF stable rate system, and other exceptions, such as Peru, were even less important.

The Canadian dollar rose from US$0.90 to about US$1.07 and thereafter fluctuated above US$1.00. But its rise hurt Canadian exports, and unemployment in Canada was relatively heavy. After more than ten years with a floating rate, Canada decided in 1962 to force the value of its dollar down. At the same time, as might have been expected, speculators began to sell Canadian dollars. Their value fell sharply until in May 1962 the government stabilized the value at a new par of US$0.925.

Opinions vary concerning the success of the Canadian experiment.[10] Some economists argue that if Canada had increased its money supply sufficiently to attain "full" employment, the floating rate would have been useful in checking "imported" inflation by discouraging too great an inflow of American investment funds. Others argue that abandonment of the floating rate was evidence of failure. In 1970, Canada again permitted its exchange rate to float. This time, other major countries also permitted their currencies to float after an attempt to maintain par values from 1970 until 1973.

ELIMINATION OF EXCHANGE CONTROLS

Because foreign exchange controls were widely regarded as a hindrance to world trade, the IMF aimed to eliminate such controls insofar as possible. However, it was recognized that controls designed to limit capital movements have a different rationale from controls affecting current account payments. Countries which could freely permit current account payments might not be able to permit withdrawals of funds which had been invested or on deposit over a long period. Countries which could permit current account payments without restriction were expected to so notify the IMF—becoming "Article VIII

---

[10]For views and comments on Canada's experience see A. F. Wynne Plumptre, *Experience with Canada's Floating Rate*, Essays in International Finance, No. 81 (Princeton, N.J.: Princeton, 1970); G. Hartley Mellish and Robert G. Hawkins, *The Stability of Exchange Rates—The Canadian Experience*, The Bulletin, Nos. 50–51 (New York: New York University Graduate School of Business Administration, 1958); Harry G. Johnson and John E. Nash, Hobart Papers 46 (London: The Institute of Economic Affairs, 1969); Paul Wonnacott, *The Canadian Dollar, 1948–1968* (Toronto: University of Toronto Press, 1965); Sydney A. Shepherd, *Foreign Exchange and Foreign Trade in Canada* (Toronto: University of Toronto Press, 1973).

countries"—while others continued to avail themselves of a transitional period exception provided in Article XIV of the IMF agreement. By 1974, only about 40 nations had become Article VIII countries, but they included the major industrialized countries.

IMF and GATT

Controls may be imposed on either *payments* or *transactions*; the former are termed *exchange controls* while the latter are usually referred to as *trade controls*. The IMF was expected to try to gain the removal of payments restrictions while another organization, GATT, became the major focus of efforts to remove restrictions on trade—both tariffs and nontariff barriers, although the original effort was directed toward tariffs. The U.S. government had made proposals during World War II for eliminating restrictions on international transactions. Subsequently, in 1947 when tariff concessions between pairs of countries were negotiated in Geneva, Switzerland, they were generalized under what is termed *most-favored-nation treatment* to become applicable to all the negotiating parties under a broad agreement known as the General Agreement on Tariffs and Trade (GATT). It had been intended that GATT would be merged into an International Trade Organization (ITO), but that organization was never established because the U.S. Congress did not ratify the agreement for its establishment. GATT has continued as an organization with rather limited powers, but a series of tariff negotiations under GATT has reduced tariffs substantially, and some progress has been made in reducing nontariff barriers. The GATT agreement required GATT to cooperate with the IMF to pursue a coordinated policy for reduction of both trade and payments barriers. Thus if BOP problems are cited by a country as a reason for imposing or increasing restrictions, GATT consults with the IMF.

Convertibility of Major European Currencies, 1958

The signing of the Treaty of Rome in 1957 provided for the establishment of a European Common Market, with gradual removal of trade barriers among the member countries. Impetus for European coordination came from both the United States and Europe. Secretary of State George Marshall's speech in June 1947 had promised U.S. aid funds if Europe would develop a plan for using such aid constructively. The Organization for European Economic Cooperation (OEEC) had been formed partly in response to this offer and partly because of the European desire for cooperation. With the addition in 1948 of West Germany to the original group of 16 countries, the organization included most of the major countries of Europe. With the exception of Greece, Iceland, Turkey, and Finland, all successfully achieved currency convertibility on current account in 1958. Greece and Turkey had problems arising from difficult economic conditions and the possibility of external forces acting against them, although they benefited from special U.S. aid under a program initiated by President Truman.

   With the action in 1958, practically all currencies extensively used in financing international trade and payments became freely convertible for current account transactions if they were not already convertible. This result must be attributed to economic recovery in Europe generally; to a new monetary policy in West Germany after 1947 which limited inflation and provided a solid foundation for growth in that country; to the U.S. aid program, especially in earlier years from 1948 to 1952; and to the activity of the IMF in consulting with countries to achieve elimination of payments restrictions.

Special Exceptions to Permit Exchange Controls

The IMF agreement recognized three special reasons for imposition of exchange controls: (1) difficulties involved in postwar recovery, (2) a need for controls on capital movements under some conditions, and (3) the possibility that a particular currency (in mind was the U.S. dollar) might become generally scarce because of great and widespread demand for it. In fact, a "scarce currency" provision in the IMF agreement permitted discriminatory controls in such an event—but the provision was not used because by the mid-1950s the period of dollar scarcity began to become the period of dollar surplus.[11]

RESOURCES OF THE IMF

The IMF was both an international consultative agency for the establishment and maintenance of stable but adjustable exchange rates and a fund which could be drawn upon to meet temporary needs instead of changing exchange par values. Understood in a special sense, the IMF was and is a bank. Banks generally make loans and in the process create money in the form of deposit accounts; Keynes's original plan for the IMF would have involved this activity. But, as the IMF was established, it simply exchanges desired currencies for local currencies of the countries wishing to "borrow"—from a fund established by contribution of currencies to the IMF under quotas set by agreement. The only difference between this process of borrowing from the IMF and purchasing foreign exchange on the private markets is that the IMF guarantees to supply the desired currency or currencies at the established par values, whereas market purchases would result, unless central banks intervened, in changes in exchange rates, with higher rates for the currencies being purchased and a lower rate for the currency of the buying country.

Quotas and Contributions

Political bargaining determined the quotas for contributions to the IMF to establish the fund. Some countries insisted that size and population were important and should be given weight in determining quota amounts, but the

[11]Yeager gives three reasons why the scarce-currency clause was not invoked: the IMF in effect rationed currencies by not granting some applications for borrowing, the American aid programs provided substantial amounts of dollars, and the kind of discriminatory controls that could have been imposed under the scarce currency clause were imposed anyway under Article XIV by many countries; see Yeager, *International Monetary Relations*, p. 401.

major factor was the extent of trade—presumably the basis for international need for specific currencies.

U.S. authorities argued for and obtained an important role for gold in the IMF; it was agreed that one-fourth of each quota should be contributed in gold, if possible, and the remaining three-fourths in a country's own currency. Since any country can create its own currency, the significant requirement was the gold contribution. This ensured continued use of gold as an international reserve asset.[12] But the importance of the dollar in world trade and its strength because of the large and increasing real output (real GNP) in the U.S. economy meant that the dollar was also an important international reserve asset under the new system—more important than it had been before World War II.

Since the IMF had only a limited amount of the currencies which were most likely to be needed (chiefly those of major trading countries), 10 leading member countries agreed in 1962 to lend the IMF a maximum of $6 billion of their currencies when needed by any of the 10 countries. This agreement was termed the General Arrangements to Borrow. It was an important and much used addition to the IMF's potential resources. The Group of Ten, as these countries came to be called, played a major role in various developments in the international monetary system in subsequent years.[13]

Before European currencies became convertible on current account in 1958, the European Payments Union (EPU), created in 1950, had acted as a clearinghouse and as a means of economizing on transfers of currencies. Each member could use claims on some members to offset debt to other members; thus only countries which were persistent net debtors with respect to all the other 16 members had to make large transfers of reserve assets. The Bank for International Settlements (BIS) acted as agent for the EPU in handling the clearing and the transfers of reserve assets. Countries owing the clearinghouse could pay partly in gold or dollars and could, up to certain quotas, incur deficits. The result was that BOP reasons for trade discrimination among the member countries were eliminated. This arrangement, like that of the General Arrangements to Borrow, supplemented the IMF's activities and helped to permit better functioning of the international monetary system.

When most European currencies became convertible on current account in 1958, the EPU was replaced by a European Monetary Agreement (EMA), under which a fund was created for temporary loans to aid in maintaining convertibility. The EMA played only a small role, however.

---

[12]By April 30, 1974, gold constituted 23 percent of total global monetary reserve assets. SDRs and unused automatic borrowing privileges from the IMF combined totaled 10 percent. The remaining 67 percent consisted of foreign exchange. Holdings of U.S. dollars constituted a little more than one half the holdings of foreign exchange, and holdings of Eurodollars another one fifth. Clearly, the system was still a gold-dollar system for the most part. See International Monetary Fund, *Annual Report*, 1974, pp. 34–36.

[13]For the text of the General Arrangements to Borrow, see IMF, *Annual Report*, 1962, pp. 232–245. The amount of $6 billion was the equivalent of the total amount to be loaned by the Group of Ten countries combined. The countries are the United States, West Germany, the United Kingdom, France, Italy, Japan, Canada, the Netherlands, Belgium, and Sweden.

Loans—Borrowing or Purchasing?

As a result of the quota contribution requirement, the IMF holds gold and currencies of member countries, the latter partly in the form of deposits in the various central banks (deposits created by the central banks) and partly in the form of non-interest-bearing notes of member countries. When demand in a given country for foreign exchange is heavy, the exchange values of foreign currencies rise. If they begin to rise more than the permitted 1 percent above par, the central bank may export gold or sell foreign exchange to prevent further rise. If it begins to run short of such reserve assets, it may "borrow" from the IMF by paying into the IMF its own currency (which it can create) and withdrawing the desired currency or currencies at the par value.[14]

Since countries normally paid one-fourth of their quotas in gold and three-fourths in their own currencies, the IMF normally held three-fourths of a country's quota in that country's currency. The remainder of the quota was termed the *gold tranche*, and this amount could be "borrowed" from the IMF without question—in effect, that amount was generally secured by gold.[15]

The intention underlying the IMF agreement was to put pressure on debtor countries to correct their BOP situations as they became worse. A limit was therefore placed on "borrowing" by specifying that the IMF would not, except under special waiver, accept more than twice any country's quota in its own currency. Since the IMF normally held three-fourths of a country's quota in that country's currency, the limitation meant that maximum borrowing without special waiver was limited to $1^1/_4$ times a country's quota. Provision was made for the IMF to permit larger borrowing under special circumstances, and here the similarity of the IMF to a bank became more evident: the IMF could decide, on the basis of its evaluation of creditworthiness, how much could be borrowed. The IMF has also provided *standby arrangements* similar to those of banks to assure countries in difficult circumstances that they could borrow specific amounts.

There were also provisions in the IMF agreement to encourage the use of gold instead of borrowing, and complex provisions for repayment of borrowings which we need not examine in detail. The major importance of the repayment provisions is the understanding that financial aid from the IMF is short-term or medium-term, generally not to exceed three to five years. The basis for Keynes's comment that the IMF should have been called a bank is clear: the IMF, like a bank, provides generally short-term financial aid in amounts which it determines on the basis of its judgment of creditworthiness (above certain minimum amounts). On the other hand, it is not a bank in that it does not lend but instead sells currencies (at established exchange rates), and it does not create money except for the SDRs mentioned earlier and discussed in some detail later in this chapter.

[14]Special rules had been applied by the Executive Directors of the IMF for the values to be used in the cases of floating currencies, such as the Canadian dollar. See IMF *Annual Report*, 1955, p. 125–127.

[15]A few countries had contributed more than one-fourth of their quotas in gold, and thus had what came to be termed *super gold tranches*. The term *tranche* means share or portion.

The IMF agreement established an international authority, to which member countries made some concessions from their sovereign powers. Veto was retained by the United States on a number of important decisions by the requirement of an 85 percent majority vote, while the United States still holds more than 15 percent of the voting power. It became difficult for countries to withdraw from the IMF, although Poland and Czechoslovakia did so at an early time. By 1974 the only nonmember countries were the Soviet bloc, mainland China, and a few with special situations—for example, North Korea. Even the Soviet bloc was not solidly outside the IMF, for Romania is a member, and it has been rumored that mainland China has considered the possibility.

EXPERIENCE OF THE IMF

The gold standard was a system of implicitly understood rules. The IMF system which replaced it is one of rules established by agreement among member countries. If the essence of the Bretton Woods system is regarded as stable but adjustable exchange rates, the system may be said to have ended in 1973; if regarded as the gold-dollar international reserve (money) system, it ended in 1971; or if regarded as the establishment of guidelines for the international monetary system by international agreement, it still continues its operation. It may be useful to review briefly the experiences of the IMF from 1946 to 1971.

Experience in the 1950s and Early 1960s

It was understood that the IMF would not finance postwar reconstruction. This was a task allocated in part to a related institution, the International Bank for Reconstruction and Development (IBRD), discussed in Chapter 12. Nor would the IMF provide for postwar aid—Marshall Plan aid alone amounted to $17 billion in four years, and the resources of the IMF at that time of only several billion dollars could not have met the need for aid funds. Occupation aid in Japan, Korea, and West Germany and special assistance by the United States to Greece and Turkey were likewise outside the scope of the IMF.

The first potential test of the IMF thus came in the early 1950s. General stability of exchange rates in that period for major industrial countries and the gradual elimination of restrictions on international payments among such countries were signs of limited success, or at least signs that the system would not break down.

A test in 1956 came from Egypt's seizure of the Suez Canal, formerly controlled by Britain. The action created serious payments problems for Britain because the closure of the canal forced the use of longer and more costly shipping routes and deprived the United Kingdom of earnings from the operation of the canal. Downward pressure on the pound was heavy.

Nevertheless, the system of stable but adjustable exchange rates, supported by drawings (borrowings) from the IMF, continued through the 1950s and 1960s. A second devaluation of sterling in 1967 was accompanied by devaluations of the currencies of a number of other member countries. There were upvaluations of the Dutch guilder and of the German mark by 5 percent in 1961, and a second upvaluation of the German mark in 1969. In spite of these changes, serious weakness in the system was not clearly apparent until 1970.

The problem may be described as either too little gold or too many U.S. dollars. Additions of gold to monetary reserves stopped in the late 1960s as industrial and hoarding demand for gold and the cessation of Soviet gold sales actually reduced monetary gold holdings in some years. The situation is shown graphically in Figure 5-2.

The other side of the problem was the abundance of U.S. dollars. Increased money supply in the United States and spending for both the Vietnam war and domestic social programs led to the increased availability of dollars. The poor performance of the U.S. stock market, especially after 1968, contributed to the desire to seek better hedges against inflation. Dollars were transferred out of the United States and became abundant in other countries, especially in Europe (the Eurodollar market for dollars on deposit in banks outside the United States is described later in Chapter 10).

SDRs

In the meantime, monetary authorities had been concerned about the lack of growth in gold holdings and the consequent slower growth in world monetary reserves than in trade. World trade had been growing at about 8 percent per year whereas gold production, even if it had all been added to monetary reserves, would have added only about $1^1/_2$ percent per year to world monetary gold stocks. An increase in the price of gold, which would have increased the *value* of gold holdings, was opposed by many economists on the grounds that (1) it would benefit primarily the three major gold producing nations (South Africa, the Soviet Union, and Canada, in that order) and (2) it would create a potential for increased inflation because at least some central banks would probably take advantage of their increased gold holdings to create more money. It was opposed by the U.S. government for an additional reason: It would have further entrenched the role of gold in the world monetary system, and U.S. officials had by that time concluded that this role should be minimized.

The need for additional liquid international reserves was met by agreement for creation by the IMF of a new form of international reserve assets—SDRs, or special drawing rights.[16] These were created and distributed, after approval of the plan by more than the required 85 percent of the voting membership of the IMF, to member countries which accepted allocations—as all but a very few did.

---

[16]Drafting of provisions for the creation of SDRs had been agreed upon at the Rio de Janeiro meeting of the IMF in September 1967, and the draft, in the form of amendments to the articles of agreement, was sent to members in 1968. It came into force on July 28, 1969, after having been accepted by over three-fifths of the members of the IMF having over four-fifths of the total voting power. The actual creation of SDRs occurred subsequent to a proposal by the Managing Director of the IMF (after consultations with members), concurred in by the Executive Directors, and approved by a majority of the members having over 85 percent of the weighted voting power. See International Monetary Fund, *Annual Report*, 1968, pp. 133–174, for lengthy details of the draft provisions and an outline of procedures.

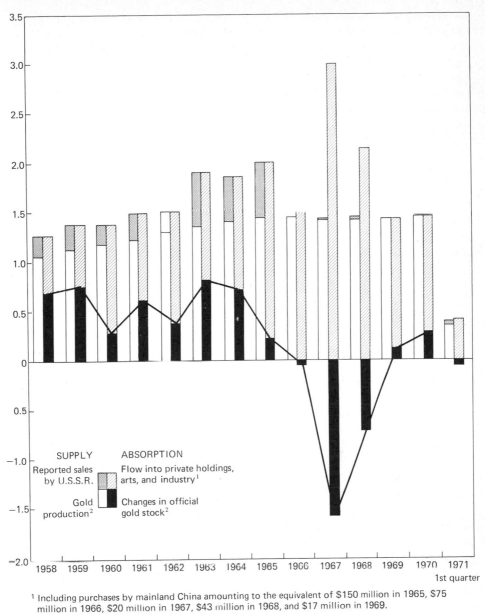

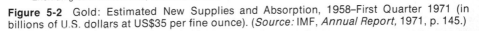

Figure 5-2 Gold: Estimated New Supplies and Absorption, 1958–First Quarter 1971 (in billions of U.S. dollars at US$35 per fine ounce). (*Source:* IMF, *Annual Report*, 1971, p. 145.)

[1] Including purchases by mainland China amounting to the equivalent of $150 million in 1965, $75 million in 1966, $20 million in 1967, $43 million in 1968, and $17 million in 1969.

[2] Excluding CMEA countries, mainland China, etc.

The SDRs were in effect paper gold since their value was guaranteed by that time in terms of gold. The creation of SDRs was money creation by an international institution—a historic event. Distribution of SDRs in January of 1970, 1971, and 1972 gave central banks a new reserve asset totaling approximately $10 billion—adding that much to world reserves. Unfortunately, at the same time world reserves were beginning to increase tremendously as the flow of dollars into foreign countries began to be absorbed by central banks and other holders. Although the creation of SDRs came just at the wrong time in this respect, it was another milestone in the long transition of money from metallic form to deposit (liability) form.

The special nature of SDRs as international reserves should be carefully noted. SDRs were to be exchanged *only* among central banks so that there was no possibility of changes in *public* demand affecting their acceptability. They were a reserve currency not a vehicle currency. Central banks were bound by a detailed agreement to accept and use SDRs under carefully specified conditions, and central banks could generally be counted on not to make speculative purchases or exchanges. Interest was paid at a nominal rate on amounts distributed and on additions to holdings and charged on amounts received in distributions and on amounts used for payments. Thus countries holding precisely the amounts distributed to them neither received nor made a net interest payment, but holders of additional amounts received net interest paid by those who held less because they had used SDRs. The interest rate was later increased to make SDRs more attractive and subsequently changed as money market interest rates fluctuated.[17]

The SDR account is separate from the general account of the IMF. Member countries made no deposits of either gold or currency to obtain SDRs—in effect, the IMF printed and distributed money of a special kind. When a central bank wished to use SDRs because its other reserves were low (the agreement specified that it would not use them simply to obtain other forms of reserve assets), it would transfer SDRs to the account of another country's central bank in exchange for convertible currencies. If no country provided these voluntarily, the IMF designated a country or countries whose BOP situations made it possible to provide SDRs. If countries violated the rules concerning use of SDRs, the IMF could offset their actions partly or wholly by directing subsequent transfers of SDRs from other countries to the violators in exchange for convertible currencies. Countries may use all available SDRs but must acquire or hold enough so that average holdings over a five-year period are at least 30 percent of the allocations they have received; thus only 70 percent of total allocations are available for permanent use. Countries designated to receive SDRs must accept them until their total holdings, including allocations, reach three times their cumulative allocations. The intention was to assure that if countries needed to use SDRs for payment there would always be countries required to accept them.

Certain special features of SDRs as money should be noted. First, they were created under an agreement among governments rather than by fiat of a single government or central bank. Second, however, they were created in limited amounts on specified occasions—not continuously under discretionary power. There have been proposals to make the IMF a world bank with full

[17]See IMF *Survey*, July 5, 1976, p. 193.

powers for continuous creation of money, but thus far these proposals are academic. Whether they will be carried into effect, and in what form, depends on the further evolution of the IMF as an international financial institution.

In spite of the special features noted above, SDRs are in a very important sense a form of money—they are an allocation of purchasing power to economic units (countries) by a central authority. When created, they expand world reserve assets. They do not necessarily increase the supply of money for commercial payments, but they constitute a means of final settlement of debt among central banks.

GOLD AND FOREIGN EXCHANGE IN INTERNATIONAL RESERVES

Gold and foreign exchange continued to be important as the major international reserve assets during the period 1946–1971, with SDRs representing only a small addition at the end of that period. Preferences of countries with respect to gold and foreign exchange as reserve assets vary. The United States still holds almost all its international reserves in the form of gold. France has generally preferred gold and at times has converted most of any foreign exchange obtained into gold. Japan, on the other hand, has held very little gold. In 1971 gold was still important, although this situation has changed, as we shall see later.

Foreign exchange was also important, and it seems probable that it will continue to be an important element in international reserve assets in the foreseeable future. Because of its wide use as a vehicle currency, the major currency held by central banks as a reserve asset has been the U.S. dollar, although small amounts of other currencies are held.

The need for reserve assets depends on the nature of reform of the international monetary system. A freely floating exchange rate system would mean no need for international reserves. To the extent that central banks intervene to moderate exchange rate fluctuations or to influence exchange rate movements in other ways, some reserves are needed. If the period of floating exchange rates for major industrial countries which began in the spring of 1973 should be terminated by a return to a system of stable but adjustable exchange rates like that which existed in the period 1946–1971, sizable reserves would be needed.

A WORD ON THE CURRENCIES OF NONMEMBER COUNTRIES[18]

Before turning to reform of the international monetary system, it is appropriate to touch on a question which may be in some readers' minds: What about exchange rates for currencies of countries which are not members of the IMF?

---

[18]This section draws very heavily on Robert Z. Aliber, *The International Money Game*, 2d ed. (New York: Basic Books, 1976), pp. 279–290.

The fact is that these currencies' exchange rates have little meaning in the international monetary system. Trade with the Soviet Union consists largely of barter of one group of commodities for another. Soviet trading agencies in New York make purchases in dollars. Purchases and sales of rubles are strictly controlled. For tourists traveling in the Soviet Union and for others who must make purchases in that country and hence must exchange dollars and other currencies for rubles, there are special exchange rates. Prices are not used in the Soviet Union to guide production, which is determined by planning. Imports, exports, and other elements in the balance of payments are also planned. As Dufey has observed, "There is no need for a special mechanism equilibrating the balance of payments, such as exchange rate changes or the public sector's international reserves; the plan equalizes exports and imports and serves as the single, all-embracing decision maker."[19]

For some time the ruble was pegged at 4 rubles to the dollar, and later it was pegged at 140 rubles per ounce of gold. Since the dollar was worth $1/_{35}$ of an ounce of gold, the ratio of rubles to dollars remained the same. In a currency reform in the early 1960s, new rubles were exchanged for old rubles at a rate of 1 to 10. This should have meant an upward revaluation of the ruble to 10 times its previous value, but the Soviet Union established a new price of 32 rubles per ounce of gold. This made the ruble theoretically worth $1.10 (instead of $2.50 at which it might have been valued). Since strict control prevents any but the hardiest of black market traders from exchanging rubles for dollars or other foreign currency at private market prices, the exchange value of the ruble is essentially meaningless. The value of the ruble in terms of goods and services can be determined by examining the prices at which goods can be bought by tourists or by ascertaining the hours of work necessary to earn the money to buy particular goods and services in Russia compared with another country.

Currencies of the countries of Eastern Europe, except Romania, have official rates and rates for tourists (different for tourists from socialist countries and from other countries). There are also black market rates, which may not be accurately reported but which can be approximated from *Pick's Currency Yearbook* and other sources. The Soviet Union is able to purchase more goods and services from these countries by using special exchange rates than it could if it used the official basic rates. Soviet tourists, including Soviet army divisions stationed in those countries, can obtain goods and services at lower cost than is indicated by the official rates. A good example is Poland. The basic rate for the Polish zloty in 1974 was 3.32 per U.S. dollar, but the socialist tourist rate was 11.42 zlotys per dollar and the capitalist tourist rate was 33.2 zlotys per dollar.

Although Yugoslavia is sometimes regarded as belonging to the Eastern European group of countries, it is an exception to many of the comments made above. It belongs to the IMF; its citizens may buy foreign currencies in regular foreign exchange markets and can travel abroad freely. True, Yugoslavia

---

[19]Gunter Dufey, "Financing East-West Business," *Columbia Journal of World Business*, Spring 1974, p. 39.

imposes import controls, but so do many countries which suffered heavily in World War II or which are still developing. Yugoslavia is part of the international monetary system; the Soviet Union and most of the Eastern European countries are not.

SUMMARY

For a quarter of a century the international monetary system for that part of the world which uses the price system to regulate economic activity was one in which exchange rates were generally stable for considerable periods, fluctuating only within narrow bands around established par values. When adjustment was necessary, devaluations occurred, and occasionally upvaluations vis-à-vis fixed values of U.S. dollars and gold.[20] There were at least discussions of such changes with the staff of the IMF—sometimes perfunctory, sometimes significant. Until such changes were made, central banks supported exchange rates as necessary, obtaining other currencies from the IMF if needed for such purpose.

A major event was the agreement for the IMF to create SDRs and to allocate them to member countries. This by no means made the IMF a full-fledged world central bank able to create money continuously and to control the world money supply. The creation of SDRs was a first venture, limited in amount, based on a large majority vote, and a one-time step although in three installments.

The IMF is (1) an institution facilitating consultation, (2) a financial intermediary providing desired currencies in exchange for a country's own currency at fixed exchange rates, (3) an overseer to some extent of the establishment of par values and of exchange rate practices in maintaining exchange rates at desired levels and in reducing or eliminating exchange controls, and (4) in creating SDRs, a central bank in a very limited way. In the long run, it is possible that the IMF may become a full-fledged central bank, creating money as an ongoing process, but this seems remote at present.

Some economists quickly proclaimed the end of the Bretton Woods system in 1971. If the essence of that system was the stable value of the U.S. dollar in terms of gold and its convertibility into gold at least for foreign central banks, the end did come in 1971. If the essence of the system was stable but adjustable exchange rates, the end, at least temporarily, came in 1973. But if the essence of the system was the establishment of an institution facilitating discussion of guidelines for central bank action and for agreement on changes in the international monetary system, the Bretton Woods era still continues. It is highly unlikely that the non-Communist world will return to a gold standard system in which basic rules are implicitly understood and followed, but it is also unlikely that—although the agreement in 1976 provided for both free and

---

[20]It is of course recognized that any devaluation is in effect an upvaluation of some other currency. But the fact that the U.S. dollar remained unchanged during this period in terms of its gold value and that changes always occurred in values of other currencies makes it convenient to refer to the devaluations of currencies other than the U.S. dollar during this time.

controlled exchange rates—the non-Communist countries will continue a "do as you please" policy in the long run. Forces for economic integration, including the activities of multinational corporations and the growing international effects of business fluctuations, probably preclude complete economic independence of nations.

Thus those concerned with international finance should analyze the possibilities for agreements which may be reached within the framework of IMF consultations and the probable effects of such agreements on exchange rates, exchange controls, and the degree of risk in foreign transactions.

QUESTIONS FOR DISCUSSION

1 Do you think that the IMF agreement successfully incorporated the best features of the gold standard, flexible exchange rates, and exchange controls? Why or why not?
2 How can a country comply with its obligations both to remove exchange restrictions and to prevent exchange transactions within its territory at rates more than 1 percent above or below par value?
3 Why is the term *borrowing* used when countries actually purchase foreign exchange from the IMF with their own currencies?
4 The IMF agreement provided that the head office of the IMF should be located in the United States. Why? It did not specify a city, but some representatives wanted it to be in New York, while the U.S. representatives wanted it to be in Washington, D.C. Why?
5 Many central banks have a degree of independence from their governments, and the IMF has a substantial degree of independence from the UN. Why?
6 What is meant by Article VIII countries in contrast to Article XIV countries?
7 Do you agree that a country may have a fundamental disequilibrium in its balance of payments without any significant outflow of reserve assets if it has serious unemployment and some downward pressure on prices and wages? Explain.
8 Do you believe that the IMF was justified in accepting par values suggested by individual countries for their own currencies between 1946 and 1948 even if it had doubts that these par values were appropriate? Why did it do this?
9 Why were the signing of the Treaty of Rome in 1957 and the convertibility of major European currencies in 1958 so important for the international monetary system?
10 What was the significance of the decision to issue SDRs? Discuss the reasons for making this decision and the results in view of subsequent developments.

SUGGESTED REFERENCES

Publications of the International Monetary Fund include reference works with which everyone concerned with international finance should have some familiarity: the *Annual Report*, the *Annual Report on Exchange Restrictions*, the *Staff Papers*, and others. The *IMF Survey*, published twice a month, enables one to keep up with current developments in international finance, with special emphasis on those in which the IMF is involved.

Special publications of the IMF which are particularly useful are J. Keith Horsefield, ed., *The International Monetary Fund, 1945–1965* (Washington, D.C.:

International Monetary Fund, 1969); Joseph Gold, *Special Drawing Rights, Character and Uses*, 2d ed. (Washington, D.C.: International Monetary Fund, 1970); and J. Marcus Fleming, *The International Monetary Fund* (Washington, D.C.: International Monetary Fund, 1964). More recent developments are covered in Margaret G. de Vries, *The International Monetary Fund, 1966–1971: The System Under Stress,* 2 Vols. (Washington, D.C.: International Monetary Fund, 1976).

On some of the technicalities related to SDRs, see Martin Barrett, "Activation of the Special Drawing Rights Facility in the IMF," Federal Reserve Bank of New York, *Monthly Review*, February 1970, pp. 40–46. For a general account of the creation of SDRs, see Fritz Machlup, *Remaking the International Monetary System: The Rio Agreement and Beyond* (Baltimore, Md.: Johns Hopkins, 1968).

For a view favorable to the Bretton Woods system, see Samuel I. Katz, *The Case for the Par Value System, 1972,* Essays in International Finance, No. 92 (Princeton, N.J.: Princeton, 1972).

For a detailed review of international monetary relations during the period covered by this chapter, see Leland B. Yeager, *International Monetary Relations*, 2d ed. (New York: Harper & Row, 1976), Chaps. 20–27.

On Canada's experimenting with a floating exchange rate, see the references cited in fn. 10.

Chapter 6

Reform of the International Monetary System Since 1971

The international monetary system which had been established under the Bretton Woods agreement of 1944 was abruptly changed in 1971 when the United States refused further convertibility of dollars into gold. Some say that the Bretton Woods system ended in 1971. Others argue that the changes were in part temporary, and in any event did not change two of the most important features of the system—international consultation concerning exchange rates and exchange controls and the presence of the IMF as a "lender of last resort" to provide foreign exchange to countries needing it without adding to pressures on exchange rates.

An even more important change occurred in 1973, when major countries permitted their currencies to float in foreign exchange markets. Again, some regarded floating as an interim measure, while others saw it as a definite end of the stable but adjustable exchange rates system.

These events of 1971 and 1973 made it clear that reform of the international monetary system was necessary. This need became more urgent when a huge increase in the price of oil in late 1973 led to major shifts in BOP positions for almost all countries. At the same time, reform became more difficult. While the oil-producing countries generally shifted to surpluses on current account, the major industrial countries encountered deficits on current account if they had not had them before 1973, and developing countries other than the oil-producing nations encountered serious current account deficits.

It was estimated that the Organization of Petroleum Exporting Countries (OPEC) would realize a current account surplus of about $55 to $60 billion in 1974 vis-à-vis the rest of the world. Many observers expressed concern that these surpluses would drain funds from the financial system of oil-importing countries, causing financial crises or perhaps even the bankruptcy of some nations. How, it was asked, could the oil-importing nations finance these enormous deficits? Before we examine this question and the problems of reform of the international monetary system, let us review some of the important events of the early 1970s.

THE EVENTS OF 1971

In mid-August 1971, after substantial pressures by foreigners to exchange dollars for gold, the U.S. government announced that it would no longer convert dollars into gold, even for official foreign holders. The "gold window" was closed.[1] Next, a 10 percent surcharge was added to the tariff on most dutiable imports. Finally, a wage-price freeze was imposed for 90 days. This later was extended into several phases of wage-price controls, which did not terminate until early 1974.[2]

These steps were taken for several purposes. Among them was the desire to stop the continued loss of U.S. gold reserves, which had fallen almost to $10 billion (from more than twice that level in the early years after World War II). Another objective was to exert pressure on certain foreign countries to upvalue their currencies in terms of the U.S. dollar, a goal not likely to be achieved through intervention in the foreign exchange market, because any attempt to reduce the value of the U.S. dollar would probably be countered by efforts of other countries to reduce the values of *their* currencies. Finally, the U.S. government wanted to show other nations that an effort was being made to control inflation. Much of the downward pressure on the U.S. dollar in foreign

---

[1]It is too soon for a definitive historical account of events of the weekend preceding Aug. 15, 1971, in Washington, D.C. The relative influence of economic and political factors is especially unclear. One writer has indicated that President Nixon and Secretary of the Treasury Connally had made the key decisions some time previously; see William Safire, *Before the Fall—An Inside View of the Pre-Watergate White House* (New York: Doubleday, 1975), p. 527.

[2]Some economists regarded wage and price controls as a *cause* of inflation, which may be somewhat startling. For a carefully worded evaluation, see the *Economic Report of the President*, February 1975, pp. 228–229, in which a slightly less firm statement is made:". . . the effects of wage and price controls . . . will be long debated and may never be resolved. . . . However, the evidence . . . does support a partial but important judgment . . . regardless of the overall effect of the program, whatever contribution it may have made was probably concentrated in its first 16 months, when the economy was operating well below its potential. As various industrial sectors reached capacity operations in 1973 under the stimulus of a booming domestic and world economy, the controls system began to obstruct normal supplier-purchaser relationships, and in some cases the controls became quite unworkable. The sharply rising costs of basic materials, often reflecting work market influences and dollar devaluation, were largely uncontrolled; and when passed through to consumers, they resulted in accelerating inflation."

exchange markets resulted from inflation in the United States becoming, during 1969, more rapid than in such countries as West Germany.

It had become increasingly clear by mid-1971 that the U.S. dollar was overvalued with respect to certain major foreign currencies, notably the Deutsche mark and the Japanese yen. The central banks of Germany and Japan, which had purchased dollars from private holders to prevent a rise in the values of their currencies and a simultaneous decline in the value of the U.S. dollar, were showing some unwillingness to continue this action. In May, the German Bundesbank (central bank) temporarily suspended foreign exchange operations. Thereafter, the Deutsche mark was allowed to rise in value, in a presumably temporary upward float. Values of currencies of the Netherlands, Switzerland, Belgium, and Austria also rose.

Meanwhile, the United States showed a merchandise trade deficit of $1.0 billion for the second quarter of 1971, while the overall BOP official settlements basis deficit rose sharply to $11.6 billion. The deterioration in the U.S. current account BOP position as well as in its official settlements balance, coupled with the unwillingness of foreign central banks in some countries to continue to accumulate dollars, led the United States to suspend the convertibility of dollars into gold. By mid-1971 convertibility would have been impossible for more than a fraction of the foreign official dollar holdings, since these totaled approximately $50 billion, almost five times the value of U.S. gold reserves. It should be noted, of course, that the United Kingdom had not had more than about 10 percent of its foreign liabilities in the form of gold reserves in the gold standard period before World War I, but that was an era of little inflation and of few significant changes in the economic positions of major countries.

Causes of the 1971 Events

These events had a number of significant causes. First, the economic recovery of Western European countries and of Japan improved their trade position with the United States and their competitive position in other world markets. Second, U.S. foreign investment outflows continued to increase as U.S. residents, both individuals and firms, bought foreign securities and made direct investments abroad. Growing economies in Western Europe and Japan offered opportunities for investment at higher expected rates of return, relative to risk, than in the United States, where real profits were under pressure from rising costs in wages and expenditures for pollution control and from rising taxes.[3] Third, the U.S. government added somewhat to the outflow of funds by sizable foreign aid and military assistance programs, although by the late 1960s these were, except for Vietnam, a relatively small factor. Fourth, the inflation rate in the United States, which had been very modest in the first half of the 1960s, rose sharply in the later 1960s as the Vietnam war and the "Great Society" social programs were financed through larger budget deficits. Sometimes it is

[3]*Economic Report of the President*, January 1976, pp. 40–41. The situation is also well described by Peter Bernstein, "Profits, Inflation, and Flag-Waving," *Morgan Guaranty Survey*, November 1976, pp. 8–15.

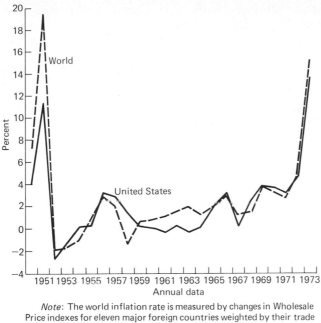

Note: The world inflation rate is measured by changes in Wholesale Price indexes for eleven major foreign countries weighted by their trade shares with the United States. The United States inflation rate is measured by changes in the Wholesale Price index.

Figure 6-1 Comparative Rates of Inflation. (*Sources:* U.S. Department of Commerce, International Monetary Fund, and Organization for Economic Cooperation and Development. Reprinted from Federal Reserve Bank of St. Louis, *Review*, May 1974, p. 15.)

assumed that inflation in the United States was greater generally than in the rest of the world. This is *not* true, as shown in Figure 6-1, but the inflation in the United States was more significant than in other countries because dollars were the most important international reserve asset and vehicle currency. As U.S. inflation became more serious, the dollar's value as a store of purchasing power came into question and gold began to seem more attractive.

Devaluation

In principle, a country may use devaluation of its currency as one means of correcting a worsening BOP position. Although there is some argument concerning the usefulness of devaluation, that option was not available to the United States under the Bretton Woods system as it operated before 1971. Other currencies were valued in terms of gold or dollars at the fixed rate of $35 per ounce of gold, and the market values of currencies other than the U.S. dollar were generally held at rates close to par values by government intervention. Unless other governments were willing not to intervene and to permit values of their currencies to rise, the United States could not meaningfully devalue as long as it was willing to convert dollars into gold at a fixed price. Even an increase in the official price of gold would in all probability have been followed by a similar increase by other governments, with no resulting change in the value of the dollar vis-à-vis other currencies. At that time most countries seemed unwilling to let their currencies rise in value, no doubt because of concern about the impact of such a rise on their export and import-competing industries.

From August to December of 1971, most major currencies were allowed to float, and, as expected, the U.S. dollar declined vis-à-vis a number of major foreign currencies. While each government retained its pre-August 1971 parity, all but the French government suspended their commitments to buy dollars at the lower limits of the exchange rate bands. In most cases the float was a "managed float," whereby central banks intervened to limit the movement of their currencies' values. During this period a number of countries imposed some trade and exchange controls, and there was concern that these measures might become sufficiently widespread to restrict world commerce. Some even envisioned another period of trade curtailment comparable to that of the 1930s. The uncertainties associated with floating rates and a fear that trade wars might precipitate a serious worldwide recession led to intensive international discussions.

The Smithsonian Agreement

These discussions culminated in the Smithsonian Agreement of December 18, 1971, which specified a new set of exchange rates for a number of major currencies, based on an official U.S. gold price of $38 per ounce. The increase in the dollar price of gold from $35 to $38 per ounce represented a 7.89 percent devaluation of the dollar vis-à-vis gold. The pound sterling and the French franc remained unchanged in value in terms of gold, but appreciated by 8.57 percent vis-à-vis the U.S. dollar. The Swiss franc, the Italian lira, and the Swedish krona were devalued slightly against gold, which reduced their effective appreciation against the U.S. dollar. The West German mark, the Japanese yen, the Dutch guilder, and the Belgian franc were revalued upward significantly in terms of gold and in terms of U.S. dollars. These changes are shown in Table 6-1.

The U.S. government had indicated that the 10 percent import duty surcharge was intended as a temporary measure; in fact, it was removed shortly after the Smithsonian Agreement was reached. It may be surmised that it had served a purpose in stimulating agreement for upvaluation of major currencies.

Although Canada permitted its dollar to continue to float in value as it had since 1970, other major countries' central banks were expected to defend the new "central rates," at least for the time being, as if they were official par values.

To make it easier to maintain market exchange rates relatively close to the central rates without constant official intervention, it was agreed that the bands around the central rates within which fluctuation was permitted would be widened to plus or minus $2^{1}/_{4}$ percent instead of only 1 percent. Thus a wider band, which many had proposed, became a reality.

Table 6-1 Currency Value Changes under Smithsonian Agreement

Currency*	Percentage appreciation against U.S. dollar
Belgian franc	11.57
British pound	8.57
French franc	8.57
German mark	13.58
Italian lira	7.48
Japanese yen	16.88
Netherlands guilder	11.57
Swedish krona	7.49
Swiss franc	6.36

*The currencies listed above, minus the Swiss franc and plus U.S. and Canadian dollars, are those of the Group of Ten major industrial countries with significant influence on exchange rate stabilization in the 1960s. Switzerland's representatives meet with those of the Group of Ten countries, but Switzerland is not a member of the IMF.

Source: Federal Reserve Bank of New York, *Monthly Review,* March 1972, p.44.

It should be noted that dollar devaluation in terms of gold was not essential to establish the new exchange rates under which the dollar depreciated, on a trade-weighted basis, approximately 12 percent. In principle, the same result could have been obtained if other countries had upvalued their currencies sufficiently in terms of U.S. dollars. The dollar price of gold has no necessary relationship to the exchange value of the U.S. dollar in terms of other currencies. Moreover, once the gold window was closed, the dollar price of gold was not meaningful in terms of a U.S. selling price for gold. The decision to devalue the dollar in terms of gold was no doubt a concession to political pressures from other countries. For example, France wanted a reduced role for the U.S. dollar in world affairs and a higher value for gold, which France held in its reserves in sizable amounts.

The Smithsonian Agreement was an important historical event in international monetary affairs, but it was intended to be an interim arrangement: it was agreed that "discussion should be promptly undertaken . . . to consider reform of the international monetary system."[4] As subsequent events soon proved, it was an overstatement to refer to it, as President Nixon did, as the "most significant monetary agreement in history."

PROBLEMS IN 1972 AND THE CRISIS OF 1973

For convenience, we may discuss the events of 1972–1973 under three major topics: the attempt to maintain a narrower band for fluctuations of European

---

[4]An interesting review of the events of this period is that of Gottfried Haberler, "Prospects for the Dollar Standard," *Lloyds Bank Review*, July 1972, pp. 1–17.

Common Market country currencies among themselves, the problems affecting the pound sterling, and the floating of all major currencies.

The Snake within the Tunnel

The European Common Market countries had announced their aim of achieving a common currency by 1980, and, even if this timing were not adhered to, they did not wish to have wide fluctuations in exchange rates among currencies which they hoped to blend into a common currency in the future. In May 1972 they agreed to a $2^1/_4$ percent band for values of their currencies relative to one another, while permitting a $4^1/_2$ percent band, as agreed at the Smithsonian meeting, for such values relative to other currencies, including the U.S. dollar. This band within a band became known as "the snake within the tunnel."

Floating of the Pound

The first major sign of trouble with the new set of exchange rates occurred in June 1972 with a speculative attack against the pound. This forced the British to abandon their commitment to a central rate and to let the pound float. Britain had agreed to keep the pound within the snake, although Britain did not join the Common Market until early in 1973. After the pound was permitted to float, other currencies came under heavy pressure as funds moved from one currency to another. Intervention by the Federal Reserve System and other central banks was necessary to maintain the Smithsonian exchange rate structure. Massive trade surpluses of Germany and Japan contributed to the view that their currencies were still undervalued, and their currency values moved sharply higher. Reports of increasing inflation in England, Italy, and France led to widespread selling of pounds, lire, and francs and consequent lower values for those currencies.

All Major Exchange Rates Float

In January 1973, the Bank of Italy acted to counter speculative pressure against the lira. It established a two-tier market in which lire for commercial payments were officially supported in value, but lire for financial payments were allowed to float. Some funds were moved from Italy to Switzerland. This created uncertainty in the market for Swiss francs, speculative demand put upward pressures on the Swiss franc, and shortly thereafter the Swiss authorities allowed it to rise above the ceiling rate.[5] Most other European currencies and the Japanese yen rose in value as speculation increased that these currencies would have to be permitted to float upward. At the same time, the U.S. Administration proposed a 10 percent further devaluation of the dollar in terms of gold, raising the price of gold to $42.22 per ounce. Congress took this action

---

[5]Switzerland, as noted, was not an IMF member, nor was it a member of most other international organizations. However, it participated in some activities of groups of countries within the IMF, and because of the location of the Bank for International Settlements (BIS) in Switzerland and the stability of the Swiss franc as an international currency, Switzerland is for its size an important country in international finance.

Note: Nominal devaluation is measured by the change in the dollar price of gold. Effective devaluation is measured by the appreciation of eleven major currencies relative to the par values which prevailed as of May 1970. The appreciation is then weighted by separate export and import shares with the United States based on 1972 trade data.

   Latest data plotted: April

Figure 6-2 Nominal and Effective Dollar Devaluation. (*Sources:* IMF and the Federal Reserve Bank of New York. Reprinted from Federal Reserve Bank of St. Louis, *Review*, May 1974, p. 16.)

later in 1973. The nominal devaluation of the dollar in terms of gold is shown in Figure 6-2. Figure 6-2 also shows the *effective* devaluation of the dollar during this period, which takes into account the floating of foreign currencies and the weight of the volume of trade in affecting changes in currency values. The trade-weighted value of the U.S. dollar fluctuated somewhat after early 1974, but in early 1977 was still 10 percent below its value before the devaluations (see Federal Reserve Bank of Chicago, *International Letter,* Apr. 1, 1977).

In March 1973, speculative movements of funds, especially from U.S. dollars into Deutsche marks, caused official closure of some foreign exchange markets. When those markets officially reopened, five European Common Market countries (Belgium, the Netherlands, West Germany, France, and Denmark) announced that they would permit their currencies to float in value vis-à-vis other currencies outside the group, but would maintain the snake. The tunnel was gone but the snake remained. However, financial problems led to France's withdrawing, rejoining, and again withdrawing from the snake during the 1972–1976 period and raised serious questions about the snake's viability. The change to a general floating of exchange rates in 1973 was perhaps more significant than the actions taken in 1971, for it signaled the end, at least for a time, of the stable but adjustable exchange rate system.

The Rise in Dollar Reserve Asset Holdings

A significant accompaniment of the other 1971–1973 events was the replacement of gold by foreign exchange, chiefly dollars, as the largest item in world monetary reserves.

Gold had become a dormant international reserve asset. It was still held but very little used. The official price of gold had been raised, but had very little meaning in view of the rise in the private market price of gold shown in Figure 6-3. The restricted supply of gold relative to the large increase in the supply of dollars was a factor in changing the value relationships. Those who valued gold highly began to believe that it was a good hedge against inflation, which dollars were not unless invested in stocks or other inflation-hedge assets and unless such assets rose in value. Stock prices in the United States fell sharply in 1973 and 1974.

As inflation mounted and became worldwide, private holders of dollars sold them. As long as central banks tried to maintain stable exchange rates, that is, until March 1973, they were forced to buy dollars from private holders. Private holders apparently believed that other assets were better as precautionary balances and as hedges against inflation. By the end of 1973, world dollar monetary reserves totaled $2^1/_2$ times as much as world gold monetary reserves, although gold had been the major international reserve asset in the 1950s and 1960s, as shown in Figure 6-4.

RECOGNIZING THE NEED FOR INTERNATIONAL MONETARY REFORM

The problems which had created the need for floating rates did not immediately disappear when rates floated. The U.S. BOP deficit did not immediately change to a surplus. As shown in Figure 6-5, U.S. exports as a percent of world trade

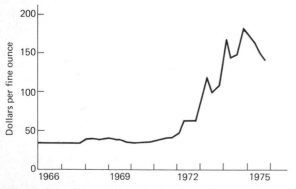

Figure 6-3 Price of Gold in London. (*Source:* Federal Reserve Bank of Dallas, *Business Review,* January 1976, p. 10.)

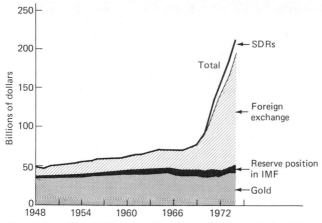

Figure 6-4 World Monetary Reserves. (*Source:* Federal Reserve Bank of Dallas, *Business Review,* January 1976, p. 7.)

continued to decline, and U.S. imports as a percent of U.S. GNP rose sharply. Upward floating of the Deutsche mark and the yen did not halt the growth in reserve assets of West Germany and Japan. The rise in the price of gold, satisfying France that at least some token of support had been given to gold as an international reserve asset, did not settle the question of gold's ultimate role in the international monetary system. Nor was the status of SDRs settled. As

Figure 6-5 Selected Measures of International Trade Performance. (*Source:* U.S. Department of Commerce and IMF. Reprinted from Federal Reserve Bank of St. Louis, *Review,* May 1975, p. 13.)

shown in Figure 6-4, they were only about 5 percent of total world monetary reserves, whereas it had been proposed that they become the major reserve asset. To be the major reserve asset in quantitative terms, their supply would have to be increased substantially, yet with the flood of dollars into the hands of central banks, there seemed to be little need to add further to world monetary reserves. One author suggested that a "second coming" of the Bretton Woods system was one possibility and that a division of the world into monetary blocs was another.[6]

Under a freely floating exchange rate system, no international reserves would have been needed, and reform might have been of small concern. But many observers doubted that governments would (or should) permit a completely free float of exchange rates. Just as governments think it necessary to take action on *domestic inflation*, which reduces the internal purchasing power of currencies, they also seem to think it necessary to control, to some degree at least, the *international* purchasing power of currencies. As stated by Alfred Hayes, exchange rates "are not like other prices, because currencies are not commodities or simple financial assets, but are crucial economic variables that help shape the economic welfare of each country and thus have to be the responsibility of governments."[7]

The virtue of the gold standard before 1914 had been that it was implicitly understood that the primary duty of central banks was to safeguard the values of currencies. With increasing emphasis on the maintenance of high levels of employment, central banks could not necessarily give first priority to the control of inflation. Moreover, although the Bretton Woods system seemed to be biased in favor of internal readjustments and stable exchange rates, in practice in many countries internal readjustments were not made, and the result was sometimes, after long delay, sizable devaluation. The Bretton Woods system was biased toward adjustment on the part of deficit countries rather than of surplus countries. As long as countries which had to adjust were those which could devalue, while the United States, which could not readily devalue, had a current account surplus, devaluations by other countries were a means of adjusting. When the United States, which had had a deficit on capital account but not on current account, began to have a deficit on current account, the system was in jeopardy. Reform involved settling two very serious and a number of minor questions. The two serious questions were: (1) Could convertibility of the U.S. dollar into some other reserve asset, for example gold, be reestablished and (2) could a mechanism be found to require adjustments by countries whose currencies should be upvalued vis-à-vis the U.S. dollar? The U.S. government desired an answer to the second question while European countries were more concerned with the first.

[6]Alexandre Kafka, *The IMF: The Second Coming*? Essays in International Finance, No. 94, July 1972 (Princeton, N.J.: Princeton, 1972).

[7]See the 12th annual Per Jacobsson lecture, August 13, 1975, by Alfred Hayes, "Emerging Arrangements in International Payments—Public and Private," as reported in IMF *Survey*, Sept. 29, 1975, pp. 282–285.

PROBLEMS OF REFORM

The problems of reforming the international monetary system could be classified in a number of ways. The authors discuss five major matters of concern:[8]

1   The need for greater flexibility in exchange rates than existed in the period 1946–1971 and, if free floating is not accepted, the need to develop guidelines for central bank intervention
2   The need (if any) for convertibility of international reserve assets of one type into other types, a special aspect of which is the question of the convertibility of U.S. dollars into gold
3   The need to define the role of SDRs, both as a "numeraire" or accounting unit and as a major or minor international reserve asset
4   The need to agree upon means of triggering readjustments in BOPs or changes in par values if par values are reestablished
5   The need to find a means to control speculative flows of short-term capital which can be increasingly disruptive to the international monetary system as world money and capital markets become more and more closely integrated

Greater Flexibility in Exchange Rates

Most observers probably agree that "permanently" fixed exchange rates, which existed under the gold standard before 1914, are now impossible. Countries differ too much in monetary policies, rates of inflation, rates of real economic growth, and extent of international capital flows to impose upon themselves the domestic adjustments necessary to maintain fixed exchange rates. This is not to say that a system of fully flexible (freely floating) exchange rates is either desirable or inevitable. There are many possible arrangements between the fixed rate system and fully flexible rate, and these are discussed below.

For What Areas are Stable Exchange Rates Appropriate?   Closely related to the question of flexibility in exchange rates is the question of the optimum currency area. What size area can advantageously adopt a stable exchange rate policy vis-à-vis other areas? Depending on the criteria used, an optimum currency area might be a single country, regions within a country, or a group of countries. The announced goal of the European Common Market countries was a single currency by 1980, which would mean no exchange rates, or in effect completely fixed rates, among the currencies of those countries.

The problem of small countries as currency areas is that they usually can

---

[8]Little effort has been made to distinguish between interim actions and those which were presumably more permanent. Existing uncertainties prevent many firm judgments concerning the permanence of specific changes. Moreover, little effort has been made to name committees which drafted particular proposals. A number of committees of the IMF acted during this period, and the principles are more significant than are specific committee names. The Outline of Reform was printed in the IMF *Survey*, June 17, 1974, pp. 193–208.

produce only a limited number of goods and services. Many goods and services must therefore be imported. Hence fluctuations in the exchange value of the currency of a small country having its own currency tend to have a drastic effect on national income. At one extreme, imports may constitute only 7 percent of the GNP of a country such as the United States, and import-competing industries only a small additional percentage. But the cost of imports for a small country may be a very large fraction of national income. Political changes in the twentieth century have in many cases reduced the size of currency areas. As former colonies and commonwealth areas split off from their former governing countries and became independent, they usually established their own monetary units and central banks.[9] This is directly opposed to the economic tendency toward growth in market size, in size of enterprises, and in areas within which capital is mobile. This conflict between political fragmentation and economic integration is a source of many problems in international finance.[10] The sales of some multinational firms have become larger than the GNPs of many single countries at the same time that the establishment of newly independent countries has created smaller areas controlled by sovereign governments.[11] Clearly, some countries are too small to benefit from flexible exchange rates and must peg their currencies to other currencies, to gold, or to some other unit, such as SDRs.

Small countries are not alone in facing the problem of the appropriate currency area. For example, Italy is a part of the Common Market, yet much of its trade is with the United States and much is with countries around the Mediterranean. Should its currency be tied to the currencies of the other Common Market countries, to the U.S. dollar, or to the currencies of Mediterranean countries?

On the other hand, many developing countries cannot maintain stable exchange rates, because they usually have rather rapid rates of inflation. This makes it necessary for them to devalue their currencies frequently or to permit them to depreciate.[12] The industrialized countries, on the other hand, have generally been presumed to be able to control inflation and to have less need for continual devaluation or currency depreciation. It is only when countries have

[9]Raymond Vernon assembled evidence that the growth of multinational enterprises combined with the small size of some nation-states has enabled those enterprises to elude the regulatory powers of some governments and sometimes to take actions overriding the principle of sovereignty, de facto if not de jure. See Raymond Vernon, *Sovereignty at Bay: The Multinational Spread of U.S. Enterprise* (New York: Basic Books, 1971).

[10]Robert Z. Aliber commented on this process as follows: "For the last hundred years, changes in technology have led to a widening of the marketplace for goods, services, and securities. For generations, the market had been smaller than the nation-state. The expansion of the boundaries of the market while the boundaries of the state remain constant has threatened the viability of both national independence and of national firms in many industries." Robert Z. Aliber, *The International Money Game* (New York: Basic Books, 1973), pp. 10–11.

[11]It is of course recognized that total sales and GNP are not precisely analogous, but the comparison is useful as a rough measure of size.

[12]See the discussion by Milton Gilbert and Gottfried Haberler in *The International Adjustment Mechanism* (Boston: Federal Reserve Bank of Boston, 1970), pp. 21–33.

more rapid inflation than related countries that they usually must devalue or depreciate their currencies. In the short run, the United States was an exception to this rule because of the wide use of the U.S. dollar as a reserve asset; the decline in purchasing power of the dollar led to a shift toward gold as a reserve asset.

Recognizing the special situations likely to be encountered by very small countries which must often peg their currencies to other currencies and by developing countries which must devalue their currencies regularly or permit them to depreciate, the following discussion is confined to the currencies of the major industrial countries.

Reasons for Some Flexibility in Exchange Rates   Keynes was among those who argued that some flexibility in exchange rates is desirable.[13] He believed that national economic policies should be insulated to some extent from external forces. If exchange rates are completely fixed, there is no insulation. Any change in external factors affects the demand for and the supply of foreign exchange and hence tends to force either internal adjustments in prices, wages, and employment or a change in the exchange rate. If the exchange value of a currency is free to fluctuate within some band, external forces do not necessarily require changes in national policies unless they are strong enough to cause the exchange rate to move outside the band. As early as 1930, Keynes argued that the margin between the gold points should be wider.[14] He was especially concerned that if a country raised interest rates for reasons of policy (for example, to control inflation), it might attract gold or other capital assets from foreign countries, thereby moderating the rise in interest rates and providing funds for spending or lending. The possible perversity of the interest rate mechanism concerned him because an inflow of capital might prolong an economic boom.

A concern of the central bankers and others who worked out the Bretton Woods agreement was competitive depreciation of currencies such as had occurred in the 1930s. Some economists believed that with flexible exchange rates speculation could be destabilizing.[15] It had also been argued that countries' independent setting of exchange rate par values had led to "subsequent disintegration," and that the cooperative establishment of par values *by agreement* was essential.[16]

These ideas were accepted by central bankers at the same time that many

---

[13]John Maynard Keynes, *A Treatise on Money*, Vol. II (New York: Harcourt, Brace, 1930), Chap. 36, especially pp. 303–304. See also his *Means to Prosperity* (New York: Harcourt, Brace, 1933), especially pp. 32–33.

[14]Keynes, op. cit., p. 320.

[15]Ragnar Nurkse, *International Currency Experience* (Geneva: League of Nations, 1944), esp. pp. 117–118. For a contrary view, see Leland B. Yeager, *International Monetary Relations* 2d ed. (New York: Harper & Row, 1976), especially pp. 328 ff. and Milton Friedman, *Essays in Positive Economics* (Chicago: University of Chicago Press, 1953), p. 176n. for comment on the influence of Nurkse's book.

[16]Nurkse, op. cit., p. 117.

economists were coming to the view that exchange rates might be relatively stable if free to fluctuate in response to market forces. If true, this removed a major argument against flexible exchange rates.[17]

A widened band appeared to some economists as both an acceptable compromise and an opportunity to test the effects of at least limited flexibility in exchange rates. It was argued that such flexibility would largely eliminate the potentially counterproductive effect of interest rate changes when deficits or surpluses existed in BOPs. A rise in interest rates, induced by slowing money supply growth to limit inflation, would not attract much foreign capital if at the same time the exchange value of the currency rose.[18] Greater flexibility in exchange rates would promote monetary independence, it was suggested.

Limited experience with floating exchange rates has not yet validated the fears of those who believed they would bring chaos, nor has it fully justified the hopes of those who believed that floating rates would improve significantly the functioning of the international monetary system. In mid-1975 there was some evidence that opinions among the academic community were turning against floating rates.[19] No international financial crisis like that of 1931 had appeared, however, and although some banks suffered foreign exchange trading losses, the number of bank failures was not large. In a period of adjustment to a major change in oil prices, perhaps it was necessary to have fluctuating exchange rates. Nevertheless, the wide fluctuations of the 1973–1976 period increased the costs of international transactions in some cases. Although increased costs could easily be passed along in such an inflationary period, less inflation would test the ability of floating rates to permit continued rapid growth in world trade and investment.[20] An important question is whether central banks can reduce uncertainty and improve the stability of floating rates by means of "managed floating."

Guidelines for Central Bank Intervention   In the Outline of Reform issued by the Committee of Twenty of the IMF in June 1974, guidelines were proposed for central bank intervention in what was then termed the interim

---

[17]Fritz Machlup presented an imposing list of economists who favored flexible exchange rates. See his *Plans for Reform of the International Monetary System*, Special Papers in International Economics, No. 3, rev. March 1964 (Princeton, N.J.: Princeton, 1964).

[18]Leland B. Yeager discussed this question at some length in his analysis of Germany's situation in the 1950s and 1960s; see his *International Monetary Relations*, Chap. 24, "The German Struggle Against Imported Inflation."

[19]See, for example, "The Drift Back to Fixed Exchange Rates," *Business Week*, June 2, 1975, in which Paul Samuelson is quoted as saying that "people selling the flexible rate system exaggerated their case," and Charles P. Kindleberger is quoted as predicting: "I am not sure how we will get there, but I am confident that we will evolve back to a fixed exchange rate system over time." In a sentence no doubt included for emphasis and drama, *Time*, July 21, 1974, p. 4, quoted an unidentified multinational firm executive as saying that "all the Harvard Business School techniques are worthless when exchange rates can move by 20 percent in a matter of months." There is a core of truth in this statement: Unless business managers understand the fundamental economics of exchange rates, training in microfinancial techniques of exchange rate forecasting is not enough. The dollar did decline in value in the foreign exchange market, at least vis-à-vis the Deutsche mark, from late 1974 to early 1975 by about 20 percent.

[20]This concern was expressed by Alfred Hayes; see fn. 7 above.

period of floating exchange rates.[21] The guidelines began by stating that "a member with a floating exchange rate should intervene on the foreign exchange market as necessary to prevent or moderate sharp and disruptive fluctuations from day to day and from week to week in the exchange value of its currency." This guideline was later supplemented by an agreement signed by representatives of France and of the United States at the Rambouillet conference of heads of state or government of France, West Germany, Italy, Japan, the United Kingdom, and the United States in November 1975.[22] The Rambouillet Declaration did not include a text of the U.S.–French agreement but indicated that "monetary authorities will act to counter disorderly market conditions or erratic fluctuations in exchange rates."

Early in 1976 a proposed new Article IV of the IMF agreement was adopted by the Interim Committee of the IMF in Jamaica. It provided that each member would "collaborate with the Fund and other members to assure orderly exchange arrangements and to promote a stable system of exchange rates."[23] The proposed article, subject to anticipated ratification by member governments, emphasized the avoidance of manipulation of exchange rates and specified that members might establish par values in terms of SDRs or some other unit (but not gold or another currency), might maintain values for their currencies in terms of the currency or currencies of another member or members, or might make other arrangements. Thus floating rates and other arrangements were legalized. At the same time, it was emphasized that exchange rate stability was related to the achievement of greater stability in underlying economic and financial conditions.

The guidelines also permitted countries to act to bring their exchange rates into some target zone after consultation with the IMF. Some observers were concerned that this might lead "to attempts to defend disequilibrium rates for long periods of time."[24] IMF "surveillance" of the target zone rates was permitted if the IMF considered movements outside the target zone inimical to the interests of other members. The tenor of the guidelines was the consideration of floating rates as a mechanism of adjustment within the framework of principles underlying an exchange rate system based on "stable but adjustable par values,"[25] but modified to "accommodate occasional perhaps inevitable (but unwelcome) bouts of managed floating."[26]

---

[21]The Committee of Twenty was an IMF committee established to draft proposals for international monetary reform. It included representatives of all IMF member countries in a manner analogous to that by which IMF Executive Directors are designated to represent countries and groups of countries. For further details, see glossary. See also *Guidelines for Exchange Market Intervention, Hearings before the Subcommittee on International Economics of the Joint Economic Committee*, 94th Cong., 2d Sess., Oct. 18, 1976.

[22]The Rambouillet Declaration is printed in IMF *Survey*, Nov. 24, 1975, p. 350.

[23]Text of the new proposed Article IV for the IMF agreement is printed in IMF *Survey*, Jan. 19, 1976, pp. 20–21.

[24]Raymond F. Mikesell and Henry N. Goldstein, *Rules for a Floating-Rate Regime*, Essays in International Finance, No. 109 (Princeton, N.J.: Princeton, 1975), p. 21.

[25]Ibid., p. 17.

[26]Wilfred Ethier and Arthur I. Bloomfield, *Managing the Managed Float*, Essays in International Finance, No. 112 (Princeton, N.J.: Princeton, 1975), p. 23.

The new article also provided that the IMF "shall exercise firm surveillance over the exchange rate policies of members, and shall adopt specific principles for the guidance of all members with respect to these policies." The surveillance by the IMF is another step toward surrender of a small amount of sovereignty to an international organization. How big this step is and what initiatives the IMF can take in its surveillance must be judged after some experience with the new article's operation. Effective surveillance involves some influence over domestic financial policies of member countries, and how far the IMF can move in this direction remains to be seen.[27]

Provision for Possible Return to Par Value System   In this context it is not surprising that the agreement reached at Jamaica also provided for the possible return to a par value system. It provided that with an 85 percent majority of total voting power, the same majority required to create SDRs, the IMF might determine that economic conditions permitted reintroduction of stable but adjustable par values. Observers have not agreed on the likelihood of such a reestablishment.[28]

There was also a provision that members must ensure that current exchange rates do not differ from par values (if these are established) by more than $4^{1}/_{2}$ percent (wider than the $2^{1}/_{4}$ percent Smithsonian band). The provision that members should not propose changes in par values except to correct a fundamental disequilibrium in their BOPs was retained, and the phrase "or to prevent the emergence of" such a disequilibrium was added. Provisions that the IMF must concur with or object to a proposed new par value within a reasonable period and that the IMF cannot object because of domestic social or political policies of the member country are similar to former provisions.

Note that since the United States has more than 15 percent of the total voting power in the IMF, it has veto power over a return to the par value system.

Convertibility of Reserve Assets

The question of *asset* convertibility of reserve assets had been pushed into the background by the events of the first half of the 1970s. *Market* convertibility of the U.S. dollar and of most other major currencies is not in question, since the countries concerned do not impose exchange controls on current account payments. Originally, asset convertibility was desired because of fear that governments in general tend to spend too much and hence to create, or induce

---

[27]A similar cautious view was expressed by Tom deVries, an Alternate Executive Director of the IMF, "Reforming International Monetary Relations—An Analysis," *Finance and Development*, September 1976, pp. 10–13. DeVries makes the point that those who believe the exchange rates should be left to "market forces" overlook the fact that government authorities, through monetary policies, affect exchange rates indirectly whether or not they do so directly. See also Charles A. Coombs, "The Realities of Managed Exchange Rates," *First Chicago World Report*, March 1977, pp. 1–3.

[28]See Citibank, *Economic Week*, Jan. 19, 1976, p. 8.

central banks to create, too much currency. During a depression this fear is far less justified, but since World War II the existence of only small recessions has created concern that greater government spending may "crowd out" desirable private borrowing and spending, or, alternatively, total spending may indeed cause inflation.[29]

The major asset into which currencies might be convertible is gold. The developments of the first half of the 1970s indicated that U.S. authorities wanted to eliminate gold from any significant role in the international monetary system. The IMF decided early in 1975 to take actions which would "ensure that the role of gold in the international monetary system would be gradually reduced." In August 1975 it was agreed to abolish the official price of $42.22 per ounce for gold. It was also agreed to terminate the obligation to use gold when possible in transactions with the IMF. Finally, it was agreed that one-sixth of the IMF's gold would be sold over a period of years at market prices, the excess over cost being used to benefit developing countries and that another one-sixth of that gold would be returned to contributing countries. These announcements were accompanied by declarations that there would be no action to peg the price of gold and that the IMF and the Group of Ten monetary authorities would not increase their gold holdings for a period of years. In September 1975 these understandings were confirmed at the IMF annual meeting.[30]

It appears that the role of gold as an international reserve asset is being greatly diminished, although both the IMF and central banks may continue to hold gold. The distribution of some gold to member countries will add to their liquid assets and make less likely the creation and allocation of additional SDRs in the foreseeable future.

Note that convertibility becomes important as the number of reserve assets increases. When gold and sterling (firmly tied to gold in value) were the only reserve assets, there was little concern about convertibility. If the role of both gold and SDRs as reserve assets is minimized, foreign exchange, largely dollars, becomes the major reserve asset, and the significance of convertibility is diminished.

The Role of SDRs: a "Numeraire" and a Reserve Asset

It is essential that acceptability of SDRs be maintained, since they are without an independent demand, such as that which exists for gold, to support their value. Action was taken in 1974 to increase the interest rate paid on SDRs from a nominal rate to 5 percent per year as a means of maintaining demand for them. It was indicated that this rate was to remain in effect as long as a

---

[29]Roger W. Spencer and William P. Yohe, "The 'Crowding Out' of Private Expenditures by Fiscal Policy Actions," Federal Reserve Bank of St. Louis, *Review*, October 1970, pp. 12–24.

[30]IMF *Survey*, Sept. 15, 1975.

Figure 6-6 International Monetary Fund SDR Valuation, July 2, 1974. *Source:* IMF *Survey,* July 8, 1974, p. 214.)

Currencies (1)	Currency components (2)	Exchange rates,* July 2, 1974 (3)	U.S. dollar equivalent (4)
U.S. Dollar	0.4000	1.00000	0.400000
Deutsche mark	0.3800	2.55750	0.148583
Pound sterling	0.0450	2.38800	0.107460
French franc	0.4400	4.81350	0.091410
Japenese yen	26.0000	285.90000	0.090941
Canadian dollar	0.0710	1.02850	0.073024
Italian lira	47.0000	646.50000	0.072699
Netherlands guilder	0.1400	2.66350	0.052562
Belgian franc	1.6000	38.10000	0.041995
Swedish krona	0.1300	4.37500	0.029714
Australian dollar	0.0120	0.67227	0.017850
Danish krone	0.1100	5.98100	0.018392
Norwegian krone	0.0990	5.44350	0.018187
Spanish peseta	1.100	57.27000	0.019207
Austrian schilling	0.2200	18.25500	0.012051
South African rand	0.0082	0.66669	0.012300

SDR 1 = US$1.206375
SDR value of US$1 = SDR 0.828930

Currency Units per SDR

Currency†	Symbol	June 28‡	July 1	July 2	July 3
Austrian schilling	S	22.0762	22.0097	22.0526	21.9857
Belgian franc	BF	45.8564	45.9249	45.9148	45.9234
Canadian dollar	Can$	1.17281	· · ·	1.16295	1.17700
Danish krone	DKr	7.23810	7.23304	7.21717	7.17950
Deutsche mark	DM	3.08222	3.06809	3.08290	3.07063
French franc	F	5.81762	5.82126	5.80570	5.80766
Italian lira	Lit	781.262	779.746	779.653	778.927
Japanese yen	Y	342.724	343.773	344.904	346.163
Netherlands guilder		3.19864	3.20316	3.21078	3.20177
Norwegian krone	NKr	6.55048	6.59386	6.56874	
Pound sterling	£	0.505066	0.505474	0.505184	0.504706
Spanish peseta	Pta	69.0213	69.0742	69.1195	69.1238
Swedish krona	SKr	5.28381	5.31489	5.28394	5.30606
U.S. dollar	$	1.20635	1.20601	1.20638	1.208670
Ecuadoran sucre	S/		30.1503	30.1595	30.2168
Irish pound	£IR		· · ·	0.505184	
Kuwaiti dinar	KD		0.351685	0.352142	0.352388
U.A.E. dirham	Dh		4.76057	4.76203	4.77107

*Quoted in terms of currency units per U.S. dollar except for the pound sterling and the Canadian dollar, which are quoted as U.S. dollars per currency unit in accordance with the practice of the market.

†The first fourteen currencies listed are those included in the basket for which the Fund has established representative rates.

‡Under Rule 0-3 before its amendment effective July 1, 1974.

Data: IMF Treasurer's Department.

weighted average of short-term interest rates in the United States, the United Kingdom, France, Germany, and Japan remained between 9 and 11 percent.[31] Subsequently, changes were made to keep the interest rate on SDRs below this weighted average of short-term interest rates, but not too far below it.

The SDR as a Unit of Account   With floating exchange rates and the dollar no longer tied to gold in value, the SDR also fluctuated in value, and it appeared that countries might not wish to hold this asset under such conditions. In June 1974 the Executive Directors of the IMF agreed on a method of valuing the SDR in terms of a "standard basket" of 16 currencies, currencies of those countries with at least 1 percent each of world exports during the years 1968–1972. Weights were assigned to each currency, generally proportional to trade, but with the U.S. dollar given greater weight (33 percent of the total) because of its widespread use. A calculation was then made of the amount of each currency which, multiplied by the weight, would result in values which when added would equal the dollar value of the SDR at the end of June 1974, taking into account the two official devaluations of the dollar. This value was $1.20635, as shown in the upper half of Figure 6-6.

From July 1, 1974, the value of the SDR has fluctuated. Each day the IMF calculates the value of an SDR by converting the specified amounts of each of the other 15 currencies into dollars at the daily exchange rate and adding these to the fraction of a dollar (40 cents) which had been decided on as part of the currency basket.[32] Thus the SDR became a multicurrency unit with a floating value, but a value more stable than that of a particular currency: if one currency depreciated, another currency necessarily appreciated. Because of the heavy weight of the dollar, its depreciation or appreciation affects the SDR more than changes in values of other currencies. Nevertheless, the new method of valuation gave the SDR increased appeal as a unit of account and as a reserve asset. Note in the upper half of Figure 6-6 that the value of the dollar in terms of SDRs, often convenient to use in accounting, was SDR 0.82893 when the new system was established.

The IMF calculated rates for the SDR against currencies other than the dollar by obtaining from individual foreign exchange markets "representative rates" reported by central banks concerned and agreed on by the IMF as being representative of market rates.[33] The rates on June 28, 1974, for 14 currencies included in the basket are shown in the lower half of Figure 6-6, with rates for those and a few other currencies for the first several days of July 1974. As representative rates were agreed on, the IMF added new currencies to its report.

---

[31]IMF *Annual Report*, 1974, pp. 51–52.

[32]The IMF made arrangements for daily reporting of exchange rates for 14 currencies from either New York, London, or Frankfurt, and for the yen from Tokyo.

[33]For details, see IMF *Survey*, July 8, 1974, pp. 213–214. See also "The SDR Rejuvenated," Chase Manhattan Bank, *Business in Brief*, October 1975, pp. 4–5.

Early in 1975 several Middle East countries announced that they would set the values of their currencies in relation to SDRs rather than to U.S. dollars. At least one bank issued CDs and made loans denominated in SDRs. Suez Canal revenues were set in terms of SDRs and so were international air transport rates.[34] The advantage for those holding or receiving funds so denominated is that the value does not fluctuate as much as it would if stated in an individual currency. Of course, countries which make payments in a mixture of currencies quite different from that used in the SDR valuation do not find the SDR very useful. But for many purposes, a multicurrency unit of account is of value to protect lenders and sellers against the decline in purchasing power of amounts held or received.[35] Buyers and borrowers accept the designation because they may obtain better terms or because they see no convenient alternative.

These changes enhanced the usefulness of SDRs as a unit of account, but did not make them a medium of exchange for the public, which was still prevented from using them. The possibility of a private market for SDRs has been discussed, but was not deemed desirable at the time of the valuation change. The Jamaica agreement specified a number of changes to broaden somewhat the use of SDRs by member countries.[36]

Gold and Foreign Exchange as Major Reserve Assets   Although SDRs have become more significant as a unit of account, gold and foreign exchange remain the major reserve assets. Foreign exchange is the major means of payment, for both central banks and the public, while gold is a potential but decreasingly important means of payment for central banks. Because of industrial and hoarding demand, the price of gold in private markets affects its monetary use. The London gold price, since the reopening of the market in 1954 after 15 years of closure, had been significant as a measure of price trends. Other markets have existed in such places as Zurich, Paris, Beirut, Kuwait, Bombay, Hong Kong, Bangkok, Singapore, Tokyo, Toronto, Mexico City, Montevideo, and Rio de Janeiro, international financial centers with good communications facilities, foreign banking institutions, no or few governmental restrictions, and a demand for gold. Private trading in gold was finally permitted in the United States at the end of 1974, but no great rush to buy gold developed in spite of its high price of about $130 to $190 per ounce in foreign markets.

Both the price of gold and its future role as a reserve asset are difficult to forecast. By 1976 central banks were free to sell gold, and major central banks had agreed not to add to their gold holdings.

---

[34]Federal Reserve Bank of San Francisco, *Business & Financial* Letter, Mar. 7, 1975.
[35]"Changes Within the Fund," *Finance and Development*, June 1976, pp. 12–13.
[36]Franco Modigliani and Hossein Askari, *The Reform of the International Payments System*, Essays in International Finance, No. 89, September 1971 (Princeton, N.J.: Princeton, 1971).

The *trend* of the price of gold has been continuously upward since about the year 1200, but there have been short declines and long periods of price stability. Clearly, gold was a hedge against inflation in the period 1968–1975, but this is no assurance that it will be such a hedge in the foreseeable future. Factors affecting the future price of gold are: (1) the apparent desire of the U.S. government and some others to reduce the role of gold in the world monetary system; (2) the supply of gold, dependent on the possibility of new discoveries or the perhaps fanciful alchemy of transforming other metals into gold; (3) the industrial and hoarding demand for gold, dependent on the rate of inflation in various countries and on the behavior of prices of other assets, chiefly stocks, held as inflation hedges; and (4) war, since in wartime gold is an easily moved asset, less subject to govermental confiscation than most other assets and likely to be readily accepted for payments.

Success in the effort to reduce the role of gold and to reduce inflation, combined with the maintenance of general world peace, could hold down the price of gold or cause it to fall for a time. Therefore, gold is probably no longer an important reserve asset, although it may continue to be held by some countries for this purpose.

If neither SDRs nor gold seem likely to be major reserve assets in the foreseeable future, there remains foreign exchange, now the bulk of world monetary reserves, as was shown in Figure 6-4. The great flood of dollars absorbed by central banks in the period 1971–1973 assured that dollars will be for some time the major reserve asset unless deliberately replaced. With freely floating exchange rates, of course, reserves would not be needed, but the promulgation of guidelines for intervention suggests that reserves remain important for intervention. If inflation in the United States continues to abate in relation to world inflation, dollars will become more desirable. A situation can be envisaged in which dollars are again recognized as the major reserve asset and continue to be the major vehicle currency, reflecting the continuing strength of the U.S. economy.

A Means of Triggering Readjustments in Exchange Rates

U.S. officials sought agreement on some means of triggering needed readjustments in currency values before consenting to the reestablishment of stable but adjustable par values. Recognizing the long delays in readjustment under the Bretton Woods system, they looked for a means of automatic or semiautomatic readjustment. But uncertainty whether deficits are "fundamental" when they do not occur every year, as in Britain, and hesitance to upvalue a currency by more than very small amounts, as in West Germany, tend to make other nations slow to adjust.[37]

---

[37]David C. Rowan, "Towards a Rational Exchange Policy: Some Reflections on the British Experience," Federal Reserve Bank of St. Louis, *Review*, April 1969, pp. 17–26.

The U.S. representative, George Shultz, presented detailed proposals at the annual IMF meeting in 1972 and in a later memorandum, specifying means of triggering adjustment on the basis of changes in levels of reserves.[38] He argued that a judgment would have to be made about necessary base levels of reserves, which would be expected to rise over time. Then a low point would be designated, perhaps at a minimum reserve level necessary to meet extreme emergencies, and a lower warning point somewhere between the base level and the low point. Similarly, an outer point would be set above the base level and an upper warning point between. When a warning point was reached, small devaluations or upvaluations would be freely permitted, and larger changes, although requiring approval of the IMF, would probably be allowed if reserves were below or above the warning points. If the low point were reached, the IMF might take stronger action to let exchange restrictions prevent further loss of reserves.

Progress toward consensus on this issue was relatively slow. Actually, the justification for using reserves as indicators of the need for adjustment is theoretically weak, since reserve levels reflect past changes. There is general agreement that (1) countries shoud adjust par values, if they exist, rather than wait until nearly all possible actions have been taken and (2) countries should upvalue as readily as they devalue. But there is not agreement concerning timing of these actions.

The lack of agreement on means of triggering readjustments is a major obstacle to reestablishment of a par value system. U.S. officials wish to be assured that adjustments will be made when necessary without long delays like those in the 1960s. On the other hand, European officials would like assurances of a relatively stable value of the dollar or of its convertibility into some asset such as gold before making decisions that might be difficult to change. This is the heart of the problem of further reform.

Control of Speculative Flows of Capital

Even in the IMF agreement, the propriety of controls to prevent speculative flows of capital was recognized. In recent years, the need for such controls has become urgent, in part because multinational firms have become increasingly proficient in managing their assets and liabilities. They may, for example, shift from dollar to Deutsche mark liabilities, with the same effect as any other movement of funds into Deutsche marks. Capital flows need not be the result of desires of speculators for gain. They may simply result from the desire of multinational firms to maximize gains and minimize losses by appropriate asset and liability management. Banks have the same objectives in managing their foreign exchange assets and liabilities.

The internationalization of both business and banking has contributed to the increase in the volume of funds that can be moved suddenly from country to country. Many such transactions were unreported. They are presumed to be

[38]*Economic Report of the President*, January 1973, pp. 160–174.

short-term capital movements because there is little evidence that they could be anything else.[39] Regulation is difficult, but control may be needed under some conditions.

Wider bands are a means of avoiding resort to controls as long as fluctuations remain within the bands. Moreover, they cause speculators to recognize the possibility of more substantial losses if exchange rates move in the unexpected direction. Adequate holdings of reserve assets also make avoiding controls possible by offsetting short-term capital flows through shifts in reserve assets.

FINANCIAL CONSEQUENCES OF THE OIL CRISIS

When an Arab-Israeli war began in October 1973, the Middle East oil producers instituted an embargo on oil shipments, aimed at nations they believed were aiding Israel. Although that embargo was removed when some steps toward peace were achieved early in 1974, the Organization of Petroleum Exporting Countries (OPEC) had meanwhile increased taxes levied on oil produced in their countries. The result was that, for most consuming countries, the cost of imported oil was increased to four or five times its previous level. Since the United States at that time imported about one-third of its oil, gasoline prices nearly doubled. The long-term petroleum supply and demand situation in the United States is shown in Figure 6-7.

[39]For one discussion of the nature of short-term capital flows in a period of international monetary change, see Donald L. Kohn, "Capital Flows in a Foreign Exchange Crisis," Federal Reserve Bank of Kansas City, *Monthly Review*, February 1973, pp. 14–23.

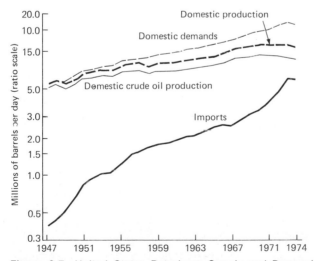

Figure 6-7 United States Petroleum Supply and Demand. (*Sources:* Bureau of Mines, 1946–1955; American Petroleum Institute, 1956–1971; and Chase Manhattan Bank, 1972–1973. Reprinted from Federal Reserve Bank of St. Louis, *Review*, May 1975, p. 13.)

Countries importing almost all the oil they consumed were much more adversely affected. Since OPEC countries usually wanted payment in either dollars or pounds, preferably dollars, this meant a huge accumulation of what became known as petrodollars in the hands of some of them.

Petrodollars

Some OPEC countries could use all their oil revenue to buy goods and services, others could not. In 1974 most of the net inflow of about $55 billion was not spent but instead was invested. Major investments were deposits in European and U.S. banks. Smaller amounts were used to purchase securities and other assets in the major industrial countries, and very small amounts were loaned to developing countries. Estimated uses of OPEC revenues in 1974 are shown in Figure 6-8.

It is evident that most OPEC surplus funds were invested in relatively safe and liquid assets, mainly deposits in Eurocurrency in European banks and dollar deposits in U.S. banks. Because of the magnitude of these deposits, there was initial concern expressed by some international bankers that the influx of petrodollars could precipitate a liquidity crisis. The basic problem was that the OPEC deposits were short-term liabilities which could be withdrawn virtually on demand. The funds were loaned to borrowers who wanted assurance that they could have the funds for longer periods. Some banks did indeed encounter difficulties, and for a time there were categories of banks in which it was considered safe, less safe, or unsafe to deposit Eurocurrency. Deposit interest spreads widened as a result, but a crisis was averted, and the process continued smoothly after a period of uncertainty.

The problem remained that countries which do not provide deposits nevertheless need funds to finance oil and other imports. What market mechanisms exist that might provide these countries with additional funds?

If the flow of funds is, say, mainly to the United States or England, interest

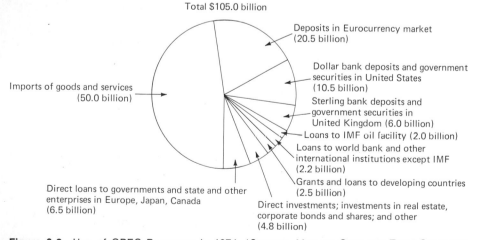

Figure 6-8 Use of OPEC Revenues in 1974. (*Source:* Morgan Guaranty Trust Company. Reprinted from Federal Reserve Bank of Dallas, *Business Review,* May 1975, p. 4.)

rates in these countries would tend to decline relative to those in other financial markets. The resulting interest rate differentials might induce OPEC officials to recycle funds to other places.

Let us suppose, however, that OPEC surplus revenues are not distributed by changes in relative interest rates. Arab investors might prefer dollar-denominated assets in the United States to others because those assets offer a better mix of safety, liquidity, and yield. The resulting increased demand for the U.S. dollar would raise its price (exchange rate) relative to foreign currencies. With some time lag, this would reduce U.S. exports and increase imports. Foreign countries would have an improved trade position vis-à-vis the United States, offsetting at least partly their trade deficit with the oil-exporting countries. The United States would have a capital account surplus with the oil-exporting countries and probably a current account deficit with both OPEC and other foreign countries. Some Arab investment in the United States did occur, although on a small scale. The specter of Arab ownership of American industries proved to be almost as disturbing as had the ownership of industries in France by U.S. firms some years earlier.[40]

While these types of adjustments might alleviate the financial strain on industrialized countries arising from higher oil prices, they are not likely to benefit the LDCs. Many poor countries cannot depend on increased exports of either goods and services or securities on a scale sufficient to finance their oil requirements. Direct loans from some OPEC countries, economic aid from some developed countries, and the special lending facility of the IMF have provided some funds to meet this problem.

IMF Lending to Avoid a Crisis

Early in 1975 a "safety net" fund arrangement was agreed to by a committee from the Organization for Economic Cooperation and Development (OECD) countries. This organization includes the Group of Ten countries plus most of the other countries of Europe except the Soviet satellite countries of Eastern Europe. The safety net arrangement was intended to aid OECD member countries with BOP deficits they are unable to finance themselves or through loans from international organizations. The fund was to be SDR 20 billion (about $25 billion at the time of the agreement), but funds were to be raised only as needed to meet requests. Countries which obtained financial aid from the fund would be required to refrain from restricting international trade, to follow economic policies aimed at reducing their BOP deficits, and to conserve energy. This fund was intended to be an addition to the credit facilities of the IMF, especially the "oil facility" established in 1974 by OPEC countries, which amounted to SDR 3 billion. In these financial arrangements, SDRs are used only as units of account; the equivalent values are provided in national currencies.

With the effort to reduce the role of gold in the international monetary system, it was agreed that the IMF would sell part of its gold (contributed by

[40]Jean-Jacques Servan Schreiber, *The American Challenge* (New York: Atheneum, 1968).

members), and that profits from the sale at the market price (much higher than the original value) would be set aside in a "trust fund" to aid low-income countries through either grants or loans.

Early in 1976, the IMF decided to temporarily increase its credit tranches to permit increased lending until proposed quota increases were approved. Readers may remember from Chapter 5 that borrowing (or buying foreign exchange) from the IMF is automatic for the first, or gold, tranche, generally 25 percent of each country's quota. Borrowing of up to four additional credit tranches is available at the IMF's discretion. The increase raised each credit tranche from 25 percent to 36.25 percent of each country's quota. If a country borrowed all four credit tranches, the IMF would then hold 75 percent of that country's quota from the country's original contribution, 25 percent from the borrowing of the gold tranche, and 145 percent from the borrowing of the four credit tranches.[41] Further borrowing is permitted by special arrangements.

Thus increased lending is to be channeled through the IMF, instead of relying on Britain for lending in crises, as in the days of the gold standard, or on the United States, as in the 1920s. Cessation of foreign lending by the United States in 1929 was a major cause of the international financial collapse in 1931.

Soon after approval of the temporary change, permitting a member country to draw from the IMF up to 145 percent of its quota, beyond the gold tranche, the IMF was confronted with Britain's need to borrow a very substantial amount. Britain could draw a total of SDR 4.06 billion (about $3.25 billion), which was 145 percent of its quota of SDR 2.8 billion, but it had already drawn some $700 million by the end of 1976. The IMF agreed early in January 1977 to a loan of SDR 3.36 billion (about $3.9 billion). Britain was required to agree to follow economic policies which, in the view of the IMF, could correct underlying economic conditions that necessitated the borrowing.

Britain also made arrangements to borrow SDR 2.56 billion (about $2.94 billion) under the General Arrangements to Borrow, in its eighth use of this agreement. Previous borrowings, all for loans to the United Kingdom or to France, had totaled $2.154 billion. Thus, with the added amount, about $5 billion of the $6 billion line of credit under the GAB had been used or committed by early 1977.[42]

The hope was that the loans to Britain, together with internal British policies agreed upon with the IMF, would tide Britain over its external financial difficulties until internal economic growth, including North Sea oil revenue, could provide the basis for a satisfactory long-run solution. The effort to coordinate national macrofinancial policies through IMF guidance was a further extension of the role of the IMF in exercising surveillance over financial policies affecting the international monetary system.[43]

---

[41]IMF *Survey*, Mar. 1, 1976, p. 67. This was a temporary increase because it was expected that BOP deficits would diminish after effects of the large oil price increase wore off.

[42]Federal Reserve Bank of Chicago, *International Letter*, Jan. 7, 1977.

[43]Evidence of the increased influence of the IMF has been noted by some observers; see, for example, "The IMF Wields Sudden New Power," *Business Week*, Mar. 28, 1977, pp. 86–90.

SOME CONCLUSIONS FROM EVENTS OF THE EARLY 1970s

Certain conclusions may be drawn from events of the early 1970s. First, it is difficult for governments to determine and to maintain equilibrium exchange rates in periods when rates of inflation vary substantially. In such periods funds shift from one currency to another, and to gold if its price seems likely to rise.

Second, the different rates of inflation, even among European Common Market countries, made it difficult to maintain the snake—that is, to tie a group of currencies together in an attempt to keep exchange rates among the group fluctuating together.

Third, although there was some initial confusion, it quickly became evident that the rise in oil prices simply meant that some oil-exporting countries were enabled to import more goods and services while others had more funds available for investment. The basic BOP identity is a truism; funds obtained must be spent or invested somewhere unless they are hoarded. The problem was whether invested funds could be smoothly recycled to countries which needed funds to pay for oil and other imports.

Fourth, wide fluctuations in exchange rates for some major currencies, for example the U.S. dollar and the Deutsche mark, made it evident that there were, at least in this period, increased costs in exchange rate changes for those engaged in world trade and investment. Such costs were perhaps easier to absorb in a period of inflation than they would be in a period of more stable prices, suggesting that the test of the effect of floating rates on world trade and investment is yet to come.

Finally, gold is probably no longer a major factor in the international monetary system, although it may still be held by governments and by the IMF.

PROSPECTS FOR FURTHER INTERNATIONAL MONETARY REFORM

The international monetary system has worked better than some had expected in a difficult period. The banking system was able to recycle petrodollars in large amounts to many countries needing funds for imports. The role of the IMF is expanding, and has become more essential than ever, as agreements become more complex. The gradual integration of the world economy has forced nations to enter into economic agreements, and the IMF has served as both a focal point for negotiations and a pool of currencies to facilitate continued lending during crises. Although such lending might be done by certain countries, as it was before 1929, or by the long-term development-lending institutions, there are reasons to separate short-term emergency lending from long-term development lending. Long-term lending institutions borrow in the capital markets and need not have great concern for liquidity. Short-term emergency lending may not effectively meet needs if it must depend on funds from long-term capital markets, which may not function properly in serious recessions or worldwide depressions. There is also merit in separating short-term emergency lending so that its problems need not concern institutions that lend for development.

Most countries have been unwilling to let their currencies float without some degree of official intervention. At the same time, some countries which were members of the European Common Market found it impossible to keep their exchange rates within the self-imposed "snake." It is premature to conclude that floating exchange rates have permanently replaced the relatively fixed rates of earlier periods.

The major conditions which might give rise to a return to stable but adjustable exchange rates are: (1) The moderation of inflation in major countries; (2) the revived desire to hold U.S. dollars as precautionary balances, with a concomitant decline in the desire to hold gold; (3) the willingness of the U.S. government to permit return to a stable but adjustable exchange rate system, which in turn depends in part on the willingness of other countries to adjust rates when necessary; and (4) a period of relative stability in the world economy, so that further major shocks like those accompanying the oil price changes are unlikely. Under these conditions another period of stable but adjustable exchange rates might be inaugurated to avoid the wide fluctuations in rates and the high costs of such fluctuations for those engaged in world trade and investment.

Such a development cannot occur unless major countries are more willing to coordinate their monetary policies. It may not occur if guidelines for central bank intervention to manage floating rates can succeed in moderating fluctuations.

Those who envision continued integration of the world economy, however, are likely to believe that floating is temporary. They are likely to foresee establishment of single currencies for certain areas and more stable rates among different currency areas. They may even foresee, in the very long run, a world central bank with power to control the money supply for a number of countries.

APPENDIX: Proposals for Reform of the International Monetary System

In the main part of this chapter, discussion focused on partly or wholly accepted measures for reform and on those under active consideration. Extensive discussion for many years, however, dealt with other proposals not now actively supported in official meetings. Nevertheless, coverage would be incomplete if we failed to mention them at all. Therefore this appendix mentions some of the major proposals.

Machlup classified these proposals into five main groups: (1) extension of the gold-exchange (gold-dollar?) standard; (2) mutual assistance among central banks; (3)

centralization of monetary reserves and reserve creation; (4) increase in the price of gold; and (5) freely flexible exchange rates.[44] We follow his classification.

Extension of the Gold Exchange Standard

It would be possible for the gold exchange standard to be extended by either the continuously increasing use of the U.S. dollar as a reserve asset or by the extension of the gold exchange standard to include other currencies as major reserve assets. The first alternative may yet survive, and no more comment on it seems necessary than was made in the chapter. If dollar creation can be controlled, foreign countries may eventually accept dollars as the major reserve asset. A financially responsible U.S. government is required for this.[45] One leading economist, for a time a member of the President's Council of Economic Advisers, with responsibilities in the area of international finance asked and answered the question: "Will the United States come round to using fiscal means to suppress excess demand? The answer is surely 'yes.'"[46]

Some favored adding to holdings of currencies other than the dollar and the pound as reserve assets.[47] The system would necessitate holdings of other foreign currencies by the central banks of the United States and of the United Kingdom. This is not necessarily harmful, and has in fact been done to some extent. The Federal Reserve System has purchased currencies in small amounts. But one is reminded of the period of bimetallism: even two kinds of money were one too many, and Gresham's law began to take effect, with the metal having the lesser market but the same nominal value being used in reserves and in payments, and the other metal being hoarded. Adding other currencies as reserve assets multiplies the problem of maintaining confidence in the equivalent value of all types of reserve assets.

Mutual Assistance Among Central Banks

Mutual assistance among central banks has been involved in the purchases of foreign currencies by the Federal Reserve System, and in swap arrangements among central banks. The swap arrangements increase reserves for one central bank when needed, and return them to another central bank at another time. This is helpful and will certainly continue. It is not fundamental reform.[48]

---

[44]See the work by Machlup referred to in fn. 17. For a different and thought-provoking approach, see Richard E. Caves and Ronald W. Jones, *World Trade and Payments* (Boston: Little, Brown, 1973), Chap. 20, "Reserves and Liquidity: External Balance from an International Viewpoint."

[45]The United States must have a slower rate of inflation than most or all the other major industrialized countries, or an equal but very moderate rate—so that the dollar remains relatively stable in purchasing power, compared to other currencies. The U.S. balance of payments deficit must be of a size not adding to world reserve assets more than can be absorbed voluntarily by private holders and central banks together. The precise limit or range of this amount is not known, but can be determined in practice with further research.

[46]Ezra Solomon, "Monetary Policy and Credit Allocation—The Basic Issue," in *Credit Allocation Techniques and Monetary Policy* (Boston: Federal Reserve Bank of Boston, 1973), p. 13.

[47]See the references to their writings in Machlup, op. cit., pp. 24–30.

[48]See the regular reports entitled "Treasury and Federal Reserve Foreign Exchange Operations" in the Federal Reserve Bank of New York *Monthly Review*; for example, Charles A. Coombs and Scott E. Pardee, "Treasury and Federal Reserve Foreign Exchange Operations," Federal Reserve Bank of New York, *Monthly Review*, March 1975, pp. 39–56.

Centralization of International Monetary Reserves

The most significant reform proposal extensively discussed, but not treated in the body of the chapter, is the proposal for centralization of international reserves and for the regular creation of reserve assets by an international institution. The two major proponents of this proposal were Keynes, who argued that overdraft facilities should be available to deficit countries at their initiative, and Triffin, who proposed the creation of reserves by an international institution, presumably (probably?) the IMF, through open market operations or some variant.[49]

Keynes made his proposal in connection with the plans for establishing the IMF. Since the IMF was not established in that form, his proposal has only historical interest. The basic question was: Would this amount to the control of the world central bank by borrowing countries and would such a situation be desirable?

The Triffin proposals have been extensively discussed, partly as a result of a series of books by Robert Triffin. Essentially, his plan was the creation of international reserves through a form of open market operations, like that by which the Federal Reserve System now controls the monetary base for the U.S. money supply. Except for the creation of SDRs, a limited activity, the present activity of international institutions involves credit but not money. Triffin, on the other hand, proposed the creation of international money by an international institution.

Only those well versed in monetary theory are likely to emphasize the difference. Money is more important than other financial assets either because of its use for payments or because it is closely correlated with total spending and income so that increases in the money supply are followed by increases in total spending and income. Early monetary theory emphasized the first reason. Some modern monetary theorists, notably Milton Friedman and associated economists, emphasize the second. If money is important as a cause of changes in business activity, as Friedman seems to have convinced most theorists, then changes such as those proposed by Triffin are major steps. Because of the implications for the relinquishment of sovereignty and the important relationship to business activity, many view such steps as unlikely in the foreseeable future, although perhaps possible in the long run.

Increase in the Price of Gold

Some suggest that one way to create more reserves without such a step is simply to increase the price of gold. Although two increases occurred in the period 1971–1973, and although the private market price soared to unexpected heights, it seems unlikely that this will happen again. It is contrary to U.S. government policy and has been strongly advocated only by representatives of France. More important, it is contrary to the long-run trend for governments to make more rather than less effort to control the money supply in order to control changes in levels of income and business activity. Arguments that an increase in the price of gold benefits the major gold producers, such as South Africa, the Soviet Union, and Canada, are secondary. Secondary also is the argument that raising the price of gold is inflationary, since this result depends on the timing and amount of the price increase and the use of the additional gold reserves (both newly produced gold and additional gold in monetary value terms) by central banks. It is

[49]For Keynes's views on this proposal, see the discussion in Machlup, op. cit., pp. 39–45. For Triffin's views, refer to a number of his many books. For a brief treatment, which may be supplemented by further reading in his works, see Robert Triffin, *The Evolution of the International Monetary System: Historical Reappraisal and Future Perspectives*, Princeton Studies in International Finance, No. 12 (Princeton, N.J.: Princeton, 1964).

not likely that governments and/or central banks will move toward abandoning discretionary control of the money supply. It is not likely that this control will be transferred to an international institution, nor that it will be abandoned for an unvarying "rule" like that proposed by Milton Friedman.

Freely Flexible Exchange Rates

Flexible exchange rates were discussed in the body of the chapter, but one further comment should be made. Although widening of bands around par values was discussed, the related proposal for crawling pegs was not.[50] One way of making a system of floating or managed floating rates adjustable in small steps is to impose limits or rules concerning the extent of exchange rate changes. These limits or rules could affect amounts of change, timing or frequency of change, and events or conditions that might trigger changes in exchange rate par values. A crawling peg may be advantageous for smaller and more open economies with large volumes of foreign trade relative to their sizes. Such economies are not large enough to justify a fixed rate of exchange for the domestic currency. A small country which exports primarily, say, bananas, and which establishes a fixed par value for its currency, has succeeded in stabilizing its currency in terms of the price of bananas! A crawling peg may also be advantageous for developing countries with significant rates of voluntary or involuntary inflation, requiring regular devaluations of the currency.

QUESTIONS FOR DISCUSSION

1 To what extent do you think the actions of August 15, 1971, by the U.S. government were precipitated by international factors? Explain.

2 What was accomplished by the Smithsonian Agreement of December 18, 1971?

3 Some economists have stated that the events of 1971 were tantamount to the death of the Bretton Woods international monetary system. It should be evident that this is not the view of the authors. Discuss both interpretations, indicating the basis for interpreting that year as the end of that system, and the basis for the alternative interpretation, that although a basic change occurred, the system remained intact. Note that in answering this question, you must define what is essential in the Bretton Woods system; if that is gone, clearly the system is dead.

4 Present the arguments for a wider band around par values.

5 Evaluate the experience with floating exchange rates since early 1973, and compare it with the experience in the 1930s.

6 What is the significance of the move of a few countries to tie their currencies to SDRs instead of to dollars?

7 Compare the views of Keynes and Triffin about an international central bank with regular (day-to-day) reserve-creating power.

8 Do you agree with the comment in the appendix that the crawling peg proposal has merit for many LDCs? Why or why not?

9 Do you regard SDRs as reserve assets which promote an economically efficient use of resources? (See the book by Caves and Jones referred to in fn. 22, pp. 430–431.)

10 What do you think are the most likely next steps in the reform of the international monetary system? Why?

[50]John H. Williamson, *The Crawling Peg*, Essays in International Finance, No. 50 (Princeton, N.J.: Princeton, 1965).

SUGGESTED REFERENCES

Plans for reform of the international monetary system were detailed with thoroughness in Fritz Machlup, *Plans for Reform of the International Monetary System*, Special Papers in International Economics, No. 3, rev. (Princeton, N.J.: Princeton, 1964). The proposals for widening the exchange rate "band" were likewise thoroughly analyzed in George N. Halm, *The "Band" Proposal: The Limits of Permissible Exchange Rate Variations*, Special Papers in International Economics, No. 6 (Princeton, N.J.: Princeton, 1965).

The influential work by Ragnar Nurkse, *International Currency Experience* (Geneva: League of Nations, 1944) should be read to understand the reasons why countries' representatives adopted a fixed (but adjustable) exchange rate system at Bretton Woods.

Details of changes in the international monetary system from the U.S. viewpoint were well summarized in chapters in the *Economic Report of the President* for 1972, 1973, 1974, and 1975.

Varying views on the international monetary system were presented at a conference in October 1969, the proceedings of which were published in *The International Adjustment Mechanism* (Boston: Federal Reserve Bank of Boston, 1970). Especially, Professor Friedman clearly presented the view that adjustment has not been successful, and Mr. Gilbert almost as effectively presented the view that it has often been successful, although not for the United States and the United Kingdom. Gilbert argued strongly that there just was not enough gold. To understand his view, which could not be fully presented in the space available, it is helpful to read his *The Gold-Dollar System: Conditions of Equilibrium and the Price of Gold*, Essays in International Finance, No. 70 (Princeton, N.J.: Princeton, 1968).

Everyone should read the Outline of Reform in the IMF *Survey*, June 17, 1974, even if one almost goes to sleep in doing so.

Because moderation may be a virtue, the authors recommend Anthony Lanyi, *The Case for Floating Exchange Rates Reconsidered*, Essays in International Finance, No. 72 (Princeton, N.J.: Princeton, 1969).

The changing role of gold is reviewed in Adrian W. Throop, "Decline and Fall of the Gold Standard," Federal Reserve Bank of Dallas, *Business Review*, January 1976, pp. 1–11.

A perceptive review of diagnoses of the need for reform of the international monetary system and of the pros and cons of the various proposals for reform is provided in Leland B. Yeager, *International Monetary Relations*, 2d ed. (New York: Harper & Row, 1976), chaps. 28–32. Yeager's conclusions are quite different from those of some economists whose theories are reviewed in Chapter 9. Yeager argues that either monetary independence or fixed exchange rates must be sacrificed. If, as Aliber suggests, monetary independence is likely to require wide fluctuations in exchange rates, the whole argument requires restatement, and the goals of a degree of integration of economic policies of the countries of the industrialized world and stable but adjustable exchange rates may be consistent.

For the steps taken in the IMF toward reform of the international monetary system, see the IMF *Survey*, especially July 8, 1974 (basket valuation of SDRs), Sept. 15, 1975 (Interim Committee report on gold), Nov. 24, 1975 (Rambouillet meeting agreement), Jan. 19, 1976 (Jamaica report of the Interim Committee), Feb. 2, 1976 (increase in credit tranches), and Apr. 5, 1976 (Board of Governors approval of increase in quotas in IMF).

A brief appraisal of the Jamaica agreement as the culmination of negotiations beginning in 1971 may be found in Norman S. Fieleke, "International Monetary Reform: The Jamaica Composite," Federal Reserve Bank of Boston, *New England Economic Review*, March–April 1976, pp. 57–62. Also interesting are the views of eight economists presented in Edward M. Bernstein et al., *Reflections on Jamaica*, Essays in International Finance, No. 115 (Princeton, N.J.: Princeton, 1976). Bernstein concludes that the IMF may "grow steadily in stature as the international monetary authority," but others view the result much less favorably. Machlup, for example, concludes that "the important principles were lost in the shuffle, or deliberately dropped."

Some interesting speculation on future reform of the IMF is presented in Alexandre Kafka, *The International Monetary Fund: Reform without Reconstruction?* Essays in International Finance, No. 118 (Princeton, N.J.: Princeton, 1976). Kafka thinks that rate flexibility, convertibility, restrictions, the intervention system, the dollar overhang, the use of SDRs, and liquidity may all be modified. He also suggests that the dollar overhang—the great amount of U.S. dollars held by central banks in relation to the former size of their holdings—may simply disappear with continuing inflation (*à quelque chose malheur est bon*).

A detailed discussion of the changes in the international monetary system from 1945 to 1976 is provided by Robert Solomon, *The International Monetary System, 1945–1976: An Insider's View* (New York: Harper & Row, 1976). An academic view of the period is provided by Robert J. Carbaugh and Liang-Shing Fan, *The International Monetary System: History, Institutions, Analyses* (Lawrence, Kan.: The Regents Press of Kansas, 1976).

A good review of OPEC's situation is covered briefly in D. K. Osborne, "Prospects for the OPEC Cartel," Federal Reserve Bank of Dallas, *Review*, January 1977, pp. 1–7. His conclusion: "OPEC . . . will die. The only questions are how and when."

Part Three

International Banking, Exchange Rates, and Money Markets

For a long time commercial banks have been an essential part of the international payments mechanism. International payments, like domestic payments, are generally made by requesting banks to transfer ownership of deposits. Transfers are made by drafts or cable or, more recently, by telephone, instead of by checks (one form of draft). But the essential elements are the same. Moreover, banks obtain additional deposits in foreign banks (foreign exchange) from their central banks, just as they obtain more reserves domestically. Central banks make final settlements by shifting reserve assets. When one country's currency constitutes a reserve asset, as sterling did before World War I, or dollars and sterling since that war, settlements by that country may involve either an outflow of reserve assets or an increase in its liquid liabilities to foreigners.

In addition to handling the international payments mechanism, commercial banks provide a number of services intended to reduce risks in obtaining payments for international transactions. These are discussed in Chapter 7.

Gradually, as their customers expanded their international activities, banks did the same to serve those customers. Banks have now become international, lending and investing *in* many countries as well as handling payments *between* countries. This shift in activity in international banking is the subject of Chapter 8.

Exchange rates are essentially prices determined by private supply and demand alone or in combination with government intervention in some form. The determination of exchange rates is discussed in Chapter 9. The basic determinant is the change in purchasing power of various currencies, which in turn reflects varying rates of inflation and real growth. Purchasing power parity is thus fundamental to the analysis and forecast of exchange rate determination, but other factors are also considered in the discussion of exchange rates in Chapter 9.

For a long time commercial banks have participated to some degree in foreign as well as in domestic money markets. Their effect was usually minor. With the advent of Eurodollars (dollar deposits outside the United States), a truly international money market came into existence. Because banks in Europe sought additional deposits, they did not wish their governments to restrict this market; and the United States, having no sovereignty in Europe, was not in a position to do so. Although some regulation was finally imposed, the Eurodollar market remained relatively free, and fortunately could accept some of the funds obtained by the OPEC countries from petroleum sales, providing, at least temporarily, liquidity and safety. A smaller Asian dollar market developed in the Pacific area. Both are parts of what might properly be termed the offshore currency market, including deposits in pounds, marks, Swiss francs, and other currencies outside the countries issuing them. This market affords an alternative to national markets for depositing, lending, and borrowing. These markets and the interest rate interrelationships among money markets are discussed in Chapter 10.

Chapter 7

International Banking

As we have seen in Part Two, central banks have the obligation to arrange final settlements for international debts. Most international payments by individuals and firms, however, are handled through commercial banks which provide financial instruments quite similar to those used in domestic transactions. Banks also help reduce risks associated with international transactions. Finally, they are important lenders to those engaged in foreign trade and to business firms located and operating abroad. The discussion in this chapter is generally applicable to banks in any country, although when specific details seem necessary, reference is to banks in the United States.

THE ROLES OF COMMERCIAL BANKS IN INTERNATIONAL FINANCE

It may be useful to elaborate briefly on the three major roles of commercial banks in international transactions: operating the payments mechanism, helping to reduce risks, and extending credit. The domestic and international payments and lending operations are quite similar; helping to reduce risk is far more important in international than in domestic banking.

The International Payments Mechanism

Essentially, banks operate the international payments mechanism by maintaining deposits in banks abroad and accepting deposits of foreign banks and by debiting and crediting these accounts when payments are made. Thus, if an importer wants to pay for goods imported, the firm may obtain a bank draft from a bank, paying in local currency. The draft may be in local or foreign currency. Either the importer or the bank may send the draft to the exporter. If the draft is in the importer's currency, the exporter usually exchanges it for local currency, and the bank which pays him obtains reimbursement by sending the draft back for deposit credit in a bank in the importer's country. If the draft is in the exporter's currency, it is usually deducted from the deposit account maintained by the importer's bank in a bank in the exporter's country.

If payments equal receipts, as they do if there is equilibrium in the BOP, deposit accounts in general remain at the initial level, although some banks find deposits increased and some find them reduced. By using telegraph and telephone services, banks can make transfers very quickly, at small cost per unit of currency transferred to those making payments.

Currencies in which payments are very frequently made are termed *vehicle* currencies. If U.S. exporters normally price exports in dollars and are paid in dollars, and if Japanese exporters price goods in dollars for sale to the United States, payments are made in both directions by additions to and subtractions from deposits maintained by Japanese banks in U.S. banks. To the extent that this occurs, conversions of one currency into another (foreign exchange transactions) take place in Japan, not in the United States.

Reducing Risks in International Transactions

A major means to reduce risks in international transactions is the *letter of credit.* Letters of credit assure beneficiaries—for example, exporters—that banks will pay them upon presentation of the proper documents before a specified time limit. Thus exporters are assured that neither financial difficulties of importers or other purchasers nor BOP problems which may cause governments to restrict payments will prevent them from receiving funds. The latter risk has usually been the more significant because creditworthiness can be investigated and credit refused for those not meeting specified standards. Moreover, most international importing firms have strong credit. But most firms are not able to analyze BOP situations precisely and to predict the imposition of government controls. Governments impose controls when necessary but are reluctant to impose controls which prevent *banks* from honoring commitments already made. Generally, governments permit banks to honor letters of credit already issued, although they may restrict further issue. Thus the letter of credit becomes a strong force in reducing risks of obtaining payments and a device to permit a freer flow of international commerce.

Banks also reduce risks by providing, for some currencies, contracts to buy or sell "forward" exchange—foreign currency to be delivered at a specified time in the future at a price agreed upon at the time of the contract.

This eliminates the risk that an exchange rate may rise, which would increase costs for importers and others making payments. It also eliminates the risk that an exchange rate may fall, which would reduce receipts of exporters and others who receive payments. By selling foreign exchange at a specified discount, the discount on selling forward exchange, an exporter máy avoid the risk of a larger cost if the exchange rate falls sharply.

Extension of Credit

Banks also extend credit for international transactions and for business activity within foreign countries. They make loans to importers and exporters and provide special forms of credit convenient to those engaged in international business. This chapter focuses on loans made in connection with international transactions and on loans extended from bank home offices to firms, financial institutions, governments, and government agencies in foreign countries. In recent years banks have become more active in operating branches and subsidiaries in foreign countries, and in making loans through such offices. This phase of credit extension is discussed in Chapter 8.

INTERNATIONAL BANKING DEPARTMENTS OF BANKS

Financing international transactions is usually sufficiently different from other work of a bank to warrant a separate international banking department as soon as volume justifies cost. One reason to establish a separate department is that personnel must be specially trained in the nomenclature, procedures, and legal aspects of international banking. Another reason is to make it easier to determine profitability. In the early days of international banking in the United States, the profits realized in international banking departments (then known as foreign departments) were usually minimal. These departments were often maintained as a service to business customers, and, since banks made profits on their loans and services to such customers, profiting on international banking services was not considered important. This situation has changed in recent years because some U.S. banks made from 40 to 60 percent of their total net profits from international banking alone.

Reducing Financial Risks[1]

A major part of the work of international banking departments has been to reduce risks in international transactions by issuing letters of credit, by selling and buying forward exchange contracts, and in other ways.

Letters of Credit and Power of Banks to Issue Them   The issuance of letters of credit by banks has a long history but an unclear legal basis. It is now accepted, however, that banks have this power, although in many cases not authorized by specific legislation.

[1]For a much more detailed discussion of matters included in this section, see Charles N. Henning, *International Finance* (New York: Harper & Row, 1958), Chaps. 3–8, 11, 14.

Courts have often held that although banks have the power to lend money, they may *not* lend their "credit." That is, they do not have the power to make guarantees for others. Clearly, letters of credit are very similar to, if they are not in fact, guarantees. They state that if certain specified conditions are met banks will honor drafts drawn upon them by beneficiaries of the letters of credit. In effect, payment is guaranteed by banks if the conditions are met.[2] Courts have denied banks the right to give guarantees because of the danger that more guarantees might be made than could be fulfilled, since they require no immediate cash outlays and no creation of deposits which show as liabilities on bank balance sheets. Letters of credit are one exception; the power to issue them has come to be regarded as inherent or implied. This does not give banks the right to give other guarantees, although one other exception arose out of the Dixon Irmaos case discussed in the appendix to this chapter.

Section 13 of the Federal Reserve Act included the power for member banks to accept drafts drawn on them. Acceptance indicates that banks will pay the drafts, and specifies the date of payment; if the draft is drawn payable 30 days after sight, it is payable 30 days after a bank accepts it. The power to issue letters of credit stating that drafts would be honored was legally held to be implied. Since 1913, therefore, there has been no question of the power of member banks, including all national banks, to issue letters of credit. Some writers have urged that it is not desirable to limit a power of banks simply because, if carried too far, it might be abused. Any industry, even a regulated industry like banking, needs freedom to develop new techniques, methods, and instruments in order to increase its effectiveness.

Because the power to issue letters of credit is not based on specific legislation, discussion of this power is relevant. If banks change their methods and develop new techniques, issues which appeared to be legally settled may come into question again.

Letters of credit issued in international banking are chiefly *commercial documentary letters of credit.* They are commercial as distinct from travelers' and other letters of credit which may be issued by a bank apart from its international operations. They are documentary because in most cases drafts are honored only when presented with specified documents in proper form covering the transactions. Nondocumentary credits, or *finance bills,* are an alternative to borrowing on promissory notes. They have the advantage of being bank obligations and hence are safe, so they may be marketed even when it might be impossible to sell the promissory notes of many business firms in the commercial paper market. Because they are safe, almost never encountering default, interest rates on them may be lower than on other short-term instruments in periods of rising interest rates, if fears of default on some instruments begin to affect yields.

---

[2]The most logical view of the letter of credit under contract law theory is that the payment of commission to the opening bank by the importer or other party requesting the opening of the letter of credit is the consideration for the letter of credit, even though the agreement of the bank is to make payment to the beneficiary, usually the exporter. See Herman N. Finkelstein, *Legal Aspects of Commercial Letters of Credit* (New York: Columbia, 1930), pp. 284–295.

Because bank acceptances are marketable, banks themselves need not advance funds; hence acceptances are a source of funds even when banks are "loaned up." Bank acceptances need not necessarily be related to international transactions, although in the past they usually have been.

Advantages of Letters of Credit   The major advantages of letters of credit accrue to beneficiaries, and in international transactions beneficiaries are usually exporters. Exporters are almost completely assured of payment if they meet specified conditions under letters of credit. Moreover, they can obtain funds as soon as they have the necessary documents—usually those covering shipment and insurance of goods—and need not wait, even if importers are granted credit permitting delay of payment for some period. The major risk faced by exporters is that governments may impose restrictions preventing payment by firms. This risk is almost eliminated by letters of credit; cases in which governments have prevented banks from honoring letters of credit already issued are very few. Similarly, only in special conditions such as war or revolution is it likely that a bank *cannot* pay, and there are means of specifying that in such cases another bank in another country must pay.

Importers also obtain advantages. Letters of credit assure importers that exporters will not be paid unless they provide certain documents and until these are carefully examined by a bank. Including among the required documents certain certificates of quantity, quality, or grade, protects importers further. Note, however, that this protection is limited to examination of documents. No one would expect employees of banks to open and examine contents of boxes or crates, and even if they did, they would seldom know whether quality was as specified. Even with a letter of credit, a shipment may arrive containing only sawdust, if an exporter is dishonest.[3]

Another advantage to importers is that it may be cheaper to finance under a letter of credit than by borrowing. Moreover, under provisions of letters of credit, banks sometimes extend credit to importers which might otherwise be difficult to obtain. This possible advantage also exists for exporters.

The Simplest Case—the Circular Negotiation Letter of Credit   A clear understanding of letters of credit may best be obtained by examining simple cases first. Perhaps the simplest case is that of a letter of credit requested by an importer from his bank and sent by that bank to the beneficiary, the exporter. The importer, in applying for the letter of credit, signs a letter of credit agreement to provide the funds necessary to honor the letter of credit on or before the due date, and to pay required fees. The bank, termed the *opening bank,* "opens" the letter of credit, specifying on it the amount, terms, documents necessary, length of time for which it is valid, and other conditions;

---

[3]*Sztejn v. Schroder Banking Corporation,* 177 Misc. 719, 31 N.Y. Supp. 2d 631 (Sup. Ct. N.Y. Cty. 1941) is the leading case in establishing the principle that drafts must be honored unless fraud is discovered before the drafts have been honored. For more discussion, see Henry Harfield, *Bank Credits and Acceptances,* 5th ed. (New York: Ronald, 1974), pp. 81–83.

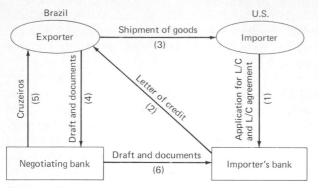

Steps in this transaction are as follows:

1 Importer applies to opening bank for L/C and signs L/C agreement.

2 Opening bank opens L/C and sends it directly to exporter.

3 Exporter examines L/C, finds it satisfactory, prepares goods for shipment, and ships them.

4 Exporter brings draft and necesssary documents (bill of lading, commercial invoice, and others) to selected negotiating bank. (*Note:* if this occurs very long after step 3, the drafts become what banks term "stale drafts," since the goods may reach the port of destination and be subject to damage while on the docks.)

5 Negotiating bank examines documents carefully and if satisfied pays exporter, normally in exporter's currency.

6 Negotiating bank sends draft and documents to opening bank.

7 Opening bank examines draft and documents, and if they are satisfactory, documents may be given to the importer, perhaps in exchange for a trust receipt. If the draft is a sight draft, the bank pays it, usually simply by crediting the deposit of the negotiating bank maintained in the opening bank, if such a deposit exists. If the draft is a time draft, the opening bank accepts it, stamping and dating it, and may either purchase it itself if it wishes to hold additional bank acceptances, or sell it in the acceptance market. If the draft is sold in the market, the bank must honor it at maturity. In either case, the importer must provide the necessary funds.

Figure 7-1   A Circular Negotiation Letter of Credit.

and sends it to the beneficiary. Three parties are involved, as shown in Figure 7-1; the importer (sometimes called the account party), the opening bank, and the beneficiary (the exporter).

Such a letter of credit is termed a *circular* letter of credit because it can "circulate," being available for use by the beneficiary whenever he wishes, if banks are willing to honor the drafts that the exporter draws. The exporter may go to any bank to obtain funds under such a letter of credit, and the bank, if willing, *negotiates* the draft or drafts, paying usually in the exporter's currency regardless of the currency in which the draft is drawn. This type of letter of credit is therefore especially useful when there are rapidly changing floating exchange rates. Under such conditions an exporter may be able to obtain a slightly more favorable exchange rate from one bank than from another. The bank examines the documents, determines that they meet the conditions specified in the letter of credit, and pays the exporter. The bank is termed a *negotiating bank,* since the drafts are negotiable instruments. The bank obtains a profit, usually, by buying drafts at a somewhat lower rate than that at which it would sell similar drafts to importers or others with payments to make. It sends· the drafts and documents to the opening bank for payment, usually debiting the opening bank's account if the drafts were drawn in the currency of the country of the negotiating bank, or debiting its own deposit account in the opening bank or another bank in the same country if the drafts were drawn in the currency of that country.

Specially Advised Letters of Credit   Frequently it is convenient to send letters of credit to beneficiaries *through* banks, which are then termed *notifying* or *advising banks,* because banks frequently communicate with each other, and their personnel understand letters of credit. In such cases the notifying or advising banks have no responsibility, nor do they receive fees. They try, of course, to send the letters of credit to the beneficiaries in correct form. Under the rules of the Uniform Customs and Practice for Documentary Credits fixed by the International Chamber of Commerce, notifying banks are not responsible for errors. The situation is shown in Figure 7-2. The letter of credit is known as a *specially advised* letter of credit. The use of an advising bank often

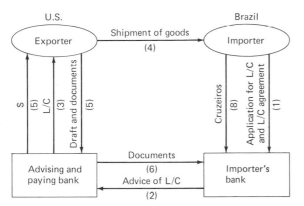

Steps in this transaction are as follows:

    1 Importer applies to opening bank for L/C and signs L/C agreement.

    2 Opening bank agrees to open L/C and sends a notice to this effect to the advising and paying bank, which has been selected in advance.

    3 Advising and paying bank prepares L/C, normally on its own stationery form (but the form indicates that the importer's bank is the opening bank and that drafts are to be drawn on the paying bank and will be honored by it).

    4 Exporter examines the L/C, finds it satisfactory, and ships goods.

    5 Exporter brings draft and necessary documents to paying bank and obtains dollars.

    6 Paying bank, having examined documents carefully and paid exporter when assured that all documents are in order, sends documents to opening bank.

    7 Paying bank reimburses itself, usually by debiting the deposit account of the opening bank if that bank maintains such an account in the paying bank.

    8 Importer provides funds to opening bank before specified date.

Variations may of course occur in these steps; the above list is illustrative. Since step 7 usually involves simply bank accounting entries, it is not shown in the diagram.

Figure 7-2   A Specially Advised Straight Letter of Credit.

involves more than convenience, for many letters of credit designate advising banks as *paying banks,* in which case they receive fees. In these situations the letters of credit indicate that drafts are to be drawn on the paying banks, which will honor them. Frequently the message from an opening bank comes to a paying bank by cable or telex, and the paying bank prepares the letter of credit on its own stationery. The form indicates that drafts are to be drawn on the paying bank, which clearly incurs some risk. If it pays drafts in error, the opening bank may refuse to reimburse it; hence the fee for acting as a paying bank.

Letters of credit that involve paying banks are termed *straight* or *domiciled* letters of credit. Figure 7-3 illustrates such a letter of credit. Note that drafts are drawn at 90 days' sight on Crocker National Bank, the paying bank. A "full set" means all the signed, hence negotiable, copies; clean means no indication of damaged goods, and on-board means indication that the goods were on board a steamship or motor vessel. Note the provision referring to Uniform Customs and Practice for Documentary Credits.

The advantage of such letters of credit is that exporters are assured of obtaining payment quickly from banks near them, usually banks with which they have already been dealing. Drafts drawn on those banks are drawn in the national currency, and no foreign exchange transaction is involved for the exporter. Hence this type of letter of credit is frequently used for U.S. exporters. It is sometimes inaccurately called an *export letter of credit* because it is so frequently used for U.S. exports, but clearly, it is an import letter of credit for importers in other countries.

Drafts drawn under such letters of credit may be discounted; in such cases exporters are paying part of the cost of financing the transactions. In other cases the letters of credit, termed "cash against documents" letters of credit, provide for cash in full to exporters. Just after World War II, it was common for U.S. exporters to require foreign importers to have their banks open specially advised straight letters of credit, with drafts payable at U.S. banks, cash against documents. Exporters could insist on such letters of credit because in a sellers' market they were able to force foreign importers to bear the entire cost of financing.

Irrevocable and Revocable Letters of Credit   Most letters of credit issued today are *irrevocable.* They cannot be revoked before a specified date without prior notice to beneficiaries. Some *revocable* letters of credit are issued, which may be revoked at any time without notice to beneficiaries, giving exporters little assurance of receiving payment. Notice must be given in such cases to advising banks if these are involved. Although such letters of credit are not now common, they may be used in some situations.[4] For example, exporters

---

[4]Ernest D. Shaw, *Practical Aspects of Commercial Letters of Credit* (New York: Irving Trust Company, 1963) points out that the revocable letter of credit is better for exporters than open credit to the buyer, even if drafts under the open credit are collected through banking channels, since under a revocable letter of credit the buyer is arranging the financing, whereas in the other case the exporter must arrange it if needed.

ADVICE OF CORRESPONDENT'S
IRREVOCABLE STRAIGHT CREDIT

[X] P.O. BOX 38010
SAN FRANCISCO, CALIFORNIA 94138

[ ] P.O. BOX 2861
LOS ANGELES, CALIFORNIA 90051

[ ] P.O. BOX 1550
SAN DIEGO, CALIFORNIA 92112

CROCKER NATIONAL BANK
INTERNATIONAL BANKING DEPARTMENT

L C NO. 0002

NAME OF BANK
ESTABLISHING THIS CREDIT

OUR ADVICE
NO. X1234

DATE March 7, 1974

GENTLEMEN:

WE HAVE RECEIVED A **cable** DATED **March 7, 1974** FROM THE ABOVE NAMED BANK

REQUESTING US TO INFORM YOU THAT THEY HAVE OPENED THEIR IRREVOCABLE LETTER OF CREDIT NO 0002

IN YOUR FAVOR, DETAILS OF WHICH ARE GIVEN BELOW

AMOUNT (NOT EXCEEDING) US$5,000.00 (Five thousand and no/100 U.S. Dollars)

FOR ACCOUNT OF Brazilian Importing Company, 000 Miraflores Avenue, Rio de Janeiro, Brazil

DRAFT(S) TO BE DRAWN IN DUPLICATE AT 90 days sight ON Crocker National Bank San Francisco, California

AND MUST BE MARKED 'DRAWN UNDER Rio Banking Company, Rio de Janeiro, Brazil, L/C No.0002

DATED March 7, 1974

THIS CREDIT EXPIRES AT THIS OFFICE ON October 31, 1974

DOCUMENTS TO ACCOMPANY DRAFT(S) (COMPLETE SETS UNLESS OTHERWISE STATED) CONSISTING OF

Signed Commercial Invoice in quintuplicate.
Full set of clean "on board" ocean Bills of Lading made out to order of shipper, blank endorsed, marked "Freight Prepaid" and "Notify Brazilian Importing Company, 000 Miraflores Avenue, Rio de Janeiro, Brazil."
Insurance Policy in duplicate, endorsed in blank for 110% of the CIF invoice value.
Packing List in triplicate.

EVIDENCING SHIPMENT OF: 2,000 Transistor Radios, @US$2.50 each CIF Rio de Janeiro, shipped from San Francisco, California, to Rio de Janeiro, Brazil, no later than October 25, 1974.

Partial shipments are not permitted. Transhipment is not permitted.

This letter of credit is transferable.

THIS LETTER OF ADVICE MUST ACCOMPANY YOUR DRAFT(S) WHEN PRESENTED FOR NEGOTIATION AND THE AMOUNT OF EACH NEGOTIATION MUST BE ENDORSED HEREON. UNLESS OTHERWISE EXPRESSLY STATED THIS CREDIT IS SUBJECT TO THE UNIFORM CUSTOMS AND PRACTICE FOR DOCUMENTARY CREDITS FIXED BY THE INTERNATIONAL CHAMBER OF COMMERCE. IF THIS CREDIT WAS OPENED BY CABLE, WE RESERVE THE RIGHT TO MAKE ANY SUCH CORRECTIONS AS MAY BE NECESSARY TO CONFORM WITH THE TERMS OF THE MAIL CONFIRMATION

THE ABOVE NAMED CORRESPONDENT ENGAGES WITH YOU THAT ALL DRAFTS DRAWN UNDER AND IN COMPLIANCE WITH THE TERMS OF THIS CREDIT WILL BE DULY HONORED UPON PRESENTATION TO US OF THE DOCUMENTS AS SPECIFIED

THIS LETTER IS SOLELY AN ADVICE OF CREDIT ESTABLISHED BY THE ABOVE NAMED BANK AND CONVEYS NO ENGAGEMENT OF THE PART OF CROCKER NATIONAL BANK.

NOTE: Documents must conform strictly with the terms of the Credit. If you are unable to comply with its terms, please communicate with your customer promptly with a view to having the condition changed.

THE DESCRIPTION OF THE MERCHANDISE MENTIONED ABOVE MUST BE DESCRIBED IN EXACTLY THAT FORM IN YOUR DOCUMENTS.

16-159 (REV. 1-74)

CROCKER NATIONAL BANK

Bob Barker
AUTHORIZED SIGNATURE

Figure 7-3

may want letters of credit open for as long as one or two years, to make a number of shipments. Banks may hesitate to have irrevocable credits open for so long, since economic conditions may change. Similarly, a letter of credit opened to permit payment for engineering or consulting services over a period of years under drafts drawn by the engineers or consultants may be revocable.

Sight and Time Drafts—Bank Acceptances Drafts may be sight or time drafts, depending on specification in the letters of credit. If sight drafts are drawn, payment is made on sight, and the drafts are of no further use except to be filed. If time drafts are drawn, however, they are accepted by the paying or opening bank. Acceptance is shown by a stamp including the word "accepted" and the date. Since time drafts have 30, 60, 90, or more days to maturity, they are bank obligations from the date of acceptance to the date of maturity, and are known as *bank acceptances.* They are safe; they are liquid because they may be sold, being discounted, of course, for the time remaining until maturity; and they provide a yield for the holder, in the form of the difference between maturity value and the discounted amount. They must be discounted in the country of the bank on which they are drawn, at the rate of discount then existing in that country. Hence a bank that buys time drafts from exporters must buy them at exchange rates below those which it pays for sight drafts, because it must allow for the fact that such drafts must be sent to the opening bank's country and discounted to obtain cash immediately or held to obtain full maturity value. Acceptances may be bought by the accepting banks themselves, if they wish to hold liquid assets of this type, or may be sold in the acceptance market. The creation and handling of a bank acceptance is shown in diagram form in Figure 7-4.

Forward Exchange Contracts For many currencies there is sufficient supply and demand that banks offer *forward* (future) exchange contracts to sell or buy a specified currency at a specified rate, delivery to be made at a specified future time, usually not more than 180 days from the contract date. Traditionally, banks offer these contracts primarily as a service to customers, so that exporters who have drawn time drafts or expect to draw them may sell them forward, thus being assured of the price to be received. Likewise, importers may buy forward exchange, thus being assured of the price they must pay for purchases when required. The determination of exchange rates, both for exchange for immediate delivery and for forward exchange, is discussed more fully in Chapter 9. Here we may simply note that banks usually try to offset purchases of foreign exchange for immediate delivery with equal sales, and purchases of foreign exchange for future delivery with equal sales of forward exchange. If this cannot be done, because of insufficient supply or demand, they usually still try to offset excess spot (current) purchases with excess forward sales, and then arrange *swaps* with other banks to sell the same amounts spot and buy them forward, thus making their total spot purchases

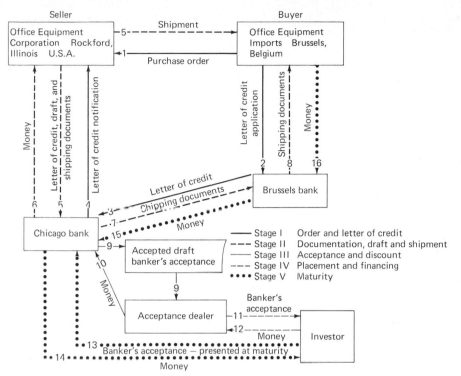

Figure 7-4 A banker's acceptance is created, discounted, sold, and paid at maturity. (*Source:* Federal Reserve Bank of Chicago, *Business Conditions,* May 1976, p. 5.)

equal to their total spot sales and their total forward purchases equal to their total forward sales. Assuming that they had the desired amounts of foreign balances before entering into these transactions, their balances remain at the desired levels. Moreover, they do not even have *temporary* excess balances, as they would have if they bought more spot exchange than they sold and simply offset that by excess forward sales.

In the period of floating exchange rates in 1973 and following years, banks sometimes forgot these rules, and managers sometimes sold currencies in larger amounts than they bought or bought more than they sold. After all, should they not try to sell a currency which seemed likely to float downward in value? Shouldn't they "roll over" their inventory of weak currencies? Sometimes when large losses occurred, trading was labeled as unauthorized, and perhaps it was. But floating rates encouraged risk-taking because they encouraged attempts to avoid losses, and even traders who might not have sought gains were tempted to try to avoid losses.

Use of Bank Acceptances

As shown, time drafts led to creation of bank acceptances. A bank acceptance is illustrated in Figure 7-5, in which the draft is drawn payable 90 days after

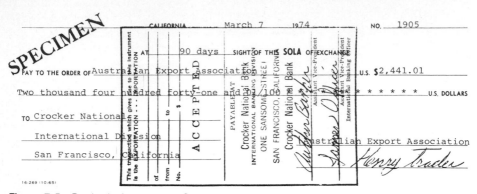

Figure 7-5 Banker's Acceptance Created under a Letter of Credit.

sight, that is, 90 days after acceptance. Note that the stamp also has space to indicate the nature of the transaction giving rise to the acceptance.

The Federal Reserve System tried to lay down rather strict rules concerning acceptances which were "eligible" for rediscount at Federal Reserve Banks. Because of the danger that banks might create more acceptances than they could honor, an effort was made to require banks to retain evidence in their files that eligible acceptances arose out of warehousing or shipment of goods. An exception was made for drafts drawn by banks in certain countries having seasonal exports, because it was recognized that such banks needed funds when imports were normal but exports were small, and that such funds could be repaid when exports were seasonally large. In recent years some large banks in money market centers have accepted drafts drawn on them by customers who wanted funds for working capital. Such accepted drafts could be sold in the money market, and if other investors (not banks) bought them, *bank* funds were not used. Thus some credit escaped from the controls on bank credit imposed by the Federal Reserve System. Because this could lead to undesired expansion of credit, the Federal Reserve System imposed a basic 5 percent reserve requirement against such acceptances in June 1973, and an additional 3 percent on additional acceptances of this type later.[5]

It is important to remember that drafts accepted by financial institutions were widely used in British international finance for many years. Acceptances were understood in financial circles and were generally regarded as almost riskless. In these circumstances it may not be surprising that foreign funds are frequently attracted to a country for the purchase of bank acceptances. When credit is tight and borrowing demand is heavy, with interest rates rising, there may be an inflow of foreign funds for the purchase of bank acceptances. This may be advantageous if the country has less than full employment, since it

[5]See Charles N. Henning, William Pigott, and Robert Haney Scott, *Financial Markets and the Economy* (Englewood Cliffs, N.J.: Prentice-Hall, 1975), p. 198; see also *Money Market Handbook for the Short-Term Investor,* 3d ed. (New York: Brown Brothers Harriman and Company, 1970), p. 38.

tends to prevent interest rates from rising and provides funds for borrowers. However, if full employment has been attained or if inflation is a problem, the inflow of capital may be disadvantageous because it tends to offset efforts of the central bank to control credit expansion.

A recent example illustrates the use of bank acceptances in periods of rising trade and high interest rates. The volume of bank acceptances outstanding more than doubled in 1974 as banks tried to finance a growing volume of trade, especially imports by Japan, through acceptances of U.S. banks. Investors found the relatively high yield on bank acceptances, together with the low risk, attractive. It seems likely that in periods like 1974, when interest rates are relatively high, further increases in volume of bank acceptances outstanding will occur.

When international trade is being financed, there is always a choice whether to have drafts drawn on the opening bank, frequently in the importer's country; on a bank in the exporter's country; or on a bank in a third country. The rise in bank acceptances outstanding in 1974 reflected in good part the fact that the cost of acceptances by banks in Japan would have been higher than for those created in the United States. The existence of a developed market for bank acceptances in the United States was also a factor.[6]

It should be kept in mind that U.S. banks are subject to state laws, and most states impose usury limitations on interest rates on loans. Most international loans do not have this interest rate limitation. Hence, in a period of high interest rates, international loans may be especially profitable, and it may also be possible, concomitantly, to pay relatively high rates of interest on bank acceptances.

Handling International Payments

Since the volume of currency (paper money and coin) used in international payments is relatively small, banks handle most international payments in the form of various types of orders to transfer deposits. This is similar to handling checks for domestic payments, but there is more variety in the form of payment order. Telephone requests and cable transfers are frequently used, especially for larger payments; sight drafts may be used, and are frequently sold by banks for smaller and medium-sized payments. Sight drafts and time drafts drawn by exporters and others are purchased by banks, but if these drafts are drawn on business firms or individuals, banks must then carry out the process of making the transfer called by those on whom the original drafts were

---

[6]The Federal Reserve System discounts bank acceptances to provide funds to banks and also purchases them in its open market operations, as a part of its support for the market for bank acceptances. In 1974 it changed its rules to make more acceptances eligible for purchase even if they were not available for discount. Eligibility for purchase makes an acceptance also eligible as collateral for an advance to a member bank, so that such banks may thus obtain funds from the Federal Reserve System if they have acceptances eligible for purchase by the System. See Ralph T. Helfrich, "Trading in Bank Acceptances: A View from the Acceptance Desk of the Federal Reserve Bank of New York," Federal Reserve Bank of New York, *Monthly Review,* February 1976, pp. 51–57.

drawn. That is, an importer on whom a time draft is drawn must at the maturity of that draft arrange with a bank to remit payment to the drawer.

Clearly, with a variety of instruments being purchased and sold at a number of locations in a bank—in the international banking department, in other locations in the head office, and in branches—centralization of control is needed. The task of keeping track of the bank's foreign exchange "position" is even more complex in some ways than that of keeping current on its "money position" (deposit with the Federal Reserve Bank). Not only are numerous currencies involved, but exchange payable in London is not the equivalent of exchange payable in Liverpool, and the purchase and sale of forward exchange add other complications. Time differences add other problems, for transactions with some areas may be impossible at a time when other areas are in the midst of heavy trading activity.

International payments may be made in local or foreign currency. If the transfer is in local currency, the recipient is likely to exchange the funds for his own currency. The bank which does this for him receives the draft, which adds to its deposit balance in the bank that made out the draft. When drafts are in foreign currency, those making payments usually pay their banks by permitting their deposit accounts to be reduced, and the banks in turn authorize, through the draft, a reduction in their balances maintained abroad.

Credit and Collection Services[7]

Banks also serve as collecting agents for drafts drawn by exporters and others on those obligated to make payments to them. In this connection it may be useful to make a distinction among "cashing," "purchasing," "discounting," and "collecting" drafts. Banks *cash* drafts if the drafts are in local currency and are drawn on them, usually as either paying or confirming banks, if not as opening banks. No charge is made to parties cashing drafts because the financing costs of opening and confirming letters of credit have already been paid, or will be paid, by importers. Drafts are *purchased* if they are in foreign currencies; they are usually exchanged for local currency, either paper money or deposit credit, at an appropriate exchange rate. Drafts are *discounted* if they are in local currency, but are time drafts; the party discounting the draft is paying the cost of obtaining funds before the maturity date of the drafts. When drafts are purchased, they are purchased at a slightly lower exchange rate if they are time drafts than if they are sight drafts, to allow for the cost of discounting them in foreign countries in order to obtain funds immediately.

In *collecting* drafts, banks simply act as agents. They may advance funds against the drafts, either total, a percentage, or a percentage of all pending collections. The drawer is liable for return of such advances if drafts are not honored. Banks do not take title to drafts when they collect them. However, since they incur trouble and expense, they expect a fee. They may also be

---

[7]For more detailed discussion of this topic, see Henning, op. cit., Chap. 14.

unwilling to handle drafts if the credit risk which they believe to exist in the drawers is unduly great.

Technical matters arise in connection with the collection of drafts, such as whether the drafts are D/A (documents to be surrendered to drawees on acceptance of drafts) or D/P (documents to be surrendered on payment). An "in case of need" party may be designated for consultation in case of rebates, refusal to honor drafts for the full amounts, or other difficulties. Drafts must usually be *protested* if they are not honored, by filing notarized certificates establishing that drafts were dishonored and letting interested parties know this in case they wish to take some legal action, such as making effort to collect debts owed to them by drawees of dishonored drafts.

Foreign Exchange Trading

As banks become more involved in international activities, foreign exchange trading becomes a more important part of their work. Small sales and purchases of drafts for importers, exporters, and travelers are not trading in any extensive sense. But as the volume of such activity increases, banks need to buy and sell foreign currencies in order to add to or reduce their balances abroad. They are not generally presumed to engage in this activity for speculation, but if a currency is falling in value, they might want to sell it simply to reduce foreign exchange losses.

Trading is usually centralized, with one person designated as the trader, or the head trader. Since most trading in large amounts is now done by telephone, telex, or cable, traders must be able to make instantaneous judgments whether to buy or sell. Although personnel in the investment departments of banks are in a similar position in making judgments on the purchase and sale of bonds when prices vary, foreign exchange traders are frequently forced to make judgments concerning currencies which may be devalued by as much as half, or may float downward or upward by large percentages. Foreign exchange traders have no assurance that currencies which fall or rise will return to their former values, and they have only general guides, discussed in Chapter 9, to the trend values around which currencies may fluctuate. Buying and selling foreign exchange is in this respect much more like trading in stocks than in bonds.

Since foreign exchange markets are connected by excellent communications networks, it is generally assumed that any divergence of a given currency's value in one market from its value at the same time in another market will be met by instant *arbitrage* to take advantage of the opportunity for profit. If the value of the pound were higher in London than in New York, pounds would be bought in New York and sold in London (actually, the proper designation is that dollars would be bought in London, for which pounds would be offered). The price difference, minus the communications costs, would be the profit over marginal cost.

Clearly, also, currencies should be obtainable through third currencies at the same rate at which they are obtainable directly. If not, perhaps because of government controls on trading, *broken cross rates* exist.

Although the foreign exchange trader must have knowledge of economics and especially of the BOP analysis discussed in Chapters 2 and 3, and also of conditions in the countries in whose currencies he trades, he usually does not have time for extensive analysis when trading. Thus trading is a combination of knowledge and judgment; it is to some extent an art rather than a science.

Other Activities

The international banking departments can and usually do act in many other ways. For example, they give information on foreign exchange rates, exchange control regulations, and foreign credit and trade, and advise customers on accounting and tax problems related to foreign exchange; they assist customers in foreign trade development, and they give general advice to customers on many types of international activities.

RECENT DEVELOPMENTS IN INTERNATIONAL BANKING

It should be evident that the work of international banking departments has generally been related to international trade and payments by individuals and business firms. International investments by banks themselves may be made by the investment departments of banks or by international banking departments. Banks which establish offices overseas, whether branches, subsidiaries, or affiliates, engage in many other activities, discussed in Chapter 8. But in recent years more nontraditional activities—primarily lending—have been engaged in by banks without necessarily involving overseas offices.

Nonrecourse Export Financing

Nonrecourse export financing has become more common as banks have sought means of attracting customers. Such financing reduces risks for international trade firms because they have no further potential liability for drafts once sold to banks. Their cash flow is speeded up and they may be enabled to increase sales by offering attractive credit terms. Banks engaging in nonrecourse export financing are clearly taking some additional risk, but it may be minimal. The buying of receivables of business firms (termed *factoring*) involves more risk, since the bank does not have the evidence of specific transactions in the form of drafts and accompanying documents to help them collect receivables from importers.

Business firms which receive nonrecourse export financing obtain off-statement financing of foreign receivables: the foreign receivables do not appear on their financial statements. This may in turn enable them to qualify for additional credit.

Banks obtain higher interest rates for nonrecourse financing; hence usually more profit. Some government programs are available to reduce risk: protection may be had through Foreign Credit Insurance Association (FCIA) short-term comprehensive policies issued to firms and assigned to banks, or banks themselves may obtain such credit insurance policies. For medium-term financing, there are FCIA medium-term credit insurance policies and coverage offered by the Export-Import Bank.[8]

Direct Overseas Lending

It is only a small step from lending to exporters to direct overseas lending, but most banks did not engage in that activity until recently unless they had overseas offices. In recent years banks have recognized that with higher interest rates in many foreign countries than in the United States, U.S. banks can profitably lend overseas if they exercise care in examining the credit, foreign exchange rate, and political risks involved. Loans may be made to overseas subsidiaries of American firms, to local foreign firms, to foreign governments and government agencies, and to foreign financial institutions.

Banking Practices   In direct overseas lending, U.S. banks encounter a number of differences in practices that must be taken into account. For example, many firms especially in Europe are accustomed to overdraft borrowing, in which they are permitted to borrow simply by reducing their deposit balances below zero, a practice not generally permitted in the United States. Firms are, moreover, not accustomed to compensating balances, which are peculiar to U.S. banking. Foreign firms are also generally accustomed to borrowing chiefly on the security of assets, not on the basis of projected income or cash flow, while U.S. banks have become accustomed to this basis for lending, because income or cash flow is the source of repayment for many loans. Finally, little differentiation is made in many countries among short-term, medium-term, and long-term lending, whereas U.S. banks normally make many short-term loans and restrict the volume of their medium-term or so-called term loans.

Legal Differences   Legal restrictions not normally imposed in the United States complicate foreign lending. For example, a firm in a foreign country which borrows from a U.S. bank may be required to deposit a part of the loan with the central bank in the firm's country. This of course increases the cost of borrowing, but it may still be cheaper to borrow from a U.S. bank if local interest rates are extremely high.

Loan agreements often cause difficulty because it is customary in many

---

[8]John Mathis, ed., *Offshore Lending by U.S. Commercial Banks* (Washington, D.C. and Philadelphia: Bankers' Association for Foreign Trade and Robert Morris Associates, 1975), pp. 110–111. In recent years, because countries with centrally planned economies have not had enough foreign exchange to pay cash for their purchases, some special methods of financing such purchases have developed. Information concerning these methods is very scattered, but for one summary see Michael P. McNamara, "Current Trends in Financing U.S. Trade with Eastern Europe," master's degree research report, Graduate School of Business Administration, University of Washington, Seattle, 1977. In one method, termed *forfaiting*, exporters accept notes receivable from importers and discount them at banks. The discount is sizable because the banks acquire the notes without recourse, but exporters seem to have been able to increase prices sufficiently to cover the difference between the discount and the interest received on the notes.

countries to make medium-term loans without restrictive covenants specifying limitations on borrowers' activities to protect their repayment ability. If collateral is required and involves documents creating liens on assets, care must be taken that the documents are in proper form recognized under local laws.

Taxes   Many countries impose withholding taxes on interest paid to foreign banks. U.S. banks receiving interest have thus already paid the withheld tax on this foreign income. They may deduct such taxes from their foreign income when computing taxes due the U.S. government provided that they keep adequate records to substantiate the facts. If borrowers maintain dollar accounts in U.S. banks, they may pay withholding taxes themselves and mail the tax receipts to the banks. The banks can then reimburse the borrowers for the tax payments by crediting their accounts, which they had previously debited for the full amount of interest due. Tax treaties may reduce withholdings and some U.S. banks may be able to make loans through their overseas branches, subsidiaries, or affiliates in countries which have tax treaties with the borrowers' countries. This involves overseas banking, discussed in Chapter 8.

Accounting Differences   Accounting practices such as rules relating to depreciation and valuation of assets vary among countries, and financial statements must be examined in the light of the rules prevailing in borrowers' countries. This matter is discussed in more detail in Chapter 16.

Government Agency Loan Participation   Participation of a government agency such as the Export-Import Bank may be especially advantageous because, in addition to providing part of the total loan, and perhaps accepting later repayment in order to permit earlier repayment to banks, the agency's interest rates may be lower than those for the remainder of the loan. Moreover, interest paid by borrowers to such agencies may not be subject to withholding taxes.

Loans to Foreign Governments, Agencies, and Financial Institutions   Relevant financial analysis includes examination of the borrowing countries' BOP positions, not only in the case of loans to private firms, but in the case of loans to governments and government agencies. Lending to governments may be less risky than lending to private firms because governments may impose restrictions which prevent private firms from repaying loans, whereas in loans to governments there is normally the promise of the government not to do this. Even so, of course, there is the question whether a government which defaults will permit itself to be sued and whether it can be forced to pay even if it does permit suit and even if a judgment is won. Legal opinion is desirable on the existence of consent by borrowing governments to limitations on their sovereign immunity so that lenders can collect debts.

Because of differences between U.S. and foreign financial institutions' statements, they often cannot easily be compared with U.S. statements for purposes of credit analysis. Comparisons may be useful among similar institutions in the same country, but risk usually cannot be as clearly judged as for U.S. domestic loans.

All these factors combined mean that credit, foreign exchange rate, and political risks are greater and profits thus more variable on foreign than on domestic loans. Banks making foreign loans must be prepared to accept this variability and to exercise caution.[9] The term *country risk* has become common as a general term covering the risks encountered. Since these risks become especially important in lending to LDCs, they are discussed further in Chapter 20.

INTERNATIONAL BANKING IN PERSPECTIVE

International banking activity basically arises from needs of bank customers to finance their transactions. As long as most customers of U.S. banks who desired international financing were engaged primarily in foreign trade, the activities of international banking departments in financing trade served business adequately. As multinational firms became more important and as even medium-sized firms began to operate in foreign countries, firms began to desire banking services *in* those countries. They could turn to local banks or to offices of other foreign banks, and this possibility led U.S. banks to establish more foreign branches and subsidiaries in competition.

U.S. banks began to recognize, as economic fluctuations moderated after World War II, that overseas lending directly from home offices could be profitable and that risks could be accepted without encountering losses so great as to eliminate profit. There were and are special risks involved because of legal, tax, accounting, and banking practice differences, and because of the intrusion of the principle of governmental sovereignty. But increased knowledge of foreign countries, the need for loans in such countries, and some reduction in risks as economic growth occurred led to overseas lending by U.S. banks at relatively high interest rates. International lending increased just as international investment in foreign government securities had developed earlier.

APPENDIX: Some Technical Aspects of the Work of International Banking

International banking is a specialized field with many technicalities. While these cannot be examined in detail, the person who desires a general knowledge of international

---

[9]So far, losses on such loans have been very few and the problem seems to be rescheduling repayments rather than outright defaults; see Nicholas Sargen, "Commercial Bank Lending to Developing Countries," Federal Reserve Bank of San Francisco, *Economic Review,* Spring 1976, pp. 20–31. See also Nicholas P. Sargen, "Country Risk," Federal Reserve Bank of San Francisco, *Business & Financial Letter,* Mar. 18, 1977.

finance should appreciate some of the more important situations giving rise to the need for special techniques.

This appendix includes discussion of the following topics: confirming letters of credit; simple and reimbursement letters of credit; liabilities of banks under letters of credit; the right of recourse; authorities to purchase (a special form of letter of credit); the problem of precise conformity to the wording of letters of credit and the problem of bank guarantees as illustrated by the Dixon Irmaos case; the use of trust receipts; and special arrangements for providing payment, in advance of shipment of goods, to exporters, to manufacturers, and to other parties.

A general understanding of the circumstances in which these topics are significant is useful to both bankers and international traders.

Confirmed Letters of Credit

Sometimes exporters feel that there are risks even with specially advised straight letters of credit. There might be a war or revolution in the country of the opening bank, or the bank might fail before documents were presented to it. War or revolution is more common than bank failure, especially in the field of international banking, but recently there have been a few bank failures.

If an exporter wants further assurance, the importer may be asked in advance to obtain a confirmed letter of credit, opened as usual by the opening bank, but also confirmed by a *confirming bank*. Usually the confirming bank is located in the exporter's country, and may be the exporter's bank. If confirmation was not requested initially, it may be obtained, for a fee, after the exporter's receipt of the letter of credit. The confirming bank has the same liability as the opening bank to honor the drafts drawn under the letter of credit, and this adds to the assurance that payment will be received. An intelligent exporter, of course, will ask for confirmation only when he believes there is significant risk; otherwise it is not worth the cost.[10] Risk is greatest, of course, when war or revolution prevents banks from paying, and when banks do not have deposit accounts in banks in the exporter's country. If they have such deposit accounts, the exporters' banks may pay the exporters and exercise the right of offset to deduct reimbursement from the accounts of the opening banks.

Simple and Reimbursement Letters of Credit

An opening bank must reimburse a paying or confirming bank, and the simplest way is to permit the paying or confirming bank to deduct from a deposit account maintained in it by the opening bank. Letters of credit handled in this way are termed *simple*.

If such an account is not maintained, the paying or confirming bank may be reimbursed by drawing a draft on some other bank, which in turn obtains reimbursement from the opening bank. Opening banks are likely to have deposits in New York or San Francisco or Chicago banks even if they do not have accounts in other U.S. cities. Letters of credit which involve this means of providing funds are termed *reimbursement* letters of credit. A negotiating bank may negotiate an exporter's draft drawn on the opening bank, obtaining reimbursement directly by having the opening bank credit the deposit account maintained in it by the negotiating bank. Or it may discount the exporter's draft and then draw its own reimbursement draft on the opening bank.

---

[10]Shaw, op. cit., noted that if the confirming bank is in the exporter's country or state and does not pay when the exporter believes that it should pay, the exporter can sue in *local* courts, which may be advantageous.

Liabilities of Banks under L/Cs

Although liability under a letter of credit is contingent until the beneficiary asks for payment, many banks prefer to record an actual liability. "Liability Under Letters of Credit" or similar accounts are credited, and "Customers' Liabilities Under Letters of Credit" or similar accounts are debited to indicate importers' liability to provide funds. When drafts are presented, such entries can be reversed, with appropriate entries for payments to exporters, reimbursement from opening banks, fees for services, and so on. If drafts are accepted, an actual liability of a specific type comes into existence. Credit is made to an account such as "Liability Under Acceptances Outstanding," and debit to an account such as "Customers' Liabilities Under Acceptances."

If an opening bank becomes insolvent after the drawing and negotiation of drafts, a negotiating bank has recourse to the drawer (the exporter). This is discussed in more detail below. Some legal cases indicate that if the importer already provided some funds to the opening bank, the drawer of the draft would rank as a preferred creditor of the bank with respect to such funds. A buyer sometimes supplies enough funds to pay the entire draft, and in that case can hardly rank as anything other than simply a general creditor of the bank. This is not usually done; most letters of credit are issued in consideration of the importer's promise (in a letter of credit agreement) to provide the funds when due. A confirming bank, of course, must honor drafts even if the opening bank has failed. In theory, the confirming bank is only a general creditor of the opening bank, but it may have a special position because of the right of setoff (the right to offset its liability to honor the drafts by its claim on deposits held in it by the opening bank). It was reported that in one recent case such right was exercised, even though other creditors of the insolvent bank could not be paid at that time and had potential losses.

Recourse

When a draft is discounted (if in local currency) or purchased (if in a foreign currency), there may be a right of recourse to prior endorsers, if any, or to the drawer (the exporter in our examples). It should be clear that recourse only exists for an *intermediary* party such as a negotiating bank. Neither a paying bank nor an opening bank has a right of recourse, because these banks have agreed to pay and are not intermediaries. A confirming bank may have recourse if it negotiates drafts drawn on the opening bank, but unless refusal of the opening bank to pay is justified, the confirming bank's right of recourse is offset by its own obligation to pay, and hence is of no significance.

Strict conformity to law is essential if a right of recourse to the drawer or to prior endorsers is to be protected. If, for example, a draft is "dishonored" (payment is refused), it may be necessary to protest it. This is just one example of the necessity of strict conformity with every word of a document, and with each relevant law.

Authorities to Purchase

Letters of credit authorize drafts to be drawn on banks. In countries in which bank acceptances are readily marketable, paying or negotiating banks can obtain funds quickly by instructing the opening bank to purchase the acceptance or sell it in the market. If there is no market, or a poor market, for bank acceptances, this may not be possible. In these circumstances, in some countries, a slightly different document termed an *authority to purchase* (A/P) is used. Drafts are drawn on importers (not on banks), but banks promise, in the A/P forms, to honor the drafts. Originally, the drafts were drawn with recourse to the drawer (the exporter), but this gave no firm assurance of payment. Gradually it came to be generally specified that the drafts should be *without* recourse. Keep in mind that without this specification recourse would exist, because the drafts are drawn on importers and the banks are thus intermediary parties. In effect, the modern A/P is similar to a letter of credit, except for the drafts on importers. Nevertheless banks pay, and consider themselves obligated to pay. Typically, the exporter obtains full cash value of a draft, and the paying or negotiating bank is reimbursed by debiting the account of the opening bank. Thus the opening bank actually advances the funds, instead of funds being advanced by some purchaser of a bank acceptance.

A common practice in connection with A/Ps is to include a provision termed the Far Eastern interest clause (because these documents are most commonly used in trade with the Philippines and some other Far Eastern areas). This provision specifies that the importer must pay interest on the drafts from the date they are drawn or negotiated to the approximate due date for return of the proceeds to the paying or negotiating bank. This is the length of time for which the opening bank advances funds, and the clause is a means of requiring importers to pay interest for this period. Importers usually find the interest rate lower than for a local loan in their own country. Since the opening banks are often (although not always) branches of foreign banks in the Philippines or other Far Eastern area, they are satisfied with a moderate rate of interest comparable to that obtained in their home countries. This usage of A/Ps may eventually be modified or die out, but for some time it has been a convenient way of assuring exporters of payment by banks, and requiring importers to pay interest on the funds advanced.[11]

An Illustration of Complexities

A well-known legal case may illustrate the complexities of some transactions involving letters of credit. An exporter in Brazil shipped cotton to Belgium in 1940, under a letter of credit opened by Chase Manhattan Bank at the request of a Belgian bank. The exporter was paid by a Brazilian bank. Documents were forwarded to Morgan Guaranty Trust Company (correspondent bank for the Brazilian bank), and Morgan Guaranty presented the draft and documents to Chase, with a request for payment and a guarantee that Chase would suffer no harm if some signed copies of some documents were later presented by someone else. (Some signed copies were not among the documents forwarded to Morgan Guaranty.) Chase refused to pay on the grounds that (1) the letter of credit called for a "full set" of documents (meaning *all* the signed copies), and some were not presented and (2) guarantees by banks are illegal. The real reason for Chase's unwillingness to pay was, perhaps, that war had begun in Western Europe, the Germans had occupied Belgium, and neither the importer nor the Belgian bank could or would pay the drafts. After long legal action, the highest court which heard such cases decided that Chase must pay, on the grounds that (1) for any other bank or any other party to suffer loss would have been inequitable—only if the Belgian bank could have been forced to pay would an equitable result have been attained and (2) although guarantees by banks are illegal, guarantees by banks for this purpose had been given for years in New York and had become a customary thing—hence payment could not be refused. The case is of special interest becuase it established two important precedents: (1) that guarantees of this kind (although not, by this decision, of any other kind) can be offered

---

[11]In ibid. it is pointed out that for exporters and paying banks, it would be preferable if drafts were drawn on the paying banks.

by banks and (2) that in this type of case, a letter of credit need not be explicitly followed in every respect, although under any other circumstances, even a minor variation from the terms of a letter of credit could invalidate a transaction.[12]

Trust Receipts

As the documents covering an international transaction pass from one party to another, the *negotiable* documents (bills of lading, insurance policies, sometimes others) pass title to the merchandise, insurance on it, and so on. Thus banks are protected by collateral during such transactions. When merchandise reaches its destination, however, and title is transferred to the importer; or if it is unloaded at an intermediate point for storage, processing, or some other reason, the bank does not have a satisfactory collateral document unless it can use a trust receipt. Payment may not be due from the importer for some time and the bank may want protection of its claims.

A Uniform Trust Receipts Act and then the Uniform Commercial Code furnished this protection. The Uniform Commercial Code did not provide for new collateral documents, but set up the conditions under which claims exist. There is the delivery of goods, documents, or instruments (in international trade, normally documents, in most cases a negotiable bill of lading) to the debtor (the importer), and the bank has and retains a "security interest" because of the funds owed to it. The bank may "perfect" its security interest by filing with the appropriate local government office a financing statement, which continues its security interest beyond the short period for which it is automatic. Since the goods need not be kept in a warehouse (as was required when warehouse receipts were used), and the importer need not already have taken title (as was necessary for an enforceable chattel mortgage), the conditions specified by the Uniform Commercial Code are very appropriate for trust receipts. Note that the bank retains a security interest, not ownership; it can claim only funds owed to it, not the full selling price of the goods if sold, unless they sell for the amount of the debt or less. The importer is free to process, warehouse, or sell the goods, and funds from their sale may enable him to pay the bank.

One problem with trust receipts is that the legislation covering them is essentially Anglo-American, and although similar legislation has been adopted in a number of countries, there are many countries, especially those influenced by the Napoleonic Code of law, in which trust receipts are not recognized.[13] The law of hypothecation must therefore be followed in these countries. Banks must be careful that goods are not unloaded in such a country during transit unless hypothecation is carried out, if they wish to preserve intact their legal claim.

Special Arrangements for Payments

Letters of credit can be modified and supplemented in many ways to meet special needs. An exporter may obtain, by consent of all concerned parties, an amendment to a letter of credit. If it is desired to assure someone from whom an exporter buys goods, perhaps

---

[12]*Dixon Irmaos & Compania, Ltda. v. The Chase Manhattan Bank of the City of New York* (C.C.A 2d 1944) 144 F. 2d 759, cert. denied 324 U.S. 850. For further discussion of the case, see Henry Harfield, "American Law as Affecting Foreign Trade," in *International Banking and Foreign Trade* (London: Europa, 1956) and the references cited there, as well as Henry Harfield, *Bank Credits and Acceptances,* 5th ed., pp. 112, 173.

[13]For a general review, see Roy P. M. Carlson, Trust Receipts in International Banking, unpublished research report (Seattle: Pacific Coast Banking School, 1963).

a manufacturer, of payment, arrangements can be made for assignment of the letter of credit to the vendor. The letter of credit is simply written to "X Co. or assigns." Such transfer can be made only once. The disadvantage to export middlemen is that the suppliers then know the final destination and price of the goods, and may thereafter deal directly. Similarly, an assignment of proceeds of a letter of credit may be executed. This is even less satisfactory, because there is no assurance that a prior assignment has not been made. A pledge of a letter of credit has only negative value; hence is not very useful. It prevents the exporter from obtaining funds under a letter of credit while it is pledged, but does not assure the manufacturer of funds.

The most common provisions for assuring payment to suppliers, or interim payments to the exporters themselves so that they can buy for cash, are "red clause letters of credit" and "back-to-back" or overlying and underlying letters of credit.

Red clause letters of credit include a clause specifying that the paying bank may, at its discretion, make cash advances to the beneficiary against *clean* drafts (no documents). This clause was necessary because sometimes exporters must purchase goods for cash in countries where the use of credit is limited. Conditions for advances may be imposed, and interest is paid on the advances. Red clauses may be written as "progress payments" clauses to provide for interim payments to the manufacturer when a manufacturing process is lengthy.

Back-to-back letters of credit are letters of credit issued by banks usually located near the beneficiaries of the original letters of credit. The back-to-back letter of credit is issued in favor of the manufacturer or other party desiring assurance of payment. Some bankers use the term only when the back-to-back letters of credit are almost identical, preferring another designation if terms are not almost identical.[14] Actually, exporters often want letters of credit which are not quite identical, because the initial letter of credit provides for ocean shipment, and the second letter of credit provides for land shipment from the manufacturer, as shown in Figure 7-6. The risk for the bank opening

---

[14]Shaw, op. cit., indicates that a "true back-to-back credit" should not have more than the following four differences from the underlying credit: (1) the one who requests the credit is the exporter instead of the importer; (2) the beneficiary is the manufacturer instead of the exporter; (3) the amount is somewhat less, to allow for profit of the exporter; and (4) the time of validity is reduced a few days to allow for document substitution.

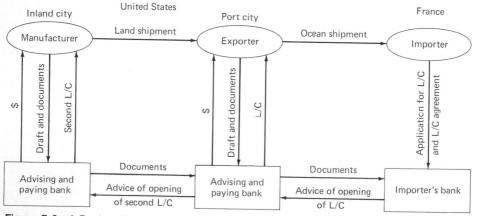

Figure 7-6 A Back-to-Back Letter of Credit.

such a letter of credit is somewhat increased. The most common risk is that a dock strike or other situation may prevent overseas shipment, forestalling payment to the exporter under the initial letter of credit. If the exporter cannot be paid, it may be impossible to pay the manufacturer. Although these situations are not as common as those discussed in the chapter, they illustrate the flexibility of and the problems connected with letters of credit.

QUESTIONS FOR DISCUSSION

1 Why are authorities to purchase (A/Ps) used in some areas instead of ordinary letters of credit?
2 What was important about the Dixon Irmaos case as a case establishing precedents in the law concerning international financing?
3 When are circular negotiation letters of credit likely to be advantageous for exporters? Why?
4 What reasons can you think of for the tremendous expansion in the volume of bank acceptances outstanding in the United States in 1974?
5 What risks are reduced by obtaining a letter of credit? When would you expect letters of credit to be more widely used? Why?
6 What is the right of recourse? Who may have recourse on whom? Explain fully.
7 Some types of letters of credit were characterized as involving "cash against documents" and were common under certain conditions. Under what conditions do you think they were used, and why?
8 Some bankers say, "We must sell foreign exchange (deposits) which are likely to decline in value and purchase currencies which are likely to rise in value." Evaluate this view.
9 Why is the *financing* of international transactions legally separated from the marketing and delivery of the goods?
10 Explain the nature of a trust receipt and the reasons for its development in connection with foreign trade financing. Can it also be used in connection with domestic transactions? Explain.

PROBLEMS

1 Assume that an export firm receives a large order for goods and that only part of the order can be filled from goods in inventory. Merchandise needed to fill the remainder of the order may be purchased from an inland supplier, but the supplier wants assurance of payment before shipping such goods. The supplier would like to be paid at the time of shipment. The letter of credit received by the exporter from the importer's bank specified that payments for drafts are to be made against a full set of on-board bills of lading, "partial shipments not permitted." What actions could the exporter take to fill the order and meet the terms of the letter of credit? What risk does the exporter incur? What is your recommendation of the best way to handle this situation, and why?
2 An exporter in Brazil finds that the exchange rate at which U.S. dollar drafts received can be converted into Brazilian cruzeiros varies from bank to bank and from time to time because of changes in the value of the cruzeiro. What kind of letter of credit should the exporter ask an importer to provide in order that the

exporter may obtain the advantage of the best rate at a given time? Explain your answer.

3 A U.S. exporter received an order from a Philippine importer. The importer was willing to pay against D/P sight drafts (documents to be delivered to the importer against payment). The exporter knew that this importer had an excellent credit rating. Tying up funds in receivables might force the exporter to seek a loan from a bank. Moreover, the exporter was uneasy about these terms. Advise him what factors he should examine before accepting this or similar orders. Are there risks or costs other than that of obtaining a bank loan, and if so what are they?

4 A U.S. import firm applies to its bank for a letter of credit for an import shipment and is asked to indicate on the application form the following things, among others: (1) whether the credit should be revocable or irrevocable, (2) the name and address of the beneficiary of the letter of credit and the tenor of the drafts, (3) the party on whom the drafts are to be drawn, (4) the documents required, (5) the latest permissible date for negotiation of the drafts, and (6) who is to obtain insurance on the merchandise. What considerations determine the answer to each of these questions?

5 The Philippine Importing Company imported merchandise valued at $6,200, under an A/P containing the Far Eastern clause. Drafts were to be drawn at 90 days' sight. Transit time to Manila may be assumed to be 5 days. The Far Eastern interest rate at that time was 5 percent per year, and the exchange rate for the Philippine peso was 50 U.S. cents per peso. What did the Philippine Importing Company have to pay to its bank, in pesos? (Assume there was no fee for opening the A/P.) Show your calculation. On whom were the drafts drawn? Would you expect the Philippine bank which opened the A/P to have recourse to the exporter if the Philippine Importing Company failed to pay? Why or why not?

6 Suppose that, as an exporter, you receive a number of letters of credit, each containing different wording. Explain in each of the following different cases what you know from the wording, quoted in each case from a letter of credit:

a "This letter is solely an advice and carries no engagement by us."

b Letter of credit from Barclay's Bank containing the wording "we hereby authorize you to value on Seattle-First National Bank."

c "We hereby agree with you and negotiating banks or bankers that drafts drawn under and in compliance with the terms of this credit shall be duly honored on due presentation to the drawee."

d "We are instructed to advise you of the establishment by the Bank of Tokyo of their irrevocable credit in your favor. . . . This letter is solely an advice and conveys no engagement by us."

e "This advice, revocable at any time without notice, is for your guidance only in preparing drafts and documents and conveys no engagement or obligation on our part or on the part of our abovementioned correspondent."

f Letter of credit from Irving Trust Company including this wording: "At the request of Barclay's Bank, London, we hereby authorize you to draw on us. . . . We engage with you that drafts drawn in conformity with the conditions of this credit will be duly honored by us."

g A letter of credit from Seattle-First National Bank indicating that a letter of credit has been opened by the Fuji Bank, Tokyo, and stating that "the above correspondent engages with you that all drafts drawn under and in compliance with the terms of this credit will be duly honored. We confirm the credit and thereby undertake that all drafts drawn and presented as above specified will be duly honored by us."

7 Suppose that you, as a Hong Kong exporter, receive a letter of credit from Seattle-First National Bank stating that "this is a confirmation of a credit cabled through Citibank, Hong Kong. . . . We hereby authorize you to value on Seattle-First National Bank. . . . Drafts to be negotiated not later than June 1." What do you know from this wording?

8 Suppose that, as a U.S. exporter, you receive a letter from the Bank of America, N.T.&S.A., stating that "we are requested by the Philippine Bank to inform you that they have established their irrevocable Authority to Purchase in your favor . . . available by your drafts in duplicate on Philippine Importing Company, Manila, without recourse." What do you know from this wording?

9 What difference does it make to you if you receive one letter of credit containing the wording "we engage with you" and another containing the wording "we engage with drawers, endorsers, and bona fide holders"? Assume first that you are an exporter, then assume that you are a banker.

10 Explain in each case what must be done to meet the following conditions specified in a letter of credit:
   a "Full set of clean bills of lading endorsed in blank."
   b "Partial shipments not allowed."
   c "Bills of lading made out to order of shipper."
   d "Drafts without recourse." (If this wording were *not* included, what party or parties could have recourse to the exporter if the drawee did not pay—an opening bank? A negotiating bank? A paying bank? Others?)

SUGGESTED REFERENCES

Charles N. Henning, *International Finance* (New York: Harper & Row, 1958), Chaps. 3–11 and 14 provides detailed coverage of procedures used in international banking departments. Francis A. Lees, *International Banking and Finance* (New York: Wiley, 1974) discusses the operations of large (especially U.S.) banks in international finance. An earlier publication, William S. Shaterian, *Export-Import Banking,* 2d ed. (New York: Ronald, 1956), although out of date, contains information that is still useful.

An authoritative discussion of letters of credit is found in Henry Harfield, *Bank Credits and Acceptances,* 5th ed. (New York: Ronald, 1974). For a less legalistic discussion, see Ernest D. Shaw, *Practical Aspects of Letters of Credit* (New York: Irving Trust Company, 1963).

Recent developments in international banking were reviewed in special sections in *Business Week* in 1973 and in 1975: "The New Banking," Sept. 15, 1973, and "The Great Banking Retreat," Apr. 21, 1975.

Practices of banks in making offshore loans, whether from offices in the United States or from overseas offices, are described in some detail in F. John Mathis, ed., *Offshore Lending by U.S. Commercial Banks* (Washington, D.C. and Philadelphia: Bankers' Association for Foreign Trade and Robert Morris Associates, 1975).

One useful booklet containing many details about the handling of letters of credit and collection of drafts, together with sample L/C forms, is *Man-on-the-Spot Around the World* (San Francisco: Bank of America, September 1976).

Chapter 8

Overseas Banking

The discussion in the preceding chapter focused on the international banking activities of banks in their home countries, with some emphasis on the United States. Banks also carry on activities overseas. Overseas banking has been conducted for centuries, and British and Dutch banks were conspicuous by their presence in many areas. Many of these areas were parts of their colonial empires or commonwealth territories; some were countries with trade ties to Britain or to the Netherlands. Some other countries, such as France, engaged in overseas banking on a lesser scale.

United States banks carried on very little activity overseas before 1914 or even between the World Wars. Only three U.S. banks established a sizable number of branches abroad. Foreign banks in the United States were likewise not very important.

After World War II, however, U.S. banks found that many business firms had overseas branches or affiliates. These branches and affiliates needed financial services which could best be provided by banks located nearby. When they sought services from U.S. banks, they sometimes found them unavailable. They were tempted to and frequently did seek services from banks in the countries where they were operating. This trend forced U.S. banks to reconsider the desirability of establishing branches, subsidiaries, or affiliates abroad. Although multinational firms are the prime example of firms whose need for services forced U.S. banks to expand overseas, many small and medium-sized firms, whose overseas activities were hardly numerous or extensive enough to justify calling them multinational, needed banking services in countries where they did business. They were, in fact, sometimes in greater need of aid than were larger firms.

As U.S. banks expanded overseas to meet the needs of their customers' overseas branches, subsidiaries, and affiliates, they found that profitable loans could also be made to local foreign firms, foreign governments and agencies, and foreign financial institutions through overseas bank branches and subsidiaries. Most countries of the world have higher interest rates than the United States, partly because they have generally had more inflation. Thus in the 1950s and 1960s, the field of overseas banking began to seem inviting, and by the early 1970s, U.S. banks, with more than 600 branches overseas, were more important in this field than were banks of any other country. Partly for this reason, this chapter emphasizes overseas operations of U.S. banks and activities of foreign banks in the United States.

OVERSEAS ACTIVITIES OF U.S. BANKS—ORGANIZATIONAL STRUCTURE

All the activities discussed in Chapter 7 could be and were carried out by many banks without banking offices abroad. Banks made arrangements, by letters or more formal agreements, with correspondent banks to handle transactions for them. Deposits were maintained in correspondent banks, investments in money markets were made for banks by their correspondents, and drafts and letters of credit were handled through this system

For many years, only a few U.S. banks went further than this in overseas activities. Three major banks established a number of branches, and a few banks had other forms of overseas offices and perhaps one branch for each bank, but with limited activity. The next few paragraphs consider successively correspondent relationships; foreign branches; Edge Act subsidiaries and their offices; and foreign subsidiaries of U.S. banks, their Edge Act subsidiaries, and their holding companies. The organizational structure which may exist is shown in Figure 8-1, although not all of these forms need exist for any individual bank.

Correspondent Relationships

Correspondent relationships can be formed very simply by an exchange of letters specifying activities to be carried out, conditions to be followed, and fees to be paid. The relationships may be formalized in more detailed agreements if desired.

Such relationships are useful, indeed essential, in handling international payments, letters of credit, and other instruments described in Chapter 7. They are also useful in that instructions can be given to correspondent banks concerning the investment of funds in short-term foreign government securities and related money market instruments. Such services, however, have become less and less necessary as communications have improved so that trading in

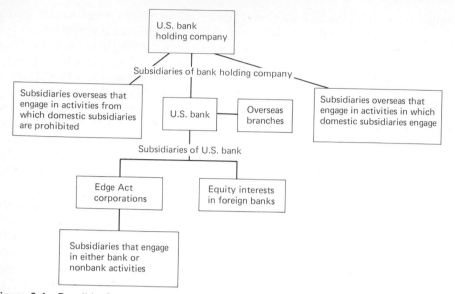

Figure 8-1 Possible Organizational Structure of U.S. Banks and Their Affiliates Overseas. (Modified slightly from Federal Reserve Bank of Chicago, *Business Conditions*, October 1974.)

foreign money markets is possible directly from head offices of U.S. banks.

Operating through correspondent banks was satisfactory for some activities, but became less and less so as U.S. banks became more active overseas. Correspondent banks, after all, were interested primarily in their own benefits. Although they were willing to perform services for U.S. banks, they were unlikely to be very *active* on their behalf or to do more than perform adequately the designated, largely routine duties. There is, however, no substitute for personal inspection of a credit situation, and banks began to realize that they needed their own personnel abroad. As the importance of international activity became more apparent, U.S. banks looked for other methods of handling overseas business.

Foreign Branches

The establishment of foreign branches in large numbers by many U.S. banks is very recent. As late as 1965, only 13 U.S. banks had foreign branches; by 1975, more than 100 banks had, although many were only nominal branch offices. Nevertheless, by 1974 U.S. banks held abroad more than one-fifth as much as the total assets they held in the United States. A few banks had as many as half of their total employees working overseas, and a few obtained more than half of their total net income from overseas activities.

From a legal viewpoint, branches are an integral part of a bank. Their creditors have claims on assets of the bank as a whole, and creditors of the head office have claims on branch assets. Of course, it is not often that such claims are exercised. Deposits of all branches, including foreign branches, are part of total deposits of a bank and reserve requirements are related to such total deposits. Moreover, branches are subject to all the legal limitations which exist for U.S. banks. The Comptroller of the Currency is responsible, as might be expected, for examination of overseas branches of national banks, while state banking authorities share jurisdiction with the Board of Governors of the Federal Reserve System over activities of state-chartered member bank branches abroad. Granting power to open a branch abroad is reserved to the Board of Governors of the Federal Reserve System.

In practice, because of the principle of governmental sovereignty, it is not always possible for Comptroller's office or Federal Reserve examiners to examine foreign branches as they would wish. Procedures have been devised in recent years to improve the information on the condition of foreign branches, but there may still sometimes be inadequate data.

For a long time, branches could not engage in activities forbidden to banks in the United States, but in 1962 the Board of Governors was permitted to allow overseas branches to engage in activities "usual" in connection with banking in countries where the branches operate. However, both nonfinancial activities and investment banking (underwriting, selling, or distributing securities) were still prohibited.

Branches have an advantage in name identification with the main bank, and one major disadvantage was reduced by the change mentioned in the preceding paragraph. Other major disadvantages of branches are the cost of establishing them and the fact that they still cannot engage in investment banking and some other activities.

Edge Act Subsidiaries

The Edge Act was passed in 1919 as a means of permitting U.S. banks to operate overseas and to engage in activities which they could not conduct within the United States. Edge Act corporations operate under federal charter, and need not be owned, even in part, by banks, although most of them are. Banks may invest an equity of not more than 10 percent of their capital in Edge Act subsidiaries. There is still a small number of "agreement corporations" with state charters, which operate in a manner similar to Edge Act corporations under agreements between them and the Board of Governors of the Federal Reserve System.[1]

An Edge Act corporation may engage only in international banking, but it may have an office in the United States. These offices may not engage in banking other than that incidental to their foreign operations. A bank may have as many as five Edge Act subsidiaries. Establishment of an office in a U.S. city for each Edge Act subsidiary allows a large bank to have offices in a number of states outside that in which it operates. This is especially useful in serving large

---

[1]"International Banking—Structural Aspects of Regulation," Federal Reserve Bank of Chicago, *Business Conditions*, October 1974, pp. 3–11.

multinational firms. With the Edge Act offices in different cities, the market for banking services to large corporations with international operations has become in effect a national market. Although these offices cannot engage in business except that incidental to their international operations, they can accept deposits related to their international operations, refer customers to their parent banks, and in other ways permit these banks to obtain business in states where they are not chartered.[2] This increases competitive pressure on banks in various cities in the United States. Edge subsidiaries of large multinational banks can inform customers on exchange rates, exchange controls, international money and capital markets, and accounting and tax regulations, matters about which local banks may not be fully informed. Moreover, the Edge subsidiaries can direct customers to their parent banks, which often can make much larger loans than can banks in some regions of the United States. The parent banks can provide worldwide service; for example, Citibank had, in 1975, nearly 250 branches in nearly 60 countries, and Edge Act subsidiary offices in Chicago, Los Angeles, Miami, and San Francisco. Additionally, it had international banking subsidiaries in more than 15 countries. Its Edge Act subsidiary with an office in Houston, Texas, was an investment Edge Act subsidiary—not engaged in accepting deposits.

The Board of Governors of the Federal Reserve System has permitted Edge Act subsidiary offices overseas to engage in many activities usual in connection with banking in various countries, even though U.S. banks may not engage in such acitivities. Some countries allow foreign banks to carry on activities forbidden to their own banks; Edge subsidiaries are free to engage in activities closely related to banking. The Board of Governors has prohibited activities not generally regarded as closely related to banking, for example, issuing general insurance.

This power to engage in activities common in foreign countries but not possible for U.S. banks is the chief advantage of Edge Act subsidiaries in foreign countries. Some broadening of powers of branches reduced this advantage, but the advantage of separate corporate structure remained, and also that of being permitted to establish a U.S. office outside the state in which the parent bank was chartered.[3]

Foreign Subsidiaries

The most interesting development in recent years is the expansion of overseas banking through equity participation by U.S. banks in foreign banks, and by

---

[2]Martin Mayer, *The Bankers* (New York: Weybright and Talley, 1974) commented that "Bank of America has an Edge Act subsidiary on Broad Street [in New York] with 900 employees and $1 billion in assets—mostly [acquired with funds from] noninsured deposits" (p. 436).

[3]"Edge Corporations: A Microcosm of International Banking Trends," Federal Reserve Bank of Richmond, *Monthly Review*, September 1973, pp. 15–16. See also "New Edge Offices Participate in Expanding International Banking Market," Federal Reserve Bank of Dallas, *Business Review*, March 1976, pp. 1–5.

U.S. bank holding companies in both foreign banks and nonbank financial institutions.

When a U.S. bank or Edge Act subsidiary or a U.S. bank holding company wishes permission to engage in equity participation in a foreign bank or, in the case of holding companies, in a foreign nonbank financial institution, the Board of Governors considers the effect this activity may have on (1) the solvency of the U.S. bank, if a bank has made the application; (2) the concentration of economic power; and (3) the competitive position of U.S. banking organizations vis-à-vis their foreign competitors. The Board has some leeway, since it may determine either whether most evidence indicates no significant adverse effects or whether evidence *does* indicate adverse effects. A major refusal was that of the application of the Bankamerica Corporation (the bank holding company which owns the Bank of America in California) and the Allstate Insurance Company for a joint foreign venture in insurance in 1974. The denial was predicated upon both a possible increase in concentration of economic power and the bank's need for a stronger capital base before engaging in such activity.[4]

The Board's cautious strategy is intended to minimize risks to U.S. banking through its overseas activities and to maintain the separation between banking and commerce traditional in the United States. In this sentence banking is used broadly to mean financial activity; in the narrower sense of institutions which accept deposits (the legal definition of banks in many states), former limitations have largely been removed. Edge Act companies, for example, formerly had to be either banking (deposit-accepting) or financing companies; now they may be both, although they need not be. If they accept deposits they must meet certain requirements designed to insure the safety of depositors' money.

Since Edge Act subsidiaries may purchase equities (stocks) in some countries and engage in other activities prohibited to banks in the United States, they require specially trained personnel and an organizational structure different from that of domestic banks. Investment knowledge may be more important than ability to analyze loans, and such differences lead to other characteristics in the foreign subsidiaries of banks.[5]

Venture Banking

The volume of activities in which multinational firms are often engaged and the need for international cooperation in some projects have led to consortia of banks to provide funds. Often funds are needed in several different currencies and the firms engaged in a project may be domiciled in several different countries. Moreover, banks themselves sometimes take equity participation in

[4]*Federal Reserve Bulletin*, July 1974, pp. 517–519.

[5]See, for example, Dean A. Dudley, "Evolution of a Financial Institution: The Edge Subsidiary," unpublished doctoral dissertation, University of Washington, Seattle, 1965.

projects, which gives them a stronger interest in the success of the projects than they might have had as lenders only.

These consortia activities have been termed venture banking by some.[6] Venture banking is likely to be especially important in financing economic development, when large projects and multinational financing are involved. Although many economic activities can be financed in developing countries by local financial institutions, creating wealth in forms different from those of the past may be beyond the capacity of local banks to finance; indeed, it may be beyond the capacity of many multinational banks. Some projects are larger than any one bank can or should finance. Banks may be aided in these endeavors by long-term lending institutions, including international institutions such as the World Bank and its affiliates, discussed in Chapter 12. International capital must be mobilized in some manner if such projects are to be carried out; venture banking is one way for banks to play an important part.

OVERSEAS ACTIVITIES OF U.S. BANKS—FINANCIAL PRACTICES

Not only has U.S. overseas banking grown remarkably in the past two decades, but also practices have changed significantly. A transfer of financial technology from the United States to foreign countries has often occurred, as banks have taken practices developed in the United States and adapted them to foreign environments. In other cases new practices have been developed to serve multinational firms and others.

Reasons for Expansion of Branch Networks

Restraints on capital outflows from the United States during the 1960s and early 1970s, discussed in more detail in Chapter 13, created additional requirements for funds for overseas affiliates and subsidiaries of U.S. firms. Since they could not obtain enough funds from the United States, they turned to other sources. Moreover, some countries restricted the amounts of earnings which business firms might retain for reinvestment purposes, and this also led to increased borrowing. It became evident that additional foreign offices of U.S. banks could tap foreign funds (whether in dollars or other currencies) and lend them to U.S. foreign subsidiaries and affiliates. Later, lending to foreign local firms, governments, and financial institutions became important.

Regulation Q limiting interest rates that banks can pay on time deposits, and the law prohibiting payment in the United States of interest on deposits withdrawable with less than 30 days' notice were additional incentives for establishment of overseas facilities. In most countries, interest can be paid on all deposits.

Appropriate hours for banking was important in locating overseas facilities. The overlap in business hours between England and various centers on the

---

[6]Louis J. Mulkern, "Venture Banking," *University of Washington Business Review,* Summer 1970. pp. 31–36.

continent, in addition to the availability of trained personnel, made London especially convenient for offices to make loans and accept deposits.

In some years, deposits accumulated or created in foreign branch and subsidiary offices were returned as loans to U.S. bank home offices for lending within the United States, as tight money and high interest rates on money market instruments discouraged the placement of time deposit funds in U.S. banks, and forced them to seek other sources of funds.

For these and other reasons, the number of U.S. branches abroad nearly tripled in the decade from 1965 to 1975, the most rapid growth being in Europe and the next most rapid in Asia.

Although tight money and high interest rates occurred in 1973–1974 as well as in earlier years, by that time the Federal Reserve System had suspended Regulation Q ceilings on interest rates on large-denomination CDs, and banks no longer greatly needed to borrow from their foreign offices. Thus the funds deposited in the foreign offices were almost fully available for lending in foreign countries.

"Shell" Branches

A substantial number of "shell" branches were created, principally in the Caribbean area. Shell branches have no contact with the local public, and the offices and staffs may be supplied under contract by other parties. Such branches provide foreign headquarters and places of transaction for many international banking activities. Low taxes in some areas, such as the Caribbean countries, are advantageous. Deposits recorded for shell branches were organized by banks with no other overseas facilities, and some were part of worldwide banking office networks.

Negotiable CDs

One instance of exporting innovations was the development of negotiable CDs in dollars at foreign branch offices. Development of a secondary market for such CDs made them attractive, and enabled branch offices to gain substantial amounts of deposits.

Branches accepted deposits in local currencies as well as in dollars, thus obtaining funds which could be used to finance local currency requirements of U.S. subsidiaries and also to lend to local firms.

Chase Manhattan Bank led the way in obtaining permission to offer CDs denominated in SDRs, as indicated in Chapter 6. This attracted holders who feared greater depreciation of other currencies and believed that the SDRs, once they had been valued in a basket of 16 currencies in 1974, would be more stable than single currencies.

Thus foreign offices of U.S. banks attracted business from those who desired liquid, low-risk assets.

Multicurrency Loans

Firms could borrow from U.S. bank branch offices either in dollars (*Eurodollars,* as they came to be called, because they were dollars in Europe or elsewhere, not in the United States) or in local currencies. In fact, after restrictions were removed early in 1974, firms could use the facilities of such bank offices to obtain loans directly from the United States if that seemed more desirable.

From lending in dollars and in local currencies, it was but a small step to making multicurrency loans. Such loans are useful when firms need different currencies and wish to borrow partly in one currency and partly in others. Multicurrency loans are also useful when exchange rates vary, so that obtaining a particular currency might be more costly for borrowers with payments to make in various currencies. Of course, banks which make multicurrency loans must be sure that they can obtain the currencies when needed. This may create problems at times of BOP difficulties in particular countries which impose exchange controls.

A later development was the introduction by some banks of loans denominated in SDRs. Because SDRs fluctuated less than many individual currencies, these loans were useful in reducing risks to borrowers of having to repay more than they borrowed when the foreign exchange cost of a particular borrowed currency rose.

Syndication of Eurocurrency Loans[7]

As larger loans became customary for multinational firms, and sometimes for governments and government agencies, even large banks hesitated to permit their branches and subsidiaries to grant the entire amounts requested. Instead, they began to join with other banks' branches and subsidiaries to make syndicated loans. Larger loans were possible with the spreading of risks, and management fees and publicity could be obtained by banks. In the case of intermediate-term loans, it became customary to set floating interest rates after the pattern of the domestic multibank floating rate term loan in the United States. Medium-term loans of 3 to 15 years maturity were made. The interest rate was often specified as a spread above the interbank offering rate. The base rate was generally the London interbank offering rate (LIBO or LIBOR). Since LIBO sometimes fluctuated between 6 and 14 percent, its fluctuation was often more important than the spread above it.

Usually, a leading bank office syndicated a loan, "sourcing" the loan (finding the potential borrower and the banks to participate), structuring it, selling it, and servicing it. Syndicate leaders enjoyed prestige while participating banks gained exposure and made portions of loans with less risk than if they had made loans without participation.

Structuring such loans meant establishing terms including maturity, amortization schedules, grace periods, and prepayment provisions, as well as the rate spread. It also meant setting management and commitment fees and

---

[7]This section draws heavily on Robert N. See, "Syndication," Chap. 9 in F. John Mathis, ed., *Offshore Lending by U.S. Commercial Banks* (Washington, D.C. and Philadelphia: Bankers' Association for Foreign Trade and Robert Morris Associates, 1975), pp. 151–165.

designating legal clauses to be included in loan agreements. The following are examples of such clauses, illustrating the problems to be provided for: (1) cross-default clauses giving banks a right to first claim on repayment sources, (2) reserve requirement clauses similar to compensating balance requirements but permitting banks to levy on the reserves, (3) dollar availability clauses protecting banks against nonavailability of dollars for repayment if the loan was made or was to be repaid in dollars, (4) judgment currency clauses designating currencies in which judgments might be paid if obtained, (5) clauses allocating tax credits, (6) jurisdictional clauses to establish places of jurisdiction for settling claims, and (7) clauses specifying uses of proceeds and events which would be deemed to be default.

Syndicates could be "best effort" syndicates, firm commitment syndicates, or syndicates in which certain amounts were advanced with rights to participate in the remainder of the loan at a later time.

In the foregoing discussion, banks were intermediate-term lenders, and the syndication of the loans did not quite involve the banks in what may be termed investment banking, the development of which we discuss in a later section.

Cash Flow Financing

Inevitably, U.S. bank practices such as cash flow financing crept into lending overseas. Most European lending is based on collateral in the form of specified assets, but U.S. banks for many years have based much of their lending on anticipated income or expected cash flow. Borrowing firms were asked to prepare pro forma cash flow statements, or bank lending officers developed their own estimated figures for such statements. Clearly, the source of repayment of medium-term loans is almost always cash flow; few firms would be forced to sell equipment or other assets to repay loans. The practice of cash flow financing is sound banking practice provided the term loans are not so large in volume or so long in maturity that banks find it difficult to meet depositors' requests for withdrawal.

Shifts in Borrowing-Lending Relationships

The shift from U.S. bank head office borrowing from foreign branches to other sources of funds has already been mentioned. As loan demand fell in the United States in the 1973–1975 recession, U.S. banks began to supply more funds to their overseas offices and to purchase bank acceptances. This made more funds available for the syndicated loans described above. Most funds were first provided to branches in England and in the Caribbean area, since these were to some extent money management centers because of the lack of restrictions on capital flows and the excellent communications network.

The strain in international banking markets resulting from foreign exchange losses by some banks and the failure of the I.D. Herstatt bank in Germany stimulated the flow of funds overseas. Depositors began to feel that there was substantial risk in depositing funds in dollars in European banks; and interest rates on such deposits, and hence on loans, rose to a substantial premium over U.S. interest rates. The demand for loans was heavy, in part because of demand by countries with deficits caused by payments for importing oil at much higher prices than before, and also because of demand by developing countries, including some oil exporters.

We must conclude that without government restrictions interest rate differentials induce flows of bank funds. Thus efforts to keep interest rates low within a country in order, say, to encourage economic recovery may lead to an outflow of funds for foreign lending and hence to at least temporarily decreased availability of funds within the country which tries to keep its interest rates low.

Merchant Banking

The most significant difference between activities of U.S. bank and bank holding company subsidiaries overseas and activities of U.S. banks and bank holding companies in the United States may be the trend toward what may in very general terms be called merchant banking overseas. Merchant banking means offering total financial services to business firms. This includes both short-term and intermediate-term lending and services to facilitate business firm current asset management, which banks have long offered; and long-term lending, placement of securities, and financial advisory service, which have been prohibited to banks in the United States since the 1930s.

Because of problems which arose in the early 1930s from banks having been engaged in both long-term and short-term financing of business firms, banks were not allowed to engage in both commercial banking and what is termed investment banking by the Banking Act of 1933.[8] Investment activities of commercial banks on their own behalf have been limited since then to a narrow range, including the purchase of top-grade corporate bonds, municipal securities, and U.S. government securities. In practice banks buy very few corporate bonds because of the extra effort of security analysis compared to government securities. Investment activities of commercial banks on behalf of others were limited to underwriting government securities and certain categories of state and local government securities.

U.S. commercial banks have long been prohibited from purchasing equity securities (stocks), and if they happen to acquire stocks, for example by taking title to stocks which were collateral for defaulted loans, national banks must dispose of them within five years. For most state banks there are similar provisions.

Clearly, in long-term lending, purchase of long-term business securities, and purchase of investments other than top-grade bonds, risks are greater than they are in short-term lending and purchase of high-grade bonds. The banking legislation of the 1930s prevented U.S. banks from assuming such risks. There

---

[8]This act is also known as the Glass-Steagall Act (of 1933) and is so called in a number of publications. Some confusion is caused by the fact that there was also a Glass-Steagall Act in 1932, with provisions related to other matters.

are also substantial risks in owning stocks; an example is the fluctuation in stock market prices in 1973–1976.

The underwriting and placement of long-term business securities also may involve commercial banks in activities which risk depositors' funds. There is temptation for the underwriting and placement divisions of banks, if they exist, to urge the commercial banking divisions to buy securities being underwritten and marketed.

Nevertheless, banks in foreign countries are often permitted to engage in both types of activities. In Germany, banks act in commercial banking, investment banking, and stock brokerage. Beyond that, they often exercise direct management control over firms, through the ownership of stock.

With the establishment of Edge Act subsidiaries and subsidiaries of bank holding companies abroad, and the acquisition of equity in foreign banking institutions, U.S. bank holding company affiliates could undertake some or all of the investment banking activities allowed in foreign countries. Branches of U.S. banks could not do this because they were integral parts of U.S. banks and bound by U.S. banking laws, as subsidiaries were not.

An example of an overseas subsidiary which is attempting to engage in merchant banking activities is Citicorp International Bank Ltd., known as CIBL. It is a subsidiary of Citicorp, the holding company which owns Citibank, the leading U.S. bank in international banking. CIBL has been very active in syndicating loans and is interested in Eurobond underwriting and dealing. Although the oil crisis which began in 1973 and the Herstatt and Franklin National Bank failures in 1974 made bankers cautious about new activities, it is likely that if conditions become more stable, overseas subsidiaries of U.S. banks will gradually enlarge their "merchant banking."

Leasing

Many activities of subsidiaries of U.S. banks or holding companies are similar to nontraditional banking activities of banks or their subsidiaries or holding companies in the United States, and need no further comment. Leasing, however, is a special case.

Leasing in international banking may provide flexibility by permitting firms which lease equipment or other assets to make periodic lease payments in one of several currencies for some of which interest rates are lower and expected exchange rate movements favorable.

Leasing in international banking also involves special factors because of differences in international accounting practices, tax laws, and legal provisions. The implications of these differences for firms which lease equipment are discussed in more detail in Part Five after the discussion of accounting and tax differences, but one example of an accounting difference may be useful. The leasing agreement may designate a lessor in a country in which rapid depreciation is permissible. An example of a tax factor is an arrangement for the lessee to be located in a country with no tax withholding on lease payments to a lessor in a foreign country, thus freeing the lessee's funds for immediate use. Finally, an example of a legal difference is that options to purchase equipment at the end of the lease period at "fair market value" are often deemed to be leases under U.S. law, but in the United Kingdom they are treated as conditional sales.[9] Under a lease, the lessor may take depreciation on the property; under a conditional sale, the lessee (conditional purchaser) may take it.

It should be clear that the growth of multinational firms and the consequent awareness of U.S. banks of opportunities for profits overseas have led banks into diverse fields of overseas banking activity. Although the 1973–1975 period provided some serious challenges and forced some cutbacks, it is likely that overseas banking will resume its expansion both in areas served and in types of activities.

OPERATIONS AND REGULATION OF FOREIGN BANKING IN THE UNITED STATES

Foreign banks have found it increasingly profitable in recent years to engage in overseas banking, especially in the United States. Earlier, their primary motive was to provide a full range of financial services to the U.S. subsidiaries of home-based customer firms. In short, the banks followed their corporate clients to the United States. More recently, foreign banks have tried to compete effectively for the loan and deposit business of U.S. firms. In a few instances, most notably in California, foreign banks have also offered retail banking services, just as U.S. banks have offered such services in other countries (for example, the Familien Bank, or Family Bank, subsidiary of Chase Manhattan in Germany).[10]

There are, however, other reasons for the expansion of foreign banking in the United States. U.S. offices of foreign banks serve several specific purposes. They provide a means of obtaining dollar deposits to meet dollar obligations, such as withdrawals of Eurodollar deposits. They may use dollars deposited, or purchased in the U.S. money market, to lend to customers of their parent banks or to branches in other foreign countries—especially useful if regulations in those countries prohibit conversion of local currency into U.S. dollars. They can invest surplus liquid funds in the U.S. money market when interest rates are higher than in their home countries. Many foreign banks can underwrite securities, and it is advantageous for them to have offices in the United States, so they can observe and participate in the U.S. capital market. They can also participate directly in "clearing" dollar transactions, instead of doing this through U.S. correspondent banks. Finally, they can finance their own industrial firms as those firms make direct investments in the United States, but at the same time they can establish relationships with U.S. firms. They are sometimes

[9]Rita M. Rodriguez and E. Eugene Carter, *International Financial Management* (Englewood Cliffs, N.J.: Prentice-Hall, 1976), p. 490.

[10]"Merchant Banking," *Business Week*, Apr. 19, 1976, pp. 54–104, especially p. 94.

able to ease the entry of U.S. firms into countries which were former European colonies.[11]

If they simply desire contact with U.S. firms, they may establish *represent-ative* offices, which do not carry on any banking business. If they wish to make loans but do not seek deposits, they may establish *agency offices.* If they wish to handle both loans and deposits, they must establish either a *branch* or a *subsidiary*, if permitted. A subsidiary may seek FDIC insurance of deposits. Some foreign banks have established *investment companies* in New York, to secure close connections with the capital market.

The regulation of foreign banking in the United States has rested primarily with state governments. A foreign bank may obtain from a state a charter for an agency (which does not accept deposits), a branch (which does), or a subsidiary, which usually engages in general banking. A number of states have permitted this; among them the important states of New York, Illinois, and California.[12] The Federal Reserve System and other federal banking authori-ties generally have no jurisdiction over foreign bank agencies and branches; since 1970 the Board of Governors of the Federal Reserve System has had certain jurisdiction over foreign bank subsidiaries.[13] It prohibits control of banks in more than one state by such subsidiaries except in instances in which "grandfather clauses" permit this. It also restricts nonbank subsidiaries to activities permissible for U.S. subsidiaries of bank holding companies.

Proposals for Federal Control

In 1976 legislation was being considered which would extend federal control over foreign banking in the United States.[14] One set of proposals, which emanated from the Federal Reserve System, was embodied in the Foreign Bank Act of 1975. This bill provided that foreign and domestic banks be treated generally alike with respect to both privileges and restrictions. Specifically, foreign banking facilities would be covered by federal regulations on reserve requirements, permissible banking activities, Federal Deposit Insurance Cor-

[11]For more elaboration on the purposes of foreign banks in establishing offices in the United States, see Joseph G. Kvasnicka, "International Banking: Part II," Federal Reserve Bank of Chicago, *Business Conditions,* March 1976, pp. 3–11.

[12]Illinois law governing foreign bank branches was liberalized in 1973, and almost 20 licenses were granted in about a year. Before 1973 some state-chartered subsidiaries of foreign banks had been established. See Allen Frankel, "International Banking—Structural Aspects of Regulation, op. cit., p 10. Also see a selected bibliography on foreign banks in the United States, Federal Reserve Bank of Chicago, *International Letter,* Supplement to No. 218, Apr. 18, 1975.

[13]See Fred H. Klopstock, "Foreign Banks in the United States: Scope and Growth of Operations," Federal Reserve Bank of New York, *Monthly Review,* June 1973, pp. 140–154, and Bruce J. Sommers, "Foreign Banking in the United States: Movement Toward Federal Regula-tion," Federal Reserve Bank of Richmond, *Economic Review,* January–February 1976, pp. 3–7.

[14]Currently, branches and agencies of foreign banks in the United States are not subject to federal regulation, supervision, or examination. Requiring all foreign banking facilities to take the form of subsidiaries would be one way of subjecting all such facilities to federal regulation.

poration insurance (as applied to insured banks in the United States) and some other requirements.

Another proposal, somewhat more restrictive, was contained in a report based on the Financial Institutions and the Nation's Economy (FINE) study of 1975, conducted for Congress. All foreign entites that accept deposits would be required to take the form of subsidiaries, state chartering of foreign banks would be abolished, and all supervisory functions would be transferred to a newly created agency.[15] Further, foreign banks would not be allowed to engage in underwriting or equity investment activities, as they now may in some states.

Although the Foreign Banking Act and the proposal based on the FINE study differ somewhat in their provisions, both would consolidate control over foreign banking at the national level. Two major arguments have been advanced to support this step. First, federal regulation would enhance the effectiveness of monetary policy. Under present arrangements the states have primary jurisdiction over foreign banking operations.[16] Some states are restrictive.[17] However, all states' powers are limited, and they do not have responsibility for the nation's monetary policy. Since foreign banks control over 6 percent of total bank assets in the United States and the dollar amount doubled from 1963 to 1975, this is important. George W. Mitchell, Vice Chairman, Board of Governors of the Federal Reserve System, expressed concern as follows:

> The United States is virtually the only country that does not have central bank control over the activities of foreign banks within its borders. This situation creates a gap in the Federal Reserve's control over domestic monetary conditions that will inevitably widen and increase in importance as foreign banks' activities continue to grow.[18]

It is of course true that the Federal Reserve System does not control reserve requirements for nonmember U.S. banks—another gap in federal control. But nonmember banks usually keep their reserves in the form of deposits with member banks who keep them with larger banks, usually members of the Federal Reserve System. Thus indirectly the Federal Reserve System has some control in this area, although it has noted in recent years that

[15]Since there was no grandfather clause envisaged, all present foreign bank branches and agencies would have to close, and only offices which became part of subsidiaries would exist.

[16]It is legally possible for a foreign bank to obtain a federal charter, under provision of the National Banking Act and its amendments, but the requirement that all directors of a national bank must be U.S. citizens in effect eliminates foreign banks from this option.

[17]Only 10 states have explicit laws permitting operations by foreign banks. Such operations are entirely prohibited in 16 states, quite in contrast to the situation faced by U.S. banks abroad, where they can, if permitted to operate in a country, generally operate in almost any location. In 24 states there is no legislation on foreign banks.

[18]Statement by George W. Mitchell, Vice Chairman, Board of Governors of the Federal Reserve System, before the Subcommittee on Financial Institutions of the Committee on Banking, Housing, and Urban Affairs, U.S. Senate, Jan. 28, 1976.

some changes in money supply result from its lack of control over reserves of nonmember banks.

The second argument in favor of federal regulation is that foreign and domestic banks should be treated alike to foster competition and to improve the allocation of financial resources. At present foreign banks have the advantages of lower reserve requirements in some instances and engagement in some activities not permitted to U.S. banks, to give two examples. But they are more restricted in other ways; they cannot operate at all in most states, and branches cannot offer FDIC deposit insurance to their depositors. The argument is that regulation should be made uniform insofar as possible to reduce discrimination both in favor of and against foreign banks. It is unlikely that uniformity can be attained under present institutional arrangements in which foreign banks may be treated liberally in some states and restrictively in others, and in which federal control is imposed only on foreign subsidiaries, rather than on all forms of foreign banking activities. Even the control over foreign subsidiaries by the Federal Reserve System is limited in purpose. In the dual banking system in the United States, if state legislation seems unduly restrictive to banks, they have the alternative of converting to national charters, and vice versa. This alternative is not now open to foreign banks.

Standardization of regulation would have the effect of dealing similarly with all banks. Since U.S. banks operate abroad extensively and have now far more assets than foreign banks have in the United States, dealing with foreign banks in the United States in what is perceived to be an arbitrary or unduly restrictive manner might invite retaliation by foreign countries.[19]

A third alternative in regulation, for which no specific legislation for foreign banks was under consideration in early 1976, would be a liberalization of banking regulations to permit foreign banks to carry out many of the activities which they may conduct in their own countries. At the same time it would probably be necessary to liberalize provisions for U.S. banks. One liberalization would be to allow U.S. and foreign banks to engage in interstate banking, now possible de jure for only one U.S. bank, under a grandfather clause, although possible de facto through the use of Edge Act offices. A second liberalization would be to define time deposits as those requiring one day's notice for withdrawal instead of 30 days, permitting U.S. banks to compete more effectively for international deposits, on which interst can be paid in most countries whether they are time or demand deposits. A third liberalization, which is probably beyond what officials would now acquiesce in, would be to permit merchant banking in the United States, so that both U.S. and foreign banks might engage in a full range of financing for business firms.

The Federal Reserve System proposal permits existing interstate banking by foreign banks to continue under a grandfather provision but prevents any

---

[19]In 1975 U.S. banks had about three times as much in assets overseas as foreign banks had in assets in the United States.

further extension. Legislation is proposed to allow banks to pay interest on demand deposits; if this applied to foreign banks, the second liberalization would be accomplished. It is difficult to judge whether repeal of other provisions of the banking legislation of the mid-1930s to permit broader activities by banks is desirable. The currently favorable economic picture in Germany, in which banks not only provide long-term financing to industry but also own a substantial part of industry, is not conclusive.

Criteria for Judging a Regulatory Framework

The possible effect of regulation of foreign banking in the United States on foreign regulation of U.S. banking overseas is one criterion for evaluating a set of regulations. Other criteria include the safety of depositors' funds and of funds provided by other creditors of banks and the influence of the regulations on competition. This influence includes not only the effect on competition between foreign and U.S. banks, but also on competition between large and small U.S. banks and between U.S. and foreign industry. Foreign direct investment in the United States might be facilitated by an expansion of foreign banking activity in the United States, thus increasing both financial and industrial competition in the same way that the entry of U.S. firms and banks into foreign markets in the 1960s and early 1970s stimulated competition in those markets.

This is not to say that such criteria will be intelligently and logically applied. Legislation sometimes takes forms that are inefficient or counterproductive. But it is important that careful thought be given to these questions. Regulation of international banking, if properly carried out, may promote a healthy environment for international finance, trade, and investment.

TECHNOLOGICAL DEVELOPMENTS AND OVERSEAS BANKING

An electronic funds transfer system is being developed in the United States and in some foreign countries. This system is expected to reduce the use of checks, although it is unlikely that any country will become a "checkless society." Use of coins and paper money will probably also diminish, as point-of-sale (POS) terminals come into use. At such terminals payments can be made electronically and immediately in retail establishments or other places of purchase.

Technology is now available so that payment transfers can be made automatically by telephone; thus many international banking transactions can take place without branches and subsidiaries. U.S. banks, for example, can deal directly with foreign depositors and transfer funds by telephone or cable.

Ultimately, the effective market for the home office of any large bank, for many banking transactions, may be the world. Competition could become far more intense. To the extent that U.S. banks are more efficient than other banks, they may grow rapidly. They have one advantage over other banks in such competition: the U.S. dollar is likely to remain a preferred currency, and although banks in other countries may accept deposits denominated in U.S. dollars (sometimes termed Eurodollar or Asian dollar deposits), dollar deposits in the United States have some advantages. Dollar deposits outside the United States also would have a disadvantage for some foreigners, of course, if international conflict or other reasons were to cause the U.S. government to block deposit balances in the United States.

The importance of these developments is that banks create money, and banking is therefore a sensitive industry, which foreigners are permitted to enter only within limits. Controlling the creation of money is an important part of national policy. Most countries have some concern about their money supplies and the role of banks, domestic or foreign, in creating money. Yet if technology makes it possible to carry out transactions in foreign countries without offices there, regulation and control by governments is more difficult.[20]

The outcome is in doubt in the conflict between technological forces which increase the size both of firms, financial and nonfinancial, and of markets on the one hand, and nationalistic forces which limit the size of firms and markets on the other hand. Because nationalistic forces might create another depression like that of the 1930s, it is to be hoped that in the long run some limitations on nationalistic control may emerge. This means relinquishing part of the sovereign powers of governments, to either an international agency or some forum of consultation and agreement among governments. The long-run reform of the international monetary system discussed in Chapter 6 may ultimately produce willingness to agree on sufficient coordination of monetary policies to prevent disruption of trade and investment patterns and imposition of exchange controls in major industrialized countries. The alternative is the possibility of serious recessions or depressions in which world trade and investment suffer more than domestic business activity, as they did in the 1930s vis-à-vis U.S. business activity.

THE ROLE OF INTERNATIONAL BANKING IN FINANCIAL DEVELOPMENT

International banking has three important roles: (1) financing international transactions, its oldest traditional activity; (2) financing business activity in various countries; and (3) the nontraditional activity of bringing together equity and debt capital for projects which could not be financed in the country or countries in which they are to be developed. As noted in Part Four, individual financial institutions are too small to finance some of these projects, especially when risk and the need for diversification of assets are considered. International financial institutions are often limited in not being able to provide or to generate equity capital. Banks, through international banking activities, especially those such as syndication of loans, merchant banking, and venture

[20]Cf. Robert Z. Aliber, *The International Money Game*, 2d ed. (New York: Basic Books, 1976), Chap. 13, "Banking on the Wire."

banking, have an opportunity to help in the huge task of development of lower-income countries. This means cooperation as well as competition among international banks. An international financial cartel could have power inimical to development, yet cooperation is needed in sharing risks and technology.

The future of international banking is surely most favorable. The need for capital is great, even in the United States, if business activity is to continue to grow. The alternative is unemployment in the industrialized countries and more starvation in many LDCs. Banks have an important task and an opportunity for profit. The growth of financial institutions and markets in developing countries is an essential part of their economic development, and recent studies have emphasized the role of finance in development, as detailed to some extent in Chapter 20.

SUMMARY

The operations of U.S. banks overseas and of foreign banks in the United States were both at a crossroads in the mid-1970s. Some U.S. banks were finding that a large part of their net income could be obtained by operating in the three-fourths of the world (in income) outside the United States. The continued spread of multinational firms presents greater opportunity for overseas banking, as does the growth of industries in developing countries, especially where banking systems are not well developed. At the same time, some indications of restriction on foreign banking activities are surfacing. Of course, nations realize that restrictions may bring retaliation, as in the case of trade and exchange controls, and there is some reluctance to invite such retaliation. Moreover, countries sometimes avoid controls because they are not strong enough to impose controls without incurring adverse effects. In some industries, multinational firms may simply move to neighboring countries, reducing GNP in countries which adopt restrictions.[21]

It is to be hoped that governments will be able to avoid the widespread erection of additional barriers to international banking. If at the same time the risks involved in international banking in a period of floating exchange rates can be moderated by central bank intervention, or if there is a return to a relatively stable par value system for the major industrialized countries, the growth of trade and investment on a worldwide basis may be facilitated by increased competition in international banking.

QUESTIONS FOR DISCUSSION

1   What was the major advantage of Edge Act subsidiaries when they were first authorized? Why do you think banks have found it advantageous to continue to establish such subsidiaries in recent years?

[21]Compare Raymond Vernon, *Sovereignty at Bay* (New York: Basic Books, 1971) and the more critical view of Richard J. Barnet and Ronald E. Muller, *Global Reach: The Power of the Multinational Corporation* (New York: Simon and Schuster, 1974).

2 Evaluate the criteria which the Board of Governors of the Federal Reserve System uses in granting or denying applications for international banking activities.

3 What are the significant characteristics of venture banking?

4 What is the importance of the bank holding company in the spread of U.S. overseas banking?

5 Discuss the nature of more restrictive treatment, "equal treatment," and more liberal regulation of foreign banks in the U.S., as directions in which regulation might evolve.

6 Why do you think *federal* control of foreign banking in the United States is only now being considered?

7 Explain how safety of depositors and competition among banks may be affected by controls over foreign banking in the United States.

8 Why may technological developments lead to more worldwide competition among major banks?

9 Do you see any signs of blurring of the distinction between commercial banks and several other types of financial institutions, in the international field?

10 Do you agree with the authors that overseas banking is at a cross-roads, and that the path it will take may not be clear for several years or more? Why or why not?

PROBLEM

Assume that a fairly large (in the top 50) U.S. bank has been making some term loans to financial institutions in Brazil but has not had any other participation in lending to or in Brazil and has had no overseas banking activity in that country. Suppose that the following alternatives are suggested: (1) cease making such loans, (2) continue making such loans but make no other attempt to become active in Brazil, (3) establish a branch bank office in Brazil, (4) establish a representative office in Brazil, (5) acquire partial ownership of an investment bank in Brazil, or (6) acquire a partial ownership of a *financeira* in Brazil. What considerations can you think of that should be weighed by the bank's officials in making a decision on these alternatives? Investment banks in Brazil have many similarities to investment houses in the United States, and *financeiras* have many similarities to finance companies.

SUGGESTED REFERENCES

Sources of information on overseas banking are scattered. The book by Francis A. Lees, referred to in the suggested references at the end of Chapter 7, is valuable.

For one view of the alternatives in regulation of foreign banks, see Francis A. Lees, "Which Route for Foreign Bank Regulation?" *Bankers Magazine,* Autumn 1974, pp. 53–57. For a detailed discussion of the activities of foreign banks in the United States leading to probable changes in regulation, see Robert Brasch, "Foreign Banks in the United States at a Crossroads," unpublished research report, Pacific Coast Banking School, 1974.

Martin Mayer, *The Bankers* (New York: Weybright and Talley, 1974) has some throught-provoking sections on international banking.

For brief reviews of some recent developments in overseas banking by U.S. banks, see Allen B. Frankel, "International Banking: Part I," Federal Reserve Bank of Chicago, *Business Conditions,* September 1975, pp. 3–9, and the interesting discussion of some of the nontraditional activities of U.S. banks abroad in "The Lessons Banks Learned from Overseas Misadventures," *Business Week,* Apr. 19, 1976, pp. 100–104.

Regulation of foreign banking in the United States in early 1976 was described by Bruce J. Summers, "Foreign Banking in the United States: Movement Toward Federal Regulation," Federal Reserve Bank of Richmond, *Economic Review,* January–February 1976, pp. 3–7. See also Joseph Kvasnicka, "International Banking: Part II," Federal Reserve Bank of Chicago, *Business Conditions,* March 1976, pp. 3–11; and Robert Johnston, "Proposals for Federal Control of Foreign Banks," Federal Reserve Bank of San Francisco, *Economic Review,* Spring 1976, pp. 32–39.

Chapter 9

Exchange Rates

Thus far in this book it has generally been assumed that exchange rates are either determined, like other prices, by supply and demand, or somehow controlled by government actions. In this chapter specific attention is given to the nature of the market for foreign exchange, the market determination of rates, exchange controls, the pros and cons of flexible exchange rates, the optimum currency area within which a single currency (no exchange rate) may be desirable, and the theory of the determination of exchange rates. The chapter concludes with a quick glance at the exchange rate situation in the 1970s.

THE MECHANICS OF FOREIGN EXCHANGE DEALINGS

We begin with some discussion of the mechanics of foreign exchange dealings because of the general unfamiliarity with the foreign exchange market and because the terms used will be helpful in later discussion.

The New York Foreign Exchange Market

New York is the major U.S. financial center and the hub of the foreign exchange market. In other countries foreign exchange markets are generally located in the major financial centers. Although banks are the most important buyers and sellers of foreign exchange, business firms are becoming more and more important. The major oil firms are particularly significant. For example, oil firms supply sterling from their sterling earnings and buy sterling to use in certain payments. Over time, it has become customary for world markets for certain commodities to become centered in certain countries and for sales of many commodities to be priced in specific currencies, thus giving rise to foreign exchange dealings as importers of those commodities buy the currencies and exporters frequently sell them.

For foreign exchange, there is no specific trading place like the New York Stock Exchange. Participants simply arrange deals by telephone. No rules define who may participate, but there is an informal code of ethics and business standards, and institutions often, for example, discourage individuals from purchases or sales deemed speculative.[1] Banks usually deal with brokers, of whom there are a relatively small number, some specializing in particular currencies. The time of trading is important. The usual hours are 9 A.M. to 5 P.M. in New York, but the important relationship is the overlap of about 3 hours of trading time in New York and London. Similarly, Singapore has some advantage over Hong Kong because of time overlaps of trading hours. The significance of the time difference resulting in the cessation of European trading and banking several hours before the end of such activity in New York was brought to attention in the well-publicized closure of the Herstatt bank in Germany. Banks which had delivered marks to the Herstatt bank in the morning, German time, found that it had been closed by the German authorities before the anticipated offsetting delivery of U.S. dollars from Herstatt's funds in a New York bank could be made to the banks which had provided marks. Closure of the Herstatt bank created a potential for heavy losses, but subsequent recoveries reduced the losses to small amounts.

Of course, banks in most parts of the country buy and sell foreign exchange, usually in smaller amounts than are traded in New York. Purchases may involve, for example, sterling drafts bought from exporters. If purchases and sales of sterling do not match, and if the bank does not wish to increase or reduce its holdings of sterling balances, it buys or sells sufficient exchange in the New York market to balance the amounts. Thus the New York market becomes the place where trading occurs to balance other trading, and therefore the place where, at the margin, exchange rates are affected.

When time drafts are purchased another factor is involved. A time draft, when purchased, must be sent to the drawee bank or firm for acceptance. Cash can then be obtained by discounting the accepted draft (termed a *bank acceptance* if drawn on and accepted by a bank), but it must be discounted in the country of acceptance. Banks must know or estimate what the discount rate will be when the draft arrives for acceptance and discount. Sometimes rates of discount have been quoted on a "to arrive" basis, valid for one or two days.[2] Otherwise banks must estimate the rate and allow for the discount in quoting an

---

[1] For an example of such actions, see "Ken and Joan Morse," Rita M. Rodriguez and E. Eugene Carter, *International Financial Management* (Englewood Cliffs, N.J.: Prentice-Hall, 1976), pp. 115–121. Ken and Joan were discouraged at some institutions and found difficulty in meeting minimum collateral requirements in other markets, in their attempt to sell foreign exchange short.

[2] William S. Shaterian, *Export-Import Banking*, 2d ed. (New York: Ronald, 1956), p. 251.

exchange rate at which they purchase such drafts if the drafts are in foreign currency. Changes in discount rates are seldom likely to be substantial over the short periods of time involved.

Banks operating in the foreign exchange market deal chiefly in deposits in foreign banks and in instruments such as sight and time drafts which will normally be deposited in bank accounts or will reduce such accounts. Their transactions in foreign paper money and coins are usually small, often for travelers and others who need small amounts. Foreign stocks and bonds, denominated in foreign currencies, are generally not included in foreign exchange, as the term is usually used, although they can be sold in securities markets and thus converted into bank deposits.

Bank Foreign Exchange "Traders"

In major banks, some person is designated as the foreign exchange trader, or chief trader if there are many. Traders have a trading room with excellent communications, similar to the bond trading rooms used by the investment officers of the same banks. Traders make bids and offers to brokers and to banks domestically and abroad by teletype, telephone, and cable.

Each bank has a foreign exchange *position*—the net balance at any point in time after purchases and sales up to that point. Most banks try to keep an approximate balance of purchases and sales unless they wish for some reason to increase or reduce their deposit balances held abroad. Banks establish limits for variations in positions, but recognize that it would be difficult to keep a position at precisely the same level at all times. The limits are of concern to top management of banks because a large position, whether *long* or *short*, could cause heavy losses. Yet traders must have some leeway for handling transactions. Proper control of positions requires careful specification of rules by management, and even so, traders sometimes make errors or exceed their limits because of a desire to make gains.[3]

At any given time, there are purchases not yet added to accounts abroad and sales not yet deducted from these accounts. As indicated in later discussion, a balance may be negligible in the long run, but long (positive) or short (negative, sales exceeding purchases) for short periods. Moreover, balances in, for example, London are not precisely the same for some purposes as balances in Liverpool. Therefore control of the foreign exchange position requires precise and detailed records, yet decisions to buy or sell foreign exchange must be made almost instantaneously. A telephone offer must frequently be responded to within minutes at most.

Traders, like other professionals, have their own jargon. For example, a trader may inquire on the phone, "What's sterling?" (meaning, what is the

---

[3]For an example of newspaper and magazine reports concerning losses by a branch of Citibank located in Belgium, see Rodriguez and Carter, op. cit., pp. 132–138. Losses occurred both in current trading and in the closing of the position by the bank when it felt that further losses might result. The reports reveal the need for appropriate accounting controls in home offices of banks to detect both undesirable overall foreign exchange positions and positions taken by each trader.

exchange rate for sterling). A broker may answer "75-77" (meaning, $1.9077 is the rate at which sterling may be bought and $1.9075 is the rate for selling). The trader may then say, "I'll take 100,000 at the middle" (meaning that the trader will buy £100,000 at $1.9076), "if that is real" (meaning, if the broker actually has the exchange for sale). If the broker has the exchange, the purchase is made. If there is a firm sale offer from another bank, the broker contacts that bank, which normally has made the firm offer valid for a short time. The broker may say to the offering bank's trader, "75 bid for 100,000" (meaning a bid of $1.9075, allowing $0.0001 for the broker's commission). The selling trader may say, "OK, who receives?" Only then is the trader told to whom the foreign exchange is to be delivered. In that way individual banks protect their orders and offers so that other traders do not know which banks are buying and selling or how much (since that knowledge might lead them to suspect inside information or a "feel for the market" on the part of certain banks).

Although traders carefully analyze BOPs and much economic information related to world financial conditions, their purchases and sales must usually be made on the basis of almost instantaneous judgment. It should be easy to see how errors or misjudgments may lead to losses.

The Basic Rate of Exchange

On any particular day there are slight differences among a number of exchange rates for any single currency. Banks sell cable transfers and sight drafts, and buy sight drafts and time drafts; the rates on these instruments are slightly different. They also buy and sell travelers' checks, foreign money orders, and other instruments. It seems plausible that there should be one *basic* rate, from which other rates differ enough to allow for the time difference, profit, or other factor causing a particular rate to vary from the basic rate.

Today it is generally accepted that the cable or telephone transfer rate is the basic rate.[4] This may be the same rate at which banks sell sight drafts or slightly higher. If a significant time is required for a sight draft to be sent to a foreign country and paid, the rate may be slightly lower than for a telephone transfer because for a short time the bank's balances abroad will not be reduced, as they will immediately with a cable or telephone transfer. Thus banks may lose a small amount of interest in selling cable transfers rather than sight drafts. Banks in need of foreign balances buy foreign exchange from other banks, at those banks' selling rates (ignoring brokers' commissions). Generally, central banks compile and publish representative exchange rates each day; these are an average of sampled rates at specific times. In the United States, rates are compiled by the Federal Reserve Bank of New York at noon, and that bank reports "noon buying rates" in published statistics.[5] Reference is

---

[4]This was true even before World War II. See Frank A. Southard, *Foreign Exchange Practice and Policy* (New York: McGraw-Hill, 1940), p. 82.

[5]See table in issues of the *Federal Reserve Bulletin*.

often made to *the* exchange rate on a given day, and such rates are convenient indicators of "the" exchange rate.

Clearly, rates for sterling should be the same in New York and in London. If for a moment they are not, traders can profit from *arbitrage*; they can buy in whichever city sterling is cheaper and sell in whichever city its value is higher. Note that if they "buy" sterling in London, they actually sell dollars, acquiring sterling. In such cases, arbitrage means selling dollars in London, acquiring sterling there, and selling sterling in New York. With continual improvement in communications, opportunities for arbitrage are infrequent, but its possibility keeps rates generally the same in major centers.

So-called *cross rates* should also be consistent. If rates for sterling in New York, dollars in London, francs in New York, and dollars in Paris are all specified, the rate for sterling in Paris is a cross rate. If cross rates are not consistent, opportunities for arbitrage exist. Sometimes cross rates are inconsistent or *broken* because governments intervene or restrict fluctuation of certain rates. Such broken cross rates are a form of undesirable price discrimination or desirable selectivity, depending on one's viewpoint. The IMF has regarded them as discriminatory and has opposed them.

Wholesale and Retail Rates

When foreign exchange is bought or sold in small amounts, "retail" rates are quoted, generally higher (if selling rates) or lower (if buying rates) than the current wholesale rates. Margins are sufficient that banks are not likely to suffer losses on retail sales or purchases even if wholesale rates fluctuate. Retail rates are adjusted as often as necessary by sending new rate sheets to the offices involved.

The traveler, for example, who wants a small amount of Japanese yen to pay taxicab fares when first arriving in Japan is not likely to be disturbed about having to pay a relatively higher retail rate. Rates for travelers' checks may be slightly different from other rates, for reasons not always obvious. A country may wish to encourage incoming tourists or there may be reasons less plausible and sometimes less reasonable, such as favoritism for travelers' checks issued by a particular institution.

All the wholesale and retail rates discussed so far are termed *spot* rates. They are all rates for immediate delivery of foreign exchange—financial assets denominated in foreign currencies. Even if the assets are time drafts, they are promptly delivered to purchasers. All these rates are distinct from *forward* rates for delivery of foreign exchange at a specified *future* time, as discussed later in this chapter. Forward rates are set at the time contracts are made to deliver the exchange at some future date.

Quotation of Rates

Foreign exchange rates are quoted in the New York market by the *direct* method: a foreign currency is quoted as having a value of so many cents or dollars and cents per unit. In Britain, however, it has been customary to quote rates by the *indirect* method: the pound sterling is quoted as having a value of so many units of each foreign currency. Remember, therefore, that a rate of $2.01 in London is a *lower* value for the dollar than a rate of $2.00, since the pound is worth $2.01 instead of $2.00. For some currencies rates are quoted in terms of premiums and discounts. A one percent premium in Canada means that it takes Can$1.01 to purchase US$1.00. This is equivalent to a discount of 0.9 percent in the United States.

Par Values and Market Rates

Par values may be established by governments as desired rates around which it is hoped that market rates will fluctuate. Under the gold standard, the relative gold contents of two currencies established the par values; if the pound was worth 4.8665 times as much fine gold as the dollar, the par value of the pound was $4.8665. During the Bretton Woods era, from 1946 to 1971, it was customary to set par values for other currencies in terms of either gold or U.S. dollars, the U.S. dollar having a fixed value of $1/35$ of an ounce of gold. If par values exist, as they may in the future if agreement to reestablish them is reached, they would be the same as market values only at certain times. Market values would fluctuate around them, either without any limit other than the forces of demand and supply or within limits created by government intervention.

THE MARKET DETERMINATION OF EXCHANGE RATES[6]

Exchange rates are prices of one currency in terms of another. Since in international finance "currency" is generally defined as money and other short-term financial assets denominated in a particular monetary unit, trading in foreign exchange usually means trading in claims on bank deposits and other short-term financial instruments.

Exchange rates indicate the *international* value of money in terms of purchasing power, and changes in exchange rates indicate changes in this value, while changes in the *domestic* value of money are indicated by the reciprocal of some price level index.[7]

In a free foreign exchange market, exchange rates are determined by

[6]This section draws on Charles N. Henning, *International Finance* (New York: Harper & Row, 1958), Chap. 12; basic principles involved have changed very little.

[7]A source of confusion is the tendency of some to refer to interest rates as prices for money; interest rates are prices for the *use* of money. The price of money is the reciprocal of some index of the price level—or, more properly, changes in the price or value of money are indicated by changes in the reciprocal of some index of the price level. When the money supply increases, the price of money falls, other things being equal, as might be expected. When the money supply increases, although interest rates may at first fall, they later *rise* as income effects and possibly inflation effects lead to increased demand for funds. This has recently been emphasized again by Milton Friedman, "Discussion," *American Economic Review*, Papers and Proceedings, May 1975, pp. 176–179, especially p. 176.

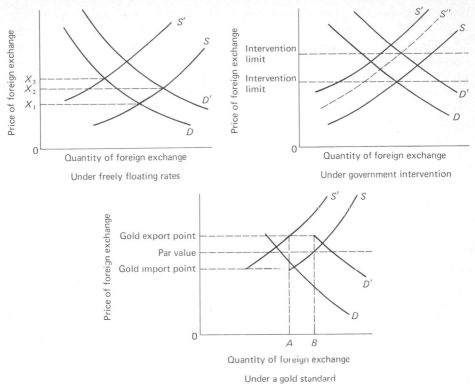

Figure 9-1   Market Determination of Exchange Rates.

supply and demand, like other free market prices. Figure 9-1 shows the market determination of exchange rates under three conditions: (1) under freely floating rates, (2) when governments intervene at certain points to prevent wider fluctuations in exchange rates, and (3) under a gold standard. Figure 9-1*a* shows the determination of freely floating rates.[8] If D is the demand curve and S is the supply curve, the equilibrium exchange rate is at x_1. If it is below that point it will rise because of an excess of demand over supply, and if it is above that point it will fall because of an excess of supply over demand. If the demand curve shifts to D', the equilibrium exchange rate rises to x_2. If the supply curve should then shift to S', the equilibrium exchange rate would rise still farther, to x_3.

Figure 9-1*b* illustrates the situation when there is government intervention. If D and S are the demand and supply curves, there is no need for government action because the equilibrium rate is close to but not below the lower intervention point. If the demand curve shifts to D', the exchange rate rises, but

---

[8]The terms *floating* and *flexible* are often used interchangeably. Sometimes, however, floating refers to a situation in which a government intervenes whenever an exchange rate fluctuates beyond certain limits, while flexible rates refer to a situation in which very wide fluctuations in rates may occur.

there is no need for government action. If, however, the supply curve then shifts from S to S', government action occurs because otherwise the equilibrium rate would rise above the upper intervention level. The government supplies foreign exchange from reserves to shift the supply curve at least to S'', so that the equilibrium rate is at but not above the upper intervention level. Governments may vary the intervention levels, depending on how wide a range of fluctuation of the exchange rate is thought desirable. Most frequently, the purpose of the government in intervening is to prevent temporary factors from causing shifts in demand and supply curves which in turn cause fluctuations in exchange rates which may be detrimental to activities of those engaged in foreign trade and investment.

For completeness and to contrast the situations of government intervention and gold standard effects, Figure 9-1c illustrates the situation when there was a gold standard. There was then, in effect, under normal conditions, no demand for foreign exchange above the gold export point, and no supply of foreign exchange below the gold import point. Foreign currency could be obtained by acquiring gold, insuring it and shipping it abroad, and exchanging it there for foreign currency at the par value rate. Under those conditions there was no reason for purchasing foreign exchange at a rate above the gold export point, which was par value, determined by relative gold content of the two currencies, plus cost of insuring and shipping enough gold to purchase a unit of foreign currency. If D' and S', for example, were the demand and supply curves, an amount of foreign exchange equal to AB would be obtained by shipping gold, so that in effect only an amount of foreign exchange equal to OA would be demanded in the foreign exchange market.[9] Essentially, government intervention and the gold standard accomplish similar results, but the gold standard relied on a fixed price of gold and at least partly on private rather than government action in shipping gold.

Figure 9-1b illustrates the situation now existing. Under both the gold standard and government intervention (unless extremely strict), market determination of exchange rates occurs within some range. The range under the gold standard was quite narrow, whereas under government intervention it may be as wide as governments believe desirable. Of course, in unusual circumstances the gold standard did not keep exchange rates from wide fluctuations. When war broke out in 1914, it was very costly and sometimes impossible to ship gold, and hence foreign exchange rates rose far above the gold export point in New York.

Demand for Foreign Exchange

Demand for foreign exchange may come from individuals or firms having to make payments to foreigners in foreign currencies. Of course, if an American

---

[9]Instead of gold being shipped, title to it may be transferred. Moreover, if banks had deposits in a gold standard country, they could regard those deposits as equivalent to gold reserves, even though they did not convert them into gold.

firm buys goods priced in U.S. dollars, it has no need for the foreign exchange market. Both an increase in imports of goods priced in foreign currencies and a rise in prices of such goods may cause the demand curve for foreign exchange to shift to the right, although how much rightward shift may occur when import prices rise depends on elasticity of demand for such imports.

Potentially, demand for foreign currency could arise from any debit item in the U.S. BOP: purchases of goods and services, gifts and grants, loans, and investments. Because of the general acceptability of the U.S. dollar, payments are often made in dollars, and hence demand for foreign exchange in the U.S. market is rather "thin" for many currencies. On the other hand, in such cases the market for U.S. dollars may be important in foreign countries, since many exporters and others must sell U.S. dollars to obtain local currency to pay cost of goods sold, wages, and so on.

Because demand for oil was relatively price inelastic, the rise in oil prices in 1973 caused a large increase in demand for dollars by Japan, by European countries, and by other countries which needed dollars to pay for oil, because petroleum exporting countries usually desired payment in dollars. There was at the same time a shift in the supply of dollars because the United States paid more for oil imports. This made more dollars available to oil exporting countries. The oil exporting countries made some of these dollars available for exchange into other currencies in foreign exchange markets by increasing their purchases of goods and services from countries other than the United States.[10]

Supply of Foreign Exchange

The supply of foreign exchange comes from exporters who draw drafts in foreign currencies, from sellers of securities who do the same, from travelers cashing travelers' checks denominated in foreign currencies, and so on. Again, because of the general acceptability of the U.S. dollar, the supply of such instruments in the U.S. foreign exchange market is not extremely large. American exporters, for example, in selling to many countries are likely to price their goods in U.S. dollars and to draw drafts in U.S. dollars to obtain payment.

Thus the use of the U.S. dollar as a vehicle currency means that foreign exchange markets in other countries are more important than they otherwise might be.

Any person or institution holding financial assets denominated in foreign currencies can furnish a supply of foreign exchange. As multinational firms have become more and more important and have come to operate in many countries, they have accumulated sizable balances in many currencies. Sometimes the view is expressed in the financial press that such developments may explain much of the increased volatility of foreign exchange rates in recent

[10]The total result cannot be specified until it is known what OPEC countries did with their dollar oil receipts. If they invested them in nondollar countries or used them to purchase goods and services from nondollar countries, their actions added to the supply of dollars and to the demand for nondollar currencies.

years. An opposing view is that this practice by multinational firms is relatively unimportant, because they hold balances, in all probability, chiefly for transactions purposes, and hence shifting balances from one currency to another would be inconvenient. It is suggested instead that they may influence supply and demand for foreign exchange, and hence exchange rates, by changing the currencies in which their *liabilities* are denominated. Treasurers of multinational firms may decide to replace maturing dollar-denominated debt, for example, with borrowing in Deutsche marks. If dollars are sold to pay off the existing debt and if Deutsche marks are demanded by firms wishing to borrow in that currency, the transactions could put downward pressure on the dollar in foreign exchange markets, with a rise in the value of the Deutsche mark.

With the acceptance of floating exchange rates for many major currencies in 1973, both the volatility of exchange rates and the costs of making foreign exchange transactions generally increased, although increases varied with different pairs of currencies. Sometimes the U.S. dollar, for example, depreciated as much as 2 percent in one week.[11] It is difficult to ascribe that much change in so short a time to changes in trade patterns. Volatility of exchange rates in the 1973–1976 period is shown in Figure 9-2. It is not clear whether this increased volatility is a temporary condition, nor is it clear that increased transactions costs have significantly discouraged foreign trade and investments. However, any expectation that fluctuations would be minor was not fulfilled. It is difficult to attribute this to government intervention, although there has been such intervention, because governments intervene to *prevent* sharp rises or rapid declines in exchange rates. The greater volatility of exchange rates after 1973 is important in formulating the theory of the determination of exchange rates, discussed later in this chapter.

Market Rates under Normal Conditions

It is expected that, within the relevant range, demand curves for foreign exchange are downward sloping and supply curves are upward sloping, so that in the absence of intervention the exchange rate tends to move toward equilibrium at the intersection of the demand and supply curves. As previously noted, the equilibrium point need not be *at* par value when par values exist. Historically, governments established par values believed to be appropriate in the light of the various factors affecting supply and demand. As supply and demand change, par values can become inappropriate. As the history of the Bretton Woods period demonstrates, governments were often reluctant to change par values even when they were clearly inappropriate; and if the situation was doubtful, they generally did not make a change. With floating exchange rates since 1973, par values for major currencies are not specified, but the 1976 agreement on a provision for possible restoration of a par value system in the future leaves open the question whether par values may ever be reinstituted and be important.

[11]"The Drift Back to Fixed Exchange Rates," *Business Week*, June 2, 1975, pp. 60–63.

Backward-Sloping Supply Curves and the Stability Conditions

The foreign exchange market is unusual because the demand for pounds, for example, *constitutes* the supply of dollars. With downward-sloping demand curves, which seem logically necessary to assume, it is easy to show that supply curves in all foreign exchange markets would be backward sloping at some points.[12] There might be a second equilibrium point, therefore, at which both demand and supply would be greater below the equilibrium point and less above it. At one time it was suggested that this might account for instability of exchange rates under some conditions, if a rate began to fall from an unstable equilibrium. Since supply and demand could not cause a rate to remain at an unstable equilibrium, it seems likely that a rate could be in such a position only if held there by government intervention. If the intervention ceased, the exchange rate might fall drastically. This could account for sharp declines in rates in a few limited conditions. However, it is generally agreed that unstable equilibrium points, although theoretically possible, are probably rarely encountered.[13] The range within which rates fluctuate may very rarely include unstable equilibrium points. Hence the determination of foreign exchange rates is usually analyzed under the normal assumption that supply and demand curves have upward and downward slopes, respectively. Volatility of exchange rates is not explained, except possibly in *very* rare cases, by unstable equilibrium points in foreign exchange markets.

EXCHANGE CONTROLS

Exchange controls vary widely in both aims and methods. Let us consider first the arguments for and against exchange controls and then the purposes they may serve.

Pros and Cons of Exchange Controls

There is wide agreement on the undesirability of exchange controls, except when necessary to control capital movements. Exchange controls affecting payments for current account BOP items are generally condemned, and fixed official exchange rates recognized as emergency measures. Rationing of foreign exchange by governments, and especially rate discrimination among different groups of buyers and sellers of foreign exchange, are as much detested as price controls, and for the same reasons. They distort production and trade and prevent the free operation of the forces of supply and demand in directing

---

[12]The stability conditions are discussed in detail in Leland B. Yeager, *International Monetary Relations*, 2d ed. (New York: Harper & Row, 1976), Chap. 8.

[13]In Chap. 3 it was indicated that the Marshall-Lerner condition, if satisfied, leads to a stable equilibrium in the foreign exchange market, and that the Marshall-Lerner condition is probably easily satisfied by supply and demand for foreign exchange arising from trade in goods and services. This is because the Marshall-Lerner condition requires only that the elasticity of home demand for imports plus the elasticity of the foreign supply of such goods and services be greater than one. Demand and supply for such imports are both likely to be at least somewhat elastic.

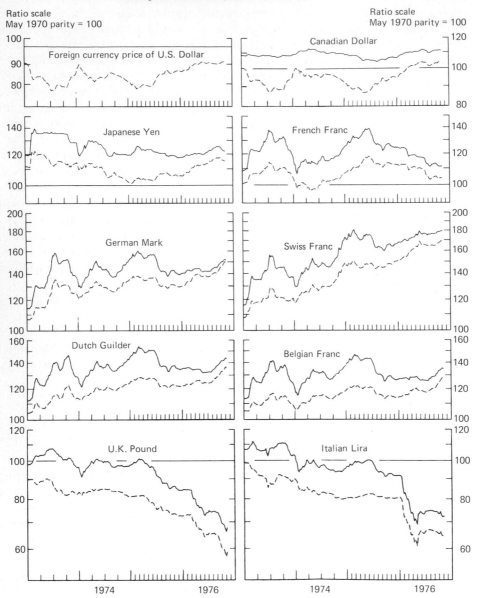

SPOT EXCHANGE RATES
Indexes of dollar prices of foreign currencies (solid line)
and trade-weighted average values (dashed line)
average for week ending Wednesday

Figure 9-2   Selected Exchange Rates. (*Source:* Federal Reserve Bank of Chicago, *International Letter*, Nov. 26, 1976.)

3-MONTH FORWARD EXCHANGE RATES
Premium (+), or discount (−)
averages for week ending Wednesday

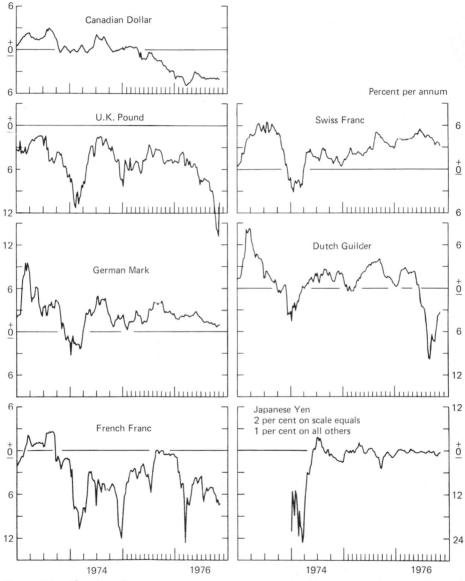

Figure 9-2 *(Continued)*

economic effort, which is generally accepted as desirable except in centrally planned economies.

On the question of government intervention in foreign exchange markets, however, there is much less agreement. Those who advocate freely flexible rates are, of course, opposed to any intervention to limit exchange rate movements. Others argue that at times it may be useful for governments to intervene, and indeed Chapter 6 showed that guidelines in IMF agreements in recent years *require* or urge intervention under certain conditions. The rationale for this view is that intervention may tend (1) to offset destabilizing speculative activity in foreign exchange markets and (2) to cushion or eliminate repercussions on the domestic economy from foreign economic developments, or both. Opponents of this view argue that there is little evidence that governments can identify destabilizing exchange rate changes promptly and that there is a possibility that government intervention may itself be destabilizing in the market. Further, many dispute the effectiveness of government intervention in foreign exchange markets in cushioning economies from foreign economic developments. If foreign exchange rates are not allowed to perform their market function, adjustments in liquidity, income, and prices inevitably occur, as shown earlier.

Increasing economic integration of major countries causes many to argue that some coordination of economic policies and rates of change in economic variables in major countries is necessary. Such coordination might reduce volatility of exchange rates. But it is not clear what conditions may encourage central banks to attempt to coordinate basic monetary policies.

Current Purposes and Methods of Exchange Controls

Once exchange controls have been introduced—usually for BOP purposes—it is difficult to abandon them. The need for controls implies a large difference between supply of and demand for foreign exchange at the prevailing rate, and abandonment of controls would probably greatly alter the exchange value of a country's currency. Exchange controls are used for several purposes: (1) countries which desire rapid economic development need exchange controls to prevent capital flight, which causes BOP disequilibrium, and to avoid depreciation of the currency, which might lead to more inflation; (2) controls facilitate national planning by insulating an economy from foreign repercussions; (3) exchange controls may be used as an alternative to tariffs and nontariff trade barriers to limit imports and thus protect domestic industry; and finally, (4) controls allow sale of foreign exchange by a government agency at a higher price than that at which the agency purchases foreign exchange, providing some government revenue.[14]

Since governments want foreign exchange received by exporters and others to be available for purchase of essential imports, they usually require the surrender of such foreign exchange to a government agency. Since exchange

---

[14]For a more detailed discussion, see Franklin R. Root, *International Trade and Investment*, 3d ed. (Cincinnati: South-Western, 1973), Chap. 14, "Exchange Control and Its Effects."

transactions are for the most part handled through banks, governments can enforce such rules by requiring banks to obtain necessary evidence of surrender of foreign exchange by exporters.

In regulating the availability of foreign exchange to importers and others who need it, governments can make individual allocations, establish exchange quotas and license systems, prohibit the allocation of foreign exchange for certain purposes, and in other ways channel to desired purposes the limited amount of foreign exchange available.

In multiple-rate systems of exchange control, the rates themselves are used as devices to control allocation of foreign exchange. Some countries have, in effect, a two-rate system by having a wide spread between foreign exchange selling and buying rates. Others have a single fixed rate which may be used for designated purposes such as current account payments, and a fluctuating rate used for other purposes such as capital account transactions. Sometimes exporters and others are permitted to sell at fluctuating rates different proportions of the amounts of foreign exchange obtained, depending on the source. Thus exporters of certain products may be encouraged and others discouraged.

When countries impose exchange controls, they usually do so because imports or other debit items in the BOP exceed exports or other credit items (excluding settlement items). Thus trade is reduced to the level of the lower amount. Some countries still have what are termed bilateral payments agreements, under which specified deficits may occur between two countries. For deficits larger than those specified, payment must usually be in U.S. dollars or some other generally acceptable currency. The main use of bilateral payments agreements in recent years has been between developing countries and countries with centrally planned economies. Multiple-rate exchange control systems exist almost entirely in developing countries.

Since the IMF was established, most developed countries have eliminated exchange controls on current account transactions. Only five countries still retained the Article XIV status permitting such controls at the end of 1974.[15] Almost all countries, however, retain exchange controls in some form on capital account transactions; the only exceptions at the end of 1974 were a group of Middle East and other oil exporting countries (Bahrain, Ecuador, Indonesia, Iran, Kuwait, Oman, Qatar, Saudi Arabia, and the United Arab Emirates), certain European countries (Belgium-Luxembourg, West Germany, Netherlands), some Central and South American countries (Bolivia, Guatemala, Honduras, Mexico, Nicaragua, Panama), Canada, Hong Kong, Malaysia, and the United States. Lebanon was also in the group at that time.[16]

---

[15]The five countries were Finland, Greece, New Zealand, Portugal, and Spain. Austria, France, and the United Kingdom have imposed such restrictions also, although they had agreed not to do so. Readers may remember that countries agreeing not to impose such controls are classified as Article VIII countries, having accepted obligations to permit currency convertibility on current account under Article VIII of the IMF agreement.

[16]Details concerning exchange controls and payments of each country which is a member of the IMF are reported in the *Annual Report on Exchange Restrictions* published by the IMF.

In exporting to countries in which exchange controls on current account transactions exist, exporters generally find it useful to request letters of credit. Services of larger banks are also useful in keeping exporters informed concerning the nature of such controls.

Controls on capital account transactions are of more interest to firms making foreign investments, both direct and portfolio, since they may wish to repatriate interest, dividends, or profits, or even to sell investments (termed *divestment*) and repatriate the proceeds.

FORWARD EXCHANGE

Exchange risk exists to some extent in any system in which exchange rates may fluctuate, even by small amounts. Since a single world currency is not likely to come into existence in the foreseeable future, and since freely fluctuating exchange rates may not be permitted by governments, the choice probably lies between a degree of flexibility in exchange rates with some government intervention, and a system of fixed rates in which adjustments are made from time to time.

In either event there is some risk of exchange losses. Risk is inherent to some degree in all business activity, and perhaps it is not desirable to eliminate all risk, for in so doing businesses which face no risk or less risk are in effect being subsidized.

However, it is possible for those engaged in foreign trade, in contrast to those making long-term foreign investments, to avoid exchange risk if they wish, by paying for its elimination. Remember that risk is the degree to which prices or returns vary; by paying a fixed amount, traders may avoid the risk of wider variation. An exporter who expects to be paid in pounds sterling could borrow in London and sell the proceeds for U.S. dollars, repaying the loan with the sterling he will later receive. The cost of this type of hedge is the interest cost.

The more common manner of hedging, however, when it is available, is to enter into a forward contract for sale or purchase of foreign exchange to be delivered later, at a price agreed upon in the contract. If an exporter who expects to be paid in a foreign currency can contract with a bank or other institution at a specified price or exchange rate, the exporter knows that loss is limited to the amount by which such price is below the present exchange rate (if it is). Similarly, suppose that an importer must pay for goods priced in a foreign currency. If the importer can enter into a contract with a bank to buy foreign exchange from the bank at an agreed price, the loss is limited to the amount by which that price is above the current exchange rate (if it is) at the time of the contract. Since a forward rate can be either above or below the spot rate, an exporter could gain or lose, as could an importer. Of course, if the forward rate were above the spot rate, it would normally mean that those in the market judged the exchange rate likely to rise. Exporters might conclude that it was unnecessary in such circumstances to seek to avoid risk of a decline in the exchange rate. In fact, in any situation, exporters and importers sometimes prefer to take the risk, hoping that the exchange rate will move in a direction favorable to them.

In the Bretton Woods era, when other currencies were related to stable values of U.S. dollars and of gold, it was much more common to devalue than to upvalue currencies of European countries; hence forward rates were usually below spot rates for such currencies in the New York market.

Forward rates are specified for the time at which the exchange is to be delivered—30 days forward, 60 days forward, and so on. If a pegged, or fixed but adjustable, exchange rate is deemed likely to be devalued, the discount on forward exchange may be quite sizable. If countries could be counted on to maintain exchange rates as they did in the period of the gold standard, risk would be small. But if they cannot be counted on to do this, risk under a system of fixed but adjustable exchange rates may be as great as or greater than under a system of flexible exchange rates.

Traders buying or selling goods or services priced in currencies of small countries may have a disadvantage because forward markets for little-used currencies cannot be expected to be very broad or deep, and may not exist at all. Longer-term investors face some disadvantage because forward contracts generally do not exceed 180 days in maturity. In theory, if they invest in major countries, they can eliminate most exchange risk by selling exchange forward for 90 days and then renewing the forward contract every 90 days, but the cost may be prohibitive.

Lenders exporting capital in the form either of loans or investments, if they wish to protect themselves against exchange risk can sell the borrowing country's currency forward. Since they buy the borrowing country's currency in order to invest, the purchase of foreign currency to make a foreign investment is offset by sale of foreign currency in the forward contract. To the extent that lenders do this, there is no *net* outflow of capital at all, in the long run.

Exchange instability is to some extent a deterrent to international capital movements. This is true whether the instability results from flexible exchange rates or from adjustments, even though infrequent, in fixed but adjustable exchange rates.

Nature of Forward Contracts

Forward contracts are simply agreements to buy or sell foreign exchange, at a rate agreed to on the date of the contracts, with the exchange deliverable 30 days, 60 days, or some other specified time in the future. Banks sometimes offer contracts under which exporters or importers may deliver or take delivery of foreign exchange any time during a week, a fortnight, or a month. They also buy and sell odd-denomination amounts.

Forward rates are often quoted as discounts from or premiums over the basic spot rate. If there is any likelihood of depreciation or devaluation of a currency, it is probable that the forward rate will be at a discount. Some risk is involved for banks, because firms may default on delivering or taking delivery of the exchange. Hence careful evaluation of credit is necessary. A margin in the form of a cash deposit may be required.

As in other instances of risk avoidance, a business firm or individual uses forward exchange contracts when the risk is deemed to be such that hedging is desirable. Mistakes may be made, of course. But it would be foolish for an importer to buy forward exchange when there is little likelihood of the exchange rate rising, just as it is foolish for an exporter to require a letter of credit when there is little likelihood of any government restriction on foreign exchange payments or other risk and when the credit standing of the importer is excellent.

Exporters can sometimes compensate for the cost of protection against exchange risk by raising foreign currency prices at which they sell. Exchange risk avoidance in the form of making forward contracts is a cost of doing business.

However, the forward market can be used by speculators as well as by exporters and importers. In fact, an exporter or an importer may be a speculator. Speculators are simply those who enter a market because of belief that their forecasts of expected prices or rates are reasonably accurate, so that they may profit. Forward exchange arrangements are contracts in which a speculator who buys forward exchange, perhaps with only a small down payment, can gain if the exchange rate rises above the rate at which the forward exchange was purchased. Similarly, a risk averter who hedges by buying forward exchange may gain by being able to buy exchange at the forward rate instead of at the higher future rate if the future spot rate rises above the current forward rate.[17] Despite some similarity to insurance, we should note that forward exchange agreements are simply contracts from which *both* parties may gain—importers from buying forward exchange at a lower rate than they would have had to pay if they had waited, and sellers of forward exchange from the premium of the forward rate over the spot rate.[18]

Banks normally are not expected to be speculators, although in periods of flexible exchange rates they may believe that they should sell currencies which seem likely to depreciate in value. In an efficient market, one cannot predict short-term fluctuations in rates, since all predictable influences have been taken into account by well-informed market participants.

In attempting to avoid speculative activity, banks normally buy and sell equal amounts of each foreign currency in which they deal, once they have established their desired foreign exchange positions. Forward sales do not precisely offset risk involved in spot purchases, however, so banks which have bought spot exchange and sold forward exchange buy forward exchange and sell spot exchange simultaneously in the same amounts. The previous spot

[17]See Egon Sohmen, *International Monetary Problems and the Foreign Exchanges*, Special Papers in International Economics, No. 4 (Princeton, N.J.: Princeton, 1963), p. 56, and *Flexible Exchange Rates* (Chicago: University of Chicago Press, 1961).

[18]It should be noted that ongoing export and import firms may not gain, because the forward exchange rate usually fluctuates at least as much as the spot rate.

purchases are offset by the spot sales, and the previous forward sales by the forward purchases.

Forward and Spot Rate Relationships

Those who invest in foreign countries to obtain higher short-term interest rates must pay the discount (assuming there is one) when selling forward exchange to protect themselves against the risk that the exchange rate may fall before they have returned their funds to their home country. Investment protected by forward sales is termed *covered investment,* or *interest arbitrage.* The net gain is normally the difference in interest rates minus the discount on the sale of forward exchange, the latter expressed as a percentage per year. Thus this type of capital outflow occurs only when the interest rate differential is greater than the discount on forward exchange.

The situation with respect to covered foreign investment is shown in Figure 9-3. Only when the algebraic sum of the two rate differentials is in the cross-hatched area, as, for example, at point *A*, will an outflow of this type of investment occur. Only when the algebraic sum of the two rate differentials is in the diagonally-lined area, for example at point *B*, will an inflow occur.

Note that the occurrence of this type of investment widens the spread between spot and forward rates through purchases of spot exchange and sales of forward exchange. It also reduces the interest rate differential by removing investment funds from the home country and investing them in the foreign country. This removes the opportunity for such investment by changing the spreads—reducing the spread between spot and forward rates and widening the spread between home country interest rates and foreign country interest rates. Point *A* moves from *A* to *A'*.

Central Bank Activity

Central banks can, if they wish, vary the conditions under which they are willing to provide forward cover, and thus encourage or discourage short-term

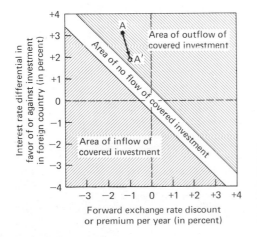

Figure 9-3 Forward Exchange Rate Discounts and Premiums, Interest Rate Differentials, and Flows of Covered Investment. (Modified from diagram in Alan R. Holmes and Francis H. Schott, *The New York Foreign Exchange Market,* Federal Reserve Bank of New York, 1965, p. 54.)

fund flows by their actions related to forward rates.[19] In a country in which open market operations cannot be used effectively because of inadequate development of a market for government securities, the central bank may contract to deliver forward local currency at a lower than normal rate. Banks are tempted to buy forward exchange at this lower rate, but must sell local currency (buy foreign currency) to cover. This means a flow of funds out of the country, reducing the money supply under some circumstances. The central bank can increase the money supply by opposite action.

Central banks may also buy local currency forward, hoping to raise the forward value of the local currency. This narrows the spread between the forward rate and the spot rate, tempting some banks to acquire spot local currency by selling spot foreign exchange. This raises the spot rate for local currency; the central bank would probably do this when the spot rate was weak and needed support, and when, perhaps, the central bank did not have enough foreign exchange to support the rate directly. Although it might appear in such a situation that the currency was strengthening, it would actually be weakening except for the support of actions of the central bank. Thus, although it might be presumed that a forward rate would be a useful guide to forecasting future spot rates, it *may* be misleading. Changes in the "normal" spread or discount on forward exchange may alert traders in foreign exchange to the possibility of changes in spot rates, and may induce them to examine the basic factors likely to determine the trend in spot rates.

Factors Determining Forward Rates

In general, forward rates are determined simultaneously by three factors: (1) the rate which would be necessary to eliminate profit on covered interest arbitrage, (2) the spot rate expected at future dates by speculators, and (3) the forward rate which would be necessary to equate the demand for and supply of foreign exchange by commercial hedges. This is because there are three basic sources of demand and supply for forward exchange: (1) the demand or supply by those seeking covered investment, chiefly banks; (2) speculators, who may buy forward exchange if they expect the future spot rate to be higher than the present forward rate, since they can sell exchange delivered to them, presumably, at the expected spot rate; and (3) commercial traders, engaged in import and export business, who buy and sell forward exchange when they think it necessary to hedge against the risk of exchange rate fluctuation.[20] This general conclusion will be helpful to us later in examining the possibility of forecasting exchange rates and the various means which might be used in attempts to forecast. Those questions are deferred to Chapter 14.

---

[19]Wilson B. Brown, "The Forward Exchange Rate as a Forecasting Tool," *University of Washington Business Review*, Winter 1971, pp. 48–58.

[20]The simultaneous and consistent determination of forward rates by possible profit on covered investment, the spot rate expected in the future by speculators, and the forward rate necessary to equate supply of and demand for forward exchange by hedgers is elegantly shown by Ian Giddy, "An Integrated Theory of Exchange Rate Equilibrium," *Journal of Financial and Quantitative Analysis*, December 1976, pp. 883–892.

Before completing the discussion of exchange rates, however, three other topics must be covered: the pros and cons of freely flexible exchange rates, which have generally been favored by a majority of economists and opposed by a majority of central bankers; the question of the optimum size for a currency area; and the factors determining the long-run level of exchange rates. Short-term forecasting must be based on an understanding of the factors determining long-run levels, since these are fundamental. The question of the optimum size of a currency area is important because we need to ask why, for example, the dollar has essentially one value within the United States, but may fluctuate in relation to currency in areas outside U.S. borders. Would a single currency be desirable for Europe? For the European Common Market? Is a fixed rate desirable for a very small country, or is its area too small to be suitable? The question of optimum size of currency areas is related to the pros and cons of flexible exchange rates, although flexible rates might be suitable for large countries and not for small ones, or not under all conditions.

THE PROS AND CONS OF FLEXIBLE EXCHANGE RATES

Economists have argued for a long time about the desirability of fixed versus flexible exchange rates. Because most officials concerned with establishment of exchange rates concluded in the early 1940s that flexible exchange rates were undesirable, the Bretton Woods system envisaged changes in exchange rates only when there were "fundamental disequilibria" in BOPs. Actually, in amplitude of variation, flexible rates may vary less than fixed but adjustable rates over a period of time. Moreover, as Machlup pointed out, there are many different situations: rates may be completely flexible, determined by private market forces; or rates may be fixed, with government intervention to maintain them. Between these extremes, which are rarely found empirically, there may be government intervention maintaining fixed rates in a general way, but permitting fluctuation within a predetermined *band*. There may also be a managed float, with government intervention to cause changes in the exchange rate in the desired direction.[21]

The Case for Fixed Exchange Rates

The arguments for fixed exchange rates have been, as Harry Johnson has written, "part of a more general argument for national economic policies conducive to international economic integration."[22] Fixed exchange rates are equivalent to a single currency: they simplify profit-maximizing calculations of traders, facilitate competition, and promote the integration of the whole area of fixed exchange rates into a connected series of markets. Since it must be recognized that factors of production are usually not completely free to move

---

[21]Fritz Machlup, "Round Table on Exchange Rate Policy," *American Economic Review*, Papers and Proceedings, May 1969, pp. 366–369.

[22]Harry G. Johnson, "The Case for Flexible Exchange Rates, 1969," Federal Reserve Bank of St. Louis, *Review*, June 1969, pp. 12–24; see p. 14.

internationally, and even trade in goods and services is limited to some extent, the conditions for fixed exchange rates are not as suitable as for a single currency within a given country. Nevertheless, it may be argued that the need for economic integration and the benefits of connected competitive markets are sufficiently strong to justify fixed exchange rates among major industrialized countries. Hardly anyone argues for fixed exchange rates for less developed countries, for their monetary and fiscal systems and the degree of inflation likely to exist in them may not be conducive to fixed exchange rates. For major industrialized countries, fixed exchange rates, even if adjustable from time to time, imply a degree of coordination in monetary and fiscal policies and hence in inflation and interest rates, and probably in the general timing of fluctuation in overall economic activity.

Also, some economists believe that fixed exchange rates are a form of discipline over nations in the group of countries with fixed rates. A country's policy actions may be inhibited if it recognizes that they are likely to cause a devaluation. Friedrich A. von Hayek, recent Nobel prize winner in economics, put the case bluntly: "Present unemployment is the direct and necessary consequence of what we have been calling a full employment policy . . . inflation is solely and entirely a question of the quantity of money . . . fixed exchange rates may be inferior to an ideal policy, but nonetheless may be absolutely essential to protect governments against a kind of pressure which is bound to be imposed upon them if they have freedom to act in these respects."[23] He argued that if the public believes that unemployment can be significantly reduced by tax cuts or expenditure increases, democratic governments cannot resist the pressure to take such measures, and central banks cannot resist the pressure to accommodate the added demand for funds by increasing the money supply. Hayek regarded the gold standard and fixed exchange rates as factors enabling central banks to resist, to some extent, the constant pressure to increase the money supply faster than the combined increase in productivity and the labor force, which leads to increased real output.

In addition, those who favor fixed exchange rates argue that flexible rates cause undue risk and hardship for international trade and investment, because of the uncertainty of changes in exchange rates and the consequent uncertainty of revenues, costs, and net returns. On the other hand, there may be adverse consequences for business firms engaged in international transactions if fixed rates are accompanied by exchange controls or other restrictions.

The Case for Flexible Exchange Rates

Advocates of freely flexible exchange rates argue, first, that such a system solves BOP problems. It eliminates chronic deficits or surpluses in BOPs, and

---

[23]Friedrich A. von Hayek, "World Inflationary Recession" in First National Bank of Chicago *Report*, May 1975.

governments are free "to use their instruments of domestic policy for the pursuit of domestic objectives."[24] Those nations whose governments believe that they need to accept some degree of inflation to achieve higher employment would be able to do so without BOP deficit problems, and nations which fear inflation would be able to take steps to restrain it without the problem of huge BOP surpluses.

This leads to a second, broader argument for flexible exchange rates: such a situation would enhance world trade and investment by removing needs for tariffs, exchange controls, and other controls on BOP items. The case for flexible exchange rates derives from the argument that free markets, whether in commodities or in foreign exchange, will establish rates which will equate supply and demand. If rates are fixed, they may be above or below the equilibrium level, and in either case controls may be needed.

Third, it is argued that fluctuations in exchange rates, under a flexible exchange rate system, would not be so great as to disrupt international trade and investment. Those who favor flexible exchange rates have argued that if exchange markets were free, and if speculators were well informed, they would buy foreign exchange when a rate is below the equilibrium rate, hoping to profit by its rise, and would sell when a rate is above the equilibrium rate, taking a profit. Likewise, when a rate is above the equilibrium rate, they would sell short, selling exchange which they do not have, for later delivery, and then buy and deliver the foreign exchange when the rate fell, making a profit. Milton Friedman, also a Nobel prize winner, has probably been the most ardent advocate of this view. It is similar to the argument that activities of speculators tend to stabilize prices in the stock market. However, it is strengthened by pointing out that, unlike the stock market, in the foreign exchange market many exchange transactions *must* be carried out for current trade and services payments. Thus any speculative errors or excesses, leading to volatility of rates, affect only some but not all transactions.[25] It should therefore be possible to forecast the long-run levels of exchange rates, based upon fundamental factors, and short-run fluctuations should not be excessive. It is also true that speculative buying and selling are equally easy in the foreign exchange market, whereas in the stock market there are rules tightly restricting short selling. Short selling must be done with borrowed stock, and borrowing stock may at times be limited or impossible.[26]

The argument boils down to this: if speculators are relatively free in the

---

[24]Harry G. Johnson, op. cit., p. 18.

[25]See Leland B. Yeager, *International Monetary Relations*, 2d ed., pp. 246–248.

[26]There is a difference between short selling of foreign exchange and short selling of stocks, land, or other commodities: stocks, land, or commodities, if they are not already owned, must be borrowed in order to sell short. Foreign exchange need not be; it can always be bought for delivery on the due date. Stocks, commodities, and especially land are limited in supply. The long-term trend in land prices should always be upward, if economies have rising nominal income. So should the long-run value of stocks, in general, and of many commodities. For some commodities, however, substitutes can be found—for example, the substitution of nylon, rayon, and polyester for silk and other fibers.

foreign exchange market to express either bullish or bearish views, the pressures from both sides should prevent the development of speculative excesses.

Fourth, it has been argued that pegged (or stable but adjustable) exchange rates involve costs: there is the cost of holding international reserves to use in stabilizing exchange rates, the social cost of an exchange rate which is not always the optimum from a free market point of view, and the social cost of reducing somewhat the risks involved in international transactions. Under fixed exchange risks some costs are paid in part by society as a whole rather than by those engaged in international transactions.[27]

Finally, it has been argued that opportunities for hedging, previously discussed, are available to reduce the risk for foreign traders. It should be mentioned that such opportunity does not eliminate other risks—for example, the risks in developing a line of exports and then finding that movements in exchange rates have made this line unprofitable. Nor does it eliminate risks for long-term investment, for means of hedging are not easily extendable beyond relatively short periods. On the other hand, long-term investors have some opportunity to shift the forms of their investments, for example from bonds to stocks, since different rates of inflation resulting in changes in exchange rates would tend to be offset in the long run by changing monetary values of stocks.[28]

Before concluding the arguments for flexible exchange rates, two exceptions may be noted. First, it was difficult for a country like the United States to vary the exchange value of the dollar, since other countries pegged their exchange rates to the dollar. Only by pressure and by obtaining agreement, as described in Chapter 6, could the United States devalue its own currency relative to other currencies. Devaluation vis-à-vis gold would not have been enough, if other countries also had devalued vis-à-vis gold by the same percentage.

Second, small countries which export principally one or a small number of commodities might find flexible exchange rates more detrimental than useful. Stability of the values of the currencies of such countries in terms of command over goods bought from foreign countries is probably more important than freedom for autonomous domestic monetary and fiscal policy. Such countries may wish to peg the values of their currencies to the currency of a major

[27]These points are developed in detail in Anthony Lanyi, *The Case for Floating Exchange Rates Reconsidered*, Essays in International Finance, No. 72 (Princeton: Princeton, 1969).

[28]It is assumed that in the long run stocks are a hedge against inflation. If this is not so, much of financial theory is destroyed, since it is assumed that risks on stocks are higher than on bonds and risk is compensated for by higher yields. It has been demonstrated quite conclusively that bond yield rates rise in periods of inflation. Belief in the effectiveness of stocks as a hedge against inflation was damaged by the experience of 1967–1975, but this is only an 8-year period. See "The Long-Term Case for Stocks," *Fortune*, December 1974, pp. 97, 100, 102. For a review of the shorter-run position of stocks as an inflation hedge, see Frank K. Reilly, *Companies and Common Stocks as Inflation Hedges*, New York University, Bulletin 1975-2 (New York: New York University, 1975).

country with which they carry on a substantial trade, and many have done so since 1973.

Evaluation of the Pros and Cons of Flexible Rates

Against the economic benefits of flexible exchange rates—and they are admittedly not overwhelming, since there are both benefits and costs—must be set the political costs of a flexible rate system. Exchange rates, like general price levels, are so pervasive in their effects that it seems unlikely that governments will permit freely fluctuating exchange rates, just as they will try to avoid rapid inflation or extensive deflation. Admittedly, they may not be able to take effective steps in all circumstances. If it is granted that government intervention is likely to occur, the practical possibility of freely flexible exchange rates is very limited.

Stable but adjustable exchange rates are a compromise between the fixed rates of the gold standard of the period 1880–1914 and the freely flexible exchange rates desired by some economists. The authors are inclined to accept the view outlined by one group of economists:

> The conference by implication was agreed that a mixed exchange system would emerge in the future, thus reconciling the two apparently opposing views on the desirability of fixed rates. Advocates of floating rates conceded that a regime in which every national currency floated independently could lead to a chaotic destruction of the use of money in international exchange or, more probably, to an increased international use of the dollar and one or two other currencies in private market transactions. On the other hand, it was also recognized that a universal system of fixed exchange rates would not be compatible with independent national rates of inflation. Countries could accept binding rules for fixed rates only if they were prepared to adapt their own monetary policies to the monetary policy of the currency area and accept the common rate of inflation.[29]

We might add that if individual countries pursue very different policies, especially monetary policies, the choice may not be fixed versus flexible rates but floating rates versus fixed rates plus stringent controls. The real question is the willingness of governments to accept a degree of coordination of monetary policies of major countries as a basis for a system providing relative stability for exchange rates.

If a dollar standard is accepted, it means that U.S. monetary policy is also accepted as a dominant factor in the world economy. Convertibility of dollars into some international asset other than currencies limits the complete independence of U.S. monetary policy.

This would not rule out the establishment of single currencies in limited areas, possibly the European Common Market, if the political conditions necessary for harmonization of government policies within that area can be attained.

---

[29]*The Santa Colomba Conclusions 1975*, First Chicago Report, August 1975, p. 9.

It should be noted that the arguments for flexible exchange rates are directly contrary to Nurkse's analysis, discussed in Chapter 4. Nurkse's analysis has been dismissed by many as less applicable today, since the world does not face the serious depression faced in the 1930s, and therefore the impetus to engage in competitive depreciation of currencies is less. Some observers also dismiss Nurkse's analysis on the ground that it applied to a *dirty* float—one in which governments intervened—whereas what is desired is a clean float.

Floating rates since 1973 caused some economists to be less sanguine about the desirability of flexible exchange rates.[30] Transitory news events seemed to be accompanied by relatively wide fluctuations in exchange rates, and devaluation did not always seem to improve trade balances.

The strongest argument against flexible exchange rates in recent years is that advanced by Mundell and Laffer. They argue that changes in currency values do not affect relative prices of commodities, and that any short-run price advantage gained by devaluation or depreciation of a currency is soon offset by more inflation in the devaluing country. With devaluation, prices of imported goods and of their domestic substitutes rise. Moreover, funds received in payment for exports may add to the money supply unless this is offset by central bank actions. Their analysis amounts to the argument that relative prices of goods and services depend on productivity (output per worker-hour) rather than on currency value fluctuations. Countries in which productivity is increasing only slowly cannot fundamentally affect their situation by allowing their currencies to depreciate.

In this view, the only fundamental solution to the problem of simultaneous inflation and recession is "a ceiling on the growth of world liquidity and more stimulus to production."[31] Mundell argues that tax cuts may be necessary in countries experiencing recessions, but that such tax cuts cannot be fully effective unless they stimulate production by increasing profits—cuts in corporate income taxes, the investment tax credit, and so on.

THE OPTIMUM CURRENCY AREA

Since one extreme would be a world currency, with no exchange rates—in effect, fixed rates throughout the world—and the other extreme would be a different currency for each small area (at the ultimate limit, for each individual), it is appropriate to ask, what is the optimum size for a currency area?

It is generally agreed that having one currency used throughout the United

---

[30]"The Drift Back to Fixed Exchange Rates," *Business Week*, June 2, 1975, pp. 60–63. Samuelson, for example, is quoted as saying that "people selling the flexible rate system exaggerated their case; the idea that elasticities of demand are great enough to restore equilibrium is malarkey"; and Kindleberger, who favored fixed rates to some extent much earlier, is quoted as saying that "I am confident that we will evolve back to a fixed exchange rate system over time."

[31]Robert A. Mundell, "World Money and the Optimum Policy Mix," in First National Bank of Chicago *Report*, May 1975.

States is preferable to having a New England dollar, an Appalachian dollar, and so on. The European Common Market countries hoped to achieve a single currency unit by the end of the 1970s, but this now appears unlikely. With a single currency, there would be a large, integrated market within which dealings in foreign exchange would be eliminated for international transactions. Two types of criteria have been suggested as bases for determining the characteristics of an optimum currency area.

One economist has argued that if factors of production, such as labor and capital, can move to all parts of an area relatively freely, one currency for the whole area is preferable to a number of currencies with exchange rates indicating their relative values. If one part of such an area has a recession because products in which that region specializes are in less demand, factors of production can move to other regions, and the advantage of a single currency in eliminating foreign exchange trading costs is significant.[32]

Another economist suggested that a more important question is whether a large percentage of all commodities and services produced in a country or area are traded with other areas. If so, exchange rate changes accomplish little in altering relative prices, and they reduce the usefulness of money as a store of value.[33] Under these conditions a single currency for a broader area is desirable. The country may wish to peg its currency to the value of the currency of another country with which there is a large volume of trade in order to obtain the advantage of stability in the value of its currency in terms of the currency of the country with which it trades significantly. If a country or area is small and a large proportion of its output enters international trade, the area may be too small to gain advantage from having flexible exchange rates between its currency and those of its trading partners. On the other hand, if a country or area is relatively large, and if only a small fraction of its output enters international trade, although a fall in the value of the currency could cause a rise in prices of imports and of import-competing goods and services, it might have little effect on prices of nontraded goods and services. Thus the effect on the domestic price level in general might be small. If monetary and fiscal policy are relied on to reduce spending in order to stabilize the exchange rate, it may be necessary to cause a reduction in prices of nontraded goods in order to achieve this goal. Since labor costs are a large component in prices (labor receiving, in the United States, for example, about three-fourths of national income), there might have to be a significant cut in money wages. The tail, as McKinnon put it, would be wagging the dog, since relatively small BOP items would determine policy affecting domestic goods and services prices. Thus in this case it might *not* be desirable to have a single currency for an area including more than this single country.

---

[32]Robert A. Mundell, "A Theory of Optimum Currency Areas," *American Economic Review*, September 1961, pp. 657–665.

[33]Ronald McKinnon, "Optimum Currency Areas," *American Economic Review*, September 1963, pp. 717–725.

Determination of an optimum size of currency area is difficult and no definitive answer has been generally accepted. Yet the question is not academic. When an important "outer exchange rate" or "outrate" changes, what policy should a country follow? For example, when the mark-dollar rate changes, what policy should Italy follow? Should it maintain the lira-dollar rate, maintain the lira-mark rate, adopt an in-between policy, or let the exchange value of the lira fluctuate? Should Italy be a part of the dollar currency area, be a part of the European Common Market currency area, adopt a compromise course, or accept a flexible exchange rate?

"The essence of a currency area is an acceptance of a common set of targets with respect to inflation, interest rates, and exchange rates."[34] Reform of the international monetary system in the direction of again forming a large area of fixed but adjustable exchange rates would reduce uncertainty with respect to long-term interest rates and exchange rates. Such uncertainty can make it difficult to obtain needed capital in certain areas, and this in turn can generate levels of unemployment above desired percentages of the labor force. Yet differences in inflation rates and in interest rates and the desire for independence for monetary policy have prevented such a step in international monetary reform.

THE THEORY OF EXCHANGE RATE DETERMINATION

It is now time to recapitulate and complete the theory of exchange rate determination.

Short-Term Fluctuations in Exchange Rates

Earlier in this chapter it was shown that equilibrium values of (1) spot exchange rates, (2) interest rate differentials minus the cost of forward cover, and (3) forward exchange rates are mutually determined. Thus in an efficient market the forward premium or discount would equal the interest rate differential between two countries, plus or minus the rate of change in the spot exchange rate. The expected rate of depreciation or appreciation of an exchange rate would be equal to the interest rate differential and the forward premium or discount would equal the expected rate of depreciation or appreciation of the exchange rate. This is an application of Irving Fisher's interest rate parity theorem to international transactions. Sometimes the term "Fisher open" is used to contrast this application with the application of the same principle to a "closed" economy (one with no international transactions).[35]

Unless there is predictable intervention by central banks, the interest rate differential is the best forecaster of the future spot rate and the forward rate is

[34]*The Santa Colomba Conclusions 1975*, First Chicago Report, August 1975, p. 11.

[35]Giddy integrated the short-run equilibrium interest rate parity theorem, the interest rate theory of exchange rate expectations, and the forward rate theory of exchange rate expectations with the long-run purchasing power parity theorem in the classic article referred to in footnote 20.

the best forecaster of the future spot rate over time. In short-term fluctuations, in efficient markets, forecasting may not be possible, since fluctuations should be random. That is, in efficient markets participants presumably take into account in establishing the rates at any time all information, including predictable events, then available. Unpredictable events affecting rates cannot be taken into account, and unpredictable events are by definition random.

Long-Term Fluctuations in Exchange Rates

In the long run, account must be taken of the long-run trend in exchange rates, which exists even if short-term fluctuations are random. (Technically, such a situation is termed a submartingale; it also exists in stock markets, where short-term fluctuations in stock prices are random but there is a long-term trend in prices.) The trend is derived primarily from changes in inflation rates in the two countries concerned. The reason for this is that if there are no trade barriers and no capital controls, equilibrium in the exchange rate exists when prices for the same goods and services or the same basket of goods and services in different markets (different countries) are the same when translated at current (spot) exchange rates. In the long run, differences in inflation in different countries would tend to cause offsetting changes in exchange rates which would restore equilibrium.

Seven factors can be identified which may cause changes in exchange rates:

1 Differences in rates of inflation among nations
2 Differences in rates of growth of real income among nations
3 Changes in interest rate differentials
4 Fear of controls which may confiscate wealth or prevent its use or transfer
5 Speculation motivated by expectation of changes in exchange rates
6 Changes in economic situations of nations or in comparative advantage, caused by such things as important discoveries of natural resources, increase in size of market, reduction in tariff barriers, and so on
7 Changes in tastes

In the long run, all except the first of these should be of minor importance in determining exchange rates. Differences in rates of growth in real income must be reflected in prices (inflation or deflation) to affect trade, and even if capital movements cause temporary departures from rates reflecting relative price changes, trade should change in such a way as to restore equality of prices of goods and services in different countries when translated at current exchange rates.

Purchasing Power Parity Theory The theory that exchange rates in the long run move toward equilibrium positions in which prices of goods and services in different countries, translated at current exchange rates, are the same, has been known as purchasing power parity theory.

In absolute form this proposition is difficult to verify. If $12^{1}/_{2}$ Mexican pesos buy the same basket of goods and services as a dollar, the dollar should be worth $12^{1}/_{2}$ pesos. But this presumes that a basket of goods and services can be identified, prices of these goods and services measured and weighted, and a resulting ratio of purchasing power of currencies determined. Such calculations are difficult.

It is easier, however, to obtain price level indexes for countries, determine a year or period in which it is believed that the exchange rate reflected approximate purchasing power parity, and then determine the changes in price levels in the countries since that year or period. This relative form of purchasing power parity calculation can be the basis for predicting long-run levels of exchange rates, and for forecasting approximate levels to which currencies will be devalued or upvalued if par values exist and it becomes necessary to change them.[36]

The exchange rate should equal the exchange rate in a base year or period times the ratio of country A's price level now to its price level in the base year divided by the ratio of country B's price level now to its price level in the base year. Price levels in the base year can be treated as 100. If country A had, over a period of time, inflation which raised its price level from 100 to 200, and if country B had inflation which raised its price level from 100 to 300, purchasing power parity for country B's currency in terms of country A's currency should be 200/100 divided by 300/100, or 200/300, or 2/3. With the change in price levels, a unit of country B's currency would buy 2/3 as much as in the base year, compared to country A's currency. If country A had no inflation and country B's price level doubled, the value of country B's currency in terms of country A's should be 100/100 divided by 200/100, or 1/2; country B's currency would buy half as much when translated into country A's currency as it had in the base period.

For a historical example, take the stabilization of the French franc in 1926. The average exchange rate for the French franc during 1913 was 19.3 cents, and it was generally accepted that 1913 could be considered a base year in which the exchange rate was approximately at purchasing power parity level. United States prices were at an index of 143 in 1926 (1913 equals 100) while French prices were at an index of 722 in the last four months of 1926. Thus the

---

[36]Both the absolute and relative versions of the purchasing power parity theory were advanced by Gustav Cassel, in a number of writings. See, for example, *Money and Foreign Exchange After 1914* (New York: Macmillan, 1927) and *The Theory of Social Economy* (New York: Harcourt, Brace, 1934). Cassel's idea was not entirely new, since it can be found in economic theory much earlier. But Cassel revived it and made it popular. The absolute version tended to be ignored for reasons indicated in this chapter and also because high tariffs imposed in one country could invalidate it, whereas such tariffs, if they remained in force unchanged for a considerable period of time, would not invalidate the relative form of the theory. For a modern use of the absolute version, however, see H. S. Houthakker, "Exchange Rate Adjustment," in U.S. Congress, Joint Economic Committee, *Factors Affecting the United States Balance of Payments* (Washington, D.C.: Government Printing Office, 1962, pp. 289–304).

calculation is 143/100 divided by 722/100, or 143/722; multiply this by 19.3 cents and the result is 3.82 cents. The French franc was actually stabilized at 3.92 to 3.98 cents, not far from its purchasing power value.

Again, after World War II, there was no commercial exchange rate for the Japanese yen because Japan had not traded with the United States during the war. It was calculated that in 1949 the purchasing power parity value of the Japanese yen was about 350 yen to the dollar. The commercial exchange rate established at that time, 360 yen to the dollar, was maintained until 1971.

On the other hand, calculation of purchasing power parity for the British pound showed that it should have been revalued upward in the late 1940s. Instead, it was devalued by 30 percent in 1949. In this instance purchasing power parity was not a good guide to the appropriate value for the currency. The importance of capital transactions in Britain's balance of payments was great, and loss of foreign investment income after World War II was also important. These factors tended to depress the value of the pound in the short run. In the long run the movement of prices made a lower value for the pound appropriate in terms of purchasing power parity.

For 30 countries, Yeager found that post-World War II exchange rates, using a prewar base period, were never lower than 80 percent or more than 200 percent of purchasing power parity. The ratio of actual rates to purchasing power parity was within the range of 75 to 125 percent for three quarters of the countries, and within 80 to 120 percent for two thirds of the countries.[37] Much earlier, Frank Graham had found that in the early 1920s actual exchange rates did not vary by more than 35 percent from purchasing power parity values in 97 percent of the country-months' rates in his sample. Variation was not over 25 percent in 91.5 percent of the country-months' rates. Some variation is not surprising since random fluctuations occur in the short run, and purchasing power parity theory merely predicts the long-term *trend*; at any given time, a rate may by random fluctuation be above or below the trend.

Defects of Purchasing Power Parity Theory   In evaluating these results further, it may be helpful to consider some of the defects of purchasing power parity theory. First, it is difficult to identify an appropriate base period in which it can be justifiably assumed that the exchange rate was at purchasing power parity. Second, many goods are home goods, not traded goods. Their prices ideally should not be included in an index of purchasing power change, since they do not enter into supply of and demand for foreign exchange arising from trade. Moreover, whether goods are traded or not changes to some extent from time to time. Third, there are statistical defects in price indexes. This not only makes it difficult to calculate purchasing power parity, but it may also explain some of the discrepancies found in empirical attempts to test the theory.

---

[37]Leland B. Yeager, *International Monetary Relations*, 2d ed., p. 222. Yeager was influential in reviving the consideration given to purchasing power parity theory; see Leland B. Yeager, "A Rehabilitation of Purchasing Power Parity," *Journal of Political Economy*, December 1958, pp. 516–530.

Fourth, tariffs and transportation costs change, and these changes should be incorporated into changes in the purchasing power indexes, but normally this is not done because of the difficulty of obtaining data and making the calculations. Finally, and perhaps most important, purchasing power parity indexes measure only the point of equilibrium in the long-run trend in the movement of exchange rates; they take no account of random fluctuations around the trend. The same is true of theories of trend in stock market prices.

Thus in some cases purchasing power parity calculations may be quite wrong in predicting current and immediate future values for currencies.[38]

Additional Considerations   Consideration has been given to factors other than purchasing power parity which may influence the establishment of a new par value for a currency when a devaluation or upvaluation occurs. A country must consider the value of its international reserve assets and their adequacy to meet emergency needs, both before and after devaluation. Moreover, any country which has debt denominated in foreign currencies must consider the size of such foreign debt both before and after revaluation. Devaluation would increase its size in terms of local currency and might create too great a burden of interest and principal repayment. Finally, the psychological effects of a revaluation must be considered. It would be unfortunate, for example, for a government to devalue its currency too little and then have to devalue again in a short time. Hence a devaluation may be slightly greater than necessary, in order to avoid the possibility of a second devaluation if error had occurred. Trading partners of a devaluing country may object to a devaluation if it is too large, however, because it might give too much advantage, in the long run, to the devaluing country's exports.

Monetary Policy Independence under Floating Exchange Rates

We can now consider some implications of the theory of prices, interest rates, and exchange rates for independence of monetary policy under floating exchange rates. This involves the interest rate parity theorem, purchasing power parity theory, and also the quantity theory of money.

Proponents of flexible exchange rates argue that flexibility in rates is necessary if independent monetary policies are to be used in different countries for different domestic purposes. They also argue, however, that speculation will stabilize exchange rates enough that their fluctuations will not be seriously detrimental to world trade and investment. Robert Aliber has suggested that, on the contrary, greater uncertainty concerning exchange rates and greater

[38]According to the calculations reported in Lloyd A. Metzler, "Exchange Rates and the International Monetary Fund," in *International Monetary Policies*, Postwar Economic Studies, No. 7 (Washington, D.C.: Board of Governors of the Federal Reserve System, 1947), the parity rate for the pound sterling would have been either $4.6759 or $5.4946 per pound, depending on the price index used. The rate announced by the IMF was $4.03, and devaluation to $2.80 occurred approximately two years after the date of Metzler's calculations.

volatility in rates are *essential* under flexible rates to permit different monetary policies to be effective for different domestic purposes.[39] Let us examine the basis of his argument.

It is useful to begin with generally accepted long-run relationships. First, when there is full employment, meaning some minimum level of unemployment, a money supply increase tends to raise prices approximately proportionately, because velocity of circulation of money does not change very much, and at full employment real GNP cannot change very much. Since MV equals PT, where MV is the money supply times its velocity of circulation, and PT is nominal GNP, a change in the money supply leads to an approximately proportionate change in prices in the same direction. This proposition is termed the quantity theory of money.

Second, interest rates rise in the long run when money supply increases, and they rise by roughly the same percentage as prices. This is because both lenders and borrowers add an inflation premium to interest rates. Lenders do this to retain their previous *real* rate of return, and borrowers do it because, with rising prices, they expect a nominal profit enough higher than before to enable them to pay the same real rate of interest as before when borrowing funds. This is Fisherian interest rate theory.

In short-run analysis, two models may be considered, that of Keynes and that of Nurkse. Keynes assumed a considerable amount of unemployment and argued that in the short run a money supply increase would usually cause a fall in the interest rate by making more funds available for lending. He argued that, in an open economy involved in international transactions, the exchange value of the local currency would fall in the short run because of capital outflow caused by the fall in the domestic interest rate (assuming that interest rates in other countries did not change). Because Keynes assumed a constant price level when there was considerable unemployment, but also assumed that the exchange value of the local currency would fall, his model involved deviation from the purchasing power parity theorem. Moreover, since he argued that interest rates would fall but that at the same time the exchange value of the currency would fall, his model involved deviation from the interest rate parity theorem. Remember that this theorem states that investors will arbitrage away any differences in yields from interest rates in different countries, on securities with comparable risks, unless the differences are *offset* by changes in exchange rates. This theorem is termed "Fisher open" by some economists, as already noted. To offset a fall in the interest rate, the exchange value of the currency would have to *rise*.

Nurkse accepted the Keynesian theory that a money supply increase would in the short run cause interest rates to fall. He assumed, as did Keynes, that this would lead to a fall in the exchange value of the local currency because of capital outflow. But he argued that prices would rise because of a rise in

[39]Robert Z. Aliber, "Monetary Independence under Floating Exchange Rates," *Journal of Finance*, May 1975, pp. 365–376.

prices of imported goods, which would lead to rises in prices of import-competing goods. Thus the purchasing power parity theorem might hold. Nurkse further argued, along the lines of modern theory, that exchange rates are determined in the short run by *anticipated* exchange rates. Those dealing in foreign exchange markets would expect the exchange value of the local currency to fall because of outflow of capital and, extrapolating this fall, they would move capital abroad. Thus Nurkse's model, like that of Keynes, involves deviation from the interest rate parity theorem.

Aliber used the Keynesian and Nurksian models to suggest that if monetary policy different from that in other countries is to be effective, there *must* be *uncertainty* about movements in exchange rates when monetary policy changes. Otherwise, a money supply increase causing interest rates to fall would, if nothing else occurred, also cause an outflow of capital. But an outflow of capital would prevent interest rates from falling in comparison with interest rates in other countries. If that occurred, the change in monetary policy would be ineffective, since if interest rates remained at their former level, investment, consumption, and GNP would not be stimulated. If, however, because of uncertainty concerning volatility of exchange rates, foreign and domestic securities were *not* perfect substitutes, so that investors would *not* arbitrage away differences in interest rates, monetary policy *could* be effective. The purchasing power parity theorem could hold, as in Nurkse's model, but there would be deviation from the interest rate parity theorem.

We now see the significance of Nurkse's analysis, presented in Chapter 4. With floating exchange rates, there is uncertainty about fluctuations in exchange rates, and therefore foreign and domestic securities are *not* perfect substitutes. Thus investors may *not* fully arbitrage away any changes in differences between interest rates in different countries, and independent monetary policies may be effective. Fisher open does not hold, in Nurksian analysis. Independent monetary policies could not be effective if uncertainty concerning exchange rates were not inherent in a floating rate system.

The differences in the models may be more readily perceived by examining Figure 9-4. Classical theory assumed full employment and hence no changes in *real* variables or in the BOP as a result of a money supply change. In the Keynesian model real output would rise with a money supply increase but it is not clear what would happen to net exports. Imports would rise because of rise in income, but whether exports would rise more than imports is uncertain. In the Nurksian model, the expected exchange rate would fluctuate more than the spot rate, arising from and causing a substantial outflow of capital. The resulting fall in the exchange value of the local currency would lead to a rise in net exports. Foreign countries would use at least some of the borrowed funds to purchase goods from the country which increased its money supply. The effect of a money supply increase on real output would be amplified.

The reasoning thus far implies that uncertainty about exchange rates is necessarily greater under floating rates than under pegged rates if monetary policies differ, and that the uncertainty is what permits different monetary

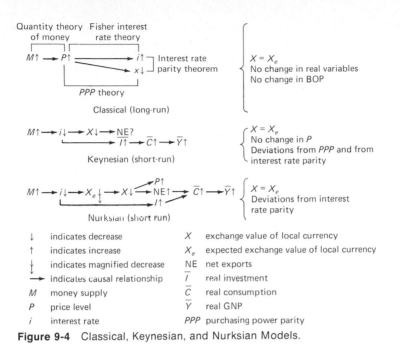

Figure 9-4 Classical, Keynesian, and Nurksian Models.

policies to be effective. It also implies that pegged rates require some degree of coordination of monetary policies among major countries and that flexible exchange rates definitely impose greater burdens on international trade and investment.

Aliber presented evidence that uncertainty concerning exchange rates has been greater under floating rates than under stable but adjustable rates. In particular, restrictive monetary policy in Germany in 1973 led to far more appreciation of the mark than might have been predicted from purchasing power parity. There was heavy capital inflow into Germany as investors apparently anticipated an appreciation of the mark. There was a deviation from interest rate parity; flow of capital did not arbitrage away the difference in interest rates. Speculation in marks was destabilizing, increasing fluctuation in exchange rates; the German mark appreciated 20 percent in several months.

THE EXCHANGE RATE SITUATION SINCE 1970

We may now quickly review other aspects of the exchange rate situation since 1970. Changes in par values in 1971 led to adoption of various policies concerning exchange rates. Since 1973 the world situation has been a mixture of floating rates, pegged rates, controlled rates, and mixtures of these arrangements adopted by various countries. Many currencies are subject to exchange controls.

The absorption approach developed in Chapter 3 may be used advantageously in analyzing the exchange rate situation in the early 1970s. It may be remembered that Alexander argued that current account deficits indicate an excess of absorption (spending) relative to output. Under such a condition a country's BOP position can be improved only by increasing real GNP relative to real absorption. Alexander argued that it is difficult to believe that devaluation is likely to have this effect in significant degree.[40] An excess of absorption over GNP means an excess of domestic investment over saving.[41] If devaluation is to improve a BOP situation in such circumstances, it must either increase saving or decrease domestic investment, or both, or it must increase saving more than investment. When expenditures exceed GNP, individuals and business firms are reducing their cash balances, and with smaller cash balances the same volume of domestic spending can continue only with an increase in the velocity of circulation of money or an increase in the money supply. Thus the analysis leads to a focus on the monetary approach.

Policy conclusions of some economists may be related to this view. An example is the argument of Mundell.[42] He argued that until about 1960 two undervalued assets, gold and U.S. dollars, served as money for the world economy. The value of the U.S. dollar in the foreign exchange market was below what it should have been in terms of purchasing power parity, since the United States had less inflation than any major industrial country. After 1965, the U.S. dollar became overvalued in the foreign exchange market relative to gold, as the rate of increase in the money supply in the United States rose. The easy money policy of the Federal Reserve System (needed to meet government spending) led to a glut of dollars in the world economy. With the breakdown of the Bretton Woods system, there was no ceiling on world monetary reserves, because there was no reason for private parties to continue to hold U.S. dollars in excess of desired transactions balances. Until 1973, dollars sold by private parties were purchased by central banks, and total world reserves shot up, as shown in Figure 9-5. Almost all of the increase was in foreign exchange, chiefly U.S. dollars. The result was the world inflation of 1973 and 1974, which abated only slowly thereafter in most countries.

Mundell's solution was twofold: (1) put a ceiling on the growth of the *world* money supply, in which he included Eurodollars as well as dollars held in the United States, and (2) stimulate production in the United States through tax cuts for business firms, designed to induce them to increase output and employment and to reduce the outward flow of capital from the United States resulting from the undervalued dollar. Capital outflow again emerged as a result of the devaluations of 1971 and 1973 and speculation against the dollar after 1973.

---

[40]S. S. Alexander, "Effects of a Devaluation on a Trade Balance," IMF *Staff Papers*, April 1952, pp. 263–278, and "Effects of a Devaluation: A Simplified Synthesis of Elasticities and Absorption Approaches," *American Economic Review*, March 1959, pp. 22–42.

[41]J. Black, "A Savings and Investment Approach to Devaluation," *Economic Journal*, June 1959, pp. 267–274.

[42]A very clear statement of these views is Robert Mundell, "World Money and the Optimum Policy Mix," First National Bank of Chicago *Report*, May 1975.

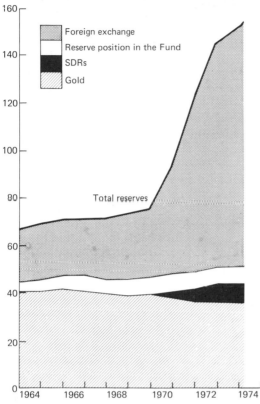

Figure 9-5 Level and Composition of Reserves, End of Period, 1963–First Quarter 1974 (in billions of SDRs). (*Source:* IMF, *Annual Report*, 1974, p. 33.)

Michael Keran has suggested that both the world inflation of 1973–1974 and the simultaneous recession in the United States in 1973–1975 may be explained by the fact that the world money supply increased much more rapidly than the U.S. money supply.[43] The increase in the world money supply led to world inflation. World inflation caused a resumption of inflation in the United States because of the rapid rise in prices of goods imported into this country (not only oil, but also many other products) and the rapid rise in prices of U.S. export goods because of increased foreign demand—for example, for food. The less rapid increase in the U.S. money supply led to slower increase in output in the United States and to some shifts from home goods production to export goods production. Thus world inflation, U.S. inflation, and simultaneously a U.S. recession are not inconsistent.

Keran found that an equation which included the U.S. money supply and a measure of world money supply (he used monetary reserves of major industrial countries as a proxy for world money supply) accurately tracked the trend of

[43]Michael W. Keran, "Towards an Explanation of Simultaneous Inflation-Recession," Federal Reserve Bank of San Francisco, *Economic Review*, Spring 1975, pp. 18–30.

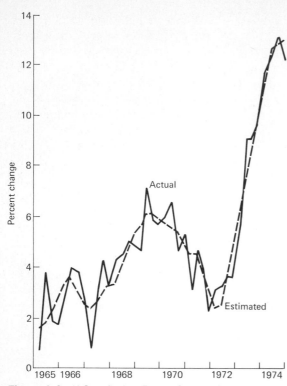

Figure 9-6   U.S. Inflation Rate. (*Source:* Federal Reserve Bank of San Francisco, *Business Review*, Spring 1975, p. 26.)

U.S. inflation after 1965 and predicted the rapid inflation of 1973–1974, as shown in Figure 9-6.

He also answered two anticipated questions: (1) Why must world money supply now be included as a determinant of U.S. inflation when it was not so included in the past, and when past U.S. inflation had been relatively accurately predicted by using only *domestic* money supply as the major determinant? (2) If world money supply increases faster than domestic money supply, why does this not lead to higher world prices (quantity theory of money) and a BOP surplus for the United States, and hence, with floating exchange rates, an appreciation of the U.S. dollar, offsetting for the United States the influence of the rise in world prices? In other words, why didn't purchasing power parity theory work to determine the exchange rate for the U.S. dollar? He answered the first question by pointing out that only recently has the world money supply, as measured by the proxy of world monetary reserves, risen so dramatically. Its past influence was little different from that of domestic money supply. He answered the second question by arguing that capital flows adverse to the dollar were important in determining the exchange value of the U.S. dollar after early 1973, and that this is why it did not rise in value, but fell.

Keran's imaginative and provocative analysis is plausible although not conclusive. It might be inferred from his analysis that, in the absence of additional major changes, inflation in the United States might slow down, and the exchange value of the dollar might then rise in line with long-run purchasing power parity. This may have been what was occurring in the mid-1970s.

To summarize: it appears that the glut of dollars depressed the value of the U.S. dollar in world foreign exchange markets. Relatively low returns on financial assets in the United States led to anticipation of future low returns and further depressed demand for U.S. dollars. It might be inferred that if inflation moderates in the United States and if U.S. productivity resumes its long-run rate of increase, the long-run equilibrium value of the U.S. dollar in foreign exchange markets should rise from the levels of the mid-1970s. Concomitantly, returns on financial assets in the United States should rise and this should attract world capital to the United States, contributing to the rise in the value of the U.S. dollar. The next decade will be an interesting period in which to see whether these possibilities are realized.

One further point should be made. International capital flows cannot be analyzed simply in terms of relative changes in interest rates. The theory of financial decisions based on expected returns discounted at appropriate interest rates is examined in Parts Four and Five. This analysis helps to illuminate the problem of financing economic development and the outlook for world finance, discussed in Part Six.

QUESTIONS FOR DISCUSSION

1 Explain exactly why the rate at which time drafts are purchased by banks from exporters and others must be below the rate at which sight drafts are purchased in similar transactions.
2 What is the difference between the margin established in the situation in question 1 and the "discount" on drafts drawn on local currency and sold to banks?
3 Does a foreign exchange trader make his profit (if any) from sale of one currency and purchase of another, or must he calculate his profit from the price at which he purchased a currency and the price at which he sold it? Explain your answer.
4 Precisely what is meant by *spot* exchange rates? Exactly how do they differ from forward rates?
5 What is the distinction between the par value of a currency, established with the IMF if a country is a member, and the market value of the currency?
6 Construct an example to indicate the possibility of backward-sloping sections of supply curves in the foreign exchange market.
7 What are the arguments for and against flexible exchange rates? Offer your evaluation of the conclusion quoted in the chapter from *The Santa Colomba Conclusions 1975* that a mixed system is likely to emerge in the future.
8 Do you think it likely that the usefulness of purchasing power parity calculations in determining appropriate par values when these are established has increased in the last half century or diminished? Why?
9 In what ways is the foreign exchange market analogous to the stock market? In

what ways is it different? To what extent are exchange rates influenced by anticipated income, discounted at some appropriate interest rate?

10 What are the reasons for a single currency in the United States, but not including Canada? What would be the advantage of including Canada in a single currency area, if it were agreeable to Canadians? Would the same arguments apply to the inclusion of Mexico? Explain.

PROBLEM

Prepare an analysis of the downward float of the Mexican peso in the latter half of 1976, using theory explained in this chapter, and considering the various factors which probably caused this float. Should this float have been foreseen? If so, when? Give evidence that it should or should not have been. Then trace subsequent developments concerning the exchange value of the peso. Finally, consider the factors affecting the peso's future value, and comment on any possible trend which you can foresee.

In view of purchasing power parity changes between the Mexican peso and the U.S. dollar and in view of interest rates in the United States and in Mexico, what comment can you make about interest rate parity theory for the period 1955–1975, as respects this particular currency and relative interest rates?

SUGGESTED REFERENCES

For a detailed discussion of foreign exchange and foreign exchange markets, see Norman Crump, *The ABC of the Foreign Exchanges*, 13th ed. (London: Macmillan, 1963). An interesting historical review is Paul Einzig, *The History of Foreign Exchange* (London: Macmillan, 1962). For the more practical aspects, see the booklet by Alan R. Holmes and Francis H. Schott, *The New York Foreign Exchange Market* (New York: Federal Reserve Bank of New York, 1965).

Leland B. Yeager, *International Monetary Relations*, 2d ed. (New York: Harper & Row, 1976), Chaps. 11–14 presents thorough coverage of many of the issues discussed in this chapter. Charles N. Henning, *International Finance* (New York: Harper & Row, 1958), Chaps. 12 and 13, is still useful for discussion of some of these topics.

A good, brief, and recent discussion of purchasing power parity is contained in Richard E. Caves and Ronald W. Jones, *World Trade and Payments: An Introduction* (Boston: Little, Brown, 1973), pp. 333–339.

The theoretical arguments for flexible exchange rates were set forth by Milton Friedman, *Essays in Positive Economics* (Chicago: University of Chicago Press, 1953). The argument was further elaborated by Egon Sohmen, *Flexible Exchange Rates* (Chicago: University of Chicago Press, 1961). Opposing arguments are more scattered. Among older writings, Benjamin M. Anderson, *Economics and the Public Welfare* (Princeton: Van Nostrand, 1949) is notable, and the awarding of the Nobel prize to Friedrich A. von Hayek focused attention on his writings; see the reference to him in fn. 23 in this chapter. See also Samuel I. Katz, *The Case for the Par Value System, 1972*, Essays in International Finance, No. 92 (Princeton: Princeton, 1972). Katz argued that the par value system gave governments the option of choosing either demand-management policies or exchange rate policies in dealing with situations involving both internal and external stabilization problems.

A highly theoretical but stimulating discussion of the foreign exchange market is Jerome L. Stein, *The Nature and Efficiency of the Foreign Exchange Market*, Essays in International Finance, No. 40 (Princeton: Princeton, 1962).

A detailed discussion of the situation in foreign exchange markets after 1973 is Samuel I. Katz, *'Managed Floating' as an Interim International Exchange Rate Regime, 1973–1975*, New York University, Bulletin 1975-3 (New York: New York University, 1975).

Laffer's view that devaluation leads primarily to inflation in the devaluing country inspired a number of different views and criticisms; for a brief discussion see Arthur B. Laffer, "The Bitter Fruits of Devaluation," *Wall Street Journal*, Jan. 10, 1974, p. 10, and the letters from Milton Friedman, Gottfried Haberler, Henry M. Goldstein, and Victor A. Mack, *Wall Street Journal*, Feb. 5, 1974, p. 16. The argument of Michael Keran (see the reference in fn. 43) points out some specific reasons why the cause of world inflation may have been the sharp increase in the world money supply together with capital flows adverse to the dollar. In this context devaluation is less important and perhaps unnecessary to the argument. Clearly, currency depreciation means higher prices for some or all imports, but this is not proof that devaluation *causes* inflation. With fixed exchange rates, some inflationary pressure is absorbed by increased imports, which may lead to some inflation in foreign countries. With currency depreciation, net imports are presumably reduced. The *cause* of the inflation is monetary and fiscal policies; exchange rate policies simply determine whether the inflation is confined to the one country or "exported" in part to other countries. For careful analysis of this, see Hang-Sheng Cheng, "Depreciation=Inflation?" Federal Reserve Bank of San Francisco, *Business & Financial Letter,* May 20, 1977.

Chapter 10

International Financial Centers and Money Markets

For many years foreign lenders and borrowers have participated, usually on a relatively small scale, in financial markets of a number of countries.[1] In many places in the world international financial centers developed where there was extensive activity in international finance by both domestic and foreign financial institutions.[2] Until the 1950s, in spite of the existence of such centers, there were no truly international financial markets; there were no financial markets in currencies traded outside their countries of origin.

The first truly international money market was the Eurodollar market, so named because some European banks, at first chiefly British banks in London, began to accept deposits and make loans denominated in U.S. dollars. Later, these and other banks began to accept deposits in other currencies, for example, sterling, Deutsche marks, and Swiss francs, in each case outside the country of the currency involved. The term Eurocurrency or Eurocurrencies became more appropriate than Eurodollars to designate these markets. Still later, markets for these currencies developed outside Europe, in such places as

---

[1]For a discussion of foreign participation in money and capital markets, see Roland I. Robinson, *Money and Capital Markets* (New York: McGraw-Hill, 1964), pp. 340 ff. At the time that book was published, the Eurodollar market was much less important than now.

[2]For two recent studies, see Charles P. Kindleberger, "The Formation of Financial Centers: A Study in Comparative Economic History," Massachusetts Institute of Technology, Department of Economics, *Working Paper No. 114*, August 1973; and Harry G. Johnson, "Panama as a Regional Financial Center," *Economic Development and Cultural Change*, January 1976, pp. 261–286.

the Caribbean area and Panama, and in certain financial centers elsewhere. The entire market might better be called the offshore or external currency market, but the earlier names are likely to remain widely used.

Bonds denominated in currencies other than that of the country in which the bonds were issued also came into existence, with the development of what came to be termed the Eurobond market. Discussion of that market is deferred to Chapter 12 with other discussion of long-term investment.

MONEY AND MONEY MARKETS

Clarification concerning the terms money and money markets may be helpful in understanding the nature of the Eurodollar market.

Money

Money is generally defined in one of two ways: (1) The older definition of money is that it is whatever is used for final settlement of debts; (2) a more recent definition is that money is that aggregate of liquid assets which has the best correlation of changes in its stock with changes in business activity or GNP. The first definition of money limits it generally to currency (meaning coins and paper money) and demand deposits, since almost all final settlement of debts occurs through transfer of those assets. Purchases made on credit, including the use of bank and other credit cards, require payment of money narrowly defined for final settlement of the debt created. Money narrowly defined has come to be designated as M_1 (coins and paper money alone are sometimes designated as M_0).

The second definition does not clearly circumscribe what should be included in money, but M_1 plus time deposits in commercial banks minus large (over $100,000 each) negotiable CDs has come to be widely used as an aggregate meeting the conditions of the second definition, and has been designated as M_2. Large negotiable CDs are excluded because they are in the nature of money market instruments like Treasury bills and other short-term debt instruments; time deposits in commercial banks can be quickly converted into demand deposits and then used for spending.

Other definitions of money exist. An example is M_3, which is M_2 plus accounts held in mutual savings banks, savings and loan associations, and credit unions.

The reason for concern about a precise definition of money is that money is either used for spending (M_1), is readily converted into assets which can be so used (the remainder of M_2, time deposits in commercial banks), or perhaps can significantly influence spending because it constitutes relatively liquid wealth. Since total spending equals total income (national income or GNP), control of the size of the stock of money might permit control of total spending and hence of GNP. Of course, turnover or velocity of money is also important, and velocity varies, especially in the short run. Hence control over the stock of money does not necessarily mean control over spending in the short run.

Monetarist economists emphasize the importance of variations in the size of the money stock in the long run, and tend to prefer a fixed rate of growth in the money stock. Nonmonetarist economists tend to emphasize the variations in velocity and to prefer a discretionary monetary policy aimed at achieving a desired rate of increase in spending by careful control of the size of the money stock, but with attention also given to variations in velocity and to interest rates.

Recently, the nature of money as a means of final settlement of debts has begun to change somewhat. Mutual savings banks and savings and loan associations in the United States have begun to institute means of paying certain bills directly from funds held in those institutions. As an electronic funds transfer system (EFTS) comes into general use, it may be possible to make payments from such funds as easily as from demand deposits in banks, depending on the position which nonbank institutions attain in EFTS. The history of money has been a long history of change in the instruments used to settle debts; the importance of demand deposits increased greatly over a long period of years as checks became more widely used. This process still continues. In some countries checks are still very little used, and a shift to checks could take place for a considerable time. Thus, unfortunately, what is money may be subject to institutional factors.

One final point should be made concerning the use of the terms money supply or money stock. Money stock is technically more correct, since what is meant is the entire stock of money available in a country or other area. Money supply does not mean supply offered for exchange, as is the case when the term supply is used in supply and demand analysis of prices. Thus when there is discussion of the supply of and demand for money, supply means the total stock of money, whether used for payments or held for transactions, precautionary, or speculative purposes. The theory that interest rates are determined by liquidity preference, or the demand for money relative to its stock, is thus a stock theory, not a flow theory.[3]

Money Markets

Financial markets are often designated as money markets or capital markets. The former are the markets in which short-term financial assets are accepted by lenders, while borrowers obtain money. The latter are the longer-term markets in which long-term financial assets, such as bonds, mortgages, and stocks, are issued and traded. Although the distinction between short-term and long-term markets is arbitrary, money markets are usually defined as those in which instruments traded mature within one year. Capital markets involve instruments which mature in more than one year.

Thus money markets are not markets for money, but markets for short-term credit instruments: that is, they are markets in which lenders offer

[3]Relationships of the theories of interest to money market concepts are discussed in Charles N. Henning, William Pigott, and Robert Haney Scott, *Financial Markets and the Economy* (Englewood Cliffs, N.J.: Prentice-Hall, 1975), Chap. 9, "The Money Market," and Chap. 12, "The Determination of the Level of Interest Rates."

money and borrowers obtain money in exchange for short-term debt instruments. The debt instruments may be obligations of the government, such as Treasury bills (short-term government securities); obligations of banks, such as CDs and bank acceptances; or obligations of business firms or certain types of financial institutions, such as commercial paper.

The "loanable funds" theory—that short-term interest rates are determined by the supply of and demand for funds in money markets—is a flow theory. It is easily understandable because it states that short-term interest rates are determined by the supply of funds flowing into money markets from lenders and by the demand for funds as evidenced by the short-term credit instruments offered by holders or issuers of such instruments (borrowers).

A final source of confusion is the use of such a term as "tight money."[4] Tight money does not mean a relatively high demand for money in the sense in which that phrase is used in the liquidity preference theory of interest rates. It means a relatively high demand for *loanable funds* by borrowers relative to the supply of loanable funds from lenders, and hence relatively high interest rates.

With these comments concerning definitions of terms in mind, we discuss first the foreign influences in domestic money markets, especially in the U.S. money market, and then an international money market, the Eurodollar market, which developed after World War II.

FOREIGN INFLUENCES IN DOMESTIC MONEY MARKETS

Foreign influences in domestic money markets must always be considered in any complete analysis of such markets. Although the major part of the supply of funds may come from saving out of prior income and creation of new money by commercial banks, foreigners provide part of the supply of loanable funds. Foreigners also create part of the demand for such funds by offering short-term debt instruments for purchase.

Only a thin line, if any, separates demand deposits from money market instruments such as time deposits. In the United States, payment of interest on demand deposits by banks has been prohibited since the 1930s, although legislation has been proposed to again permit such payment of interest. When foreigners supply funds to the United States and hold demand deposits, it is generally assumed that their motive is to hold transactions balances—deposits which they need for making payments. In foreign countries in which interest is paid on demand deposits, it is not so easy to determine whether the balances are held for transactions or for other purposes, presumably for interest income.

Transactions Balances

Foreigners who hold demand deposits are holding part of the narrowly defined money supply (M_1), and in fact their deposits are counted as part of the U.S. money supply whether the demand deposits are held in commercial banks or in Federal Reserve Banks. Foreign banks need dollar deposits so that they can

---

[4]"Use of the Word 'Money,' " Federal Reserve Bank of St. Louis, *Review*, October 1963, p. 7.

easily make payments to U.S. firms and individuals, and large foreign firms may hold deposits for the same purpose. Central banks and governments need dollar deposits, the former for foreign exchange operations and the latter usually for purchases of goods and services. Because relatively large dollar balances are held by foreigners, the dollar has come to be the most important *vehicle* currency (used for payments by private parties), *reserve* currency (held by central banks or governments for emergency use), and *intervention* currency (sold by foreign central banks to purchase and thus support the exchange value of their own currencies, or bought when they wish to dispose of their own currencies to prevent a rise in their exchange values).

Foreign Lending

In addition to transactions and precautionary purposes, money and other short-term assets are held by foreigners for other motives—to gain interest income, presumably higher than in their own countries; to profit from a rise in the exchange value of the U.S. dollar; to avoid losses from devaluation or depreciation of foreign currencies or from confiscation of financial assets; and perhaps for other reasons. Desire for income, desire for profit from an anticipated rise in value, and fear of loss or confiscation of assets all play a part in short-term capital flows. The first may be termed interest arbitrage, the second speculation, and the third capital flight. A final motive may be a desire for liquidity; if the supply of liquid assets in foreign countries is relatively small, foreigners may send funds to the United States to acquire liquid assets (demand deposits or money market instruments).

Even if interest rates are higher in one country than in another, leading to a flow of funds to the country with higher interest rates, there is usually some risk involved that the exchange value of the currency of the country with relatively high interest rates may fall. If such a fall occurs, it could well offset the gain from the higher interest rate when funds are returned to the home countries. Hence such investment of money market funds is likely to be *covered* investment, in which dollar exchange is sold forward at the same time that spot dollars are purchased to invest in, say, the U.S. money market. Banks are the institutions most likely to be involved in this type of investment, because they typically have large amounts of funds which they wish to hold in liquid form to meet possible needs, but on which they nevertheless wish to earn the highest possible short-term interest rate.

Business firms engage in some investing of this type. They also at times hold foreign currencies in the form of accounts receivable, whenever they sell on credit and price the sales in foreign currencies. Unlike other short-term capital flows, accounts receivable normally do not appear in BOPs, because data on short-term capital flows are collected from banks rather than from business firms.

Foreign Borrowing

Why do firms and banks from foreign countries borrow in the short-term market? Until recently, the amount of such borrowing was not large, because business firms usually dealt with banks they were familiar with. The increase in offshore lending by U.S. commercial banks has made loans to foreign firms, financial institutions, and governments and government agencies more significant. Even so, there has generally been more concern with foreign lending in the money market than with foreign borrowing. It has been assumed that relatively low short-term interest rates are likely to result in a fall in the supply of funds from foreigners and hence perhaps a fall in the exchange value of a country's currency. Short-term interest rates are usually low during recessions, and central banks are tempted to try to raise them as a means of supporting the exchange value of the currency, unless they are permitting the exchange rate to float. Raising long-term interest rates would discourage investment, and this is not desired; but raising short-term rates might attract foreign funds, and hence provide additional funds for investment, as well as support the exchange value of the currency.

Although the IMF does not usually directly enter foreign exchange markets, it does hold balances in the form of deposits or credits payable in deposits in the central banks of member countries. When countries wish to borrow from the IMF to meet emergency needs, they supply more of their own currencies to the IMF and withdraw from the IMF the currencies which they need. This increases their central banks' holdings of the needed currencies. As their central banks use those currencies, the funds get into private hands and are used or can be used to make payments for goods, services, and financial assets. Thus the money supply in the hands of the public tends to rise in a country whose currency is loaned to other countries' central banks, and the exchange value of that country's currency tends to rise in the short run. Of course, its exchange value may fall in the long run if the increase in the money supply leads to inflation and if long-run trends in exchange rates do in fact correlate with purchasing power parity.

If all countries wanted dollars, as almost all did in the years just after World War II, we might have had the "scarce currency" situation envisioned in the IMF agreement. However, the United States at that time provided dollars in the form of a loan to Britain, Marshall Plan aid to Europe, aid to Greece and Turkey, and occupation funds spent in Germany, Japan, and Korea, thus creating greater stability; and the scarce currency provisions were never brought into force.

INTERNATIONAL FINANCIAL CENTERS

Before discussing the Eurodollar market and the reasons for its centering in London, it will be helpful to discuss international financial centers and the factors that have influenced their growth.

Some cities have developed into major international financial centers because they have major financial institutions such as banks, insurance companies, and securities dealers; foreign banks participate in their activities; they provide a sizable market for foreign exchange; and they have good communications facilities and related institutions and activities needed for international financing. Some of the related institutions are shipping companies, commodity brokers, and accounting and legal firms. An international financial center also almost always has a relatively favorable regulatory environment, with only limited formal restraint on financial transactions exercised by the government, and a currency that is relatively widely accepted or at least convertible into widely accepted currencies.

London as a Major International Financial Center

London achieved preeminence as the world international financial center in the eighteenth and nineteenth centuries and has maintained its prominence since that time. Even today, although New York is a major international financial center, there are many ways in which London's position is equally significant. It has an important private gold market, and its banks and dealers trade in foreign exchange on a very large scale.

London's financial institutions which are engaged in international finance are supported by a unique infrastructure of accounting, legal, insuring, shipping, and securities firms. To take one well-known example, Lloyd's of London is a household word in insurance.

The British government has encouraged the further development of London as an international financial center, partly because the income from banking and related services helps Britain's BOP position.[5]

Regulation of financial activities is characterized by a minimum of formal requirements. Enterprises which want to carry on banking activities must obtain permission from the Department of Trade and Industry, and banks (both British and foreign) which wish to deal in foreign exchange must obtain permission from the British central bank, the Bank of England. But much limitation is simply traditional; by custom, banks engage in banking but not in commerce and industry. There is no banking act similar to the National Banking Act in the United States.

The Bank of England is responsible for the coordination and implementation of monetary policy. General monetary policy is formulated by the Treasury under the Chancellor of the Exchequer. The Bank of England was nationalized in 1946, but the Treasury does not appear to use very extensively its power to issue directives to the bank.

Banking in Britain is similar in many ways to banking in the United States. The payments mechanism is more advanced in some ways, since standing orders can be used to make periodic payments and one check plus instructions can be used to have banks make payments to various parties. A major difference is the concentration of British banking in a few banks. The four largest clearing banks—major banks which act as clearing banks for payments

---

[5]For discussion of benefits and costs of international financial activity in Britain, see Benjamin J. Cohen, "Sterling and the City," *The Banker*, February 1970, pp. 183–193; "The Benefits and Costs of Sterling," *Euromoney*, September 1969, pp. 10–12; and "Measuring the Benefits and Costs of Sterling," *Euromoney*, April 1970, pp. 39–43. Although most of Cohen's analysis concerns benefits of sterling as an international currency, he discusses other financial activity, including activity in the Eurodollar market.

to and from other banks and other financial institutions through accounts maintained with the Bank of England—hold about five-eighths of the total deposits of residents of the United Kingdom. (In the United States, the largest 25 banks hold less than half of total deposits.) Other banks, termed merchant banks, are not legally defined, but generally specialize in some type of financial activity and clear their payments through the clearing banks. Other enterprises may be licensed by the Department of Trade and Industry to act as banks, but usually also specialize in their financial activities; an example is hire purchase or sales finance and consumer loan companies.[6]

Most international banking is carried out by overseas banks operating in London and extensively in foreign countries. Some of these banks are now owned by the clearing banks; an example is Barclays International. Hongkong and Shanghai Bank, still considered a British bank although registered in Hong Kong, is independent. These banks are active on an almost worldwide basis, which is true of only a few U.S. banks. For example, Barclays Bank operates in about 50 countries compared to about 100 countries for Citibank, but there are a number of other British banks with activities in many countries.

London's importance as an international financial center does not rest entirely on the activities of British banks. By the end of 1974 nearly 250 foreign banks from more than 50 countries operated in London.

Bank for International Settlements (BIS) data show foreign currency deposit liabilities of banks in the United Kingdom to be about half of the total of banks in major European countries which hold such deposits. About three-fourths of the Eurocurrency deposits in the United Kingdom are Eurodollars, as discussed in the next section of this chapter. U.S. banks operating in the United Kingdom have about 40 percent of total Eurocurrency deposits.

Other Important International Financial Centers

Many other international financial centers have developed, and in every major country there are international financial centers which are the focus of foreign exchange dealings in those countries. New York as an international financial center was described in Chapter 9.[7] Paris, Zurich, Luxembourg, and some other centers in Europe are especially important. Beirut in the Middle East for a long time was a center for international banking and for foreign exchange and gold dealings; with civil war in Lebanon in 1975, there has been considerable discussion of other potential centers in the general area—for example, Cairo, Bahrain, and Teheran.[8]

---

[6]A useful brief description of the types of financial intermediaries in London may be found in William M. Weiant, *London—An Examination of an International Financial Center* (New York: Blyth Eastman Dillon, 1975).

[7]In addition to New York, the West Coast of the United States has recently developed into a regional international center: see Hang-Sheng Cheng, "U.S. West Coast as an International Financial Center," Federal Reserve Bank of San Francisco, *Economic Review*, Spring 1976, pp. 9–19.

[8]See, for example, Monroe J. Haegele, "Iran's Potential as a Financial Center," *International Finance*, Chase Manhattan Bank, Feb. 23, 1976, pp. 7–8.

Hong Kong, Singapore, and Tokyo are important international financial centers in Asia. The role of Singapore is described later in this chapter in the section on Asian financial centers.

Panama, in Central America, is a center of some importance, as is Nassau, in the Bahamas in the Caribbean.

The importance of relative freedom from strict government control and of stability and strength of the local currency cannot be overemphasized as factors in the development of international financial centers, although volume of commerce and availability of related activities such as legal services are significant.

Some international financial centers, for example, Nassau and the Cayman Islands in the Caribbean, are centers because of favorable tax laws. Such centers have little potential for development into major international financial centers, and may lose importance if tax havens become sufficiently annoying to major countries to cause changes in tax laws in those countries, reducing or eliminating the use of tax havens.

Financial centers in Switzerland, Germany, and some other places are limited to some extent by actions of the governments to discourage inflows of potentially disruptive funds. These countries have feared that inflows of funds may cause "imported inflation," and they are also somewhat fearful of potential problems arising if such funds are later withdrawn.

EURODOLLARS

Dollars deposited in banks in countries outside the United States are generally termed Eurodollars; sometimes the term Asian dollars has been applied to dollars deposited in Asia. The term Eurodollar is still somewhat appropriate since most of the deposits are in European banks.[9]

Origin of the Eurodollar Market

To understand why the Eurodollar market came into existence and grew as rapidly as it did after the 1950s, it is useful to begin with the concept of financial intermediation. Financial institutions enable borrowers to obtain loanable funds provided by ultimate lenders or created by banks. As intermediaries, financial institutions provide financial assets, such as bank deposits, which meet lenders' desires for safety, liquidity, and income. At the same time, they hold financial assets which meet borrowers' desires for funds at minimum interest rates for the term of borrowing and the risks involved. Banks and all

---

[9]The story that the name Eurodollars arose from deposit of funds coming from a Paris bank which served the Russian state bank is labeled as "possibly apocryphal but nevertheless plausible" in Joseph C. Kvasnicka, "Eurodollars—An Important Source of Funds for American Banks," Federal Reserve Bank of Chicago, *Business Conditions*, June 1969, pp. 9–20. He indicated that a major supplier of dollar deposits to European banks in the early 1950s was a bank in Paris which served the Russian state bank; this Banque Commerciale pour l'Europe du Nord, S.A., whose international cable code was "Eurobank," naturally used its cable code in international transfers of dollars, and foreign bankers came to refer to dollar deposits obtained from it as "Eurodollars."

other major financial institutions are intermediaries; banks are unique because they both accept funds and create deposits, and once they have created demand deposits the public cannot, with minor exceptions, reduce the amount of such deposits in existence.

Effective Intermediation The major reason for the establishment and growth of the Eurodollar market was the effective intermediation by European, especially British, banks. They were able to offer to hold deposits from lenders in the form of Eurodollar deposits at attractive interest rates. They also offered a high degree of safety and liquidity. On the other hand, they were able to make loans which borrowers sought at relatively low interest rates. Resulting profit margins of the banks were rather narrow, but as the volume of activity increased, total profits became sizable. The spread between loan rates and deposit interest rates was generally much smaller than the corresponding spread for U.S. banks.

Several other factors contributed to growth of the Eurodollar market and should not be ignored.

Deposit Interest Rate Ceilings in the United States Ceilings on interest rates which could be paid by U.S. banks on time deposits contributed to the growth of the Eurodollar market because they prevented U.S. banks from competing for the deposits. The United States imposed, in the 1930s, along with the prohibition of payment of interest on demand deposits, a provision for interest rate ceilings for time deposits. Ceiling rates were specified by the Federal Reserve System through Regulation Q. The announced reason for the rate ceilings was to prevent banks from paying too much interest on deposits and thus being tempted to make risky loans on which they could charge high interest rates in an attempt to increase profits. As time passed, it became evident that ceiling rates were also needed for interest rates paid by savings and loan associations and mutual savings banks unless such institutions were to be enabled to attract large amounts of funds away from commercial banks. In order to somewhat favor the housing industry, these institutions were permitted to pay slightly more interest than commercial banks.

Because higher interest rates could be obtained in London on deposits denominated in dollars, it was advantageous for Americans and foreigners who had deposits in the United States to transfer funds. In the 1960s regulations were imposed to prevent such transfers by Americans, but restrictions could not be imposed on foreigners without making the dollar an "inconvertible" currency; under the IMF agreement a government could not impose restrictions on current account payments to foreign countries if its currency were to be deemed convertible.

The Desire of British Banks to Maintain Their Position A second factor contributing to the development of the Eurodollar market was the desire of British banks to maintain their position in international financial markets. As financing in sterling declined, it appeared that British banks might lose this position. But the position could be maintained if substantial financing were done through the United Kingdom, even if not in sterling. By offering to hold Eurodollar deposits, British banks attracted funds, both because the banks were well known and of high standing, and because the deposits could be in dollars, which were desired because of their wide use and generally high status. The British government did not interfere with the banks' effort, as it might have done by using exchange controls.

Fear of Blocking of Balances Held in the United States   A third factor contributing to growth of Eurodollar deposits in some instances was that some who held or received dollars (that is, deposits in U.S. banks or claims on such deposits) feared that these deposits might be blocked or frozen in the event of international conflict.[10] How important this factor may have been is not clear; in any event, it was rather small and operated only in certain instances. The British government was not likely to restrict deposits, since growth of such deposits was a means of maintaining foreign income generated from banking and related services, and such income helped Britain's BOP.

Confidence in the Vehicle Currency   A fourth factor in the development of the Eurodollar market was that confidence in the U.S. dollar, the major vehicle currency, was sufficient to encourage those who made Eurodollar deposits to believe that risk of long-run decline in their value was not great enough to cause them to refrain from holding such deposits.

Some have argued that a deficit in the U.S. BOP was also essential for the development of the Eurodollar market, but this is not theoretically correct.[11] Foreigners could hold dollars for liquidity, transactions, or investment and still make a separate decision to place these dollars in banks outside the United States. Of course, one factor was that large U.S. BOP deficits meant the transfer of large dollar balances to foreigners, since this provided dollar balances which foreigners could then decide to hold, to spend, or to place elsewhere. With removal of controls on Americans placing funds abroad, the growth of the Eurodollar market depends also on decisions by Americans.

Nature of the Eurodollar Market

The Eurodollar market developed rapidly, and soon billions of dollars were on deposit in London and in other centers. Banks in other European countries, and

---

[10]Onc authority states that Communist-controlled banks were prominent among early depositors in the Eurodollar market, and that "the view was widely held that the main object was to conceal from the American authorities the size of their dollar holdings by disguising them as the holdings of London or Paris banks. In redepositing their dollars, Communist banks wished to safeguard themselves against the risk of a seizure of their funds by the United States authorities in case of an aggravation of the Cold War." See Paul Einzig, *The Euro-Dollar System,* 5th ed. (New York: St. Martin's Press, 1973), p. 30.

[11]Carl H. Stem, "The Euro-Dollar System: An Analysis of its Credit Function and Impact on the International Financial Position in the United States," unpublished doctoral dissertation, Harvard University, 1968.

later elsewhere, found they could obtain funds for lending by accepting such deposits. The lack of regulation, almost a sine qua non for the market's existence, encouraged transfers of funds whenever advantageous. With lack of regulation, governments had no regulatory reason to collect data; hence estimates of the size of the Eurodollar market usually used are those provided by the Bank for International Settlements (BIS) and by Morgan Guaranty Trust Company.

How Eurodollar Deposits Come into Existence   To understand the origin of Eurodollar deposits, examine Figure 10-1. Part *a* shows the most common way in which Eurodollar deposits arise. A person or institution having a deposit in a U.S. bank withdraws it and transfers the funds to a Eurodollar account in a London bank (1). The London bank thus obtains a deposit in a U.S. bank (2). Ownership of the deposit is transferred to the London bank. The total amount of deposits in the United States does not change, but obviously the transactions velocity of money in the United States increases.[12] Since most Eurodollar deposits arc time deposits, there is little or no change in the money supply in the United Kingdom, if money supply means M_1.

Milton Friedman tried to show that the process of adding to Eurodollars is very much like the process of creation of money by banks.[13] If depositors feel that interest rates in U.S. banks are too low and thereupon transfer accounts to, say, London branches of those banks, in which higher interest can be paid, new Eurodollar deposits come into existence without any change in total liabilities of the U.S. banks. This is shown in Figure 10-1*b*.

It seems likely, however, that in most cases Eurodollar deposits in foreign branches do not arise in this manner, but arc sought by the branches, which may not know the source of the deposits until they have obtained them.[14] Thus branches may acquire deposits formerly held in their own home offices or may not. In any event, when a foreign branch of a U.S. bank obtains Eurodollar deposits, it obtains title simultaneously to a demand deposit in a U.S. bank. Unless this bank is the branch's parent bank, transfer of title to the demand deposit requires a shift of funds on deposit in a Federal Reserve Bank, from the bank in which the deposit was formerly held to the branch's parent bank. This is shown in entries (1) and (2) in Figure 10-1*c*.

Borrowing of Eurodollars by U.S. Banks   When U.S. banks encountered a situation of tight money in the late 1960s, some of them turned for loans to their

---

[12]Transactions velocity is the rate of turnover of money for all transactions in which money is used. For demand deposits it is, with minor qualifications, bank debits (checks and withdrawals) divided by the average money stock outstanding during a period. Whether or not an increase in transactions velocity involves an increase in income velocity of money and hence a rise in GNP depends on whether or not the shift in ownership of deposits results in more spending for goods and services.

[13]Milton Friedman, "The Euro-Dollar Market: Some First Principles," *Morgan Guaranty Survey,* October 1969, pp. 4–14; reprinted in Federal Reserve Bank of St. Louis, *Review,* July 1971, pp. 16–24.

[14]Joseph G. Kvasnicka, op. cit.

(a)

U.S. bank

Deposits	−(1)
	+(2)
	−(3)
	+(3)

London bank

		Eurodollar deposits	+(1)
(2)+	Reserves (deposits in U.S. banks)		
(3)−			
(3)+	Loans (repayable in dollars)		

(b)

U.S. bank

Time deposits	−(1)
Due to London branch	+(2)

London branch of U.S. bank

		Eurodollar deposits	+(1)
(2)+	Due from home office		

(c)

First U.S. bank

(3)+ Reserve (deposit in Federal Reserve Bank)	
	Eurodollar borrowings +(3)

London branch of first U.S. bank

		Eurodollar deposits	+(1)
(2)+	Reserves (deposits in second U.S. bank)		
(3)−			
(3)+	Due from home office		

Second U.S. bank

(1)− Reserve (deposit in Federal Reserve Bank)	Time deposits −(1)
(2)−	Deposits of branch of first U.S. bank +(2)
(3)−	U.S. bank −(3)

Figure 10-1 Eurodollar Deposits.

foreign branches. By borrowing Eurodollar deposits from their foreign branches, they could obtain funds in the form of deposits in Federal Reserve Banks which were reserves and which, if not needed as reserves, could be used for lending. At the same time required reserves were unchanged because the Eurodollar borrowings were liabilities but not deposits. Also, they did not have to pay deposit insurance premiums on such funds. Later, the Federal Reserve System imposed certain reserve requirements on Eurodollar borrowings, to prevent large increases in such borrowings. Basically, such borrowings shift reserves from other banks to the banks which borrow. The effects of borrowing Eurodollars are shown in entry (3) in Figure 10-1c.

The Eurodollars obtained by the parent bank were treated as items in process of collection. These could be deducted from reported demand deposits in accordance with the regular rules for computing net demand deposits subject to reserve requirements.[15] At the maturity of the Eurodollar loan, the parent bank could repay by issuing a check to its branch office; this check was also not subject to reserve requirements, nor was it included in demand deposits, so that the original deduction was not canceled when the loan was repaid. Not only did this result in lower required reserves for the bank, but in understatement of the demand deposit portion of the money supply, until the Federal Reserve System changed regulations to prevent this. It may be useful to note that changes in practices such as these may cause errors in money supply figures which may in turn cause errors in monetary policy actions.

Interbank Eurodollar Deposits There is a large volume of interbank Eurodollar deposits. A bank which obtains Eurodollar deposits need not itself make loans with the funds corresponding to the deposits. It may find, for example, that there is not a strong demand for loans in its location at a particular time. It may therefore redeposit funds in other Eurodollar banks, perhaps in other countries. Those banks in turn may lend or redeposit the funds. Since margins between the rate of interest paid on the original deposits and the rates paid on redeposited funds are likely to narrow as redeposits are made, this chain is not likely to continue indefinitely.[16]

Are Eurodollar Deposits Money? We have noted that shifting funds from banks in the United States to Eurodollar deposits does not directly cause any change in the size of the money supply in the United States, defined as M_1.

---

[15]Thursday overnight loans, as they were called, provided funds which counted as reserves for three days (Friday, Saturday, and Sunday) in computing average reserves held during a week. The loans could be repaid on Friday with clearinghouse checks issued on that day but not collected in Federal funds (that is, not causing a reduction in the bank's deposit at the district Federal Reserve Bank) until Monday. For further details, see Vincent G. Massaro, "Eurodollars and U.S. Banks," *Conference Board Record*, October 1970, pp. 15–22.

[16]As Fritz Machlup noted, interbank deposits do not have the same significance as deposits by nonbank parties, and should be reported separately in the statistics; see his "Euro-Dollar Creation: A Mystery Story," *Banca Nazionale del Lavoro Quarterly Review*, September 1970, pp. 219–260, and "Euro-Dollars, Once Again," op. cit., June 1972, pp. 119–137.

Since most Eurodollar deposits are held for investment and not as transactions balances, even though they are short-term liquid investments, it is not clear that they may properly be classified as part of the money supply in the United Kingdom or in other countries in which they are held. Moreover, they are not easily transferred into demand deposits and then spent, as time deposits in the United States frequently are; hence there is not that justification for including them in M_2.

On the other hand, if money is defined as an aggregate of liquid assets, changes in which correlate well with changes in prices or in nominal GNP, there may be justification for considering Eurocurrency deposits to be money. A study by Chase Econometric Associates found that for 11 major countries, changes in a weighted average price index correlated better with changes in M_1 plus Eurocurrencies or with changes in M_2 plus Eurocurrencies than with either M_1 or M_2 alone.[17] Whether Eurocurrencies may be termed money is thus somewhat controversial. In any event, however, they are not included in M_1 and are not normally included in M_2.

The Eurodollar Deposit Multiplier   Another question has been the size of the Eurodollar deposit multiplier, that is, the amount of Eurodollar deposits resulting from an inflow of $1 of Eurodollar deposits from the United States. Some have assumed that because European banks hold very small reserves against Eurodollars, a very large multiplier could exist, analogous to the multiplier for demand deposits in the United States.[18] But if European banks do not create Eurodollars by making loans, but instead simply transfer title to deposits held in the United States to borrowers, the multiplier must be quite small. It has been argued that it must be between zero and unity unless there is redepositing of Eurodollars into the market by central banks, and that even when such redepositing occurs the Eurodollar deposit multiplier is probably not high.[19]

Since Eurodollar deposits are chiefly time deposits, they do not have to be held by anyone, and could be repatriated to the United States if conditions

[17]"Money Growth Feeds World Inflation," Chase Manhattan Bank, *Business in Brief*, April 1976. The 11 countries were the Group of Ten countries minus Sweden, plus Spain and Mexico.

[18]The money multiplier within a country is the money stock divided by the monetary base, currency plus bank reserves. The size of this multiplier is affected by percentages of reserves actually held by banks, the ratio of currency to demand deposits, and the ratio of other deposits (time and government deposits) to demand deposits held by the public. See Henning, Pigott, and Scott, op. cit., Chap. 4.

[19]For a clear presentation of this argument, see John Hewson and Eisuke Sakakibara, "The Euro-Dollar Deposit Multiplier: A Portfolio Approach," IMF *Staff Papers*, July 1974, pp. 307–328. They argue that Eurodollar deposits exist in an unregulated competitive situation in which portfolio choices by depositors and borrowers should affect interest rates, whereas demand deposits (the major part of M_1) in the United States, for example, exist in a situation in which the only significant portfolio choice for depositors is between demand deposits and time deposits in commercial banks, and in which interest rate restrictions limit fluctuations in interest rates. (Keep in mind that a shift of deposits from a demand deposit account in a commercial bank to an account in a savings and loan association does *not* change the total amount of demand deposits, but merely shifts the title to some deposits to a savings and loan association.)

justified this. Increased interest rates in the United States might result in such a shift. Second, most Eurodollar loans are made to borrowers who use the funds to make payments, and there is no reason to believe that the recipients of the payments will *necessarily* redeposit the funds in the Eurodollar market. Leakages must be high.[20] If people try to get rid of money (M_1) by lending or spending it, the money is still held by someone; in this sense it is impossible under most conditions for the public to reduce the money supply through these means. But this is not true of either Eurodollar deposits or Eurodollar loans.

The fact that reserve requirements in Europe against Eurodollar deposits may be very low is not relevant to the question of deposit creation. Of course, if banks were extending loans in their own currencies and adding to deposit accounts of borrowers, it would be relevant. But in the Eurodollar market, banks are lending deposits held in the United States, exchanging claims on U.S. banks for claims on Eurodollar borrowers. What borrowers do with the funds is generally not known, but there is no reason to believe that large amounts are likely to be redeposited in the Eurodollar market.

Eurodollar Depositors Central banks were originally among the most important Eurodollar depositors and they are still of some importance. They may acquire Eurodollars when dollars are sold by private parties who wish to acquire, for example, Deutsche marks. They have also indirectly supplied dollars to the Eurodollar market by lending dollars to commercial banks in their own countries; the commercial banks then placed the dollars on deposit in Eurodollar banks. When some Eurodollar borrowers sold the dollars to obtain Deutsche marks, the dollars returned to the central banks in a vicious circle.

Central banks may also sell dollars to commercial banks and offer to repurchase them in the future at attractive rates. This reduces the forward discount on dollars and thus enables banks to earn higher returns on their Eurodollar investments. This action may also result in a vicious circle, however, since dollars are or may be sold short by speculators without covering the exchange risk, because they believe it to be small or nonexistent. The dollars then may come back to the central banks if they buy dollars to stabilize exchange rates.

Commercial banks are also major depositors in the Eurodollar market. The absence of broad, varied domestic money markets in a number of European countries increases the appeal of the Eurodollar market. Banks may borrow Eurodollars and lend them to other banks. If the deposit maturities are shorter than the borrowing maturities, it is helpful to the banks which do the borrowing and lending. They may also dispose of funds in the Eurodollar market when interest rates in their own countries are relatively low, especially if other

---

[20]This was an important part of the response to Milton Friedman by Fred H. Klopstock, "Money Creation in the Euro-Dollar Market—A Note on Professor Friedman's Views," Federal Reserve Bank of New York, *Monthly Review*, January 1970, pp. 12–15. The argument is well summarized in G. Walter Woodworth, "Understanding the Euro-Dollar Market," *The Bankers Magazine*, Autumn 1971.

countries have higher interest rates, perhaps because they are not in the same phase of the business cycle.

Nonbank financial institutions and multinational firms are also depositors in the Eurodollar market. United States residents, both individuals and firms, were originally depositors, although this flow of funds ceased during the period of controls on U.S. outflow of capital (1963–1974). Recently Eurodollar short-term floating rate notes issued by banks and purchased by MNCs have been a convenient medium for investment of liquid funds. The floating rate is tied to LIBOR, but the notes sometimes have a fixed minimum yield rate; see *Business Week,* Feb. 21, 1977, p. 67.

Since Eurodollar deposits are primarily short-term investment funds rather than transactions balances, it seems likely that transfers occur from short-term money market instruments and time deposits in the United States to demand deposits in the United States and then into Eurodollars. If this is true, addition to Eurodollar deposits is limited to some extent by the fact that demand deposits in the United States have higher reserve requirements than time deposits, while money market instruments require no reserves. This assumes, of course, no change in Federal Reserve policy, since such a change could encourage further expansion of the Eurodollar market or could restrict expansion. The reader should note carefully that the *ultimate* source of net Eurodollar deposits is deposits or currency held in the United States, except when or if banks in Europe or elsewhere create Eurodollars.

Eurodollar Loans   Eurodollar banks which have deposits make loans to obtain income; the loans are generally repayable in dollars. See the entries marked (3) under London bank in Figure 10-1a. Loans are usually short-term, although gradually the percentage of intermediate-term loans has increased as the demand for them has been strong. As this occurs, banks incur a liquidity risk.

Borrowers in the Eurodollar market when it first developed were largely firms which needed financing for foreign trade. A large amount of world trade, perhaps as much as one-fifth or even one-fourth, is still financed through Eurodollars. But as the market has developed, many other opportunities for lending have been found. Loans to U.S. banks, to British local government authorities, to Communist governments, to the Belgian Treasury (which is restricted in obtaining funds from the Belgian central bank), and other loans are made.

Business loans are usually made only to companies with excellent credit standing. Short-term loans are usually extended to multinational companies and other firms under established lines of credit in much the same way as such loans are made in the United States. Loans may also be made on special bases, to bridge a time gap until the acquisition of other funds, such as proceeds from an issue of bonds. Parent company guarantees may be requested from subsidiaries. Lending banks must be assured of firms' abilities to generate sufficient cash flow in dollars, or currencies unquestionably convertible into dollars, to pay off the loans at maturity. Exchange controls and the possibility of their imposition present serious problems.

As the market has developed, banks have begun to make medium-term credits. Some are revolving credits, with a confirmed line of credit for a specified amount for a period of three to five years. A major advantage of revolving credits is that banks can usually terminate unused portions of such credits if necessary.[21]

Term loans, with an initial maturity of more than one year, usually involve an appropriate amortization schedule. Sometimes interest rates are adjustable every six months, coinciding with the issue by the banks of 6-month certificates of deposit. Fixed-rate term loans may be made, however, if cash flows are accurately predictable. Prepayment penalties may be included in loan agreements.

Branches of U.S. banks were exempt from imposing the Interest Equalization Tax, which existed from 1963 to 1974 and was intended to eliminate the interest advantage of foreign over domestic lending. This and other barriers to foreign lending and investing were removed in 1974.

Loan agreements often include provisions to protect banks against any taxes which may be imposed. They also usually include clauses to protect borrowers from paying income withholding taxes on interest paid to banks.

Japanese banks and firms became important as borrowers. In early 1975, for example, firms and agencies in the United Kingdom, Sweden, and Japan, and subsidiaries of U.S. firms, were the largest borrowers in developed countries. Among developing countries, major borrowings were made by firms and agencies located in Brazil, the Republic of Korea, and Mexico. Loans were also made to Hungary, the Soviet Union, and other Communist countries. Very few loans were made, however, to the lower-income developing countries in Africa and Asia, and the problems of financing economic development in LDCs are serious.

Eurodollar Deposit and Loan Interest Rates　It should be clear from the foregoing discussion that there are two sets of interest rates: Eurodollar deposit interest rates and Eurodollar loan interest rates. The latter are higher to meet administrative costs of loans and to make profits. In general, deposits in the Eurodollar market had to involve higher interest rates than similar deposits in the United States. United States deposit interest rate ceilings, toward which most actual rates moved, thus set a floor for Eurodollar deposit interest rates generally. Figure 10-2 shows comparisons of Eurodollar deposit and loan interest rates with CD and prime loan interest rates in the United States.[22]

Some economists have presumed that the major determinant of Eurodollar

[21]For some details on Eurodollar loans, see *Euro-Dollar Financing, A Guide for Multinational Companies*, 2d ed. (New York: Chase Manhattan Bank, 1968), and 3d ed. (1974).

[22]Useful data may be found in *Borrowing in International Capital Markets* (Washington, D.C.: International Bank for Reconstruction and Development), quarterly.

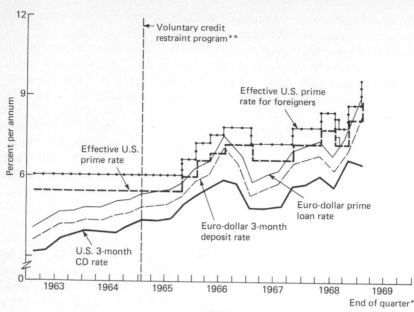

Figure 10-2 Eurodollar and U.S. Deposit and Loan Rates. (*Source*: Federal Reserve Bank of Boston, *New England Economic Review*, May/June 1969, p. 6.)

NOTES

*All data are for end of quarter except figures for 1963 which are the rates in effect at mid-month in March, June, September and December.

**The voluntary credit restraint program announced in February 1965 greatly limits the availability of U. S. bank loans to foreigners.

U. S. 3-Month CD Rate: Secondary market rate for 3-month CD's at the ask. Source: Salomon Brothers & Hutzler, *An Analytical Record of Yields and Yield Spreads*, New York (1969).

Euro-dollar 3-Month Deposit Rate: Euro-dollar rates in London at the ask. Source: Salomon Brothers & Hutzler, *op. cit.*

Euro-dollar Prime Loan Rate: Based on Euro-dollar 3-month deposit rates with the addition of a ½ percentage point margin. Although this margin may vary over time, Ernest Bloch (*Euro-dollars: An Emerging International Money Market*, New York, C. J. Devine Institute of Finance, 1966) and Paul Einzig (*op. cit.*) have suggested that this figure is a good estimate of the margin applied to loans to prime borrowers. Source: Salomon Brothers & Hutzler, *op. cit.*

Effective U. S. Prime Rate: U. S. prime rate plus 20 percent to include the cost of maintaining compensatory balances. Sources: Factor for compensatory balances is based on Oscar Altman, "Foreign Markets for Dollars, Sterling and Other Currencies," International Monetary Fund *Staff Papers*, VIII (Dec. 1961) (See also Morgan Guaranty Trust Company, *The Financing of Business with Euro-dollars*, New York, 1967, which suggests a factor of "about 15 per cent."); data for the U. S. prime rate are from the *Federal Reserve Bulletin*.

Effective U. S. Prime Rate for Foreigners: U. S. prime rate plus the additional ½ percentage point required for short-term loans to prime non-residents plus 20 percent to include the cost of maintaining compensatory balances. These figures do not include the Interest Equalization Tax, effective after June 1963, which applies to bank loans of more than 1 year. Sources: Margin for non-resident borrowers, statement by William McChesney Martin, Chairman of the Board of Governors of the Federal Reserve System, during hearings on higher interest rates on time deposits of foreign governments before the U. S. House of Representatives, Committee on Banking and Currency, in July 1962, quoted by Carl Stem, *op. cit.*; see in addition sources given for effective U. S. prime rate.

deposit interest rates, subject to the floor set by U.S. CD rates, is the U.S. Treasury bill rate. The reasoning is that since almost all Eurodollar holders could be influenced by the Treasury bill rate, while only some Treasury bill holders could be influenced by Eurodollar rates, causation must run from the Treasury bill rate to the Eurodollar rate.[23] Evidence in the later 1950s and the

[23]Patric H. Hendershott, "The Structure of International Interest Rates: The U.S. Treasury Bill Rate and the Eurodollar Deposit Rate," *Journal of Finance*, September 1967, pp. 455–465. See also Georg Rich, "A Theoretical and Empirical Analysis of the Euro-Dollar Market," *Journal of Money, Credit, and Banking*, August 1972, pp. 616–635.

first half of the 1960s indicated that the Eurodollar deposit interest rate adjusted to changes in the U.S. Treasury bill rate after about one year. From this it may be inferred that in that period an attempt to raise the Treasury bill rate to retain foreign funds in the United States could have been successful temporarily at least.

Eurodollar interest rates on loans must generally be less than similar rates in the United States, because firms of high credit standing can generally borrow in the United States except when foreign lending is restricted and hence would not generally borrow in Europe if the cost were higher.[24]

The floor on deposit interest rates and the ceiling on loan interest rates mean that profit margins are narrow. Sizable volume, lack of statutory reserve requirements, and other factors maintain the Eurodollar market in spite of relatively narrow profit margins.

The 6-month London interbank rate (LIBO or LIBOR) is regarded as a fundamental rate in the Eurodollar market for comparison. Loans are typically made at 1 or $1^1/_4$ percent above the LIBO rate. Japanese banks, which accumulated large Eurodollar deposits in 1971–1973, sometimes made loans at lower rates, to dispose of their deposit funds. With the problem after 1973 of paying higher prices for petroleum, Japanese banks needed funds, and were out of the lending activity temporarily. United States banks tried to attract funds from OPEC countries and to "recycle" them to Japanese banks, as discussed at the end of this chapter.

The need for loans to finance development projects, public enterprises and large multinational firms, and for BOP purposes, creates a demand for large loans, often too large for one bank safely to undertake. Syndicated loans are common. Banks which originate such loans and manage the syndicates receive fees. Financial institutions may be established especially to engage in such activities. For example, Citicorp International Bank Limited, a foreign subsidiary of Citicorp, the holding company which owns Citibank, was formed especially to act as a merchant bank, to syndicate loans, and to engage in other activities, such as underwriting sales of new securities, facilitating business mergers, and dealing in money markets.

Banks which have Eurodollar deposits are to some extent borrowing short-term and lending intermediate-term. In mid-1974, for example, 17 percent of the Eurodollar deposits of London banks were less than 8 days in maturity, while 21 percent of their Eurodollar loans were similarly short-term in nature. At the other end of the maturity scale, only 6 percent of deposits but 18 percent of Eurodollar loans were over 1 year in maturity. A number of loans have maturities as long as 10 years. They are usually amortized, so that the principal is repaid in installments, but in some cases no principal repayment is required for as much as 5 years.

---

[24]For proper comparison the U.S. prime loan rate must be increased by 15 or 20 percent because U.S. banks usually require compensating balances of that size in making such loans, thus making the effective rate higher. European banks do not usually follow this practice. The proper rate for comparison may not be the prime rate, because many foreign firms are not sufficiently well known in the United States to be granted the prime rate when borrowing.

Eurodollars and Monetary Policy in Europe[25]

The Eurodollar market permits investors who hold dollars to place those assets in European banks without incurring any exchange risk. The accompanying expansion of international banking has increased the rapid spread of information to investors. Eurodollar banks can lend funds received as a result of Eurodollar deposits to local, known institutions, or they can relend the funds abroad. Loans to U.S. banks are also easily made. Although Federal Reserve changes in regulations limited the appetite of U.S. banks for borrowing Eurodollars in 1973–1974, there was some borrowing at that time. Governments have hesitated to regulate their banks too strictly, for they must compete with foreign Eurodollar banks. Since the Eurodollar market divides risks between the Eurodollar banks and the depositors, it encourages movement of funds.

These movements of funds may be quite contrary to monetary policy goals of specific countries and their central banks. Yet central bank tools in Europe are often not adequate to offset the flow of funds. For example, if both banks and their customers can borrow in the Eurodollar market, how effective are central bank discount rates? If open market operations were as heavily used in Europe as in the United States, the situation would be somewhat different. In fact, the attraction of Eurodollars may limit the development of open markets for government securities: banks and nonbank financial institutions and corporations may be reluctant to buy government securities instead of holding Eurodollar loans or deposits in other banks.

Governments have several options: (1) impose capital movements controls—but this is notoriously ineffective; (2) use monetary policy for international matters and use fiscal policy actions for domestic purposes (but can fiscal policy be flexible enough and effective enough?); (3) use intervention in the forward exchange market to reduce the covered interest rate incentive for capital flows—but this may be difficult; or (4) give up their commitment to fixed exchange rates and adopt floating rates.

In a system of floating rates, borrowing Eurodollars provides funds to meet BOP deficits (such as those caused by higher oil prices) and at the same time supports the exchange rates for the currencies of the borrowing countries. Floating rates may make domestic monetary policy more effective. If tight money policies raise interest rates, the resulting inflow of capital (which would tend to offset the rise in rates) will be limited because the flow of funds into the country will be limited by its tendency to raise the exchange rate.

Trends in the Eurodollar Market

The growth of the Eurocurrency market was temporarily halted in 1974, but it appears likely to resume and to continue. Oil-producing nations are likely to deposit a substantial fraction of their accumulations of dollar funds in the

---

[25]Many points in this section are discussed in more detail in Jane Sneddon Little, "The Impact of the Eurodollar Market on the Effectiveness of Monetary Policy in the United States and Abroad," Federal Reserve Bank of Boston, *New England Economic Review*, March/April 1975, pp. 3–19.

Eurocurrency market, and these funds, although nominally short-term, may in fact be long-term until OPEC countries find other investment opportunities which they regard as more suitable.

With the removal of restrictions on outward foreign investment by the United States in early 1974, it was thought by some that foreigners might borrow more in the United States, reducing the relative importance of the Eurodollar market. So far this has not happened on a large scale.

Because London is the most important center of the Eurocurrency market, Britain's economic problems and rate of economic growth are significant to the growth of the Eurocurrency market. But the international financial markets were relatively unscathed in the difficult year of 1974, despite two well-publicized bank failures (Bankhaus Herstatt in Germany and Franklin National Bank in the United States). The role of the dollar as the leading international currency has been maintained in general, and although bank failures were followed by a marked widening of interest rate spreads, with substantially higher deposit interest rates paid by banks of lesser standing than the leading banks, the outlook for the foreseeable future seems relatively favorable.

ASIAN FINANCIAL CENTERS

Many regard all areas in which offshore currencies are held as part of one total market. Since deposits in the Bahamas and in some other places are primarily made on the basis of tax advantages, there may be no reason to regard them as separate markets. However, some believe that sources and uses of funds in the offshore currency market in Asia are sufficiently different from those in other areas to give that market a separate designation, the Asian dollar market or Asian currency market.

An offshore currency market developed in the late 1960s in Singapore. Singapore had, of course, important international entrepôt trade, an excellent communications network, and important banks. It also had a stable government and its currency was one of two in Asia, the other being the Japanese yen, which had attained the status of being convertible under terms of Article VIII of the IMF agreement.

Reasons for Development of Singapore as a Financial Center

Four possible reasons may be suggested for development of this market in Singapore. When the branch of the Bank of America there proposed to the Singapore government that taxes and restrictions be relaxed so that dollar accounts could be held in that branch, the Singapore government agreed, first, perhaps because Asian dollar deposits would be likely to attract other deposits, bring increased banking activity, and attract income from tourism, other services, and so on. Second, Singapore would gain both publicity and prestige by being the Asian dollar market center. Third, it might also gain a degree of additional political security, since the existence of foreign deposits and foreign banks in Singapore might build up support for its neutrality and existence as a trade and financial center. Finally, Southeast Asia is in need of large amounts of capital for economic development. Singapore, almost at the center of this important area, is a logical place for the financing of such development.

Development Lending in Southeast Asia

The market is still quite small, perhaps about one-twentieth of the size of the rest of the offshore currency market. Nevertheless, it is an interesting beginning in a swelling flow of funds into the development of Southeast Asia. With the end of the Vietnam War, although the actions of the governments in Vietnam, Cambodia, and Laos cannot easily be predicted, the development of Southeast Asia (including Singapore, Malaysia, Thailand, Indonesia, and the Philippines, and possibly Burma, as well as what was at one time Indochina) could proceed at a more rapid pace.

As the market developed, rates in it and in the rest of the offshore currency market became more competitive for instruments of equal maturities, which suggests that the Asian currency market may be simply an extension of the market elsewhere. In 1973, however, the Asian market began to be a net receiver of funds from Europe instead of a net supplier of funds to Europe. This suggests that a market was developing with a capability of attracting funds for investment in Asia, which might therefore be considered a separate market.[26]

The market offers deposit options of varying maturities; a negotiable certificate of deposit was introduced in 1970, and medium-term and long-term as well as short-term loans are made.[27] A number of bond issues have been floated; some term these Asian dollar bonds, although others regard this activity as simply part of the Eurobond market.[28] Thus this market has provided increased liquidity and has begun to promote trade and investment in Asia. It has also served to generate closer economic cooperation.[29]

Hong Kong and Tokyo as Potential Offshore Currency Market Centers

Some believe that neither Hong Kong nor Tokyo, the two centers in Asia with potential as offshore currency market centers, is likely to develop in that way.[30] Singapore has certain advantages: a relatively free economic climate; working hours which overlap with those in major financial centers in Europe, which is

[26]Stanley A. Lance, "The Singapore Asian Currency Market: Structure, Development and Prospects," unpublished master's degree report (Seattle: Graduate School of Business Administration, University of Washington, 1975). See also Robert F. Emery, *The Asian Dollar Market*, Board of Governors of the Federal Reserve System, International Finance Discussion Papers, No. 71, November 1975.

[27]Dick Wilson, "First Big Asian Dollar Loans," *The Bankers*, August 1972, p. 1084; Dick Wilson, "Singapore Widens Its Lead," *Far Eastern Economic Review*, Apr. 1, 1972, p. 61; *The Straits Times*, Mar. 22, 1974, p. 16; *International Reports*, Apr. 4, 1975, pp. 324–325.

[28]Y. S. Park, "Asian Dollar Market," *Asian Forum*, January–March 1973, pp. 77–78; *The Straits Times*, Dec. 7, 1973, p. 15.

[29]*The Asian Dollar Market* (Singapore: Citibank, 1973).

[30]See, for example, Mark Borzuk, "The Future Development of Offshore Capital Markets in Asia," *Columbia Journal of World Business*, Spring 1974, pp. 48–59.

not true either for Hong Kong or Tokyo; rapid economic growth combined with BOP surpluses; and relatively low taxes on financial activity.[31] However, the fluidity of economic and political conditions in Asia makes forecasting difficult. Tokyo has Asia's largest capital market and Hong Kong the second largest. Hong Kong's economy depends heavily on foreign trade and it has no central bank. Thus independent macroeconomic management through monetary policy is not attempted and adjustment is left primarily to market forces. Singapore has a monetary authority, the Monetary Authority of Singapore (MAS), but in the long run Singapore's money supply is largely determined by the BOP.

City-states, small territories dominated by single cities which contain most of the inhabitants, are old forms of political organization. In the modern world they are scarce; Monaco and San Marino in Europe may be mentioned. The virtual autonomy of Hong Kong, even though it is still nominally a British colony, and the independence of Singapore since its separation from Malaysia in 1965, give these two city-states the possibility and the need to develop their economies. Since they have almost no natural resources, they must rely on trade and services, including finance, as bulwarks of their economies.[32]

Tokyo, as capital of the largest economic power in Asia, is in a different category. Japan is a major source of funds for the economic development of much of the rest of Asia. Japan clearly has the technology, communications, infrastructure, and ability to develop a major international financial center— and in many ways Tokyo already is such a center. The barriers to further development are largely political (desire to restrict foreign investment to a certain extent) and perhaps cultural (a lingering desire for a degree of isolation).

In spite of these barriers, the Pacific Basin region is likely to be influenced more heavily by Japan. Japan constitutes the major market for raw materials produced in much of the rest of the Pacific Basin, and for some of the semimanufactured goods and manufactured products as well. Most of the other countries in the area cannot produce at comparable cost many of the products in which Japan excels.

Financial markets in the Pacific Basin are much less developed than those in Europe. In the growth and development of financial markets in the area, there is an important role for Japanese financial institutions.

EURODOLLARS, "PETRODOLLARS," AND THE INTERNATIONAL MONETARY SYSTEM

As readers might surmise from the discussion of international monetary reform in Chapter 6, the rise in oil prices and the portfolio preferences of the OPEC countries, especially the Arab members of OPEC, created serious strains on

---

[31]Mishio Ishihara, "Asian Currency Market Shows Potential for Continued Rapid Growth," IMF *Survey*, Jan. 6, 1975, pp. 12–13.

[32]A very helpful booklet is Theodore Geiger and Frances M. Geiger, *Tales of Two City-States: The Development Progress of Hong Kong and Singapore*, Studies in Development Progress, No. 3 (Washington, D.C.: National Planning Association, 1973).

the Eurodollar market. The Eurodollar market is a major financial intermediary system through which funds received by OPEC countries can be "recycled" for loans to those countries which need funds, their needs having increased greatly with the increased prices for oil. Oil trade deficits in total are equal to oil receipts, which can be spent for goods and services or reinvested; hence the recycling is possible, but problems arise in the difference in investor preferences concerning liquidity and risk.

Difficult problems have arisen from the OPEC, especially Arab, preference for depositing funds in the highest-rated banks and in short-term maturities. Banks can refuse deposits if they appear to be too great for the banks to dispose of through appropriate loans. Banks can also reduce deposit interest rates and increase loan interest rates to widen their spreads to compensate for increased risk, but they may thus cause a slowdown in growth of the Eurodollar market. Another problem is the difficulty of oil-consuming countries, especially low-income deficit countries, in making interest payments and repaying loans when they have other BOP deficits. Individual banks which encounter difficulties because of unsound loans or liquidity problems can turn to central banks in their countries as lenders of last resort.

Thus although the rise in oil prices reduces real income for oil-consuming countries and so may cause recession, financing oil payments is basically feasible for the developed countries. Real income may be lower for a time and economic growth may be slower for a long period, but the problems are not insurmountable.[33]

THE OUTLOOK FOR INTERNATIONAL MONEY MARKETS

What are the conditions for continued existence of the Eurodollar market? If the view of that market now taken by many is correct, the major reason for its existence is the competitive ability of banks outside the United States to attract time deposits and to lend the funds profitably. They are able to do this because of (1) the general absence of statutory reserve requirements against Eurodollar deposits, which permits them to lend all but small fractions of the reserves acquired when Eurodollar deposits are obtained; (2) ceilings on time-deposit interest rates in the United States, which limit interest payments compared to those outside the United States; (3) some tax advantages because of lower corporate income taxes and some other lower taxes on banks in countries other than the United States; (4) the generally large size of both Eurodollar deposits and Eurodollar loans, which permits greater profits per dollar of funds; and (5) very limited government controls which might interfere with flows of funds. There may be other less evident factors.

Changes such as the elimination of Regulation Q ceilings on interest on time deposits in the United States might adversely affect the Eurodollar market, but unless a number of the above conditions change, the Eurodollar

---

[33]For similar views and further elaboration see "The Eurodollar Market's Big Test," First National City Bank, *Monthly Economic Letter*, July 1974, pp. 9–15.

market will probably continue to be important. Thus it is likely that international money markets will be important in international finance, at least in the short-run future.

International money markets increase the flow of capital among countries. They also reduce the spread among interest rates in various countries. They are likely to survive as long as there are areas or countries which impose a less onerous degree of regulation on banking than other countries. It seems very unlikely that all countries will impose regulations strict enough to destroy such markets, nor does it seem likely that all countries will impose the same degree of regulation.[34]

With electronic funds transfer systems, banks will have less need for offices in a particular country to deal in that country's currency. As one author puts it

> The costs and the inconvenience of using banks based in distant locations will decline. Inevitably, the change in the technology of payments will enlarge the market for major banks across the national borders; U.S. banks will find it easier to attract foreign customers and foreign banks will find it easier to attract U.S. customers and international banking will expand.[35]

In such a market, U.S. banks will have some advantages because of their size, their efficiency, and their possession of the preferred currency. If U.S. regulation of banking should be liberalized, especially by eliminating ceilings on interest rates paid on time deposits and the prohibition of payment of interest on demand deposits, it is possible that a larger share of the international money market will be shifted to U.S. banks.

Britain and possibly some other countries, to retain the advantage of income from banking and other international services, must offer a relatively free climate for such activity, with a minimum of regulation. British banking activities do not necessarily depend on sterling being a major vehicle currency.

It will be interesting to see the result of the conflict between nationalistic policies, based in part on a desire to control monetary policy and economic activity within each country, and the opposing thrust of technology toward international, worldwide operations. We live in an exciting age for students of and participants in international business and banking.

QUESTIONS FOR DISCUSSION

1 Money markets are usually distinguished from capital markets, the line usually being drawn at one-year maturities. Discuss other distinguishing features of money markets as compared with capital markets, insofar as you understand them.

[34]Robert Z. Aliber, "Towards a Theory of International Banking," Federal Reserve Bank of San Francisco, *Economic Review*, Spring 1976, p. 5. See also his *International Money Game* (New York: Basic Books, 1973), Chap. 12, "Banking on the Wire."

[35]Aliber, "Towards a Theory of International Banking," op. cit., p. 5.

2 In what types of instruments are foreigners most likely to invest in the U.S. money market? Why?

3 Explain the role of the U.S. dollar as a *vehicle* currency, as a *reserve* currency, and as an *intervention* currency.

4 Central banks are sometimes said to try to "twist" the yield curve (the graph indicating yields for financial assets of the same general type but of varying maturities, on the same day) to prevent outflow of funds during recessions. How might they try to do this, to what extent do you think it possible for them to be successful if they try, and what are they trying to accomplish?

5 Discuss the relative advantages and disadvantages of the following as international financial centers: London, Paris, Zurich, Beirut, Hong Kong, Singapore, Tokyo, Panama, Nassau, New York, San Francisco, and Honolulu.

6 Discuss the three major factors causing the development of the Eurocurrency market. Why three and not four?

7 Discuss the development of a "quality spread" in Eurodollar deposit interest rates in 1974, and compare it with the quality spread which also developed in U.S. money market interest rates in the same period.

8 What are the arguments for and against the position that the multiplier for total Eurocurrency deposits based on existing Eurocurrency deposits is quite small?

9 Can the Asian currency market be regarded as independent or separate from the Eurocurrency market? Give reasons.

10 Evaluate the risk involved in borrowing short and lending long (or intermediate-term) by banks in the Eurocurrency market.

SUGGESTED REFERENCES

For a brief review of the U.S. money market and the relationship of the Eurocurrency market to it, see Charles N. Henning, William Pigott, and Robert Haney Scott, *Financial Markets and the Economy* (Englewood Cliffs, N.J.: Prentice-Hall, 1975), Chap. 9, "The Money Market." For recent concern about how money should be defined, see Carl M. Gambs, "Money—A Changing Concept in a Changing World," Federal Reserve Bank of Kansas City, *Monthly Review,* January 1977, pp. 3–12.

The role of international financial centers and their formation has been neglected in recent regional economic theory as well as in financial development theory. One exception is Charles P. Kindleberger, *The Formation of Financial Centers: A Study in Comparative Economic History*, Princeton Studies in International Finance, No. 36 (Princeton: Princeton, 1974). See also the shorter articles by Hang-Sheng Cheng, "U.S. West Coast as an International Financial Center," Federal Reserve Bank of San Francisco, *Economic Review*, Spring 1976, pp. 9–19, and Harry G. Johnson, "Panama as a Regional Financial Center," *Economic Development and Cultural Change*, January 1976, pp. 261–286.

Relatively brief accounts of the Eurocurrency market are Jane Sneddon Little, "The Euro-Dollar Market: Its Nature and Impact," Federal Reserve Bank of Boston, *New England Economic Review*, May/June 1969, pp. 2–31; and G. Walter Woodworth, "Understanding the Euro-Dollar Market," *The Bankers Magazine*, Autumn 1971. Longer discussions include Paul Einzig, *The Euro-Dollar System*, 5th ed. (New York: St. Martin's, 1973); Klaus Friedrich, *The Euro-Dollar System*, Program on Comparative Economic Development (Ithaca, N.Y.: Cornell University, 1968); Geoffrey Bell, *The Eurodollar Market and the International Financial System* (New York: Halsted, 1973);

and Jane Sneddon Little, *Euro-Dollars: The Money Market Gypsies* (New York: Harper & Row, 1975).

The size of the Eurodollar market is estimated by the Bank for International Settlements (BIS) and published data may be found in its *Annual Reports*; estimates are also made by Morgan Guaranty Trust Company and published in *World Financial Markets*.

Valuable analytical studies in addition to those cited in footnotes include Gunter Dufey and Ian H. Giddy, *Credit Creation and the Growth of the Eurodollar Market*, Research Paper No. 127, Columbia School of Business, Columbia University, July 1976, and John Hewson and Eisuke Sakakibara, "A Qualitative Analysis of Euro-Currency Controls," *Journal of Finance*, May 1975, pp. 377–400.

On Asian financial centers, see Robert F. Emery, "The Asian Dollar Market," Board of Governors of the Federal Reserve System, International Finance Discussion Papers, No. 71, November 1975, and other references cited in footnotes. See also Theodore Geiger and Frances M. Geiger, *Tales of Two-City States: The Development Progress of Hong Kong and Singapore,* Studies in Development Progress, No. 3 (Washington, D.C.: National Planning Association, 1973).

John R. Karlik, *Some Questions and Brief Answers about the Eurodollar Market,* Staff Study, Joint Economic Committee, 95th Cong., 1st Sess., Feb. 7, 1977, is very helpful on a number of points.

Part Four

International Long-Term Investment

We have now discussed the international monetary system and international banking, exchange rates, and money markets—short-term international finance. In the next three chapters we examine international long-term investment.

In Chapter 11 we distinguish between portfolio investment, in which investors seek return, liquidity, and safety, but not control, and direct investment in which managerial control is obtained. Before World War I most investment was portfolio investment, as Britain, the leading creditor nation, used retained earnings in large part to finance domestic investment, and British investors found investment in colonial areas attractive. Shifting of the burden of international lending to the United States after World War I meant a shift to inexperienced investors, many losses, and a sudden termination of lending when the stock market crash in 1929 was followed by the Great Depression. After World War II direct investment became more important than portfolio investment. Differences in causes of the two types of investment are examined.

Chapter 12 concerns the ways in which various institutions and markets have facilitated the expansion of international investment. Prominent among them is the World Bank Group; a very important development is the growth of the Eurobond market as an international long-term capital market.

In Chapter 13 the focus is on *effects* of international long-term investment. Those engaged in international finance need to understand the social effects of international investment—effects on other items in the BOP, on domestic employment, on the transfer of technology, on interest rates, and on other economic variables. Because some effects of international investment were deemed undesirable, controls on such investment have been maintained by some countries and were imposed for a decade (1963–1974) by the United States.

Chapter 11

Nature and Causes of International Long-Term Investment

Chapters 9 and 10 discussed flows of funds from one country to another to obtain foreign currency (money) and to invest in short-term financial assets, the development of international financial centers, and the international market for short-term financial assets. International *long-term* investment is made in capital market assets—bonds, stocks, mortgages, and real capital assets (acquisition of plant, equipment, and inventory abroad, and of firms owning such assets).

International short-term investment involves for the most part an international flow of funds. International long-term investment may also involve such a flow of funds or it may occur simply because income (earnings) on foreign investments is reinvested, or because long-term assets held in foreign investments increase in value (capital gains). Retained earnings of foreign subsidiaries and profits of foreign branches may be reinvested without any flow of capital from one country to another, and capital gains may also increase values of foreign investments, especially of stocks and of real capital assets.

Intermediate-term investment is generally included in the discussion in this chapter. It has already been mentioned in such things as Eurocredits, and some intermediate-term lending is carried out by banks and other institutions discussed in Chapters 7–10. Indeed, there is no firmly established dividing line between intermediate- and long-term, and although 20-year loans are clearly long-term and 3-year loans are clearly intermediate-term, there is some fuzziness in the range between 5-year and 10-year maturities.

NATURE OF INTERNATIONAL LONG-TERM INVESTMENT

Many firms engage in both international trade and international investment. Investors, however, may have no connection with trade, being interested simply in the profitable use of funds, or they may be business firms with operations in more than one country. Foreign operations of such firms may be initiated by flows of investment, and a flow of investment may be maintained. Once foreign operations have been established, however, the flow of investment may sometimes decline sharply or cease, as the firm begins to rely on local sources for additional investment funds.

In this section, we are concerned with the causes and effects of flows of investment funds. In later chapters we deal with questions arising in financing the operations of firms, both in foreign trade and in foreign operations—in the case of multinational firms, in many countries. Foreign operations may be conducted by branches, subsidiaries, or affiliated firms. Forms of organization may be affected by legal factors, government restraints, and costs. The definition of a multinational firm is not entirely clear, and some firms are on the borderline of this category, but the large firms which operate in a number of countries are generally recognized as multinational. The headquarters of such firms may be in one of the countries in which they operate, and the firm may generally be regarded as belonging to that country. On the other hand, the location of the headquarters is not necessarily the determining factor in the attitudes of the managements of such firms. Managements may be concerned with the growth and profits of the firms as entities, and may in fact, in some cases, consider the locations of headquarters to be fortuitous.[1]

---

[1]The president of Chas. Pfizer & Co. stated the development of the attitude of a multinational firm in this way: "For a company . . . which has already realized a good share of its potential in the U.S. marketplace or for a less mature company which discovers an outstanding new product that will attract strong demand everywhere, the case for world-wide marketing seems almost irresistible. To leave competitors to enjoy the growth potentialities abroad would be to concede to them substantial earnings which they can use to compete more effectively everywhere, including the domestic market. For such a company, a beginning is made with exports. But more importantly, the company will inevitably be drawn to make direct investments, first in marketing facilities, sales offices and warehouses and then, as necessary, with plants. . . . In these circumstances, the company finds that it has not just grown—it has been transformed. In making direct investments abroad, it has become multinational. In such a situation, though the headquarters of the company is in the United States and though it has the large U.S. market at hand, it must now be organized as a world enterprise. The company's assets and efforts must now be managed multinationally, in accordance with market opportunities wherever they may be." Speech delivered at the semiannual meeting and midyear conference of the Manufacturing Chemists' Association, Inc., New York City, Nov. 21, 1967.

In an age in which multinational firms have become important, much international capital flow may really be *intrafirm* transfer, but much, of course, is external.

Portfolio Investment

The distinction between portfolio investment and direct investment is very significant, for the causes of each are quite different.

The distinction between long-term and short-term portfolio investment may not be very meaningful; short-term investments may be rolled over in such a way as to become long-term. In fact, some argue that portfolio investment really need not be divided into long-term and short-term. There are two arguments against this view, however: (1) some causes of short-term portfolio investment may not apply to long-term portfolio investment—for example, the need of short-term assets for working balances, and (2) more important, short-term investment is influenced by short-term interest rates, while long-term investment is influenced by long-term interest rates. Short-term rates and long-term rates have quite different determinants. Short-term rates are determined chiefly by monetary policy actions, variations in business borrowing resulting from business fluctuations, and government short-term borrowing. Long-term rates, on the other hand, are determined largely by productivity of capital and saving (which determine the basic "real" interest rate) together with an inflation premium, which gives lenders added return to offset inflation.

In the 1920s, most U.S. international investment flow was portfolio investment—investment by those who sought return, safety, and liquidity in investments, without a significant degree of management control. Most of it was bond investment, although stock investment also became important.[2]

International portfolio investment has the same basic causes as domestic portfolio investment: desires for yield, safety, and liquidity. The risks are often greater, and there are additional risks, such as the possibility of changes in exchange rates, wars and revolutions, confiscation of holdings by foreign governments, and blocking of payment of dividends and interest and of remittance of profits to home offices. The flow of information is usually not as complete; hence investors may act with greater uncertainty because of lack of information.

Portfolio investors in bonds receive no more than the stated yields, over the life of the securities, but they may receive less. Hence risk affects them asymmetrically, and it seems probable that they should demand a risk premium. This has tended to discourage portfolio investment except in utilities and in government agencies, where risk of loss is less than in other fields. To encourage portfolio investment, international lending institutions have offered

[2]In the late 1920s, foreign bonds offered in the U.S. capital market amounted to about one-third as much in volume as total domestic corporate bonds offered in that market. See Hal B. Lary and associates, *The United States in the World Economy*, Economic Series No. 23, U.S. Department of Commerce, Bureau of Foreign and Domestic Commerce (Washington, D.C.: Government Printing Office, 1943), especially pp. 95–99.

their own securities; the institutions then use the funds to make loans, and various protective provisions reduce risk of loss.

Direct Investment

Direct investment is that made as equity, through purchases of stocks; acquisition of entire firms; or establishment of branches, affiliates, or subsidiaries. It is not clear how much equity in a firm must be owned to gain control. The U.S. Department of Commerce has adopted as a guideline the acquisition of 10 percent or more of the equity by a U.S. resident or an affiliated group of U.S. residents, or the ownership of 50 percent of the voting stock by U.S. residents.[3] Whether this is the most appropriate dividing line is not certain, but the Commerce Department figures must be used generally as statistical data.

Branches, subsidiaries, or affiliated firms which are direct investments may grow through retention of earnings, with or without capital flows. Such additions to investment are not reported as capital flows in the U.S. BOP, as noted in Chapter 2. Hence BOP figures, even if added year by year, understate the total of U.S. foreign investment.[4] In fact, BOP figures are not a good measure of direct foreign investment, since at best they indicate the portion financed from the United States.

Before the Great Depression, U.S. long-term portfolio investment abroad probably exceeded U.S. direct investment abroad, as indicated in Table 11-1. In the decade of the 1930s, portfolio investment declined, and net long-term investment dropped sharply as a flight of capital occurred from Europe and elsewhere to the United States, much of it in gold. By 1945, both direct and portfolio investment had increased slightly, and net long-term investment had increased sharply in percentage. Long-term inflow of investment into the United States was no greater than it had been before World War II. Portfolio investment outflow was less. In the 1930s there had been a wave of defaults on foreign bonds owned by Americans. Almost 40 percent of the total foreign dollar bonds outstanding were in default, and this experience of lenders in the United States had a lasting negative effect.[5]

U.S. long-term direct investment abroad, which was less than $1 billion in the early 1950s, began to increase in the middle of the decade, and reached $3 billion to $5 billion a year in the late 1960s and early 1970s. Foreign long-term direct investment in the United States did not significantly exceed $1 billion in any year until 1973. Foreign portfolio investment in the United States,

---

[3]For a discussion of the classification, see *The Balance of Payments Statistics of the United States*, Report of the Review Committee for Balance of Payments Statistics to the Bureau of the Budget (Washington, D.C.: Government Printing Office, 1965), pp. 62–63.

[4]The report of the review committee recognized that retained earnings should be included, but pleaded inadequacy of timely data by area as the reason for omission; see *The Balance of Payments Statistics of the United States*, p. 64.

[5]Sir Arthur Salter, Director of the Economic and Finance Section of the League of Nations for a decade, wrote that "with the exception of loans recommended by the League of Nations and the central banks, the *bulk* of the foreign loans in these years to public authorities in debtor countries would better not have been made" (*Recovery*, London, Reynal and Hitchcock, 1932).

Table 11-1   United States Capital Flows for Selected Years
(In Billions of Dollars)

	1929	1939	1945	1947
Long-term outflow				
Direct (book value)	7.6	7.3	8.1	9.4
Portfolio	7.8	4.1	5.6	5.6
Long-term inflow				
Direct (book value)	1.4	2.9	2.7	2.6
Portfolio	4.5	5.8	5.8	4.8
Net long-term outflow	9.5	2.7	5.2	7.6
Short-term outflow	1.6	1.1	0.9	1.4
Short-term inflow	3.0	3.8	5.7	5.1
Net short-term inflow	1.4	2.7	4.8	3.7
Net outflow, private	8.1	3.0	0.4	3.9
Government, long-term	n/a*	n/a	2.1	11.3§
Government short-term outflow	n/a	n/a	0.6	0.4
Government short-term inflow	n/a	n/a	3.1	3.5
Net government flow, total	n/a	n/a	−1.4‡	8.2
Total net flow	+8.1†	+3.0	−1.0	+12.1

* Not available.
† + indicates net outflow.
‡ − indicates net inflow.
§ Includes $3.4 billion paid on subscriptions to International Monetary Funds and to World Bank.
Source: Cleona Lewis, *The United States and Foreign Investment Problems* (Washington, D.C.: The Brooking Institution, 1948), pp. 26, 32.

however, was larger; net portfolio investment reached nearly $4 billion a year in 1972 and 1973, as foreigners purchased U.S. securities.

To understand the factors affecting long-term investment flows, we must examine some of the conditions underlying such investment over the past century.

INTERNATIONAL CAPITAL FLOWS

Although international capital flows have occurred for centuries, we are most concerned with the conditions in the period since about 1880. In the times of colonial empires, large commercial companies such as the British East India Company, the Dutch East India Company, and Hudson's Bay Company engaged in both trade and investment in large areas. Colonies were often sources of raw materials for countries which governed them. There was no reason for encouraging in colonies development of industries which might compete with those in the governing countries, and such industries were usually not developed.

Britain's Experience as a Creditor Nation before 1914

The great creditor nation in the last part of the nineteenth century was Britain. Large-scale foreign lending and investing by Britain began about the middle of the nineteenth century, a period of somewhat greater political stability than since World War I. Much of the investment was in the production of raw materials, including food, which Britain needed. In exchange, Britain shipped manufactured goods to foreign countries. Because much of domestic output in Britain was financed by plowing back profits, British investors could choose primarily between domestic investment in government securities and foreign investment. In foreign investment, although risks were greater, returns were also much higher, and it appears that returns more than compensated for the risks. As described in Chapter 4, world currencies of major countries were tied to gold, and exchange rates were generally stable. Transfer restrictions and exchange controls were minimal.

Britain, as a matter of policy, had no tariffs and trade restrictions, nor were foreign loans tied to the purchase of British goods. Imports were between one-fourth and one-third of national income. From 1880 to 1913 the value of British investment overseas nearly tripled. Income from these investments increased much more rapidly than national income. Foreign bonds yielded, in the period 1870–1880, 5.5 percent, and other foreign securities 7 percent, compared to a yield of 3.8 percent on Consols (British government perpetual bonds). Even in the early twentieth century, the yield on foreign securities averaged 5.2 percent compared with about 3 percent on Consols and 3.5 percent on domestic securities in general.

More than one-third of British investment, by 1913, was in the United States and Canada; nearly half is accounted for if investments in Australia and New Zealand are included; and over half if India is also included. This investment was both direct and portfolio. Sometimes British firms, such as those which built and operated railroads in China and in Argentina, issued bonds, so that investors made portfolio investments in firms with direct investments. Railway securities were the most important, accounting for 40 percent of the total. Loans to government authorities accounted for another 30 percent. Basically, capital was provided for what is now often termed the social infrastructure; only a small part of the investment was in manufacturing.

An important aspect of British foreign investment was that much of the earnings on such investment was balanced in the British BOP by an excess of imports over exports. Investment bankers in Britain were careful to make sound loans and investments, and losses were minimal. This meant that borrowing by foreign governments as well as by enterprises could be repaid from the proceeds of new loans, which could be obtained easily in most cases because the old loans had been repaid on time.

Most short-term financing for international transactions was carried out in London, through an elaborate system of bank acceptances, discounted in the market. London's international banking system and related institutions prospered on this basis, and the payments into the accepting houses by importers from countries all over the world roughly balanced the debt owed by the accepting houses on accepted bills. One evidence of the satisfactory nature of this situation was the rise in the value of the pound sterling to $7 at the outbreak of World War I, as importers provided funds to meet maturing acceptances, and those who held pounds did not attempt to withdraw their funds.

For much of the period under discussion, development of industry in Britain was financed out of profits. There was little need of funds from investors for domestic investment until the beginning of the twentieth century. Since fixed debt of domestic industry was relatively small, chances of bankruptcies were minimal.

For all of this period earnings from foreign investments were greater than average annual exports of capital. In other words, total capital exports could be financed out of the returns on former investment.

America's Experience as a Creditor Nation after 1918

World War I ended the period in which Britain was the world's major creditor nation. Britain's war costs and loss of some foreign investments were so great that it was no longer in a position to lend abroad on a large scale. America began to assume the role of the leading creditor nation, whereas before World War I, the United States was a net importer of capital rather than a net lender. The financial system in the United States was largely developed to finance *domestic* industry, as befitted a country which began its existence with no industry and very little money. (The major characteristic of finance in early America was the need for money—a shortage of British currency, which was used widely, was supplemented by various means, and finally by the issue of Continental currency.)

The history of American banking was a history of loans made to finance enterprise. Often these were "bad" loans, in the sense that they could not be repaid. Although this resulted in periods of "bad banking" (including the era termed that of "wildcat banking"), the expansion of money probably served the country well.[6]

The American banking system, however, was not well suited to financing foreign investment. Nor was its long-term capital system well established. Thus when World War I dramatically changed the British position, when the new regime in Russia repudiated former debt, when Britain had accumulated war debts to foreign countries, and when Europe needed reconstruction, America's inexperience in foreign lending resulted in much of the funds for foreign investment from America being channeled through Britain, which in turn loaned to the continent of Europe as it had done earlier.

---

[6]Paul B. Trescott wrote: "It was no accident that the century of free banking coincided with the most rapid and revolutionary period of the nation's economic development. . . . Free banking was symptomatic of the spirit of enterprise which provided the driving force for economic growth and change, and it contributed directly to that force" [*Financing American Enterprise* (New York: Harper & Row, 1963), p. 265]. And Kenneth Boulding concluded that "the United States has had in the past a worse record of bank failures, but on the other hand, the local banks have been more active in promoting and encouraging local enterprise, and it may well be that the greater dynamism of the American economy may be in part a result of the high degree of local autonomy in the banking system" [*Principles of Economic Policy* (New York: Prentice-Hall, 1958), pp. 229–230].

The suddenness of the opening up of new opportunity for foreign investment may have contributed to the poor judgment in making such investment. Investment banks with little knowledge in this field engaged in fierce competition, with little analysis of investment quality.

Funds were invested in foreign securities in relatively large amounts. About half of U.S. investment in the interwar period (1919–1939) was direct. Most of the rest was in dollar bonds (U.S. investors were not accustomed to investing in foreign-currency financial assets). These bonds were issued chiefly by governments, or with government guarantees, in Canada, Germany, the remainder of Western Europe, and Latin America. Because borrowers were chiefly governments, individual firms which obtained funds indirectly were under little pressure to use the funds carefully. And because governments were the major borrowers, lenders (investors) had some feeling of security or safety based on the foreign government obligation to repay.

The major creditor nations in this period were the United States, Britain (which still retained some capability for foreign lending), and France. Investments were heavily in Europe and Latin America. Europe is not a net exporter, in general, of food or raw materials, and in this period it was not a net exporter of most manufactured goods. Thus, while exports had provided earnings to repay loans in the period of heavy British investment, they were far less adequate to do so in the 1920s. A substantial portion of the proceeds of loans were used for municipal projects and for rearmament—neither of which is productive in the sense of producing exports or output which could be sold to repay loans.

One burst of such lending in 1919–1920 was temporarily restrained by the U.S. recession of 1920–1921, in which commodity prices fell drastically, and banks found that letters of credit indeed carried obligations. As many importers found reasons to default on their obligations to provide funds to meet drafts, the legal technicalities of letters of credit became painfully clear to banks, and losses were severe.

This period of largely short-term lending was followed, after recovery in the United States from the recession of 1920–1921, by a period of growing long-term foreign investment. This culminated in the crash of 1929, in which brokers' loans (in part by banks, in large part through banks, by "others") clearly were no longer the secondary reserves which they had seemed. Although, as indicated in Chapter 4, the stock market crash probably did not cause the Depression, it undoubtedly made it more severe.

With the Depression of the 1930s, U.S. foreign investment declined sharply. At the same time, the worldwide character of the Depression reduced income in many countries, and defaults on foreign borrowing were numerous. Incidentally, the sharp rise in U.S. tariff rates in the Smoot-Hawley tariff of 1930 was not helpful, since it prevented borrowing countries from selling as much goods in the United States, and hence reduced their ability to repay loans. More than half the dollar bonds issued by European countries were in default by 1934, and more than 80 percent of the bonds issued in Latin American countries. It should be noted, of course, that many countries did not default. But inevitably, investors remembered the substantial losses, and were chary of investing in foreign securities for many years.[7]

Status of Long-Term International Capital Flows at the End of World War II

It is not surprising that in the early years after World War II there was almost no outflow at all of portfolio investment from the United States. (The purchase of World Bank securities, and the consequent lending by that bank, discussed later in this chapter, is excluded from this comment.) Redemptions of existing bonds exceeded sales of new bonds. Direct investment occurred on a modest scale—but chiefly in Canada, Latin America, and the Middle East. Three-fourths of such new investment was in the petroleum industry. Most of it came from undistributed domestic profits of parent companies with foreign subsidiaries. Very few countries other than the United States were able to make any significant contribution to foreign investment, and most refused even to permit the World Bank to lend the money which they had contributed to that bank. To quote one leading authority, "private foreign investment (in which the general investor risks his money) either in portfolio or in direct investment has been practically non-existent."[8]

The outbreak of the Korean conflict in June 1950 increased the impediments to foreign investment and postponed its revival. A continuation of government foreign lending as well as foreign grant aid was made inevitable. Military expenditures in Korea and economic aid for Korea were obviously necessary to meet the goal of containment of the invasion from the north.

The problem of reviving private foreign investment, which had been foreseen as difficult, was made much more difficult. Nevertheless, during the 1950s and 1960s, a broad expansion of foreign investment occurred. Most of it took place because of such incentives as exploitation of salable natural resources, for example, oil, rising profits in growing markets, and gradual reduction of risk.

The expansion of international long-term investment did not begin very auspiciously and for a number of years obstacles to it were so great that little progress could be made.

At this point it is important to examine the theoretical reasons for international flows of capital. These factors are somewhat different for portfolio investment and for direct investment and hence are treated separately.

---

[7]For a lengthy discussion, see John F. Madden, Marcus Nadler, and Harry C. Sauvain, *America's Experience as a Creditor Nation* (New York: Prentice-Hall, 1937).

[8]Sir Arthur Salter, *Foreign Investment*, Essays in International Finance, No. 12 (Princeton: Princeton, 1951), p. 38.

CAUSES OF PRIVATE LONG-TERM INTERNATIONAL PORTFOLIO LENDING AND INVESTING

Since portfolio investment does not involve control of management, such investment should depend chiefly on yield. Portfolio investment by U.S. residents, the major source of capital in the early postwar years, was small, and did not expand for some time. It did not consistently exceed $1 billion on a net basis until 1968. Direct investment became more important, as shown in Table 11-2. The lesser importance of portfolio investment, in contrast to its dominance in the period of major British investment, must be explained.

Interest Rate Differences—A Flow Theory

Early theory of international capital movements focused mainly on differences in interest rates as the cause. Long-term capital movements were assumed to occur because of the attraction of higher interest rates, and equilibrium was temporarily achieved, in the received theory, by short-term capital movements which served to offset the long-term capital flows temporarily. Thus long-term borrowing was offset by temporary deposit of the borrowed funds in the lending country, until the funds were needed for investment.[9]

A small extension of theory is required to include differences in yields on stocks, for which both dividend yields and capital gains must be taken into

[9]The writings of Kindleberger and Iversen were important in developing the analysis. See Charles P. Kindleberger, *International Short-Term Capital Movements* (New York: Columbia, 1937) and Carl Iversen, *International Capital Movements* (London: Oxford, 1936).

Table 11-2 United States Long-Term Investment for Selected Years

(In Billions of Dollars)

	U.S. long-term direct investment abroad	Foreign long-term direct investment in the U.S.	Net portfolio investment
1950	−0.6*	0.1	−0.3
1955	−0.8	0.2	0.2
1960	−1.7	0.1	0.4
1965	−3.5	0.1	−1.1
1970	−4.4	1.0	1.2
1971	−4.9	−0.1	1.3
1972	−3.4	0.2	3.7
1973	−4.0	1.9	3.8

*− indicates outflow.
Source: International Economic Report of the President, 1974 (Washington, D.C.: Government Printing Office, 1974).

account. There is no fundamental difference in this respect between foreign investment and domestic investment.

Finance has been plagued by the use of two different meanings for the term *capital*: on the one hand, financial assets, and on the other hand, real capital assets, goods which provide services over time. If capital flow refers to the flow of real capital assets, there is substantial evidence over the long run to support the flow theory.[10] But a flow theory may not be applicable to short-run financial capital movements.

Moreover, this flow type of theory alone does not explain why interest rates remain higher in some countries than in others, or why there are (as indicated in Table 11-2) simultaneous flows of capital in opposite directions. If differences in interest rates alone were the explanation, the flow should be in the direction of countries having the highest interest rate and it should continue until rate differences disappear.

Risk and Return—A Portfolio Adjustment Theory

Recent theory of capital movements centers on two variables, return and risk, and attempts to integrate them in a portfolio adjustment theory. Risk is variability of the return on an investment.[11] Two stocks may have the same long-term yield on the average, yet one may vary widely in yearly return while the other may have a relatively stable return. The former stock is said to be more risky. The degree of risk may be judged by some measure of variation in return, such as standard deviation or variance.[12]

Investors are assumed to have various preferences concerning return and risk, but it is generally assumed that, for any group of investors, their willingness to accept increased risk is accompanied by a desire for increased return. Some groups of investors may have preferences such that they are unwilling to accept high risks; other may be willing to accept such risks if returns are high. If preferences of various groups of investors are plotted by the lines labeled *I* in Figure 11-1 and if the rates of return on three securities

[10]See, for example, Bertil Ohlin, *Interregional and International Trade* (Cambridge, Mass.: Harvard, 1957), especially pp. 335, 406. See also the evidence in Herbert Feis, *Europe the World's Banker, 1870–1914* (New Haven, Conn.: Yale, 1930).

[11]For a good discussion of some of these points, see Herbert G. Grubel, "Internationally Diversified Portfolios: Welfare Gains and Capital Flows," *American Economic Review*, December 1968, pp. 1299–1314.

[12]When any variable has different probabilities of occurring at different levels, an *expected value* can be calculated as an average of the various levels weighted by the probabilities of occurrence. This is in a sense the most probable amount. Standard deviation is the square root of the squares of the differences of each amount from the expected value, each being weighted by the probability of its occurring. Standard deviation is a useful measure of risk or variation when expected values of different variables are the same, but if they are different, a *coefficient of variation* is more useful. This is the standard deviation divided by the expected value; it provides a measure of *relative* variance. These concepts are discussed in many texts on financial management; see, for example, James C. Van Horne, *Fundamentals of Financial Management*, 2d ed. (Englewood Cliffs, N.J.: Prentice-Hall, 1974), pp. 206–207.

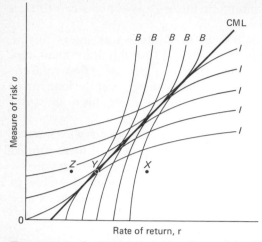

Figure 11-1 Capital Market Line Formed by Tangencies of Portfolio Frontier Lines of Investors and Borrowers.

having the same degree of risk are plotted as X, Y, and Z, any investment with expected return and risk Z or Y would be rejected by an individual investor or a group of investors in favor of investment X. Competition among investors, however, would tend to cause them to accept less return with a given degree of risk, and hence to purchase investment Y. However, given their risk-return preference limits, as indicated by the curved lines I, they would not purchase investment Z.

On the other side of trading in capital assets, borrowers presumably have different preferences. It may be assumed that borrowers would like to obtain funds by offering the lowest possible yield and will offer higher yields with increased risk, but that there are limits to the increase in yield that they will offer with increase in risk. Hence their preference frontiers may be delineated by curves marked B. Borrowers would not offer securities with a risk and return indicated by X. Although they would prefer to offer securities with risk and return indicated by Z, competition would force them to offer securities with risk and return indicated by a point close to Y.

The Capital Asset Pricing Model (CAPM)   With many groups of borrowers and of investors, having different risk and return preferences, trading would tend to occur in investments lying along the "investment frontier" representing the lowest rates of return investors are willing to accept with given risks and the greatest returns borrowers are willing to offer with given risks. This line has been termed a capital market line (CML)—see Figure 11-1—and the resulting model a capital asset pricing model (CAPM). The capital market line indicates risks and returns on traded securities. The lowest rate of return available is that on a riskless asset. Other capital assets have both higher yields and greater degrees of risk.[13]

It must be assumed that investors hold portfolios of capital assets—that is, that they do not hold one single asset, but many. A basic reason for this is that diversification reduces risk. However, it must be noted that there may be systematic risk in the market. The market as a whole, or a portfolio selected to represent the market, may fluctuate in a certain manner. Such systematic risk cannot be eliminated by diversification as nonsystematic risk can.

A measure of the extent to which return on one investment fluctuates with (covaries with) the market as a whole is termed *covariance.* If a portfolio of investments has a covariance such that it fluctuates precisely with the market as a whole, holding that portfolio can eliminate all nonsystematic risk.

Foreign securities may not fluctuate in value in the same manner as domestic securities, since they are influenced by other factors. Economic conditions may be improving in some countries while they are declining in others. Hence it may be possible to reduce risk still further by including foreign securities in a portfolio. International diversification in portfolios may eliminate risk which cannot be eliminated by domestic diversification.

An International Capital Asset Pricing Model (ICAPM)   It should be possible to develop an international capital asset pricing model (ICAPM) comparable to the capital asset pricing model (CAPM). However, certain obstacles make the task complex. First, interest rates on what are viewed as riskless assets in different countries vary, and there may not be a universal riskless asset. Second, the international capital market is to some extent segmented. For various reasons, investors cannot or do not trade in foreign stocks to the same extent as they trade in domestic stocks. Reasons may be lack of information or various types of restrictions. Third, exchange rate risk exists. This means that investors in different countries face different risks in purchasing the same securities.

If instantaneous adjustment in exchange rates were assumed, so that purchasing power parity were instantly reached, exchange risk would be irrelevant. But it is realistic to assume that capital flows react more swiftly to changes in prices and in expected exchange rates than do current account transactions. Purchasing power parity can be expected to be attained, if at all, only in long-run trends, as we found in Chapter 9. Thus with exchange risk, investors of different nationalities are likely to hold different portfolios.

If investors could trade continuously, they could engage in continuous hedging, and exchange risk would become irrelevant. But it is not realistic to assume that continuous trading is possible.

[13]The analysis was first presented in William F. Sharpe, "Capital Asset Prices: A Theory of Market Equilibrium under Conditions of Risk," *Journal of Finance*, September 1964, pp. 425–442.

Thus an ICAPM developed on the assumption that there is no exchange risk is probably unrealistic. Various other possible ICAPMs could be developed on different assumptions concerning segmentation of international capital markets or on trading at either discrete or stochastic intervals.[14]

It has been pointed out that different models require different tests. A model which is independent of exchange risk can be tested by regressions involving returns on securities, betas (covariances), and international market indexes, either alone or with country market indexes. If segmentation of capital markets is assumed, regression of each return on a given security with all national indexes would probably be necessary.

Although some research indicates that investors can reduce risk by diversifying their portfolios internationally so that results are consistent with an ICAPM, the precise form of a proper ICAPM has yet to be defined. Further testing of models based on various assumptions about exchange risk, segmentation of international capital markets, and continuous trading is necessary.

Liquidity—A Special Form of Risk Reduction

Liquidity in financial assets reduces the risk that there may be variability in return if it is necessary at some time before maturity to sell the assets. Prices of nonliquid assets may vary widely if sold at given times. A long-term bond may have a low net return or even a loss if sold when its price is low (net return being the interest income minus the capital loss on the sale). But this simply means that there is variability in the return to the time of desired sale. Liquidity means little risk of this type; lack of liquidity is simply a special form of risk. Liquidity preference is a type of behavior toward risk: those who have a liquidity preference prefer short-term or otherwise liquid securities because this form of risk is less for such securities. (There is also the income risk: for an investor who desires long-term yield, a short-term security may mature and have to be replaced by a security with less yield, if interest rates have fallen. But it is usually assumed that the risk of lack of liquidity is important to more investors than is the converse risk. Moreover, in a period of inflation, long-term decline in interest rates is clearly unlikely.)

In the general theory of interest, a liquidity premium has been postulated by many economists. This means *generally* lower interest rates for short-term

---

[14]A clear discussion may be found in Michael Adler and Bernard Dumas, "Optimal International Acquisitions," *Journal of Finance*, March 1975, pp. 1–19. For other useful references, see especially Bruno H. Solnik, "International Pricing of Risk: An Empirical Investigation of the World Capital Market Structure," *Journal of Finance*, May 1974, pp. 365–378; Bruno H. Solnik, "An Equilibrium Model of the International Capital Market," Research Paper No. 129, Graduate School of Business, Stanford University, October 1972; Bruno H. Solnik, "An International Market Model of Security Price Behavior," Graduate School of Business Research Paper, Stanford University, September 1972, forthcoming in the *Journal of Financial and Quantitative Analysis*; and Haim Levy and Marshall Sarnat, "International Diversification of Investment Portfolios," *American Economic Review*, September 1970, pp. 668–675.

securities than for long-term securities, or at least lower rates for such securities than there would have been without the liquidity premium.

Growth in Portfolios (Wealth)

The fourth factor affecting portfolio investment is the size of financial asset portfolios held by investors. When portfolios increase in size, investors may wish to add to their holdings of foreign securities to maintain the same percentage of such securities in their portfolios (and hence the same prospect for higher return and the same degree of risk, assuming that risks in various countries did not change). Economic growth in a country may therefore cause a flow of portfolio investment to foreign countries, even if neither yields nor risks change.

Thus we have identified four major factors as basic causes of international portfolio investment: yield differentials, risk differences, liquidity differences, and differences in rates of economic growth. These provide a more adequate explanation of capital flows than the theory that capital movements are induced by interest rate differences alone.

CAUSES OF PRIVATE LONG-TERM INTERNATIONAL DIRECT INVESTMENT

Even if yields, risk, and wealth were the main factors causing international direct investment, these factors would play a different role in causing direct investment from their role in causing portfolio investment. For portfolio investors, relevant expected rates of return and risks are those on foreign *securities*; for direct investors, they are the expected rates of *profit* and risks associated with operating a foreign subsidiary or at least having some degree of managerial control.

To some extent, portfolio and direct investment may substitute for each other. Portfolio investment reduces the supply of capital at home and increases that in foreign countries; hence it presumably substitutes to some extent for direct investment. Moreover, portfolio investment tends to increase the market values of foreign firms, increasing the cost of purchasing controlling interests in them. Finally, portfolio investment tends to increase exchange values of foreign currencies, making direct investment more costly. Sometimes most direct investment flows in one direction and most portfolio investment in another. After World War II, there was a large outflow of U.S. direct investment, especially to Europe, while at the same time there was a substantial flow of European portfolio investment to the United States. Recently a similar flow has begun to come from OPEC countries, and some direct investment from Europe and Japan can now be observed.

Most authors presume that portfolio investment would be a more efficient way than direct investment to move capital if conditions of perfect competition existed. These conditions would mean that (1) rates of return and risk on foreign equities would properly reflect rates of profit and risk in foreign enterprises; (2) enterprises in one country would not have any special advantages enabling them to operate more profitably than local firms in foreign countries; (3) the objective of both individuals and corporations would be to maximize profits; and (4) individuals and corporations would attach the same premium to exchange risks and would be equally able to cover such risks. Since, under such conditions, all international investment would be portfolio investment, the theory of direct international investment has been directed toward relaxation of one of the four above assumptions. It is recognized that foreign direct investment probably arises from imperfections either in markets for securities or in industrial markets.[15]

Imperfections in Securities Markets

If securities markets are imperfect, it may be impossible for portfolio flows to equalize rates of profit, and hence direct investment may be attracted to areas where rates of profit are relatively high. If information concerning corporations is difficult to obtain, this may discourage foreign portfolio investment. If the market for stocks is small, fluctuations in stock prices may be great. Such risks of changes in prices in the short run would be more discouraging to the portfolio investor than to the direct investor. Institutional factors, such as controls, may impede portfolio investment.

However, this explanation, while perhaps of some significance, does not seem adequate. For one thing, the United Kingdom has the best-developed securities markets in Europe, yet the amount of U.S. direct investment in the United Kingdom relative to GNP is larger than in any other country.

Advantages of Superior "Knowledge" and Economies of Scale

Direct investment is more industry-specific than portfolio investment. It is usually made, by any one corporation, in one or possibly several industries, whereas portfolio investment is usually made in a number of industries. Direct investment is also more difficult to liquidate, once made, than portfolio investment.

Thus a widely accepted theory of direct investment holds that it is a result of specific advantages such as better production technology, greater managerial skill, better organization, more knowledge, and perhaps economies of scale.[16] For these advantages to be causes of direct investment, however, such investment must be a more profitable alternative (as long as we do not relax the profit-maximizing assumption) than either exporting or selling "knowledge" to foreign local firms through licensing or other means. Licensing is of course

[15]Incisive analysis of some of these aspects is presented in Richard E. Caves and Ronald W. Jones, *World Trade and Payments* (Boston: Little, Brown, 1973), pp. 486–491.

[16]Charles P. Kindleberger, *American Business Abroad: Six Lectures on Direct Investment* (New Haven, Conn.: Yale, 1969).

fairly common. Caves has suggested that small companies may frequently license foreign firms to produce because small firms often have only a one-time advantage, while managers of larger firms may believe that they can continuously produce new knowledge and product improvements.[17]

To explain why U.S. firms are the ones which have the largest volume of direct investment, Raymond Vernon developed the product cycle theory.[18] He argued that the United States, with a large market and high per capita income, is a place in which many new products are first introduced. As production increases, U.S. firms begin exporting the new products. Then later they make direct investments abroad to take advantage of lower local production costs and to avoid losing foreign markets to local (foreign) firms. Hymer and Rowthorn have also argued that U.S. direct foreign investment is of this defensive nature, but they said that the reason was a desire to maintain the share of U.S. firms in world markets at a time when GNP in the United States was not increasing as rapidly as elsewhere.[19]

Oligopoly and Growth

Other authors have stressed oligopoly and the desire to prevent entrance of new competitors, while some authors have emphasized growth rather than profit as a motive for expansion, relaxing the profit-maximizing assumption.[20] However, if industrial concentration is a cause of foreign investment, why have European firms made much less foreign direct investment than U.S. firms, in spite of the fact that the degree of industrial concentration in Europe is greater than in the United States?

Exchange Rate Risks

Aliber advanced a theory which combined elements of financial capital budgeting theory with a theory about exchange rates.[21] He argued that direct foreign investment may occur because source-country firms discount the same expected stream of income at a lower rate than do host-country firms. This could of course be combined with the idea that the expected stream of income may be greater because of semimonopolistic advantages. Interest and profit rates are higher in weak-currency countries than in strong-currency areas. If markets were perfect, exchange risk would offset the lower discount rate, discouraging investment in weak-currency areas. Aliber argued, however, that

---

[17]Richard E. Caves, "International Corporations: The Industrial Economics of Foreign Investment," *Economica*, new series, 1971, pp. 1–27.

[18]Raymond Vernon, "International Investment and International Trade in the Product Cycle," *Quarterly Journal of Economics*, May 1966, pp. 190–207.

[19]Stephen H. Hymer and Robert Rowthorn, "Multinational Corporations and International Oligopoly: The Non-American Challenge," in Charles P. Kindleberger, ed., *The International Corporation: A Symposium* (Cambridge, Mass.: M.I.T., 1970), pp. 57–91.

[20]See Bela Balassa, "American Direct Investment in the Common Market," *Banca Nazionale del Lavora Quarterly Review*, June 1966, pp. 121–146.

[21]Robert Z. Aliber, "A Theory of Direct Foreign Investment," in Charles P. Kindleberger, ed., *The International Corporation: A Symposium*, pp. 17–34.

this need not occur, and that a source-country firm might issue securities in its own market, at the source-country yield rate, and buy a foreign firm having the same expected income stream. The foreign firm would have a lower present value for the expected income stream because it would discount it at a higher rate.

When the U.S. dollar was a strong currency, empirical data seemed to support Aliber's argument to some extent. When the dollar weakened, some authors found Aliber's argument more difficult to accept.[22] One might, of course, take the view that the long-run outlook for the U.S. dollar is still that it is a strong currency, because the United States has less inflation than almost any other major country. However, the facts that *net* foreign investment by the United Kingdom increased when sterling was weak and that countries with strong currencies, such as Germany, had large net inflows of direct investment seem to provide evidence against Aliber's view.

Nevertheless, it does seem clear that capital can generally be raised more cheaply in the United States than in other countries. Why can't foreign firms take advantage of this, and thus discount their expected income streams at lower rates? Of course, when controls prevented them from borrowing in the United States, the reason was obvious. Perhaps the registration regulations and costs imposed by the Securities and Exchange Commission (SEC) constitute a barrier to foreign borrowing which prevents foreign firms from using a low-cost source of capital.

SUMMARY

When Britain was no longer the greatest creditor nation, after World War I, the United States began to be the major source of international capital outflows. But the United States had relatively short experience in this activity, and many investments were made without much investigation. Thus when losses accumulated on such investments and at the same time the crash in the stock market in 1929 was followed by the Great Depression, U.S. international lending and investing almost ceased. There was almost no source of funds for meeting cyclical needs and no significant lender of last resort. This undoubtedly contributed to the severity and worldwide character of the Great Depression.

Private long-term international portfolio lending and investing is probably best explained by some variation of the capital asset pricing model, which regards lending and investment as forms of adjustment of portfolios in view of expected return and risk. Growth in portfolios (increase in wealth) is probably another independent variable determining long-term capital flows, although tests of this hypothesis have been few in number, partly because of the scarcity of data on wealth for many countries.

Direct international investment has other causes, probably arising from

---

[22]Giorgio Ragazzi, "Theories of the Determinants of Direct Foreign Investment," IMF *Staff Papers*, July 1973, pp. 471–498.

special advantages in knowledge, patents, organization, and other factors. The theory advanced by Aliber that firms in strong-currency countries (source countries) may discount future expected returns on investment at lower rates than firms in weak-currency countries (host countries), for the same industries, is also a possible explanation of direct investment.

QUESTIONS FOR DISCUSSION

1 Contrast British experience as a creditor nation with that of the United States. What conclusions or tentative hypotheses can you draw from this comparison?
2 Why was world trade more adversely affected than domestic income, by the Depression in the 1930s, and international investment more adversely affected than world trade?
3 Do you think that the concept of "dollar shortage," as presented in *The United States in the World Economy*, was useful? Why or why not?
4 Why does risk make it more likely that investment will flow into *and* out of a country, whereas interest rates alone might make a one-way flow logical?
5 Does direct investment imply and require the assumption of product differentiation? Could there be direct investment and pure or perfect competition? Explain.

6 State Aliber's theory of the cause of direct investment. What evidence is available for and against that theory?
7 How could imperfections in international securities markets be a cause of international direct investment? What argument may be made against this theory?
8 What lessons of the 1920s concerning international capital flows are significant for today?
9 What effect did defaults on international investments in the 1930s have on international portfolio investments after World War II?
10 Why did a portfolio adjustment theory replace a flow theory of international portfolio investment? What problems arise in attempting to extend the capital asset pricing model to an international capital asset pricing model?

SUGGESTED REFERENCES

Excellent perspective on the status of foreign investment at the end of World War II is provided by Sir Arthur Salter, *Foreign Investment*, Essays in International Finance, No. 12 (Princeton: Princeton, 1951). For a review of the earlier role of the United States in international investment, see Cleona Lewis, *The United States and Foreign Investment Problems* (Washington, D.C.: The Brookings Institution, 1948). All the volumes of the series of reports on U.S. international transactions by the Department of Commerce are useful, but Hal B. Lary and associates, *The United States in the World Economy*, Economic Series No. 23, U.S. Department of Commerce, Bureau of Foreign and Domestic Commerce (Washington, D.C.: Government Printing Office, 1943) is invaluable. For Europe's role before World War I, see Herbert Feis, *Europe the World's Banker, 1870–1914* (New Haven, Conn.: Yale, 1930).

Extension of financial market theory from a flow theory to a risk-return portfolio selection theory was based on the contributions of James E. Tobin, "Liquidity Preference as Behavior Towards Risk," *Review of Economic Studies*, February 1958, pp. 65–86, and of Harry M. Markowitz, *Portfolio Selection: Efficient Diversification of Investments* (New York: Wiley, 1959). On the extension of such theory to international capital flows, in addition to the article by Grubel cited in fn. 11, see William H. Branson and Raymond K. Hill, Jr., "Capital Movements Among Major OECD Countries: Some Preliminary Results," *Journal of Finance*, May 1971, pp. 269–286; Chung H. Lee, "A Stock-Adjustment Analysis of Capital Movements: The United States–Canadian Case," *Journal of Political Economy*, July/August 1969, pp. 512–523; Thomas D. Willett and Francesco Forte, "Interest Rate Policy and External Balance," *Quarterly Journal of Economics*, May 1967, pp. 242–262; and Norman C. Miller and Marina von Neumann Whitman, "A Mean-Variance Analysis of United States Long-Term Portfolio Foreign Investment," ibid., May 1970, pp. 175–196.

One obstacle to the analysis of reasons for foreign portfolio investment in the United States is the lack of data for wealth in many foreign countries; some studies tried to use foreign GNP figures as proxies for wealth—see, for example, the study by Branson and Hill, cited above.

For surveys of the literature on financial capital flows, see Erich Spitaller, "A Survey of Recent Quantitative Studies of Long-Term Capital Movements," IMF *Staff Papers*, March 1971, pp. 189–220; Zoran Hodjera, "International Short-Term Capital Movements: A Survey of Theory and Empirical Analysis," IMF *Staff Papers*, November 1973, pp. 683–740; and Ralph C. Bryant, "Empirical Research on Financial Capital Flows," Board of Governors of the Federal Reserve System, Discussion Paper No. 50, July 1974.

The effect of the U.S. role as a financial center on capital flows to and from this country has been analyzed in, for example, Charles P. Kindleberger, *Balance of Payments Deficits and the International Market for Liquidity*, Essays in International Finance, No. 46 (Princeton: Princeton, 1965) and Arthur B. Laffer, "The U.S. Balance of Payments—A Financial Center View," *Law and Contemporary Problems*, Winter 1969, pp. 33–46.

The capital asset pricing model was developed in William F. Sharpe, "Capital Asset Prices: A Theory of Market Equilibrium Under Conditions of Risk," *Journal of Finance*, September 1964, pp. 425–442. Important discussions of the international capital asset pricing model include Bruno H. Solnik, "The International Pricing of Risk: An Empirical Investigation of the World Capital Market Structure," *Journal of Finance*, May 1974, pp. 365–378; Michael Adler and Bernard Dumas, "Optimal International Acquisitions," *Journal of Finance*, March 1975, pp. 1–19; and Donald R. Lessard, "World, National, and Industry Factors in Equity Returns," *Journal of Finance*, May 1974, pp. 379–391.

Chapter 12

Institutional Factors Affecting International Investment

Although risk-return relationships and special advantages in production are the basic causes of expansion of international investment, institutional factors also play a part. Development of new financial institutions and markets tends to reduce risk and increase efficiency of flow of funds from lenders to borrowers, thus facilitating investment. There may sometimes also be institutional pressure for divestment; questions related to divestment are considered at the end of this chapter.

POSTWAR EXPANSION OF INTERNATIONAL LONG-TERM INVESTMENT

A number of specific developments helped to revive long-term investment after World War II. In this section some of these developments are noted, and the roles of international long-term lending institutions, of private long-term lending and investing institutions, of investment insurance, and of the development of an international long-term capital market (the Eurobond market) are analyzed.

Resources are unequally distributed throughout the world, and one of the major reasons for direct investment has been the need for certain natural resources, especially, in recent times, petroleum and certain ores and metals. Petroleum was the first industry in which any significant postwar investment occurred, and most of the investment was direct.

A substantial number of countries succeeded in attaining rapid rates of growth in real per capita income in the postwar period. In such countries the increasing size of the market attracted direct investment. Such fields as retailing presented attractive opportunities in some countries as the increasing incomes of consumers could be spent on a greater variety of goods and services, rather than chiefly on food and housing.[1]

Finally, there was the development of regional "common" markets, of which the best example is the European Common Market. These markets were created by gradually eliminating tariffs and other barriers within them. Productive facilities established in common market areas could obtain advantages of economies of scale and of being "inside" the external tariffs of the common market. Profit differentials seemed to be inadequate, empirically, to explain the heavy United States investment in the European Common Market. Alternative or supplemental hypotheses considered size of market, growth, and tariffs. Size of market may be a factor if a certain size is necessary for the efficient introduction of technology on an appropriate scale. Growth in income may be a factor if it provides more "discretionary" spending power for consumers. Tariffs may be a factor if their elimination permits reduced selling prices for products produced within the common market area. One study, which tried to determine correlations between volume of U.S. investment in the European Common Market and all three of these variables, found statistical support for the size-of-market hypothesis but none for the tariff hypothesis.[2]

It is difficult, however, to accept the size-of-market hypothesis alone as *the* cause of foreign direct investment. If it is the size of the market which provides the inducement, why not export rather than engage in direct foreign investment? And if foreign direct investment is undertaken, why can't local firms compete? Clearly, the goods or services *can* be produced in the country; why, then, can foreign firms produce them profitably in competition with local firms? It seems that we must return to a theory based on specific market imperfections, especially for technology.

ROLE OF INTERNATIONAL LONG-TERM LENDING INSTITUTIONS

Before the usual causes of foreign investment could generate postwar investment on a significant scale, it was necessary to reduce obstacles to foreign investment. The likelihood of very slow revival of private international investment was recognized even during World War II. The outbreak of war in

[1]See, for example, Daniel Seligman, "The Maddening, Promising Mexican Market," *Fortune*, January 1956, pp. 103 ff.

[2]Anthony E. Scaperlanda and Laurence J. Mauer, "The Determinants of U.S. Direct Investment in the E.E.C.," *American Economic Review*, September 1969, pp. 558–568.

Korea in June 1950 added to the concern. But much earlier it had been generally recognized that noncommercial risks of government taxation and confiscation, risks of outbreaks of international or civil conflict, memories of past investment losses, absence of power and transportation facilities in many less-developed countries, political instability especially in newly independent countries, exchange controls and inconvertibility of currencies, and the relatively high rates of return obtainable on investment in the industrialized countries would be likely to limit private international investment.

Lack of knowledge concerning foreign investment was also a limiting factor, and the need for defense spending in industrialized countries was recognized as a competing demand for funds.

In view of these considerations, it seemed likely that local capital would be inadequate for reconstruction and development, and that foreign capital would not flow into countries in need of reconstruction and development unless risks were reduced.

The World Bank Group—IBRD, IFC, and IDA

For these reasons it was agreed at the Bretton Woods Conference in 1944 to establish an International Bank for Reconstruction and Development (IBRD) as a companion institution to the IMF. The IMF was to be (as explained in Chapter 5) an institution for the cooperative setting of exchange rates, and a short-term international banking institution to provide funds to central banks and governments to enable them to maintain fixed exchange rates during temporary BOP deficit periods. The IBRD was a long-term lending or guaranteeing institution, designed to facilitate provision of long-term capital for reconstruction and development. (Indeed, Keynes remarked that the IMF should have been called the bank, and the IBRD the fund.)

The IBRD   It was originally believed that to encourage private investment the IBRD could be simply a guaranteeing institution. This expectation was quickly shown to be in error. Guarantees were not enough to induce private investment—for one thing, because many investors remembered the government-guaranteed investments of the 1920s which had defaulted in the 1930s. The World Bank made certain loans in Europe for reconstruction, and found its resources totally inadequate for this purpose. Hence it stopped lending and reassessed its position and the means it might use to generate international investment. Funds for reconstruction in Europe were supplied by the Marshall Plan aid, on condition that European countries cooperate in programs for the use of such funds. This cooperation led to the European Common Market. When the World Bank was ready to resume activity, it was free to concentrate on lending for economic development.

However, since it had been intended that it would be primarily a guaranteeing institution, it had relatively few funds for lending. It had been established with comparatively small amounts of capital contributed by the member countries; most countries which joined the IMF joined the IBRD (membership in the IMF was a prerequisite to membership in the IBRD, since it was desired that both lending and borrowing countries should participate in the cooperative establishment of stable but adjustable exchange rates).

The capital of the IBRD was contributed in the form of a transfer to the IBRD of an amount equal to 20 percent of each country's quota—quotas being determined in the same manner as for the IMF. Of the 20 percent contribution, 2 percent had to be in gold and 18 percent in the currency of the contributing country. Countries were permitted to restrict the lending of their local currency funds by the World Bank if their governments believed that they could not appropriately make foreign loans at the time. Hence the only loanable funds possessed by the World Bank were the small total of gold contributions and the local currencies contributed by some countries, most importantly the United States, which agreed that their currencies might be used in lending.

Fortunately, provision had been made in the charter of the World Bank that it could borrow by issuing bonds. The only major capital market in which bonds could be issued at first was that of the United States. In order to induce investors to buy such bonds, at yields permitting moderate interest rates on loans and sufficient margin to cover administrative costs and to build up some reserve for loan losses, investors had to be somehow assured that the bonds had a very high degree of safety.

Fortunately again, this could be done. First, the World Bank was generally required to make loans only for *projects* for which cost and revenue estimates could be reasonably accurate. It adhered to this approach very strictly for a number of years. Second, a guarantee was required from the government of the country in which a project was to be carried out. When the World Bank loaned money to Brazil, to be paid to a Canadian firm to build electric power plants in Brazil, a guarantee for repayment of principal and interest was required from the Brazilian government. Third, an extra one percent was added to the interest rate, and this amount was put into a reserve fund and also carried in the capital account of the World Bank as a reserve. The reserve fund was to be used in case losses on loans resulted (or would result) in losses to investors in World Bank bonds. Fourth, and perhaps most important in the formative years of the World Bank, member countries were required to pay in the unpaid 80 percent of their contribution quotas in the event that funds were needed to meet losses which otherwise would fall on investors in World Bank bonds. Since the United States had a large quota, a large amount would have to be paid by the United States in such event. Thus World Bank bonds were regarded as almost as safe, or often, as safe, as U.S. government bonds. Frequently the World Bank bonds carried the same quality rating, AAA, as U.S. government bonds.[3] Additional

---

[3]World Bank bonds have generally been long-term issues, with maturities from 10 to 30 years. Recently the bank entered the intermediate-term market to widen the potential number of buyers of its bonds. The World Bank, as might be expected, has never defaulted on any bonds, and there were no defaults on any loans it made to borrowers through 1970. Every year since 1947 the World Bank has made a profit which has been used to make additional loans and to provide funds to IDA. See *World Bank and IDA: Questions and Answers* (Washington, D.C.: World Bank, 1971).

safeguards sometimes existed: If collateral seemed of value, it was supplied. Loans for building steamships in the Netherlands were collateraled by mortgage claims on the ships—easily enforceable if the ships entered the harbors of countries such as the United States.

Another task remained. The World Bank had to be sure that its bonds could be purchased by U.S. investors, since other investors could not buy them, either because of lack of funds or restrictions of their governments. Moreover, institutions rather than individuals were the major market for such bonds—their safety and liquidity, with their low yield, made them appeal to institutions more than to individuals. Institutions had to be persuaded to buy them, and legal permission for institutions to buy them had to be acquired where it did not exist. Many states had "legal lists" of investments permissible for certain types of institutions, and these had to be changed by persuading state legislatures. Also, the World Bank had to hire investment bankers to market the securities through syndicates, so that broad secondary distribution would ensure purchase of the securities by many different institutions (giving breadth and depth to the secondary market, to provide liquidity).

All these tasks were accomplished, with some difficulty, in the early 1950s, and the flow of funds to the World Bank began. By the time the tasks had been completed, problems of European reconstruction had been largely met by Marshall Plan aid funds, loans to Greece and Turkey, and other special U.S. government programs. Some reconstruction had also taken place in Japan, partly through use of occupation funds. The World Bank could turn its attention to loans for economic development, and it successfully made many such loans, with no losses.

The IFC Two problems which could not be adequately met by World Bank loans were met in part by creation of a World Bank affiliate—the International Finance Corporation (IFC). The World Bank could not lend without a government guarantee; yet, in the field of manufacturing, in contrast to the fields of electric power, railroads, irrigation, and some others, firms often either could not or did not wish to obtain government guarantees. If they did acquire such guarantees, they were likely to be subject to additional government regulation and restrictions. Nor could the World Bank supply equity capital. Risks involved in providing equity capital would have inevitably resulted in some losses; hence in diminished appeal of World Bank securities to investors. Moreover, the thought of an international institution owning and managing productive facilities in various countries was repugnant to those who believed in the power of sovereignty.

The IFC, established as a relatively small institution in 1955, was authorized to make loans without government guarantees and to purchase convertible securities, although not to buy stocks.[4] Loans could be sold, after "seasoning,"

---

[4]The IFC invests in private enterprises, not publicly owned ones, but a small percentage of government ownership does not necessarily disqualify an enterprise. See *IFC, General Policies* (Washington, D.C.: IFC, 1970), p. 3.

to private investors, and the convertibility of the securities would permit conversion into stocks by private investors if that became advantageous. The investigation by the staff (the same staff is used by the IFC and by the IBRD, to minimize adminstrative costs) would make investors aware of the characteristics of investments, and the repayment of loans through regular amortization would assure investors that continued repayment would be likely after they had purchased the securities. Incidentally, the World Bank also followed this practice when possible, selling securities to private investors, thus obtaining funds for additional loans. It also made loans jointly with private investors, often taking the later maturities in serially maturing securities, so that private investors might take the earlier maturities and be assured of earlier repayment.

IDA The World Bank and the IFC, and gradually reviving private investment in some areas, notably in the European Common Market, in parts of Latin America, and in the Middle East, did not meet the need for funds on the part of many LDCs, especially those with low per capita incomes. This led to the creation in 1960 of the International Development Association (IDA), which was chartered as another affiliate of the World Bank to lend to LDCs at relatively low rates of interest, and often at no interest for a certain period. Frequently its loans were very long-term, because the types of projects needed in many LDCs could generate income to repay borrowed funds only over long periods. The members of IDA were classified into Part I countries—comparatively developed or high-income countries—and Part II countries, those less developed. Each Part I country pays all of its subscription in convertible currency, available for lending. Part II countries pay only one-tenth of their subscriptions in convertible currencies, and the remainder in their own currencies, which may not be used for lending without their consent.

In 1964 it was agreed that there would be a general replacement of IDA's resources, paid in by the Part I countries. A second replenishment was agreed upon for effect in 1969, and there were negotiations for further replenishments. Some Part II countries take part in these. Nonmember countries (for example, Switzerland and New Zealand) have made loans to IDA on the same terms on which IDA lends at a maximum—50 years maturity, a grace period of 10 years before repayment begins, and no interest.

Some other institutions provide similar loans for LDCs. IDA has some advantages over other institutions: its loans are less likely to be politically influenced, it has the benefit of the expertise of the World Bank staff, it can readily obtain cooperation from UN agencies, and negotiations for replenishment of funds are backed by the World Bank's influence.

The World Bank Group—IBRD, IFC, and IDA—has made a significant contribution to the revival of international long-term investment. The IBRD has in the past few years moved somewhat beyond the project approach to a broader approach to lending for sectors of the economies of LDCs. Its success over a quarter of a century enables it to experiment with other types of lending, and it is to be hoped that it can make possible the financing of some investments which could not be undertaken by private investors.

The establishment of IDA points out a dilemma for the World Bank group: should it be a banklike institution, making loans only to creditworthy borrowers, or should it be a development institution, making loans in an effort to aid in the development of LDCs? What criteria should the World Bank group establish for loans? In its early years, it was essential for the World Bank to demonstrate that it made sound loans which would be repaid on time, to encourage private investors to participate in such loans and to purchase loans from the World Bank.

With the growing gap between incomes in the industrialized countries and those in the LDCs (except OPEC), the question was more frequently raised whether the World Bank group should make loans with greater emphasis on their usefulness for development. This question is discussed in more detail in Chapter 20.

The IDB and Other Regional Long-Term Lending Institutions

Regional groups of countries have, in association, created regional long-term lending institutions to assist economic development. The Inter-American Development Bank (IDB) is perhaps the best example. It makes development loans to both governments and private industry, it makes "easier" loans of the type made by IDA, and it administers special funds created by member countries for specific development purposes. An example is the Social Progress Trust Fund of $525 million to promote social development in Latin America, created by the United States under terms of the Alliance for Progress. European countries and Canada have also provided special funds. The IDB gives preference to projects which further the economic integration of Latin America. Approval of the governments of the countries in which projects are carried out is required, but government guarantees are not normally required.[5]

There are a number of other regional development banks: the Asian Development Bank, the African Development Bank, and the European Investment Bank, to mention only three. There is also a Central American Bank for Economic Integration (CABEI), which finances projects contributing to the economic integration of countries that are members of the Central American Common Market (CACM).[6]

The reason for the establishment of regional development banks is that many projects are beyond the capacity, and sometimes outside the interest, of development banks and other institutions within individual countries. The World Bank Group would not necessarily have a special interest in economic

---

[5]The IDB is potentially more subject than most of the other international lending agencies to influence by the countries which borrow from it. The U.S. Congress ordered in 1970 that its loans, with those of the other international lending agencies, be reported by the National Advisory Council on International Monetary and Financial Policies, which is supposed to integrate to some degree the international activities of government agencies and of agencies of which the U.S. government is a member. See Sidney Dell, *The Inter-American Development Bank: A Study in Development Financing* (New York: Praeger, 1972).

[6]See Ingo Walter and Hans C. Vitzthum, *The Central American Common Market: A Case Study on Economic Integration in Developing Regions*, Bulletin 44 (New York: New York University, Graduate School of Business Administration, 1967).

integration of an area, yet economic integration seems to be a means to economic development. Moreover, it is recognized that it is harder for less-developed parts of a region to obtain financial aid, and that the need to finance projects which may be in the interest of economic integration cannot very well be met by institutions located in and concerned primarily with individual countries.

ROLE OF GOVERNMENT LONG-TERM AND INTERMEDIATE-TERM LENDING INSTITUTIONS

Many governments in industrialized countries have their own lending institutions to foster long-term and intermediate-term international loans and investments. The U.S. Export-Import Bank is probably best known, but Japan has an Export-Import Bank and many other countries have similar institutions.

The Export-Import Bank

The U.S. Export-Import Bank serves several functions: it makes development loans, in many cases very similar to those made by the World Bank; it makes medium-term and short-term loans to finance exports; and it can make loans to finance imports, although this program has been dormant. The bank has capital stock and may borrow from the U.S. Treasury to obtain funds. It pays rates based on the average cost of Treasury borrowing. It formerly issued its own medium-term debt, but now borrows through the Federal Financing Bank for medium-term funds. It makes development loans with the expectation that the borrower will provide about half of the total cost in the form of equity. It also guarantees loans made by private institutions. Finally, it provides war risk and expropriation insurance for U.S. property owned by U.S. citizens and located in foreign countries.

The basic principle of the Export-Import Bank, like that of the World Bank, has been that its financing is available for generally sound projects and exports when other financing is not. Interest rates are at the usual levels for the type of transaction.

Such a bank serves some functions not served by the World Bank—it makes loans to countries that are not members of the World Bank, such as the Soviet Union; it makes tied loans specifically to finance exports; and it makes loans in which U.S. economic and/or political goals have some role, although not a predominant one.[7] In other cases loans could be obtained from either the

---

[7] The Export-Import Bank has always had some part in the facilitation of credits for the Soviet Union and Eastern Europe. Originally two Export-Import Banks were established in 1934, one specifically to facilitate trade with the Soviet Union, and they merged. Legislation prohibits credits by private entities to countries which have defaulted on obligations to the U.S. government (and this would include the Soviet Union), but this does not apply if the countries are members of the IMF (as Rumania is) or if the Export-Import Bank participates in the credit. It has been concluded by several Attorneys General that the prohibition does not apply to normal export trade credits. All the governments of Eastern Europe except Bulgaria are in default on obligations to the U.S. government.

Export-Import Bank or from the World Bank, and the choice depends on the same considerations which would prevail in seeking a loan from one or the other of two commercial banks. The Export-Import Bank did not adhere to the "project" principle as strictly as the World Bank did; some of its loans could be classified as "BOP" loans, and some as general loans not tied to a project with specific prospective revenue (for example, a loan for reconstruction after an earthquake).

The Export-Import Bank's lending authority has been extended from time to time. In 1974 the extension was in doubt for a while because of congressional desire to limit the amount of its loans to the Soviet Union. After agreement on an extension of lending authority, including a limit of $300 million on credits to the Soviet Union, the bank returned to more active lending. Its direct loan limit was changed to permit it to cover from 30 to 55 percent of the cost of exports (instead of 30 to 45 percent) and to extend guarantees up to 85 percent (instead of 45 percent).[8]

Trade credits to the Soviet Union have also been made by the Export-Import Bank of Japan. For example, a credit of $220 million was made in 1975 to finance the export of Japanese ammonia mnaufacturing facilities. Loans have also been made by consortia of private banks in Europe.

In evaluating the Export-Import Bank, keeping in mind that it is intended primarily to encourage U.S. exports, its borrowing from the Treasury in effect subsidizes exports in that the borrowing is at lower rates than could be obtained by a private or international institution. The question must then be raised, is the promotion of U.S. exports a useful function? Whatever the answer may have been under fixed exchange rates, when a BOP deficit was considered to be a significant problem, subsidization of U.S. exports in a period of floating exchange rates cannot be justified on economic grounds. To the extent that exports are subsidized, tax funds are used to distort trade patterns and thus reduce general welfare. Economists have generally argued that tariffs are harmful because they distort international trade and usually cause a reduction in trade and loss of some of its benefits. The same argument may be applied to means used to stimulate exports. They distort trade and redistribute income toward exporters.

The Export-Import Bank is useful, however, in providing medium-term financing which is not widely available from banks. In this sense it has the same function as the farm credit institutions established by the government.

AID

There is also the Agency for International Development (AID), an agency which is part of the U.S. State Department. It operates the Development Loan Program and the Cooley Loan Program. The Development Loan Program provides long-term funds to LDCs. Private companies may borrow these funds from their governments, which borrow from the Development Loan Fund

---

[8]See Federal Reserve Bank of Chicago, *International Letter*, Dec. 13, 1974, and Feb. 28, 1975.

(DLF). Maturities are longer and interest rates lower than they would be for private loans. Cooley Loan funds are local currency funds (in foreign currencies) obtained in payment for agricultural products sold by the United States under either the Mutual Security Act or the Agricultural Trade Development Assistance Act. These local currency funds are loaned to U.S. firms and subsidiaries in the countries that provided the funds by buying agricultural products from the United States. Interest rates are comparable to those in the countries concerned, and maturities are flexible.

AID is the latest in a long line of agencies responsible for U.S. foreign aid. At the time of the Marshall Plan, suggested in 1947 and implemented in 1948, the Economic Cooperation Agency (ECA) was established to handle the flow of funds to Europe. Later changes in the name and mission of the agency handling foreign aid reflected changes in priorities in U.S. foreign policy. As mutual security became important at the time of the Korean conflict, the foreign aid agency became the Mutual Security Agency (MSA) in 1951; with somewhat less emphasis on the military aspect after the Korean armistice, the new agency became the Foreign Operations Administration (FOA) in 1953; this agency was superseded by the International Cooperation Administration (ICA) in 1955; and when President Kennedy was inaugurated, the Agency for International Development (AID) was established. Reasons for name changes included gradual changes in the objectives of foreign aid; lack of clarity in objectives; a desire, especially in recent years, to coordinate all foreign aid programs, insofar as possible, in one agency; and a changing philosophy. The change in philosophy was reflected in a shift from the reconstruction of Europe (chiefly in 1948–1952) to the development of LDCs, from military security to economic development, from grants to largely loans, and to an emphasis on long-range planning and funding. The grant portion of foreign aid declined greatly, and as a percentage of GNP is now very small. Much of the grant aid was in South Korea in the period during and immediately following the Korean conflict, and in South Vietnam during the conflict there.

AID has encouraged and helped private agencies in economic development. Some activities are small but may be significant. For example, AID supported the work of the International Executive Service Corps (IESC), which supplies experienced American volunteer businessmen to advise on and aid in the development of business firms in LDCs.

ROLE OF PRIVATE LONG-TERM LENDING AND INVESTING INSTITUTIONS

As private long-term international investment began to revive in the 1950s, and bond and stock markets in the United States again began to receive issues of foreign securities, it became more feasible for private institutions to engage in international investment. The formation of the European Common Market and the achievement of convertibility of major European currencies in 1957–1958 were landmarks in the progress toward freer international investment. The main prerequisites for private international investment are free markets and minimal governmental controls. Although most private international invest-ment is carried on through direct investment by firms that have established market positions and through capital markets in which bonds and stocks may be purchased by individual and institutional investors, there is room for some specialized institutions devoted to lending for international investment.

An Equity Institution—IBEC

Although profit maximization is the assumed goal of much international investment, there is a place for private institutions with additional major purposes. A pioneer in this area is the International Basic Economy Corpora-tion (IBEC), which was founded by Nelson Rockefeller in 1947. The aim of IBEC, in addition to profit, has been to assist the development of economies in which it operates by (1) determining economic bottlenecks, (2) establishing joint economic ventures to break such bottlenecks, (3) establishing enterprises which contribute to higher living standards and lower production and distribu-tion costs, (4) selecting enterprises that complement each other, (5) encourag-ing financial participation by nationals of the countries, and (6) employing local nationals when possible, and training them for technical and managerial positions.[9] Activities of IBEC have included supermarkets, low-cost concrete housing, mutual funds designed to channel savings into effective activities, and fishing. The problems it encountered are familiar to those with experience in economic development activities: the impact of inflation on business practices; the resistance to change, not only in simple use of tools, but in concepts and attitudes toward organization; and the problems of nationalization.

Could other companies, differently managed, have had the same or better results? IBEC is essentially a family-owned company; over 70 percent of the ownership is held by the Rockefeller family and trusts for their benefit. Whether a publicly owned company could have operated as IBEC did is questionable. A basic change in attitudes, however, has made business firms more concerned about the social effects of their activities, and their social responsibilities, than they were in the 1950s. Perhaps publicly owned compa-nies could now undertake some of the nonprofit activities undertaken by IBEC.

An International Development Bank—Adela

Adela (from adelantar, to advance or progress) Investment Company, S.A., is another institution established to make long-term investments in LDCs. IBEC operates worldwide, but Adela operates only in Latin America. Its major purpose is to furnish equity capital for activities, at the same time providing technical assistance and management aid. This company has had moderate success. Adela is owned by more than 200 industrial, commercial, and financial companies from Europe, Canada, the United States, Latin America, and Japan. Adela is in effect a development bank, financing new industries to which it also

---

[9]These objectives were stated in the 1948 Annual Report of the IBEC. For longer discussion, see Wayne G. Broehl, Jr., *The Case Study of the International Basic Economy Corporation*, National Planning Association Series on United States Business Performance Abroad (New York: National Planning Association, 1968), pp. 9–11.

provides managerial assistance. Many development banks have been established in recent years in LDCs and these are discussed in more detail in Chapter 20. Adela sells its investments when this seems appropriate, and devotes the funds to new investment. Although it provides equity capital, it does not seek control or management, in this respect differing significantly from IBEC.

PICA and Others

The Private Investment Company for Asia (PICA) is a recently established private international development bank. Ownership is one-third Japanese; one-third American; and one-third European, Canadian, and Australian. Since there is great poverty and also great variation in culture and language in Asia, PICA faces a major challenge.

PICA may borrow funds and increase its capital as its operations grow. Since its shareholders are private firms and banks, it has no governmental aims, and concentrates on profitable investments in industries which may contribute to the economic development of Asia. It usually makes minority rather than majority investments in firms, and plans joint ventures with local investors and entrepreneurs.

Another recently organized private development organization, the Société Internationale Financiere pour les Investissements et le Développement en Afrique (SIFIDA), is similar in nature and operations to Adela and PICA.

INVESTMENT INSURANCE—OPIC

International investment encounters risks not found to the same extent in domestic investment: risks of expropriation, war, and inconvertibility of currencies. An insurance and guarantee program was authorized in the Economic Cooperation Act of 1948 (the Marshall Plan Act), and the program was continued by the agencies which succeeded ECA. However, at the time of writing this book it was handled by a separate agency—the Overseas Private Investment Corporation (OPIC), established in 1969, but not active until 1971.

There is some contradiction in the program; it is intended to help the economic development of LDCs, but at the same time to make the insurance program businesslike and to cover costs.[10] OPIC has reinsured in part with Lloyd's of London, but reserves of OPIC could be depleted quickly by a wave of expropriations. One way to reduce risk is to encourage business firms to engage in more joint ventures, U.S. minority interest ventures, and projects involving a nonequity role (management contracts, for example). Such activities would be less subject to risk of expropriation. Some U.S. insurance companies have discussed with OPIC the possibility of their participating with it in underwriting.

[10]"What Future for OPIC?" *Morgan Guaranty Survey*, January 1974, pp. 4–8. For the earlier history of foreign investment guarantees, see Marina von Neumann Whitman, *The United States Investment Guaranty Program and Private Foreign Investment*, Princeton Studies in International Finance, No. 9 (Princeton: Princeton, 1959).

OPIC insures only projects owned by U.S. citizens or by corporations at least 51 percent owned by U.S. citizens. Investments must be new and must be in developing countries that have signed guarantee agreements with the U.S. government. Aside from such restrictions, the major problem is the need for clarification of the conditions for payment of claims, since governments may take many actions that may or may not be included within the terms of the insurance or guarantee program.

AN INTERNATIONAL LONG-TERM CAPITAL MARKET—THE EUROBOND MARKET

As in money markets, for many years international long-term lending meant the participation, as either lenders or borrowers, of foreign firms in the domestic capital markets of leading countries. In the 1960s, however, a truly international capital market developed, just as an international money market—the Eurodollar market—had developed in the 1950s.

Eurobonds are bonds denominated in a currency other than that of the country in which they are issued. Frequently they are issued in one country for a borrowing firm located in another country, and purchased largely by buyers in still other countries.

Origin and Development of the Eurobond Market

Controls on capital outflows from the United States were a major reason for the origination of Eurobonds. Freedom from the withholding of taxes on interest income to bondholders (which was usual on bond issues sold in the United States) may have been another cause. The growing ability of Europe to buy securities was a third. Finally, the restrictions on capital movements in Europe were a fourth—because Eurobond sales were not controlled; being intended for purchase by foreigners, they did not involve an outflow of funds from the country where the sale was made.

Basically, then, restrictions confronting foreign borrowers who tried to borrow in national markets, together with the availability of offshore funds for investment in bonds in an essentially unregulated market, gave rise to a new international bond market. The restrictions have changed somewhat. In the period 1963–1974, the legal restrictions on foreign borrowing in the United States were most significant. Since 1974, it has probably been the SEC registration requirements which discourage foreign borrowers from issuing securities in this market even though interest costs are lower on comparable bond issues relative to risk.[11]

The high quality of the issues, the excellent credit standing of the borrowing firms, and the expertise of the investment houses which have marketed Eurobonds have contributed to the success of this market. Most

[11]For a careful study of differences in yields above the rate on riskless assets, comparing the U.S. bond market and the Eurobond market, see Norman Bartczak, "Measuring and Comparing the Effect of Selected Factors on the Cost of Debt Capital under Two Alternative Financial Disclosure Systems," unpublished doctoral dissertation, University of Washington, Seattle, 1977.

Eurobonds have been denominated in dollars. At some times, however, such as early 1975, denomination of bonds in Deutsche marks was common.[12] In spite of the high quality of the issues, yields are higher than on comparable bond issues in the United States. Prices (and hence yields) depend on anticipated changes in exchange rates as well as on the quality of the bonds. The exchange rate risk factor presumably contributes to the higher yields. When revaluation of the Deutsche mark was anticipated in 1969, prices of bonds denominated in that currency rose, and yields fell. Studies which did not take the anticipated revaluation of the mark into account showed unexplained yield differentials.

Present Status and Future of the Eurobond Market

The future of the Eurobond market depends on several factors: the continuation of its relative freedom from control; the desire of U.S. subsidiaries in Europe to borrow there for their local operations; the types and quality of bonds issued in the Eurobond market and the expertise in their marketing; the emergence of new European borrowers, including public agencies; and the requirements that discourage borrowing in the United States. Another factor favoring the continued existence and development of the Eurobond market is that some international issues are larger than can conveniently be marketed in any national market, even in New York.

The relatively large role of public issues in Eurobond sales in 1975 suggests that the Eurobond market may offer a means of providing capital for public projects—reminiscent of the loans of the early twentieth century. Clearly, relative rates of inflation are significant, and governments that cannot restrain inflation destroy their own credit standing and that of public agencies within their boundaries.

SEC registration requirements are probably a formidable barrier to many foreign borrowers who might otherwise borrow in the U.S. market. Much more extensive financial disclosure is required than many foreign entities are willing to give; and in some cases disclosure requirements have caused even U.S. institutions to cancel projected securities issues.

Characteristics of Securities in the Eurobond Market

Many issues of Eurobonds are, except for the place of issue, much like similar issues in the New York market. However, special characteristics of some issues merit comment. Underwriting syndicates are usually composed of investment bankers from various countries and the bonds are sold to investors in various countries. It is difficult for any country to regulate the Eurobond market as a whole because, although one country may pressure its financial institutions not to underwrite such bonds or to underwrite them only under certain conditions, it is impossible for one country to influence underwriters in many countries.

Eurobonds have been issued in the form of convertible bonds, in the form of floating rate notes, and with warrants. Convertible bonds and bonds with

---

[12]IMF *Survey*, May 12, 1975, pp. 133–136.

warrants have been popular when the U.S. stock market was rising, since at such times it was likely that conversion into stocks could bring further capital gains, and warrants would also rise in value as it became likely that the price might be reached at which warrants could be used to buy stock, which could then provide still further capital gains.

Floating rate notes, with the rate tied to the LIBO rate, were usually offered when there were downsloping yield curves. They were issued in small denominations to attract small investors who cannot make the large deposits required in the Eurodollar market. However, many such bonds were purchased by banks. For borrowers, the usual 10-year maturity on such bonds was attractive when bond financing was difficult to obtain (in tight money conditions). The cost of commissions, averaging 2 percent, however, was a deterrent—why not borrow through a syndicated Eurodollar loan at $1/2$ percent commission? The maturity was usually somewhat shorter, of course.[10]

Some firms avoided both the Eurodollar loan charges of banks and the costs of floating issues in the Eurobond market by issuing Eurodollar commercial paper. Of course, to obtain significant advantage from this, the firms had to be of such credit standing that they could easily issue such paper and had to be ready and able to roll it over to obtain any significant maturity length.

Multiple Currency Bonds   Multiple currency bonds were also issued when necessary to attract buyers. Such bonds were issued with denomination in European Units of Account (EUAs) and in European Monetary Units or European Currency Units (EMUs or ECUs). The EUA had a fixed value, originally equal to that of the U.S. dollar before the 1971 devaluation. In 1972, its value was linked to the value of the currencies of the enlarged European Common Market (nine countries instead of six), instead of the 17 countries of the older European Payments Union (EPU). A number of other changes were made.[14] The value of the EUA changed only when the values of all the reference currencies changed and when at the same time at least two-thirds of them changed in the same direction. Issuers of EUA bonds designate the currency of payment for purchasing the bonds, but buyers redeem the bonds in terms of the EUA, the value of which changes as values of the constituent currencies change. EUA values change less than the values of individual constituent currencies because some currencies rise and others fall. If one currency changes in relation to values of the other currencies, borrowers gain or lose, since they must redeem the bonds in the same amount of EUAs, but EUAs are more or less valuable in terms of their own currencies. Similarly,

---

[13]For further detail, see Yoon S. Park, *The Euro-Bond Market: Function and Structure* (New York: Praeger, 1974), pp. 24–29.

[14]The 17 countries included the original six members of the European Common Market (France, Germany, Italy, the Netherlands, Belgium, and Luxembourg), the seven members of the European Free Trade Area (Austria, Denmark, Norway, Portugal, Sweden, Switzerland, and the United Kingdom), plus Iceland, Greece, Ireland, and Turkey. Denmark, Ireland, and the United Kingdom subsequently joined the European Common Market. The European Payments Union was an agency established to help settle balances among the 17 member countries in a period in the 1950s before most of the currencies became freely convertible.

lenders may lose or gain if their currencies change in value relative to the other currencies. If the Deutsche mark rises in value, a German lender loses because he receives less in Deutsche marks than he would have received had he made the loan in that currency. Thus the EUA bond gives more stability in value than a single-currency bond, but there is chance for either borrower or lender to gain or lose.

Issues of bonds denominated in EMUs or ECUs may be paid for in any of the European Common Market country currencies, and may be redeemed by purchasers in whichever of these currencies they select. Naturally they would select the currency which has risen most in value. Thus EMU bonds are biased in favor of bond-buyers. Such bonds are therefore used when firms fear difficulty in selling bonds without some attractive feature.

Effects of Tax Laws   Tax laws caused some special provisions for international bond issues such as those in the Eurobond market. For example, U.S. firms have used domestic financing subsidiaries, usually incorporated in a state such as Delaware, to obtain funds through the issue of Eurobonds. Since the income of the financing subsidiary is foreign-derived, it can pay interest and dividends to securities purchasers abroad without withholding any tax. If proceeds of a Eurobond issue are used in the United States, U.S. firms often establish overseas finance subsidiaries to issue bonds. Since activities of overseas finance subsidiaries are conducted outside the United States, their interest income from lending the proceeds of Eurobond issues to U.S. firms is not U.S.–source income. Thus the interest income is not subject to U.S. withholding. Any change in tax laws obviously may affect the need for such activities.

Euro-Equities?   Brief mention should be made of what some have termed Euro-equities and Asian dollar bonds, both issued in recent years.[15] Some observers contend that Euro-equities is a misnomer, because although the securities are issued outside the United States, they are otherwise indistinguishable from other stocks of U.S. firms and must be traded in the U.S. stock market. Euro-equities have sometimes been evidenced by bearer depository receipts, regarded favorably by European investors. Morgan Guaranty Trust Company has issued International Depository Receipts (IDRs) interchangeable with the older American Depository Receipts (ADRs). These permit U.S. citizens to buy foreign stocks and receive dividends with no transfer of stock certificates, but only of the IDRs. It should be made clear that, although some U.S. firms or their subsidiaries have found it advantageous to issue stocks outside the United States, there is no Euro-equity market comparable to the Eurobond market.[16]

[15]For a brief discussion of one of these equities, see John F. Dunlop, "A New Form of Euro-Equity," *Euromoney*, February 1972, pp. 30–32.

[16]One writer argued that not only is there no Euro-equity market, but none is needed; see Nicholas J. Bär, "Do We Need a Euro-Equity Market?" *Euromoney*, April 1972, pp. 18–20.

Asian Dollar Bonds Asian dollar bonds, issued in the Singapore market in small amounts in the early 1970s, may grow in volume. One key factor is the availability of dollars in Asian countries for investment in such issues. With the end of the Vietnam war, economic development in many areas in Asia (if not in Vietnam, Cambodia, and Laos) requires capital and may benefit from the issue of bonds denominated in dollars. "Asian dollar bonds" may also be a misnomer, since such bonds are basically the same as other bonds issued in the Eurobond market. The growth of a market for offshore currency bonds in Asia is nevertheless of interest, and there may be capital market imperfections leading to some yield differentials. In any event, the sources and uses of funds in the Asian offshore capital asset market are worth noting in the study of the development of world financial centers.[17]

DIVESTMENT

Institutions have a degree of longevity, but there is a tendency to attribute to them a permanence which in the long run they are unlikely to have. The Christian church is an example of a very long-lived institution; most institutions have much shorter lives. Many automobile firms were established in the United States, but only four major companies survive. Even the institution of the nation-state, which has existed in its present form roughly since the Peace of Westphalia (1648) may not be permanent, although under present conditions it seems likely to continue for some time.

It is of course possible that the multinational firm will become a powerful and long-lived institution, with headquarters of various firms in various countries. It may even sometimes serve as a countervailing power against the nation-state. But it is inevitable that divestment must occasionally occur, and there may be circumstances when it is advantageous. We tend to think in terms of forced divestment—confiscation, liquidation as a result of losses like those incurred in a depression, and wartime destruction. But divestment may be voluntary, if other opportunities for the use of capital seem more profitable.

At least two economists (Paul Prebisch and Albert O. Hirschman) have suggested that an international financial intermediary be established to purchase securities of firms wishing to divest. The intermediary could hold such securities until local investors were able and willing to purchase them.[18] Such an intermediary might be established as an agency of the World Bank group or of regional banks such as the IDB.

Divestment is most likely either in countries undergoing political change that may be adverse to foreign investors or in countries where economic development has raised the levels of income and saving available for additional

---

[17]For a discussion of Singapore as a regional financial center, see Morgan Guaranty Trust Company, *World Financial Markets*, Mar. 22, 1973, pp. 8–12. On Panama, see ibid., pp. 12–13.

[18]Albert O. Hirschman, *How to Divest in Latin America, and Why*, Essays in International Finance, No. 76 (Princeton: Princeton, 1969).

investment domestically, hence reducing levels of profit for foreign investments in those countries below those formerly achieved.

For direct investment, however, the most serious problem may not be finding purchasers for the securities of firms which divest. Since foreign direct investment is usually undertaken because of quasi-monopolistic factors such as patents, quality of management, organizational excellence, and so on, the question must be asked, is it likely that such advantages can continue if local investors purchase the firms? Direct investment is not so much the result of financial factors as it is of managerial differences. Ability or willingness of local investors to purchase foreign firms may not be the key factor in maintaining profitable output. The conflict between economic viability and political nationalism is clearly evident in at least some cases, and the long-run result is difficult to forecast.

THE STATUS OF INTERNATIONAL LONG-TERM INVESTMENT

There is resentment over international long-term investment when it is too extensive, and sometimes even when it begins. The French were very conscious of American investment in Europe, and especially in France, in the 1960s.[19] Americans are very conscious of Arab investment in the United States in the 1970s.

In "one world," it would not matter very much. We are not much concerned about New York investment in San Francisco or vice versa, although occasionally there is complaint about such activity. The prospect of one world is not very bright, although the prospect for economic integration in common market areas is again improving after several difficult years caused by the international monetary upheaval of the early 1970s.

The need for economic development in order to raise incomes is so great that there is the possibility that international long-term investment may sometimes be accepted simply because it offers the possibility of increase in per capita income. Egypt may even be ready to move toward peace with Israel in order to attract more foreign capital to meet Egypt's desperate need for economic development. Of course, irrational nationalism may come, as it did with Adolf Hitler in the 1930s. But international long-term investment may be the only salvation for the low-income countries. Relief grants will not suffice; relief grants are consumed by people who produce more people who need more relief grants. Even increased production is often consumed by a growing population, with little increase in per capita income, as in some of the African nations.

A number of countries—South Korea, Taiwan, Iran, Mexico—have proved that real economic development can occur, with the encouragement of foreign investment as a major factor. Japan proved that it could occur with

[19]This was the theme of the well-known book by Jean-Jacques Servan-Schreiber, *The American Challenge* (New York: Atheneum, 1968).

little foreign investment, but Japan is a country of strong cohesiveness and singleness of purpose, and was already somewhat developed. In the LDCs foreign investment is essential, as we shall discuss in Chapter 20.

International long-term investment encounters obstacles because of wars, revolutions, confiscation of property, and inconvertibility of currencies, as well as because of "usual commercial risks." Yet it continues to increase, and the world now has far more foreign investment than in 1913, in spite of two world wars and numerous less extensive conflicts. The United States alone has, as shown in Figure 12-1, net international investment of $50 billion and foreign investment totaling about $200 billion. A long-term international capital market,

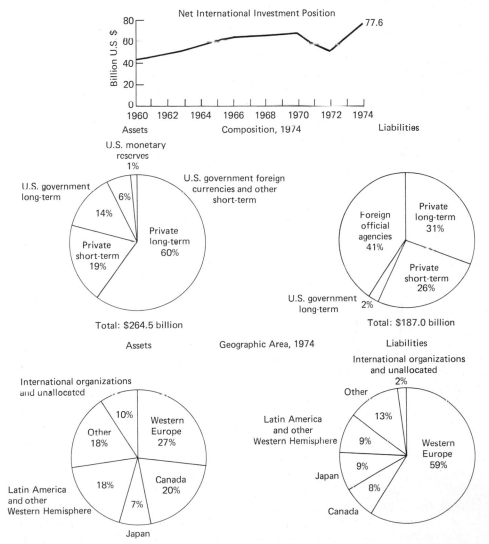

Figure 12-1 U.S. Foreign Assets and Liabilities. Securities are market value, and all others are book value. (*Source: International Economic Report of the President, 1976, p. 67.*)

the Eurobond market, has come into existence. The internationalization of U.S. banking is proceeding at a rapid pace. The economic forces leading in the direction of world economic integration may yet overcome, slowly, political forces which have created barriers. In large part, these economic forces become visible in expansion of financial activities which were essential in the development of the U.S. economy and which are the means of transferring resources and of permitting investors to hold claims on resources—essential activities for economic development.

QUESTIONS FOR DISCUSSION

1 Since charters for both were agreed upon at the same conference, it is useful to compare the nature and functions of the IMF and the IBRD. Why did Keynes remark at one time that the Fund should have been called a bank and the World Bank should have been called a fund?

2 Compare the World Bank Group and the regional long-term lending institutions.

3 Why do the international institutions not make equity investments? In what way does this hinder their facilitation of international investment?

4 Do the same arguments used to justify the establishment of the World Bank justify the existence of the Export-Import Bank? Explain.

5 What place does foreign aid (grants) have in international investment?

6 Give some examples of investment apparently undertaken because of the need for natural resources, some undertaken because of the inducement offered by growing markets, and some undertaken because of the establishment of "common market" areas.

7 How and why did the World Bank become a "model" banking institution? Is it proper to term it a "banking" institution? How has it modified its activities in the 1970s?

8 In what ways did IFC and IDA supplement World Bank activities? Do you believe that the World Bank group should change in any other ways in order to be more effective in international lending and facilitation of international investment? If so, how?

9 Evaluate the role of each of the following in stimulating international investment:
> OPIC
> Private long-term equity institutions, such as IBEC
> Private long-term lending institutions, such as Adela
> The Eurobond market

10 Does the Eurobond market have the same type of origin as the Eurodollar market? To what extent does its continued growth depend on the same factors?

SUGGESTED REFERENCES

Programs of the World Bank and its affiliates are discussed in many publications of that group of institutions. A good statement is that in *Policies and Operations, The World Bank, IDA, and IFC* (Washington, D.C.: IBRD, 1971).

Changes in the U.S. foreign aid program are clarified in Walter C. Jones, Jr., "United States Aid Programs," *Baylor Business Studies*, November–January, 1963–1964, pp. 9–35. A proposed "new approach" to foreign aid was outlined by the Report to the President from the Task Force on International Development, *U.S. Foreign Assistance in the 1970s: A New Approach* (Washington, D.C.: Government Printing Office, 1970). The case for foreign aid in helping economies reach a point at which sound bank loans and investments can easily be repaid is made by Lawrence A. Mayer, "Bringing Foreign Aid Out of Limbo," *Fortune*, March 1972, pp. 86–89, 108–117.

Many interesting events in the history of IBEC are related in Wayne G. Broehl, Jr., *The Case Study of the International Basic Economy Corporation*, National Planning Series on United States Business Performance Abroad (New York: National Planning Association, 1968).

The basic questions involved in the investment guaranty program were discussed in Marina von Neumann Whitman, *The United States Investment Guaranty Program and Private Foreign Investment*, Princeton Studies in International Finance, No. 9 (Princeton: Princeton, 1959). The basic dilemma of OPIC—economic development versus avoidance of risk—was highlighted in "What Future for OPIC?" *Morgan Guaranty Survey*, January 1974, pp. 4–8.

The Eurobond market has been analyzed in a number of books and monographs. Paul Einzig, *The Euro-Bond Market* (New York: St. Martin's, 1969), Gunter Dufey, *The Eurobond Market: Function and Future* (Seattle: Graduate School of Business Administration, University of Washington, 1969), and Yoon S. Park, *The Euro-Bond Market: Function and Structure* (New York: Praeger, 1974) are all very useful. Investor preferences and yield correlations were investigated by Robert A. Yoder, "A Study of the Eurobond Market, 1969–1972," unpublished master's degree research report, Graduate School of Business Administration, University of Washington, 1973. On a recent interesting development, the first Eurobond issue denominated in yen, see *Business Week*, Apr. 11, 1977, p. 86.

A general discussion of foreign investment problems is included in the *International Economic Report of the President* (annually since 1973).

Chapter 13

Effects of and Controls over International Long-Term Investment

We found in Part Three that there are many causes for short-term capital movements, and that such capital movements are often *results* of changes in other items in the BOP. This is particularly true for short-term capital movements into and out of major international financial centers, such as the United States. The need for transactions and compensating balances and temporary offset for long-term lending play important roles in causing short-term capital flows into and out of such centers.

Long-term capital movements tend to be *causes* rather than results of other changes in BOPs. Therefore it is important to examine the effects of long-term capital movements on other variables, and the social repercussions of such changes.

If international financial analysts were only technicians, trying to find the cheapest ways to borrow and other techniques useful in short-run financial decisions, they might have little interest in the results of long-term capital flows. But if the analyst is concerned with the financial *policy* of a firm, he or she must take into account the broader implications of its activities. The success of international firms may not depend so much on the ability of financial managers to reduce borrowing costs or to forecast exchange rates as on an understanding of long-run effects of international financial activities of firms. The international impact of international firms on BOPs, on employment, on technology transfer, and on business growth, and the resulting actions by governments and public groups may be far more significant than a few basis points saved on a bond issue. Both aspects of finance are important.

Let us begin with effects of income transfers like those involved in long-term capital movements.

THE TRANSFER PROBLEM—EFFECTS OF CURRENT INCOME TRANSFERS

Before considering long-term capital transfers involving shifts of purchasing power which are long-term but still not permanent (since loans must presumably be repaid and direct investments generate investment income), it is instructive to consider another type of transfer. This is the private remittance, the government grant, or the payment such as reparations for war damages. These transfers are intended to shift purchasing power and hence spending from one country to another. Although purchasing power is transferred through gifts and grants, transfer of *spending* means a transfer of *real assets* in the form of goods and services. A loan or a grant is of benefit when it enables a borrowing or recipient country to buy goods and services.

An increase in imports may, if exchange rates are relatively stable, lead to a loss of international reserve assets, a reduction in the money stock, a decline in prices or at least a slowing in their rate of increase, and hence a balancing outflow of exports, as was explained in Chapter 3. An income transfer in the form of remittances, grants, or reparations could have the same effects.

An increase in imports could also lead to a decline in real income in the importing country, as the increased payments for imports reduce spending within that country. The increased payments for imports shift income to foreign countries, enabling them to buy more from the country which experienced the initial increase in imports. As was explained in Chapter 3, however, the income shift is rarely alone sufficient to offset the increase in debits.

If exchange rates are not fixed, there is no reason for the price-specie flow mechanism to operate. Under floating or flexible exchange rates, however, increased imports cause a rise in foreign exchange rates and a corresponding decline in the value of the home currency. Depending on elasticities of demand and supply, there might or might not be a shift of income abroad, but it seems very unlikely that exchange rates adjust quickly enough to prevent some income shift.

The Keynes-Ohlin Debate

Note that reliance is placed on both mechanisms—price-specie flow and income shift—to cause BOP effects. In considering current income transfers, Keynes, relying only on the price-specie flow mechanism, argued that demand and supply elasticities of Germany's exports were too small to permit the expansion of German exports which was necessary if German reparations payments after World War I were to be made effective.[1] As events turned out, Keynes was correct, but his reasoning was not. German export prices did not fall, because lending to Germany was extensive, permitting the expansion of credit and maintenance of prices—in fact, helping to permit inflation. Instead of reducing prices of exports, Germany maintained them. On the other hand, the recipients of German reparations, chiefly France and Britain, did not permit an increase in spending. Instead, they used the reparations receipts as a means of reducing their own debt. As a result, the price-specie flow mechanism did not work as expected.

Ohlin, arguing as Keynes later argued in the 1930s, suggested that since Germany collected the funds for reparations payments through increased taxes, spending and income in Germany were reduced. He further argued that France and Britain would regard the reparations payments as an increase in their incomes, and on that basis there would be a multiple increase in income in those countries, and hence an increase in imports from Germany, making possible the *real* transfer of resources.[2] Although Ohlin's reasoning was logical, the results were not in accord with this scenario. United States lending to Germany permitted German imports to continue at relatively high levels, and when such lending stopped in 1929–1930, the system collapsed.

The Oil Price Increase as an Excise Tax

A similar problem arose in the 1970s with the rise in petroleum prices. This involved a transfer of income from oil-consuming countries to oil-producing countries. It was, in effect, an excise tax imposed by the oil-producing countries. In this case, the oil-consuming countries did in general somewhat reduce spending (in the recession of 1973–1975), and many of the oil-producing countries increased their spending. The funds received by a number of the Arab countries which, because of relatively small populations and low levels of economic development, did not increase spending significantly, were a problem because they had to be recycled to countries which would use them to increase their spending. Fortunately, the international monetary and banking system apparently met this severe test, partly because financial transfers *did* induce a substantial *real* transfer. Propensities to import in many OPEC countries were relatively high. Thus the long-run problem of recycling funds may not be as great as some had feared.

THE TRANSFER EFFECTS OF CAPITAL FLOWS

Turning from gifts, reparations, and taxes in the form of cartel price increases, we may note that, in the short run, long-term capital movements have the same

---

[1]John Maynard Keynes, "The German Transfer Problem," *Economic Journal,* March 1929, pp. 1–7.
[2]Bertil Ohlin, "The Reparation Problem: A Discussion," *Economic Journal,* June 1929, pp. 172–173.

effects as such transfers of income. Although the loans are expected to be repaid at some time in the (perhaps distant) future, the immediate effect is a shift in income from the lending country to the borrowing country. Capital outflows result in reduced levels of spending in the lending country, and increased levels of spending in the borrowing country. The changes may be either absolute or simply changes in *rates* of decrease or increase in spending. Shift in real income is possible unless the borrowing country is at full employment and at full capacity in plant utilization, or unless governments adopt policies to counteract the effects of the shift. American direct investment in Europe in the 1960s was clearly one cause of the relatively rapid growth in real income in Europe during that period. The United States might have had a slower rate of increase in real income than it did except for the policies adopted to increase the money supply and to reduce taxes (especially in the large tax cut of 1964).

Effects of Capital Flows with Stable Exchange Rates

With stable exchange rates, the effects of an outflow of capital should be to cause an outflow of reserve assets and the operation of the price-specie flow mechanism, and also a shift of income and the resulting income effects. Similarly, an inflow of capital should cause an inflow of reserve assets and of real income. As a result, imports should increase.

In the early part of the twentieth century, a number of economists who were students of Taussig showed that countries may borrow abroad and increase their imports, and that it was possible for the process to work very smoothly. The increased imports (debits) in the current account balanced the increased borrowing (credits) in the capital account.

Viner's study of Canadian borrowing in the period 1900–1913 is perhaps classic.[3] Canada borrowed, mainly in England. English banks made loans and placed sterling balances in the accounts of Canadian borrowers. The Canadian borrowers sold the sterling balances to their local banks to obtain Canadian dollars to use for investment at home. The Canadian banks converted the sterling balances into U.S. dollar balances by buying U.S. dollar exchange in the foreign exchange market, thus transferring the balances from London to New York. As Canadian banks needed increased reserves to lend, to meet investment needs of business, they transferred funds into Canada by purchasing Canadian dollars. Canadian business used both foreign borrowed funds and locally borrowed funds for investing. When the exchange rate for Canadian dollars in New York reached the gold export point, gold was shipped to Canada. However, an interesting aspect of the situation was that relatively little gold was shipped. Canadian banks treated deposit balances in New York as secondary reserves, and increased credit without necessarily importing gold. Money stock in Canada increased, as might have been expected from the

---

[3]Jacob Viner, *Canada's Balance of International Indebtedness, 1900–1913* (Cambridge, Mass.: Harvard, 1924).

price-specie flow mechanism described in Chapter 3, even though only a part of the change involved actual gold movement.

Viner found that, in fact, Canadian prices did rise as credit became more easily available. Although world prices generally rose, Canadian prices rose more. Moreover, Viner found that certain prices increased more than others. The greatest increase occurred, as might have been expected, in prices of goods sold domestically in Canada—home goods. Prices of Canadian exports increased less, because world market competition restrained price increases. Prices of Canadian imports increased least of all, because these prices were determined in world markets, and Canadian imports had only a small effect on such prices.

With increased money and credit in Canada, and higher prices, Canadian imports increased. The increase in imports relative to exports created a current account deficit in the BOP, offsetting the credit surplus in the capital account (long-term).

The gold standard worked as it was presumed to work, and a transfer of income to Canada enabled Canadians to purchase more imports. A capital inflow adds to income temporarily—and in the case of a long-term inflow of capital, the addition to income continues for a considerable number of years.[4]

Instead of assuming that the inflow of borrowed capital was the initiating cause, it could have been assumed that economic growth, giving rise to additional investment opportunities, was the initiating cause, and that the capital inflow was a result. It might also have been assumed that economic growth and capital inflow were both causes of expanded economic activity.[5] These assumptions make the theory more complete, and explain the increase in exports (which occurred, although it was less than the increase in imports). Without these assumptions, it might have been expected that exports would decrease.

The operations of the international mechanisms under the gold standard seemed to be remarkably smooth. Imports, money supply, and sectoral price levels behaved as expected if allowances are made for Canadian banks treating their New York dollar balances as reserves. An issue left in some doubt is whether the capital inflow or internal economic growth was the major initiating cause. Does borrowing lead to economic growth or does growth lead to borrowing? This question is discussed at more length later in this book.

Effects of Capital Flows with Flexible or Floating Exchange Rates

With floating or flexible exchange rates, the change in exchange rates rather than any flow of reserve assets is the mechanism for causing changes in other

---

[4]See the comments by Frank A. Southard, Jr., *Foreign Exchange Practice and Policy* (New York: McGraw-Hill, 1940), pp. 162–165.

[5]See James C. Ingram, "Growth in Capacity and Canada's Balance of Payments," *American Economic Review*, March 1957, pp. 93–104. See also Lloyd A. Metzler, "The Theory of International Trade," in Howard S. Ellis, ed., *A Survey of Contemporary Economics*, vol. 1 (Philadelphia: Blakiston, 1948), pp. 210–254, especially pp. 214–222.

items in the BOP after a change in capital flows. A long-term capital flow may be temporarily balanced by a short-term capital flow in the opposite direction. This countereffect may be no more than the temporary deposit of foreign borrowed funds in the lending country, before removing them for use in home investment. At some point, however, the borrowing country is likely to sell the lending country's currency to obtain home currency. With flexible exchange rates this reduces the value of the lending country's currency and raises the value of the borrowing country's currency. Of course, some funds may be quickly spent in the lending country, thus increasing that country's exports even in the short run, and partly compensating for the loan. Unless the loan is a tied loan, however, in which the borrowing country must buy from the lending country, this is likely to be only a partial offset.[6]

The depreciation of the lending country's currency was formerly regarded by economists as only temporary when the lending was a one-time flow. If the currency depreciation resulted in a matching increase in exports, the export flow would transfer the loan in real terms. The borrowing country would be enabled to buy goods. When it had purchased goods or services equal in value to the amount of the loan, this process would stop if no other changes occurred. At that time the demand for the lending country's currency to pay for such goods would fall. Changes in exchange rates were regarded as temporary fluctuations in which a lending country's currency would fall in value when loans were transferred, and rise again when the borrowing country purchased goods from the lending country. Recognition that services might be purchased instead of goods was not a significant change in the theory. Recognition that the borrowing country might buy from other countries rather than from the lending country meant only that those countries would have funds with which to buy from the lending country, and also required no basic change in the theory.

It may also be noted that heavy reliance was placed on the quantity theory of money. In the 1930s, when it appeared that the velocity of money also declined as the money stock declined, and when velocity seemed to change unpredictably at times, the quantity theory of money lost adherents. Much more emphasis was then placed on shifts of real income. Clearly, however, changes in the money stock were important in countries which attempted to spend far in excess of income. Those countries expanded their money supplies tremendously, and since no one then expected a return to "normal," speculators contributed to the fall in currency values as prices rose, by selling the home currency in the foreign exchange market (that is, by buying foreign currencies). Studies of hyperinflation, which occurred in several countries after World War II, gave a new monetarist school support for their idea that if velocity of money changes *predictably,* changes in the money stock can be used to predict changes in real income and price levels. Economic thought had come almost full circle.

---

[6]An early study was that of John H. Williams, *Argentine International Trade Under Inconvertible Paper Money, 1880–1900* (Cambridge, Mass.: Harvard, 1920). See also Charles P. Kindleberger, *International Short-Term Capital Movements* (New York: Columbia, 1937).

Extreme monetarist positions are still not widely accepted, but the argument that changes in the money stock have substantial effects on both real and nominal income (or GNP) *is* widely accepted. In modern theory, the money stock is affected through the monetary base, which is currency plus bank reserves, since bank reserves form the base for creation of money by banks. The monetary base is affected through changes in assets and liabilities of the central bank, and through changes in monetary items of the Treasury (gold holdings, issues of Treasury currency, and Treasury cash holdings in its own vaults). Reserve asset flows are significant because they affect the monetary base, and hence potentially affect the money stock. In the United States, items which affect the monetary base include gold flows, changes in holdings of foreign exchange by the Federal Reserve System, and changes in deposits held in Federal Reserve Banks by foreigners: these are the international items. In addition, of course, the monetary base is affected by changes in other assets and liabilities of the Federal Reserve System and in Treasury currency and Treasury cash.[7]

Acceptance of the monetarist viewpoint leads to emphasis on changes in the items which affect the monetary base as the significant net BOP balance. Some monetarists have stressed these as the *only* meaningful balance.[8] Many economists would not accept such an extreme position, and would argue that the current account balance, the basic balance, and other measures are useful for some purposes.

LONG-TERM INTERNATIONAL INVESTMENT AND BOPs

It would appear that the major effect of long-term international investment is to make possible an increase in income in the borrowing country, and thus an increase in imports. But this does not take into account that loans and investments, unlike gifts, grants, and reparations, are expected to be repaid at some future time. Clearly, long-term capital flows should influence investment income, an item in the current account of the BOP.

Domar's Analysis—Payback Periods

Evsey Domar was the first to analyze in detail the relationship between long-term capital flows, amounts of foreign investment already made, rates of

---

[7]For one form of current analysis, see Charles N. Henning, William Pigott, and Robert Haney Scott, *Financial Markets and the Economy* (Englewood Cliffs, N.J.: Prentice-Hall, 1975), Chap. 4.

[8]This view is advanced in Donald S. Kemp, "Balance of Payments Concepts—What Do They Really Mean?" Federal Reserve Bank of St. Louis, *Review,* July 1975, pp. 14–23. Kemp argues that the only meaningful balance in the BOP is what he terms the *money account*—for the United States, changes in primary international reserve assets plus or minus changes in foreign deposits in Federal Reserve Banks. Under floating or flexible exchange rates, he argues that no concept of balance in the BOP is meaningful. He is quite correct in asserting that concepts used in the past may now be misleading in their implications, and he has a strong basis for arguing that the money account is a useful concept. But his assertion that other balances are not economically meaningful may be regarded by many economists as extreme.

return on the capital flows, and the impact on BOPs. Domar pointed out that, given an amount of foreign investment already made, an annual addition to such investment through an outflow of long-term capital (direct or portfolio investment) would lead to an investment income return. Depending on the percentage addition to investment already existing and the percentage rate of return on such investment and on the new investment, a "payback period" could be calculated to indicate the time at which return on investment would begin to exceed the outflow of capital, if that outflow were maintained at a constant level. A constant level of capital outflow would inevitably be a declining percentage of the investment already made at any given time, while the rate of return might be presumed to remain relatively constant. If the rate of lending (the percentage of addition to investment already made) were higher than the rate of return (interest, dividends, or profits), there would be no point at which investment income would begin to exceed capital outflow, but this seemed very unlikely to occur.[9]

Norman Buchanan in fact argued that to maintain a rate of growth in investment greater than the rate of return, public investment might be necessary except for two facts: (1) total foreign investment at any time is reduced by losses, including those from expropriation, and (2) wars and inflation tend to reduce the importance of return on foreign investment as a percentage of GNP, and hence to lead to further private international investment.[10]

A payback period type of analysis was applied in some studies of United States international long-term investment in the 1960s. It was argued in one well-known study that because a point would come at which return on investment would begin to exceed capital outflow, the rising outflow need not cause more than temporary concern.[11] Unfortunately, although investment return did rise significantly, other changes in items in the U.S. BOP resulted in continuing deficits, and ultimately in a crisis in August 1971.

Bruck and Lees—A More Complex Analysis

A study by Nicholas K. Bruck and Francis A. Lees, published in 1968, used a more complex theoretical framework. Bruck and Lees pointed out that a direct long-term capital outflow would have (1) immediate effects in the form of the capital outflow itself (a debit) and related merchandise exports (credits); (2)

[9]Evsey Domar, "The Effect of Foreign Investment on the Balance of Payments," *American Economic Review*, December 1950, pp. 805–826. Domar was concerned whether there could be any net outflow of capital over and above the inflow of investment income, and suggested that government lending abroad might supplement private lending, and that low interest rates on government lending might offset higher yields on private lending, thus keeping the total investment income return below the net outflow of capital. See the excellent discussion by Norman S. Buchanan, "International Investment," in Bernard F. Haley, ed., *A Survey of Contemporary Economics*, vol. II (Homewood, Ill.: Irwin, 1952), pp. 307–350, especially pp. 320–323.

[10]Norman S. Buchanan, op. cit., p. 321.

[11]The example is Walter S. Salant and others, *The United States Balance of Payments in 1968* (Washington, D.C.: The Brookings Institution, 1963).

secondary effects, in the form of exports of materials and spare parts (credits), exports of services, including management services and patent rights (credits), and the return of earnings (credits); and (3) tertiary effects in the form of export promotion through the overseas subsidiaries, displacement of exports by production of such affiliates, and import competition from that production (receipts, reduced receipts, and payments with no clear theoretical result in either net credits or net debits in the balance of payments).[12]

Philip W. Bell added to this analysis by assuming single outflows of capital, continuous outflows, and continuously increasing outflows, and also by making empirical estimates of parameter values for rates of return on investments, percentages of earnings remitted home, fee and royalty income, and net exports as a percent of investment outstanding.[13] Unfortunately, Bell's empirical estimates were based on scanty data, and can hardly be relied on. But the effort to make such estimates was useful in indicating the analysis required.

Hufbauer-Adler and Behrman

G. C. Hufbauer and F. M. Adler expanded this model into a more complete analysis in an attempt to determine with some accuracy the effects of foreign direct investment. The results were significant for policy because of the debate concerning the imposition of controls on capital outflows, discussed later in this chapter.

In the Hufbauer-Adler model it was assumed that an outflow of capital resulted in a debit in the BOP each year as long as outflow continued, but that the debits were partly (or perhaps wholly) offset by several credits: (1) exports of capital goods, parts, and components to the overseas affiliate; (2) exports of finished goods to the affiliate for resale; (3) increased exports to the foreign economy in which the investment was made, because national income (or GNP) in that economy was increased as a result of the investment and the operation of the Keynesian multiplier; and (4) a return of earnings, royalties, and fees from the affiliate.[14] At the same time, these credits were expected to be partly offset by debits for (1) increased U.S. imports from abroad because some of the increased output in the foreign economy would be sold to the United States and (2) displacement of U.S. exports elsewhere by some production and sale of goods and/or services by the affiliate and by other facilities established as a result of increased GNP abroad.

Hufbauer and Adler developed their estimates of recoupment periods—the periods of time elapsing before net outflows of capital caused net credits equal or exceeding the outflows—on several bases. First, they made what they termed classical assumptions: that direct investment adds the invested amount

[12]Nicholas K. Bruck and Francis A. Lees, *Foreign Investment, Capital Controls, and the Balance of Payments,* Bulletins 48–49 (New York: New York University, Graduate School of Business Administration, 1968).

[13]Philip W. Bell, "Private Capital Movements and the United States Balance of Payments," *Factors Affecting the United States Balance of Payments,* Compilation of Studies Prepared for the Joint Economic Committee, U.S. Congress (Washington, D.C.: Government Printing Office, 1962).

[14]G. C. Hufbauer and F. M. Adler, *Overseas Manufacturing Investment and the Balance of Payments,* Tax Policy Research Study No. 1 (Washington, D.C.: U.S. Treasury Department, 1968).

to capital formation in the host country, and reduces it by that much at home. Second, they made what they termed reverse classical assumptions—that direct investment does not add to capital formation in the host country (presumably it substitutes for domestic investment there) and does not reduce it at home (substitution occurs at home also). Finally, they made what they termed anticlassical assumptions—that direct investment adds the invested amount to capital formation in the host country (no substitution), but causes no decline at home (substitution occurs). In their initial estimates for investment in various areas of the world, recoupment in many cases never occurred. Even with downward adjustment in the amount of export displacement, which seemed to them reasonable, recoupment periods were relatively long. These results were not necessarily an argument for controls on capital outflows, but they could be so used, since lengthy recoupment periods or no recoupment meant long or permanent excesses of debits over credits in the usual measures of deficit or surplus.

The length of the recoupment period was a problem in several ways. Over a long period of time, with firms developing new capabilities and other changes occurring, it would be unlikely that conditions would remain stable, and the basic Hufbauer-Adler model might be modified. The type of analysis suited to short periods was less suited to long ones.

Jack N. Behrman, Raymond Vernon, and others criticized the Hufbauer-Adler results on several grounds.[15] First, Behrman pointed out that U.S. foreign subsidiaries and affiliates may grow by retaining earnings and by borrowing abroad as well as by borrowing from or obtaining equity capital from the United States. Growth of foreign investment does not always imply an outflow of capital, and this should be kept in mind. Second, he argued that the rates of return used by Hufbauer and Adler were unduly low because they compared remissions of profits and interest with total investment (including retained earnings). If retained earnings were included in total investment, he argued, they should be included as returns (even though they were not remitted to the United States). Third, he argued that economic growth resulting from the increased investment *could* allow for both the sale of production arising from the investment *and* a continuation of exports to the country in which the investment was made. Fourth, he argued that foreign affiliates do not necessarily develop sources of parts and replacement equipment locally—or at least that this does not occur within any short period—and that therefore the export of parts and equipment to affiliates may continue for some time. Behrman argued that, although the results were certainly more complex than the early theories such as that of Domar had postulated, there was reason to presume that a recoupment period would be finite, and perhaps not too long in years.[16]

[15]Jack N. Behrman, *Direct Manufacturing Investment, Exports, and the Balance of Payments* (New York: National Foreign Trade Council, Inc., 1968). See also Raymond Vernon, *Sovereignty at Bay: The Multinational Spread of U.S. Enterprise* (New York: Basic Books, 1971), especially pp. 163–166 and 172–178. The discussion is based on the earlier publication by Raymond Vernon, *U.S. Controls on Foreign Direct Investment: A Reevaluation* (Financial Executives Foundation: 1969).

[16]For further discussion, see *The Multinational Corporation*, Studies on U.S. Foreign Investment, vol. 1 (Washington, D.C.: U.S. Department of Commerce, 1972), especially pp. 75–80.

The argument was significant because the case for controls on foreign direct investment (considered later in this chapter) rested on the presumption that a recoupment period was either very lengthy or infinite. As indicated in the following discussion, there are other considerations relating to controls on foreign direct investment. It does seem, however, that Hufbauer and Adler did not prove their case prima facie. Without a prima facie case, controls are much less easy to accept and support.

CAPITAL FLOWS AND INTEREST RATES

It was stated earlier that short-term capital flows might be attracted by interest rates sufficiently higher than those in other countries to more than compensate for any risk differential. Interest rates, however, cannot be presumed to be the major motive for long-term international *direct* investment unless it is presumed that the long-term rate of interest and the rate of return on real capital assets are the same, except for differentials resulting from differences in risk. It must be presumed that long-term direct investment is made to obtain a return on real capital assets—a rate of profit. If the difference between the long-term interest rate and the rate of return on real capital assets varies because of *change* in the risk involved in real investment, a widening of the differential may attract foreign investment. The supply of such funds, however, tends to reduce interest rates at any given level of GNP, by adding to the supply of funds for investment. With a rise in GNP, the partial equilibrium of a loanable funds model is not sufficient for conclusive judgment. Empirical evidence suggests that increased investment may lead to increased output (GNP) and to some degree of inflation even before full employment is reached, and that this leads to a rise in interest rates. The rise in interest rates may not be quite as great as the inflation, because part of any yields are in the form of capital gains, and since these are usually taxed at lower rates than ordinary income or not taxed at all, interest rates need not rise as much as the inflation to continue to provide the same return to lenders.

LONG-TERM INTERNATIONAL INVESTMENT AND OTHER ECONOMIC VARIABLES

Long-term international investment affects a number of economic variables not included in BOP data, the most significant being employment, business enterprise growth, and the transfer of technology.

Investment and Employment

It is clear that foreign investment tends to increase employment in the host country. But the effect of direct long-term international investment on domestic employment in the lending country has been controversial in policy discussions. It has been argued that the establishment of subsidiaries abroad may cause loss of jobs in the United States, as firms use cheap labor abroad instead of more costly labor at home, in an effort to reduce costs.

A survey of 298 firms conducted by the U.S. Department of Commerce showed that multinational firms seemed to help rather than hinder the growth of domestic employment. While total U.S. private employment grew 1.8 percent per year from 1966 to 1970, domestic employment attributed to multinational corporations increased by 2.7 percent per year.[17]

Except for the automotive agreement with Canada in 1965, which admittedly did increase imports of automobiles and parts into the United States, only a small percent of multinational firms, output is imported into the United States.[18] Most of U.S. foreign direct investment is in Canada and in Western Europe in any event, and these are not areas with very low wage costs.

It must be kept in mind that production by U.S. subsidiaries abroad increases output and income in foreign countries. This makes it possible for the foreign countries to purchase more imports, as well as more of their own products. Hence they can buy more from the United States and from other countries.[19]

Nevertheless, the eminent economist Paul Samuelson, among others, has warned that, given the basic principle of comparative advantage and the mobility of capital, American firms may find that foreign labor can be employed more efficiently in many manufacturing industries. The U.S. economy could shift somewhat toward services away from some manufacturing, with perhaps a slower increase in demand for labor. The *share* of profits and interest in GNP might increase and that of wages might decline.[20] This might make the reduction of unemployment in the United States difficult. At the same time, political factors in foreign countries may restrict the flow of investment earnings back into the United States. These trends could be quite adverse. If "nationalism impairs the successful collecting of the fruits of our foreign investments," as Samuelson puts it, the United States would find itself poorer and at the same time facing the necessity of shifting resources back into industries which had declined. There is the possibility of a significant conflict between the international flow of capital, resulting in an increase in the real standard of living of the American people, and the forces of nationalism and labor unions, which may either limit such flow and thus reduce the standard of

---

[17] *International Economic Report of the President*, 1973, p. 58.

[18] The Canada–U.S. automotive agreement of 1965 was apparently intended to integrate the two automotive markets, and to provide for eventual elimination of duties between the two countries in this field. The Canadian industry had been less efficient than the corresponding part of the U.S. industry. Canadian efficiency increased following the agreement (production rose, but employment remained about the same), and Canada gained a larger share of the market. The U.S. net export surplus of automobiles dropped sharply, but any evaluation of net effects must take into account the profit performance of Canadian subsidiaries of U.S. parent automotive firms. See Carl E. Beigie, *The Canada–U.S. Automotive Agreement: An Evaluation* (Canadian-American Committee, National Planning Association and Private Planning Association of Canada, Washington, D.C., 1970).

[19] On this basis, it has been stated that the "major premise of U.S. policy on direct investment is that the free market should determine the direction of capital flows throughout the world to maximize economic efficiency" (*International Economic Report of the President*, 1975, p. 43).

[20] Paul A. Samuelson, "International Trade for a Rich Country," *Morgan Guaranty Survey*, July 1972, pp. 3–11.

living, or may, after the flow has been permitted, limit the return of earnings on investments.

Investment and Business Enterprise Growth

The possibility and, indeed, the encouragement of international investment after World War II was one of the factors leading to the growth of what have been termed multinational corporations (MNCs). While these have many aspects (such as managerial, productive, and personnel) which cannot concern us in this book, we must note that their growth has proceeded to such an extent that business enterprise everywhere has been outgrowing national boundaries.

Both investing and host countries have had ambivalent attitudes toward this growth. Investing countries, such as the United States, have felt on the one hand that foreign investment by their firms has many favorable effects. Yet there has also been some feeling that vulnerable sectors of the U.S. economy may have to be protected against incursions that could reduce U.S. employment, and that production abroad may be one cause of some decline in the U.S. share in world exports.[21]

Host countries, on the other hand, have sometimes expressed fear that giant MNCs headquartered in the United States may gain control over large sectors of their economies. However, they have also acknowledged that multinational corporations have increased welfare and helped advance technology.

Unless direct investment by MNCs permanently displaces local business, which is not usually assumed, direct investment must add to employment in host countries. It must also generate enough exports or substitute for enough imports, depending on the kind of goods produced, to compensate for loss of income by the host country through repatriation of profits. The addition of foreign investment to local investment in host countries increases income (GNP) by some multiple of the amount of foreign investment, according to the basic Keynesian multiplier concept. Although it is not certain how this may affect net exports, since goods produced may be exported, consumed domestically without affecting imports, or consumed domestically as substitutes for imports, it seems highly probable that enough output would either be exported or consumed as a substitute for imports to offset at least the amount of profits repatriated. Profits are only a small percent of the output of any industry, and repatriated profits are less than total profits. The effect of foreign direct investment on net exports of the host country is less certain because increased income causes increased consumption, of which part is an increase in imports. However, the increase in consumption is a fraction of the increase in income and the increase in imports is a fraction of the increase in consumption. Unless these fractions are quite high, the trade balance would not shift to more imports relative to exports, because goods produced by foreign investment might be

---

[21]The U.S. share in world exports declined from a little over 16 percent in 1955 to a little over 12 percent in 1974; *International Economic Report of the President*, 1975, p. 131.

exported or consumed in place of imported goods, thus shifting the trade balance toward exports.

The financial size of MNCs is often cited in comparisons which may be dramatic but are crude at best and at worst misleading. It is pointed out that many such firms have sales larger than the GNPs of many small countries in which they do business. This comparison is very crude, since sales cannot properly be compared with GNP because the latter represents value added in production rather than total sales revenue. Findings such as that of a U.S. Tariff Commission study which reported that multinational firms controlled some $268 billion in short-term liquid assets at the end of 1971 may be used in misleading ways. It was implied in some articles that shifts of such funds from country to country might cause changes in exchange rates which could be very detrimental to some countries, especially small countries. This is misleading, however, since most firms maintain liquid assets as working balances, and cannot shift such funds to different places without considerable cost and inconvenience. Shifts in *debt* of corporations from one currency to another may affect exchange rates, but these shifts are largely in response to change in interest rate differences chiefly resulting from differences in monetary policies. Nevertheless, it is possible for multinational firms to cause adverse shifts in current account balances. The simple ploy of having all employees of such a firm order their airline tickets through the office of a subsidiary in one particular country could cause a drain of $100,000 a year from that country.[22]

The MNC with its world outlook may be a challenge to the nation-state. International organizations established since 1945 still almost entirely reflect *national* decisions by member states. The development and spread of the MNC is creating a world market in somewhat the same manner in which the development of the corporation created a national market in the United States and broke down regional barriers. International barriers are of course much stronger than regional barriers, and it appears that a long period of adjustment may be expected.

Investment and the Transfer of Technology

Direct investment inevitably involves some transfer of technology, and technological transfer may occur even from small firms through international licensing agreements. The many repercussions involve questions of technological benefit, national security, and other significant issues. A great rise in royalty and fee receipts by U.S. firms in recent years is evident in the statistics, but it is not clear what this means, since the royalties and fees may be in part other items reported as royalties and fees. The effects of technological transfer on BOPs, on employment, and on growth of enterprises are just as controversial as the effects of direct investment itself. No econometric models have been developed that can satisfactorily predict the effects. International economic reports of the President have therefore argued for a broad policy of neutrality, but with

[22] *Wall Street Journal*, Apr. 19, 1973, pp. 1, 20.

some modifications of this policy in providing for adjustments for specific industries and regions.[23]

CONTROL OF INTERNATIONAL CAPITAL FLOWS

Control by governments over capital flows has been more generally accepted as necessary then control over current account payments. Current account payments are needed for trade and other services, and are limited by the trends in such transactions. Capital flows are guided by expectations of profit, interest, or other return, or by speculative desires for gain or fears of loss. Moreover, capital flows may represent outflows of funds invested in a country long ago. It may be very difficult for a country to permit liquidation of such investment over a short period of time.

For these reasons provisions of international agreements generally included exceptions permitting exchange controls on capital movements. Moreover, when capital outflows from the United States continued to increase during the 1960s, there was consensus that these outflows should be controlled, even though studies in the late 1960s were challenged as inconclusive in demonstrating their negative effects.

Capital Outflow Restrictions in the United States

In the 1960s, when United States government officials were concerned about the continuation of deficits in the U.S. BOP (according to either of the measures described in Chapter 2), they suggested and the government imposed various restrictions and taxes to reduce particular debit items, or to increase credit items other than those classified as deficit components (outflows of reserve assets and increases in short-term liquid liabilities to foreigners). Some military dependents were brought home to reduce spending for their maintenance, allowances for duty-free imports by tourists were reduced to discourage such purchases abroad, and some efforts were made to stimulate exports. However, most of the restrictions were directed toward capital outflows, partly because these had increased rapidly and partly because it seemed more appropriate to control foreign investment than to limit imports, which would have been contrary to international agreements.

An interest equalization tax (IET) effective in 1963 was imposed to reduce purchases of foreign bonds and stocks; the tax was intended to add enough to the cost to reduce the yield to that for similar securities in the United States, hence eliminating the incentive of a yield differential for foreign investment. Canadian and even some Japanese issues were exempt, as were issues of LDCs.

In 1965, voluntary controls were established for direct foreign investment by business firms and for lending by banks. Corporations were urged to restrict

---

[23] *International Economic Report of the President*, 1975, p. 104.

foreign investment, and banks were given guidelines by the Federal Reserve System concerning amounts of lending overseas.[24]

This "voluntary" program was superseded, for direct foreign investment, by mandatory controls in 1968. The controls limited direct investments to percentages of the 1965–1966 level, with smaller percentages in Canada, Japan, Australia, and the United Kingdom than in less developed areas, and even smaller percentages in the rest of Europe. Many exceptions were allowed, and the regulations became complex, as might have been expected.

In early 1974, all these limitations were removed.[25] Clearly, they had not prevented the difficulties encountered in 1971, although it might be argued that these difficulties might have come sooner without restrictions on capital outflows.

Regulations of these types perpetuate differences in interest rates based on supply of and demand for capital. Risk differences and other factors might still cause some differences in interest rates, but the prevalence of restrictions on capital flows makes the differences greater.

Restricting the Inflow of Direct Investment

The affluence of some of the OPEC countries gave rise to a new question: would increased foreign investment in the United States be harmful? At the end of 1973 U.S. direct investment abroad was estimated at over $100 billion (book value), while foreign direct investment in the United States was estimated at less than $18 billion.[26] To the extent that foreign direct investment in the United States is undertaken by foreign firms having a special advantage in technology, or attempting to avoid trade barriers, it seems likely to supplement rather than substitute for U.S. domestic investment. It may also contribute to competition. Traditionally, both these effects have been considered beneficial.

Since the same BOP analysis applies as was used in evaluating foreign investment by U.S. firms, and since results are equally inconclusive, the Administration in 1974 concluded that the best policy was equal treatment for foreign and domestic investment. However, the federal form of government creates some special problems, since state regulations may differ from federal regulations, and special regulations may be needed for specific industries. Foreign investment in power (especially nuclear power), communications, transportation, and some fields related to national defense may require special regulation. Banking regulations have already been discussed in Chapter 8. There seem to be few other reasons for concern.[27]

---

[24]Many details of the voluntary foreign credit restraint program (VFCR) are discussed in a relatively short space in Francis A. Lees, *International Banking and Finance* (New York: Wiley, 1974), pp. 217–229.

[25]*Wall Street Journal,* Jan. 30, 1974, p. 3.

[26]*International Economic Report of the President,* 1975, p. 43.

[27]Sanford Rose, "The Misguided Furor about Investments from Abroad," *Fortune,* May 1975, pp. 170–175, 290–297.

Restrictions on Outflows from Sterling Balances

At the beginning of the twentieth century sterling was the major form of international money, with gold second. Sterling obligations were heavily short-term, and as Britain made large expenditures in both World Wars, the burden of short-term obligations increased.

Proposals to "fund" the sterling balances—that is, to turn them into long-term obligations—were advanced beginning in 1945. It has been necessary for the IMF to provide large credits for Britain, in some cases merely to enable Britain to postpone repayment of earlier credits. Devaluations of the pound in 1949 and 1967, and floating of the pound in 1970, reduced the attractiveness of sterling as international money. However, sterling is still widely used, and is unlikely to be completely abandoned unless the value of the pound falls over a long period.

In the late 1960s, arrangements with other industrialized countries provided standby credit to finance any additional net withdrawals of sterling area balances. At the same time, the United Kingdom agreed to maintain the *dollar* value of eligible official sterling reserves of sterling area countries, except for 10 percent of each country's reserves. The sterling area countries, on the other hand, pledged to keep specified percentages of their total reserves in sterling. The entire agreement was called the Basel Facility, and the standby credit to Britain was provided through the Bank for International Settlements (BIS).

The British government did not seem to have a firm policy concerning the ultimate role of sterling in the international monetary system. One course could have been to terminate the international role of sterling. Another possibility would have been to revalue gold upward and take other steps which might liquidate enough of the sterling balances that the remainder would have been convertible. A third action, or group of actions, would have involved compromises designed to maintain some modified role for sterling in the international monetary system.[28]

As an international vehicle currency, sterling continues to be important. Much world trade is priced in sterling, and private sectors of the world economy continue to hold sterling to use for payments. Sterling is less important as an intervention currency because of the predominant role of the dollar for that purpose, and it is not very important outside the sterling area as a reserve currency.

As long as sterling is an important vehicle currency, working balances in sterling are necessary. The basic problem is to separate working balances from investment balances, and to fund the latter. The line between working balances and investment balances is no easier to draw in the international field than in the domestic area, however. Keynes' distinction between "active" and "idle" money balances was useful in theory, but empirically it has been very difficult

[28]Benjamin J. Cohen, *The Reform of Sterling*, Essays in International Finance, No. 77 (Princeton: Princeton, 1969).

to make. Some provision to limit capital losses for a time on sales of sterling balances by holders might, however, permit holders themselves to make the identification as they proceed. Working balances would be held. If other balances could be eliminated without heavy capital losses, holders might be inclined to take the step of disposing of their holdings in excess of desired working balances.

Internationally then, sterling would continue to be a vehicle currency (like the dollar), but it would not be an intervention currency or an international reserve asset, nor would sterling balances be held on a large scale for investment.

Early in 1977, an agreement was reached in Basel, Switzerland, that the United States, Belgium, Canada, West Germany, Japan, the Netherlands, Sweden, and Switzerland would be prepared to lend up to $3 billion to Britain if foreign holders of sterling were to reduce their balances below levels existing in December 1976.[29] Provision was to be made for the issue of medium-term securities in sterling by Britain, so that holders of sterling balances, now generally in the form of Treasury bill holdings, might exchange bills for the medium-term securities. This would not result in any reduction in sterling balances, but would relieve the pressure of immediate withdrawals. It was reported that Britain had agreed to try to somewhat reduce official sterling holdings of foreign countries. Over time, holdings of sterling needed as working balances will rise with inflation. Holdings may also increase if North Sea oil is sold by Britain for sterling.

The agreement seemed likely to further diminish sterling as an international reserve asset, although not to eliminate it. The agreement illustrates the continuing importance of the BIS as a kind of central bank for central banks.

Other Countries' Restrictions on Capital Flows

Many countries maintain restrictions on capital flows, and often they follow a different principle from that of the United States—that flows are permissible unless specifically restricted. Many countries deem capital flows to be subject to regulation by government, and permissible only when so specified.[30]

Foreign direct investment is especially subject to restriction because governments often believe that foreign investment profits are too high (although they may in fact be high partially because of efficiency), because research and development results may not be available to the host country or its firms, because foreign investors can sometimes evade public policy guidelines of host countries, because foreign firms are to some extent controlled by their home governments, and because foreign firms may exert political influence. Direct investment thus has political force that portfolio investment is not likely to exert.

---

[29]*Wall Street Journal,* Jan. 11, 1977, p. 2, and Jan. 12, 1977, p. 16.
[30]Raymond Vernon, *The Economic Environment of International Business* (Englewood Cliffs, N.J.: Prentice-Hall, 1972), pp. 77–78.

Host countries obtain benefits from the net increase in value of output (GNP or national income). They also may tax—usually with first claim—the profits of foreign firms operating in their territories. There may be indirect benefits, too, because local firms can learn from foreign firms, leading to a general increase in productivity and output.

International direct investment is the most obvious challenge by the economic trends toward integration to the political barriers around the nation-state. This conflict is fundamental in international economics and finance. It is generally assumed that the nation-state has the greater power, but this may not be so.

SUMMARY

In this chapter we have examined the effects of long-term international investment on BOPs, interest rates, employment, the growth of business enterprise, and the transfer of technology. We found that although earlier simple analyses of BOP effects have been replaced by more complex analysis, econometric models are not yet adequate to the task of simulating long-term developments.

Thus the case for controls over international capital movements, which seemed to become stronger as the analysis of effects of such movements began, was weakened by further study. Certain exceptions may be made in strategic or monopolistic industries, but for the most part a policy of neutrality toward foreign investment in any direction seems desirable.[31]

Controls on capital outflows may be necessary for countries like Britain, with large balances due to foreigners and a currency declining in value. Outflows of capital are likely to further reduce the value of sterling, and means must be found to fund the remaining sterling balances.

Some countries have adopted the principle that foreign investment within their jurisdictions is presumed to be subject to control, and permissions are granted as a matter of privilege rather than right. This approach emphasizes the conflict between the force of economic trends toward integration of economies and the efforts of nation-states to retain barriers. A long period of adjustment appears to be in prospect.

[31]This appears to apply even to the so-called "offshore" production by U.S. firms in LDCs. A recent study by Richard W. Moxon, "The Motivation for Investment in Offshore Plants: The Case of the U.S. Electronics Industry," *Journal of International Business Studies,* Spring 1975, pp. 51–65, showed that although some particular kinds of jobs were transferred abroad and that imports into the United States did increase, these changes would probably have occurred anyway. Imports were already penetrating the U.S. market before the offshore plants were established. The study did not throw much light on whether the Kindleberger-Caves-Hymer theory or the Aliber theory of the cause of foreign direct investment was more valid. Although BOP effects in the LDCs were considered likely to be positive, the study did not investigate fully the income and import effects in the LDCs and the possible repercussions on U.S. income, employment, and the BOP. Nevertheless, this pioneering study showed that alternatives to the offshore investment were *not* likely to be more beneficial to the U.S. economy and BOP.

QUESTIONS FOR DISCUSSION

1 Keynes believed that the reparations demanded from Germany after World War I were beyond that country's capacity to pay, in terms of increased exports of goods and services. Keynes argued that German export prices would not fall enough to permit an increase in exports sufficient to make the real transfer. Actually, German export prices rose. Why?

2 Ohlin argued, with greater force of logic, that spending and income in Germany would be reduced as taxes were collected to pay reparations, while spending and income in Britain and France would increase. Ohlin was equally wrong. Why?

3 Why was the increase in petroleum prices in 1973–1974 more serious in its effects than a similar increase in a commodity produced wholly within the United States would have been?

4 How did Canada expend its money stock and increase prices without sizable gold inflows in the period 1900–1913?

5 How did the decline in the belief in the quantity theory of money affect the theory of the effects of capital flows under flexible or floating exchange rates?

6 Domar and Buchanan were both concerned about the need for government foreign lending and investment to supplement private foreign investment after World War II. Why? Were they justified in this concern?

7 The Hufbauer-Adler study was used to justify controls over U.S. foreign investment. Did it justify these controls? Why or why not?

8 Evaluate Paul Samuelson's concern about the effects of U.S. foreign investment on domestic employment.

9 Is the MNC a challenge to the nation-state? If so, which institution is likely to be dominant in the long run? Why?

10 The dangers arising from U.S. controls on foreign investment have been called "the perils of ad hoccery" by one author (see Jack N. Behrman, "Foreign Investment Muddle: The Perils of Ad Hoccery," *Columbia Journal of World Business,* Fall 1965, p. 54). Why? Is he justified? Explain.

SUGGESTED REFERENCES

Everyone concerned with international income transfers should read the classic Keynes-Ohlin debate in the *Economic Journal,* March and June 1929, pp. 1–7 and 172–173.

The growing complexity of analysis of the effects of capital flows on other items in balances of payments may be traced in Evsey Domar, "The Effect of Foreign Investment on the Balance of Payments," *American Economic Review,* December 1950, pp. 805–826; Norman S. Buchanan, "International Investment," in Bernard F. Haley, ed., *A Survey of Contemporary Economics,* vol. II (Homewood, Ill.: Irwin, 1952), pp. 307–350; Nicholas K. Bruck and Francis A. Lees, *Foreign Investment, Capital Controls, and the Balance of Payments* (New York: New York University, Graduate School of Business Administration, 1968); G. C. Hufbauer and F. M. Adler, *Overseas Manufacturing Investment and the Balance of Payments,* Tax Policy Research Study No. 1 (Washington, D.C.: U.S. Treasury Department, 1968); Jack N. Behrman, *Direct Manufacturing Investment, Exports, and the Balance of Payments* (New York: National Foreign Trade Council, Inc., 1968); and Raymond Vernon, *Sovereignty at Bay: The*

Multinational Spread of U.S. Enterprise (New York: Basic Books, 1971), pp. 163–166 and 172–178.

For reviews of economic and financial policy issues in international affairs in recent years, see the *International Economic Report of the President,* annually since 1973.

Although predicting exchange rates is almost as hazardous as predicting stock market prices (but not quite), the overvalued dollar of the 1960s is probably gone, and the undervalued dollar of 1974 is likely to disappear. The most important factors are rates of increase in the money stock and in real GNP in various countries. See Sanford Rose, "How to Think about the Dollar," *Fortune,* August 1975, pp. 117–121, 196–198.

A good description of restrictions on international capital flows in a brief space may be found in Raymond Vernon, *The Economic Environment of International Business* (Englewood Cliffs, N.J.: Prentice-Hall, 1972), pp. 74–78.

The changing role of sterling and the sterling balances is reviewed in Benjamin J. Cohen, *The Reform of Sterling,* Essays in International Finance, No. 77 (Princeton: Princeton, 1969).

Part Five

International Managerial Finance

Analysis of the problems of international financial management is based on concepts and theories developed in previous parts of this book. For example, decisions involving foreign credits require analysis of BOP situations as well as of financial statements of customers or borrowers. Methods of financing exports or imports can be evaluated on the basis of the theory and practice of international banking. Decisions on borrowing require a knowledge of the various money and capital markets, including the Eurocurrency markets.

Nevertheless, some further analysis must be made from the standpoint of individual firms. This is the view taken in this part of the book.

We first consider in Chapters 14 and 15 the responses of business firms in evaluating data on the economic environment, forecasting trends in that environment, forecasting inflation and risks of exchange rate fluctuations, and making use of means of reducing or eliminating risks. In Chapter 16, we appraise the ways in which differences in accounting systems and practices affect the usefulness of the financial information generally available to firms. In Chapter 17 we examine variations in tax systems and consider effects of these variations on business firms' actions. Finally, in Chapters 18 and 19 we analyze the financial problems of direct foreign investment (discounting cash flows and capital budgeting analysis) and the management of assets and capital structures of business firms operating internationally.

Chapter 14

Environmental Factors Affecting International Managerial Finance

Success of investments made by an individual firm, correctness of decisions to finance in one way rather than another, and profits or losses on specific transactions often depend on a knowledge of the economic environment and an ability to forecast changes in it. Some changes in the economic environment involve serious risks for firms. A firm may lose millions of dollars because of a rise in the value of the currency of a country from which it imports raw materials if financial managers of the firm did not foresee the upvaluation or appreciation of that currency. Even larger losses may occur for firms selling on credit or for banks lending to countries which encounter serious BOP difficulties, and for firms making direct investment in countries where economic trends are unfavorable.

Successive sections of this chapter include consideration of data often used to measure the economic environment, general methods used in forecasting economic trends, and an analysis of bases for changes in economic policy. Special attention is given to the problems of forecasting inflation and exchange rates.

DATA ON THE ECONOMIC ENVIRONMENT

A significant problem is obtaining data on the economic environment in foreign countries comparable to that used in analyzing and forecasting the domestic economic environment. A little reflection suggests that in addition to information published by governments and banks in individual countries, data published by the IMF, the IBRD, and the BIS may be valuable. Also, information published by such organizations as the OECD contain not only data on conditions in the member countries but forecasts. Thorough international financial analyses should not rely solely on such forecasts, but they are useful starting points.

The financial analyst should keep in mind that there are great variations in both economic conditions and rates of change in economic variables among countries, and that data must be carefully interpreted. The problem is to select data that are available and at the same time likely to be significant for forecasting other variables, such as exchange rates, of interest to international financial managers.

Variations in Economic Conditions

Wide variations in economic conditions may make actions that are appropriate in the United States quite inappropriate in some foreign countries. U.S. firms have in recent times faced no more than about 12 percent inflation a year, and that for only one year. In a number of countries inflation has jumped from a nominal rate to over 20 percent a year in one or two years.[1] Such changes necessitate careful consideration of decisions concerning management of cash balances, for example.

U.S. firms have operated in an economic environment in which rates of growth in real GNP of more than 6 or 7 percent a year are uncommon. Yet in Japan real growth continued for a number of years at 10 to 11 percent a year, and in some LDCs zero real growth is encountered. Such differences in growth make significant differences in market opportunities.

Moreover, economic changes have occurred very rapidly. The growth rate for real GDP for the 24 nations that are members of the OECD—industrialized countries—dropped from over 6 percent in 1973 to an average of approximately zero in 1974.[2] Such a rapid decline creates obvious problems for inventory management, for example.

Interpreting Economic Indicators

For many purposes, a quick review of economic indicators for a number of countries may be useful. For example, suppose that managers of a firm are considering expansion of its activities in marketing, but do not feel able to expand in more than one or two countries at a time. Economic indicators can be helpful in eliminating countries that are not likely to offer the best opportunities.

Figures for GNP or GDP are the best measure of the economic size of a

---

[1]Japan's inflation rate was less than 5 percent in 1972, over 10 percent in 1973, and over 20 percent in 1974; see IMF, *International Financial Statistics,* March 1975, p. 37.

[2]Lawrence A. Mayer, "Climbing Back from Negative Credit," *Fortune,* August 1975, pp. 150–154.

country. They represent total income generated by productive factors of the country or total income generated domestically, excluding net income from abroad (GDP). The IBRD publishes figures for GNP or GDP by country. Although some of these figures are guesstimates, they do indicate very roughly the relative size of incomes.[3] Since countries have had varying rates of inflation, it is desirable to deflate such figures to express them in constant purchasing power, as well as to convert them to U.S. dollars in some cases for easy comparison. The resulting data indicate comparative real GNP which firms' economists can refine and break down when companies are interested in specific countries.

Data on per capita GNP show the level of per capita income, and countries have been classified as developed or as developing (less developed or LDCs) on the basis of such figures. Although no precise demarcation is agreed on, a figure of $1,000 per year for per capita income has been used in recent years to separate developed from developing countries.[4] For a number of countries— Burma, Ethiopia, Haiti, Nigeria, North Vietnam, and others—data are so difficult to interpret and to convert meaningfully that for a time the IBRD did not publish figures for GNP per capita, although it made estimates of the growth rate for this indicator. Estimates of per capita income were published later. It is of course recognized that these data give a very rough indication of income.[5]

Rates of growth in GNP, in population, and in per capita GNP are the most valuable general indicators of economic growth and market potential. Countries may at times move rapidly to higher income levels. When data are available, rates of growth in the labor force (those gainfully employed plus those indicating a desire for gainful employment but not currently employed) and in productivity (increase in output per worker-hour) are significant for projections. By adding the rates of growth in the labor force and in productivity, one can project a rate of *potential* growth in GNP from a year of "full" employment, one in which employment is at the maximum level, or unemploy-

---

[3]For comments on some of the reasons why estimates are tentative and may vary widely when made by different methods, see the "Note" in the *World Bank Atlas,* 7th ed., 1972, and the "Technical Note" in the *World Bank Atlas,* 6th ed., published in *Finance and Development,* March 1972. Even if they approximate equilibrium rates, exchange rates indicate at best the values of internationally traded goods. In many countries, much of the output is consumed directly, rather than sold in markets, and the value of such output must be imputed. Between the 6th and 7th editions of the *World Bank Atlas,* a shift was made from estimates at factor cost and estimates at market prices. Estimates at factor cost had been made to avoid distortions resulting from different tax systems, but the wide use of GNP at market prices and the presence of other distortions resulted in a decision to change.

[4]In Europe, such socialist countries as Poland, Bulgaria, and Rumania, and other countries such as Greece, Spain, Portugal, Yugoslavia, and Albania were all below that line at the end of the 1960s. In all of Asia, only Israel and Japan were above the line at that time—before the great increase in oil revenue.

[5]See, for example, "World Bank Atlas," 6th ed., in *Finance and Development,* March 1972, pp. 48–60, in which figures for GNP per capita were not published for a number of countries, and *World Bank Atlas,* 7th ed. (Washington, D.C.: IBRD, 1972), in which estimates of GNP and GDP per capita were given for all countries covered.

ment at the minimum level, believed to be attainable. In doing so, of course, it is assumed that adequate capital facilities of plant and equipment are available to attain this potential, which may not always be true.

Rates of inflation—rates of increase in some index of prices—are important, but are not necessarily an indication of either rapid or slow growth in real income. Although under some conditions inflation hinders output, zero to moderate inflation seems to have little correlation with real income growth.[6] Business firms are concerned with inflation because they must devise policies for operating profitably under conditions of inflation, but they should not assume that inflation necessarily stimulates or hinders growth. In a period when inflation was generally less virulent than recently, the conclusion was reached that evidence "covering a wide range of periods and many countries shows that with price increases from zero to 6 percent per year, there is no appreciable association between the rate of growth and the rate of price change."[7] Exceptions occur with higher rates of inflation: Brazil achieved real economic growth at a rate of about 10 percent a year with persistent inflation at about 20 percent a year. A review of growth and price changes in 15 countries of North America and Europe during the period 1948–1957 indicated that the country with the most rapid annual increase in the price level, Austria, also had the highest rate of growth in per capita real product.[8]

Economic structure varies with development. As countries develop, the share of GNP contributed by agriculture, forestry, and fishing normally declines, while that contributed by industry increases, as does the share contributed by services and utilities.[9]

External dependence of a country is important in granting credit and in forecasting BOP problems. It may be measured by a number of indicators. Ratios of imports, exports, or total foreign trade to GNP indicate the importance of foreign trade, which may be especially significant if countries that are major export markets experience recessions. The size of holdings of reserve assets is important in evaluating whether a country can meet temporary BOP deficits. External debt and interest obligations, especially when denominated in foreign currencies, are significant because they must then be met from foreign currency earnings.

It should be noted that single indicators, such as debt service ratios, should never be used without consideration of related data and ratios. For example,

[6]In the United States, for example, growth was more rapid in the period 1960–1965, when inflation averaged about $1^{1}/_{2}$ percent a year, than it was in the period 1950–1959, when it averaged about $2^{1}/_{2}$ percent a year. See *Economic Report of the President*, 1975, pp. 130, 251. However, the highest growth rate in the world was maintained for some time by Japan, with a rate of inflation averaging $4^{1}/_{2}$ percent per year from 1958–1969.

[7]*Money and Credit*, The Report of the Commission on Money and Credit (Englewood Cliffs, N.J.: Prentice-Hall, 1961), p. 44.

[8]Arthur W. Marget, "Inflation: Some Lessons of Recent Foreign Experience," *American Economic Review*, May 1960, p. 211.

[9]Hollis B. Chenery, "Targets for Development," in Barbara Ward, ed., *The Widening Gap* (New York: Columbia, 1971), pp. 30–31.

debt service ratios are reported for a number of countries in *Annual Reports* of the IBRD. These are ratios of debt service actually paid to exports of goods and services, rather than ratios of the contractual debt service owed to such exports. Related factors to be considered are: stability and diversification of the country's exports, prospects for growth of exports, how far imports can be reduced without adversely affecting production, maturities of outstanding debt, amount of reserve assets held and amount of compensatory financing potentially available, and the past debt service record of the country.

When comparisons are desired, most of the indicators mentioned above are converted to dollars, if comparisons are made in that currency, by using current exchange rates. Current exchange rates reflect, as was shown in Chapter 9, the demand for and supply of foreign exchange. More relevant for income comparisons would be the purchasing power of currencies for goods and services. Such comparisons would require detailed studies; hence are seldom made. When they are made, the results sometimes differ widely from those resulting from conversion of figures at current exchange rates. For example, U.S. per capita product in 1959 was about 30 times that of India when current exchange rates were used, but a purchasing power parity calculation showed a ratio of only about 12 to 1.[10] One should therefore be cautious in interpreting figures converted into other currencies.

FORECASTING ECONOMIC TRENDS

An extensive review of forecasting business activity would be beyond the scope of this book. Some general comments may, however, point out the major problems in forecasting income, interest rates, and BOPs. Because of the importance of inflation, comments on forecasting price trends are made later. It is useful to make a distinction between economic trends dependent largely upon past data, which can therefore be forecast by using some type of econometric techniques, and such variables as prices in efficient markets. The latter cannot be forecast for the short-run future because participants in such markets have already taken into account all known data and predictable changes in making and accepting price offers. Short-run changes in prices are therefore random because they arise from unpredictable events. Technically this situation is called a martingale. Some variables may have predictable (nonrandom) long-run trends; this situation is termed a submartingale. Interest rates, discussed below, may be random in the very short term and prices in some types of markets (for example, the U.S. stock market) are probably random, but with a predictable long-run trend. As we shall see, whether short-term changes in foreign exchange rates under the managed floating system in effect after 1973 are martingales or submartingales or are predictable is still under discussion.

[10] *Finance and Development*, March 1972, p. 53.

Forecasting Income

Almost all economic forecasting begins with income forecasts, because these are more reliable than other forecasts. The most stable trends generally are in such things as labor force and productivity increases, which determine the trend in potential income or output. These seem to depend on basic factors in the cultural and social fabric, although even they may change abruptly over periods of time. Fluctuations in income, whether measured in nominal or real terms, occur as business activity falls below or rises up to or occasionally slightly above potential, since "potential" is not a precise measure. Long-term forecasts of potential income in countries such as the United States have been relatively accurate.[11] Short-term economic forecasting is subject to more error but is still fairly accurate, in real terms.[12]

Aside from purely judgmental forecasting, the major forecasting techniques include extrapolation of past trends, use of an "opportunistic" model of the economy, and use of a large-scale computer model of the economy. Studies have shown that use of a computer model improves forecasting, but only when computer results are modified by judgment. Clearly, computer models cannot, even when very large, include all the factors determining output, and changes in causal factors may change the equations used in obtaining forecasts. An "opportunistic" model in which some judgment is used can produce forecasts nearly as accurate as those derived from large-scale computer models plus the use of judgment. Hence we make further comments on opportunistic model-building.[13]

This activity begins with the Keynesian income identity, and attempts to use, for each major sector of the economy, methods of forecasting that have proved most applicable; for example, surveys of investment intentions that have been rather reliable and hence are used for forecasting plant and equipment spending. Judgment must be used because financial factors may limit the availability of funds to carry out intended spending, and rapid changes in outlook may change intentions. Analysis of budget data and current

[11]Compare, for example, "The Shape of the 1970's," *Morgan Guaranty Survey,* November 1969, pp. 3–10, and "A New Look at the Seventies," *Morgan Guaranty Survey,* February 1975, pp. 5–11. In the 1960s, two long-term forecasts were made for a rise in real GNP of 58 percent, while the actual rise was 53 percent—an error of only 5 percent in 10 years.

[12]Deborah D. Malley, "Lawrence Klein and his Forecasting Machine," *Fortune,* March 1975, pp. 152–157; Geoffrey H. Moore, "Economic Forecasting—How Good a Track Record?" *Morgan Guaranty Survey,* January 1975, pp. 5–8; and Stephen R. McNees, "How Accurate are Economic Forecasts?" Federal Reserve Bank of Boston, *New England Economic Review,* November/December 1974, pp. 2–19. Moore pointed out that the average error in forecasting nominal GNP by the President's Council of Economic Advisers from 1961 through 1974 was 1.1 percent—half as large as the error that would have occurred if it were simply assumed that there would be no change in GNP from one year to the next. However, forecasts of inflation based on the assumption that last year's rate would continue would have produced forecasts almost as accurate as those of the Council.

[13]Forecasting with the use of an "opportunistic" model is described in John P. Lewis and Robert C. Turner, *Business Conditions Analysis,* 2d ed. (New York: McGraw-Hill, 1967), pp. 363–572.

information on congressional appropriations are used to forecast government spending. Methods of relating inventory levels to sales figures are used in forecasting additions to or subtractions from inventories. Finally, consumer spending is forecast on the basis of past ratios of consumer spending to GNP, with C being treated as a percentage of Y. Accuracy can sometimes be improved by treating separately ratios of consumer spending to consumer disposable income, consumer disposable income to consumer income, and consumer income to total income. It should be obvious that the ratio of consumer disposable income to consumer income depends on tax rates, and the ratio of consumer income to total income depends on fluctuations in other types of income (corporate retained earnings, depreciation, and so on) included in GNP.

If there is any question of a turning point in business activity being reached during the forecast period, results of the forecast can be supplemented by the use of "leading indicators" developed by research on many statistical series to find those that lead, those that coincide with, and those that lag behind changes in general business activity.

Some attempts were made to develop monetarist models for economic forecasting, in spite of the fact that, being small models with only a very few equations, they could not be used for forecasting much breakdown of GNP. The failure of monetarist models, which were far less accurate than other models in the early 1970s, led to the discontinuance of their use. Hence consideration has been given above only to forecasting somehow based on Keynesian models, although these may sometimes include an extensive financial sector with equations for the determination of interest rates and intersectoral funds flows.

Forecasting BOP Items and Ratios

In the preceding section no mention was made of a method of forecasting net exports, which are one element in GNP. For the United States, NE is usually so small that it may almost be ignored—or the forecaster may assume it will not change. For many countries, however, and even for the United States in some cases, net exports or net imports become important. Essentially economists try to forecast the current account section of the BOP. For some elements of this sector, projection of past trends, with some modification for recent changes in trends, may be the best method. For exports, levels of business activity in the major export markets are important. The forecaster's task thus becomes one of forecasting activity in major markets. Sometimes the best that can be done is to take into account a few major changes and estimate their possible effect. Accuracy of forecasts of NE is generally not as high as that of other elements of GNP.

As we have already seen, forecasting the capital account section of the BOP involves forecasting the remaining sources of supply of and demand for foreign exchange. Sine capital flows depend on levels of profits and interest relative to such levels in foreign countries, and on any capital flight or speculative flows of capital which may occur, forecasting becomes extremely difficult. Moreover, it depends to some extent upon interest rates.

Forecasting Interest Rates

Interest rate forecasts are usually made on the basis of GNP forecasts. Studies have shown that the long-term interest rate rises from a "normal" level as inflation occurs, although it may rise slightly less than the rate of inflation.[14] Since it is generally believed that earnings on real capital assets must be greater than earnings on such financial assets as bonds because of greater risk and less liquidity in holding real capital assets, rates of profit may be higher than the long-term interest rate by varying amounts. In a declining economy, they could be below the long-term interest rate, but we ignore this unlikely possibility. Basically, profits are much more variable than long-term interest rates. Variability (risk) may increase or decrease; hence variation of rates of profit in relation to long-term interest rates may occur. Thus a forecast of the long-term interest rate, even if accurate, is not sufficient to forecast capital investment flows based on potential profits.

Moreover, many capital flows are short-term, and likely to be affected by short-term interest rates. Short-term interest rates fluctuate much more than long-term rates. In part this is because substantial changes in demand, supply, and prices of long-term financial assets are required to cause significant changes in long-term interest rates. In part it is because the most significant changes in demand for and supply of funds usually occur in short-term markets. For example, business firms want to borrow large sums to replenish inventories in periods of rising sales. Short-term interest rates may, in boom periods, rise above the level of long-term rates. In recessions, they are normally considerably lower. Governments may attempt to "twist yield curves"—that is, to raise short-term rates without increasing long-term rates, or vice versa. Success in this effort is in doubt, since available evidence is conflicting and other factors occur which may have caused changes in the relative rates.

In any event, short-run interest forecasts are usually made on the basis of estimates of the supply of and demand for funds, which in turn are based on the forecast of GNP and its elements. Since funds flow through financial institutions as well as directly from individuals, an attempt is usually made to estimate the flow through the various types of financial institutions. Since various limitations are imposed, in all countries, on the types of loans and investments which can be made by various institutions, estimates of the flows through institutions aid in forecasting the allocation of funds to various types of investment. Of course, heavy demand, such as that of business firms for money to buy inventory, changes particular interest rates and affects the flow of funds. Finally, it must be recognized that the central bank in any country controls the

---

[14]See, for example, M. Feldstein and O. Eckstein, "The Fundamental Determinants of the Interest Rate," *Review of Economics and Statistics*, November 1970, pp. 363–375.

money supply through some techniques affecting bank reserves and currency issue, and bank reserves in turn form the basis for expanding bank demand deposits. The rate of growth in the money supply permitted by the central bank is an important factor in the supply of funds to the financial markets.[15]

SYNCHRONIZATION OF BUSINESS CYCLES

Some economists have assumed that there has been a gradual tendency toward synchronization of business cycles as interdependence among countries has continued to increase.[16] In the past, major industrial countries have often been in different phases of the business cycle at a given time, although in the Great Depression of the 1930s most countries were in depression together.

In 1974–1975, however, it appeared that for the first time in a number of years the United States, Western Europe, and Japan were all experiencing recessions (declines in real GNP) simultaneously. In 1967 the United States had a minirecession, but both Western Europe and Japan had relatively high growth rates in real GNP. In 1970, the United States had a small recession, but again business activity in both Western Europe and Japan continued to show fairly high, though slower, rates of growth. However, in 1974 both the United States and Japan had negative real growth rates, and Western Europe's growth rate was falling sharply.[17]

Floating exchange rates were helpful in one way—shifts in values of currencies, which necessarily followed the huge rise in oil prices in late 1973, would surely have caused financial crises had countries attempted to maintain fixed exchange rates. At the same time, floating exchange rates were detrimental, because as a country's exchange rates fell its import prices rose, and inflation occurred in the import sector and in other sectors indirectly affected. Moreover, speculative capital movements caused much wider fluctuations in exchange rates than would have occurred as a result of trade movements alone.

The experience of the Great Depression taught most countries that if they attempted to solve their own business cycle problems by restricting imports and dumping exports at unrealistically low prices, they were likely to make all countries, including their own, poorer. Such actions provoke retaliation, world trade declines, and some of the benefits of trade are lost. International investment is also discouraged, and growth through such investment slows. Member countries of the Organization for Economic Cooperation and Development (OECD) pledged in May 1974, and renewed the pledge in 1975, not to

---

[15]See, for example, Salomon Brothers, *Supply and Demand for Credit*, annually.

[16]Geoffrey H. Moore, "The State of the International Business Cycle," *Business Economics*, September 1974, pp. 21–29. Wesley Mitchell discussed the reasons for the international spread of business cycles in *Business Cycles: The Problem and Its Setting* (New York: National Bureau of Economic Research, 1927), p. 446. The elaboration of the income shift mechanism in Keynesian theory provided further rationale for such a belief.

[17]Lawrence A. Mayer, op. cit., pointed out that the revival of weaker countries in Europe, such as Italy, depended in part on recovery in Germany; but German recovery depended in part on recovery in the United States.

resort to protectionism. Italy imposed some restrictions, but since these were indirect, presumably temporary, and necessitated by Italy's exceptionally difficult financial position, they were regarded as exceptions.

If integration of the world economy has proceeded so far that synchronized business cycles are likely in the future, cooperation in efforts to stabilize business activity is essential. If a number of industrialized countries are in recession at the same time, rising net exports cannot be counted on by any one of these countries to be a major factor in recovery. Synchronization of business cycles, in other words, could make countries more vulnerable to deep or prolonged recessions. It should be added, however, that the data suggesting synchronization of business cycles require careful analysis, and the trend may not have proceeded as far as suggested above.

WORLD INFLATION

Have some of the factors which seem to have led to the synchronization of business cycles also led to the spread of inflation throughout at least the industrialized world? The increase in inflation rates in industrialized countries in the 1970s can be traced in large part to the generation of moderate inflation in the United States in the late 1960s by a combination of war spending, shortages of some commodities, and rates of expansion of the money supply exceeding growth in productivity plus the growth in the labor force. Contractive monetary-fiscal policies were used in 1968–1969 to slow the inflation. At the same time, output was inevitably reduced, resulting in the recession of 1969–1970. When recovery gained speed in 1972–1973, inflation increased again.[18]

As prices of internationally traded goods rose in response to rising demand based on greater availability of money, inflation spread. With an approximately synchronous business cycle, the effects of inflation could easily be transmitted from country to country, especially in a boom period such as 1972–1973.[19] When central banks permitted exchange rates to float in early 1973, they stopped the increase in reserve assets, since they no longer needed to prevent exchange rates from floating upward.[20] However, central banks found that governments had large deficits. These deficits would have resulted in very high

[18]See "A Longer-Term Perspective on Inflation," First Chicago *Report*, September 1974, p. 3. See also Alexander Lang, "A Crisis in Critical Commodities," *Columbia Journal of World Business*, Spring 1973, pp. 43–52.

[19]Inflation in 1972–1974 was worldwide and unprecedented in extent in industrialized countries. See Samuel I. Katz, *'Managed Floating' as an Interim International Exchange Rate Regime, 1973–1975*, New York University Bulletin 1975-3 (New York University: Center for the Study of Financial Institutions, 1975), pp. 13–14.

[20]At that time, however, the Committee of the Board of Governors of the Federal Reserve System on International Monetary Reform concluded that "exchange rates must be a matter of international concern and consultation and that in the reformed system the exchange rate regime should remain based on stable but adjustable par values," while ministers of the Group of 24 countries (LDCs) also agreed that "a system of stable exchange rates based on adjustable par values expressed in SDR's constitutes an essential element of a satisfactory international monetary order." See IMF *Survey*, Apr. 9, 1973, pp. 100–101.

interest rates—hence in restraint on business recovery—unless central banks expanded money supplies. The situation was of course aggravated by the huge increase in oil prices. As indicated in Chapter 9, even in a country such as the United States, in which growth of the money supply was slower than in most countries (see Table 14-1), the rise in prices of internationally traded goods caused a rise in prices of imports and goods using imported materials. It also resulted in increased exports of goods for which prices are determined in international markets, and hence in some cases commodity shortages.

One might ask, given the theory of exchange rates developed in Chapter 9, why did not the rapid rise in the world money supply, compared to the money supply in the United States, cause more inflation abroad than here, and hence a rise in the foreign exchange value of the dollar, which would have discouraged imports? An important part of the answer is the flow of capital out of dollars and into other countries. This prevented the dollar from rising in value, and in fact caused it to fall after a time.[21] Possible explanations are: loss of foreign confidence in the ability of the U.S. government to control inflation (that is, an expected increase in inflation in the United States); the adverse impact of economic changes on rates of profit in the United States, which declined sharply from 1966 to 1970, and even by 1975 had not recovered sufficiently to restore earlier levels of profits as a percent of GNP; and the apparent ability of some countries, such as West Germany, to control inflation more effectively than the United States.

In most industrialized countries since World War II, adequacy of the stock of capital has been taken for granted; the problem has been assumed to be the need to increase demand when recessions occurred. The relatively low percent of GNP accounted for in the United States in recent years by net investment may lead to a shortage of real capital, especially in basic industries. This could lead to renewed inflation during business recoveries even if capacity in other industries and unemployed labor still remained unutilized. Slow recovery in real income in the United States accompanied by serious inflation could adversely affect other industrialized countries. The efforts of OPEC and other commodity cartels to raise prices could also drain away income from the United States, slowing recovery. For coming decades, the efforts of certain commodity-producing LDCs to obtain a redistribution of wealth in the world may be a factor in causing continued inflation and slower real growth in the industrialized countries.

GOVERNMENT POLICIES

Those who forecast the international economic environment for business firms should understand the influence of government policies. From a financial

---

[21]Sanford Rose, "How to Think About the Dollar," *Fortune*, August 1975, pp. 117–121, 196–198, pointed out that as oil-importing countries paid more for oil and depleted cash balances they sold securities, raising interest rates and creating profitable lending and investing opportunities for U.S. banks. This led to a dramatic expansion of lending by such banks. Also, countries which were anxious not to have their currencies depreciate further (especially Britain and Italy) borrowed from U.S. banks to offset debits (such as oil payments) in their BOPs.

Table 14-1 Growth Rates of Consumer Prices and Money Stock for the United States and Five Other Developed Countries, 1965–1974
(Percent change, annual rate)

Country	Consumer prices		Money stock*			
			1965 to 1970‡		1970 to 1974‡	
	1965 to 1970	1970 to 1974†	M_1	M_2	M_1	M_2
United States	4.2	6.0	5.2	7.1	5.9	9.8
Canada	3.8	6.4	8.1	10.6	19.7	16.8
France	4.4	8.0	5.3	10.8	12.1§	17.1§
Germany	2.4	6.2	6.4	12.7	9.2	14.4
Italy	3.0	9.5	15.8	13.7	21.9	21.5
Japan	5.4	11.0	15.2¶	16.5¶	24.4	22.2

*M_1 = "Money" and M_2 = "Money" plus "Quasi-Money" as they appear for each foreign country in *International Financial Statistics*, International Monetary Fund. These data are roughly equivalent in all countries.
† Change from June 1970 to June 1974.
‡ Based on average of end-of-month figures, average of first 6 months for 1974 and 12-month average for other years (except figures for the United States, which are based on averages of daily figures for December 1964 and 1970 and June 1974).
§ Change from 1970 to 1973.
¶ Change from 1966 to 1970.

Sources: Department of Labor (Bureau of Labor Statistics), Board of Governors of the Federal Reserve System and International Monetary Fund (*International Financial Statistics*); and *Economic Report of the President, 1975*, p. 133.

viewpoint, the most significant government actions are monetary policy and fiscal decisions—taxing and spending. In certain periods, incomes policies— price and wage controls and other limitations—may become important. They are likely to be used when monetary and fiscal policies seem to be unsuccessful in restraining inflation. Specific restraints in particular sectors of an economy may also be significant.

Monetary and fiscal policy affect both real income and prices. Their influence may vary because of the existence of unemployed resources and because of the ability to increase the labor force and/or productivity. Some countries can increase the labor force by permitting the entry of labor from other countries, as Germany did for some time. During recessions, such labor may become unemployed, and may even return to their countries of origin. Changes in productivity seem to be more difficult to achieve. Studies in the United States have shown that probably less than half the increase in productivity results from increased real capital investment; the other half is accounted for by improved technology, and training and education of labor. But specific government actions seem to result in only minor changes in productivity.[22]

Monetary and Fiscal Policies

Given the rates of increase in labor force and in productivity, monetary and fiscal policies are the major determinants of rates of growth in real income and in inflation. The relative importance of monetary policy versus fiscal policy is debated by monetarists and fiscalists, but it is generally agreed that both are significant. Increase in the money supply increases real output and prices in some proportion, the proportion depending on how close the economy is to "full employment" and on the rate of increase in the money supply. Rapid increase in the money supply causes some increase in prices even if much unemployment still exists. Fiscal policy changes also have some effect, since increased government spending or reduced taxes provide more income to consumers and to business.

The business economist who attempts to forecast the economic environment for his firm must, therefore, be a close observer of the operation of monetary and fiscal policy. Different definitions of the money supply, in different countries and in the same country, complicate this task. So do the complexities of transmitting changes in the monetary base to the money supply and from the money supply through financial institutions and markets and spending to national income or GNP.

It was widely assumed after Phillips' study in 1958 that there was an inflation-unemployment tradeoff, such that if inflation was slowed, unemployment would increase. But the evidence later showed that the inflation-unemployment relationship was unstable over time and different in different countries. In the United States, part of the unemployment problem arose from

---

[22]Edward F. Denison, *Sources of Economic Growth in the United States and the Alternatives Before Us* (New York: Committee for Economic Development, 1962); see especially p. 266.

a relatively rapid increase in the labor force, resulting in part from the desire of women for paid work and in part from anticipation of rising rates of inflation which induced efforts to supplement income.

In any event, rapid and sustained inflation requires a relatively rapid increase in the money supply, and fiscal deficits are usually the major cause of a rapid increase in the money supply. The degree of inflation depends largely on how much the increase in the money supply exceeds the average rate of increase in real output possible because of labor force and productivity growth. These vary from country to country; hence must be examined in any analysis of anticipated inflation.

Incomes Policies

When other policies to control inflation do not seem to work well, governments often resort to incomes policies—price and wage controls and other forms of direct limitations on income. The history of all recent efforts is that such policies temporarily slow price increases, but after a time enforcement is weakened by a combination of the desire to evade controls, the distorting effect of controls in limiting prices arbitrarily, and not recognizing the need for price increases in products in heavy demand and short supply. Inflation begins to resume the trend which could be forecast from rates of growth of money supply, labor force, and productivity.

Incomes policies may be temporarily useful when a reduction in the rate of increase in the money supply is bringing inflation under control, especially if at the same time cost-push pressures are tending to prolong it. At such times, control over wage and price increases may help to slow inflation.

Specific Constraints

Specific constraints may be easier to impose than general wage and price controls. Specific constraints on various international transactions may help, as they did in the United States in the 1960s, to temporarily reduce BOP deficits. But if the major causes of BOP deficits—fiscal deficits, rapid increase in the money supply, slow growth in productivity, and speculation against the currency in the foreign exchange market—continue, specific constraints are not likely to be successful in the long run.

Both incomes policies and specific constraints tend to distort an economy. In a market economy prices indicate which commodities are in heavy demand and short supply. As prices of particular commodities rise, their output usually increases. Controls prevent the operation of this indicator function of prices. Hence they may be in effect a cause of inflation, limiting prices and output of commodities greatly needed.[23]

[23]The manner in which prices of steel and some other basic commodities rose dramatically in 1974–1975 after having been held down by price controls in 1971–1973 is described in some detail in Edmund Faltermayer, "The Hyperinflation in Plant Construction," *Fortune*, November 1975, pp. 102–107, 202–206.

Noneconomic Constraints: Political, Social, and Cultural

Throughout the world, international business firms encounter various constraints, many of which are noneconomic. Political barriers reserve certain fields of production for local firms; social constraints prevent the hiring of certain types of workers or require the hiring of others; and cultural barriers prevent certain types of actions. Since these controls are often noneconomic, we do no more in this book on international finance than mention their existence. We limit ourselves to exploring financial factors.[24]

INFLATION

Inflation is perhaps the most important among the financial factors affecting international business, because inflation occurs at widely varying rates in different countries. Firms operating only in the United States may have encountered "double-digit" inflation only in the 1970s, while firms operating in some countries may find it endemic.

Various Degrees of Inflation

Although the following classifications are only approximate, it is evident that rates of inflation of less than 3 or 4 percent a year are largely ignored. This is in part simply because the changes resulting from such rates are modest. It is also because there are costs involved in acting to offset the effects of inflation. For example, hoarding of commodities as an inflation hedge involves costs of storage and insurance. Common stocks were often bought because they have usually been an effective hedge against inflation when rates were modest. Other attempts to hedge were not resorted to because of the effort and cost involved.

At moderate but somewhat higher rates of inflation—but still probably less than double-digit inflation—the major changes in behavior seem to be economizing on money narrowly defined, which is likely to lose value more rapidly than interest-bearing assets under this condition, and trying to increase saving in an effort to provide more adequately for precautionary balances and future retirement needs. The rate of saving by consumers tends to increase, as it has in recent years in the United States, and this may somewhat retard the upward movement in interest rates.[25] At the same time, there may be less saving by business, because accounting practices usually distort profits and show them to be higher than they actually are when inflation is fairly rapid. Business saving may in fact become inadequate to replace real capital, and a shortage of capital which may retard income growth is a possibility.

When inflation reaches double-digit levels and higher, there is likely to be a

[24]For a more extensive discussion of noneconomic constraints, see, for example, Stefan H. Robock and Kenneth Simmonds, *International Business and Multinational Enterprises* (Homewood, Ill.: Irwin, 1973), Chaps. 14–16.

[25]Personal saving in the United States in 1973–1974 averaged 8 percent of disposable personal income (DPI), in contrast to less than $5^{1}/_2$ percent in 1960–1969; *Economic Report of the President,* 1975, p. 268.

more pronounced change in behavior. Hoarding becomes worthwhile. The tendency to buy now, before prices rise, may become evident. Indexation of incomes, interest rates, and other prices becomes more common. A major problem, of course, is that although incomes of some groups may not rise proportionately with inflation, taxes in a country which uses progressive income taxes are likely to rise more than proportionately. Thus more funds are available for government spending, and there is less incentive to restrain such spending.

At some point, inflation *may* enter a phase which is termed hyperinflation. Prices rise faster and faster, eventually rising so fast that production is hindered because people are devoting so much energy to offsetting the effects of inflation. As prices rise, the value of the currency falls in the foreign exchange markets; in Germany in 1923, the mark reached a low point of 4 trillion to the U.S. dollar. But hyperinflation is very rare. It has usually occurred only in countries where, because of war or revolution, the tax system has almost completely broken down, so that money must be created to provide for much of goverment spending. In most instances of hyperinflation, the monetary system collapses, and a new monetary unit must be introduced. The obvious cases of hyperinflation are Germany in the early 1920s and Hungary, Greece, and China after World War II. Some countries, such as Brazil, have come close to hyperinflation but have stopped the rising inflationary trend and held increases in prices to more moderate percentages thereafter.

The Role of Money Supply in Inflation

Efforts to forecast short-run changes in the rate of inflation in recent years have failed dismally. While the more successful business forecasters have been able to forecast real GNP within relatively small margins of error, they have missed the extent of inflation by wide margins.[26] Thus it is usually not practicable to do more than guess the short-run changes in inflation, given the current state of the art.

It is, however, much more practicable to forecast, on the basis of certain assumptions, the long-run trend level of inflation. Major assumptions are the long-run rate of increase in the money supply and the closeness of the level of output to that possible with "full employment."

To forecast the long-run trend rate of inflation, we begin with the equation of exchange. This equation, usually written in the form $MV = PT$, has a much longer history than the Keynesian income identity discussed in Chapter 3, although it expresses the same truism—spending equals income. In this case, however, the equation includes *all* spending, not just spending for newly produced goods and services, or it may be limited to include only spending for newly produced goods and services, as the Keynesian identity is limited. M is the money supply, V is its velocity of circulation, and MV is total spending. P is

[26]For comments on the errors of economists in forecasting inflation in 1973, see Walter W. Heller, "What's Right with Economics?" *American Economic Review*, March 1975, pp. 1–26, especially pp. 15–25.

the average price level, T is the total volume of transactions counted, and PT is the total value of goods and services produced, or income, if the equation is limited to income spending. Since PT cannot be separated, because it is impossible to add wheat, automobiles, and so on, P cannot be measured. But it is convenient to measure *changes* in prices by some price index.

For the purpose of forecasting the long-run trend of inflation, it is helpful to rewrite the equation in the form $P = MV/T$ and to use rates of change for each variable. When this is done the equation becomes $dP = dM + dV - dT$.

Monetarist economists tend to assume that the rate of change in M is an independent variable and that the rate of change in V is related in some manner to the rate of change in M. Then if the rate of change in M for a period of time is known or can be assumed on the basis of predicted behavior of the monetary authority, the long-run inflation rate becomes predictable. The rate of change in T must also be projected, usually by extrapolating long-run trends in the rise in real output, given the social and cultural setting in a particular country. Productivity in the United States has increased by about 3 percent on the average, and the labor force by about $1\frac{1}{2}$ percent. Of course, in some years real output increases by 6 or 7 percent; in other years it declines. But forecasting the long-run rate of inflation may be very helpful to business firms by enabling them to plan on future price increases. For example, on the assumption that the central bank would not change the rate of increase of the money supply from its rate in the past 5 or 6 years, it was clear that the "double-digit" inflation of 1974 would decrease, probably to a range around 6 or 7 percent per year.

Other Factors Affecting Inflation

Nonmonetarist economists do not deny the role of money in inflation, but they do not give it quite as much importance as monetarists do. They emphasize the impossibility of control over the rate of increase in the money supply by the central bank if the government runs excessive deficits over long periods. They also emphasize the role of shortages of certain commodities, and factors of cost-push. If, for example, oil supplies are restricted as they were in the early 1970s, or if there are droughts and crop failures, reducing the rate of increase in the money supply is not likely to control inflation, because people tend to continue to spend for such things and for a time to increase the velocity of circulation of money. Similarly, after inflation has gained headway, if labor demands sizable wage increases, rising costs tend to push prices up, and again for a time spending may rise with an increase in the velocity of circulation of money.

In spite of such qualifications, it remains true that the long-run trends of inflation can be forecast with some accuracy on the basis of the rate of increase in the money supply. The greater or more rapid the increase in the money supply, the more significant it becomes as a cause of inflation, and for hyperinflation correlations are almost perfect.

It should be evident from the foregoing discussion that an inflation forecast is likely to be valid only for the period during which the action of the central bank can be predicted. If the central bank changes its desired rate of growth in the money supply and is able to achieve its new goal, the rate of inflation will change. Central banks may feel forced to expand money supplies more rapidly if governments borrow large sums, since otherwise interest rates reach extraordinarily high levels. Thus fiscal policy forecasts are also essential to a forecast of inflation.

EXCHANGE RATE FLUCTUATIONS

Those involved in international finance face the extra risk of exchange rate fluctuations in addition to risks of fluctuations in real income, price levels, and interest rates. We consider separately the fluctuations in exchange rates under conditions of stable but adjustable exchange rates and under conditions of managed flexible exchange rates. Because rates of inflation and other economic conditions vary from country to country, it does not seem likely that conditions can exist for a return to long-term fixed exchange rates or to a system such as the gold standard described in Chapter 4. Hence we consider stable but adjustable exchange rates. Similarly, when floating exchange rates have existed, the floats have generally been managed floats—governments have intervened to some extent. Therefore our consideration of flexible exchange rates refers primarily to periods of managed floating, although some comments are made on the possibility that complete flexibility for private market forces to determine exchange rates might be attained.

The Nature of Exchange Rate Risk

Arguments for and against stable exchange rates were considered in Chapter 9. We now view the risks from the standpoint of entrepreneurs, to evaluate the problems of forecasting changes in rates and to examine what can be done to avoid or reduce risk.

It should be clearly understood that in equilibrium, exchange rate risk would not exist. That is, assume that exchange rates immediately adjust perfectly to purchasing power parity and that interest rates immediately adjust to inflation. Then although there might be fluctuations in exchange rates, the purchasing power of any two currencies would always be the same, assuming conversion of one currency into the other at the current exchange rate. Interest rates in the two countries would be the same except for inflation premiums— differences in interest rates would equal differences in rates of change in prices. The reason is that if one country had an inflation rate 2 percent higher than the other country, interest rates in the first country would have to be 2 percent higher in order to provide sufficient purchasing power at the end of a year to enable lenders to buy as much with the principal plus interest as before. Thus exchange risk arises because there are short-term deviations both from purchasing power parity and from interest rate parity (Fisher open).

For entrepreneurs, exchange risk arises from the fact that their receipts or their assets are denominated in one currency and their profits or net worth in another. If purchasing power parity is attained, even with a lag, adjustments in prices and in exchange rates should offset each other, leaving asset values unchanged when converted at current exchange rates. With respect to cash flows, if a single transaction occurs, the forward rate can be used to measure the cost of avoiding the exchange risk. But even in such cases, forward sales or purchases can nullify exchange risk only if entrepreneurs can accurately forecast the amount of foreign currencies they wish to convert. Even those engaged in foreign trade cannot always estimate this correctly, since the foreign price or the quantity to be sold must sometimes be a random variable. Thus exchange risk is a business *cost,* causing variations in profits.[27]

One misconception may be created by the last two sentences, and it should be corrected. Although a forward discount is a cost in making a covered transaction, it is not correct to regard forward discounts as costs of making covered foreign financial investment. Thus if an investor who could lend domestically at 8 percent can lend abroad at 14 percent, he cannot regard the forward discount on covering his foreign financial investment as a cost of making that investment, except in a very naïve sense. The high interest rate abroad is no doubt a reflection of higher inflation there and the forward discount is a reflection of the risk of devaluation or depreciation of the foreign currency. In equilibrium the covered yield on the two loans would be identical.

The objective of entrepreneurs is to maximize utility (satisfaction), which is a function of possible profit and of risk.[28] When a risk can be ignored, calculation of net returns and prices for assets, either financial or real, is easy. The standard formula for capital asset pricing can be used:

$$PV = \frac{Y_1}{1+r} + \frac{Y_2}{(1+r)^2} + \cdots + \frac{Y_n}{(1+r)^n}$$

If the assets are government bonds, credit risk may usually be ignored, and today's price and the rate of discount are known. (In a few cases, of course, governments have defaulted on foreign debt obligations.) But clearly future prices of the bonds, except at the maturity date, involve risk. The rate of discount may vary even if the returns do not. If the rate of discount, r, were a random variable, risk would be high. But if r can be forecast with some accuracy, because it is the "normal" rate of interest plus an inflation premium, risk is less. Risk is greater if monetary and fiscal policies or other factors cause greater variation in interest rates over business cycles. The mean degree of risk over a cycle might be the same, but probability of gain or possibility of loss would be greater for any period less than or more than a cycle. Investors who

[27]Anthony Lanyi, *The Case for Floating Exchange Rates Reconsidered,* Essays in International Finance, No. 72 (Princeton: Princeton, 1969), p. 4.

[28]This section draws heavily upon Samuel I. Katz, *Exchange-Risk under Fixed and Flexible Exchange Rates,* New York University, Bulletins 83–84, June 1972 (New York: New York University, Institute of Finance, 1972).

try to avoid risk would be wise to hold fewer government securities under such circumstances.

When equities instead of bonds are held, Ys (incomes) become variable and hence risk is increased. There is usually also a credit risk. Therefore risk-averse individuals and institutional managers would prefer to hold smaller asset portfolios.

When two or more currencies and exchange rates are introduced, there is a third variable—the exchange risk—as well as expected profit and other risks. The rate of profit is a function of Y, PV, and X (the exchange rate), so that

$$P = \frac{(Y_{o+t} + PV_{o+t})X_{o+t} - X_o PV_o}{X_o PV_o}$$

where the time period over which profit P is calculated is $o + t$. Y and PV usually have greater variability in foreign trade and investing than in domestic trade and investing. This is because risks other than the exchange rate risk are usually greater (the present value and return on assets have greater variability).[29] Annual inflation rates, restrictions on capital repatriation and on ownership, discrimination against foreign-owned businesses, and political stability all vary greatly worldwide.

Suppose that a business is nationalized. The worst that could happen would be that no compensation would be obtained. Much more likely, the entrepreneur will obtain compensation in local currency bonds. If he could receive the bonds, sell them, and remit the proceeds promptly, no exchange risk would arise. But exchange risk may arise if he fails to remit promptly. It may also arise if measures other than total expropriation are taken by foreign governments. If they impose exchange controls, purchases of raw materials for production can be shifted from controlled but low-cost sources to noncontrolled, or less strictly controlled but higher cost, sources. When multiple exchange rates are used, all import costs for some firms may be higher, if they are required to use a higher rate in the multiple-rate structure.

Return on foreign investment combines P, a flow, with PV, the value of a stock of assets. Risk on profits is more predictable than risk on present values. Even profits cannot be precisely forecast. Of course, different entrepreneurs have different ratios of profits and assets; export and import trading firms may have almost no assets abroad, and multinational firms have large foreign asset holdings.

Sharing the Burden of Risk

It is generally assumed that commercial banks do not hold sufficient uncovered positions in foreign exchange to have much effect on exchange rates. Banks

---

[29]Robert B. Stobaugh, Jr., "How to Analyze Foreign Investment Climates," *Harvard Business Review*, September–October 1969, pp. 100–108, and "Where in the World Should we Put that Plant?" *Harvard Business Review*, January–February 1969, pp. 129–136.

facilitate transfers for customers and provide the means for customers to hedge, but they are not expected to take risks except when unavoidable. If they take small positions, this contributes to the smooth functioning of the forward market. Bank traders are usually given some freedom to maintain uncovered positions, and single banks often cannot have profitable foreign operations without taking some risks.

On the other hand, after 1971 there was an expansion of speculative activity by commercial banks. German banks especially found their lending activity domestically restricted by Bundesbank (central bank) credit policy, and sought profits in foreign exchange trading. Witnesses in U.S. Congressional hearings testified that speculating banks "were taking positions large enough to artificially influence exchange rates."[30] Foreign exchange losses were a factor in the failure of the Franklin National Bank. The failure of the Herstatt Bank before it could make delivery of foreign exchange in trades in which marks were delivered to it earlier in the day had a disruptive effect on the foreign exchange market. For a time, foreign exchange markets were thin and sensitive.

Except when banks engage in transactions based on expectations concerning future exchange rates, as some did in the early 1970s, the burden of exchange risk falls mainly on private entrepreneurs and on central banks. Under completely flexible exchange rates, central banks would not assume any of this burden. The burden of risk on the export and import sectors of economies is therefore greater under flexible rates than under stable but adjustable rates. This conclusion must be qualified, of course, if efforts of governments to resist changes in exchange rates, under stable but adjustable rate conditions, result in greater domestic inflation or deflation, since this may result in the long run in greater fluctuations in exchange rates.

Exchange Risk under Stable but Adjustable Exchange Rates

Under the gold standard system described in Chapter 4, entrepreneurs in international activities could almost ignore exchange rate risk. This diminution of risk was balanced by a greater degree of domestic risk. Business cycles had greater amplitude when macroeconomic policies were less used to minimize fluctuations. Since World War II, amplitude of business cycles has been much less than before that war.

For some transactions, forward exchange contracts can reduce risk. But as economic integration continues and political separation also continues, the volume of transactions for which forward exchange contracts are not suitable hedges will increase.

It has been pointed out by some economists that fluctuations in exchange rates may be less over a period of time under flexible exchange rates than under stable but adjustable rates. The Canadian dollar was nearly at par with the U.S.

---

[30]"International Petrodollar Crisis," *Hearings* before the Subcommittee on International Finance of the House Committee on Banking and Currency, July 9 and Aug. 13, 1974, p. 70.

dollar at the beginning of the period of floating (1950) and again in 1971. In the interim it rose to no more than $1.07 and fell to no less than 92 cents. The devaluation of many currencies in 1949 was 30 percent, approximately twice as much as the fluctuation of the Canadian dollar under floating.

On the other hand, in most LDCs with flexible exchange rates, the exchange values of the currencies have declined over time. Entrepreneurs could protect the international values of their profits and assets remitted from such countries only by raising prices in line with the inflation and the depreciation in currency values.

Upward revaluations and upward floating of exchange rates have occurred in a number of industrialized countries in recent years. This is unusual—before the Bretton Woods agreement, upvaluation through explicit action was very rare.[31] Of course, one country or a group of countries sometimes devalued, and if other countries did not do so, their currencies were in effect upvalued. But exchange risk took on a new aspect after 1971.

Under the Bretton Woods system, the narrower the band within which exchange rates were permitted to fluctuate, the more predictable the rates were, as long as the band was not shifted. Predictability *within* the band was not good unless a currency was near one edge of the band, but if the band was very narrow the small fluctuations within the band were not important. When a country's BOP situation began to weaken or strengthen, a significant change in the exchange rate became more predictable. If a BOP position seriously weakened, the question became one of whether a country would devalue or adopt some other policy, and if it did decide to devalue, the extent of the devaluation.

Some business firms and banks tried to forecast government actions. BOP analysis could tell them that devaluation was probably imminent, and the amount of the devaluation could be roughly forecast through use of purchasing power parity calculations. The major problems were timing and the possibility of adoption of an alternative policy which might forestall devaluation for some time.[32]

Forecasting Devaluations or Upvaluations   Factors to be considered in forecasting devaluations or upvaluations of currencies were in a general way well understood. First, trends and forecasts for the BOP indicated the direction of probable change, and purchasing power parity calculations indicated the general trend level to which the value of a currency was likely to be adjusted.

---

[31]*The Role of Exchange Rates in the Adjustment of International Payments* (Washington, D.C.: International Monetary Fund, 1970), p. 38.

[32]"Foreign Exchange: A Roundtable Discussion," *Wall Street Transcript,* June 24, 1974. See especially comments by Scott E. Pardee, Alan Teck, and James Burtle. See also Subcommittee on International Economics of the Joint Economic Committee of Congress Hearings, *How Well Are Fluctuating Exchange Rates Working? June 20–27, 1973* (Washington, D.C.: Government Printing Office, 1973), p. 4, where a witness stated that his firm could review the basic economic facts about a currency under stable exchange rates "and come to a pretty accurate estimate of where that currency might be headed." He added that the firm was not nearly so successful under floating rates.

Second, the value of reserve assets held relative to BOP deficits indicated need for action. The value of such assets after revaluation was also of concern because devaluation, for example, would increase the value of reserve assets, perhaps making them sufficient to meet needs. Third, the external debt of a country had to be considered since devaluation, for example, would increase the burden of such debt. Finally, timing was a consideration. For example, an upvaluation just before an election would be adverse to important sectors of the economy and thus might cause government defeat in an election. Hence upvaluation might be postponed. These basic general considerations had to be made more specific if forecasting were to be more precise.

Methods of Forecasting Revaluations   One aid to forecasting exchange rate changes was an indicator list. By watching listed indicators, it was suggested, managers could develop an estimate of the probability of a significant change in an exchange rate in a given period. The list of factors varied with different forecasters, but one list is indicative:[33]

1   Relatively low (or high) level of reserve assets, or a sharp decline (or rise) in them.
2   Persistent or sudden major imbalance in the BOP.
3   Level of foreign indebtedness and willingness of foreigners to hold the evidences of such debt.
4   Temporary normal fluctuations in the BOP.
5   Extraordinary factors, such as war, affecting the BOP.
6   Domestic rate of inflation.
7   Anticipated changes in trading partners' economies.
8   Monetary and fiscal alternatives for policy.
9   Trade, exchange, and capital controls—if used, underlying imbalance may be greater than it appears; if not being used, they may be imposed.
10   Importance of the currency in world use.
11   Importance of the country in world trade—in total or in important products.
12   Elasticities of supply and demand for trade and other BOP items.
13   Past history of changes in the value of the currency.
14   Personal philosophies or past actions of important government officials.
15   Economic philosophies of political party in power and of its supportive groups.
16   Proximity of elections.
17   Opinions of bankers and leading businessmen.
18   Large discounts or premiums in forward exchange or in a black market.
19   Unusually low or high interest rates—borrowers expecting devaluation often drive interest rates up.
20   Significant change in domestic investment and spending—expected devaluation may stimulate investment.
21   Trend of domestic real estate values—expected devaluation may stimulate investment in real estate.

[33]Christopher M. Korth, "The Future of a Currency: A Four-Step Procedure for Forecasting Change," *Business Horizons*, June 1972, pp. 67–76.

By developing estimates of the probability of a change in the exchange rate and of the relative amount of change expected if one occurs, the two probabilities may be multiplied to give an expected effect. The expected effect may be translated into an annual cost by multiplying it by the annual cash flow likely to be affected. This may be carried a step further by making an estimate of the reliability of the forecaster and an estimate of the firm's relative aggressive or defensive stance (100 being neutral) in trying to protect itself against losses resulting from exchange rate changes. Multiplying by these two additional percentages would give an estimate of the cost of not protecting against the risk. Then if the cost of protection is known, the two may be compared and the desirability of attempting to protect against risk evaluated.[34]

Another model was developed to help decide when cost of hedging might outweigh possible exchange losses or vice versa.[35] This model required a spearate decision for each time interval. In each period, if a significant change in an exchange rate did not occur, the question was then considered whether to wait for another period in the hope that (a) the hedging cost would be less and (b) a significant change in the exchange rate would not occur during that interval.

It should be clear that with these suggested methods the development of the probabilities is an art rather than a science. The factors considered do not provide a means of measuring and predicting the probability of a change in the exchange rate, but only a list of items which may be considered in estimating such probability.

Some more recent studies used the techniques of discriminant analysis in an effort to separate countries likely from those not likely to revalue. Such analysis does not predict the extent of revaluation, but may help in predicting direction and timing, since it indicates the likelihood of a revaluation in the near future. Folks and Stansell used a period of 2 years and a devaluation of 5 percent or more as measures of the time period and amount constituting a revaluation.[36] Data were collected on countries which devalued by more than 5 percent in one or two 2-year periods and on randomly selected countries which did not do so. Then a number of variables were selected on which data were readily available or easily estimated. Ratios were used to make values more comparable among countries. The ratios selected were:

1   Rate of growth of reserve assets
2   Rate of growth of M_2

[34]R. B. Shulman, "Are Foreign Exchange Risks Measurable?" *Columbia Journal of World Business*, May–June 1970, pp. 55–60.

[35]Alan C. Shapiro, "Hedging Against Devaluations—a Management Science Approach," in C. G. Alexandrides, ed., *International Business Systems Perspectives* (Atlanta, Ga.: Bureau of Business and Economic Research, Georgia State University, 1972).

[36]William R. Folks, Jr., and Stanley R. Stansell, "The Use of Discriminant Analysis in Forecasting Exchange Rate Movements," *Journal of International Business Studies*, Spring 1975, pp. 33–50.

3 Rate of increase in the consumer price index (CPI)
4 Ratio of exports to imports
5 Ratio of debt service obligations to reserve assets
6 Rate of growth of the ratio of imports to GDP—the rate of change of the marginal propensity to import (MPIm)
7 Rate of change of the central bank discount rate

Multiple discriminant analysis was then used to estimate a discriminant function in which the discriminant score is determined by the values of the significant variables multiplied by coefficients (estimated from the data set) with the appropriate algebraic sign. This model produced correct classification of 74 percent of the devaluing countries and 89 percent of the nondevaluing countries. Other tests using only data for years prior to devaluations by the experimental group of countries generally confirmed these results, thus supporting the predictive power as well as the discriminant power of the method.

In another such study, by Murenbeeld, the variables selected were:[37]

1 Rate of change in the wholesale price index (WPI)
2 Deviation of a 2-year trend in number of people employed from the 5-year trend, measured as a percent
3 Ratio of reserve assets to imports
4 Change in reserve assets over the preceding 2 years
5 Deviation of a 1-year trend in M_2 from the 5-year trend
6 Deviation of a 2-year trend in government surplus or deficit from a 5-year trend, the deviation being measured as a percent of GNP

This selective formulation was based on an attempt to measure internal equilibrium, meaning an acceptable level of inflation and unemployment; external equilibrium, meaning absence of official settlements deficits and an acceptable level of reserve assets as a percent of imports; and trends in use of the major macroeconomic policy tools, monetary and fiscal policy. Countries were divided into upvaluation, no change, and devaluation groups, and the discriminant scores were obtained. Division was made on the basis of action taken, and the data for each country were obtained for the appropriate periods preceding an action. The "no change" group was a random selection. The scores clearly discriminated among the groups; mean scores for the upvaluing group were positive, for the no change group close to zero, and for the devaluing group negative. By selecting a level of score, only 1 out of 25 cases was not correctly classified.

Murenbeeld perceptively recognized that the post-1971 (or post-1972) era is somewhat different, but he attempted to apply his method to the post–Bretton Woods system. Although he recognized that his whole model could be irrelevant in a purely floating exchange rate system, he argued that central

[37]Martin Murenbeeld, "Economic Factors for Forecasting Foreign Exchange Rate Changes," *Columbia Journal of World Business,* Summer 1975, pp. 81–95.

banks still defend currency valuation levels, although ranges of fluctuation are much wider. Sine the pace of change has accelerated (for example, the yen floated up in early 1973 and down in late 1973), he used monthly data for the post–Bretton Woods period. He considered only the Group of Ten currencies. Correct classification occurred in 26 out of 34 cases, and the 6 misclassifications all involved situations in which no change occurred.

From a theoretical viewpoint, it is interesting that he found internal equilibrium just as important a determinant of a possible exchange rate change after 1971 as before that year, but the dominant proxy had become inflation rather than unemployment. Countries about to upvalue had lower rates of inflation and more favorable trends in unemployment. However, a simple Phillips curve relationship did not prevail; countries in the upvaluation group had *both* low rates of inflation and declining rates of unemployment. Indeed, the Phillips curve, if one exists, seems to be country-specific, being much closer to the origin for upvaluing countries than for devaluing countries.

External equilibrium as measured by changes in reserve assets was as important as ever; it appears that reserve assets and central bank actions are important in the present system, which is not a pure floating system.

Murenbeeld tentatively accepted the idea that monetary policy should be used in cases of external disequilibrium and fiscal policy in cases of internal disequilibrium, on the ground that monetary policy actions change interest rates and hence affect capital flows and thus affect BOP deficits or surpluses, while fiscal policy actions affect internal demand.[38] However, he recognized that monetary policy can result in inflation or deflation, thus affecting internal demand, and fiscal policy can affect the BOP because of changes in income Y and hence in the marginal propensity to import (MPIm). Fiscal policy was an increasingly important determinant of currency strength or weakness after 1971. In the stable but adjustable rate system, unemployment and the level of reserve assets were the most important determinants of discrimination scores.

This study was significant in basing the prediction of significant changes in currency values on the underlying economic theory of the BOP and of internal income, employment, and prices. The differences in variables selected in this and in the Folks-Stansell study indicate that selection of variables is not firm. Finally, the application by Murenbeeld of his method to the post-1971 period indicates that the change in 1971 may not have been as great as some believed.[39] We now turn to the difference resulting from this change.

Exchange Risk under Floating Exchange Rates

Since no significant period of flexible exchange rates in the sense of rates without *any* government intervention has existed, exchange risk under such a

---

[38]See Robert M. Stern, *The Balance of Payments* (Chicago: Aldine, 1973), Chap. 10; J. E. Meade, *The Balance of Payments* (London: Oxford, 1951); and Robert A. Mundell, *International Economics* (New York: Macmillan, 1968).

[39]In Murenbeeld's words (op. cit., p. 83), "Many informed observers believe that a new fixed exchange rate system is a distinct possibility once the hurdles of the post–Bretton Woods realignment period have successfully been negotiated."

condition must be analyzed hypothetically. Canadian experience from 1950 to 1961 (excluding the last year of floating rates from 1961 to 1962) was one of only moderate intervention, but the Bank of Canada did intervene to smooth out fluctuations on a very short-term basis.[40]

In a smoothly functioning flexible rate system, the exchange rate would tend to settle at a level at which market participants in general had no expectation of a movement in one direction or the other.[41] If domestic policies for the management of demand in two countries were effective in preventing serious recessions and in preventing rapid inflation, exchange rates would be difficult to predict in the short run. Only if domestic demand management policies were ineffective would prediction be easier. Even so, predictability would exist only over significant periods—very short-run fluctuations could not easily be predicted.

The Efficient Market–Random Walk Hypothesis Two researchers provided impressive evidence that in periods of flexible exchange rates with some government intervention—in the 1920s and in the early 1970s—short-run exchange rate fluctuations for industrialized countries are not predictable. Giddy and Dufey tested four hypotheses: (1) exchange rate changes follow a pattern, termed a *martingale,* in which succeeding prices are not serially correlated but are not necessarily independent; (2) exchange rates follow a pattern, termed a *submartingale,* which is the same except for adjustment of the present rate for differences in interest rate yields on assets in the two currencies; (3) the forward rate can be used to predict the spot rate; and (4) time series analysis can be used to forecast spot rates.[42]

In their results, the forward rate was the worst basis for forecasting, and time series correlation was useful in only a few cases. The martingale and submartingale hypotheses were almost equally good, suggesting that interest rate differentials may be partially but not entirely taken into account.

These results are similar to those obtained in studies which support the random walk hypothesis concerning stock market prices. The hypothesis is not strictly a random walk hypothesis, since Giddy and Dufey did not necessarily assume that rates are independent. But the assumptions and results are very similar to those of the random walk theory of stock market prices: it is assumed that the foreign exchange market is one in which rates are generally free to fluctuate, that there is no monopoly, and that present rates are strongly influenced by expected future rates. In such circumstances rates (prices) fluctuate randomly in the short run. The conclusion is that under flexible rates as they have existed in practice, forecasting for the short run is not possible. It

[40]See G. Hartley Mellish and Robert C. Hawkins, *The Stability of Flexible Rates—The Canadian Experience,* New York University, Bulletins 50–51 (New York: New York University, Institute of Finance, 1968).

[41]Egon Sohmen, *Flexible Exchange Rates,* rev. ed. (Chicago: University of Chicago Press, 1969), p. 188.

[42]Ian H. Giddy and Gunter Dufey, "The Random Behavior of the Flexible Exchange Rates: Implications for Forecasting," *Journal of International Business Studies,* Spring 1975, pp. 1–32.

might be possible if one had a better model or better information than other participants in the market and exclusive use of the information, or if predictable actions of central banks in affecting exchange rates are involved. The further conclusion is that firms generally should not try to forecast very short-run changes in exchange rates in a period of floating rates, but should try to determine their economic exposure (not accounting exposure) to exchange risks and try to protect themselves against these risks when appropriate.[43]

Inability to forecast short-term fluctuations in exchange rates does not prevent forecasting of the long-run trend in exchange rates through purchasing power parity calculations, any more than a weak form of the random walk theory eliminates the possibility of fundamental analysis and forecasting of the long-term trend in the stock market. Of course, forecasts of exchange rates through the purchasing power parity theorem are based on forecasts of inflation. As shown earlier, long-run inflation can be forecast only on the basis of beliefs or assumptions about the policies of the central bank and government.

A model for intermediate-term exchange rate forecasting has been proposed and applied to quarterly data from the beginning of 1973 to mid-1976.[44] This model is interesting because it contradicts the usual BOP theory in two respects: (1) it presumes that more rapid real income growth in one country than in another will cause the first country's currency to appreciate in value, whereas conventional BOP theory presumes that more rapid real income growth will increase imports and hence, by causing a shift toward deficit in the current account, cause the currency to depreciate in value; and (2) it presumes that a rise in the interest rate which is more rapid in one country than in another will cause the value of the first country's currency to depreciate in value, whereas conventional BOP theory presumes that a more rapid increase in the interest rate will attract capital inflows and hence cause a country's currency to appreciate in value.

In this model, the rate of growth of the demand-adjusted money stock determines the expected rate of inflation; given the real interest rate, the expected rate of inflation determines the nominal interest rate; the nominal interest rate together with the level of real income determine the demand for money; given the demand for money, the nominal money stock determines the price level; and the price level relative to that in another country determines the exchange rate. Thus the ultimate determinants of an exchange rate are viewed as (1) relative money stocks (demand-adjusted), (2) relative real incomes, and (3) relative nominal interest rates. The exchange value of the currency varies inversely with the first and third and directly with the second. The resulting regression equation was fairly accurate for the U.S.–UK and U.S.–Italy

[43]Gunter Dufey and Ian H. Giddy, "Forecasting Exchange Rates in a Floating World," *Euromoney*, November 1975, p. 28–35.

[44]Thomas M. Humphrey and Thomas A. Lawler, "Factors Determining Exchange Rates: A Simple Model and Empirical Tests," Federal Reserve Bank of Richmond, *Economic Review*, May/June 1977, pp. 10–15.

exchange rates for the period, with r^2 of .87. It did not fit the data for other countries and other time periods nearly as well.

This model has not been tested sufficiently to reach any firm conclusion about its validity. Nevertheless, the ideas that relatively rapid real income growth tends to cause appreciation of a currency and that a relatively rapid rise in the interest rate tends to cause depreciation of a currency are disturbing. The interest rate proposition is somewhat confusing because it presumably refers to the long-term interest rate, whereas in BOP theory a decline in short-term rates attracts foreign capital. Moreover, if the interest rate rises concomitantly with inflation, the inflation (or the money stock growth which caused the inflation) may be the chief cause of depreciation of the currency. The real income proposition is more difficult to rationalize. A relatively rapid rise in real income should induce a rapid rise in imports and hence a shift toward depreciation of the currency. Does growth in real income stimulate growth in demand for imports or growth in demand for money? The model merits careful examination.

Forecasting Exchange Rates in a Period of Managed Floating   In spite of the evidence that short-term exchange rate fluctuations in a period of floating exchange rates, even if it is managed floating, are probably random, some still argue that they have methods which enable them to "beat the market." The method proposed by Murenbeeld, modified as he deemed appropriate for a managed floating rate situation, has already been discussed.

It was claimed that at least one other model gave excellent results, although it was tested for only a short time.[45] This model is based on a number of propositions: (1) that inflation causes imports to rise and exports to decline; (2) that real growth in income causes imports to rise and exports to fall generally, although in the case of Japan it resulted in rising exports; (3) that increased capacity utilization causes net exports to fall, because if capacity utilization rises, public and/or private consumption is rising; (4) that rising short-term interest rates cause exchange rates to rise; (5) that government deficits cause prices to rise and net exports to decline; and (6) that central bank holdings of exchange reserves may be a proxy for speculative demand for a currency.

It appears that, as in the case of methods of technical analysis of the stock market, no consensus has been reached that any particular model "beats the market," nor has it yet been concluded that they are all simply witchcraft.

Some Further Considerations   It has been suggested that under floating exchange rates after a devaluation several factors may cause wide swings in exchange rates, accentuating the J-curve effect on the trade balance (temporarily worsening rather than improving the trade balance of the devaluing

[45]John F. Norris and Michael K. Evans, "Beating the Futures Market in Foreign Exchange Rates," *Euromoney,* February 1976, pp. 62–71.

country). It has been argued that multinational firms tend to overhedge because of their accounting and control policies. Companies in devaluing countries lose on exposed assets, and conservative accounting practices tend to treat items as exposed even when there is some doubt. Hence firms may not buy a currency which is declining in value, but instead may hedge against its further decline. Also, both central banks and commercial banks seem to discourage speculation, and commercial banks find that speculation involves risks in dealing with speculators who may lose relatively large sums (relative to their net worths). Margin requirements like those in the stock market would represent an added complication. Although they may appear in time, they have not yet developed. Finally, individuals and firms seem to want a stable store of value. In a system of floating exchange rates, there is no such asset. The price of gold is uncertain. SDRs are thus far held only by central banks. Thus it seems plausible that there may be either (1) large shifts of funds from currency to currency in search of a stable store of value or (2) attempts to diversify currency holdings, thus gaining greater stability in value.[46] It is difficult to predict which behavior is more probable. Diversification is more logical, but with fluctuating values people have at times in the past shifted from one asset to another in an attempt to hold an asset with greater stability.

The first two suggestions imply the probability of wide swings in currency values, and the third implies the probability of wide random swings. This would suggest that wide fluctuations in exchange rates may be difficult to avoid under a managed floating rate system.

THE CHANGING INTERNATIONAL ENVIRONMENT OF MANAGERIAL FINANCE

Many economic variables in different countries can be forecast by econometric and/or judgmental techniques because their future values depend in some way on past values. The dependence need not be a straight-line correlation, although this is likely for such variables as consumer spending and past personal disposable income.

Short-run forecasts of other variables, such as prices, including exchange rates, when determined in efficient markets, are not likely to be possible. For the long run, only the *trend* in such variables, not the values for specific future years, may be possible to forecast.

The business firms can benefit from being able to make or to evaluate and use relatively accurate forecasts of the former category of variables. For other variables, such as prices and exchange rates under the conditions mentioned, firms could benefit from forecasting only if they had a superior model and if that model were not generally available. The desirable alternative in the absence of such a model is for firms to consider what action they might take if certain changes in prices or exchange rates should occur.

---

[46]The first alternative was suggested by James L. Burtle, "Some Problems in Living with a System of Floating Exchange Rates," *Business Economics*, May 1974, pp. 52–55.

Entrepreneurs in the international field are exposed to less risk under a stable rate system because part of the risk and cost is shifted to central banks. Losses by central banks are in the long run paid by taxpayers. In effect, the system partially subsidizes the entrepreneurs engaged in international transactions. If central banks in various countries aimed at the same rate of inflation, it probably would not matter whether there were stable or floating exchange rates. But if different rates of inflation are chosen as goals or are believed to be unavoidable, the fluctuations in monetary policy, interest rates, and expected rates of inflation are likely to produce wide volatility in exchange rates.

Whether the volatility of exchange rates is important depends partly on the importance of international transactions to an economy. But there is a more direct influence: many countries do not constitute large enough markets in themselves to allow, without exports, for the technological advantages of large-scale production. The real question becomes not stable exchange rates versus floating rates but the consolidation of groups of countries into areas having relatively stable rates within the group, but perhaps floating rates vis-à-vis outside currencies.

Some economists argue that rapid economic growth may result from expansion of the export sectors of LDCs. If so, arrangements which favor export sectors may have a value for economic development.

Greater integration of the world economy could be furthered by some agreement on procedures for controlling fluctuations in exchange rates indirectly by accommodating domestic monetary and fiscal policies to international trends. Whether this is likely remains to be seen, but it is clear that international firms face a changing international economic environment.

QUESTIONS FOR DISCUSSION

1   What reasons can you think of for the gradual synchronization of business cycles in the industralized world?
2   Monetarists argue that the inflation of the past decade was generated solely by rapid increase in the supply of money. Give some arguments tending to show that increase in money supply was not the *sole* cause.
3   Given the theory of foreign exchange rates developed in Chapter 9, why did the rapid increase in world money supply in the early 1970s, compared with the rise in the U.S. money supply, not lead to appreciation of the dollar?
4   Why have incomes policies generally failed except for short periods and under special conditions?
5   Why is indexation of many prices and incomes often accepted when inflation reaches double-digit levels?
6   Why may long-term interest rates be expected to rise by approximately as much as the rate of inflation, whereas short-term interest rates may fluctuate widely in a period of inflation?
7   Compare exchange rate risk under the Bretton Woods system with exchange rate risk under (managed) floating rates. Why are exchange rates likely to be less easy to predict under the floating rate system? Relate the discussion to the use of different monetary policies by different countries.

8 What is the difference between the feasibility of forecasting trends in GNP and even quarter-by-quarter changes in GNP and the difficulty of forecasting price changes in the stock market or exchange rate changes in the foreign exchange market?

9 Explain the theory behind Murenbeeld's selection of variables to indicate internal equilibrium or disequilibrium, variables to indicate external equilibrium or disequilibrium, and changes in monetary and fiscal policy as the major independent variables for prediction of changes in exchange rates.

10 What should you advise a company concerning the forecasting of exchange rates in a period of managed floating rates?

SUGGESTED REFERENCES

A review of the use of macroeconomic policies in affecting income and interest rates may be helpful; see, for example, Charles N. Henning, William Pigott, and Robert Haney Scott, *Financial Markets and the Economy* (Englewood Cliffs, N.J.: Prentice-Hall, 1975), Chaps. 15–17.

An extensive discussion of environmental factors affecting international business may be found in Stefan H. Robock and Kenneth Simmonds, *International Business and Multinational Enterprises* (Homewood, Ill.: Irwin, 1973), Chaps. 11–16.

Useful comparative economic data on various countries may be found in publications of the International Bank for Reconstruction and Development: *Trends in Developing Countries,* 1971; *Finance and Development,* quarterly; *World Bank Atlas,* irregularly; and a series of volumes on individual countries.

Standard statistical sources include *International Financial Statistics,* IMF, monthly; *Main Economic Indicators,* OECD, monthly; *United Nations Yearbook of National Account Statistics,* UN, annually; *Pacific Basin Economic Indicators,* Federal Reserve Bank of San Francisco, Quarterly beginning Spring 1975.

Good surveys of the general environment of international business are Raymond Vernon, *Manager in the International Economy,* 2d ed. (Englewood Cliffs, N.J.: Prentice-Hall, 1972), and *Sovereignty at Bay: The Multinational Spread of U.S. Enterprises* (New York: Basic Books, 1971). For an interesting exchange of ideas, see the review, by Peter P. Gabriel, of the second Vernon book cited, and the reply by Vernon, *Fortune,* January 1972, pp. 119–124.

On exchange risk, see especially Samuel I. Katz, *Exchange-Risk under Fixed and Flexible Exchange Rates,* New York University Bulletins 83–84, June 1972, and *'Managed Floating' as an Interim International Exchange Rate Regime, 1973–1975,* New York University, Bulletin 1975-3.

An innovative analysis of the world inflation which followed 1971 (but an analysis which builds on known and generally accepted theory) is that of Michael W. Keran, "Towards an Explanation of Simultaneous Inflation-Recession," Federal Reserve Bank of San Francisco, *Business Review,* Spring 1975, pp. 18–30. See also, in the same issue, Edward S. Shaw, "International Money and International Inflation: 1958–1973," pp. 5–17.

For views on the exchange rate system since 1973, see the *First Chicago World Report,* March 1977. Comments by Coombs, Aliber, and Hoefs are especially thought-provoking. See also *Guidelines for Exchange Market Intervention,* Hearings, Subcommittee on International Economics, Joint Economic Committee, 94th Cong., 2d Sess., Oct. 18, 1976.

Chapter 15

Protecting against Risks in International Finance

The major risks encountered in international finance may be classified as credit risks, exchange rate risks, and political risks. Credit risks mean the risks involved in selling to buyers or lending to borrowers who may not be able or willing to pay. Exchange rate risks mean the risks arising from fluctuations in exchange rates; these fluctuations may mean either gains or losses. Political risks mean risks that foreign governments will impose regulations or restrictions which could either prevent receipt of funds or confiscate assets.

WHEN TO PROTECT AGAINST RISKS

Decisions whether or not to try to protect against risks depend in part on the risk reactions of sellers, lenders, buyers, and borrowers and in part on the cost of obtaining protection against risk compared with the extent and distribution of losses anticipated.

When to Protect against Credit Risk

In the case of credit risks, the reaction to risk determines whether protection in the form of foreign credit insurance is considered, and the cost of such protection in comparison with loss experience or anticipated loss determines whether credit insurance is purchased. Future credit losses can be forecast, generally rather accurately, on the basis of past credit losses. Loss in foreign credits has generally been low; hence foreign credit insurance is not widely purchased. However, it may be advisable in certain situations.

If it can be assumed that premiums for foreign credit insurance are set competitively, it can be concluded that the premiums are enough to cover *average* credit losses plus administrative costs. Thus if credit losses were evenly distributed, there would be no reason to purchase credit insurance, just as there would be no reason to purchase fire insurance if *every* house had a small fire. Therefore, the major criterion for purchase of foreign credit insurance, if the premiums are competitively determined, is the probability that losses will be heavy for one firm considering the purchase of credit insurance and light for another or others.

When to Protect against Exchange Rate Risk[1]

In the case of exchange rate risks, we must consider three different situations: the situation faced by (1) the firm which sells chiefly in its domestic market, but occasionally exports; (2) the firm which sells regularly in the foreign market; and (3) the multinational firm, which sells in many markets in many areas.

The Occasional Exporter (or Importer)   The firm which sells chiefly domestically but occasionally exports can avoid risk of a devaluation or depreciation of foreign currency, assuming that it prices goods sold in such a currency, by selling exchange forward. Whether it should do this or not depends on the cost of such forward cover in comparison with expected profit. If the sale is profitable in spite of the reduction in profit caused by concomitant sale of forward exchange at a discount, the sale should be made and the forward exchange sold. The question that is usually not discussed is, what does the firm do if the cost of hedging is too great, and yet the firm believes that it should hedge if it makes the sale? The answer is that it should sell the product in the domestic market, as it does with most of its output in any event. Similar comments apply to the firm which occasionally imports. Its alternative, if hedging seems desirable but is too costly, is to buy in the domestic market instead of importing.

The Regular Exporter (or Importer)   The firm which sells regularly in the export market is in a different situation. Unless it sells entirely for cash or under letters of credit which provide equivalent terms, it always has some receivables. Unless the level of such receivables changes, there is no realized loss. But of course it is likely that the level of receivables will rise as a foreign currency depreciates, and this rise measures the loss incurred. More receivables that could have been converted into home currency are tied up. There will be a decreased stream of future revenues in terms of the home currency.

[1]This section draws heavily on Gunter Dufey, "Corporate Financial Policies and Floating Exchange Rates," address at the meeting of the International Fiscal Association in Rome, Italy, Oct. 14, 1974, and on Alan C. Shapiro, "Exchange Rate Changes, Inflation and the Value of the Multinational Corporation," *Journal of Fnance*, May 1975, pp. 485–502.

What can the firm do? It might be able to increase prices in the foreign currency enough to compensate, but this is not likely. If it were likely, the question could be asked, why didn't the firm raise its prices sooner? The question really is, can competitors in the foreign country increase their production without too much increase in their costs and compete more effectively? If they can, then prices cannot be raised sufficiently to compensate for the depreciation or devaluation of the foreign currency. (Clearly, if inflation affected all parties in the same way and if currency values immediately adjusted to purchasing power parties, there would be no problem.)

If the forward market had less variability than the spot exchange market, there would be an advantage to hedging through the forward market, because the probability of unpleasant surprises in movements of the forward rate would be less than that of movements in the spot rate. In the Bretton Woods era, this was not likely, because central banks concentrated most of their activity on trying to stabilize spot rates. The situation after early 1973 is not so clear. If the forward rate is more variable than the spot rate, the possibility of unfavorable surprises when hedging is greater, and hedging is not of benefit in the long run, although it might be (by chance) on some particular occasion.

What else can the firm do? It might cut costs, but it should have been trying to do this anyway, and if it is able to, that is just an accident. The firm could, however, offset the assets in its balance sheet on which returns decrease by liabilities on which payments decrease, when both are measured in home currency. If a firm has assets in the form of receivables from foreign countries, for example, and exports regularly, its best chance of offsetting possible losses is to have liabilities in those same countries' currencies in such manner that its payments in home currency will decrease. Such liabilities should have long enough maturities for the firm to make the changes necessary to offset in the long run the decreased revenue resulting from depreciation or devaluation of foreign currencies. The firm may wish to examine other markets or sources of materials used in producing its output as means of meeting the new situation.

The foregoing presumes that the firm is not able to forecast exchange rates. Of course, if the firm has a model which enables it to forecast changes in exchange rates, it may avoid exporting goods priced in a foreign currency expected to depreciate. But we noted in Chapter 14 that in a regime of floating exchange rates, even managed floating rates, forecasting may well be impossible for the short run.

The Multinational Firm   Finally, we consider the case of multinational firms. Suppose that such a firm has a subsidiary in a country which devalues its currency or permits it to depreciate. The analysis in Part One of this book enables us to conclude that a subsidiary that exports its products should perhaps be able to increase its revenue, and hence to remit even more proceeds to the parent company than before. We remember, of course, that this conclusion is somewhat uncertain, and the results of devaluations are not clearcut. If the subsidiary sells its products in the local (foreign) market, it may or may not suffer. If it obtains its raw materials, for example, from the parent company, its costs rise and its revenues, or in any event its net revenues, probably fall.

It must be concluded that the results depend on where the subsidiary sells its output, the source of its raw materials, the degree of competition in both these markets, and the degree of flexibility which the subsidiary has in changing its markets and sources of materials.

Of course, it is clear that in the long run much depends on macrofinancial policies of governments in countries in which subsidiaries operate. If such policies attempt to reduce inflation (the usual cause of currency devaluation or depreciation), demand and output may fall and profits may be restricted. A subsidiary that exports most of its output may suffer much less. If policies are ineffective in controlling inflation, there may be continued depreciation of the currency. In that case, much depends on whether profits rise as much as other forms of income. In the United States in the period 1965–1974, profits were badly hurt during the attempts to control inflation. Unless corporate income taxes are adjusted for inflation, such taxes squeeze profits when inflation occurs, partly because of inadequate depreciation charges (and therefore excessive *reported* profits) and partly because insufficient amounts are charged for inventory sold, under accounting methods usually used, as discussed in the next chapter.

Thus the situation for multinational firms is very complex with respect to expected cash flows, and a simple formula is not adequate.

How about values of assets and of equity? Assets must be judged by their capability of producing future streams of income. If the future expected stream of income increases, the economic value of both fixed assets and inventories rises. The *economic* value of current assets other than inventory may not change. However, with a probable larger volume of sales (in terms of local—foreign—currency), the subsidiary is also likely to need to hold larger cash balances. At the same time it may have more notes and accounts payable. Any *net* increase in current assets minus current liabilities involves a loss for the parent company, which must leave more funds in its subsidiary than it otherwise would.

A parent company and its subsidiaries should avoid losses if possible by arranging their assets and financing so that any decline in return on assets (profits) is offset by a decline in interest costs on liabilities.

It is important to note that what is being discussed is *economic* exposure on assets held in foreign countries minus liabilities denominated in the currencies of those countries. *Accounting* reporting of such exposure may be quite different, and frequently misleading. If accountants indicate the methods used to translate figures from one currency to another, of course, an attempt can be made to ascertain the economic exposure. Even better, as discussed in the next chapter, if accountants could be persuaded to adopt the most accurate—or perhaps we should say the least inaccurate—methods of valuation or translation it would be helpful.

For the multinational firm, then, financial adjustments are the most appropriate response to exchange rate risk. If for some reasons, such as controls on capital flows, such financial adjustments are impossible, then use of forward exchange markets is helpful.

When to Protect against Political Risks

Finally, let us consider the problem of when to attempt to protect against political risks. If markets for both real and financial capital were unrestricted, it would be possible to avoid such risk by shifting assets from one market to another. But this is not the case; it is the difficulty of shifting real capital assets and the restrictions on moving financial capital which give rise to the need for protection against political risk.

Some protection against political risks ranging from excessive taxes to total confiscation without compensation is available in the form of government guarantees. The problem of criteria for the purchase of such guarantees is difficult. First, since the guarantees are provided by a government agency, we do not know whether the premiums for such guarantees reflect the average loss for such investments plus a small charge for administrative expenses, as they would if charged by private companies. The government may not be charging enough, thus subsidizing foreign investment, or it may be charging too much, thus gaining something at the expense of those who purchase investment guarantees. Second, the experience for such guarantees has been quite short, and it is difficult to know whether it is reasonable to extrapolate such experience. Third, the incidence of investment losses because of various forms of expropriation or less severe actions which result in loss of income or wealth is very uncertain. There is little basis for prediction.

Thus it is difficult to generalize about the conditions under which a firm should purchase investment guarantees. If we assume that the premiums are set as they would be in a competitive private market, there is still the unpredictable nature of expropriative actions and the risk-averting or risk-accepting attitude of the firm. Some writers have argued that only moderate use of the guarantees has been made because they are not well publicized.[2] Other observers regard the investment guarantee program as a "limited instrument in an age of compromise," one with many inherent limitations, an instrument which can tip the scales only in marginal cases.[3] Where investment guarantees are most needed they probably cannot be obtained, and where they are available they are less needed.

PROTECTING AGAINST RISKS

We now describe some of the measures used or available for use by firms to protect against international financial risks. These include export credit insurance, actions to protect against risk of loss from exchange rate fluctuations, and

[2]Barthold W. Sorge, *United States Foreign Investment Guarantees,* Report of Management No. 14 (Los Angeles: Graduate School of Business Administration, University of Southern California, 1966).

[3]Marina von Neumann Whitman, *The United States Investment Guaranty Program and Private Foreign Investment,* Princeton Studies in International Finance, No. 9 (Princeton, 1959).

investment guarantees and other means of protecting against risks of loss from confiscation or other political actions.

Means of Protecting against Foreign Credit Risks

Two means are available for protecting against foreign credit risks: export credit insurance may be purchased, or in some cases risk may be shifted to banks if they are willing to provide nonrecourse financing for collection of drafts drawn on those from whom payments are due.

Export Credit Insurance: FCIA   Export credit insurance has been offered for many years in a number of countries, to permit exporters to insure against credit risks. Credit risks may be commercial, political, or both. The commercial risks are those of failure of the customer before payment and of protracted default. The political risks are those of expropriation, inconvertibility of currency, war or revolution, or restriction or cancellation of import licenses by governments.

If exporters sell under letters of credit as described in Chapter 7, all of these risks are assumed by banks, except in unusual cases such as the use of revocable letters of credit. But importers often do not wish to open letters of credit—perhaps because of cost, difficulty of securing letters of credit, or other reasons—and exporters may find that competition from other countries' exporters deprives them of sales unless they are willing to sell on open account or on draft terms without letters of credit.

The export credit insurance now available in the United States was introduced in 1962. It is offered by the Export-Import Bank in cooperation with an association of insurance companies termed the Foreign Credit Insurance Association (FCIA). More than 70 insurance companies have been members. The Export-Import Bank carries the political risks and the insurance companies carry the commercial risk.[4] In foreign countries practice varies, but more commonly the credit insurance is provided by the government or by a special public agency.

Exporters may purchase short-term insurance policies to cover sales to be paid for within 180 days from the time of delivery of documents, meaning the bill of lading and other documents evidencing title to the goods and other necessary matters. Exporters report and pay premiums on all their export sales except those for cash in advance and those under letters of credit, since otherwise they might report only sales to risky customers or areas. Letters of credit may sometimes exclude political risks, in which case it may be desirable to insure for such risk only. If FCIA disapproves of any foreign buyers, exporters willing to accept the risk may continue to sell to them, and they need not report such sales. FCIA establishes limits for credit, and exporters must have credit reports in their files to indicate their basis for extending credit. Other information may be needed if exporters apply for special amounts of

---

[4]*Selling Abroad with Credit Insurance* (New York: Foreign Credit Insurance Association, 1965).

credit beyond assigned limits. When accounts receivable are paid, amounts may fall to or below the credit limit; hence exporters must pay premiums on all sales, so that when many payments are received at one time, remaining receivables may be covered.

Premiums may be paid on sales contracted for but not shipped. If a buyer becomes insolvent before shipment has been made, loss may be covered by an additional premium. FCIA may, however, exclude certain markets from coverage and eliminate them from premium charges.

To put some burden on exporters so that they will make efforts to collect receivables, 10 percent (earlier 15 percent) of the commercial risk and 5 percent of the political risk are imposed on them in many countries. Countries are rated by the FCIA and exporters may be required to carry higher percentages of risk in sales to high-risk countries. Political risk alone may be covered if exporters wish to assume the commercial risk.

Medium-term policies are available for exporters shipping products on credit terms from 181 days to 5 years. Installment payments are insured, including interest to 6 percent per year on outstanding balances. Products are generally capital goods—machinery, airplanes, and so on. Exporters normally carry 10 percent of the risk, both commercial and political. Insurance is usually on a case by case basis or on sales up to credit limits to specified buyers, but a master comprehensive policy is available. As with short-term credit insurance, political risk alone may be insured if desired. Political risk coverage does not, of course, require credit information.

There are some other special policy forms, and services may be insured; consignors, lessors, and exhibitors at trade fairs may obtain political coverage.

U.S. exporters were on several occasions in the past on record in opposition to export credit insurance under government auspices. There is debate concerning its usefulness. In some periods, average export credit losses have been as low as $1/2$ percent—which may be less than the cost of export credit insurance. Procedures to obtain export credit insurance involve cost in time and effort in addition to the premiums. Exporters have also been concerned about technical features of the program. Unless delivery has been made, FCIA has taken the position that a sale has not been made. Moreover, if a buyer claims that products do not meet specifications, FCIA has taken the position that a sale has not occurred until the dispute is resolved. Improvements have been made in the program since it was introduced in 1962, and in some cases it is valuable.[5] But the burden of paperwork and delays involved make the program undesirable for some exporters.

Nonrecourse Financing by Banks   Sometimes banks purchase on a nonrecourse basis the drafts drawn by exporters on importers. This is more advantageous to exporters than export credit insurance, since all risk is

---

[5]For one view of export credit insurance, see J. Fred Weston and Bart W. Sorge, "Export Insurance—Why U.S. Lags," *Columbia Journal of World Business,* September–October 1967, pp. 67–76; see also J. Fred Weston and Bart W. Sorge, *International Managerial Finance* (Homewood, Ill.: Irwin, 1972), pp. 69–76.

transferred to the banks. Paperwork and delays are avoided. Under letters of credit there is normally no recourse, but the nonrecourse purchase of drafts without letters of credit is somewhat unusual. (Drafts are purchased under Authorities to Purchase on a nonrecourse basis, but the A/Ps are really L/Cs in these cases. They protect against credit risk unless the opening bank should fail before honoring the drafts and without sufficient deposit balance in a paying bank, if one is designated, to be seized as offset.) Whether nonrecourse financing of drafts is likely to spread depends on the willingness of banks to assume risks.

Protecting against Risk of Loss from Exchange Rate Fluctuations

It was indicated in the discussion of when to protect against the risk of loss from exchange rate fluctuations that the best form of protection was probably the matching of liabilities with assets denominated in a given currency in such a way that losses on assets would be offset by gains from reducing interest on liabilities. An alternative, when such changes seemed impossible, was shown to be the use of the forward exchange market.

Some economists have argued that under a truly flexible exchange rate system forward rates would be close to spot rates.[6] They think that wide divergence between forward and spot rates arises only because significant changes in spot exchange rates are expected. But clearly, whether forward discounts or premiums are small depends on whether different central banks' policies are similar, producing similar rates of inflation, and hence similar levels of interest rates (assuming equivalent risks on securities). Other economists believe that truly flexible exchange rates are not likely to exist because central banks would intervene. But the interference of central banks is likely to prevent fluctuations from being wider than they would otherwise be.

If interest rate differentials and differences in expected rates of change in spot exchange rates have major effects on forward rates, it may be that if independent monetary policies are pursued by different countries, interest rate differentials may be wide at times, resulting in wide differences between spot and forward rates, with a higher cost of hedging, and wide fluctuations in spot rates, with greater risk.

Some economists believe that with some additional bank resources, which should be readily forthcoming, to expand the forward market, cost of hedging should be reduced. Others, such as Paul Einzig, argue that banks have delivery risks in dealing in forward exchange even when they have no portfolio risks,

[6]This is the position taken by Egon Sohmen, "Exchange Risks and Forward Coverage in Different Monetary Systems," in *The Burgenstock Papers*, ed. by G. N. Halm (Princeton: Princeton, 1970), pp. 310–316. The expectation that forward and spot rates would be kept close together by interest arbitrage under a system of floating rates was challenged, however, by Edwin A. Reichers and Harold Van B. Cleveland, "Flexible Exchange Rates and Forward Market," in *The Burgenstock Papers*, especially pp. 327–328. We now know that in 1973–1975, forward and spot rates diverged more than they had in the past.

having offset purchases and sales.[7] Individual banks may fail to deliver. The Herstatt bank comes to mind, although its failure was to deliver spot exchange against such exchange delivered to it in another place earlier in the same day!

The evidence thus far indicates that in the period of floating exchange rates after 1973, both the amplitude of fluctuations in spot exchange rates and transactions cost increased greatly in some cases. The wider fluctuations and increased transactions costs in these cases appear to result from differences in monetary policies which give rise to different expectations concerning inflation and hence to different results in the foreign exchange market. If this evidence is further supported, we must conclude that both risks and transactions costs are greater in international trade and investments than they were in the period of stable but adjustable exchange rates.

This conclusion need not upset our earlier conclusions that in the long run purchasing power parity is the best available tool for forecasting the *trend* of exchange rates, and that the rate of increase in the money supply is the best tool for forecasting the *trend* rate of inflation. These are long-run causes and effects. But here we are concerned with the short run. If there are short-run risks in exchange rate fluctuations, what can be done about them? An unidentified executive is quoted as saying that "all the Harvard Business School techniques are worthless when exchange rates can move by 20 percent in a matter of months."[8] If those techniques were aimed at forecasting exchange rate movements, if the evidence that exchange rate movements are essentially random is correct, and if rates are more volatile in a floating rate regime, this is not surprising! In fact, we could have predicted it. When monetary policies and inflation rates differ in different countries in direction or force and in timing, rates are likely to be volatile. If the foreign exchange market is efficient, rates are likely to move randomly in the short run. And, transactions costs are higher.

What actions, then, can entrepreneurs take to reduce losses from exchange rate fluctuations when they cannot predict those fluctuations satisfactorily? (Parenthetically, we might add that the uncertainties of floating rates seem to have increased the supply of exchange rate forecasting services. Whether entrepreneurs believe them, as investors perhaps believe the short-run stock market forecasts, or whether they are simply making sure that they can say, "Well, if losses occur, we did the best we could and had the aid of the best forecasting services we could find," is not clear.) The alternatives are considered in the following paragraphs.

Postponement or Speedup of Action   It might be assumed that most entrepreneurs would reject the waiting strategy for transactions which would readily be covered in the forward market, if the cost were not excessive. If they

---

[7]Paul Einzig, *The Case Against Floating Exchanges* (London: Macmillan, 1970), especially pp. 120–121, 124.

[8]*Time,* July 21, 1975, p. 44.

wait, they are not covered. They are affected by any subsequent change in the exchange rate, and if it is in the wrong direction, they may lose. But under the Bretton Woods system, entrepreneurs frequently adopted the waiting strategy.[9] This is because the directions, if not the precise extent and timing, of exchange rate changes were sometimes predictable.

For current transactions, entrepreneurs may avoid risk by buying foreign currency likely to rise in value, if they need to make payments; and also by selling foreign currency likely to fall in value, if they expect to receive payments. Speedup of payments from a weak-currency country into a strong-currency country produces *leads;* delays of payments from a strong-currency country into a weak-currency country produces *lags.* Buyers in strong-currency countries may delay payments (add to their accounts payable) or borrow funds in the weak-currency country and make payment with such funds. Borrowing may occur in money markets or through trade credit. Buyers are investing funds in their own (strong-currency) countries and borrowing in weak-currency countries, intending to repay their debts with cheaper funds later. Of course, leads and lags may be reversed quickly if a government takes effective action to defend a weak exchange rate. It was estimated that nearly half of Britain's reserve asset losses in the mid-1967 crisis was caused by various forms of leads and lags.[10]

Limiting Net Exposed Current Assets   Business managers recognize that in addition to risks on cash flows they have risks on stocks of exposed assets held in weak-currency countries. This risk is only on *exposed* assets; liabilities in any currency are reduced in terms of other currencies by the same amount of assets if a currency's value declines. Hence by examining balance sheet positions and perhaps by offsetting some current assets by current liabilities in the same currency, and then perhaps by covering the remaining net exposure, firms may reduce risk of loss from exchange rate fluctuations. Long-term debt in a foreign currency may also be an offset to exposed assets.[11]

One writer suggested that business managers might go beyond these actions to minimize several types of adverse financial effects on assets and prices from devaluations, but this carries us into asset and liability management, which will be discussed in Chapters 18 and 19.[12] Another writer recommended that net exposed assets be measured not simply in terms of current assets, but in terms of these plus expected receipts over some

[9]Samuel I. Katz, "Leads and Lags in Sterling Payments," *Review of Economics and Statistics*, February 1973, pp. 75–80.

[10]Paul Einzig, *Foreign Currency Crises* (London: Macmillan, 1968).

[11]This action makes many subsidiaries appear to have nearly equal amounts of assets and liabilities in the local currency, with little need to hedge. See *Management Accounting Problems in Foreign Operations*, National Association of Accountants Research Report No. 36 (New York: NAA, 1960), pp. 62–63.

[12]W. Allen Sweeny, "Protective Measures Against Devaluation," *Financial Executive*, January 1968, pp. 28–37.

reasonable future period.[13] By estimating the probable extent of devaluation, the probability of its occurrence in some forecast period, the probable error of the forecast, and the degree of acceptable risk, he believed that managements could estimate risk and attitude toward risk and thus be in a position to take appropriate action.

Still another writer developed a computerized model so that a corporate treasurer might obtain an overview of the exchange risk based on probability analysis and of the various financing and hedging probabilities, with the cost of each expressed in minimum and maximum terms. On this basis a choice could be made among financing and hedging policies.[14]

Generally, no need was considered to hedge against losses on long-term assets. This is because devaluation or currency depreciation is accompanied in the long run by a roughly similar but opposite inflation. In such circumstances, more funds are needed to maintain productive capacity, through repair and maintenance of equipment and proper replacement. If selling prices are not increased, stockholders and other suppliers of capital suffer. There is no need for hedging against losses in value. There *is* need to raise prices and to adjust depreciation and inventory valuation practices.

To the extent that future exchange rate changes may be termed uncertainties rather than risks—that is, to the extent that exchange rate changes are unpredictable—such methods are of little value. Business managers can more advantageously plan courses of action to be followed *if* certain changes in exchange rates occur, rather than to attempt to predict short-term changes in exchange rates and to hedge against them. A clear distinction should be made between the situation before 1973, in which it was possible to predict a devaluation or an upvaluation, and the situation after 1973, in which there is considerable doubt about the possibility of short-run predictions of exchange rates.

Recourse to Foreign Credits The techniques involved in leads and lags are primarily aimed at protecting against cash flow losses that may occur because of lower receipts or higher payments in home currency than had previously been anticipated. The multinational firm, however, may also wish to protect against the possibility of a fall in the value of its assets located in another country if that country devalues its currency or permits it to depreciate. Such a loss will arise only if the prospective cash flows from such assets are less. The firm may also wish to protect against a rise in liabilities in another currency if a country upvalues its currency or permits it to appreciate.

---

[13]Robert B. Shulman, "Are Foreign Exchange Risks Measurable?" *Columbia Journal of World Business*, May–June 1970, pp. 55–60, and "Corporate Treatment of Exchange Risk," *Journal of International Business Studies*, Summer 1970, pp. 83–89.

[14]Bernard A. Lietaer, "Managing Risks in Foreign Exchange," *Harvard Business Review*, March–April 1970, pp. 127–138. See also Bernard A. Lietaer, *Financial Management of Foreign Exchange: An Operational Technique to Reduce Risk* (Cambridge, Mass.: M.I.T., 1971).

First, as indicated, the *economic* (as distinct from the accounting) exposure must be determined; it has already been pointed out that the economic exposure may be quite different from the accounting exposure. Once this exposure has been estimated, a firm which has net exposed liabilities in a strong-currency country may try to borrow in a weak-currency country in an amount sufficient that if the strong currency rises in value, the additional liabilities in terms of home currency will be compensated by additional liabilities in a weak-currency country, assuming that such a currency may decline in value. Borrowing in another currency creates debt which is less burdensome in local currency if the country where the subsidiary is located upvalues its currency or permits its value to appreciate.[15]

There is likely to be a cost involved, which is roughly measured by the interest rate differential. A weak currency generally is weak because the rate of inflation is or has been relatively high. If that is the case, interest rates are also relatively high, since interest rates, according to Fisherian interest rate theory, discussed in Chapter 9, tend to rise by slightly less than the rate of inflation in any country.

If management expects a currency to depreciate, it may subtract the percentage of currency depreciation expected from the nominal interest rate to obtain the effective interest rate, and if it expects a currency to appreciate, it may add that percentage of expected appreciation to the nominal interest rate to obtain the effective interest rate.[16] Subtracting one effective interest rate from the other gives the net effective interest differential (NEID). If a currency is expected to be devalued in any country, funds may be switched from a weak-currency country (by borrowing in that country) and invested in a strong-currency country. The amount to be switched is the amount of exposed assets multiplied by the expected amount (in percent) of currency depreciation, divided by the NEID. There will be a little excess net gain because there is a small gain in paying interest as well as in repaying principal.

The problem is, of course, that these methods assume that the firm can forecast exchange rate changes reasonably accurately, and we have already indicated that under some conditions this is unlikely. Moreover, of course, if the NEID is small, the amount that must be shifted is very great for a small exposure. We have also ignored transactions costs, such as loan fees.

Mobilizing Liquid Funds   Multinational firms may also mobilize corporate liquid funds in regional financial centers; this may reduce float and save interest on borrowed funds.[17] But it also has potential usefulness in making such funds

---

[15]For a more detailed presentation, see Rita M. Rodriguez and E. Eugene Carter, *International Financial Management* (Englewood Cliffs, N.J.: Prentice-Hall, 1976), pp. 209–214. See also Samuel I. Katz, *Exchange-Risk under Fixed and Flexible Exchange Rates*, pp. 54–55, for comment on borrowing abroad by German firms.

[16]Of course, as noted, in equilibrium positions the expected depreciation or appreciation rate is equal to the interest rate differential, so there should be no NEID. The existence of an NEID indicates divergence from an equilibrium position and an opportunity to shift funds.

[17]"Developments in International Money Management," *World Financial Markets,* Morgan Guaranty Trust Company, June 24, 1971, pp. 1–6; see also Katz, op. cit., pp. 55–56.

available to reduce exposure to exchange risks. By accumulating as many financial assets as possible in strong-currency countries, these assets are protected. Receivables in a weak-currency country may be reduced.

If governments do not prevent such actions, a multinational firm with a number of subsidiaries may have its subsidiaries in weak-currency countries pay intracompany accounts as soon as possible, and delay in collecting intracompany accounts receivable. Likewise it may have subsidiaries in strong-currency countries delay intracompany payments as long as possible, and collect accounts receivable from other subsidiaries of the parent company, in weak-currency countries, as soon as possible.

The costs of such actions are varied and difficult to predict. Collecting receivables quickly may conceivably lead to a reduction in sales. Delaying payment of foreign liabilities may mean foregoing cash or prompt-payment discounts. The costs cannot be fully evaluated unless the situation is known in some detail.

Use of the Forward Market   In the case of firms engaged in trade only, having no exposure of assets located in other countries, the use of the forward market may be advantageous in protecting against exchange risk. Of course, some of the actions already discussed may be less costly than use of the forward market, in which case they should be taken. Or, there may not be an adequate forward market for some currencies, or government restrictions may limit use of foward markets.

How does the firm determine the relative cost of shifting assets or liabilities from one currency to another versus using the forward market? Forward discounts are "costs" only in a special sense. If a firm sells exchange forward and if the forward rate is a good predictor of the future spot rate, all it has done is to anticipate a decline in value of the exchange in terms of other currencies, a decline that comes in any event. If a firm has liabilities in a depreciating currency to offset assets in that currency, its liabilities decline also in terms of other currencies. The firm that borrows in a weak-currency country at a higher rate of interest is also paying an additional cost, this time in interest rate. The interest rate is higher, if loan risks are equivalent, because there is more inflation in a weak-currency country, leading to a decline in the value of its currency. As it declines in value, the cost of repaying such liabilities in terms of other currencies is less, as we noted above. So a firm can hedge by keeping assets in a weak currency and keeping an equal amount of liabilities there, borrowing there as necessary in order to do this, or it can remove assets from a weak-currency country by selling forward exchange. In the one case it has a cost in terms of interest rates, in the other a cost in forward discount, if rates are at or close to equilibrium.

The *costs* of borrowing in other countries or of selling forward exchange are the transactions costs, including wider spreads between interest rates on borrowing and lending and between selling and buying forward exchange. If these are greater for one action than for the other, this should determine which action the firm will take, provided the interest rate differential equals the forward discount or premium. Interest rate parity theory tells us that the interest rate differential should equal the forward discount or premium in equilibrium, but of course in the real world conditions are not at equilibrium. The existence of disequilibrium is the second criterion for determining which action to take. At equilibrium points, one action is equivalent to the other, except for transactions costs.

It should be noted that although forward discounts are costs only in a special sense, they are generally referred to as the cost of selling forward.[18] In the floating rate period after early 1973, there have been times when the forward rate has been at a discount, but the spot rate has subsequently risen sharply instead of falling. For example, at one time during 1973 the spot rate for Japanese yen was 300.75 yen per U.S. dollar and the 6-month forward rate was 318.50 yen per dollar, but the spot rate 6 months later was 282 yen per dollar! Thus a word of caution is necessary: firms may not be able to forecast behavior of the spot rate from observation of the forward rate, and hedging or covering may be, in hindsight, the wrong thing to do.

Forward sales may be avoided at times for patriotic motives and because of public relations problems created by "speculating against the currency." But even if decisions are made on a cost and risk basis, and even under the Bretton Woods system of stable but adjustable exchange rates, it was difficult at times to know when to hedge. Although it was widely anticipated in the mid-1960s that Britain might soon devalue the pound, forward discounts for sterling remained relatively small (less than 1 percent per annum for three months forward) until 1967. Covering the risk early in 1967 would have given necessary protection at much less cost than covering the risk for the entire period of 1965–1967.[19]

Use of the forward market has so far been discussed on the assumption that a payment must be made in foreign currency later, and the payer wishes to hedge against the risk of a rise in the exchange rate, or that foreign currency is to be received later, and the receiver wishes to hedge against a possible fall in its value. The forward market can also be used in connection with lending and investing. If foreign currencies are purchased to lend to foreign subsidiaries, for example, forward exchange may be sold to avoid the risk of a decline in the rate by the time the subsidiaries have to repay, assuming relatively short-term loans. The simultaneous spot and forward transactions are often termed *swaps.*

---

[18]One writer argued that if the spot rate rose instead of falling, the rise should be added to the forward discount to determine total cost of a forward contract. See S. R. Bradford, "Measuring the Costs of Forward Exchange Contracts," *Euromoney,* August 1974, pp. 71–75. This was disputed by another writer, who argued that opportunity costs (unknown, since it was not known that the spot rate would rise) cannot be counted as costs; see Giuliano Pelli, "Thoughts on the Cost of Forward Cover in a Floating System—A Reply," *Euromoney,* November 1974, pp. 32–33. See also Steven W. Kohlhagen, "Evidence on the Cost of Forward Cover in a Floating System," *Euromoney,* September 1975, pp. 138–141. Kohlhagen agreed with Pelli, but argued that by either measure the cost of forward cover had not *generally* increased after 1973. This, however, ignores the important increases in the U.S. dollar-Deutsche mark rate and the U.S. dollar-yen rate in some cases.

[19]Robert S. Shulman, op. cit., p. 59.

The reader may remember from Chapter 7 that banks also make swaps—for example, buying spot and selling forward simultaneously in the same amounts—when they have "long" or "short" positions in a currency because, although their total purchases equaled their total sales of that currency, spot purchases exceeded spot sales.

Similarly, if a company wants to borrow in a foreign country but fears the exchange rate may rise, it may borrow the funds, sell them for local currency, and at the same time buy forward so that it will have enough foreign currency at the appropriate time to make repayment. If this is done because interest rates in the foreign country are relatively low, the transaction has sometimes been termed an *arbi-loan*—an interest arbitrage loan.[20]

Banks and other short-term lenders, of course, use covered investment in arbitraging on interest rates—in this case investing in countries in which interest rates are relatively high.

Another variation is a credit swap: a U.S. firm, for example, provides dollars to a foreign bank (depositing them in its account in a U.S. bank) in return for a loan by the foreign bank in its own currency to the U.S. company's subsidiary.[21] The subsidiary repays in the currency of the country in which it operates, and the U.S. firm is repaid in dollars. Concern about the exchange rate is eliminated. Such financing may be costly, however, since the subsidiary must pay interest on the loan, but the bank usually need not pay interest on the funds deposited in it. Moreover, the swap rate (the amount of dollars deposited to obtain a given loan amount) may be disadvantageous to the firm. An alternative would be to lend directly to the subsidiary. If there were a forward market, the company could lend and sell forward at the same time, thus hedging its risk. But for weak currencies, the forward market may be thin or nonexistent. Devaluation of downward floating may be quite likely. If downward floating or devaluation occurs, the credit swap may be less costly than direct uncovered lending—depending on the interest rate in the foreign country, the swap rate, and the extent of downward floating or devaluation. Much depends on the ability to predict the direction and degree of movement of the exchange rate. If short-term movements in exchange rates are difficult to predict, it is difficult to determine whether the credit swap would be worthwhile. Risk of loss by devaluation or downward floating before profits from operations conducted by the subsidiary are remitted cannot be avoided by the credit swap action.

In lending in countries in which indexation is widely used, it may be possible to lend funds, convert them into indexed securities, and use the securities as collateral for local loans. Since the securities are indexed, their value rises with some price index, and this rise is likely to approximately offset the decline in the exchange rate. Similarly, if a currency seems likely to be

[20]See Guenter Reimann and Edwin F. Wigglesworth, *The Challenge of International Finance* (New York: McGraw-Hill, 1966), Chap. 31.

[21]Credit swaps are discussed in detail, with some examples, in David K. Eiteman and Arthur I. Stonehill, *Multinational Business Finance* (Reading, Mass.: Addison-Wesley, 1973), pp. 272–279.

revalued upward, it may be possible to purchase securities denominated in that currency, to be used to pay for purchases of goods. By already having funds in that currency, risk of higher cost of purchasing the currency after an upward valuation is avoided. The interest on the securities compensates, at least approximately, for the loss of return on the funds in whatever use they had previously been employed. Again, these examples assume that at least the probable direction of movement in the exchange rate can be foreseen.

Protecting against Political Risks

The methods available for protecting against exchange rate risk are usually not useful for protecting against political risks because of their uncertainty. The major protections against political risks are home government guarantees and various actions, chiefly managerial and marketing, to placate host governments, to remove net assets from the possibility of host government control, or to control some other assets or activities (for example, transportation of exports) as a means of preventing foreign government expropriation. We consider home government guarantees first.

Investment Guarantees: OPIC, the Export-Import Bank, and AID   Risks faced by long-term investors include political risks in the form of possible confiscation of assets, nonconvertibility of currency, and loss of assets in war, revolutions, or insurrections. In the nineteenth century guarantees against such risks were given, but these were usually provided by the host governments, as is now the case for World Bank loans. In that period, however, the risks were chiefly of default. Money to build railroads was often provided under such guarantees. Many of these investments resulted in defaults, however.[22]

In more recent times, the increasing political separatism has meant that guarantees against political risk were more urgently needed. The important risks facing private long-term investors are that (1) countries may have financial difficulties and hence convertibility of currencies may be restricted and (2) political forces in various countries may lead to confiscation of foreign investments, either peacefully or in war or revolution.

The problem is complicated by the fact that both inconvertibility and confiscation can exist in various degrees: inconvertibility may apply only to *some* transfers of funds, and even then transfer may be possible at different exchange rates. Confiscation may range all the way from simply not providing enough electricity to permit operation of a factory, to using armed forces personnel to round up the business executives and put them on planes leaving the country.

Such risks present problems different from those of credit risks, because credit risks are insurable: credit experience, if carefully studied, can provide a reasonably accurate guide to future credit losses on large numbers of loans, and

---

[22]The background of, the basic reasons for, and the problems of investment guarantees are thoroughly discussed in Marina von Neumann Whitman, op. cit.

the insurance principle of large numbers can spread the risk. Political risks are essentially so diverse, so unique, and so lacking in relevant past experience data that there is no basis for determining proper costs of insuring against losses. Some economists have distinguished this situation as *uncertainty* instead of risk.

Something of a dilemma is created by the difficulty of providing guarantees against political risk on the one hand and the increasing need of LDCs for foreign investment as an aid to economic development on the other hand. Without guarantees, the flow of private capital into LDCs may be limited.[23]

Since an adequate actuarial basis for determining appropriate fees for investment guarantees does not exist, only a government agency can offer such guarantees—and the backing for the guarantees is public funds. Moreover, since the risks are political, guarantees by the countries in which investments are made are of little value. Guarantees must be provided, if at all, by the governments of the investing countries. While it is true that, as indicated in Chapter 12, guarantees by host governments are provided for World Bank loans, the World Bank does not make equity investments, which present greater risk than loans, and the World Bank has a degree of prestige as an international institution and influence as a major lender whose refusal to lend might be very significant in deterring other lenders. These factors make its situation very different from that of private lenders.

Investment guarantees in the United States were provided by the Agency for International Development (AID) and its predecessors, beginning with the agency which administered Marshall Plan aid. The Export-Import Bank also provided some political risk "insurance" for long-term investments, but restricted itself to insuring loans or private credits and not equity investments. Since 1969 the agency providing investment guarantees has been the Overseas Private Investment Corporation (OPIC), although OPIC was not able to begin operations until 1971.

The basic dilemma faced by OPIC has been that it was established to encourage the flow of private capital to LDCs because their need for external funds for development was recognized. At the same time, it was instructed to conduct its operations with due regard to principles of risk management. As developing countries have become sensitive about the role of foreign capital in the development of their economies, the climate for foreign investment has deteriorated in many places.

Since the purpose is to facilitate the flow of investment, guarantees are not provided for investments already made. There has also been some concern with possible effects on the U.S. BOP, as indicated in the discussion of foreign investment and the BOP in Chapter 13.

The ideal investments for which guarantees might be given would be those least subject to confiscation. These might be investments that would be of high

---

[23]The issues were clearly presented in "What Future for OPIC?" *Morgan Guaranty Survey,* January 1974, pp. 4–8.

priority to the host governments, would employ local labor and gain participation of local capital, would produce a needed commodity or service at relatively low cost, and that could be expected to generate foreign exchange earnings and thus help the BOP situation of the developing country. They might also be investments made in politically stable host countries.

Clearly, however, OPIC is of little value if its guarantees are limited to the safest investments in the safest places. Yet concern about the financial liabilities to which OPIC may be exposed, although its early losses were small, and some question about the basic premise that foreign capital helps economic development, made OPIC controversial.

There has been some discussion of participation of insurance companies, as has occurred with the export credit insurance program, and some actual reinsurance by them has occurred. Other industrialized countries have established programs similar to that of OPIC. Whether investment guarantees facilitate a useful flow of investment into LDCs is an important question. OPIC's experience has not yet been long enough to answer it.

Part of the problem is that risks and losses are difficult to define precisely. What is expropriation? Is it expropriation if taxes are raised so high that an investment is no longer profitable? Is it expropriation if investors are prevented from receiving dividends, or from selling their shares? What if a government refused to provide enough electric power to a plant owned by foreign investors? (This last example is not deemed expropriation by OPIC.) When does civil strife become insurrection or revolution?[24] What if an investment is profitable, and most of the earnings are retained, but after a number of years convertibility of the sales proceeds of the investment is desired?

The programs for direct investment and many types of other investments, including loans, are technically termed insurance, although as indicated the appropriate fees cannot accurately be determined actuarially. OPIC also has programs that protect investors against all risks. These are termed guarantees, and apply only to portfolio investments. Investment guarantees for housing, chiefly for pilot housing projects in Latin America, have also been offered by AID. The guarantees also cover risks of loss from devaluations, commercial failures, and defaults. Guarantees are available only for investments in countries that have entered into guarantee agreements with the United States.

Investment insurance or guarantee programs are simply one factor in facilitating international capital flows. They are seldom decisive. The possibility of adequate return must exist in any event if investments are to be made; and informational and other factors are important. However, investment guarantees have a small role to play, and have been of some value.

Other Actions to Protect against Risk of Confiscation   In the early part of the colonial era, foreign companies such as the British East India Company

---

[24]See the detailed discussion of risks covered and fees charged in J. Fred Weston and Bart W. Sorge, *International Managerial Finance*, pp. 76–93. Many of the details change with changing prices and political conditions.

were given charters that stipulated their rights and responsibilities. After World War I, firms engaging in foreign investment began to negotiate agreements with host-country governments. United Fruit Company operated under a number of such agreements with Latin American countries.

As political separatism has increased, such agreements have often been more difficult to negotiate and sometimes have not been honored by host governments. In other countries, agreements are negotiated and contain very specific provisions—for example, in Japan, India, and Mexico. Business firms have found in many countries that they must adjust to the priorities and values of the host countries.

Some economists have proposed that firms undertaking foreign investment plan to sell the foreign investments to local nationals after some time, as indicated in Chapter 13. But affiliates that have been sold are not integrated into the former company and thus may suffer organizational and marketing difficulties. Sales prices are almost impossible to set beforehand and difficult to negotiate at the time of sale. Moreover, foreign investments may not be made if their life is known to be limited.[25]

Companies may take various actions to placate host governments, such as buying materials from local sources. They may also build refining plants in politically safe areas and attempt to control transportation as a means of avoiding expropriation. Their control of processes, whether patented or not, is helpful to them. They may engage in joint ventures instead of owning subsidiaries. Or they may license the use of processes, thus avoiding the need to commit large amounts of funds.

Since most of the foregoing actions are managerial or marketing rather than specifically financial, we merely mention them to illustrate some of the possibilities. Financially, companies may use devices such as higher ratios of debt to equity than normal; these are discussed in more detail in Chapter 19.

SUMMARY

A firm should purchase foreign credit insurance if it has reason to believe that its foreign credit losses may be greater than such losses for an average firm. Since loss experience of this type for U.S. firms has been generally low, such insurance is not widely purchased; it has been estimated that only 2 or 3 percent of exports are so insured. Nonrecourse financing by banks, if available, may be preferable, since banks may, as specialists in credit, be able to charge relatively low fees for such financing.

The *occasional* exporter or importer can protect against exchange rate risk by using the forward market if sales are profitable in spite of the "cost" of such action. The *regular* exporter or importer cannot do this, because the forward rate is usually likely to fluctuate just as much as or more than the spot rate, and

[25]Jack N. Behrman, "International Divestment: Panacea or Pitfall," *Looking Ahead*, National Planning Association, November–December 1970. Behrman emphasizes these and other disadvantages of planned disinvestment.

continual use of the forward market therefore does not protect. The best means of protecting may be to offset the economic value of receivables in a given country by the economic cost of payables in the same country, so that in terms of home currency both the value of assets and the amount to be paid to liquidate liabilities is reduced in the event of depreciation of the foreign currency. For the *multinational firm,* the situation is much more complex. The answer depends on where subsidiaries sell their products, their sources of raw materials, the degree of competition in both of these markets, and the degree of flexibility which subsidiaries have in changing markets and sources of materials.

The financial manager must judge values of assets by their capability of producing streams of future income, and liabilities by the streams of payments necessary to liquidate them. These calculations determine *economic* exposure, which may differ substantially from *accounting* exposure, especially if assets are valued at historical costs in a period of inflation (or deflation) and if values are translated from one currency into another from such values.

Political risks are not properly risks, but *uncertainties.* That is, they cannot be predicted in the same way as fires or credit losses and hence cannot be precisely offset in measurable ways. Thus the best form of action may be to remove net assets from the jurisdiction of foreign governments, to placate foreign governments in various ways, or to gain control of other parts of the production and distribution process as a means of leverage. Investment guarantees by home governments are another means of protection, but they are often not obtainable where they are most needed and are less needed where they are available. Hence they may tip the scales in marginal situations, which is their chief value.

There is evidence that the exchange rate situation has changed radically in the 1970s, and that in the short run floating exchange rates fluctuate randomly, much as stock market prices do. If so, there is not much use in trying to forecast short-run changes in exchange rates, and business firms would do better to focus attention on what they should do *if* certain changes occur. Nevertheless, services which claim the ability to forecast exchange rates are selling well, which may mean simply that company treasurers want to be able to shift the blame if forecasts are wrong.

If exchange rate changes *can* be forecast, even roughly, then postponement or speedup of payments or collections, limiting net exposed current assets, recourse to foreign credits, and mobilizing liquid funds in strong-currency financial centers may be useful actions. Use of the forward market may be advantageous if exchange rates are not in equilibrium positions; if they are, forward discounts or premiums are equal to interest rate differentials, and which method to use may be determined by transaction costs.

However, there are indirect factors which may have to be considered: (1) the effect on attitudes of creditors and investors of increased borrowing if that borrowing shows on balance sheets, that is, if it is not carried out and repayment made between balance sheet dates, and (2) whether a firm wishes to offset *accounting* exposure in contrast to economic exposure because foreign exchange losses shown on accounting income statements again may be regarded unfavorably by creditors and investors. There is also the fact that access to financial markets in some countries may be closed to some firms.

Increasing political fragmentation of the world has increased political risks at the same time that economic integration has increased. Since political risks are not properly risks but uncertainties, essentially unpredictable, fees for investment guarantees cannot be set on an accurate economic basis. Moreover, expropriation and related political actions are difficult to define and specify, and there are disagreements between firms and government agencies concerning such guarantees. It is probably correct to regard investment guarantees as a "limited instrument in an age of compromise," useful in marginal situations.

Finally, it is worth emphasizing that the shift to floating exchange rates increased risk and hence the cost of transactions for international activities. Under the par-value system, as long as par values were maintained, central banks shared risks with international firms. Although it has been argued that when par values changed, international firms were subject to wide variations in exchange rates, this is not the same as saying that they were exposed to large risks, because devaluations and upvaluations were *predictable,* except perhaps in timing. The basic reason for floating rates was the desire of national governments to have different employment and price level priorities. It is therefore likely that international monetary negotiations will aim at arrangements to accommodate differentials in rates of increase in productivity and in inflation among major countries. Exchange rate uncertainty can probably be reduced only if there is more similarity among major countries in their goals related to employment and inflation.

QUESTIONS FOR DISCUSSION

1   Why is it desirable for business firms to purchase fire insurance, even if losses from fires in a particular city are *on the average* quite low, whereas there may be less reason to purchase foreign credit insurance, even though credit losses may on the *average* be of some significance?

2   What should an occasional exporter do if a sale priced in a foreign currency seems to be unprofitable when taking into account the need, as the firm's managers see it, to cover the risk by selling exchange in the forward market, against the exchange to be received later in spot exchange? Why?

3   Why is the regular exporter (or importer) in a different position from the occasional exporter (or importer)?

4   Why is it stated that investment guarantees are most needed for situations for which they generally cannot be obtained, and are available for situations for which they are less needed? Does this destroy the value of investment guarantees? Why or why not?

5   Could nonrecourse financing by banks of drafts drawn by exporters be cheaper for exporters than obtaining foreign credit insurance? If so, why?

6   Why have some writers argued that *in general* fluctuations in spot and in forward

exchange rates do not seem to have increased greatly in amplitude after 1973, while other writers argue that in some cases they have done so? In what cases? For what possible reason?

7 Suggest some reasons why *economic* exposure may differ from *accounting* exposure in foreign exchange. (This question anticipates the discussion in Chapter 16, but it is of value to try to answer it now.)

8 Reconcile if you can the acceptance of purchasing power parity theory for the long run with acceptance of the efficient market–random walk behavior of floating exchange rates in the short run.

9 How would *you* resolve the "dilemma of OPIC"?

10 Why may a firm *not* decide to borrow in a weak-currency country even though from a cost standpoint this alternative may seem desirable? Why may it decide to hedge against *accounting* exposure even when this differs from *economic* exposure? Are these decisions rational?

PROBLEMS

1 Assume that a U.S. firm has a subsidiary in Mexico. For various reasons the firm does not wish to borrow or lend in Mexico nor to sell Mexican pesos forward. Assume that the subsidiary has $100,000 in exposed net assets in pesos. Assume also that the parent firm expects a depreciation of the pound sterling by 10 percent and an appreciation of the Dutch guilder by 6 percent. Finally, assume that interest rates for 1-year loans are 15 percent in Britain and 9 percent in the Netherlands.
   a How much would the firm need to borrow in Britain and invest in the Netherlands in order to approximately offset its potential loss on the depreciation of the peso?
   b How much additional gain would the firm realize? Show your calculations. Explain why the firm gains more than the amount it needs to offset its expected translation loss.

2 Assume that a U.S. firm has a subsidiary in Britain which is expected to have a net asset exposure of £1 million a year from now. Assume that the pound is expected to depreciate from $2 to $1.80 during the year.
   a How much loss can the firm expect (unrealized loss, but a loss showing on its consolidated accounting statements) a year from now?
   b If the forward rate currently is $2 and the spot rate is $2 for the pound sterling, how much should the firm buy in the spot market and sell in the forward market to offset its translation loss on assets?
   c If the forward rate currently is $1.80 and the spot rate is $2, what should the firm do? Why?

3 A firm exports occasionally to England. It expects a depreciation of the pound sterling. Discount on forward pounds is 4 percent, and a sale would still be profitable even if the exporter sold forward the sterling to be received. What should the firm do? Suppose that the discount on sterling is 10 percent, making the sale unprofitable. What should the firm do? Why?

4 Assume that the corporate income tax rate is 50 percent and that the inflation rate is 10 percent. Assume that a firm records inventory as acquired before the beginning of the period. Assume also that sales are $100,000; inventory cost is $60,000; and selling and administrative costs are $30,000. If inventory prices rise in line with other prices,

how much more tax does the firm pay than it would pay if it valued inventory on a current cost basis? Assume sales are made regularly through the year. What rate of tax is the firm paying on the profit which *would* have been recorded if the inventory had been valued at replacement cost?

5 Assume that an exporter sold $100,000 worth of goods, priced in yen, to a Japanese importer at a time when the spot rate was 300.75 yen per U.S. dollar and the six-month forward rate was 318.50 yen per dollar. Assume that the firm sold on six-month credit terms, and hedged by selling yen forward. If the spot rate six months later was 282 yen per dollar, how much was the "cost" to the exporter? How much was received, in dollars, for the forward sale of the yen? How much had to be paid for the yen to deliver yen sold forward? Should the exporter have hedged? Why or why not?

SUGGESTED REFERENCES

Among the most useful references on the problem of when to protect against foreign exchange rate fluctuation risk under floating rates are two articles by Gunter Dufey: an address to the meeting of the International Fiscal Association in Rome, Italy, Oct. 14, 1974, entitled "Corporate Financial Policies and Floating Exchange Rates" and "Corporate Finance and Exchange Rate Management," *Financial Management,* Summer 1972, pp. 51–57, and an article by Alan C. Shapiro, "Exchange Rate Changes, Inflation, and the Value of the Multinational Corporation," *Journal of Finance,* May 1975, pp. 485–502. See also Robert K. Ankrom, "Top Level Approach to the Foreign Exchange Problem," *Harvard Business Review,* July–August 1974, pp. 79–99.

Harold J. Heck, *The International Business Environment* (New York: American Management Association, 1969) indicates (p. 102) some reasons for the lack of use of export credit insurance in the United States: such insurance is not needed for shipments by government departments or agencies, bulk commodities sold for cash or on very short terms, shipments to U.S. subsidiaries, large companies which can self-insure, or shipments to Canada in many cases. See also Stanley E. Hollis, *Guide to Export Credit Insurance* (New York: Foreign Credit Insurance Association, 1971).

On investment guarantee in the United States, see *An Introduction to OPIC* (Washington, D.C.: OPIC, 1973).

For a survey of some cases of expropriation, see J. Frederick Truitt, "Expropriation of Foreign Investment: Summary of the Post–World War II Experience of American and British Investors in the Less Developed Countries," *Journal of International Business Studies,* Fall 1970, pp. 21–34. See also Stefan H. Robock, "Political Risk: Identification and Assessment," *Columbia Journal of World Business,* July–August 1971, pp. 6–20.

A comprehensive view of exchange risk under the par value system and under the floating rates existing after early 1973 is provided by Samuel I. Katz, *Exchange-Risk under Fixed and Flexible Exchange Rates,* New York University, Institute of Finance Bulletins 83–84, 1972. His 78 footnotes provide a helpful guide to other readings on particular points.

Chapter 16

Some Accounting Factors
Affecting International
Financial Operations

Accounting for multinational corporations involves all the problems associated with providing meaningful financial information on the activities of large, diversified industrial organizations. In addition, there are the specific differences associated with operating across political and cultural boundaries, and the influence which these may have on the quality and validity of reported values. Clearly, a full discussion of the problems of accounting at an international level cannot be undertaken in a single chapter or section of a book such as this. Courses in international accounting are becoming more common, and may be expected to review in greater detail a variety of problems in that area.

Nevertheless, any discussion of international business finance would be incomplete unless it contained at least an overview of some current accounting and financial reporting problems of companies operating internationally. Some of these special problems which have significant impact on financial decisions are discussed in this chapter.

The accounting function in multinational corporations is complicated by two types of problems. First, multinational corporations operate in many countries and hence face many different economic conditions, so that accounting practices which might be satisfactory in one situation are not necessarily satisfactory in others. Second, there are special problems involved in accounting for transactions across national boundaries—transfer pricing, inventory in transit for long periods, customs duties and taxes, questions of the significance of equity and debt ratios in the context of different capital markets, the relevance of financial data derived from accounts recorded in countries with varying rates of inflation, and the related problem of currency translation.

In addition, there are the problems of comparability of accounting information produced in countries whose philosophies of accounting differ significantly.

ACCOUNTING SYSTEMS

Gerhard G. Mueller, in his pioneering book in the field of international accounting, identified four characteristics which might differentiate accounting systems and the development of accounting principles in various countries:[1]

1 Accounting within a macroeconomic framework
2 A microeconomic approach to accounting
3 Accounting as an independent discipline
4 Uniform accounting

These four approaches have influenced accounting development in individual countries in varying degrees. Communist countries like the Soviet Union have adopted a basically macroeconomic approach coupled with the use of uniform accounting, while countries like the United States have adopted an approach in which accounting is recognized as an independent discipline. The different approaches are not necessarily identified with either socialism or capitalism, but rather can be found as influences in the accounting systems of many countries irrespective of their political and social philosophies and systems.

To make the four characteristics more concrete, the influence of each in some representative countries is outlined briefly in the following paragraphs. It should be understood, however, that no country is a pure example of one of these characteristics, since many influences contribute to the development of accounting in any country.

Sweden is an example of those countries that have been much concerned with economic fluctuations, which is understandable in view of the Swedish economy's dependence on international trade and consequently on economic fluctuations in other countries. The Swedish government has adopted policies designed to mitigate the disturbing effects of economic fluctuations. To some extent accounting rules have been tailored to require information helpful in implementing these policies and aiding firms to take actions to moderate the effects of fluctuations in business activity. Those who determine economic policies for the government need data on economic transactions of the business

---

[1]Gerhard G. Mueller, *International Accounting* (New York: Macmillan, 1967).

sector in forms suited to their needs, and companies have been required to publish, in addition to financial statements, annual business reports giving information on the positions of the companies, employment, total remuneration paid, and so on.[2]

The Netherlands is one country in which accounting thought has been heavily influenced by microeconomic theory, and an economic theory of value has led to the use of replacement value accounting by at least one major Dutch multinational firm.[3] In microeconomic theory, the value of any good at any moment is the value that would be lost if that good were not held by the firm. If something is sold or lost (by fire, flood, wearing out, obsolescence, etc.), the firm has lost a value that can generally be regained only by purchase or manufacture of an identical good, or one as nearly the same as possible. Thus the value of any good is its *replacement value*.[4] It is assumed that business firms are focal points of business activity and that their policies are designed to ensure their survival by maximizing profits. It is also assumed that costs of replacement are calculated on the basis of the present value of the stream of income expected to be obtained from use of an asset, the stream of income being discounted at an appropriate rate of interest. Thus if certain types of equipment are expected to produce a larger future income stream, producers will bid up the prices of such equipment. Similarly, if—to take an extreme example—some equipment is totally obsolete, it may have no value. Historical costs are irrelevant. Application of replacement value principles by N. V. Philips' Gloeilampenfabrieken has been described in some detail in writings.[5] The same principles of replacement value may be applied to the value of money and to monetary assets and liabilities. If the future income (purchasing power) expected to be obtained from money falls as prices rise, the value of monetary assets falls. The value of liabilities also falls, so that there is a gain on liabilities offsetting the loss on monetary assets. Since these gains and losses are in purchasing power and not in monetary units, they need not be taken into account in financial statements prepared in monetary units, as is generally the case. But of course if a firm holds more monetary assets than liabilities, it tends to lose in a period of inflation; and if it finances acquisition of real assets by borrowing, the increase in value (replacement cost) of real assets will be reflected in successive balance sheets.[6]

In some countries, such as the United States, accounting is treated as an independent discipline. Development of accounting standards has largely been

[2]Gerhard G. Mueller, *Accounting Practices in Sweden* (Seattle: University of Washington, College of Business Administration, 1962).

[3]Gerhard G. Mueller, *Accounting Practices in the Netherlands* (Seattle: University of Washington, College of Business Administration, 1962).

[4]The theory underlying replacement value accounting is explained by Abram Mey, *On the Application of Business Economics and Replacement Value Accounting in the Netherlands* (Seattle: University of Washington, Graduate School of Business Administration, 1970).

[5]A. Goudeket, "An Application of Replacement Value Theory," *The Journal of Accountancy*, July 1960, pp. 37–47.

[6]Armen A. Alchian and Reuben A. Kessel, "Redistribution of Wealth through Inflation," *Science*, Sept. 4, 1959, pp. 535–539.

left to the accounting practitioners' associations, and government agencies, even when they have power to require use of certain accounting principles, generally have accepted accounting statements prepared under principles agreed upon by the associations. In the United States, this has often meant that the American Institute of CPAs (AICPA) has indicated two or more alternative methods as being "generally accepted." Principles used by one firm need not be used by another—one firm may use first-in, first-out (FIFO) inventory valuation in determining cost of goods sold, and another may use last-in, first-out (LIFO). Firms may shift from FIFO to LIFO, although it is suggested that they should indicate clearly their basis for doing so. They may shift only part of their operations to a new method of valuation.

In some countries uniform accounting systems have been adopted. Examples are France, Germany, and Argentina. Uniform accounting systems have often been developed in countries in which *companies laws* have been promulgated. Such laws regulate various matters concerning companies, including rights of stockholders, rules concerning disclosure of financial information, and rules for preparation of financial statements. The United States does not have such a body of national legislation. Germany, to cite one example, has. Because of experience with financial excesses in the late 1920s and in the ensuing depression, German legislation is concerned with conservative valuation techniques, independent audits, and sufficient disclosure of financial conditions.[7] Germans have been much concerned about inflation ever since their experience of hyperinflation in the early 1920s. Since World War II, inflation in Germany has generally been moderate. German law has permitted extreme conservatism in valuation of fixed assets. One writer states that, in his opinion, in the past German accounting practice actually placed the "profit or loss calculation completely at the mercy of the balance sheet" because balance sheet values were conservatively determined, by the use of either hidden or open reserves, and there was "no choice other than 'forcing' the profit or loss determination."[8] A number of recent changes modify the situation, but the past situation serves as an example of significant differences in accounting practices among countries.

Some countries, such as Japan, give evidence of influences from several outside sources, notably the United States after World War II.[9] The mixture of influences produced a number of inconsistencies. Thus the Ministry of Finance published many opinions over time in an effort to rationalize accounting practices in Japan, but while, for example, one opinion introduced the concept of systematic depreciation, the tax law at the time still recognized voluntary depreciation.

It should be clear from the foregoing examples that companies operating

[7]Gerhard G. Mueller, *Accounting Practices in Germany* (Seattle: University of Washington, College of Business Administration, 1964).
[8]Ibid., p. 26.
[9]Gerhard G. Mueller and Hiroshi Yoshida, *Accounting Practices in Japan* (Seattle: University of Washington, Graduate School of Business Administration, 1968).

internationally must consider financial problems arising from the variation among countries of accounting definitions of income, standards for valuation of fixed assets, inventory cost practices, and rules for financial disclosure, among other things.

THE COMPATIBILITY PROBLEM

Because of variations in accounting systems from country to country, and the resulting differences in accounting practices, data on operations in one country may not be compatible with that from others. Considerable strides have been made in narrowing the gap between accounting standards internationally as the result of meetings and cooperation between the institutes of accountants in the more important trading countries of the West. The International Accounting Standards Committee, which is made up of representatives from these institutes, has a number of problem areas under discussion and at the time of writing had issued two statements of accounting standards: No. 1, Disclosure of Accounting Policies, and No. 2, Valuation and Presentation of Inventories in the Context of the Historical Cost System. These are binding standards to which the members of the subscribing institutes of accountants have undertaken to conform; and as they are added to in the future, differences among accounting practices in countries concerned should be materially narrowed. To the extent that these are also the major international trading and investing countries of the West, the beneficial influence of international standards on the production of compatible and meaningful financial information for incorporation into consolidated statements and for use in comparisons is likely to be very significant. It is perhaps worth noting in this context that, while we naturally tend to view the problems of multinational financial reporting chiefly in terms of the informational needs of the external investing public, the real scope for regularizing accounting procedures lies at the managerial accounting level.[10] As multinational firms continue to be involved in the day-to-day problems of providing managerial financial information by foreign subsidiaries, many of the problems of compatibility in utilizing information produced in countries with such diverse standards as those of, for example, France and the United Kingdom, begin to resolve themselves.

The compatibility problem is likely to be most significant, while it continues, for operations in the United States, in the countries of continental Europe, in the United Kingdom, and in Japan. For companies operating subsidiaries in developing countries or LDCs, it is likely in many cases that standards of accounting used in the home country may be imposed on those subsidiaries' operations. It should be noted that compatibility is a problem not only for companies wishing to compare and/or consolidate their subsidiaries' statements, but for anyone wishing to compare, for example, a German, a French, and a U.S. chemical company. This problem is very difficult because

[10]National Association of Accountants, *Management Accounting for Multinational Corporations*, vols. 1 and 2.

the reader of the statements may have far less knowledge than a parent company about the methods used in preparing the statements.

It cannot be assumed that all problems related to differences in accounting practices will vanish quickly. In the United States, for example, establishment of accounting principles has generally been left to the discretion of the American Institute of Certified Public Accountants (AICPA). Although the Securities and Exchange Commission (SEC) has some powers in connection with its regulation of issues of new securities, and some of its officials on occasion have indicated a desire to impose changes, the SEC has generally issued regulations which affirmed guidelines previously developed and published by the AICPA's Accounting Principles Board (APB), later the Financial Accounting Standards Board (FASB). However, the relatively slow development of principles by the AICPA and the allowance of alternative financial reporting principles has frequently been criticized in recent years. In the United Kingdom, company law changes which may affect accounting practices are generally drafted pursuant to a report of a committee appointed with members from the House of Lords, the House of Commons, government officials, attorneys, accountants, and business leaders. In Germany, drafts of company law changes are prepared in the Ministry of Justice, but opportunity is given for comments by interested parties, including accountants, before passage of a law.

However much the actions of accounting groups and of multinational companies may succeed in achieving a measure of standardization in accounting systems, two problems have particular relevance for comparison of financial results in subsidiaries operating in different countries and for incorporation of data into consolidated statements. These are the manner in which foreign currencies are translated into home country currency and the treatment of financial impacts of different rates of inflation in different countries. Hence more attention is given to the translation problem and the inflation accounting problem in the following pages than is perhaps warranted by their importance in the total picture of international accounting.

THE TRANSLATION PROBLEM

Companies may wish to translate financial statements or data from a foreign currency into their local currency either for preparing consolidated financial statements or for comparisons of financial results. In many countries (occasionally in the United States) particular items (for example, certain exports) are denominated in values expressed in foreign currencies, and the values must be translated to determine total financial statement values even for domestic firms. The term *conversion* is purposely avoided since we are not considering the conversion of one currency into another, but simply restatement of values for comparison or consolidation.

In the United States, if a company owns foreign subsidiaries, and if it owns more than 50 percent of the equity in particular subsidiaries, it may decide whether to consolidate the financial statements of the subsidiary with those of the parent company. It could, of course, translate and consolidate data for subsidiaries in which it owns less than 50 percent of the equity, but in the United States it is not the practice to do this, for published statements. To compare data, however, translation may be desirable for management.

In the United Kingdom, firms must consolidate statements not only when companies own over 50 percent of the equity in subsidiaries, but if they own as little as 25 percent, provided that they have effective control over the subsidiaries.

Consolidation of accounting statements of subsidiaries was uncommon in France before 1971. Since that time, parent companies have had to either publish consolidated statements or provide information which shows parent company equity in first-tier subsidiaries.

In Germany it is required that consolidated balance sheets, income statement, and management reports be published if a company owns more than 50 percent of a subsidiary,[11] but foreign subsidiaries' accounts are not normally consolidated.

Companies in all countries may be moved in the direction of more consolidation and fuller disclosure, however, by the need for capital, the example of financial disclosure in prospectuses issued in the Eurobond market, and stricter legislation.[12]

The merits of consolidation may be considered from two viewpoints: (1) that of disclosure and (2) that of management. From the disclosure viewpoint, failure to consolidate statements may permit a parent company to show profits on sales which include sales to unconsolidated subsidiaries, which may in turn have losses on resale, perhaps after further processing, of the same products. The question is, is a firm making profits through sales of products to another part of the same total firm? On the other hand, consolidation may hide the fact that profits of some subsidiaries are not available to the parent firm because of exchange controls in the countries where the subsidiaries operate. Consolidation shows total profits, but if some of those profits cannot be freely used, the information may be misleading. From the managerial standpoint, if management does not know what consolidated income is, it cannot effectively plan for maximization of income of the total firm. Again, however, since some profits may be subject to exchange controls and other restrictions by governments of countries where subsidiaries operate, management cannot count on such profits in the same way that it can count on profits in the home country. Thus there are both merits and problems in consolidation of financial statements.

In view of the compatibility problem, consolidated statements may not accurately reflect income and asset values on the same basis for a parent company as for its subsidiaries. MNCs may feel that it is necessary to make

[11]Anita I. Tyra, *Companies Laws and Financial Reporting* (Seattle: Graduate School of Business Administration, University of Washington, 1971).

[12]As late as 1967, about 15 percent of *Fortune's* list of the 200 largest industrial companies outside the United States still carried a footnote "not fully consolidated" or "parent company figures only." One Swiss company worth over 400 million francs on a consolidated basis would have been worth only 60 million francs on an unconsolidated basis. See Robert Ball, "The Declining Art of Concealing the Figures," *Fortune*, Sept. 15, 1967, pp. 136–139, 160–171.

adjustments in statements of subsidiaries before consolidating them. For instance, depreciation may be increased or reduced to express it at standard rates used by a parent company. Many other adjustments may be made, and afterward figures may be translated into the currency of the country of the parent company for consolidation. Even so, the resulting consolidated statements may not be adequate for management purposes, and additional information may be required.

Usefulness of Translation

Usefulness of translation may be considered from the viewpoints of creditors of a subsidiary, creditors of the parent company, stockholders of either, or management of the parent company. Although other parties may be interested, these are the primary groups concerned.

Creditors   Consolidated statements are useful to creditors of subsidiaries primarily because debt of subsidiaries is very often guaranteed by parent companies, implicitly if not explicitly. Parent companies are not likely in many cases to permit subsidiaries to default, although this may occur. Obviously if subsidiaries' debt is explicitly guaranteed by parent companies, the consolidated statements are of interest to creditors of the subsidiaries.

Creditors of parent companies are primarily interested in unconsolidated financial statements of the parent companies, since in most cases such creditors receive payments from income generated by the assets of the parent companies. A subsidiary may have potential for generating income in the currency of the parent company, and hence may be of interest, but unless this is true, consideration must be given to the convertibility of earnings of a subsidiary into the currency of its parent company.

Stockholders   Outside stockholders of a subsidiary (the minority interest if the subsidiary is owned more than 50 percent by the parent company) are not likely to have a direct interest in consolidated statements. But they may have an indirect interest because such statements indicate the financial strength of the firm, including the subsidiary. Whether the subsidiary could obtain financial assistance from the parent company in the event of need may depend on the financial strength of the parent company. Moreover, minority stockholders of the subsidiary may be interested in comparisons of financial ratios or of policies, such as that on dividends.

Management   Management needs financial data to judge total asset values and total income, and to make decisions concerning pricing, production, marketing, and dividend policies, among others. For these purposes its interest parallels that of stockholders of the parent company, although management is more directly concerned and is usually active in using the information, while stockholders may be inactive. Management also uses financial statements and other financial information in evaluating performance. For this purpose, the statements of individual subsidiaries may be as useful as or more useful than consolidated statements, and translation into the currency of the parent company may not add to their usefulness. Since the currency of the parent company is more familiar to its management, however, it may wish to use statements in that currency. If so, translation is important.

For judging total asset and net worth values, financial statements are not likely to be very useful, whether translated or not. The use of historical costs of fixed assets in many countries, price level adjustments in others, and varying methods of computing depreciation makes asset values as shown on balance sheets of questionable usefulness for management.

In translated statements, there are likely to be gains or losses resulting from changes in currency values over time. Although changes in the value of money are normally not recognized in domestic accounting, changes in the value of money internationally (changes in exchange rates) must be recognized in consolidated statements; if an exchange rate changes, any net excess of either assets or liabilities translated at the new rate shows a gain or loss. Thus translation serves to measure exposure to exchange rate risk, but the exposure measured is *accounting* exposure, not *economic* exposure, and varies with the accounting rules used for translation.

It should be clear that translation has value for some users of financial information and under some circumstances. It should also be clear that unsound rules for translation can provide very misleading information when exchange rates have changed as much as they have recently.

Translation of Foreign Currency Values

The purpose of translation is to properly reflect values originally reported in one currency but translated into another, but what is proper reflection?

The view of economists is that the value of any asset is the present value of expected future income from that asset discounted at an appropriate rate of interest. This was indicated in the section on accounting valuation in the Netherlands; in that country accounting theory is strongly influenced by microeconomic theory. Note that discounting at an interest rate does not necessarily imply a "time preference" for present over future income.[13] It merely indicates that some assets yield income over a period of time, that the income can be expressed in terms of percent per year, and that the present value of the assets must therefore be less than the future value. Assets are acquired and held because they are productive, generating future cash flows

---

[13]Interest rate theorists such as Irving Fisher argued that present consumption is valued more highly than future consumption, and that people must be compensated for this time preference to induce them to save. Of course, interest rates must be determined by the supply of saving as well as by the demand for funds, but it is not necessary to assume that people save because they receive interest. Economists such as Pigou argued that many people save because they desire to hold wealth, and economists such as Henry Simons and Frank H. Knight completely rejected the notion of time preference. Pigou noted that people may save even at zero interest. These views were summarized by Samuel B. Chase, Jr., *Asset Prices in Economic Analysis* (Berkeley and Los Angeles: University of California Press, 1963), pp. 14–21. The more important determinant of interest rates is probably the demand for funds, which is based on the profitability of the use of borrowed funds—basically, on productivity in relation to the cost of borrowed funds.

which can be termed interest or a rate of yield, expressed as a percentage per year.

According to this view historical cost has little to do with value. A firm that can produce only one product, for which there is little or no demand, and that owns facilities that cannot be converted to any other use has little or no value. Although such an extreme is unlikely in reality, some wineries in the United States after World War II, when it again became possible to obtain imported wines in larger quantities, were very close to this situation. Banks found themselves with some very doubtful loans to companies owning those wineries.

In this view, the best indication of the value of an asset is the present value of the cash flows expected to be obtained. In efficient markets, competition would cause prices of assets to equal their values; thus the *replacement cost* of an asset would generally be close to the economic value of the asset. From the economic view, any asset should be valued at its correct value, insofar as this is determinable, and then if translation is necessary values should be translated at current exchange rates.

Many accountants have long resisted this approach. Their argument has been based on the premise that accountants should deal with objectively determinable data and should avoid judgments insofar as possible. Historical costs of assets are more objectively determinable in most cases than replacement values, because historical costs can usually be determined from records. Replacement costs of real capital assets are especially likely to be matters of judgment because they vary so much, and there may not be active markets in which the cost of replacing particular assets can be objectively determined.

On the basis of their view, accountants argued for a long time that historical exchange rates should be used in translation when this was possible without being clearly erroneous. This was presumed to be true for fixed assets. If fixed assets were valued in the original currencies at historical costs, then they should be translated at historical exchange rates—at the exchange rates in effect at the time the assets were acquired. Otherwise their values might appear to decline every year if, for example, a currency was devalued or floated downward every year.

However, current proposals in both the United States and the United Kingdom regarding the use of replacement cost and current value accounting could, if implemented, remove some of the objections to current rate translation. The SEC announced in the spring of 1976 that the 1,000 largest U.S. firms would be required in annual reports beginning with those for 1976 to indicate in some way the replacement values of their inventories and plant and equipment.[14] The British Sandilands Committee report, discussed later, proposed current value accounting as a general practice.

---

[14]*Business Week*, Apr. 5, 1976, p. 38. It appeared that the estimates might, at least at first, be required only in reports filed with the SEC. Some argued that if investors saw these cost estimates they might assign lower values to companies' stocks, since depreciation of higher replacement costs would mean less profits than had been reported. Others argued that this should be recognized and that on that basis Congress should be asked to permit depreciation of amounts reflecting capital costs, thus reducing taxes. See *Wall Street Journal*, Nov. 23, 1976, p. 2.

Current-Noncurrent Translation   For a long time, the approved rule in translation was in general to translate current assets and liabilities at current exchange rates, and noncurrent assets and liabilities, and net worth, at historic rates—at the rates at which the assets were acquired, liabilities incurred, or net worth established.[15]

Under this rule monetary assets, such as cash and accounts receivable, are translated at current rates. Inventories are also translated at current rates, although this involves some problems, as shown later. Fixed assets, however, are translated at the rates in effect when they were acquired.

Short-term debt is translated at the current rate, whether it is in local or foreign currency. (Of course, if it is in the currency of the parent company's country, it need not be translated.) Debt in a currency which has risen in value thus increases, certainly in terms of a local currency which has been devalued and perhaps also in terms of the currency of the parent company's country.

Long-term debt in local currency or in foreign currencies has traditionally been translated at historic rates. But this creates problems: isn't the subsidiary's debt greater if, for example, it is denominated in a foreign currency which has not been devalued, but the currency of the country in which the subsidiary is located has been devalued?[16] Moreover, if long-term debt has been translated at historic rates in a country where inflation has been serious, repayment at maturity causes a sudden large increase in net worth if the debt was in local currency. This increase actually occurred over a long period of time, as the debt obligation was reduced in terms of the values of assets in the subsidiary's country. But if historical exchange rates are used for translation, the debt is not reduced until it is repaid, and repayment of debt causes a sudden decline in long-term liabilities.

Translation of inventory at current exchange rates sometimes creates problems. For example, if inventory is imported from countries that have not devalued their currencies, but the country where the subsidiary is located has devalued its currency, inventory value is reduced when its value is translated; yet the cost of replacing such inventory may have risen. One may also ask whether the inventory can be sold at a price high enough to maintain existing profit margins, with the increased cost of obtaining new inventory. If prices cannot be increased—whether because of price controls or for some other reason—it is *not* logical to use historic exchange rates for translation.

Invested capital (capital stock and other elements of net worth) is translated at historic rates—that is, what it was worth at the time of investment—and some accountants see no reason to change this value. Of course, there may be exchange translation gains or losses which should be recognized in some manner. There has been considerable controversy about

[15]Chap. 12, *Accounting Research Bulletin 43* (New York: AICPA, 1953).

[16]Translation of long-term debt at the current exchange rate was advocated by Samuel R. Hepworth, *Reporting Foreign Operations* (Ann Arbor: University of Michigan, School of Business Administration, 1956). See also Paul Grady, *Inventory of Generally Accepted Accounting Principles for Business Enterprise*, Accounting Research Study No. 7 (New York: AICPA, 1965).

whether these gains or losses should be recognized in income statements, and in particular whether losses should be recognized but recognition of gains postponed in some circumstances. Retained earnings are translated at exchange rates of the years in which they were retained.

In the income statement, the current-noncurrent view has been that most items should be translated at the average rate of exchange prevailing during the period. The Institute of Chartered Accountants in England and Wales and a Canadian research study pointed out, however, that if a substantial devaluation or revaluation of a currency occurred, profits (income and expenses) would be translated at different rates before and after the date of devaluation or revaluation.[17] If values of inventories used are not translated at current rates, as they may not be if translation at these rates seems to create problems, cost of goods sold may be translated at historic rates.

Monetary-Nonmonetary Translation   Because current-noncurrent translation gave rise to some problems, other rules have been advocated and used. In the United Kingdom it was common to use current rates to translate all items, and this was also the case in many parts of Continental Europe and the British Commonwealth, but was not accepted practice in the United States.[18] In the United States, the monetary-nonmonetary rule became commonly used.[19]

Under the monetary-nonmonetary rule, assets in foreign currency or those whose values are to be realized in specified amounts of foreign currency are translated at current exchange rates. In general, all liabilities are also translated at current rates. On the other hand, assets which change in value (price), such as inventories and fixed assets, and also net worth, are translated at historic exchange rates.

[17]Accounting Principles Board Opinion No. 6 stated that "translation of long-term receivables and long-term liabilities at current exchange rates is appropriate in many circumstances." In effect, this modification of *Accounting Research Bulletin 43* moved in the direction of the use of the monetary-nonmonetary method of translation. Because of the extensive changes in foreign currency values in 1971, the APB issued an exposure draft in December 1971, proposing that companies using the monetary-nonmonetary method defer exchange adjustments insofar as these adjustments did not exceed those attributable to long-term debt. Because of uncertainty concerning the actual practices of firms in translation, the Financial Accounting Standards Board issued, in December 1973, Statement No. 1, "Disclosure of Foreign Currency Translation Information," requiring clear specification of methods used in translating foreign currency values.

[18]Professor J. F. Flower of the University of Bristol, England, tried to argue that using current rates for all items seemed to give results in accord with common sense, but he admitted that in effect that method upvalued fixed assets when an exchange rate appreciated, and reduced their value if the exchange rate depreciated. The problem is clearly valuation, not translation. See J. F. Flower, "Coping with Currency Fluctuations in Company Accounts," *Euromoney*, May 1974, pp. 14–19, and June 1974, pp. 44–48.

[19]See the comments of Frank S. Capin, "Are Historical Costs Outdated?" *Chartered Accountants Magazine*, September 1973, pp. 45–48, and Perry Mason, *Price Level Changes and Financial Statements—Basic Concepts and Methods* (New York: American Accounting Association, 1956). For a review of the translation problem which includes a useful bibliography, see Siegfried J. Cronauer, "Foreign Financial Statement Translation in an Economic Framework," unpublished master's degree research report, Graduate School of Business Administration, University of Washington, Seattle, 1975.

A significant problem arises in connection with the use of the monetary-nonmonetary rule, however. Most companies are likely to have more liabilities than monetary assets at the time of a host-country currency devaluation, especially if they have followed practices designed to minimize exchange risk, as discussed in Chapter 15. This results in an exchange gain from translation. At the same time, if costs of goods sold and depreciation are translated at historic rates, income statements for periods after devaluation will probably show losses when translated, because these heavy charges will reduce net income. There is a further complication. Balance sheets after translation by this method might show exchange gains if liabilities exceed monetary assets. How balance sheets after translation might show exchange gains but income statements after translation might show exchange losses is difficult to understand!

FASB Statement No. 8 and the Temporal Rule   The Financial Accounting Standards Board (FASB) in the United States issued in autumn 1975 Statement No. 8, requiring translation of foreign currency values according to the temporal rule, effective for fiscal years beginning after January 1, 1976.[20] Recalculation of earlier statements was encouraged. The purpose was to require translation such that restating items in U.S. dollars would not affect the measurement bases for assets or liabilities, nor the time for recording revenues and expenses. It was required that before translation, statements to be consolidated should be prepared or revised in accordance with U.S. generally accepted accounting principles. Then, in general, the measurement basis used originally was to determine the exchange rate used for translation. For example, if fixed assets were valued at historical costs, their values were to be translated at historical rates. Under generally accepted U.S. accounting principles the temporal rule has results quite similar, in many cases, to those obtained by the monetary-nonmonetary rule. In a few cases special changes are necessary: for example, inventories must be valued in *U.S. dollars* at cost or market, whichever is lower, even if this did not result from translation. Figure 16-1 shows currency translation treatment suggested for a variety of assets and liabilities.

The statement also required that exchange gains and losses resulting from translation enter into determination of income in the current period, and not be deferred.[21] This part of the statement has given rise to much discussion and objection, because in a period of floating exchange rates exchange gains and losses may fluctuate significantly from one quarter to the next, so that even a

---

[20]It has been pointed out that the shift to the monetary-nonmonetary method occurred in part because the dollar began to weaken against foreign currencies, and therefore the older method lost its conservative appeal. The problem is the lack of a theoretical basis for the monetary-nonmonetary method as well as for the older current-noncurrent method. See FASB, *Statement of Financial Accounting Standards No. 8* (Stamford, Conn.: FASB, 1975), p. 58.

[21]The FASB recognized difficulties in making accounting changes compatible with expected economic effects; see ibid., pp. 44–51. The Board felt that compatibility could be achieved only with a change in underlying accounting valuation principles, which it felt went beyond the scope of Statement No. 8.

	Translation rates	
	Current	**Historical**
Assets		
Cash on hand and demand and time deposits	X	
Marketable equity securities:		
Carried at cost		X
Carried at current market price	X	
Accounts and notes receivable and related unearned		
discount	X	
Allowance for doubtful accounts and notes receivable	X	
Inventories:		
Carried at cost		X
Carried at current replacement price or current selling		
price	X	
Carried at net realizable value	X	
Carried at contract price (produced under fixed price		
contracts)	X	
Prepaid insurance, advertising, and rent		X
Refundable deposits	X	
Advances to unconsolidated subsidiaries	X	
Property, plant, and equipment		X
Accumulated depreciation of property, plant, and equipment		X
Cash surrender value of life insurance	X	
Patents, trademarks, licenses, and formulas		X
Goodwill		X
Other intangible assets		X
Liabilities		
Accounts and notes payable and overdrafts	X	
Accrued expenses payable	X	
Accrued losses on firm purchase commitments	X	
Refundable deposits	X	
Deferred income		X
Bonds payable or other long-term debt	X	
Unamortized premium or discount on bonds or notes payable	X	
Convertible bonds payable	X	
Accrued pension obligations	X	
Obligations under warranties	X	

Figure 16-1   Rates Used to Translate Assets and Liabilities. (*Source*: FASB Statement No. 8, p. 20.)

company which has little change in its earnings from one year to the next may have significant variation from quarter to quarter within a year.[22]

It was acknowledged that averaging and approximation may be necessary for historical rates. Earlier financial statements are to be restated if practicable.

[22]See, for example, *Business Week,* Apr. 12, 1976, pp. 28–29. Continental Can Co.'s originally reported earnings for the third and fourth quarters of 1975 were $1.33 and $0.75; as restated under the new rule, they were $1.80 and $0.65.

Deferred taxes may be translated at current rates. Gains or losses on forward exchange contracts are deferred when the contracts are intended as hedges against identifiable foreign currency commitments.

Disclosure of exchange gain or loss taken into account in determining net income for a period is required either in financial statements or in notes appended to the statements. Financial statements are not to be adjusted for exchange rate changes occurring after statement dates, although disclosure of such changes and their effects, if significant, may be necessary.

A typical business transaction which could give rise to a currency translation gain or loss is the purchase or sale of merchandise abroad by a company domiciled in the United States, the price being quoted in foreign currency. Suppose that a U.S. company orders a consignment of china tableware from a United Kingdom manufacturer, the value of the order being £100,000 sterling. Assume the goods are delivered on June 1 and invoiced at the quoted price, payable within 30 days. Assume further that the selling price on June 1 for bank cable transfers in the United States for payment abroad is $1.80 to £1. Then assume that the U.S. company purchased pounds on July 1 for payment to the United Kingdom, the price paid being the spot rate on that day, $1.70 to £1.

The dollar cost of the purchase was 100,000 × $1.80, or $180,000, on June 1, and this is the value at which the transaction should be recorded in the company's books. The bookkeeping entry would be to debit inventory account and credit accounts payable:

Inventory	$180,000	
Accounts Payable		$180,000

Purchase of china tableware from U.K. manufacturer for $100,000. Translation rate June 1, $1.80 to £1.

Since by July 1 the cost of £100,000 sterling amounted to only $170,000 (100,000 × $1.70), it could be argued that the cost of inventory purchased should be adjusted to this actual amount payable. Some companies have adopted such an approach in the past. However, FASB Statement No. 8 requires the separate disclosure of gains or losses on currency translation and currency transactions. The appropriate bookkeeping entries to record the payment therefore are:

Accounts Payable	$180,000	
Cash		$170,000
Currency Exchange Gains		10,000

Had the exchange rate moved against the dollar during the 30-day period, there would have been a Currency Exchange Loss, shown as a debit.

In order to avoid risks of exchange losses such as that possible if the dollar's value fell relative to that of the pound, the U.S. company could hedge by buying sterling for forward delivery, making the contract on June 1 for delivery July 1 (or June 30). If the rate for sterling, for a 30-day forward contract, was $1.82, the U.S. company could elect to pay $182,000 for £100,000 to be delivered in 30 days. The bookkeeping entry on June 1 would be:

Forward Exchange Investment Contract	$180,000	
Interest on Forward Exchange	2,000	
Contract Payable		$182,000

On July 1 the forward exchange would be delivered and the United Kingdom supplier paid, the bookkeeping entries being:

Contract Payable	$182,000	
Investment in Sterling	180,000	
Forward Exchange Investment Contract		$180,000
Cash		182,000
Accounts Payable	$180,000	
Investment in Sterling		180,000

Since the company had hedged to avoid exchange risk, it would show no exchange loss (or gain), but would show an item of $2,000 for premium on forward exchange.

Thus at least for the time being the accounting profession in the United States has moved to a rule which translates values in such a way as to retain the method of valuation originally used to measure items in foreign statements, and to a requirement for showing foreign exchange gains and losses in the current period. The temporal rule can be used with various methods of valuation—for example, historical cost, current replacement cost, or current selling price. With the accounting principles generally used in the United States, the results of the temporal rule and the monetary-nonmonetary rule are quite similar, but they would not be similar if a different method of valuation were used. The FASB indicated that it believed it to be a virtue of the temporal rule that it is compatible with different methods of valuation of items, although of course with the use of other methods of valuation, results of the temporal rule would differ from those obtained with the monetary-nonmonetary rule.[23]

FASB Statement No. 8 has generated controversy among accountants and MNC officials, chiefly about the requirement that translation gains or losses be recognized in income statements for the quarters in which they occur. This produces gyrations in profits if currency values fluctuate widely. Moreover, if a company borrows in local currency to finance additions to inventory, it shows a translation gain if the local currency depreciates in value. But later, as inventory is sold and charged as part of the cost of goods sold, since it was valued at cost and is translated at historic rates, the firm shows translation losses because sales are translated at current rates. A company having equal amounts of current assets and current liabilities and operating chiefly within a

[23]FASB, *Statement No. 8,* pp. 56–57.

given national environment shows translation losses or gains because inventory, although a current asset, is generally valued at cost and therefore under FASB 8 is translated at historic exchange rates. If a currency depreciates, inventory, translated at historic rates, does not fall in value when translated into dollars, while other current assets and all current liabilities are translated into fewer dollars. Of course, a company which bought raw materials outside the country in which it operated would show different results.

It should be noted that translation gains and losses are not likely to result in tax changes if taxes paid by the subsidiary are credited against U.S. taxes of the parent company, since there is no change in the subsidiary's earnings in local currency. Investors may not place a different value on the stock of the company; some studies have shown that investors do not seem to be influenced by accounting changes unless they affect taxes.

Companies which have sizable long-term debt in local currency and which formerly used the current-noncurrent convention face a problem. Clearly, if the currency value fluctuates they will show translation gains or losses. Yet why should they hedge against such gains or losses when the liabilities are long-term and thus need not be paid until far in the future, when the currency's value may be quite different? Some such firms may follow the example of Ramada Inns, which reportedly began to finance the building of hotels in foreign countries by borrowing in U.S. dollars instead of borrowing local currencies in the foreign countries.

Translation under Fixed or Multiple Exchange Rates   When exchange rates are fixed but are inappropriate as indications of the market values of currencies under free market conditions, no translation rules provide adequate translation of values. This is because the exchange rates themselves are inadequate. In the absence of a free exchange market, there may be no way of determining with any assurance the appropriate exchange rate to be used, if a powerful government maintains a disequilibrium exchange rate through the force of regulations.

Volatile exchange rates may also create problems, although in this case the problems arise from the difficulty of keeping careful records of the exchange rate fluctuations and of the items to be translated at various rates. Inaccuracies could in theory be avoided, but in practice they are likely to occur.

Multiple exchange rates give rise to even more problems. Which rate is appropriate? If a payment exchange rate can be identified, there is some justification for using the identified rate. FASB Statement No. 8 suggests that the rate at which particular transactions *could* be settled on their dates be used. For asset and liability items, it suggests that the rate applicable to currency conversion for dividend remittances be used. If payment exchange rates cannot be identified, the question of which among multiple exchange rates should be used is difficult to answer. It must simply be admitted that under multiple exchange rates, translation which accurately measures values is extremely difficult.

Evaluation of Translation Rules   Translation rules represent one type of price index adjustment of historical costs and values. The price index used is the exchange rate. It is usually applied either to current assets and liabilities but not to noncurrent ones, or to monetary assets and liabilities but not to nonmonetary ones. Thus historic values for some items, but not for others, are restated in terms of changed price relationships.

From the viewpoint of economic and financial theory, none of the standard rules for translation is adequate, and if inflation is or has been rapid, the theoretical inadequacy becomes significant in practice. This is because, in a period of inflation, values in local currency are not correct in terms of economic value under most accounting practices; hence rules for translation of some values at one rate and some values at other rates simply compound the error.

The monetary-nonmonetary rule is probably better than the current-noncurrent rule in permitting long-term debt to be translated at current rates, but it has disadvantages equally as serious as those of the current-noncurrent rule. From an economic viewpoint, if values are correctly stated, current exchange rates can be used for translation of all items. What is necessary for correct valuation is indicated in later sections of this chapter.

Translation of foreign values at current exchange rates results in foreign exchange gains or losses if exchange rates change. Thus the decision about which items to translate at current rates indicates a judgment on which items are exposed to risk. If prices of fixed assets and inventories rise (in the long run, at least) when the exchange value of a currency falls, use of historical rates to translate values of such items is appropriate because the lower exchange rate and the higher prices offset each other. The presumption underlying this decision is that purchasing power parity holds, at least in the long run.

When monetary items are translated at current rates, the implication is that interest rate parity theory (Fisher open) does not hold, for if it did, cumulative interest revenue or expense to the maturity of any financial asset would include an amount equal to any gain or loss from exchange rate changes (ignoring cash balances on which interest is not received). As we found in earlier chapters, purchasing power parity and Fisher open are logically related, and in equilibrium *both* should hold.

Aliber and Stickney presented evidence that, for developed countries, deviations from Fisher open have been smaller than deviations from purchasing power parity, but that, with one exception, deviations from Fisher open for LDCs have been larger than from purchasing power parity.[24] They also presented evidence showing that the longer the period, the smaller the deviations from both parities. Thus noncurrent assets and liabilities, which are generally held for long periods, are not much exposed to exchange losses or gains in developed countries, but are more exposed in LDCs. Since the holding

---

[24]Robert Z. Aliber and Clyde P. Stickney, "Accounting Measures of Foreign Exchange Exposure: The Long and Short of It," *Accounting Review*, January 1975, pp. 44–57.

period for current assets and liabilities is presumably short, they are most exposed in both groups of countries. However, if their amounts are relatively constant, they may in effect be viewed as being held for long periods, and hence exposure may be considered to be small.

The implication of this study is that the significant factors are the location of the assets and liabilities and the planning horizon of the firm. Over short periods, all items are exposed to exchange risk, and items in LDCs are more exposed than items held in developed countries, for most periods.

In view of such considerations, and of the problem of inflation accounting, discussed below, it is unlikely that we have heard the last word on the translation problem, although for the time being FASB Statement No. 8 must be understood and generally followed by U.S. firms.

INFLATION AND ACCOUNTING

We now turn to the problem arising because many countries have different rates of inflation. The prevalence of inflation in recent years and the variation of rates of inflation from time to time and in different countries has dramatized a problem which has existed for a long time but which has become increasingly important in recent years, and especially since 1965, when major industrialized countries have all experienced significant inflation.

Three questions may be raised: (1) Do the values of nonmonetary assets and equity change when the purchasing power of money changes? (2) Does the value of money and other financial assets change when prices change? (3) Is it proper to continue to present financial data in monetary units that have changed in purchasing power?

Economic Value

We return again to economic value. Economically, the value of any good is the cost to the individual or firm if that good is somehow lost. Values of goods held (wealth) change over time as net income is obtained or losses occur. Income is obtained when the individual or firm has wealth which he, she, or the firm can spend and still be as well off as before. Thus inventory sold constitutes a loss of value equivalent to the cost of replacing it, and depreciation and other capital consumption allowances should allow for the cost of replacing capital assets which wear out, are lost, or are destroyed by fire, flood, or other events. Only after such costs are covered by income is *net* income obtained.

The value of money certainly falls in terms of purchasing power when inflation occurs. However, the value of money changes in terms of purchasing power differently for different individuals and firms. The Consumer Price Index (CPI) in the United States is one measure of change in the purchasing power of money for a basket of goods purchased by certain groups of wage earners. It is by no means the appropriate index to measure the change in purchasing power of other groups.

For these reasons it is probably desirable to continue to present financial data in monetary units, even though drastically changed in purchasing power.

The application of these principles to the presentation of financial statements causes serious problems in periods of rapid inflation. Problems would also be caused in periods of deflation, but the latest such period for most countries was 1929–1933. The problems arising from changes in economic values in a period of inflation and the customary methods of accounting are probably most serious in connection with the values of inventories and of fixed assets. We therefore consider these separately.

The Inventory Problem

Inventories are often calculated by businessmen in physical rather than in value terms. They have so many cars in inventory, so many bolts of cloth, or so many steel bars. In these terms no problem arises, but for financial statements values must be assigned to inventories. The accountant's penchant for recorded values led him to use cost values. But if cost values are used for inventory sold in a period of inflation, cost of goods sold does not include an amount sufficient to replace the inventory sold. Therefore, in economic terms profits are *overstated* in the sense that there is not as much addition to the value of the firm (equity) as was reported. To keep the value of equity the same, enough cost should have been recorded to equal the replacement value of inventory sold.

Full discussion of tax questions is deferred to Chapter 17, but note that companies which can use either of two methods of valuation for tax purposes and choose a method that overstates profits, pay higher taxes because they show higher income. The higher income might increase the value of their stocks in the stock market if investors, unaware of the overstatement, take the reported profits at face value.[25]

FIFO and LIFO   Accountants in the United States generally recognize two methods of valuation of the cost of goods sold: first-in, first-out (FIFO), in which the cost of inventory purchased at the earliest date is used first, and last-in, first-out (LIFO), in which the cost of the inventory purchased last is used first. In a period of inflation, LIFO comes closer to valuing the cost of inventory sold at its replacement value than does FIFO, although in rapid inflation neither may accurately reflect replacement value.

Business firms obviously reduce reported profits, and hence taxes, by using LIFO valuations in a period of inflation. Yet many firms have continued to use FIFO inventory valuations. Aside from conservatism and resistance to change, another argument may be advanced for this usage: corporate officers may fear that reporting lower profits would cause investors to hesitate to buy a

[25]It has been suggested that (1) investors do not reduce the price they will pay for the stock of a company which has shown less profit because of changing its method of calculating cost of goods sold and (2) somewhat tentatively, the prices of the stocks of companies using straight-line depreciation in reports to stockholders instead of accelerated depreciation methods (while still using accelerated depreciation for tax purposes) seem only temporarily to improve. See Henry C. Wallich and Mable I. Wallich, "Profits Aren't as Good as they Look," *Fortune*, March 1974, pp. 126–129, 172.

company's stock, and this may cause the price of the stock to fall. Does this in fact occur? One research study reported that shifting from FIFO to LIFO did not reduce the price of a company's stock; investors seemed to be sophisticated enough to recognize that shifting from FIFO to LIFO only reduced *reported* profits.

Inventory Valuation Adjustment in National Income Accounting In the United States, economists who prepare estimates of GNP make an inventory valuation adjustment to attempt to adjust the cost of inventory sold to its replacement value. For firms using LIFO accounting procedures, the adjustment may be rather small. For firms using FIFO accounting procedures, it is larger. Moreover, since firms are permitted to shift from FIFO to LIFO for part or all of their operations, it is very difficult for economists to make the appropriate adjustments. Consequently, values of inventory used in sales and hence values of remaining inventories are likely to be misstated. This evidently occurred in 1973–1974, and the result was probably understatement of the value of inventories held. Then when business firms decided, in the latter part of 1974, that inventories were too large, they cut back sharply. The result was an acute recession.

Profits reported in GNP data are less, because of the inventory valuation adjustment, than profits reported by individual corporations would be if totaled. As inflation accelerates, the discrepancy becomes larger. Since dividends are correctly reported as monetary values, the discrepancy appears in *retained earnings*—earnings not paid out in the form of dividends.

The significance of this may be appreciated by considering one example. The profits reported by corporations before taxes for 1973 were $123 billion, but after the inventory valuation adjustment they were only $105 billion—an adjustment of $18 billion. If profits were valued on an after-tax basis, the difference would have been greater. The inventory valuation adjustment for 1973 reduced subsequent profits to very low levels. In countries where inflation was more rapid than in the United States, the difference would have been greater.

Replacement Value Accounting for Inventories If replacement values were used for valuation of inventories, inventories would be revalued upward as prices rose. The resulting gain could not be labeled income, since the company did not obtain this by selling goods or services. It would be set aside in a special account. Then as goods were sold, their current replacement values would be counted as part of the cost of goods sold.

Valuation of Fixed Assets

In most industrialized countries, fixed assets are still valued at historical costs minus depreciation. Although depreciation may be calculated at rates that vary depending on a number of methods of calculation, the total amount to be depreciated usually cannot exceed the cost of the assets. Upward revaluations of assets have, of course, been made in some countries, and then depreciation over the life of the asset is greater.

What applies to inventories also applies to fixed assets. If general prices rise, it is quite likely that the replacement values of fixed assets will rise also. If these assets must be replaced, the cost is higher than the historical cost at which they were purchased. Replacement value accounting would value fixed assets at replacement cost, again placing the gain in value in a special account.

Then depreciation could be charged against the revalued assets. Depreciation allowances would be larger and profits smaller. Essentially, when inflation occurs, monetary values of nonmonetary assets rise, but this does not increase the wealth of business firms, since their assets are needed, and if they wear out or are lost they must be replaced. More must be set aside from gross income for this purpose before it can legitimately be said that there are profits in the sense of an addition to real wealth.

Because of difficulties of estimating depreciation and of determining replacement values, national income accountants in the United States did not for a time attempt to determine replacement values for fixed assets as they did for inventory, but the severity of inflation in 1973–1975 caused them to make such estimates. Economist George Terborgh of the Machinery and Allied Products Institute estimated that in 1973 additional depreciation of $7 billion should have been charged.[26] This would have reduced profits before taxes from $105 billion to $98 billion. Since the corporate tax liability was $50 billion and dividends were $30 billion, this left retained earnings, with proper depreciation, of only $18 billion, as compared to $27 billion in 1965 when there was negligible inflation.

Price Level Adjustments in Accounting

A partial but somewhat inaccurate correction is the use of price level adjustments in accounting. Price level adjustment is a technique useful in adjusting national income data. It is less useful in adjusting corporate financial statement figures because there is no reason to believe that changes in values of fixed assets and inventories are necessarily the same as changes in the general price level. Price level adjustment is a second-best technique.

Nevertheless, in countries that have had serious inflation, it has been recognized that inflation leads to overtaxation and a reduction in the stock of capital. Brazil has required that depreciable assets and the related figure showing accumulated depreciation be revalued annually, using a government price index.[27] Argentina has permitted revaluations in which net book values of fixed assets were multiplied by a government-supplied coefficient to determine a "revaluation increment." The revaluation increment has then been amortized separately from the depreciation of assets on a historical cost basis.

[26]Ibid. See also *Economic Report of the President,* 1976, Table B-8 and similar data in that report for following years.
[27]On Brazil, see Dale Fieldcamp, "International Accounting in an Inflationary Economy," *International Journal of Accounting,* Fall 1968, pp. 155–168.

One variation of the price level adjustment technique is to adjust on the basis of special price indexes, such as indexes for prices of machinery, equipment, and new nonresidential construction. This technique has reportedly been used by at least one major firm in Canada.[28] Another company has computed its own price indexes.

In other instances companies have used independent appraisers to make estimates of replacement values. Philips Company, in the Netherlands, uses a combination of general price indexes, its own price indexes, and appraisal. It also goes one step further by attempting to evaluate the effects of technological change, which may actually result in decline in value of some inventories.[29]

Replacement Value Accounting, Inflation, and the Translation Problem

Widespread use of replacement value accounting would bring accounting practices in periods of inflation into line with economic theory, in this respect. Gains from increases in prices of nonmonetary assets would be recognized, whether realized or not, although they would be shown separately from operating income. Under present accounting practices such gains are not generally shown unless realized, and then they are often included with operating income. An example is the gain on inventory resulting from price increases. Such gain is not income in the sense of funds which can be spent, still leaving the firm as wealthy as before.

Replacement value accounting would eliminate much of the translation problem. After inventories and fixed assets were valued at replacement costs, they could be translated in value at current exchange rates. Similarly, by restating depreciation amounts to depreciate replacement values instead of historical costs, they could be translated at current exchange rates.

The force of conservatism and the cost of developing replacement value estimates delay the application of replacement value accounting, and if inflation moderates the need for it is less apparent. One study indicated that developing replacement value based year-end financial statements might take 160 hours for an average firm in the first year, and 55 or 60 hours in subsequent years.[30]

In the United States, although there has been some discussion of the use of replacement value accounting, and the SEC, as noted, decided to require replacement value estimates at least in reports filed with it, no broad-scale change to this kind of accounting had been made when the writing of this book was completed.

In the United Kingdom, an Inflation Accounting Committee chaired by F. E. P. Sandilands met during 1974 and the first half of 1975. The major

[28]L. S. Rosen, *Current Value Accounting and Price-Level Restatements* (Toronto: Canadian Institute of Chartered Accountants, 1971).

[29]*Solving Accounting Problems for Worldwide Operations* (New York: Business International Corporation, 1974), p. 111.

[30]R. C. Dockweiler, "The Practicability of Developing Multiple Financial Statements," *Accounting Review*, October 1969, pp. 729–742.

recommendation of that committee was the use of "current cost accounting." Value to a business of any asset held by a company was defined as "the loss the company would suffer if it were deprived of the asset."[31] As the report pointed out, in most cases this would be equal to the cost of replacing the asset. It recommended that total gains for a year should be reported, but that operating gains should be separated from gains resulting from holding nonmonetary assets and extraordinary gains realized on sales of items not a part of a company's normal output. It was argued that this would make a clear distinction between "gains which are due to a company's productive efforts and gains due to luck or skill in the timing of purchases of assets during a period of inflation."[32] The Sandilands Committee rejected the use of supplementary financial statements containing figures adjusted to current purchasing power by using a price index. Reasons were that (1) no price index is equally useful (or even valid) for all firms, (2) expressing financial statements in units of current purchasing power (base-year pounds, or base-year dollars in the United States) would be confusing to many who use financial statements, and (3) in the long run current purchasing power figures do not remedy the defects of historic cost accounting. The Committee did recommend that the Government Statistical Service develop price indexes for capital expenditures for plant and machinery specific to particular industries. This would aid companies in estimating replacement values.

In view of the persistence of relatively rapid inflation in industrialized countries, and recommendations such as that of the Sandilands Committee, replacement value accounting may gain wider use more quickly than it would have under conditions existing in the 1950s and early 1960s.

FINANCIAL REPORTING

Those concerned with international finance and accounting may expect to find many variations in forms of financial reporting in different countries. Many of these variations are simply changes in form, which may leave the reader of financial statements disoriented for a time until he grasps the differences from forms used in his own country.[33] These differences need not detain us because they are not substantive. Several characteristics of accounting statements in countries other than the United States have substantive effects, however, and are therefore worth noting.

Reserves and Earnings

In many countries various reserves are established, often to smooth out earnings from year to year. Reserves for contingencies may be established in

---

[31]*Inflation Accounting, A Brief Guide to the Report of the Inflation Accounting Committee,* Cmd 6225 (London: Her Majesty's Stationery Office, 1975), p. 6.

[32]Ibid., p. 8.

[33]David K. Eiteman and Arthur I. Stonehill, *Multinational Business Finance* (Reading, Mass.: Addison-Wesley, 1973), pp. 336–337.

years when earnings are high, to be drawn upon in years when earnings are lower.

In some countries, it is general practice to dispose of all earnings by specific appropriations. Unallocated retained earnings may be very small. Sometimes allocations are made at stockholders' meetings after the publication of annual reports, and special memoranda must be obtained for information on disposition of earnings.

Financial Disclosure

Many countries' firms disclose less financial data and provide less information concerning such matters as methods of valuation of assets, methods of calculating depreciation, and the generation of income than do U.S. firms. Secrecy is traditional in some countries. Beyond tradition, the reasons for continuing to disclose only a minimum amount of information are the absence of legal requirements like those of the Securities and Exchange Commission (SEC) in the United States; the lack of pressure from creditors, banks, and stockholders; the lack of need for public equity financing; and the related lack of extensive equity markets. It is likely, therefore, that as capital markets develop breadth and depth in Europe, as stockholders become more numerous and important, and as other conditions requiring disclosure of financial information become more widespread, more information will be provided in foreign financial statements than in the past.

Practices in some countries may include use of such methods as accelerated depreciation in determining valuations of assets in published statements; whereas in the United States firms generally use such methods for tax purposes only, and use straight-line depreciation in most instances in published statements. However, in countries other than the United States, methods of calculating depreciation often are not explained in financial statements, so that users of such statements may not be aware of the calculation methods.

Since subsidiaries need not be consolidated in some countries even if a majority of the stock of a subsidiary is owned by the parent company, the earning power of unconsolidated subsidiaries may be concealed.

Auditing

Auditing standards vary widely. Physical inventory examination may not be required and accounts receivable may not be confirmed. Use of sampling procedures for verification of the data is not uniform. In some countries auditors have no special qualifications.

On the other hand, since U.S. public accounting firms have opened offices in many countries around the world, U.S. subsidiaries in many countries may be audited by the same firms that audit the parent companies. As their services are increasingly used by business firms in foreign countries, it is likely that auditing standards will tend toward somewhat greater uniformity.

The comments made in this section are not intended to do any more than make the reader aware of the need for careful analysis of foreign financial statements, and to comment on a few of the differences commonly found in comparing such statements with financial statements of U.S. firms. The field of international accounting merits separate study and these comments can do no more than create an awareness of some of the problems of incomplete information; lack of comparability of data; and effects of varying economic conditions, especially inflation.

CHANGING INTERNATIONAL CONDITIONS AND ACCOUNTING FOR INTERNATIONAL OPERATIONS

Changing international financial conditions inevitably influence accounting for international operations and accounting in general. The rapid inflation of the decade after 1965 led to widespread discussion and hundreds of articles in accounting journals concerning means of making adjustments required by inflation. The growth of MNCs and the internationalization of banks and of public accounting firms increased the use of foreign financial information. The need to consolidate financial statements brought the translation problem to the forefront and also stimulated thinking about the use of historical cost and price data.

The development of MNCs and the internationalization of banks and of public accounting firms represent part of the process of economic integration. Although some foreign regulation of multinational firms has begun to develop, limiting such integration, the general trend has been toward greater participation in international financial activity by larger firms.

Although this integration may not lead to complete standardization of accounting systems, it does lead to comparisons and modifications. Mobility of labor and capital make it more difficult to retain significant differences in accounting and taxation. It is probable that study, comparison, and modification will continue. The direction of change is likely to be toward increasing similarity of accounting practices, although at times exceptions to this trend may arise from problems faced by certain countries.

The change in the 1970s from conditions of stable exchange rates to floating rates for the major industrialized countries made problems of translation and valuation of assets of much more concern.[34] While exchange rates fluctuated in the 1930s and have generally fluctuated for LDCs, the worldwide inflation of the 1970s created a new situation. Although inflation occurred in most countries, currency floating was upward as well as downward. If those economists who foresee continuing inflation are correct, proper accounting under inflation is probably the most significant problem in international accounting.

[34]See, for example, "Focus on Balance Sheet Reform," *Business Week*, June 7, 1976, pp. 52–60. For U.S. Steel Co., plant and equipment, stated on the balance sheet at slightly under $4 billion, became over $8 billion restated at estimated replacement cost in 1973, and after-tax income for 1973, originally reported at $367 million for that year, became a loss of $374 million after restatement of asset figures, according to one financial analyst.

APPENDIX: The Purchasing-Power–Accrual Concept of Income

In this chapter, the capital maintenance concept of income, deriving from such economists as Hicks and Pigou, was adopted rather than the purchasing-power–accrual concept. Under the latter, not only should values of real assets be adjusted to reflect replacement costs, but changes in values of monetary items (financial assets and liabilities) should also be recognized in accounting statements to reflect changes in purchasing power.

There is disagreement on this, especially since the purchasing-power–accrual concept clearly relates to what are frequently *unrealized* gains and losses—for example, declines in bond values which are losses for the bondholders and gains for companies which have issued bonds. In the case of inventory, inventory sold is clearly realization, and hence an inventory valuation adjustment is appropriate. It is perhaps debatable whether using up part of plant and equipment through depreciation is realization. An adjustment to reflect replacement cost might be debatable even if one argued that adjustment should not be made for unrealized gains.[35]

Using the capital maintenance concept of income, changes in values of financial assets and liabilities could be ignored, as the British Sandilands Committee recommended, or could be handled through a LIFO procedure. The basic postulate is the "going concern" assumption that businesses are in certain lines of activity and generally have no intention of purchasing their debt prematurely. As Shoven and Bulow pointed out, some firms do this when they can purchase the bonds at discounts. But it is still argued by many that even if adjustment should be made for changes in the real burden of *servicing* debt, as proposed in the FASB exposure draft cited above, adjustments should not be made for changes in market value of debt on the ground that *most* firms intend debt, once issued, to be outstanding until maturity or call dates, and hence market values at intervening dates are irrelevant. Assuming no default, bond values will return to par at maturity or to call price at call dates.

Whatever may be the outcome of the discussion of the purchasing-power–accrual concept of income, many would agree with the comment of Gramlich in discussion of the Shoven-Bulow article that an "inflation-adjusted capital maintenance concept would be a long step in the right direction."

QUESTIONS FOR DISCUSSION

1 Discuss possible reasons for variations in accounting principles and practices such as those observed in comparing Sweden, the Netherlands, West Germany, and the United States.

---

[35]A very useful discussion of the purchasing-power–accrual concept of income, with empirical estimates of changes needed in U.S. income figures to make adjustments in recent years, is contained in John B. Shoven and Jeremy I. Bulow, "Inflation Accounting and Nonfinancial Corporate Profits: Financial Assets and Liabilities," *Brookings Papers on Economic Activity*, 1976, No. 1 (Washington, D.C.: The Brookings Institution, 1976), pp. 15–66. For a discussion of the two concepts, see an earlier article by Shoven and Bulow, "Inflation Accounting and Nonfinancial Corporate Profits: Physical Assets," *Brookings Papers on Economic Activity*, 1975, No. 3. For an early discussion of the capital maintenance concept of income, see A. C. Pigou, "Maintaining Capital Intact," *Economica*, n.s., vol. 8, August 1944. See also the FASB, Proposed Statement of Financial Accounting Standards (Exposure Draft), "Financial Reporting in Units of General Purchasing Power," Dec. 31, 1974.

2 What are arguments for current-noncurrent translation versus monetary-nonmonetary translation? What are the arguments for the monetary-nonmonetary translation?

3 Why do multiple exchange rates make any translation of currency values likely to be erroneous?

4 Why does inflation result in a serious overstatement of profits if traditional accounting methods are used?

5 LIFO inventory accounting results in valuations for cost of goods sold which are closer to economic values than those resulting from FIFO inventory accounting in a period of inflation. Why does LIFO inventory accounting not necessarily result in valuations equivalent to economic values?

6 Why do national income accountants not attempt to adjust values of fixed assets to approximate replacement values, although they do attempt to make such an adjustment for inventory values?

7 Why is price level adjustment characterized in the chapter as a "second-best technique" for correcting values of fixed assets, inventories, and other items in periods of inflation?

8 Why is it stated that replacement value accounting would eliminate much of the translation problem?

9 Is the lack of extensive disclosure of information in financial statements in many European countries and the failure to develop broad and deep capital markets in those countries a "chicken and egg" question? Explain.

10 What effect is the opening of worldwide offices by major U.S. public accounting firms likely to have on auditing standards in various countries?

PROBLEMS

1 Assume that a U.S. firm bought chemicals from Germany for DM100,000 on April 1, payment to be made within 30 days. Assume that the DM rate was $0.35 on April 1 and $0.40 on May 1. Further assume that the company paid on May 1, by bank remittance to Germany. Show the proper accounting entries according to the rules of FASB No. 8.

2 The Philips Co., in the Netherlands, uses replacement values for its inventories and plant and equipment in its financial statements. In a period of inflation such as the past decade, what are the effects of this on (a) its assets, (b) its net worth, and (c) its rate of profit? Compare each with the result if the firm had used historical cost values.

3 Several years ago when inflation was quite rapid, Standard Oil Co. of California shifted some valuations of inventory from FIFO to LIFO. What was the effect of this change on the company's (a) asset values, (b) net worth, and (c) rate of profit?

4 Would the rules for translation of assets and liabilities shown in Figure 16-1 be applicable if replacement values were used for fixed assets and inventories instead of historical costs? Explain necessary changes, if any.

5 Would you expect a firm to be able to borrow long-term funds at a lower rate in New York than in the Eurobond market, assuming that it could borrow in both markets? What factors, including accounting factors, make a difference in the interest rate? As a corporate treasurer of a multinational firm, what factors other than the interest rate might you consider in your choice of where to borrow?

6 The group vice-president for international operations of Barber-Greene Co., a U.S.

firm making heavy machinery, with large operations in both Brazil and Britain, is reported to have stated that in one year the company lost $1.4 million on exchange rate fluctuations but even after that experience was not hedging against exchange rate risk. Argue for or against his view that hedging was not justified.

7 Memorex Co. was reported to have been starting a hedging program after the issuance of FASB No. 8, and Westinghouse Corp. subsidiaries to have remitted more dividends to the United States from countries in which currency values were declining. Comment on these financial actions—their usefulness, their cost (if any), and the side effects on things other than financial statements of the companies.

8 If your company had a subsidiary in an LDC, and you read the article by Aliber and Stickney, what questions might be raised in your mind concerning hedging against exposure to exchange risks on net assets of your subsidiary?

SUGGESTED REFERENCES

Useful sources on international accounting in general are Gerhard G. Mueller, *International Accounting* (New York: Macmillan, 1967) and Kenneth B. Berg, Gerhard G. Mueller, and Lauren M. Walker, eds., *Readings in International Accounting* (Boston: Houghton Mifflin, 1969).

For one concise explanation of the rationale for using historical costs, see *Report of the Company Law Committee* (London: H. M.'s Stationery Office, 1962), p. 130.

The view that long-run exchange rates are determined primarily by rates of inflation is expressed in *Foreign Exchange Exposure Management* (New York: Chemical Bank, 1972); see especially p. 87. See also the view expressed by Robert Gayton, "Foreign Accounts Translation: A Valuation Problem," *Journal of Accountancy*, June 1973, pp. 69–70. Criticism of purchasing power parities as vague and uncertain indicators of current exchange rate levels has been expressed by Paul Einzig, *A Textbook on Foreign Exchange* (New York: St. Martin's, 1966); see especially p. 126.

A very thorough review of the translation problem is provided by R. MacDonald Parkinson, FCA, *Translation of Foreign Currencies* (Toronto: Canadian Institute of Chartered Accountants, 1972). One should not overlook Samuel R. Hepworth, *Reporting Foreign Operations* (Ann Arbor: University of Michigan, School of Business Administration, 1956), and his criticisms of current-noncurrent translation. See also Donald J. Hayes, "Translating Foreign Currencies," *Harvard Business Review*, January–February 1972, pp. 6–18, and Gerhard G. Mueller, "Are Traditional Foreign Exchange Translation Methods Obsolete?" *California Management Review*, Summer 1965, pp. 42–43.

For the text of FASB 8 and the reasoning underlying its provisions, see Statement of Financial Accounting Standards No. 8 (Stamford, Conn.: FASB, 1975). For discussion of the ensuing controversy, see "FASB 8: A Spirited Accounting Controversy," *Morgan Guaranty Survey,* July 1976, pp. 7–11, and Linda Snyder, "Have the Accountants Really Hurt the Multinationals?" *Fortune*, February 1977, pp. 85–89.

Implications of both current value (replacement value) accounting and purchasing power accrual accounting are discussed by Richard W. Kopcke, "Current Accounting Practices and Proposals for Reform," Federal Reserve Bank of Boston, *New England Economic Review,* September/October 1976, pp. 3–29.

M. Edgar Barrett, "Annual Report Disclosure: Are American Reports Superior?

Journal of International Business Studies, Fall 1975, pp. 15–24, questions the superiority of American financial disclosure in annual reports, particularly vis-à-vis that of British reports.

Problems arising in making public figures for capital replacement costs were indicated in a number of articles in the *Wall Street Journal* and elsewhere; see, for example, *Wall Street Journal,* Nov. 23, 1976, p. 2, and Apr. 6, 1977, p. 9.

Chapter 17

Some Tax Considerations
Affecting International
Operations

It is sometimes said that only two things are certain—death and taxes. Almost all governments tax: they tax individual and corporate income, property, sales, value added, specific sales such as those of liquor or cigarettes (excise taxes), imports (import duties), and other transfers of funds, such as inheritances. In this chapter we discuss some effects of general levels and types of taxes on international business operations, some effects of taxes on forms of organization for overseas operations, "tax havens," and tax incentives for certain types of international operations.

LEVELS AND TYPES OF TAXATION

Since most international business operations are carried on by corporations, we are concerned with corporate taxes—primarily corporate income taxes. It should be made clear that in the final analysis corporations do not *pay* taxes—they only *collect* them.[1] Ultimately, *people* pay taxes. Corporations may collect taxes from customers by raising prices or from their stockholders by reducing dividends or by reducing retained earnings (thus leading to smaller capital gains for stockholders in most cases). They may also collect taxes, possibly, from their employees by bargaining with them for smaller wage

[1]This point is made very clearly by Robert Z. Aliber, *The International Money Game*, 2d ed. (New York: Basic Books, 1976), pp. 189–190.

increases than the employees might otherwise obtain. Most economists have argued that it is probable that *most* of the taxes imposed on corporations are collected from customers by raising prices. The theory of the incidence of corporate taxation is a complex and unsettled one, and fortunately we need not enter that morass. It should, however, be recognized that taxing corporations is not an *alternative* to taxing people, but a *means* of taxing people—and it may not be a very good means because we really are not certain which people we are taxing.

It might seem from the foregoing comments that corporations might be indifferent to taxes. But collecting taxes, however it occurs, is an onerous chore for them, and when taxes are raised they may have difficulties in determining the best means of making changes in their prices, wages, dividend policies, and retained earnings. Moreover, if a tax seems to affect one group of corporations more heavily than another, it is disadvantageous. Hence corporations are very much concerned about taxes, even though in the final analysis their customers, their stockholders, or their employees pay them.

Differences in Levels of Taxes

Corporations pay a great variety of taxes, including property taxes, payroll taxes, a capital tax on invested capital, stamp and registration taxes on such transactions as transfers of documents (including stock certificates) and of real estate, and taxes on registrations of agreements of various types. Many of these taxes are relatively small. If taxes are paid by all firms, they may be passed on to consumers in prices charged. Thus the major consideration is corporate income taxes and special forms of taxes such as the value-added tax (VAT), which is widely used in Europe.

It might appear that U.S. corporations have a heavier income tax burden than other corporations, and indeed in some respects this view is justified. Many industrialized countries have lower rates, grant more relief to those who receive dividends or give corporations credit for taxes paid by dividend recipients, and treat capital gains more generously than the United States does. Corporate taxes provide about one-sixth of U.S. tax revenue compared to less than 10 percent in major European countries.[2] Further, although total taxes of all kinds are a smaller percentage of GNP in the United States than in such countries, corporate taxes as a percent of GNP are higher. This is misleading, however, because European government spending constitutes a higher percent of GNP than does U.S. government spending and because corporations in Europe produce a smaller percentage of GNP—partly because more industry is government-owned in Europe.

Corporate income tax *rates* are higher in the United States than in most countries, currently being at 48 percent for most corporations; whereas in Europe they are generally in the 40 to 50 percent range. In some countries of Europe, such as Switzerland and Italy, they are significantly lower. There are some countries which have very high corporate income tax rates; India is an

[2]See ibid., pp. 185–192.

example. The rate is 55 percent for domestic corporations and for foreign companies which have made arrangements to pay dividends in India, and 70 percent for other foreign companies.

Many questions must be answered, however, before we can conclude that higher rates in any country represent a greater burden: Are definitions of taxable income the same; do countries permit more rapid depreciation, and therefore lower taxes as long as capital investment is growing; do they permit depreciation of replacement cost instead of historical cost; and are the tax rates actually paid the same as those on the tax schedules? It appears that the answers to these questions generally indicate that European taxes are lower in fact as well as in scheduled rates than those in the United States, but the difference in many cases may be no more than a few percentage points.

As indicated, it is generally presumed that in many cases corporations are able to raise prices to recoup taxes paid. A firm's position in international competition is weaker if it must raise prices more to offset higher taxes. But it is not likely that changes in tax rates have much impact on selling prices. Profits are a small percent of sales. Hence even a large increase in the tax rate would not result in a large change in selling prices. If firms have a ratio of profits to sales of 4 percent (approximately the average for U.S. firms), even the introduction of a 50 percent tax on profits would raise selling prices by only 4 percent if the tax were entirely passed on to consumers in the form of higher prices.[3]

LDCs frequently have lower rates of corporate income tax than developed countries. Their governments do not provide some of the services that governments provide in developed countries, and they have less need for tax revenue until development occurs and creates needs for added services. Lower corporate tax rates may induce foreign investment, which may aid in development. LDCs, in order to attract foreign investment, often provide "tax holidays" for the first few years. But their tax rates have been increasing. Since some countries, including the United States, tax foreign-earned income but reduce the tax by the amount of tax paid to foreign governments, there may be a reason for other governments to raise their tax levels to that established in the United States.[4] If companies are to be taxed at that rate in any event, governments may argue that they might as well obtain the revenue, instead of the U.S. government.

---

[3]Ibid., p. 190.

[4]There seems to be no international law preventing double taxation of income, once by the country in which a corporation is domiciled or chartered and again by a country in which income is earned. See Walter A. Slowinski, "United States Taxation of Foreign Source Income," in *Taxes and International Business* (New York: National Association of Manufacturers, 1965), p. 7. However, it is usual to permit credit for taxes paid to foreign governments, and some countries, such as the Netherlands, Belgium, and France, have exempted foreign-earned income from tax or taxed it at a lower rate. Some countries, such as the United Kingdom, Canada, Australia, and New Zealand, have based taxation on the location of control of a corporation rather than on its place of incorporation. Taxes are changing rapidly, and statements made in this chapter must be regarded as indications; the most recent regulations should be checked. A convenient source is the publications of the international accounting firms, some of which are mentioned in the suggested references, although even these may be out of date on occasion.

In spite of the differences in tax rates around the world, the probability that much of the corporate income tax is shifted to consumers through price increases, and the relatively small effect of tax differences on selling prices, suggest that the major differences causing the flow of world trade and investment are those in the distribution of factors of production of various types and qualities and the resulting differences in *costs*. More petroleum or a substitute for it as a source of energy *could* be produced in the United States, but the cost would be quite high under present conditions. Hence the United States continues to import a sizable fraction of the petroleum it consumes and has difficulty in formulating and agreeing upon an energy policy that would lead to greater self-sufficiency at higher cost. The higher cost of petroleum after 1973 meant a reduction in the attainable real standard of living. Contemplation of an even greater reduction in that standard causes hesitation in developing a policy which clearly will involve some sacrifice.

Differences in Types of Taxes

Differences in types of taxes may play some role in affecting world trade and investment. A popular tax in Europe in recent years has been the value-added tax (VAT).[5] This is a sales tax collected at each stage of production or distribution. Growers, manufacturers, wholesalers, and retailers each contribute some portion of the value (price) at which products are finally sold to consumers. This value-added tax has made a significant change in the European tax system. From the standpoint of international business operations, the most significant aspect is that, under rules of the General Agreement on Tariffs and Trade (GATT), such a tax may be rebated on exports and levied on imports; whereas direct taxes such as income taxes may not be rebated. VAT is neutral as between imported and home-produced goods, but to the extent that VAT has substituted for other taxes which might not be rebated, its rebate may make European exports more competitive in the United States. It must be recognized, of course, that the sales tax, used quite heavily by state and local governments in the United States, militates against imported goods that are dutiable, because it is levied on the selling price of the goods (including import duty). Thus it is not clear to what extent, if any, VAT may cause U.S. goods to be less competitive in Europe; nor is it clear to what extent if at all European goods may be more competitive in the United States.

[5]Various arguments have been used for the value-added tax. It is certainly preferable to some types of turnover tax, which force companies to integrate vertically to avoid taxes on taxes. It is relatively acceptable politically, and it cannot be avoided by such devices as large expense accounts or heavy interest on debt. It taxes unprofitable firms as much as profitable ones, forcing less profitable firms to improve or fail more quickly, thus probably improving economic allocation of resources. It is fairly easy to understand and collect. The major argument against it is that it is regressive: it taxes consumption and therefore bears more heavily on lower income individuals than on those with higher incomes. See Dan Throop Smith, "Value-Added Tax: the Case For," *Harvard Business Review*, November–December 1970, pp. 77–85; Richard W. Lindholm, "Toward a New Philosophy of Taxation," *Morgan Guaranty Survey*, January 1972, pp. 3–8; Stanley S. Surrey, "Value-Added Tax: the Case Against," *Harvard Business Review*, November–December 1970, pp. 86–94; and "The Trouble with the Value-Added Tax," *Business Week*, Apr. 17, 1971, p. 100.

TAX DIFFERENCES AND FORM OF CORPORATE ORGANIZATION

Tax differences are one factor which may be important in selecting a form of organization for overseas operations. Taxes affect foreign branches and foreign subsidiaries differently; hence these are considered separately.

Foreign Branches

Branches overseas are the simplest form of overseas operation, and the least complex from a tax viewpoint. Branch profits are fully taxed at the same rate as all corporate profits, and branch losses are fully deductible. Unfortunately for branch operations, some countries establish a relationship between a branch's profits and the profits of the total company, and tax branches on the basis of this relationship for a period of years until operations of the firm are reexamined by the foreign government. Thus if branch profits drop sharply, the tax may remain the same for a year or so in spite of the decline in profits.

Taxes paid to foreign countries by branches of U.S. firms operating abroad may be deducted from taxes paid by the parent companies to the U.S. government.

From a financial viewpoint, foreign branches have two disadvantages. First, if they incur more losses than they can absorb, the parent company itself suffers a loss. Second, the establishment of foreign branches often forces corporations to disclose to foreign governments financial details of their worldwide operations; whereas establishment of a foreign subsidiary would require disclosure of information on only that subsidiary.

Branches have a tax advantage, however, since if it is expected that they may incur losses the first few years of operation, consolidation of their losses with the profits of the parent company reduces the latter and therefore reduces taxes payable. When a branch becomes profitable, it may in some cases be desirable to transfer its assets to a foreign subsidiary corporation already established or established at the time of transfer. As indicated below, there are instances when a foreign subsidiary can defer tax on income not remitted in the form of dividends, although this possibility of tax deferral has been reduced in recent years.

Foreign Subsidiaries

For these and other reasons, multinational firms often conduct their overseas operations, or part of them, through the establishment of foreign subsidiaries. Because of the importance of U.S. firms among MNCs, we examine U.S. taxes on foreign corporate income.[6] Before 1962, there was a clear advantage in establishing foreign subsidiaries, because income from their operations was not

---

[6]For a lengthier discussion than is given here, see David K. Eiteman and Arthur I. Stonehill, *Multinational Business Finance* (Reading, Mass.: Addison-Wesley, 1973), pp. 152–159, selections reprinted from *Information Guide for U.S. Corporations Doing Business Abroad* (New York: Price Waterhouse, 1972).

taxed until remitted to the United States. Corporations could sharply reduce their taxes by establishing subsidiaries in countries with relatively low rates of taxation which taxed corporations only on income earned in the country of incorporation.

The purpose of the Revenue Act of 1962 with respect to foreign income was to tax income of foreign subsidiaries of U.S. firms when the income was earned, under certain conditions, regardless of whether or not the income was remitted to the United States in the form of dividends. Some argued that the United States had no right to tax income until received in the United States, but the opposing argument was that foreign subsidiaries often ask the U.S. government for help in case of, for example, threat of expropriation, and if help is justified so are taxes. A further purpose of the act was to tax certain income when earned, because deferment of realization and remittance of income reduced taxes in effect, even if the taxes were subsequently paid, because the funds could still be used to generate further earnings until the tax was paid. We next examine the specific provisions of the 1962 act.

CFCs   The Revenue Act of 1962 made important changes. In that act, a U.S.–controlled foreign corporation (CFC) was defined as one of which more than 50 percent of the voting stock was owned by U.S. stockholders (including corporations), each owning 10 percent or more of the total voting stock. Subsidiaries of the CFC are considered to be CFCs if more than 50 percent of the *value* of the equity is owned by U.S. residents (including corporations). A foreign subsidiary of a CFC might be deemed to be a CFC even if none of its voting stock were owned by the first CFC, provided that more than half its total stock (voting and nonvoting) were owned by the first CFC. Also, a U.S. corporation might own 90 percent of the total equity in a foreign subsidiary, but that subsidiary would not be considered a CFC for tax purposes unless the U.S. corporation owned more than 50 percent of the *voting* stock. However, a subsidiary of that subsidiary would be considered a CFC if the first subsidiary owned 55.6 percent or more of the total equity in the second subsidiary, because the U.S. corporation owns 90 percent of the equity in the first subsidiary, which in turn owns 55.6 percent of the equity in the second subsidiary, and 90 percent of 55.6 percent is more than half. Whether the first subsidiary is considered a CFC or not, taxes must be paid by the U.S. corporation on the income of the second subsidiary if the income is taxable.

Taxable Income of CFCs   Income of a CFC is taxable if its income in three designated categories exceeds 30 percent of its total income. If these categories of income exceed 70 percent of its total income, all its income is taxable. Between 30 percent and 70 percent, its income is taxed on the basis of the percentage of designated income to total income. The three categories of income are identified in the Internal Revenue Code in paragraphs designated by Subpart F, and hence this income is often termed Subpart F income. The three categories are: (1) foreign *personal* holding company income, including dividends, interest, oil lease rents, and gains from sale or exchange of securities or from trading in commodity futures; (2) foreign-based company *sales* income, including profits, commissions, and other income on purchases and sales; and (3) income from technical, managerial, scientific, engineering, commercial, or other services performed *outside* the CFC's country of incorporation. Income taxable under Subpart F is treated as if it were income distributed to the shareholder or shareholders (the parent company or the individual owners) as dividends.

A foreign corporation is a personal holding company if more than half its stock is owned directly or indirectly by or for not more than 5 individuals who are U.S. citizens or permanent residents; or if at least 60 percent of gross income the first year and 50 percent in subsequent years is foreign personal holding company income.

Sales of goods to customers in the country of incorporation of a CFC are *not* considered as foreign-based company sales income, nor are services performed in the country of incorporation. If an MNC establishes subsidiaries in all the foreign countries in which it does business, it may thereby escape U.S. taxes on income earned from sales in all those countries unless income is remitted as dividends or interest.

Figure 17-1 is intended to clarify the concepts of CFCs and of taxable income of CFCs.

Subpart F income from investments in LDCs could be excluded and not reported if that income was reinvested in the LDC.[7] There were also certain exclusions for income from shipping and for export trade income. The latter is discussed later in this chapter.

U.S. corporations which own CFCs may avoid an immediate tax on part of their income from the CFCs if the CFCs distribute some required percentage of their income. This is because, as indicated above, the law was intended to penalize deferment of realization of income. The required percentage to be distributed depends on the relationship between the income tax rate in the country of incorporation of a CFC and the U.S. tax rate. If the foreign tax rate is as high as the U.S. tax rate, no distribution is necessary to avoid immediate tax.

Credit for Foreign Income Tax Paid   The income which may be subject to U.S. income tax is foreign income *before* taxes. Companies are given credit,

---

[7]For tax purposes, Executive Order 11071, Dec. 27, 1962, defined LDCs as all countries *except* (1) countries within the Sino-Soviet bloc; (2) Australia, Austria, Belgium, Canada, Denmark, France, Federal Republic of Germany (West Germany), Hong Kong, Italy, Japan, Liechtenstein, Luxembourg, Monaco, Netherlands, New Zealand, Norway, Union of South Africa, San Marino, Spain, Sweden, Switzerland, and the United Kingdom; (3) overseas territories of countries other than those within the Sino-Soviet bloc; and (4) the United States, Puerto Rico, and U.S. possessions. For purposes of that order, countries within the Sino-Soviet bloc were defined as Albania, Bulgaria, mainland China, Cuba, Czechoslovakia, Hungary, North Korea, Outer Mongolia, Poland, Rumania, East Germany and the Soviet sector of Berlin, Tibet, the U.S.S.R., and "any part of Vietnam which is dominated or controlled by international communism." Estonia, Latvia, and Lithuania were also listed as countries within the Sino-Soviet bloc.

Figure 17-1 CFCs and Taxable Income of CFCs.

Foreign companies owned by U.S. residents (individuals or corporations) are designated as CFCs if:

1 More than 50 percent of the total voting stock is owned by U.S. residents (individuals or corporations), each owning at least 10 percent.

2 They are subsidiaries or sub-subsidiaries of companies owned at least partly by U.S. residents, if more than 50 percent of the value of the total equity (voting plus nonvoting stock) is owned by U.S. residents.

Thus if a U.S. firm owned 49 percent of the voting stock of a foreign company and 95 percent of the nonvoting stock, and if the value of the voting stock were 10 percent of total equity value and that of the nonvoting stock 90 percent of total equity value, the subsidiary, although largely owned by the U.S. firm, would not be a CFC.

If that subsidiary itself had a subsidiary of which it owned 60 percent of the total equity, that sub-subsidiary would be a CFC, because the U.S. firm would own 90.4 percent of the total value of the subsidiary, which in turn would own 60 percent of the sub-subsidiary, so that the U.S. parent firm would own 90.4 percent of 60 percent of the sub-subsidiary—54.24 percent, or more than 50 percent.

Income of CFCs is taxable if:

1 It is foreign personal holding company income, including unearned income such as dividends, interest, oil lease rents, and gains from the sale or exchange of securities or from trading in commodity futures.

2 It is foreign-based company sales income, including profits, commissions, and other income derived from buying and selling goods; however, (a) transactions in which a related (controlled) corporation is not a party and (b) transactions carried out entirely in the country of incorporation are excluded.

3 It is foreign-based company service income, including income from performance of technical, managerial, engineering, scientific, commercial or other services for a related person (or company) and outside the country of incorporation.

4 Such income is at least 30 percent of the total income of the foreign-based company.

If such income is 70 percent or more of the total income, all income of the company is taxed; if it is between 30 percent and 70 percent, tax is based on the percentage.

however, for income tax paid to foreign countries, dollar for dollar, up to the amount of the U.S. tax. When corporations receive dividends from foreign subsidiaries, they pay taxes on the gross dividends, including any taxes withheld by the foreign country; but the withheld taxes are credited against the tax otherwise to be paid. Corporations may also, if they own 10 percent or more of a subsidiary, credit a portion of the subsidiary's earnings as taxes *deemed* as paid by the subsidiary. The portion is the ratio of the dividend to the profits of the subsidiary. In the case of subsidiaries incorporated in the LDCs, the profits used in the calculation may be profits before taxes, resulting in a lower ratio of dividend to profits and hence in a lower tax deemed to have been paid; but the tax deemed paid is *not* included in the income on which U.S. tax is paid, and hence if tax rates in LDCs are relatively low, less U.S. tax is paid.

Assume a fully owned foreign subsidiary in a developed country, and assume that withholding tax is 10 percent of dividends paid. Then the income to be taxed is the before-tax income of the subsidiary. Direct credit is given for the tax withheld, and indirect credit for the ratio of dividends paid to after-tax income times the amount of tax paid in the foreign country. The dividends plus the direct credit plus the indirect credit equal the taxable income. The indirect credit is not available if the parent company owns less than 10 percent of the subsidiary.

The general effect of the foreign tax credit provisions is to limit the combined U.S. and foreign tax paid to the U.S. rate or the foreign rate, whichever is higher. If the foreign rate is higher, which is rather unusual, some "excess foreign tax paid" is available to carry back or forward to other years or to average out with other foreign taxes for the same year.

Capital Gains on Sales of Ownership in CFCs   Although in the U.S. tax system, capital gains are taxed at a lower rate than other income if assets have been held more than a specified period (formerly 6 months, but changed to one year), the Revenue Act of 1962 provided that part of the capital gain on sale of an interest in a CFC is treated as ordinary income if the interest is greater than 10 percent. The seller is taxed at the regular income tax rate on the amount of the share (percentage interest in the company) of accumulated profits which could have been received during the period the ownership interest was held. Any excess gain is taxed as long-term capital gain.

Allocation of Income and Expenses   Under Section 482 of the Internal Revenue Code, the Internal Revenue Service may allocate income and expenses among firms owned or controlled by the same interests if this is necessary to prevent evasion of taxes or to reflect clearly the proper allocation of income and therefore of tax. This provision has raised some difficult questions. For example, is research carried on in the United States by a parent company an expense of that company or is it in part an expense of foreign subsidiaries of that company which also benefit from the research? Charging the research as an expense of the parent company reduces U.S. income tax; charging part of it as an expense of foreign subsidiaries increases U.S. income tax and reduces tax on income of the subsidiaries, but the latter is usually credited against the U.S. tax liability.

DOUBLE TAXATION OF CORPORATE INCOME

Tax treaties between countries mitigate or remove the liability of taxpayers, including corporations, for double taxation of foreign income—that is, for being taxed on the same income both in the country of origin and in the country in which the person or corporation resides or has its headquarters. However, the degree to which such tax treaties actually result in total elimination of double taxation may be affected by the characteristics of tax systems operating in different countries. Countries use three basic methods of taxing income paid out as dividends and income held as retained earnings. These have been termed the independent entity method (sometimes called the classical method), the split rate or double rate method, and the dividend credit or imputation method.

Under the independent entity method, the same rate of tax is applied to distributed and to retained profits, and profits distributed as dividends are separately taxed as income received by stockholders. Under this system distributed profits are in effect taxed twice. This is the system used domestically in the United States.

The split rate system applies a lower rate of tax to distributed profits than to retained earnings, and dividends are then taxed separately as income of stockholders. In Germany the rate on undistributed income has been 51 percent and the rate on distributed income 15 percent, for corporations with unrestricted tax liability. Japan has taxed undistributed income at 40 percent and distributed income at 30 percent.[8]

Under the dividend credit or imputation system, the same rate of tax is applied to distributed as to undistributed profits, and dividends are taxed as income of stockholders, but double taxation is eliminated by allowing the tax paid on distributed profits as a credit against tax payable on total corporate profits. France, which followed the principle of territoriality, taxing income only when it was realized in France, permitted 95% of the dividends from a subsidiary company generally to be excluded from taxable income of the parent company. Since dividends from many corporations must be "grossed up" by 50 percent for the credit, tax is actually paid on $7^1/_2$ percent of the dividends. France also taxed long-term capital gains at only 10 percent.

Thus individual companies find the amount of their total tax liability is affected by the systems of taxation found in host countries, even though tax treaties enable them to credit tax paid on income abroad against their tax liability in their home countries. In particular, it is possible that MNCs may be at a disadvantage because of double incidence of withholding taxes— subsidiaries' dividends to parent companies being subjected to withholding taxes in foreign countries and dividends paid by parent companies to stockholders being subjected to withholding taxes in home countries. Even when all the tax on corporate profits and of the foreign withholding tax can be removed by means of a credit against the parent company's domestic tax liability, as is the case for American multinational firms, there may be adverse side effects on cash flows of the organization as a whole since tax credits at home are dependent on *prior* tax liabilities abroad. Against this possibility, of course, there may be set the cash flow advantages which can accrue to MNCs that establish subsidiaries in all the countries where they do business. Many of these countries have lower rates of corporate tax than the United States. To the extent that companies escape the U.S. tax on income earned through operations in those countries, as noted above, they are of course free to use the funds for further investment in operations of their foreign subsidiaries. When such profits are remitted to the United States they become subject to tax. The ability to *delay* the time at which profits are subject to U.S. tax is a considerable

---

[8]See, for example, the publications of Ernst & Ernst and of Haskins and Sells referred to in the suggested references.

benefit. Even though the ultimate tax liability of an MNC may closely approximate that of a domestic corporation with a comparable profit record, the cash flow implications for each may be quite different.

It is clear that accountants and tax lawyers often must be consulted to determine the most advantageous conditions, especially in complex cases. The financial manager in overseas operations should understand the general rules sufficiently to know the basis for decisions and to recognize situations when consultation is desirable.

TAXES ON BANKS

The general rules for taxation of income of banks are similar to those for the taxation of nonfinancial corporations, although there are many details which may change the precise tax liability.

Banks, however, are subject to a special limitation which has the effect of a tax in reducing their income.[9] Banks are permitted to create money, and the cost of creating money is quite small. Creating money is a valuable privilege. For this privilege, banks are limited in other ways. Since they have in effect a monopoly on the creation of money in the form of demand deposits, although thrift institutions in the United States are now beginning to intrude on this monopoly, it might be expected that they could have high profits. They do not have unusually high profits, however. One reason is that they are subject to reserve requirements, which force them to keep certain percentages of their assets in nonearning form (cash in vault, deposits in Federal Reserve Banks, or in some cases deposits in correspondent banks). Central banks use the required reserves as leverage points to control the money supply by raising or reducing *actual* reserves above or below the required level. For this purpose any level of reserve requirement somewhat above zero would be adequate. Or banks could be permitted to place these assets in some form on which they could earn interest.

Banking is more mobile than most industries, and with the development of electronic funds transfer systems, banks will be able to deal with customers almost anywhere in the world. This is obviously true for large loan customers. It can also be true for depositors, however. Banks may establish offices which do not maintain deposit accounts but seek deposits of individuals for their parent banks. Thereafter communications between depositors and banks through some means of rapid communication such as telephones can provide all services depositors may desire. Taxing banks more heavily in one country than in another, or imposing heavier reserve requirements, may make them less competitive. More customers may turn to banks in countries where banks are taxed less or have lower reserve requirements.

It is not necessarily implied that banks, which are in effect taxed more heavily because they must meet higher reserve requirements, make less profit.

[9]This is emphasized by Aliber, op. cit., pp. 196–197.

There may be sufficient competition to force profits to a competitive level, in which case profits cannot be lower or banks will cease to operate. On the other hand, there are some reasons for arguing that since entry into banking is limited, banks may have a degree of monopoly. The evidence of high monopoly profits is not very convincing, it must be admitted. But even if banks do not enjoy monopoly profits, higher reserve requirements mean more nonearning assets and hence necessitate higher interest rate charges on loans to provide the same interest income on assets. Banks in countries with lower reserve requirements may be able to charge lower interest rates on loans, and in fact we found in Chapter 10 that this is part of the reason for the growth of the Eurodollar market. Of course, banks having high reserve requirements might charge higher interest on loans and pay higher interest rates on deposits, making the same profit margin, but Regulation Q in the United States limits interest paid on time deposits, and payment of interest on demand deposits has been prohibited. This also has been a contributing factor in the growth of the Eurodollar market.

TAX TREATIES

In the early 1970s, the United States had tax treaties with nearly two dozen countries, including the major industrialized countries where tax rates are relatively high and therefore likely to be more burdensome. Foreign tax credits avoid double taxation to some extent, but tax treaties may allocate certain types of income to be taxed by certain countries, making it unnecessary for such income to be reported in other countries. They may also reduce or eliminate withholding taxes on income, which are likely to be burdensome because they are imposed on gross income and may be far greater than the tax finally levied on net income.

If there were no tax treaties, income of exporters who sell to customers in foreign countries might be taxed by the foreign countries on the ground that the exporter is doing business there. This is especially likely if the exporter maintains warehouses or other facilities. Business firms which do not have what is termed a "permanent establishment" in a foreign country may be exempted from taxation by tax treaties. It is important for firms to determine whether they meet the conditions for exemption.

Treaties usually reduce withholding taxes on dividends and often eliminate withholding taxes on interest and royalties. The U.S. normal withholding rate of 30 percent on certain payments to nonresidents is often reduced to 15 percent on dividends and eliminated on interest and royalties. In the absence of a tax treaty, operation of a branch may be more advantageous than operation of a foreign subsidiary, for which withholding taxes on dividends remitted and interest paid to the parent company might be high.

Treaties also usually exempt individuals from taxation in a country if they are in that country temporarily, say for 6 months. This is useful for employees sent on temporary assignments only.

Treaties negotiated with LDCs sometimes have tax incentives for U.S. investors, in the form of a 7 percent tax credit on the amount of U.S. investment by an enterprise in the LDC.

TAX MORALITY

There is of course the question of tax morality. In some countries firms do not pay full tax rates because they do not declare all their income, or because they reduce tax payments in other ways. Corporations operating in those countries must decide whether to make full disclosure or to attempt some tax evasion, even if minor.[10] Tax evasion occurs in all countries, but is undoubtedly more widespread in some countries than in others. Small efforts to avoid taxes or to obtain favors, such as the *mordida* (little bite) in Latin America, *baksheesh* in the Middle East, or the *pot de vin* (jug of wine) in France may be so embedded in cultures that they are difficult to eliminate. Infractions of foreign laws are not infractions of U.S. laws, but the Internal Revenue Service can attempt to eliminate any illegal spending abroad from tax deductions claimed in the United States.

SUBSIDIARIES IN TAX HAVENS

In some countries taxes on corporations are low. These countries are not among the major industrialized countries, and operations there are not large. They can, however, be used as tax havens by shifting income to subsidiaries located in them. This can be done through what is known as *transfer pricing*—the pricing of goods or services by a company to its affiliates. By varying the prices charged and paid, companies can shift a larger part of their incomes to affiliates in tax havens. Switzerland, Curacao, Panama, Kuwait, the Bahamas, Liechtenstein, and other small countries have served as tax havens.[11]

Why Tax Havens Exist

From a financial standpoint, in addition to having relatively low tax rates on corporate income or sales income and a low dividend withholding tax on income paid out to stockholders, a tax haven must have a stable government, facilities necessary for financial services (including good communications facilities), and a stable currency so that funds accumulated in the tax haven can be remitted to the parent corporation or elsewhere without restriction.[12]

If tax havens become important enough to cause serious losses of income to governments, more effort will be devoted to reducing their availability. The

[10]For reasons why businesses need not feel, "when in Rome, do as the Romans do," see Thomas Griffith, "Payoff is not 'Accepted Practice,'" *Fortune*, August 1975, pp. 122–125, 200–205.

[11]See Roger Beardwood, "Sophistication Comes to the Tax Havens," *Fortune*, February 1969, pp. 95–98, 173–174, 178.

[12]See the further discussion in David K. Eiteman and Arthur I. Stonehill, op. cit., pp. 150–151.

mobility of some sources of income is such, however, that it is unlikely that all tax havens can be eliminated. Tax havens are valuable to their governments because, although they have lower taxes than other countries, their taxes are high enough to more than compensate them for the services they provide for subsidiaries operating there.

Tax Havens and Offshore Funds

In the late 1960s, much interest was aroused by what were termed offshore funds. Offshore funds were intended to attract investors, other than Americans, to invest in American stocks. They were generally incorporated in tax haven countries, to limit the taxes they would have to pay. It was stated that they did not sell securities to U.S. citizens.

The success of the offshore funds was the result of rising prices (until about 1968) in the U.S. stock market; inadequacy in European capital markets, which could not provide investors with investments that would induce them to purchase securities; the ingenuity of some of the creators of the funds (Bernie Cornfeld, who established Investors Overseas Services, is the outstanding example); and the general attractiveness to foreigners of investing in the United States. The existence of tax havens in which many of these funds could incorporate was probably simply a fortunate accident for them.

Another fortunate development for them was the Foreign Investors Tax Act of 1966, which reduced taxes for foreign investors in U.S. securities, under certain conditions, on income generated in the United States.

Economic prosperity in West Germany, and West Germany's BOP surplus, also helped the offshore funds. Germany was, as a result, glad to see some of the BOP surplus used for investment in the United States. That was preferable to larger increases in foreign exchange holdings, which increased the base of the money supply and tended to cause inflation in West Germany.

Many of the offshore funds suffered heavily in the wake of the decline in the U.S. stock market after 1967.[13] Ineffective management or manipulations contributed to the downfall of some. This somewhat disillusioned Europeans who had invested in the United States. But the inflation which began in 1965; the following of accounting rules which hid the decline of corporate profits; and the rise in interest rates, which increased the discount rate for present values of expected earnings on stocks, were major causes of the difficulties of all mutual funds.

TAX INCENTIVES FOR SPECIAL CORPORATIONS

Governments have sometimes decided that they should encourage certain forms of business activity in certain areas by reducing taxes. For U.S. firms, three situations are discussed briefly in this section to indicate the general nature of these incentives as they apply to international business activities.

---

[13]Philip Siekman, "The Offshore Funds are in Dangerous Waters," *Fortune*, August 1970, pp. 118–120, 158–160.

Western Hemisphere Trade Corporations (WHTCs)

To encourage American businesses to trade with and/or locate in LDCs in the Western Hemisphere, special tax incentives were provided for businesses which carry on trade almost exclusively in that area. In general, these reduce the maximum tax rate on corporate income from 48 percent to about 34 percent.[14]

Western Hemisphere Trade Corporations (WHTCs) must be domestic U.S. corporations; they must conduct all their business in the Western Hemisphere; they must obtain at least 95 percent of their gross income from sources outside the United States; and they must obtain at least 90 percent of their gross income from the conduct of trade or business. Note that these companies may trade in the United States as well as in the rest of the Western Hemisphere, but only 5 percent or less of their income may be derived in the United States.

There have been cases, such as that of Eli Lilly, in which corporations or their subsidiaries sold to their WHTC subsidiaries at transfer prices which did not allow for profits—thus channeling income into the WHTCs for taxation at lower rates. In the Lilly case the Internal Revenue Service reallocated income to Eli Lilly and the Court of Claims Commissioner rejected the company's refund suit for the resulting additional taxes.

Domestic International Sales Corporations (DISCs)

Because of a desire to increase U.S. exports as the 1970s began, the Revenue Act of 1971 provided special taxation for Domestic International Sales Corporations (DISCs).[15] Because U.S. subsidiaries operating abroad can defer tax on undistributed income as described earlier in this chapter, there was thought to be an incentive to produce abroad instead of exporting. As imports began to exceed exports, tax provisions were devised to encourage export firms.

DISCs could be established as special companies; at least 95 percent of gross receipts of such companies had to consist of "qualified export receipts" and at least 95 percent of year-end assets had to be "qualified export assets." Qualified export receipts were defined as income from exports, receipts from lease of export property for use by lessees outside the United States, and certain related income. Qualified export assets were defined as export property—property produced in the United States and held for export, assets used in connection with exporting, and accounts receivable arising from exports, plus working capital reasonably needed for operations. DISCs were not taxed, but it was assumed that 50 percent of their income was distributed to

---

[14]For detailed information on this and other special tax incentives, see, for example, *Information Guide for U.S. Corporations Doing Business Abroad* (New York: Price Waterhouse, 1972).

[15]For a brief article, see Robert Feinschreiber, "DISC: A New Export Tax Incentive," *Financial Executive*," April 1972, pp. 66–70.

stockholders (generally parent firms), which were taxed on actual or assumed distribution. Rather complex rules were established to govern intercompany pricing so that companies operating in the United States could not use transfer pricing to shift income to affiliated DISCs and thus escape taxes.

DISCs were permitted to lend their tax deferred income (termed tax deferred because the tax would be paid by stockholders if the DISCs were liquidated or if they no longer qualified as DISCs) to parent manufacturing companies to finance increases in U.S. exports. Rather complex rules governed such loans, to make it likely that the funds would indeed generate increases in U.S. exports. In most cases a DISC is owned by one corporation, usually a large firm.

A study by the U.S. Treasury Department concluded that DISCs have considerably increased U.S. exports. But another study by the Library of Congress Staff began by assuming that DISCs could increase exports only if the tax saving were "passed through" to foreign buyers, reducing prices on sales to them. The extent of increase in exports was assumed to depend on the price elasticity of foreign demand for U.S. products. Thus it is questionable whether the revenue lost by the Treasury was offset by enough benefit to justify existence of DISCs.

Members of GATT other than the United States have been critical of DISCs from the beginning. When GATT was established, it was presumed by economists that indirect taxes such as sales taxes were passed on to consumers but that direct taxes, such as corporate income taxes, were not. On that presumption a sales tax (including VAT) would raise prices on all goods on which it was levied, but a corporate income tax would not. European members of GATT argued that VAT is neutral between imports and home-produced goods: all goods sold within a country, whether home-produced or imported, are taxed. If it were assumed that VAT was passed on to consumers, the rebate of VAT on exports was not a subsidy, but merely omission of a tax levied on domestic consumers but obviously not levied on foreign consumers. However, VAT often substituted for a corporate income tax or part of it, and in that case the rebate of a tax on exports, which had substituted for one which could not be rebated, constituted in effect a subsidy.

Since the time of the formation of GATT, the theory of the incidence of taxation has changed. Some economists always argued that corporate income taxes are largely passed on to consumers in the form of higher prices, and in recent years evidence has indicated that is probably true.[16] If so, rebates of VAT and reductions in corporate income tax would stand on the same footing. Nevertheless, a committee of GATT in late 1976 concluded that DISCs were contrary to GATT rules, while VAT presumably was not.

Under floating exchange rates there is less reason for the United States or any country to provide export incentives. If such incentives are needed, a

---

[16]See, for example, M. Kryzniak and R. A. Musgrave, *The Shifting of the Corporate Income Tax* (Baltimore: Johns Hopkins, 1963).

downward float of the exchange value of the currency may achieve the result of increasing exports. Moreover, it may be that export subsidies subsidize some exports at the expense of others, thus being a cost to the public for no benefit. Under floating exchange rates, if U.S. exports increase, so does demand for dollars by foreigners, to pay for those exports. Such an increase in demand causes the value of the dollar to rise, discouraging all U.S. exports to some extent.

These doubts about the desirability of DISCs combined with the opposition of other GATT member countries cast doubt on their continuation. Some reports indicated that Congress was likely to eliminate DISCs.[17]

Other Special Cases

Before DISCs were authorized, some tax reductions were granted to Export Trade Corporations. Subpart F income of a CFC which expanded its exports of U.S. products was reduced by a part of the firm's export trade income. The benefits were also provided for Less Developed Country Corporations which obtained most of their income from LDCs and had most of their assets in such countries. Place of incorporation was not a determining factor.

Tax benefits are also available for corporations which carry on most of their activity in U.S. possessions. Income earned by such corporations is not subject to tax on income earned outside the United States unless the income is received in the United States.

Evaluation of the Incentives

There has been much argument concerning the merits of these special provisions, especially those for DISCs. We evaluate such provisions in the light of BOP, exchange rate, and capital movement theory developed earlier.

If rates of inflation among industrialized countries are roughly comparable, exchange rates can be fixed but adjustable, and there will be no need for special incentives for exports. Adjustments in exchange rates will be necessary when changes in productivity have accumulated enough so that one or more countries are significantly more competitive with other countries than they have been in the past. If rates of inflation vary significantly, exchange rates must float or par values must be adjusted frequently.

Under floating rates exchange risk is increased, and the volume of world trade and investment is presumably reduced from levels it would otherwise attain. If floating rates are accepted, there is no need for export incentives.

If the adverse effect of floating rates on world trade and investment is deemed sufficient to restore fixed but adjustable exchange rates, export incentives still serve no purpose that cannot be better accomplished by competitive efforts to improve efficiency. If efficiency cannot be increased as rapidly in some countries as in others, exchange rates may from time to time have to be adjusted.

[17]*Wall Street Journal*, Jan. 5, 1977, p. 1.

Since trade and investment are based on the principle of comparative advantage, there is no need to worry about a country being priced out of many markets, because it is still advantageous for it to sell (export) those goods and services in which it has the least comparative disadvantage. Only if one country or one group of countries had an *equal* comparative advantage in all products would we need to be concerned about loss of markets by other countries, and this situation seems very unlikely.

WITHHOLDING TAXES AND FINANCE SUBSIDIARIES

Since many countries require withholding of taxes on payments of interest and dividends to foreign individuals or corporations, there are advantages in establishing corporations—finance subsidiaries—to advance funds and receive interest and dividends in such a manner as to minimize withholding taxes. In the United States, for example, a finance subsidiary need not withhold income tax on its interest and dividend receipts if less than 20 percent of its income is derived from activities within the United States. Hence a foreign-based subsidiary may be used to finance foreign activities and subsidiaries. On the other hand, if funds are borrowed for use in financing activities in the United States, they may be borrowed from a domestic financing subsidiary or from one established in, say, the Netherlands Antilles; treaty provisions exempt interest payments to the United States from the Netherlands Antilles from withholding. Any interest payments from finance subsidiaries abroad to subsidiaries in other countries would, of course, be subject to withholding taxes in various countries, depending on treaties with those countries.

TAXATION OF FOREIGN FIRMS IN THE UNITED STATES

A foreign corporation carrying on business activities in the United States is taxed at the U.S. tax rate on corporate income. This prevents the creation of foreign subsidiaries by U.S. firms to carry on business in the United States, and taxes foreign corporations' income from activities in the United States at the same rate as for domestic corporations operating here.

Foreign companies operating in the United States are taxed only on income received from U.S. sources. Moreover, when provided by a tax treaty, they are taxed only if they operate "permanent establishments." A draft convention of the OECD defined permanent establishment negatively, by indicating what types of operations should not be considered as permanent establishments, and the United States has begun to use this definition. The maintenance of inventory solely for storage, display, or delivery; holding goods only for processing by another enterprise; and having a place of business only for buying goods or for collecting information are *not* counted as maintenance of a permanent establishment. Aliens and foreign corporations not engaged in business in the United States but receiving income in the form of dividends, interest, rents, or royalties are taxed at 30 percent of the income, or at a lower rate if negotiated by a tax treaty. Corporations chartered in the United States may credit against their U.S. tax the income tax, or tax in lieu of income tax, paid to a foreign country.

SUMMARY

Although there are many types of taxes, those which seem likely to influence the volume and value of international trade and investment are primarily corporate income taxes and, in the case of banks, reserve requirements which are similar to a tax. Since corporations ultimately only *collect* taxes, there is a presumption that the corporate income tax is inherently a poor tax, but it is widely used; hence the arguments for and against its use are somewhat academic. In any event, they are not our concern in this book.

We noted in the preceding chapter that inflation together with the accounting methods now generally used tends to increase corporate income taxes and hence to slow the growth of business activity by somewhat reducing business saving. The reduction shows up in smaller amounts of retained earnings. We also noted that there are recommendations, such as those of the Sandilands Committee in the United Kingdom, to change accounting practices to replacement value accounting. This change would permit better distinction between profits from productive efforts and those resulting from changes in asset values during inflation. Income taxes would also be reduced if such accounting were accepted for tax purposes.

Although inflation and accounting methods have a significant effect on reported profits, it does not appear that differences in levels of taxation have very significant effects on volume or direction of world trade and investment.

Taxation is, of course, important to particular firms, and may be very significant for a choice between the establishment of branches or of subsidiaries, as well as for locations of branches and subsidiaries.

Reserve requirements affect bank profits, but the changing technology of money transfers is likely to enlarge the geographic area in which banks compete, and banks may be able to induce customers to come to them. In theory, there is no reason why the market area for any medium-sized or large bank could not be the world or a large part of it. Major determinants of the competitive position of banks are likely to be size, efficiency, and association with a desired currency (the U.S. dollar?), rather than taxes or restrictions. The conflict between the economic thrust toward a more competitive world economy and the political effort to maintain national differences, including those in fiscal and monetary policies, is nowhere clearer than in international banking.

Tax havens have had some importance in attracting firms to establish subsidiaries for tax reasons. The importance of tax havens has, however, been diminished by changes in tax laws. It is likely that, if tax havens seem important to major governments, further tax law modifications will occur.

An interesting special case of tax incentives is provided by the authorization of DISCs to encourage U.S. exports. Fundamental theory tells us that the most important long-run determinant of exchange rates is purchasing power parity. However, since capital movements are important in BOPs, short-run values of exchange rates are heavily influenced by expected rates, and in an efficient foreign exchange market this means that short-term changes in exchange rates are probably random—unpredictable. Thus although a currency such as the U.S. dollar may fluctuate in value in the short run, its value in the long run is determined primarily by U.S. fiscal and monetary policy. Unless such policies result in rapid inflation in the United States relative to inflation in other countries, the dollar is likely to be the preferred currency in the long run. Small trade deficits would be offset by foreign investment in the United States.

The importance of different tax systems would increase significantly only if the trend toward world economic integration resulted in drastic reduction in barriers to the mobility of capital and labor. Movements of capital and labor would reduce cost differences, which are now the major factor in trade. The reduction of cost differences would make tax differences more important. Under present conditions, tax differences are of some significance to individual firms, but do not appear to be a major determinant of the volume, direction, or rate of growth of world trade and investment.

QUESTIONS FOR DISCUSSION

1 Do you agree that differences in tax rates among countries are not likely to have very much effect on the total volume or direction of world trade and investment? Why or why not?

2 Why do you think the U.S. government restricted the provisions permitting deferral of tax on income not remitted to the United States, with certain exceptions?

3 Why may reserve requirements be regarded as the equivalent of a tax on banks? Aren't reserve requirements needed to meet liquidity needs? Since they provide no tax revenue, what arguments are there for maintaining reserve requirements?

4 On the basis of the discussion in the chapter, what future do you anticipate for tax havens? Are they likely to proliferate? Why or why not?

5 In your opinion, is it likely that another development like the spread of the offshore mutual funds in the late 1960s may occur in the future? What are the significant conditions which could give rise to such a development?

6 There has been much argument about the desirability of continuing legislation providing tax incentives for DISCs. Why?

7 What is the importance of the changing technology of money transfers for international banking? What effect may it have on taxation of banks, and on general legislation restricting activities of foreign banks?

8 What effect is the spread of multinational firms and the internationalization of banks and public accounting firms likely to have on international accounting, and what feedback effect is this in turn likely to have on international business and finance?

9 The statement is made in the text that short-run values of exchange rates are heavily influenced by expected rates and that in an efficient foreign exchange market this means that short-term changes in exchange rates are probably unpredictable. Explain exactly why you do or do not agree.

10 Evaluate the following statement. Monetary and fiscal policy determine inflation,

inflation determines exchange rates in the long run, and if inflation were moderate or negligible in major countries, long-run relative levels of exchange rates would change very little. Hence there is little need for tax incentive to encourage exports.

PROBLEMS

1 Assume that a fully owned foreign subsidiary located in a developed country has taxable income in that country of $100 million. Assume that the rate of income tax there is 40 percent and that dividends of $20 million were declared. Assume that the withholding tax rate for dividends is 10 percent. How much tax would the parent company owe to the U.S. government on the subsidiary's income?

2 Approximately how much tax would be owed under tax laws in effect in the early 1970s if the subsidiary in problem 1 were located in an LDC, received 80 percent or more of its income in LDCs, and used 80 percent or more of its assets in LDCs?

3 How much tax would be owed if the subsidiary were located in a developed country in which the tax rate was 48 percent (the same as the U.S. rate at that time)?

4 Does the value-added tax (VAT), if any, paid by a subsidiary count as income tax paid? Explain.

5 What tax and tax-related factors might a company consider in deciding whether to operate a foreign activity as a branch or as a subsidiary?

6 How much tax would an individual pay if he sold for $150,000 a 10 percent interest in a CFC which he had purchased 3 years earlier for $100,000? Assume that profits of the CFC in the 3-year period were $30,000 for the 3 years in total, and that the individual's margin income tax rate is 42 percent.

7 Suppose that a parent company formed a DISC subsidiary. Explain how the parent company and the DISC might avoid almost permanently paying tax on the half of the DISC's earnings not taxed immediately.

8 A finance subsidiary incorporated outside the United States need not withhold income tax on interest or dividend payments provided that it derives less than 20 percent of its gross income outside the United States (hence such subsidiaries are often called *80-20 corporations*). Explain the situations in which use of such a subsidiary would be advantageous.

SUGGESTED REFERENCES

A good brief treatment of taxation of international business may be found in Harold J. Heck, *The International Business Investment: A Management Guide* (New York: American Management Association, 1969), Chap. 9, "Taxation of International Business."

Standard references on U.S. taxation of foreign income include Lawrence B. Krause and Kenneth W. Dam, *Federal Tax Treatment of Foreign Income* (Washington, D.C.: The Brookings Institution, 1964) and Peggy B. Musgrave, *United States Taxation of Foreign Investment Income* (Cambridge, Mass.: International Tax Program, Harvard Law School, 1969). See also Michael J. McIntyre, *United States Taxation of Foreign Income with Special Emphasis on Private Investments in Developing Countries* (Cambridge, Mass.: International Tax Program, Harvard Law School, 1975) and the article by J. Peter Gaskins, "Taxation of Foreign Source Income," *Financial Analysts Journal*, September/October 1973, pp. 55–64.

A review of the impact of taxes on foreign operations is found in Paul Seghers, *Tax Considerations in Organizing Foreign Operations* (New York: American Management Association, 1967).

Details on taxes for firms engaged in international business may be found in booklets issued by major accounting firms; an example is the *Information Guide for U.S. Corporations Doing Business Abroad*, Price Waterhouse. General features of tax systems in various major countries may be found in booklets prepared by these firms; examples are Haskins and Sells, *International Tax and Business Service*, loose leaf, by country for major countries, and Ernst & Ernst, *International Business Series*, booklets for individual major countries.

For a brief discussion of VAT, see C. Lowell Harriss, "Value-Added Taxation," *Columbia Journal of World Business*, July–August 1971, pp. 78–86. Harriss was somewhat favorable toward VAT. For detailed discussion of VAT as applied in Brazil and as it might be applied in other LDCs, see Michele Guerard, "The Brazilian State Value-Added Tax." IMF *Staff Papers*, March 1973, pp. 118–169; and George E. Lent, Milka Casanegra, and Michele Guerard, "The Value-Added Tax in Developing Countries," IMF *Staff Papers*, July 1973, pp. 318–378.

On international finance subsidiaries, see Herbert C. Rosenberg and Stuart P. Singer, "Selecting an International Finance Subsidiary: A Review of Available Methods," *Journal of Taxation*, May 1969, pp. 296–298.

On the purpose of legislation permitting establishment of DISCs, see the *Economic Report of the President*, January 1972, pp. 167–168. An excellent article clarifying the arguments for and against DISCs is Joseph G. Kvasnicka and Jack L. Hervey, "Promoting U.S. Exports through DISCs," Federal Reserve Bank of Chicago, *Business Conditions*, October 1976, pp. 3–9. For more detailed legal discussion, see Arthur J. Rothkopf, "DISC: Qualifying under the New Export Income Laws, Advantages and Hazards," *Journal of Taxation*, March 1972, pp. 130–139. See also *DISC: A Handbook for Exporters*, U.S. Treasury Department, 1972.

For a general survey of taxation focusing on the integration of corporate and individual income taxes and attempts to avoid international double taxation, see Mitsuo Sato and Richard M. Bird, "International Aspects of the Taxation of Corporations and Shareholders," IMF *Staff Papers*, July 1975, pp. 384–455.

Chapter 18

Evaluating International Investment Opportunities

Principles of financial management are basically the same for international as for domestic investments. We begin with a brief review of some fundamentals of financial management and of the general method of evaluating investment opportunities. This is followed by a discussion of the cost of capital for foreign investments, with special attention to costs in the great variety of sources from which foreign subsidiaries may obtain funds. Then we consider the financial impact of mergers, acquisitions, and joint ventures. Finally, several aspects of international investments are considered which give rise to problems that do not surface in a domestic context. Important among these are changing exchange rates, political risks, different tax policies in different countries, and differences in inflation rates.

SOME FUNDAMENTALS OF FINANCIAL MANAGEMENT

People make financial decisions within the confines of two constraints: the wealth they own and the prices that markets set on financial and real investments. Individuals must decide how much of their income they will consume during a period and how much of it they will save (invest). They must also decide how much and what types of borrowing they will do. These decisions, taken together, determine their net worth in future periods.

Managers of business firms must make decisions about investing, about the amount and types of financing of such investment, and about the amount of the firms' incomes to be retained or to be paid out to owners in the form of dividends. It is assumed in finance, as in other branches of economics, that managers act in the interests of owners. Owners are affected by the stream of payments which they receive and also by changes in the values of the firms they own. So another question is, how is the value of a firm determined in the capital markets? Knowing that, we can then determine how financial decisions affect this value.

It is generally assumed, unless otherwise specified, that capital markets are highly competitive or sufficiently close to perfectly competitive that they can be treated as such for most purposes. The concept of efficient capital markets is a key concept in all modern financial theory: capital markets are assumed to be efficient in the sense that participants are well informed, the markets are not dominated by monopoly, and hence prices are established by supply and demand in the light of all known facts. Under these conditions prices move randomly, because only new and unpredictable information can change the valuations of participants.

It should be evident that time and timing are very important in financial management. The essential characteristic of a financial asset is that it serves to provide utility or income for a period of time. Similarly, real capital assets— plant, equipment, and inventories—also provide services (income) over time. Time periods, such as years or quarters, are essential in our analysis. It is also important to distinguish, as was done earlier in BOP analysis, between stocks and flows—stocks of assets held at a given time and flows of income or expenditure during periods of time.

Economic income was concisely defined by John R. Hicks: an individual's income is "the maximum value which he can consume during a week and still be as well off at the end of the week as he was in the beginning."[1] Accounting income may differ from economic income because accountants are not always able to measure income accurately or because they have adopted rules not suited to such measurement.

When we consider income of business firms, changes in value arising from price changes must be considered somewhat differently from other gains or losses. If we ignore transactions costs, an individual can sell some assets such as stocks or bonds if they have risen in value, and consume any resulting rise in value (capital gain) and still be as well off as before. But if we assume that a firm is in a particular line of business, the firm cannot sell part of its normal inventory stock and fixed assets and consume the income and still be as well off

---

[1]John R. Hicks, *Value and Capital*, 2d ed. (London: Oxford, 1946), p. 172.

as it was, because it must replace inventory and fixed assets to continue in business. Clearly, a rise in the value of equipment is a capital gain, and hence an increase in wealth. But it is not income that can be spent and still leave a firm as well off as it was before. Real capital must be maintained in normal amounts needed for the usual levels of production. This is the capital maintenance concept of income.[2] Over a period of time, if the value of real assets rises, providing capital gains, depreciation of fixed assets and replacement cost of inventory must rise concomitantly so that these costs over a period of time offset the rise in value of assets, leaving no increase in net income. For a business firm, then, income is the stream of receipts from sale of output less the costs of producing that output, and those costs include replacement cost of inventory and depreciation on replacement values of fixed assets.

Wealth is the present value of income expected to be received in the future. Since assets are productive—for example, a man using machinery can produce more products than a man using only his hands—a person who wishes to maximize wealth will invest in assets that have the highest return, and will invest in such assets as long as that return exceeds the cost of such investment. He or she will value such assets by discounting expected future incomes at some interest rate. The value of an asset times the interest rate equals the expected future income, and the expected future income divided by the rate of interest equals the present value of the asset.[3]

Managers of firms try to maximize their firms' net worth (wealth)—the present value of expected income. Most income is reflected in incoming cash flows, and such cash flows may then be used to increase holdings of assets with the highest yields consistent with other needs, such as those for working balances, liquidity, and safety.

It is generally assumed that business firms, or more properly their managers and employees, develop expertise in certain lines of productive effort; hence they obtain higher returns by investing in assets useful in such productive effort than by investing in financial assets. Financial institutions, in contrast, have expertise in investment in financial assets. Presumably, therefore, investment in money and other financial assets is made by nonfinancial firms only to the extent that it provides utility justifying the investment in assets having a lower yield—in the case of money, perhaps zero yield. Money has a utility as a convenient means of making payments.

Investment by firms in inventory and fixed assets should be made by selecting from various opportunities those with the highest present values of the future incomes expected from them. Dividend policy need not be relevant

---

[2]The capital maintenance concept of income was discussed in some detail in the chapter on accounting factors affecting international finance, Chap. 16.

[3]This statement must be modified to take care of two complications: (1) interest is usually compounded over some time period, and this compounding must be taken into account, and (2) for some assets, such as real capital assets and stocks, returns may vary significantly from period to period.

to investment decisions because it determines only the distribution of income to owners—whether it is to be in the form of dividends or capital gains. Like individuals, firms are constrained by wealth and the investment opportunities which they encounter. Firms may borrow in order to invest or they may spend their income on real investment. Interest must be paid on borrowing.

THE INVESTMENT DECISION: A REVIEW OF FIRST PRINCIPLES

Certain basic elements concern anyone contemplating an investment. Government authorities about to construct a public facility should try to quantify a benefit/cost ratio; that is, they should list and evaluate the prospective benefits of the project, attach dollar values to them, and compare them with all the costs to be incurred, both explicit and implicit. Businessmen should do the same. For them the benefit is measured by the expected cash flows, including that from the "terminal" or "scrap" value of the assets, and the principal cost is the earning potential of the funds in an alternative use—the "opportunity cost" of the project. Since these same basic elements should enter any government or private investment decision, whether domestic or international, it is useful to review their details briefly.

Capital budgeting is familiar to every finance student and to treat its many ramifications would require an entire book. This review is not designed to be comprehensive, but to provide a common ground for considering the international aspects of capital budgeting decisions. First, these decisions involve a comparison of projected cash outflows with projected cash inflows. Second, for proper evaluation of these cash flows it is necessary to choose a proper "discount" rate, or rate at which a future expected cash flow is discounted to compare it with a cash flow presently available. Third, with cash flows properly evaluated it is possible to construct decision rules, thus guiding prospective investors, whether firms or individuals, in investment decisions.

Evaluation of Cash Flows

Let us assume that a particular firm produces nuts and bolts—fasteners, as they are called in the trade—so that managerial personnel have some expertise in and knowledge of the world market for such products and the kinds of equipment, buildings, and materials required, along with the costs of necessary inputs to the production process. Firms that already make fasteners in the United States are most likely to be the firms that look for overseas opportunities to make and sell fasteners because they already have a certain human capital wrapped up in this business. Managers of firms making tires in the United States would have to hire persons with outside experience to evaluate the profit potential in the fastener business, and since hiring such personnel involves some risk we usually find that investments are made by people already knowledgeable in a field or in related fields.

Assume that managers of a firm estimate that if a factory were built it would cost a total of $1.5 million. This original cost or original cash outflow would pay for construction of the building, purchase and installation of machinery, payment of legal and architects' fees, and all other expenses incidental to establishment of an operating business. Let *OC* stand for this cash outflow.

Marketing managers and production personnel then estimate for a variety of output levels the selling prices that the firm can charge. While there will be some variability in estimates of sales and prices, eventually a best estimate must be selected. Assume that this estimate is that the expected gross revenues from sales of nuts and bolts over the next 10 years will be $1 million each year. From these expected gross revenues we must subtract expected operating costs to arrive at a figure for expected net revenue.

With these figures, after subtracting operating costs of $800 thousand from expected gross revenue of $1 million each year, we expect net revenue of $200 thousand each year over the 10-year horizon. At the end of this period we expect to sell the used machinery and factory building for $500,000. This $500,000 scrap value is simply a "best estimate."

Operating Costs Operating costs require special attention because not all costs usually considered in determining net profits are considered in present calculations. We need an estimate of net cash inflows, not net profits.

To compute net profit we would deduct depreciation of the plant and equipment, in most cases according to some schedule established by accountants as appropriate for tax and other purposes. But in the present analysis we do not deduct depreciation. Depreciation deductions are intended to prevent us from considering revenue as profit unless we have first provided for replacement of physical assets at the end of the period—in this case 10 years. They are intended, in Hicks' words, to ensure that the firm will then be as well off, and as able to produce nuts and bolts, as it was before.

A second expense always included in profit and loss statements is interest charges incurred on borrowed funds. We must distinguish between funds borrowed to provide the initial cash outflow and funds borrowed for day-to-day operations. The latter are necessary for operations, and interest paid on such borrowings, together with that received on funds temporarily invested in financial assets, are included in operating revenues and costs. If the project were financed by an initial bond issue of $1.5 million, interest charges on this bond issue would not be included and would not reduce net revenue estimates because, as shown below, it is by comparing such charges with expected net revenues that decisions may be made on whether or not projects should be undertaken.

The Present Value of the Stream of Net Revenue In our example the net revenue expected at the end of the first year is $200,000. What is this worth today? That is, what is the *present value* of this amount? The answer is provided by the formula PV equals $Y/1$ plus i, in which PV is the present value, Y is the income expected, and i is the market rate of interest or discount. The formula may also be written $PV(1 + i) = Y$; the present value plus the interest on that amount equals the total to be received. If i is 6 percent, PV is $200,000/1.06, or about $188,679; if I invest $188,679 at 6 percent, I will have approximately $200,000 at the end of a year.

The value of the $200,000 expected after two years is $PV_2 = Y_2/(1 + i)^2$; $1 + i$ must be squared because it is presumed that interest is compounded each year. If it is compounded more often, there are more periods comprising two years. The value of all the expected net cash inflows over 10 years, including the cash flow from the scrap value of the plant, is given by the formula:

$$PV = PV_1 + PV_2 + \cdots + PV_{10}$$

$$= \frac{Y_1}{(1+i)} + \frac{Y_2}{(1+i)^2} + \cdots + \frac{Y_{10} + \text{scrap value}}{(1+i)^{10}}$$

or

$$1,751,214 = \frac{200,000}{1.06} + \frac{200,000}{(1.06)^2} + \cdots + \frac{700,000}{(1.06)^{10}}$$

In general notation we might write

$$PV = \sum_{j=1}^{n} \frac{Y_j}{(1 + i)^j}$$

for an investment. This is how managers must evaluate or estimate the present value of future expected cash flows.

One final comment should be made about evaluation of costs and net receipts: if an investment project is an *addition* to an existing plant, then estimates of costs should include only those *additional* costs required for expanding production, and estimates of revenues should include only those additional revenues expected because of additional sales.

Choosing a Discount Rate

In the example the manufacturers of fasteners used a discount rate of 6 percent to find a present value of $1,751,214. If they had used a 5 percent rate, the present value would have been $1,851,304, and if they had used a 10 percent rate, it would have been $1,421,685. Present value varies *inversely* with the discount rate and *directly* with expected revenues. The discount rate the managers must choose is the "cost of capital" for the firm. Let us evaluate this cost of capital.

Steps in Estimating Cost of Capital   A reliable procedure in estimating cost of capital includes three steps: (1) setting a minimum value for cost of capital by using the rate of interest or yield on default-free government securities of the appropriate maturity; (2) adding to this an appropriate allowance for risk, since returns on real capital investments are more variable than returns on investments in government securities; and (3) adding an additional amount if the size of the borrowing is such that the firm's credit position changes and lenders may regard investment in it as more risky.

If a firm has idle funds, it might wish to invest them in safe earning assets. One such asset is a government bond. Different risks are associated with different investments, and investment in government bonds carries the risk that their prices may fall. But government bonds do not have a risk of default unless a revolution occurs which destroys the present government. This is because any government, having sovereign powers, can control the money supply and taxes so that any bonds issued can be paid off at maturity. The purchasing power of the money received by bondholders at maturity may be much less because of inflation, but the risk of default is absent. If the current yield on 10-year government bonds is 6 percent, this is the lowest rate that should be used as the cost of capital, because this yield can be obtained by investing the funds in default-free bonds.[4]

Estimates of future sales revenues and operating costs are just that— estimates. They are the best guesses of managers who evaluate the profitability of investments. One could ask such managers for high and low estimates, and the spread between such estimates could tell a decision maker something about the risk involved in establishing the new fastener operation.[5] The wider the range or standard deviation, the riskier the project. If all estimates are 5 percent, the investment is not very profitable, according to the estimates, but it is not risky. On the other hand, if one estimate is 20 percent and another estimate is 2 percent, the investment is quite risky.

The most common way of dealing with this risk is to observe yields on investments by "typical" firms in the fastener business for some years. If 10 percent is the historical average, then it may be assumed that it probably takes 10 percent to retain investors in this business. If competition prevailed, and if 10 percent were more than sufficient, new firms would begin operations and presumably the rate of return would fall as output increased. For a long time in the United States, according to extensive studies, the return on stocks (a proxy

---

[4]It is presumed that the yield of 6 percent includes an allowance for expected inflation—an "inflation premium" arising out of uniformly held expectations of inflation. As indicated in earlier chapters, Irving Fisher showed that this premium should be approximately equal to the expected rate of inflation. The expected rate is generally measured indirectly as an average of the past rates for some time, with more recent rates weighted more heavily.

[5]The range, standard deviation, or some other measure of dispersion of the estimated net revenues is used to measure risk.

for investment in real capital assets) averaged 9 percent a year, assuming the dividends were reinvested, while interest on high-grade corporate bonds averaged 5 percent a year—a 4 percent spread for risk.

The risk premium for a particular industry, however, may be so high that businessmen may think that government bond yields could vary between 6 and 9 percent without having any effect on their investment decisions. This may be true for a very high percentage of all investments, but there is always a group of marginal projects under consideration, which would be affected by changes in market interest rate levels. The greater the risk associated with an investment, the greater the discount rate that decision makers should use. This has significant implications for international investments.

Sometimes a firm has an established credit line which calls for loans to it at, say, 2 percent above the prime rate (the rate charged by leading banks and hence by other banks to their "best" customers). When projects undertaken by such a firm require large financial investment, the credit capacity of the firm becomes strained. As this occurs, it is likely that the effective cost of capital rises and a higher discount rate is applied. Thus to the risk-free interest rate we must add a risk premium for the risk inherent in the proposed project and perhaps an additional premium for the increased risk of default by the firm.

The Weighted Average Cost of Capital   If a new fastener factory requires an original cash outflow of $1.5 million for construction and if $250,000 of this is to be supplied by retained earnings, $1 million by issuing bonds, and $250,000 from the sale of new equity capital (stock), the cost of each form of financing should be weighted by the amount done in that form. It is generally presumed that the opportunity cost of retained earnings is the rate being earned currently; unless the firm can earn that rate on new projects, it should not retain the earnings. Thus the cost of retained earnings might be 12 percent if that rate were being earned by the firm currently. Including a risk premium, 8 percent might be required on bonds sold in the capital market. Finally, since profits are taxed at approximately 50 percent, in order to pay 12 percent to stockholders the firm would have to earn 24 percent on funds supplied by stockholders who purchase new stock. The weighted cost of capital would be 12 percent on one quarter of $1 million, 8 percent on $1 million, and 24 percent on one quarter of $1 million, or $11\frac{1}{3}$ percent. The average cost of capital and some additional problems concerning changes in the cost of capital as debt/equity ratios change are discussed in Chapter 19.

The Decision Rules

Armed with these estimates of operating costs, revenues, and the firm's cost of capital, the final decision to build or not to build a new fastener factory can be made on a financial basis by applying a simple rule. If *PV*, the present value of the expected future net cash inflows, discounted by an interest rate which reflects the firm's cost of capital, is greater than the original cost *OC* required to build the new plant, then the investment is a profitable one, and the managers may decide to proceed. Thus the rule is: if $PV > OC$, proceed; if $PV < OC$, abandon the project. In our example the project would be abandoned because the present value of expected cash inflows discounted at 10 percent is $1,421,685 and the cost is $1,500,000. Discounted at $11^{1}/_{3}$ percent, present value would be even lower; the project does not appear likely to generate enough cash inflows to yield enough to meet the cost of the capital involved.

An alternative rule can be stated by comparing the cost of capital with the "internal rate of return."[6] In the above example cost of capital was designated as i; let us designate the internal rate of return as r.

$$OC = \frac{Y_1}{(1+r)} + \frac{Y_2}{(1+r)^2} + \cdots + \frac{Y_n + \text{scrap value}}{(1+r)^n}$$

or let

$$\$1,500,000 = \frac{\$200,000}{(1+r)} + \frac{\$200,000}{(1+r)^2} + \cdots + \frac{\$700,000}{(1+r)^{10}}$$

In this case r is 8.93 percent. That is, the income stream of $200,000 per year from a $1.5 million investment means that this investment has an effective yield of 8.93 percent over the life of the project. Now the decision rule is that if $r > i$, the project may proceed; if $r < i$, the project should be abandoned. Since the weighted average cost of capital, i, was 11.33 percent and r was only 8.93 percent, the project should be abandoned.

There are many complexities in applying these rules, and we now turn to the complexities often encountered when making international investments.

AMENDING INPUTS TO THE DECISION RULES FOR INTERNATIONAL INVESTMENTS

Inputs for the decision rules can be quite complicated for both domestic and international investments. We do not review these complications in detail, but examine major inputs affected by special considerations in the case of international investments.

The Investigative Process

The theory of the entrepreneurial process is that businessmen who are free to begin producing commodities observe that profits are being made by existing

---

[6]In specific instances the two rules may not be equivalent. Sometimes ambiguous results are found when using internal rate of return, especially when returns are negative in some years and positive in others. For comparison of the rules, see any standard text on financial management, for example, James C. Van Horne, *Financial Management and Policy*, 2d ed. (Englewood Cliffs, N.J.: Prentice-Hall, 1971), Chap. 3, especially Appendix B.

producers and believe that their ability to compete for these profits will lead to efficient utilization of resources. It is clear that someone in a firm's management thinks, "There's a profit to be made in doing this." Typically, managers of firms think along the lines of producing abroad the products they have been producing domestically. Diversification does occur, but usually people think in terms of expanding their activities in lines in which they have expertise. Once management thinks, "there's a profit to be made," the investigative process begins.

One research study of management practices by Yair Aharoni indicated that the first phase of the investigative process for an international investment is usually carried out in the parent company's offices.[7] In a rough and very general way, local office managers estimate the size of the market for a product and evaluate the company's resources that are especially suited to the necessary tasks. Also a very general estimate of the risk associated with the project is made. If the project idea passes three general tests—(1) the product has a good market, (2) the firm's personnel have expertise for the tasks, and (3) the perceived risk is not too great—then one or more executives of the firm usually go abroad for an on-the-spot study of the feasibility of the project.

Market information available to firms considering projects in developed countries is usually far superior to that available in LDCs. Certainly, obtaining a market data base, using indicators mentioned in Chapter 14 among others, is a matter of high priority.

There is a widely recognized human tendency to become attached to something that one studies in depth. So it is with the investigative process. The executive who goes abroad to study the feasibility of a project is more likely to come home supporting it. A bias favorable to the project is likely to develop, especially if the executive is well hosted by local government officials who wish to encourage foreign investment and by local businessmen who may be able to increase their own earnings by doing business with new foreign firms. Some observers believe that the biases may become strong enough to render the decision rules above relatively unimportant in decision making. Authors of one article found that financial investment criteria were often used for small projects, and that for large projects they ". . . were used only as a rough screening device to prevent obviously unprofitable projects from wasting the time of the board of directors."[8]

Of course, if good profit potential is very obvious, there is little reason to develop detailed estimates of costs and revenues before making a decision to proceed. In these cases only "rough screening devices" are required. A familiar expression is, "Let's sharpen our pencils and see how it looks on the bottom line." That is, let's make detailed estimates to determine the expected financial

[7]Yair Aharoni, *The Foreign Investment Decision Process* (Boston: Graduate School of Business Administration, Harvard, 1966).

[8]Arthur Stonehill and Leonard Nathanson, "Capital Budgeting and the Multinational Corporation," *California Management Review*, Summer 1968, pp. 39–54, especially p. 40.

result. The more "iffy" the project, the sharper the pencils should be. It would not be surprising to find that, empirically, a very large percentage of the foreign investments made by U.S. firms are made without undergoing the specific, sophisticated, and detailed computations called for in the decision rules above. One would expect careful "pencil sharpening" only for "marginal" projects. Thus our discussion is meant primarily for marginal projects, to indicate what kinds of considerations should go into their acceptance or rejection.

Whose Cash Flows?

Cash flows may differ in the currency of the subsidiary's country from their amounts in the currency of the parent company's country. Since repatriation of funds may be restricted, cash flows to the parent may also differ from those to the subsidiary. We have already discussed the conditions under which exchange rate gains or losses may be significant. Concerning cash flows to the parent company, although they may be desired by some parent companies and their stockholders, multinational companies may have stockholders in many countries. In some cases it may be possible to pay stockholders in a given country from earnings of investments in that country. Moreover, MNCs need be concerned about stockholders only to the extent that dividend payments of an appropriate level be maintained. An MNC which expects to continue investing in a country and earning profits may not be particularly concerned about being prevented from remitting all the profits to its "home" country. Thus, although a categorical answer cannot be given, it is quite possible that managers need be concerned only with cash flows in the subsidiary's country, and that the question of repatriation of profits to the parent company can be ignored.

Factors Affecting the Cost of Capital

The decision rules require an estimate of the weighted average cost of capital—the average interest rate and the average rate of earnings on equity—that must be paid to the suppliers of capital.[9] The cost rate is used either for comparison with the internal rate of return calculated from the expected net income stream or as the discount rate for computation of the present value of the expected income stream. The latter is generally regarded as preferable. The cost of capital is determined in the broad market for financial assets—primarily stocks, bonds, and mortgages. Short-term instruments, such as promissory notes for loans, would not be so generally used in obtaining funds to initiate a major project. Note that the cost of capital used is the cost to the unit making the investment, frequently a foreign subsidiary of a U.S. firm, although it may

---

[9]We recognize the controversy in financial management theory concerning the valuation of the firm based on expected dividends and based on expected future earnings. We accept basically the view of Miller and Modigliani that present and expected future earnings are the main determinant of value, but we are aware of the possibility that dividend policy may have some effect on value. For a discussion of the controversy, see, for example, Van Horne, op. cit., Chap. 9.

be the parent U.S. company, especially if that firm is establishing a new subsidiary and providing it with some equity capital.[10]

Sources of Funds   There is some confusion about sources and uses of funds, especially in connection with the use of these terms in accounting. In economic usage, funds is an abstract term to denote whatever may be obtained by borrowing, issuing equity securities, or obtaining net income from sales and retaining the earnings. Having obtained "funds" in these ways, the "funds" are then used by firms to acquire assets—cash and other liquid assets, receivables, inventory, or fixed assets.[11]

In general, funds are classified as internally or externally generated. Internally generated funds means net profits after taxes and dividends, generally referred to as undistributed profits, plus capital consumption allowances (depreciation and other noncash charges) which were charged against profits.[12] Such charges do not cause an outflow of funds from firms, and thus funds are still available for any desired use, and in fact no doubt have been put to some use. We use the term funds as an abstraction because we do not in fact know in what assets the funds have been embodied.

In national income accounts in the United States in 1976, total corporate profits were shown as total profits reported by corporations, with an inventory valuation adjustment of the inventory component of cost of goods sold to reflect the replacement cost of inventory instead of either LIFO or FIFO cost. (As shown in earlier chapters, LIFO cost is much closer to replacement cost in a period of inflation.) There is also a capital consumption adjustment shown to reflect depreciation of replacement cost.[13]

[10]There is no question about the cost of externally borrowed funds; it is the cost the subsidiary has to pay if it borrows. But there may be a question about equity capital obtained from a parent company. Rodriquez and Carter (*International Financial Management*, Englewood Cliffs, N. J.: Prentice-Hall, 1976, pp. 328–331) argue that the cost is properly the rate the subsidiary would have to earn in the country where it is operating, not the parent company's cost of capital. Yet some firms use the latter; and one might ask, why should a parent company with a cost of capital of, say, 12 percent, not invest in a subsidiary in return for a yield of more than 12 percent? Of course, if the subsidiary is making the investment and is putting in equity capital, it should earn on that equity capital what it must earn on other equity capital, and the more equity capital it has, the higher its weighted average cost of capital, in all probability.

[11]Because its meaning is not precise, some accountants would prefer to abandon the term funds. See, for example, *Research in Accounting Measurement*, Papers given at the Seminar on Basic Research in Accounting Measurement, Graduate School of Business, Stanford University, March 1965 (American Accounting Association, 1966), especially the statement by Robert T. Sprouse on p. 104. Sprouse was criticizing the fact that accountants sometimes referred to assets held as funds. In economics, "funds" is a pure abstraction, used because sources of funds such as bond issues or sale of new stock need not generate cash, but may in some cases directly provide fixed assets. Funds obtained from various sources are used to increase holdings of cash, other liquid assets, inventory, and/or fixed assets.

[12]*Economic Report of the President*, January 1976, table B-78, p. 263. Our examples refer to corporate profits because of the importance of corporations in the economy.

[13]Ibid., table B-8, p. 180. These adjustments reduced reported 1975 profits after taxes from $60.4 billion to $43.4 billion. The adjustment for 1974 was even larger, reducing reported profits from $61.1 billion to $20.5 billion.

External sources of funds mean primarily the money and capital markets in which funds can be borrowed and additional stock issued, usually for cash but sometimes in exchange for physical assets.

Choice of a Discount Rate and Evaluation of Expected Cash Flows   Managers of international firms can determine costs of capital from various sources as indicated above, and they can also evaluate the risks involved. They must then, after evaluation of expected cash outflows and inflows, choose a discount rate for the expected net cash inflows.

The question may be raised whether greater reliance on foreign earnings, as is especially the case with multinational firms, may increase the cost of equity capital because of greater risk. Because accounting reports do not always disclose such things as contingent parent company tax liabilities on earnings retained abroad, and do not disclose a number of other facts concerning international operations, investors may not be fully informed concerning risks involved. There is evidence, referred to below, however, that international diversification reduces risk for investors. One study, the results of which are consistent with this evidence, showed that firms with relatively large international operations had statistically significantly higher price-earnings ratios (lower cost of equity capital) than firms in the same industries with less international involvement.[14] This difference did not seem to be correlated with higher rates of growth in sales, earnings, dividends, or return on investment.

Eiteman and Stonehill suggested that investors may not discount foreign risks sufficiently, and supported this view by citing a study of market performance of five Cuban stocks traded on the New York Stock Exchange or on the American Stock Exchange from 1955 to 1961.[15] These stock prices did not seriously decline in the period of Fidel Castro's takeover in Cuba nor during the attempted Bay of Pigs invasion which failed in 1961. Such an assumption of failure of investors to take into account known factors is contrary to the theory of efficient capital markets, and although such cases may exist, one must be cautious in assuming lack of knowledge on the basis of a small number of studies. Isolated instances of investors or traders ignoring evidence of economic and political changes are not unknown, of course; an example is the foreign exchange trading losses by Citibank's Belgian office on forward sales of sterling in the presumed hope that the forward spread would narrow, when it was generally accepted that the pound was likely to decline.

Cash outflows include investments in plant and equipment, including land if acquired, and necessary working capital. After operations begin, there are likely to be additional cash outflows for importing raw materials; to pay for power, labor, and overhead; and to pay fees and taxes.

---

[14]Ted Kohers, A Comparison of Performance Between U.S. Multinational Corporations and U.S. Domestic Corporations, unpublished doctoral dissertation, College of Business Administration, University of Oregon, 1970.

[15]David K. Eiteman, "American Portfolio Investor Discounting of Political and Social Risks in Cuban Securities," *Quarterly Review of Economics and Business*, May 1962, pp. 89–98.

Cash inflows come primarily from sales revenues, but the "terminal" value of the investment at a selected future date is also an expected cash inflow. No new principles are involved in evaluation other than those ordinarily used in evaluating similar flows in domestic investment. But one matter of special concern is the ability of the parent company to repatriate funds. If cash inflows are received, can the firm expect to repatriate as much of them as it desires? If there is an expected net terminal value, can the parent firm expect to sell what remains of the plant and equipment in the host country and repatriate all the funds received? This aspect of cash flows is peculiar to foreign investment decisions, and is discussed later.

In general, it is probable that only part of the resources for a project are supplied from the investor country in the form of equity and loans. Subsidiaries usually borrow some capital locally and may obtain some local equity capital. The latter becomes more likely as countries insist on local participation in ownership.

Funds expected to be remitted back to the investment source country will include—for calculation—management and engineering fees, commissions, repayment of loans with interest, dividends after deduction of withholding taxes, and the terminal value. How much can actually be remitted depends on host-country regulations and other factors. All flows must be converted to investor-country currency at some exchange rate. One possibility is that the plant is sold to host-country investors at the end of the specified time at its terminal value and the proceeds then converted into investor-country currency.

The discount rate used in determining net present value in investor-country currency is crucial. Eiteman and Stonehill viewed it according to the possible use of the investing firm's own cost of capital as a discount rate; the use of an arbitrarily higher rate to be sure that the project is justified; or the use of a rate increased above the cost of capital rate to allow for risks of exchange rate fluctuation and of political actions detrimental to the firm's return from the investment.[16]

It has been argued that it is incorrect to use a rate higher than the cost of capital rate to discount net cash flows exclusive of the terminal value, because in most instances risks are much greater further into the future than in the first few years of a planned investment. That is, the necessary risk premium may not be very great for cash flows expected in the first few years. If insurance is available for exchange risks and/or political risks as discussed in Chapter 15, or if risks can otherwise be hedged, the cost of hedging may be a measure of the amount by which cash flows could decrease. It would then be appropriate to use the cost of capital rate as a discount rate for the cash flows.

Firms may reduce risks by diversification. Indeed, if it is assumed that individuals are deterred to some extent from international diversification of their investment portfolios—for example, by lack of sufficient information—it is possible that diversification by corporations gives their stockholders benefits

---

[16]Eiteman and Stonehill, op. cit., pp. 206–208.

they could not attain under present conditions by investing in, for example, international mutual funds. Our review of the capital asset pricing model in Chapter 11 led to the conclusion that in efficient capital markets investors could seek maximum return with a given risk, or minimum risk with a given return. An efficient portfolio which met one of these goals could be obtained with a separate decision on the suitable amount of borrowed or loaned funds. In efficient markets capital asset prices would be "efficient," and changes in such prices would be random.

There is some evidence that capital markets are less efficient outside than within the United States.[17] There is also the question whether project diversification, in location or in type of output, is similar in result to securities diversification.[18]

To the extent that diversification results in a lower cost of capital because the premium for risk need not be so great, it is possible that MNCs may have an advantage in being able to use a lower cost-of-capital discount rate.

Alternative Sources of Funds in International Finance

Some funds are internally generated as always, but the international firm has a number of other sources: intracompany equity contributions and loans; borrowing from local bank offices, whether of local or of multinational banks; finance subsidiaries which specialize in raising funds for multinational firm subsidiaries; the Eurocurrency markets and the Eurobond market; and the U.S. money and capital markets.

Internally Generated Funds Roughly half of all funds obtained by U.S. foreign subsidiaries are internally generated, although the percentage is lower for petroleum affiliates than for others. Dividends approximately equal retained earnings; thus about half of after-tax profits are retained within overseas firms for use in continuing and expanding activities. Again, petroleum companies are an exception. Their subsidiaries remit most of their earnings after depreciation and taxes to their parent companies and then borrow in the United States if necessary.[19]

Except for the unusual depression years of the 1930s, the ratio of dividends to earnings (sometimes called the payout ratio) for domestic U.S. firms has been just below 50 percent. This is about the same as it is for overseas subsidiaries and affiliates. Theoretically, after-tax earnings should be paid out in dividends to the stockholders if funds cannot be used more profitably within

[17]See, for example, Bruno Solnik, *European Capital Markets* (Lexington, Mass.: D. C. Heath/Lexington Books, 1973) and John G. McDonald, "French Mutual Fund Performance: Evaluation of Internationally Diversified Portfolios," *Journal of Finance*, December 1973, pp. 1161–1180.

[18]On the benefit of international diversification of investor portfolios, see, for example, Bruno H. Solnik, "Why not Diversify Internationally rather than Domestically?" *Financial Analysts Journal*, July/August 1974, pp. 48–54, and Donald R. Lessard, "World, Country, and Industry Relationships in Equity Returns: Implications for Risk Reduction through International Diversification," *Financial Analysts Journal*, January/February 1976, pp. 32–38.

[19]For basic data see *Survey of Current Business* and *U.S. Direct Investments Abroad 1966* (Washington, D.C.: Government Printing Office, 1971 and 1972).

a company than they could if the stockholders placed them elsewhere. Retention of earnings, however, saves the cost of distribution of dividends and the cost of sale of new stock to obtain funds if opportunities arise which appear likely to yield a sufficient return. Hence retention of funds may be justified in some cases even if prospective investment opportunities with adequate yields are not immediately in sight.

Subsidiaries of U.S. firms which are located overseas usually rely somewhat less on internal sources of funds than on intracompany and external sources discussed below. This may reflect the desire of management in U.S. parent companies to repatriate funds whenever possible in view of the ever-present possibility that the local political and economic climate may change and that restrictions may be placed on the outflow of funds, or that such restrictions may be tightened. On the other hand, laws relating to depreciation allowances differ widely from country to country, and many countries have more liberal depreciation allowances for taxation than the United States. Accelerated depreciation reduces current tax liabilities and thus more after-tax earnings are available for dividends or retention. Thus depreciation laws and the desire of management to repatriate funds affect the volume of internally generated funds used for further investment.

Intracompany Sources of Funds   Overseas subsidiaries may obtain funds from their parent companies or from other subsidiaries of the parent companies. The funds may be transferred in cash or in the form of inventory or other physical assets.

Supplying physical assets without payment is a special form of lending. It may be an extremely convenient form when parent companies can supply specialized equipment of their own manufacture. One fastener company sells not only the nuts and bolts it produces but also the machinery to produce them. This company sends its machines to production factories in Ireland, England, Brazil, and other countries where they have their own subsidiaries. In such cases the terms of credit are completely flexible and can be arranged by simple internal accounting without the formality that accompanies the supplying of equity capital or loans.

Equity contributions may be made for the establishment of foreign subsidiaries or for acquisition of ownership and control of existing firms in which an initial portfolio investment has already been made. The equity contribution may be in cash or in physical assets. It is evident that any national program aimed at controlling the outflow of foreign investment should take into account the possibility of investment by supplying physical assets, but often only cash investment is controlled.

One reason for acquiring total ownership or a controlling interest in a foreign subsidiary is the desire to rationalize worldwide production and marketing by the total firm—parent company plus subsidiaries and affiliates. If this is done, profit maximization for the total firm takes precedence over profit maximization for a subsidiary, because less profit in one subsidiary may coexist with even greater profit in another. Transfer pricing decisions may be made so as to channel more profits into countries with lower taxes; this reduces the profits of subsidiaries operating in other countries. Considerations of this type were said to have influenced the decision of Ford Motor Company to purchase the relatively large British minority interest in Ford, Ltd., in 1961, in spite of the adverse impact this purchase had on the U.S. BOP at the time, and the ire it raised among those desiring to control foreign investment outflow from the United States. General Motors has generally avoided joint ventures involving foreign interests so that it can maximize gain for the total firm, and Frederic G. Donner, a former chairman of the company, has argued that production, dividend, and pricing decisions based on worldwide results are desirable in the interests of economic efficiency.[20]

Loans from parent companies are a convenient way to finance needs of subsidiaries without the formalities and difficulties of external borrowing. Since the Internal Revenue Act of 1962, U.S. firms receiving repayment of such loans must show the Internal Revenue Service that the funds obtained *are* loan repayments and not return of equity capital funds. Otherwise the IRS may treat the funds as "constructive dividends" and tax them as received earned income of the parent companies. Thus to some extent informal parent company advances are discouraged by the tax law and formal loans are more common.

Another inducement for firms to make loans rather than to invest equity capital is that foreign exchange controls imposed in foreign countries often make it easier to remit funds for loan repayments than for return of equity capital.

Conceptually there is no difference between intracompany equity investment and loans, but unless the need for capital is believed to be very long-run or permanent, parent companies usually wish to advance the funds as loans so that repayment is relatively easier and less costly in tax liabilities and so on. Greater reliance on loans than on provision of equity may often make foreign subsidiaries seem to be undercapitalized by the usual standards.[21]

Loans to a subsidiary from other subsidiaries and affiliates can be obtained in the same ways as from the parent company—through informal loans, through direct formal loans, or through transfers of physical assets with delayed payment therefor. It seems probable that even if such loans are made, the parent company can more efficiently collect information concerning the best possibilities for obtaining funds, and can best designate sources for lending and borrowing. Countries relatively short of capital may not want local subsidiaries to finance expansion of subsidiaries in other countries and may impose restrictions on such lending. Again, economic integration may be hindered by political fragmentation.

The amount of the loan obtained from a parent company or from another subsidiary is the required amount of local currency converted from dollars or another currency at the current exchange rate. The cost is (1) the after-tax cost

[20]Frederic G. Donner, "The World-Wide Corporation in a Modern Economy," Address at the 8th International Congress of Accountants, Waldorf-Astoria Hotel, New York, Sept. 27, 1962.

[21]Stefan H. Robock and Kenneth Simmonds, *International Business and Multinational Enterprises* (Homewood, Ill.: Irwin, 1973), p. 496.

of the funds at the rate at which it is assumed the lender can borrow (if it is desired to compare with other borrowing costs) plus (2) the interest on the same amount at the interest rates charged to the subsidiary by the lender (with the difference that the after-tax cost in this case is determined by the subsidiary's tax rate) minus (3) the after-tax cost of the interest paid to the parent company by the subsidiary (the tax rate in this case being the rate imposed on foreign income received) and minus (4) the tax gain by the subsidiary if the local currency depreciates during the term of the loan, resulting in a tax-deductible exchange loss.[22]

External Sources of Funds: Local Bank Offices   Short-term borrowing may be used pending receipt of funds from a bond issue or in some other circumstances. Such borrowing is likely to be from commercial banks, as it is in the United States, but the choice of banks is wider. The choice includes local banks, parent company banks' branch offices or Edge Act subsidiary offices, and third-country bank offices. Advantages of each may be readily deduced from the analysis of such banking in Chapter 8. In some countries, financial institutions may carry out functions which would be handled separately by nonbank financial institutions in the United States. Especially important in some countries are the development banks, which engage in development lending and often provide a buffer against losses by ultimate lenders when loans are made to new industries.

Local bank managers are likely to have better knowledge of local business conditions and practices, while managers of multinational bank offices are likely to have more knowledge concerning all types of financing. Moreover, the latter have advantages in being able to minimize float in international transfers of funds and in being able to provide information concerning currency and regulatory conditions in various countries. For these reasons many firms find an advantage in having two banking connections, one with a local bank and one with a multinational bank.

Long-term borrowing from banks cannot generally be done unless the banks are involved in some sort of consortium or venture banking activity to provide full financing with the aid of institutions better able than banks to engage in long-term financing. Medium-term financing, however, is provided by banks. Since equity investments may be made by Edge Act offices when local laws permit local banks to do this, Edge Act offices may provide long-term funds, including equity. Edge Act companies that do not engage in deposit banking can invest up to half of their capital and surplus in a single venture.

---

[22]The analysis of cost follows that of Alan C. Shapiro, "Evaluating Financing Costs for Multinational Subsidiaries," *Journal of International Business Studies*, Fall 1975, pp. 25–32. To find after-tax cost, multiply the amount by one minus the appropriate tax rate. To find lender's currency amount, multiply by the current exchange rate. To find amount of interest paid, multiply by the exchange rate at maturity, on the assumption that interest is paid at that time. To find tax gain, multiply by the difference between the exchange rate at the time of the loan and at its maturity and multiply this result by the appropriate tax rate. Tax gain, of course, cannot be determined at the time a loan is made, but it can be estimated if the firm's managers believe they can forecast the future exchange rate.

Two variations on the form of local loans may be mentioned: the *discounting of bills* and the *swap loan*. Discounting of bills is quite common in some countries in Europe and Latin America. Drafts are drawn on customers and discounted at banks. Although this is done in the United States on occasion, it is not common. A related means of obtaining funds in Europe is the factoring of receivables; the receivables are discounted with or without recourse—that is, with or without a claim against the firm which discounted the receivables on its balance sheet, in the event that all receivables cannot be collected. Since charges for discounting of receivables may include costs of credit investigation and of collection as well as an interest rate which includes a premium for risk of default, the cost is not properly comparable with other interest costs unless the pure interest cost portion of the charge is identified.

Swap loans are loans in which a parent company provides funds in its home country to a foreign bank; one of the foreign bank's offices lends the equivalent amount, translated at the appropriate exchange rate, to a foreign subsidiary of the parent company. When the loan matures, the funds are returned to the parent company and the loan is repaid by the borrowing subsidiary. These loans have been common in certain countries, especially in Latin America. However, Latin American governments may quickly change the conditions under which swap loans may be made. Usually no interest is paid on the funds provided by the parent company.

Nearly one-fourth of the firms in a survey by Robbins and Stobaugh favored local borrowing regardless of interest rate differentials.[23] On the other hand, some companies have favored local borrowing primarily when the risk of decline in the value of the local currency seemed great.[24]

The after-tax dollar cost of local borrowing may be calculated for comparison with the cost of an intracompany loan by using the appropriate local interest rate, the exchange rate expected at the maturity of the loan to translate interest paid into dollars, and the subsidiary's tax rate. To this should be added any exchange loss; or any exchange gain should be subtracted.

For swaps, the interest cost is (1) the cost of the funds provided to the bank by the parent company plus (2) the interest cost paid by the subsidiary. To this must be added any swap conversion cost, and any exchange gain must be subtracted. If the local currency has fallen in value, more local currency is needed to repay the parent company's loan. (In effect, it is assumed that the bank has received funds from the parent company and has used the equivalent amount of funds, translated at the current exchange rate, in its own country and must give back more local currency in order to give back the same amount as received of the parent company's currency.)

[23]Sidney M. Robbins and Robert B. Stobaugh, "Financing Foreign Affiliates," *Financial Management*, Winter 1972, pp. 56–65.

[24]Newton H. Hoyt, Jr., "The Management of Currency Exchange Risk by the Singer Company," *Financial Management*, Spring 1972, pp. 13–20.

External Sources of Funds: Finance Subsidiaries Firms may also borrow locally from U.S. or European finance subsidiaries which raise funds for industrial corporations. This is advantageous when funds are needed for foreign subsidiaries and when the finance subsidiaries are incorporated outside the United States, especially when controls are imposed on capital outflows. Borrowing from offshore finance subsidiaries is also advantageous if they are incorporated in "tax haven" countries as discussed in Chapter 17; and it may be useful if they are incorporated in Delaware or some other state with minimum corporate regulatory requirements. An interesting example of a use of a Delaware-incorporated finance subsidiary is the sale by a Baxter Laboratories subsidiary of 375,000 shares of convertible preferred stock in 1971 through a syndicate in Europe. This stock is an example of a U.S. dollar equity issued outside the United States, but it hardly represents a true Euro-equity since there is no separate Euro-equity market like the Eurobond market [25]

Finance subsidiaries are likely to use the facilities of the Eurodollar and Eurobond markets because (1) those markets provide funds in widely acceptable currencies such as the U.S. dollar, (2) the cost of funds in those markets may be relatively low because of their efficiency, and (3) those markets are free of extensive regulation. Although those markets grew out of various forces discussed in Chapters 10 and 13, activities of finance subsidiaries have strengthened them.

External Sources of Funds: Eurocurrency Markets and Eurobond Markets Most securities issued in the Eurobond market are debt issues, while borrowing in the Eurodollar market is in the form of loans. Debt securities may be issued in bearer form to appeal to European investors accustomed to this form. Loans by Eurodollar banks are often made on an overdraft basis, and the requirement of compensating balances, common in the United States, is not usual. Presence or absence of a compensating balance requirement should be taken into account in determining the effective interest rate, but this is difficult because it is not often known how much balance would be held by a firm in any event because of its need for a working balance. Interest on such a balance cannot properly be deemed an *additional* cost to the firm.

Frequently business firms, especially in LDCs, need "package" financing, including both short-term and long-term funds. These can be supplied by consortia of banks and perhaps by other institutions so that individual banks can avoid the risks inherent in large long-term commitments. Eurodollar loans are usually made to "prime" borrowers (those with the best credit ratings), in relatively large amounts (generally $0.5 million or more), and on an unsecured basis. Costs of borrowing are reduced because risk is relatively low, cost per dollar of loan is relatively low because of the large size of loans involved, and the absence of collateral eliminates its handling costs.

[25]Cf. "Now We Have the Euroequity," *Corporate Financing*, January–February 1972, pp. 9–10 and the discussion in Chap. 12.

Eurodollar loans may be for as little as one day, as in the case of one bank lending to another which has a very short-term need for cash, for example, to meet a reserve requirement; or they may be for as much as 5 years or longer. Banks making Eurodollar loans must be reasonably sure that the borrower will be able to repay in the currency loaned, usually dollars, but sometimes Deutsche marks, Swiss francs, or other widely accepted currencies. Borrowing in the Eurodollar market by U.S. subsidiaries may require a guarantee by the parent firm to assure that *dollars* will be available for repayment when due. For other firms, prior arrangements with government authorities may be necessary to assure banks that repayment in dollars will be permitted by the governments involved.

Borrowing in the Eurobond market involves the issue of long-term bonds in dollars, in some special currency unit, or in the currency of another country outside the country in which the security is issued. Interest costs have typically been lower than for borrowing in local European markets, although higher than for borrowing in the United States. Subsidiaries of U.S. firms began to make significant use of the Eurobond market after restrictions were imposed on their borrowing in the United States. Since removal of these restrictions early in 1974, there has been some return of U.S. subsidiaries to borrowing in New York. On the other hand, after some initial decline, the Eurobond market somewhat surprisingly revived. This was partly because of an increase in borrowing by local government units in Europe, but the need for somewhat less disclosure of financial information in the Eurobond market than in the U.S. capital market may also have been a factor. An explanation of the apparently lower cost in the U.S. capital market and the concomitant revival of the Eurobond market is needed, and differences in disclosure may be part of the explanation.[26]

As noted, U.S. finance subsidiaries have been active in Eurobond offerings. While U.S. restrictions on foreign investment were in effect, special authorization for such issues was granted. Interest payments were usually free of U.S. withholding taxes, and the finance subsidiaries paid minimal taxes. Although the finance subsidiaries are usually subsidiaries of U.S. firms, the interest equalization tax (IET), while it was in effect, discouraged purchase of the bonds by American investors. At the same time, the issues did not have to be registered with the Securities and Exchange Commission, a time-consuming and costly process, and they were exempt from regulation under the Investment Company Act of 1940.

The cost of borrowing in the Eurocurrency markets, for comparison, is the after-tax cost of the needed amount in local currency translated into dollars,

[26]For some views and evidence on disclosure, see, for example, Gerhard G. Mueller, "An International View of Accounting and Disclosure," *International Journal of Accounting*, Fall 1972, pp. 117–134; Frederick D. S. Choi, "Financial Disclosure and Entry to the European Capital Market," *Journal of Accounting Research*, Autumn 1973, pp. 159–175; Frederick D. S. Choi, "Financial Disclosure in Relation to the European Capital Market," *International Journal of Accounting*, Fall 1973, pp. 53–66; and M. Edgar Barrett, "Annual Report Disclosure: Are American Reports Superior?" *Journal of International Business Studies*, Fall 1975, pp. 15–24.

the tax rate in this case being that of the borrowing subsidiary. From this cost should be subtracted any tax gain (or a tax loss should be added.)

External Sources of Funds: The U.S. Money and Capital Markets   With the relaxation of U.S. controls on foreign investment in early 1974, foreign subsidiaries of U.S. firms are again able to borrow in the U.S. money and capital markets. If dollar funds are needed, this may be desirable if cost is less than in the Eurocurrency or Eurobond markets. When dollar funds are not needed, the exchange risk (that is, the risk of a change in the exchange rate in a direction making repayment of loans in dollars more costly in local currency) may offset the higher cost of borrowing funds in Europe.

Since funds borrowed in the United States are normally repaid in U.S. dollars, a firm may wish to hedge by buying forward exchange for delivery to it at the loan maturity date. This is analogous to the covering of foreign investments by banks through sale of forward exchange. The same principles concerning hedging apply.[27]

Mergers, Acquisitions, and Joint Ventures

Firms operating internationally have often expanded their activities through mergers and acquisitions, but only recently has much analysis of this type of action been published. Anti-foreign attitudes have sometimes delayed or even prevented such actions, but a number of acquisitions have occurred. General Electric's acquisition of a dominant interest in Machines Bull in France is one example. After initial refusal of the French government to grant approval, General Electric finally gained a 50 percent interest, which later became approximately a 66 percent interest.[28] Acquisitions have run in both directions. An example of the opposite direction is the acquisition of 40 percent of Libby, McNeill's stock by Nestlé, the Swiss firm.

Major problems in acquisitions can arise from differences in accounting practices and in such financial matters as dividend policies. The American practice of disclosing a substantial amount of financial information concerning companies that are acquired as well as for firms already owned may create opposition from host-country managements. Divergencies between U.S. government policies and managements of U.S. firms that try to conform to such policies, on the one hand, and foreign countries' policies and their attitudes that companies operating in their countries should conform to those policies, on the other hand, also sometimes create problems.

In one survey of 90 acquisitions by 27 American MNCs, it appeared that horizontal integration produced slightly better results than vertical integration, that the success of an acquisition was highly correlated with the GNP of the

---

[27]The term "arbi-loan" has been used for this procedure; see David K. Eiteman and Arthur I. Stonehill, *Multinational Business Finance* (Reading, Mass.: Addison-Wesley, 1973), p. 271, and the reference source cited there.

[28]Walter Guzzardi, Jr., "Why the Climate is Changing for U.S. Investment," *Fortune*, Sept. 15, 1967, pp. 113–117, 206–212.

host country, and that in the past acquisitions have tended to have lower payoffs than other types of investment in Europe.[29]

In many acquisitions joint ventures are involved. Host-country nationals retain partial control of the subsidiaries. In some countries, in fact, it is almost impossible to operate on any other basis—Japan and Mexico are examples. Joint ventures may minimize complaints about American domination and lead to a desirable sharing of risks. On the other hand, joint ventures are like partnerships in most respects, and when partners' views differ on policy issues, it may be difficult to arrange satisfactory compromises.

Joint ventures have been entered into by many American companies even when not required by host government policies. They are desirable because they provide valuable know-how as well as indirectly providing financing of investment projects. Financial aid is likely to be even more important for European multinational firms than for American firms, since many European countries still impose rather strict limitations on outflows of capital. To the extent that financing is jointly provided, foreign exchange control risks of companies entering a market are reduced.

A strong argument in favor of joint ventures has been that local partners can reduce political pressures against companies and provide positive political influence leading to good public relations. But this argument may be faulty. Usually political problems become paramount when some profound sociological or economic changes occur in host countries. The local partner is usually a member of the local elite, and if the elite are replaced, partners may become political liabilities instead of assets. An independently owned and operated subsidiary *may*, however, be able to remain aloof from domestic political unrest.

As benefits from an inflow of foreign investment decrease, host countries, especially LDCs, may wish to increase their citizens' shares of ownership in foreign firms. As indicated in Chapter 17, U.S. tax laws limit foreign tax credits for parent companies to situations in which a specified minimum ownership share exists. There may, therefore, be conflict concerning changes in ownership shares. Specific issues on which views may differ include dividend policy (local stockholders often desiring increased dividends because in many countries investors buy stocks for income rather than for capital gains); transfer pricing policy (because transfer prices may, in the interest of the MNC as a whole, for tax benefits or other advantages, reduce profits in some subsidiaries); and political issues.

In an interesting article, Lawrence C. Franko wrote that joint ventures have been widely accepted in LDCs although some are rejected.[30] Franko

---

[29]John Kitching, "Winning and Losing with European Acquisitions," *Harvard Business Review*, March–April 1974, pp. 124–136. The quotation is from p. 136. This survey was judgmental in the sense that it was a sampling of executive opinions in which success of acquisition was rated. It would be desirable if other measures could be used to give more assurance of objectivity, but the survey is interesting nevertheless.

[30]Lawrence G. Franko, "International Joint Ventures in Developing Countries: Mystique and Reality," *Law and Policy in International Business*, Spring 1974, pp. 315–336.

found that single-product firms were more successful than vertically integrated firms with production networks across international boundaries. He also expressed the opinion that although foreigners are attracted to joint ventures in the hope of acquiring skills, it is not necessary now to formalize a business relationship in this way in order to transfer knowledge from one country to another.

In joint ventures, the local interests may be held by local individual stockholders, private firms, or government companies. Many industries in some countries are publicly owned and joint ventures with participation by local government-owned companies are becoming more common. In some cases consortia composed of a number of companies, some private and some publicly owned, may be appropriate.[31]

Transnational consortia with a more defensive purpose have also been a feature of the European scene. Most of these consortia have involved the merger of two medium-large groups incorporated in different countries. The essence of such arrangements has been that the new organizations should have unified management structures without the subordination of either partner company to the other. The purpose has often been to fend off competition from American MNCs. Methods of organizing such mergers have generally been the creation of holding companies or the use of interlocking stock ownership.[32] Naturally there is nothing to prevent such consortia being formed across wider frontiers, and they are politically attractive to countries that welcome American connections but fear economic domination by MNCs.

EFFECTS OF DIFFERENCES IN RISKS, TAXES, AND INFLATION RATES

In an excellent summary article on the sources of funds for foreign investments, Robbins and Stobaugh make a provocative statement in their conclusions: ". . . the number of alternatives is so great that the manager copes by adopting simplifying decision rules."[33] They note that managements set debt/equity ratios (a subject discussed in Chapter 19), set limits on the extent of intersubsidiary financing, and seem to favor short-term local borrowing whenever suitable.

These statements, which are probably well founded, challenge those who would introduce greater precision into foreign investment decision rules. Complex situations require simplification of rules, although modern data processing techniques can assist managements in handling more complicated situations. It is not our purpose here to present a comprehensive model, but merely to stress the nature of the more important considerations that should be

[31]Consortia of multinational banks were discussed in Chap. 8.

[32]Christopher Layton, *Cross-Frontier Mergers in Europe* (Bath, U.K.: Bath University Press, 1971).

[33]Sidney M. Robbins and Robert B. Stobaugh, "Financing Foreign Affiliates," *Financial Management*, Winter 1972, pp. 56–65; see also their *Money in the Multinational Enterprise: A Study of Financial Policy* (New York: Basic Books, 1973).

explicitly introduced into a decision model concerned with international investments. Others have already begun to formalize these considerations.[34]

We briefly but explicitly consider (1) exchange rates, (2) tax differences, (3) political risks, and (4) changes in rates of inflation. In spite of the existence of these risks, a recent survey of 298 U.S. parent companies with 5,237 majority-owned affiliates indicated that these companies had higher rates of return on the average than all U.S. manufacturing firms, evidently because of the greater share of foreign-source income in these parent companies' earnings.[35] Of course, a higher rate of return is to be expected if lenders and investing companies perceive added risks and require higher rates of return to compensate for them. We do not know whether the higher observed returns are greater than or less than the losses which may in the long run result from these risks.

Recent authors have contended that international diversification can help reduce risk. To the extent that business cycles are not synchronized in various countries, systematic risk is reduced if asset portfolios cross international boundaries. Alan K. Severn surveyed investor evaluation of risk in firms and found that ". . . a typical firm in my sample was accorded a capitalization rate about 10 basis points [one-tenth of one percent] lower than what it would have been if all income had been subject to the degree of risk which it experienced domestically."[36]

Although diversification may reduce risk, we must recognize the special risks inherent in international investments and search for the net effect of these various risks.

Exchange Risk

In an article designed ". . . to develop relatively formal decision rules for managing the risk of exchange rate change," William R. Folks, Jr., focused discussion chiefly on the effect of exchange rate changes on asset evaluation rather than on effect on the flow of funds across international borders.[37] For the decision rules, the manager must make estimates of the returns that will be forthcoming from an investment and of the currency in which such net earnings will accrue. If the foreign currency is expected to depreciate and if it is expected that earnings will be repatriated, then obviously the dollars available for stockholders are reduced. We have seen that in the floating rate situation it

---

[34]In addition to the article by Shapiro cited in fn. 22, see Walter N. Ness, "A Linear Programming Approach to Financing the Multinational Corporation," *Financial Management*, Winter 1972, pp. 88–100.

[35]Robert B. Leftwich, "U.S. Multinational Companies: Profitability, Financial Leverage, and Effective Income Tax Rates," *Survey of Current Business*, May 1974, pp. 27–36.

[36]Alan K. Severn, "Investor Evaluation and Foreign and Domestic Risk," *Journal of Finance*, May 1974, pp. 545–550. See also the discussion of organization of business firms for purposes of instituting area diversification in John M. Stopford and Louis T. Wells, Jr., *Managing the Multinational Enterprise: Organization of the Firm and Ownership of the Subsidiaries* (New York: Basic Books, 1972), especially Chap. 4.

[37]William R. Folks, Jr., "Decision Analysis for Exchange Risk Management," *Financial Management*, Winter 1972, pp. 101–112.

is generally the case that depreciation or appreciation cannot be predicted in the short run. However, in some situations actions of central banks may make changes in exchange rates predictable. The important thing is for managers to evaluate reality and judge whether the situation is one of an efficient foreign exchange market, in which case they should not attempt to predict, or whether it is one of official intervention, which may permit prediction.

If exchange rate risk is believed to exist, it may be appropriate to attach a risk premium to the cost of capital when evaluating foreign investment decisions. By lowering present value, the risk premium may lead to rejection of some proposed projects. A premium may already have been introduced into the cost of borrowed funds if investors perceive risk in the investments to be made by a firm. Even in this case, a risk premium may be appropriate for the cost of retained earnings, but of course unless new foreign investments are being undertaken, it may be presumed that this premium already exists in the rate being earned on such funds.

Tax Differences

It is clearly necessary to know tax rates in host countries to estimate earnings flows. Income is sometimes exempted from taxes for some years to encourage investments. Income may be taxed on a cash or on an accrual basis, in which case it is taxed as earned, without waiting until it has been remitted to the parent company. There is also the question, how is the corporate entity defined for taxation? Including foreign branches as part of the corporate entity may enable a corporation to deduct losses in unprofitable branches from profits in other locations. Finally, there is the question of how dual taxation is eliminated or reduced. Most countries recognize that a firm should not be taxed twice on the same income, but as indicated in Chapter 17 there are a number of ways to give credit for taxes already paid. Finally, the existence of tax treaties affects taxes. In some cases, if operations are kept within certain limits, tax treaties may eliminate the necessity for filing tax returns in some countries. With knowledge concerning tax provisions and rates, managers can adjust expected cash flow streams; this information must be revised regularly because of constant change in tax legislation and administrative rules.

For our purposes, we must now consider the tax risk—the risk that a government may change its tax policy in a way unfavorable to foreign firms. This risk applies to both domestic and international operations. As far as we know, it has never been formally introduced into the investment decision rule criteria. No doubt, tax changes in some countries are more significant and perhaps less predictable than in others. Tax change risks are part of political risks assumed in doing business in foreign countries.

Political Risks

The existence of various political risks may introduce modifications into investment evaluation. Political risks include relatively mild actions such as small increases in taxes; moderate actions such as restrictions on remittances of profits; and extreme actions such as confiscation of property, sometimes without compensation, and often with inadequate compensation. A high risk premium in the cost of capital rate may eliminate consideration of new projects in some countries because risks are evaluated as very signficant.

If there is a risk that remittances of profits may be restricted, then earnings of subsidiaries beyond permitted remittance levels must be reinvested in host countries. Managers must estimate the rate which may be earned on such reinvested funds. Resulting expected returns may be included as part of total expected return on the project. This does not necessarily nor usually increase expected return, however, because the usual calculations assume that all earnings are reinvested at the rate being earned by the firm. The rate which can be earned on funds reinvested in host countries may be different; it is likely to be lower, especially if the funds are invested in short-term securities. If operating net cash inflows over a specified period, terminal value at the end of the period, and returns on reinvested funds are combined, a *terminal rate of return* can be calculated. The usual calculation is a rate of return based on the presumption that earnings are reinvested at the current rate of return. The terminal rate of return is based on the assumption that they are reinvested at a different rate. Finally, managers might wish to calculate a rate of return on the assumption that funds cannot be reinvested at all, but are simply blocked in the host country. Such calculations may yield different evaluations of different projects, depending on whether it is assumed that earnings can be reinvested at the current rate of return, that they cannot be reinvested at all, or that they can be reinvested at some rate different from the current rate of return. If the rate of return is quite high, blocking repatriation of earnings may be significant, and may lead managers to choose other investments on which the rate of return is not so high. This is especially likely if a high return is anticipated in the first few years, and a much lower rate of return in succeeding years.[38]

If an MNC has sufficient diversification, it can assign a probability to confiscation or other serious reduction in value of investments based on the likelihood of confiscation or a similar action occurring. If, for example, a firm has investments in 50 countries and if we can assume for a moment that these investments are equal, then the probability of confiscation might be based on past history in the same manner that fire insurance premiums are based on past history of fires. If confiscation has occurred in two countries, then the cost of capital rate should be increased by approximately 2/50, or 1/25, as a risk premium for such political risk. Actual situations are not as simple as this, but the example may illustrate the manner in which the problem may be considered.

Differences in Inflation Rates

Following Fisher's theory, we assume that interest rates include an inflation premium approximately equal to the rate of inflation. If rates of inflation are the same in host countries and in source countries, the same premium will be

---

[38]A pro forma example is given by Rita M. Rodriguez and E. Eugene Carter, *International Financial Management* (Englewood Cliffs, N.J.: Prentice-Hall, 1976), p. 312.

included in interest rates in both. If real interest rates were the same before inflation, nominal interest rates will rise with inflation, but will continue to be the same in different countries. If, however, there is more rapid inflation in one country than in another, we must consider purchasing power parity theory and "Fisher open." If purchasing power parity theory is valid, the exchange value of a currency will fall in proportion to increasing inflation. If Fisher open is valid, the accumulated interest agio will equal the accumulated exchange rate agio, and funds invested in a country experiencing rapid inflation will gain from interest what they lose when translated at lower exchange rates.

The question that managers must examine, then, is whether purchasing power parity theory and Fisher open are likely to hold during the period under consideration. If they do, inflation and interest rate changes are relevant, but to take advantage of this situation managers must be able to predict the nature of variations from purchasing power parity and from Fisher open. If inflation is correctly anticipated, these principles are likely to hold. Recent analyses have stressed the problems arising from unanticipated inflation, such as that of the last decade. With perfectly anticipated inflation, all prices, including interest rates (the prices for the use of money for periods of time) rise proportionately. Even money balances receive interest, and hence do not fall in value. Money balances may not receive interest, and hence lose value, tending to cause a shift in asset portfolios toward human and physical wealth, which rises in value. The inflation which has occurred has not been perfectly anticipated, and not only money but also other relatively "safe" assets such as short-term government securities and especially long-term government securities have lost value. Since most people are averse to risk, the riskiness of hitherto safe assets (the variability in their loss of value) causes investors to shift to other assets. But some other assets also become more risky in periods of variable inflation. Stocks of firms which encounter a degree of risk tend to be avoided, and their prices fall. Stocks therefore do not gain in value at the same rate as inflation, and are not a good hedge in such periods. The liquidity premium on short-term securities, raising their prices and reducing their yields, tends to increase, while short-term interest rates become more variable. The premium in the yield on long-term securities increases. In other words, long-term capital becomes more costly relative to short-term capital and to consumption. Sale of new securities is discouraged. Meanwhile, taxes, which are generally fixed as percentages of reported income, rise as reported income rises. The share of GNP accruing to government rises. The impact of this is adverse to private investment. Financial institutions whose portfolios consist largely of fixed-income securities suffer disintermediation.[39] All these changes result in unexpected variations in prices and interest rates; and certainly in the relatively short run (up to a decade), purchasing power parity and Fisher open may not hold. If so, it may be necessary for financial managers to evaluate expected rates of inflation in various countries to determine whether there are significant variations from

---

[39]This analysis draws heavily on Edward S. Shaw, "Inflation, Finance and Capital Markets," Federal Reserve Bank of San Francisco, *Economic Review*, December 1975, pp. 5–20.

purchasing power parity and from Fisher open. Thus different rates of inflation may significantly complicate life for international financial managers. Whether governments can take appropriate measures to curb unanticipated inflation is not yet clear.[40]

SUMMARY

In this chapter we reviewed fundamentals of financial management: the nature of income as a surplus beyond what is needed to maintain capital, the valuation of the business firm in terms of discounting expected future net cash inflows, and the choice of an appropriate rate of discount.

The concept of weighted average cost of capital was used in examining various sources of capital for international firms. The wide variety of such sources available to international firms was discussed from the aspect of the determination of costs and the characteristics of methods of obtaining funds from various sources.

Third, we examined the likelihood of benefits of international diversification by international firms and the means of diversifying and expanding through acquisitions, mergers, and joint ventures.

Finally, we discussed the impact of (1) exchange rate changes as a form of risk, (2) political risks, (3) tax differences, and (4) differences in rates of inflation on evaluation for foreign investment decisions. We found that although in theory a perfectly anticipated inflation might be irrelevant, the unanticipated or "dirty" inflation prevailing during the last decade and at some times in the past has been significant because it reduced the real value of money and caused a shift away from all assets perceived as risky—including, of course, real capital assets and stocks. Whether efforts of governments to "clean up" such inflation by such means as indexing, to dampen it by recessions, or to fight it by increasing real output can succeed is not yet clear.

APPENDIX: Dollar Cost of a Parent Company Loan to a Subsidiary

This appendix gives a method for determining the dollar cost of a parent company loan to a subsidiary as one example of the method of determining cost of funds. The method is based on calculations given in the article by Alan Shapiro cited in footnote 22, but the notation has been somewhat simplified.

First the following terms are defined:

[40]Such inflation may be curbed either by slow growth of money supply and moderate fiscal deficits, with a consequently rather high cost in unemployment, or by efforts to increase real output, primarily by raising the after-tax yield on investments. Reducing corporate income taxes, investment tax credits, and other similar actions are means to this end. Most observers also agree that government budget surpluses as the economy reaches levels approaching "full" employment are also essential, to avoid crowding out private investment.

C the dollar cost of a $1 loan for one year (cost of a $1 million loan would be $1 million $\times$ C) by a U.S. parent company to a subsidiary in Great Britain

E_0 the exchange rate when the loan is made

E_1 the exchange rate a year later

r_p the U.S. parent company's annual cost of debt in percent

r_{us} interest rate charged by the parent company to the subsidiary

t_{gb} subsidiary's effective tax rate in Great Britain

t_p parent company's effective tax rate on income from subsidiary

t_{us} parent company's effective tax rate on domestic income

Using these definitions we can express the dollar cost of a one-year loan of $1 by the parent company to the subsidiary as

$$C = \underbrace{E_0 r_p(1 - t_{us})}_{\substack{\text{Parent's} \\ \text{interest} \\ \text{cost}}} + \underbrace{E_0 r_{us}(1 - t_{gb})}_{\substack{\text{Subsidiary's} \\ \text{interest} \\ \text{cost}}} - \underbrace{E_0 r_{us}(1 - t_p)}_{\substack{\text{Parent's} \\ \text{interest} \\ \text{income}}} - \underbrace{(E_0 - E_1)t_{gb}}_{\substack{\text{Tax gain} \\ \text{on exchange} \\ \text{loss}}}$$

The first term is the parent's interest charge. If E_0 is $2 per pound sterling, if the tax rate on domestic income for the parent company is 50 percent, and if the parent's debt cost is 10 percent, then the interest charge for $1 is

$$E_0 r_p(1 - t_{us}) = \$2 \times .10(1 - .5) = \$.20 \times .50 = \$0.10$$

Thus the cost is 10 percent.

The second term shows the subsidiary's interest cost. If the subsidiary must pay, say, 20 percent, and the tax rate it must pay is 60 percent, then the subsidiary's interest cost is

$$E_0 r_{us}(1 - t_{gb}) = \$2 \times .20(1 - .6) = \$.40 \times .40 = \$0.16, \text{ or 16 percent}$$

The third term is the parent company's interest income. If t_p is the tax rate on foreign-source income and this is 40 percent, then

$$E_0 r_{us}(1 - t_p) = \$2 \times .20(1 - .4) = \$.4 \times .6 = \$.24, \text{ or 24 percent}$$

The fourth term is the tax gain or loss on the exchange rate change which is expected to occur. If the pound is expected to drop from $2.00 to $1.50, then E_1 is $1.50 and the fourth term is

$$(E_0 - E_1)t_{gb} = (\$2 - \$1.5).60 = \$.5 \times .6 = \$0.30$$

or 30 percent gain. In this case there is a tax gain because the loss on the exchange rate change is tax deductible.

Thus $C = .10 + .16 - .24 - .30 = .26 - .54 = -.28$, or *minus* 28 percent. The sizable depreciation of the pound assumed in the example has led to financial gain from borrowing from the parent company. If no exchange rate change took place, then $C = .10 + .16 - .24 = .26 - .24 = 2$ percent, or $0.02 on each dollar of loan. This low rate, 2 percent, comes about because of different tax rates in the two countries and the ability of firms to deduct interest expense from income before taxes.

The formulas change with different sources of borrowing, but from this example we can see the principles of estimating dollar cost of loans or of borrowing. By estimating C's for a variety of sources, it should be possible to determine the lowest cost. Dealing with a one-year loan simplifies the formulation greatly but does not affect the principles, and the use of calculators or computers can enable us to deal with more complex situations.

QUESTIONS FOR DISCUSSION

1 Explain the meaning and importance of Hicks' definition of income. If wealth is the present value of expected future income, how does inflation affect wealth? Should an increase in wealth arising from inflation be regarded as an increase in profits? Why or why not?

2 Would you expect retained earnings in most cases to have a higher or lower cost than borrowed funds? Why?

3 Why do you think that oil companies repatriate most of the earnings from their foreign subsidiaries?

4 Should profit maximization be in the interest of a total multinational firm or should each subsidiary of such a firm attempt to maximize its own profit? Give reasons for your answer.

5 Discuss some possible advantages and disadvantages of each of the following external sources of funds for foreign subsidiaries: (a) local bank offices; (b) the Eurocurrency and Eurobond markets, directly and through finance subsidiaries; and (c) the U.S. money and capital markets.

6 What factors may make the discount rate used in evaluating a firm's foreign investments higher (or lower) than the firm's cost of capital?

7 Can you suggest why acquisitions might tend to have lower payoff rates than other types of investment in Europe? What are the *financial* advantages and disadvantages of joint ventures?

8 How do you evaluate the evidence that stocks issued by firms with relatively large international operations statistically have significantly higher price-earnings ratios than firms in the same industries with less international involvement?

9 Why may *systematic* risk be reduced by international diversification?

10 What is meant by a "terminal rate of return"? and why may it be important in evaluating a foreign investment?

PROBLEMS

1 Determine the dollar cost of a $1 million, one-year loan to a subsidiary in Germany of a U.S. parent company when the mark's value is $0.40 but the mark is expected to appreciate during the year to $0.50. Let r_{us} be 10 percent, r_p 12 percent, t_g 40 percent, and t_{us} 50 percent.

2 Explain why in Problem 1 the interest rate used for r_p is the rate at which the parent company can borrow funds rather than its cost of capital.

3 One author gives an example of a parent company loan made at 10 percent, which is also the cost of borrowing by the parent company, and a Eurodollar loan available at 11 percent. Verify that the parent company loan is cheaper. Then from the

knowledge of the Eurodollar market gained from Chapter 10, comment on the likelihood of the interest rate relationship being as stated.

4 Assume that a parent company earns 12 percent on equity and invests in a new foreign subsidiary. In the country in which the subsidiary begins operating, it is estimated that a similar firm would earn 15 percent. What is the proper cost of the equity capital contributed by the parent company to the subsidiary? Why?

5 What is the probable effect of unanticipated inflation, which is also somewhat variable, on estimates of present value of new investment projects? Explain how this effect occurs.

SUGGESTED REFERENCES

Fundamentals of financial management are well set forth at a fairly high analytical level in the early chapters of Charles W. Haley and Lawrence D. Schall, *The Theory of Financial Decisions* (New York: McGraw-Hill, 1973). See also their *Introduction to Financial Management* (New York: McGraw-Hill, 1977).

A number of books with much wider scope, dealing with many aspects of international enterprises, have sections on financial policies and practices. Among these the following merit special mention: Michael Z. Brooke and H. Lee Remmers, *The Strategy of Multinational Enterprise: Organization and Finance* (New York: American Elsevier, 1970); J. Stopford and L. Wells, *Managing the Multinational Enterprise* (New York: Basic Books, 1972); and R. Hal Mason, Robert R. Miller, and Dale R. Weigel, *The Economics of International Business* (New York: Wiley, 1975).

A recent empirical study of the handling of financial matters in multinational companies which is of considerable interest is Sidney M. Robbins and Robert B. Stobaugh, *Money in the Multinational Enterprise: A Study of Financial Policy* (New York: Basic Books, 1973). A useful government report is *The Multinational Corporation: Studies on U.S. Foreign Investment*, vols. 1 and 2 (Washington, D.C.: Government Printing Office, 1973).

Among periodicals, the *Survey of Current Business* is an invaluable source of data on financing corporations, domestic and multinational; it contains, for example, the Leftwich article referred to in fn. 35. Readers may also refer to *Financing Foreign Operations* (New York: Business International), a continually updated source.

On economic elements which may contribute to foreign investment decisions, see Richard E. Caves, "International Corporations: The Industrial Economics of Foreign Investment," *Economica*, February 1971, pp. 1–27. See also W. Dickerson Hogue, "The Foreign Investment Decision Making Process," *Association for Education in International Business Proceedings*, Dec. 29, 1967, pp. 1–2, and Thomas Horst, "Firm and Industry Determinants of the Decision to Invest Abroad: An Empirical Study," *Review of Economics and Statistics*, August 1972, pp. 258–265.

A warning on the difficulties of measuring profitability of foreign subsidiaries is given in Sidney M. Robbins and Robert B. Stobaugh, "The Bent Measuring Stick for Foreign Subsidiaries," *Harvard Business Review*, September–October 1973, pp. 80–88.

On transnational enterprises, in addition to the reference cited in fn. 32, see Michael B. Stewart, "Transnational Enterprise: The European Challenge," *Columbia Journal of World Business*, July–August 1972, pp. 5–13.

On borrowing in various markets, there are many rather interesting discussions; examples are P. Henry Mueller, "How to Borrow Abroad from a U.S. Bank," *Journal of Commercial Bank Lending*, March 1973, pp. 32–43; Ian Giddy, "The Blossoming of the

Eurobond Market," *Columbia Journal of World Business*, Winter 1975, pp. 66–76; and A. W. Clements, "Markets and Those Who Make Them—A User's View," *Euromoney*, August 1975, pp. 42–48. The Winter 1975 issue of the *Columbia Journal of World Business* was devoted to international banking, and many of the articles are significant; see especially those by Thomas on international lending by regional U.S. banks, by Ruckdeschel on risk in such lending, and the article by Rudy on global planning in multinational banking.

On finance subsidiaries, see the article by Rosenberg and Singer referred to in the suggested references for Chap. 17 and also Johannes Semler, "Advantages and Disadvantages of Forming Finance Subsidiaries Abroad," *Euromoney*, June 1974, pp. 56–59.

On capital budgeting in multinational firms, see Dileep R. Mehta, "Capital Budget Procedures for a Multinational Firm," in Sethi and Holton, eds. *Management of the Multinationals* (New York: Free Press, 1974), pp. 272–291.

Finally, although the emphasis is on finance within a country, the December 1975 issue of the *Economic Review* of the Federal Reserve Bank of San Francisco is "must" reading, especially the article by Edward S. Shaw cited in fn. 39.

Chapter 19

The Finance Function in International Operations

The previous chapter contained a discussion of capital budgeting decisions for foreign investments. These are decisions made rather infrequently, when new investments are considered and when long-term borrowing is necessary. The day-to-day handling of the finance function in international operations is analyzed in this chapter. The finance function involves decisions concerning optimal capital structure, working capital management, and policies governing remittances of funds. After these have been considered, we devote a short section to financial control. Such control has implications that are broader than the financial aspects, but we confine our discussion primarily to financial questions: what forms of financial control and organization for control are likely to be best for making optimal decisions on capital structure, working capital management, and remittance policies? First we need a framework for analysis of the finance function in international operations.

A FRAMEWORK FOR ANALYSIS OF THE FINANCE FUNCTION

As always, the unifying theme guiding management is the long-run maximization of return to the owners of the firm—the stockholders. To the extent that a firm's managers can use assets, liabilities, and equity to increase the firm's net worth, they should do so. This means, for example, placing the firm's cash balances in accounts that earn the highest rate of interest consistent with needed liquidity, keeping funds in the "right" currencies, and being able to transfer funds to locations where needed.

In international finance, the underlying determinants of financial decisions are an analysis of cash flows expected, as in domestic finance, *plus* a foreign exchange management posture. In international finance it must be recognized that decisions concerning both liabilities and assets change not only the asset-liability position but also the foreign exchange position. Easier terms for credit sales may increase both total revenue and profits, but may also result in an increase in assets exposed to risk of loss in the event of a currency depreciation or devaluation.

Bases for Analysis

Certain assumptions and principles constitute bases for analyzing the finance function in international finance. First, it must be assumed that forecasts of cash flows can be made that are sufficiently accurate to be useful.

Second, a time interval for forecasting cash flows must be chosen. A year is usually convenient because it is sufficient for some short-term variations to offset each other. The longer the time interval, the less exposure is likely to be in most cases, because over long periods purchasing power parity and Fisher open are more nearly valid. However, forecasts of cash flows for longer periods than one year are likely to be greatly in error.

Third, a unit of account should be convenient. This may be the currency of the country in which the headquarters of the MNC is located. Since most multinational corporate headquarters are located in the United States, the U.S. dollar is a convenient unit of account. Other currencies are therefore, in this case, translated into U.S. dollars.

Fourth, economic exposure rather than accounting exposure to exchange rate risk should be considered, although if it is found that economic exposure is not likely to be significant it may be convenient to adjust to reduce accounting exposure. Economic exposure exists to the extent that there are systematic deviations from purchasing power parity and from Fisher open. If purchasing power parity theory is valid in the long run, then in the long run nonmonetary assets are not exposed, because prices of such assets rise in proportion to depreciation of the local currency in the foreign exchange market and vice versa. Similarly, if Fisher open is valid in the long run, interest returns and payments will compensate for the effect of changes in exchange values on monetary assets and on returns on these assets. Hence the measure of economic exposure is the extent of systematic deviations from purchasing power parity and from Fisher open. The only exception to this generalization is the holding of money narrowly defined (M_1) when interest is not paid on such assets. This applies to holdings of coins and paper money generally, and to holdings of demand deposits in the United States since 1933.

Firms may have their economic income exposed to risk without holding any foreign currency assets. For example, exporters who expect to receive payment in foreign currencies may receive less if such currencies depreciate. Again, however, if purchasing power parity holds in the long run, prices will increase proportionately to the currency depreciation.

Estimating economic risk exposure involves estimating future values for nonmonetary assets, for monetary assets and liabilities, and for income and payment streams.[1] For nonmonetary assets, the exposure is the difference between the rise in prices of assets and the depreciation of local currency. If these exactly offset each other (that is, if purchasing power parity holds), there is no exposure on these assets. For monetary assets and for liabilities, a net position must be determined; then the anticipated gain or loss from exchange rate changes must be compared with the gain or loss from changes in cumulative interest payments. If these are equal, no exposure is indicated. This means that if Fisher open holds there is no exposure except, as noted, for amounts held in non-interest-bearing assets.

It should be noted that, following the discussion in Chapter 16, the simplest analysis results if replacement values are used for valuation and current exchange rates for translation. It should also be noted that in the long run, if it is assumed that purchasing power parity and Fisher open are generally valid, the firm is not exposed in the economic sense, no matter what accounting conventions are used. It has been shown that these theories are more nearly valid for the long than for the short run. So changes in accounting rules are more significant for the short run than for the long run. If firms wish to reduce accounting exposure, they can do so by making appropriate changes in the mix of assets and liabilities. For example, when FASB 8 required translation of inventory values at historic rates (presuming the inventories were valued at historic rates), the resulting accounting exposure could be eliminated by changing debt in foreign currency by an appropriate amount.

If interest rate differentials and forward rates are generally unbiased indicators of future spot rates, there is really no reason for choosing a particular position. Hence the firm might just as well maintain a position that is unexposed according to the accounting rules currently in effect. Indeed, the results of recent studies uncover no evidence of significant systematic deviations from Fisher open.[2] These results support the proposition that the forward rate is an *unbiased* predictor of the future spot rate. These data are consistent with the findings of Giddy and Dufey, reported in Chapter 14, that during the floating rate period since 1973 the forward rate, although an unbiased predictor, was not a *good* predictor of future spot rates. Giddy and Dufey found, we may remind the reader, that the spot rate was the best predictor of the future spot rate, since changes in exchange rates in the short run were random.

What do managers do with evidence like this? It seems to indicate that

---

[1] An excellent analysis of economic exposure is contained in Robert Z. Aliber, *The Short Guide to Corporate International Finance*, mimeographed, Chicago, 1975, Chap. 9.

[2] Ibid., Chap. 6. See also Steven W. Kohlhagen, "The Performance of the Foreign Exchange Markets: 1971–1974," *Journal of International Business Studies*, Fall 1975, pp. 33–39.

over the long run the risks even out so that no net profits can consistently be made by changing asset and liability mixes to avoid exposure. Managers, however, are charged with current responsibility and feel that they must do what they can to offset the adverse effects of short-run changes in exchange rates. Managers will doubtless continue to try to avoid risks, and will pay large fees to consultants who claim to be able to forecast exchange rates, just as some investors pay large fees to investor services who claim to be able to forecast short-run movements in stock market prices.

Data for Analysis

The firm needs to forecast possible economic exposure under various assumed conditions, and to simulate results on a "what if" basis. It is probably not possible to predict short-term exchange rate changes in a floating rate system.[3] Hence the company must evaluate possibilities and be prepared for actions should these possibilities materialize. It must also examine the various countries where it operates to determine whether purchasing power parity and Fisher open appear to be valid for those countries.

The firm needs a forecast of flow of funds and of assets and liabilities in each currency; it needs to determine aggregate exposure and exposure in each currency; and it needs to forecast its rate of return on assets in each currency. Additionally, it needs a forecast of interest rates for borrowing and investing in each possible source of funds and in each possible location for investment; initial spot exchange rates for currencies involved; and initial forward exchange rates for currencies involved. These data should be provided by the firm's management information system.

Alternative Scenarios

Since short-term prediction of prices and interest rates is likely to be "dubious or even dangerous," what is then needed is development of alternative scenarios, so that actions may be taken when necessary. The alternative scenarios might include a "most likely" scenario, a "no change" scenario, and another possibility, probably one quite different from that deemed most likely.

The likelihood of changes in constraints such as borrowing restrictions, tariff and exchange controls, limitations on cash transfers and other remittances, and taxes must be considered.

One objective of a firm's management is to borrow at the lowest possible effective rate if cash flow forecasts indicate that funds may be needed; another objective is to invest at the highest effective rate if there are surplus funds.[4] Cash flow forecasts may indicate a need for borrowing by one subsidiary and

---

[3]Andreas R. Prindl, "Guidelines for MNC Money Managers," *Harvard Business Review,* January–February 1976, pp. 73–80; "Most observers would agree that attempts to predict short-term rates in today's market are dubious and even dangerous" (p. 75).

[4]Some qualifications should be inserted. For example, a conservative attitude in protecting credit relationships may be desirable in view of the possibility of "credit crunches" and other special situations. See ibid.

surplus funds for investment by another. Thus a cash flow forecast may show that expected internally-generated funds are insufficient in one subsidiary to provide for expected increases in cash holdings, accounts receivable, inventories, and so on. In another subsidiary the reverse may be true. In some cases transactions between subsidiaries may be permissible and desirable; in other cases they must be avoided. After making a decision on this question, the firm can compute costs and returns by combining borrowing and investing decisions and effective interest rates. The lowest cost of funds among various financial markets and types of borrowing may be determined from interest rate and tax data as indicated in Chapter 18. This may be done for the "most likely" scenario, the "no change" scenario, and a third scenario.

Exposure forecasts combined with the changes resulting from financing and investing provide forecasts of exposure after such actions. Because of the financing and investing, there will be foreign exchange translation gains or losses. Exposure forecasts should be made in economic terms if financial managers believe there are significant long-term or medium-term deviations from purchasing power parity and Fisher open. For example, for many years before the downward float of the Mexican peso in the late summer of 1976, investments in Mexican peso assets would have yielded far more than would have been expected in terms of theory. If, on the other hand, such deviations are not believed to be significant, accounting exposure should be measured, and means of reducing such exposure may be adopted if other factors warrant.

Also the cost of hedging can be forecast for alternative policies in which it might be carried out. Under some policies hedging may not be desired, and in such cases there is of course no hedging cost.

Depending on the management information capability of the firm, and the extent of its computer facilities, it may be feasible to generate a number of possible scenarios and to have figures on these available to managers for their decisions. But nothing can substitute for the judgment of managers in evaluating forecasts of cash flows, exchange rates (spot and forward), and interest rates.

There is no doubt that improved management information systems can provide significant aid to managers by indicating the possibilities inherent in various scenarios. But the future is not known. Simply consider the fact that many of the things we now take for granted, including jet airplanes and nuclear power, were not even mentioned in the 1939 World's Fair, which attempted to show trends in industry and inventions. How do we deal with the uncertain future? We do the best we can by applying our subjective estimate of probabilities to possible events.

Suppose, for example, that we believe that a year from now a certain currency will depreciate by 10 percent. Let us say we have confidence in this outcome in the sense that we are 50 percent certain that it will occur, so that it has a ".5 probability" of occurring. We might also assign a ".3 probability" to the outcome of no change in the exchange rate, and a ".2 probability" to the upvaluation of the currency. We might call these three partial scenarios A, B, and C.

Next, let us assume that we might take three policy positions: an aggressive position, a "no exposure" position, and a "do nothing" position. An aggressive position means that strong action is taken to offset the expected depreciation, even to the extent of taking a short position in the currency in order to offset all translation losses. A no exposure policy means that for all currencies other than the unit of account, action is taken to reduce exposure to zero. The third policy is a foreign exchange management decision to do nothing. It implicitly reflects an acceptance of purchasing power parity and Fisher open, and it is a decision to ignore possible translation losses that may result from positions remaining in a currency after borrowing from the least costly source, on the ground that such losses will probably be random, with losses in one period being made up by gains in another. Thus we have three policies, each of which can be considered in conjunction with each of the three scenarios. The numbers in the cells in Figure 19-1 indicate dollar losses or gains from the outcome of the scenario combined with the policy.

It is now possible to use a decision rule to choose the best policy. The rule is to accept the policy that provides the highest expected value. That is, we multiply each cell outcome by the subjective probability we attached to that scenario. This probability is our belief in the likelihood of the outcome. We multiply each expected loss or gain by its probability and obtain figures shown in the right-hand part of Figure 19-2.

From this example we can see that policy 2, no exposure, gives the highest expected value, since it shows the least expected loss. It is also possible to vary the probabilities to see how strength of belief in the likelihood of various outcomes affects those outcomes, and to find sets of probabilities that give equal expected outcomes. Then we can see whether management's probabilities clearly differ.

All of this use of game-theoretic, strategy-choice manipulation is merely one means of formalizing and quantifying the problem to simplify it to assist management, and so that quantitative possible results replace vague feelings. Of course, the quantitative results depend on the probabilities assigned to outcomes, and if these are wrong, the strategies are wrong. The primary advantage of the effort is to show how far wrong things will go if a policy is wrong. Assignment of probabilities is still based on analyses of factors likely to affect the outcome; and the analyses must be based on a wide range of data and

	Scenarios		
Policies	**A**	**B**	**C**
1 Aggressive	0	−10	−25
2 No exposure	−5	−2	0
3 No change	−15	0	+2

Figure 19-1 Losses or Gains from Different Policies toward Exchange Rate Changes under Different Exchange Rate Scenarios.

Policies	Scenario results times probabilities			Expected values of outcomes
	A	B	C	
1	$0 \times .5$	$-10 \times .3$	$-25 \times .2$	$0 - 3 - 12.5 = -15.5$
2	$-5 \times .5$	$-2 \times .3$	$0 \times .2$	$-2.5 - 0.6 + 0 = -3.1$
3	$-15 \times .5$	$0 \times .3$	$2 \times .2$	$-7.5 + 0 + .4 = -7.1$

Figure 19-2 Expected Values of Outcomes of Different Policies toward Exchange Rate Changes under Different Exchange Rate Scenarios.

may not be quantifiable because so many data are involved and so many possibilities arise. Sometimes corporate treasurers purchase services which provide highly complex evaluations of probabilities and forecasts simply in order to be able to say that they spared no effort to find a correct decision—especially if there is a possibility of making wrong decisions. In the period of floating rates, when the evidence shows that short-term prediction is not possible, treasurers have turned more and more to high-priced consultants!

OPTIMAL CAPITAL STRUCTURE: DEBT/EQUITY RATIOS

In discussing the criteria for making optimal investment decisions in the preceding chapter, the concept of a weighted average cost of capital was introduced. If funds required exceed the amount available through retained earnings, then issue of debt and possibly equity securities may be necessary. The cost of each of these three sources of funds varies and managers must use some weighted average cost of funds in their investment decisions. Here we examine in more detail the reasons for a difference between the cost of equity and the cost of debt, and examine reasons for establishing optimum debt/equity ratios. If debt is a less expensive source of funds, why would a firm ever choose to increase its equity?

Graphing the Debt/Equity Decision

We begin with a very simple exposition. Let the straight line in Figure 19-3 represent the possible ways of dividing a firm's capital between debt and

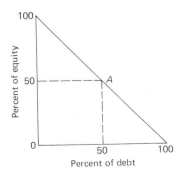

Figure 19-3 Proportions of Debt and Equity in Capital Structure of Firm.

equity. On the vertical axis at point E, the entire capital is in the form of equity; at point A it is divided equally between debt and equity; and at point D all of it is in the form of debt. The line clearly has a slope of -1 and any point on it represents some division of capital between debt and equity. This line is the debt/equity possibility line.[5]

In Figure 19-4 we have superimposed a set of three iso-yield curves on the line in Figure 19-3. Each represents a different rate of return on equity. This is the rate management wishes to maximize. The highest return on equity in this example is at point B, where the debt/equity ratio is 75/25.

What would happen if the debt/equity ratio were reduced to 1/1, as it would be at point A? In our diagram the yield is 8 percent instead of 10 percent. Why are the iso-yield curves drawn in the shape shown? Why does the rate of return on equity fall as the debt/equity ratio rises above 3 to 1? First, as the debt ratio rises there is an effective reduction in taxes because interest on debt is tax-deductible. Shouldn't the rate rise instead of fall? Yes, but there is an offsetting factor. Bondholders view a higher debt/equity ratio as making their investment more risky and therefore they require a higher interest rate for investing in the firm's bonds. Risk is greater because if a firm encountered financial difficulties, it would have fewer equity funds against which to charge losses and costs of paying interest on bonds. Default might occur. Securities rating services, such as Moody's and Standard and Poor's, may lower the ratings on the firm's bonds. The fall in return implies that the tax advantage is more than offset by the greater risk, which requires a higher interest cost on bonds.

Why does the rate of return fall as the debt/equity ratio moves in the other direction? Here the answer is primarily taxes, but of course, as the debt/equity ratio falls, the higher cost of equity is incurred on a greater proportion of the firm's capital. Equity pays a higher return because of the greater risk involved.

[5]A slope of −1 means that for a dollar fall in debt there is a dollar increase in equity to keep total capital the same.

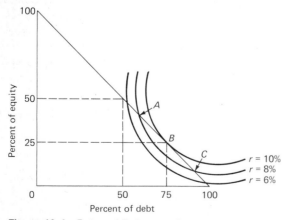

Figure 19-4 Rates of Return on Investment and Debt/Equity Ratios.

One further bit of analysis may be useful. Consider a horizontal movement from a point such as *b* to point *B*. At point *b* the capital budget is smaller. Movement from *b* to *B* represents an increase in debt with no change in the amount of equity. This is an increase in leverage. To some extent increased leverage may increase the rate of return on equity; but it is obvious from Figure 19-4 that continued increase in leverage would at some point result in a decline in the rate of return because of increased risk.

The Controversy over the Optimal Debt/Equity Ratio

A different point of view was taken by Miller and Modigliani, who argued that there is no optimal debt/equity ratio, but later modified this position to concede that when taxes are taken into account they cause the appearance of such a ratio.[6]

The more traditional view, in line with our analysis, was taken by such researchers as Armen Alchian, Reuben Kessel, and Ezra Solomon. Alchian and Kessel observed that debtor firms, that is, firms having relatively high ratios of debt to equity, are more favorably affected by inflation than other firms.[7] This is especially true if such firms are net monetary debtors—that is, if monetary liabilities (notes and accounts payable, bonds outstanding, etc.) exceed monetary assets (cash, marketable securities, notes and accounts receivable, etc.). Growth companies are typically high-leverage, high debt/equity ratio firms. In growth companies earnings grow rapidly, and as earnings accrue debt can be paid off if desired. In other words, Alchian and Kessel applied to firms the old, well-known theorem that debtors benefit from inflation because their incomes rise and they thus have more funds to pay off their debt.

Ezra Solomon pointed out that, regardless of theory, there seem to be debt/equity ratios that investors regard as optimal for different groups of firms.[8] Empirical work has confirmed Solomon's view. Although this question is not completely settled, studies seem to indicate that cost of debt, although it may be relatively constant for some substantial increase in the debt/equity ratio, begins to rise at some point.

In any event we have to recognize that tax factors do, in general, cause both a difference between the cost of debt and of equity and a change in the weighted average cost of capital as debt/equity ratios change.

In international finance, some additional factors may affect the optimal capital structure. The existence of risk of depreciation of currencies may lead a firm's managers to borrow more in currencies that may depreciate. These are usually currencies of countries where inflation rates are relatively high, and

[6]Merton H. Miller and Franco Modigliani, "Corporate Income Taxes and the Cost of Capital: A Correction," *American Economic Review,* June 1963, pp. 433–443.

[7]Armen A. Alchian and Reuben A. Kessel, "Effects of Inflation," *Journal of Political Economy,* December 1962, and Reuben A. Kessel, "Inflation-Caused Wealth Redistribution: A Test of a Hypothesis," *American Economic Review,* March 1956, pp. 128–141. See also Barthold W. Sorge, "The Prevention of Losses in Foreign Operations," Ph.D. dissertation, UCLA, 1965.

[8]Ezra Solomon, *The Theory of Financial Management* (New York: Columbia, 1963).

firms benefit by borrowing in those countries. This may bias the capital structure toward a higher debt/equity ratio.

Also, if exchange controls exist, they usually make it easier to make remittances involving payment of interest on borrowed funds than to remit dividends, and hence this also may bias the capital structure toward a higher debt/equity ratio.

In addition, the existence of substantial amounts of nonguaranteed debt to foreign individuals or institutions by firms or the government may make investors regard the BOP position of a country as risky, and hence may force up the cost of borrowing by firms in that country. The example of Italy in the mid-1970s comes readily to mind.

Too, existence of political risk of confiscation or of less drastic measures may make firms reluctant to have more than minimum equity in case of possible expropriation or other action adverse to equity positions.

Some studies have been made to try to determine whether the type of industry or size of firm significantly affects debt/equity ratios. One such study concluded that they do not.[9] This is not surprising, since the major factor is likely to be risk, although it might perhaps have been expected that industries and size of firm might be proxies for risk.

Country versus Industry Norms for Debt/Equity Ratios

Stonehill and Stitzel investigated the question of country versus industry norms for debt/equity ratios and found significantly different country norms.[10] They did not find support in the evidence for worldwide industry norms. But, even if there were such norms in the absence of taxes, they would be distorted by the variety of different tax treatments. In Greece, for example, not only are firms allowed to deduct interest on debt as a business expense, thus creating a bias favorable to debt financing, but interest receipts by investors are not subject to income tax while dividend receipts are taxable, except for a nominal amount that is exempt. Thus it is not surprising to find high debt/equity ratios in Greece, as shown in Table 19-1. Commercial attachés at the American Embassy in Athens have reported that these high ratios have led many potential foreign investors and foreign traders who were not fully informed to shy away from business in Greece, being fearful that equity was insufficient and hence that there was risk that Greek firms could not meet obligations.[11]

Robbins and Stobaugh concluded that U.S. companies ". . . generally use more equity than required to meet governmental regulations. As a result, these

[9]Lee Remmers, Arthur Stonehill, Richard Wright, and Theo Beekhuisen, "Industry and Size as Debt Ratio Determinants in Manufacturing Internationally," *Financial Management*, Summer 1974, pp. 24–32.

[10]Arthur Stonehill and Thomas Stitzel, "Financial Structure and Multinational Corporations," *California Management Review*, Fall 1969, pp. 92–95.

[11]R. H. Scott, Current Financial Issues in Greece, unpublished monograph, Center for Planning and Economic Research, Athens, 1974. The Athens Stock Exchange has also been adversely affected by the discriminatory tax treatment of dividend income. See N. A. Nicharchos, *The Stock Market in Greece* (Athens: Athens Stock Exchange, 1972).

Table 19-1 Estimated Debt/Equity Ratios, Selected Years and Countries*

Country	Year	Equity capital, %	Debt capital, %
Greece	1965	32.6	67.4
	1966	31.6	68.4
	1967	30.2	69.8
Germany	1965	46.3	53.7
France	1966	47.7	52.3
Italy	1967	33.6	63.4
Japan	1966	23.6	76.4
England	1966	57.6	42.4
United States	1966	58.9	41.1

*Ratios as of December 31 of respective years; data from Statistical Service of Greece, "Results of the Industrial Survey of the Year 1968," Federation of Greek Industrialists, "The Greek Industry," and Commission des Communautés Européennes, "La Politique Industrielle de la Communauté," Bruxelles, Belgium.

firms are losing profits by paying more U.S. taxes than would result from alternative financing methods."[12]

Differences in inflation rates clearly have an impact on debt/equity ratios. The short-run effect of inflation in the United States, for example, has clearly been adverse to stock prices, and hence has tended to increase the cost of equity capital. On the other hand, there is evidence that in the long run—perhaps over periods of 15 years or more—stocks do in fact provide a hedge against inflation, and the cost of equity capital falls.[13]

Differences in depreciation policies are also important for the debt/equity ratio. If depreciation were allowed on a replacement cost basis, more equity would be retained in periods of inflation, and this together with the revaluation of real assets would reduce the debt/equity ratio. Returns on equity would be lower and so would taxes.

Differences in capital markets also affect debt/equity ratios. The major markets for debt and equity securities have long been those of the United States and the United Kingdom. In other European countries various controls in capital markets have restricted their growth, and in LDCs such markets are small. In many countries financial markets are too small to accommodate large securities issues, partly because some countries lack institutions such as pension funds, trust departments of banks, and mutual funds which can purchase large amounts of securities; and partly because individuals in many countries do not have sufficient funds available for investment or have not had experience in investing in such securities.

[12]Sidney M. Robbins and Robert B. Stobaugh, "Financing Foreign Affiliates," *Financial Management*, Winter 1972, especially p. 58.

[13]Phillip Cagan, "Common Stock Values and Inflation—The Historical Record," National Bureau Report Supplement No. 13 (New York: National Bureau of Economic Research, March 1974). See also Frank K. Reilly, *Companies and Common Stocks as Inflation Hedges,* The Bulletin, New York University, 1975.

The increase in dollar funds outside the United States and the development of the Eurobond market made it possible for investors to buy Eurobonds, avoiding controls imposed in individual countries. Firms and government agencies in various countries have been able to tap this pool of funds by selling Eurobonds. Denominating such bonds in U.S. dollars, Deutsche marks, multiple currency units, and certain other currencies has been attractive to investors. It is possible that the rapid growth of the Eurobond market has hindered further growth of equity capital markets in Europe and perhaps tended to increase debt/equity ratios.

Stonehill and Stitzel argued that international subsidiaries should be encouraged to adopt financing norms appropriate to local norms and to cash flow patterns in the countries in which they operate. Loans from parent companies were excluded on the ground that they are frequently regarded as equivalent to equity investment by investors in countries where the subsidiaries operate. They argued that this approach would avoid some criticism of foreign-controlled companies not having a "fair share" of risk capital, and that it would permit managers of subsidiaries more easily to compare their own rates of return on equity with those of other local firms.

Carried to an extreme, this argument would permit both extremely high and extremely low debt/equity ratios. Very high ratios are characteristic of Japan, for example, as indicated in Table 19-1. In Japan banks are both lenders and owners of equity, and this may reduce concern about debt/equity ratios. Few observers accept the "local norm" approach to capital structure for subsidiaries of MNCs in general, because there is no reason to believe that local norms would be optimal for parent companies in different cases. Eiteman and Stonehill took the position that multinational firms ought to adopt financial structures optimal for their own operations, not necessarily structures appropriate for particular countries in which subsidiaries operate.[14] Theoretically, global firms have comparative advantages because of economies of scale, diversification, and other factors, and they should adopt overall debt/equity structures appropriate to their own situations. As a practical matter, using local standards would make it difficult to compare results of operations of different "multinational firms because of their geographical heterogeneity."[15]

WORKING CAPITAL MANAGEMENT

Working capital management involves financial decisions concerning the amounts to be held as working capital and the forms in which they should be held. In international finance, the *places* in which working capital is held are also important because changes in exchange rates may change translated values of working capital.

---

[14]David K. Eiteman and Arthur I. Stonehill, *Multinational Business Finance* (Reading, Mass.: Addison-Wesley, 1973), p. 224.
[15]Ibid., p. 225.

The Monetary Balance Approach versus the Economic Exposure Approach

In balance sheets in general, monetary items (all liabilities and all assets except inventory and fixed assets, roughly) are most affected by inflation. The real value of monetary asset items is reduced in inflation, and liabilities are more easily repaid. The research of Alchian and Kessel in the late 1950s tended to show, as noted, that firms which are net monetary debtors benefit from inflation. Hence there might be advantages, if inflation can be forecast, in reducing values of monetary assets and increasing liabilities as inflation occurs. For example, if a company has net monetary assets and its managers expect inflation, they might allow such assets to fall to the absolute minimum necessary levels and invest the funds in inventory and/or equipment. They might also borrow additional sums and use them for that purpose.

The cost of borrowing would be iA, where i is the interest rate and A is the amount of net monetary assets, if the aim were to achieve monetary balance. If it is assumed that the exchange value of the currency declines as inflation occurs, but not at precisely the same rate (that is, if purchasing power parity does not precisely hold in the short run), the loss from a change in the exchange rate would be $A\left(\dfrac{1}{x_0} - \dfrac{1}{x_1}\right)$, where x_0 is the exchange rate at the beginning of a period and x_1 is the rate at the end. So if $\dfrac{iA}{x_1} < A\left(\dfrac{1}{x_0} - \dfrac{1}{x_1}\right)$, it is worthwhile to borrow if the aim of achieving monetary balance is a desirable goal.

We must distinguish carefully between effects within the country in which a firm or subsidiary operates and effects on exposure to exchange risk. We have already seen that achieving monetary balance reduces *accounting* exposure but does not necessarily affect *economic* exposure. As shown earlier, the latter is not affected if it can be assumed that purchasing power parity and Fisher open are valid. This is not always the case, and therefore there are instances in which economic exposure may be affected by reducing monetary assets and increasing liabilities. But this must be distinguished from the effects within the country in which the firm operates. Within the country, these actions usually protect against effects of inflation. From an international financial viewpoint, there is no point in borrowing in a particular country because it is experiencing inflation if interest rates in that country are rising and the exchange rate is falling concomitantly with the inflation. But domestically, increasing borrowing and reducing monetary assets may be an inflation hedge.

If it does seem desirable from an international financial viewpoint to borrow in certain countries because purchasing power parity and Fisher open do not seem likely to hold for some period of time, there are also other alternatives. One is to make appropriate intracompany fund transfers from subsidiaries in which it is desired to reduce monetary assets because inflation and devaluation or downward floating of the currency are expected. Intracompany fund transfers are of course made for many reasons, including payment of dividends and interest, repayment of loans, payment of royalty and licensing fees, and compensation for technical service and management fees. Moreover, goods and services are traded on an intracompany basis.

Transfer pricing, mentioned earlier, often becomes significant. Transfer prices may be adjusted, raising them on purchases or lowering them on sales to transfer funds outward. Governments have become very watchful of this form of fund transfer because taxes may be avoided and because flows of capital out of a country may occur when governments do not desire it.

Tax differences are another reason for fund transfers. Foreign exchange gains may be taxed at higher rates in one country than in another; hence it may be desirable to make payments so that gains are recorded, when possible, in countries with lower rates.

Fund transfers entail costs. For example, reduction in receivables may also reduce sales. Leads and lags involve costs if, for example, funds must be borrowed to make payments promptly, presumably before an anticipated devaluation or downward floating of a currency. The question may reasonably be raised whether such costs are justified simply to show smaller foreign exchange losses in accounting statements.

Finally, undesired foreign exchange exposure may be hedged. It may be possible to offset an expected translation loss on exposed assets by a realized exchange gain. If a decline in an exchange rate can be forecast, it may be possible to sell forward and then buy foreign exchange to deliver to meet the forward contract after the spot rate has declined. Hedging may also be accomplished by borrowing in a currency expected to decline in value and investing the proceeds in a currency not expected to change in value. Repayment of the borrowed funds after the decline, assuming it occurs, may be made with funds acquired by selling the stable currency investment.

The difficulty of forecasting exchange rate changes in the period of floating rates since 1973 throws doubt on the effectiveness of these techniques in many instances. Since the financial market hedging assumes that Fisher open does not hold, the question must be raised whether, in particular instances, deviations from Fisher open are sufficient to justify hedging. In some cases they may be. The important task of financial managers is to identify such cases: *When* do government restrictions and other factors invalidate the conclusions applicable when efficient markets exist?

Managing Cash Balances

For MNCs, cash balances should be concentrated in places offering the greatest safety, return, and liquidity. Political stability, ready convertibility of currency, stability of exchange value of the currency, and absence of government restrictions, plus technical factors such as adequacy of communications facilities and availability of ancillary services, are all to be considered. For MNCs it may be advantageous that financial planning, including that for allocation of cash balances, be done at parent company headquarters. However, many countries restrict flows of funds for such purposes, and it may therefore be impossible to achieve optimum allocation of cash balances.

Cash Needs Just as for domestic operations, cash is held for both transactions and precautionary purposes. Standard minimum inventory principles apply. Many countries use currency (paper money and coin) much more widely than the United States, and it may therefore be necessary to have more currency and fewer demand deposits in various countries than would be held in the United States. With such qualifications, minimum cash need is essentially an inventory problem, discussed in detail in books on financial managment.[16]

Liquid Asset Investments Liquid assets held for precautionary purposes should in most cases be invested in money market instruments or time deposits in banks in order to obtain safety, adequate return, and appropriate liquidity. A centralized handling of liquid funds not needed for transactions may be worthwhile in obtaining advantages of scale of funds and of centralized information. Funds in a central pool can be transferred to a subsidiary in need of cash, using wire transfer to minimize delay. Holding funds in a central pool may minimize the total amount of funds held, since it is unlikely that funds will be needed by all subsidiaries at the same time. If each subsidiary held its own precautionary funds, it would have to hold some minimum amount. Central money pools are usually held in countries with major money centers and strong currencies: the United States and Britain have been such centers, but at times Germany or other countries may qualify. Funds may also be held in tax-haven countries, and in Eurodollars if rates are attractive.

Exchange restrictions may not permit central pooling of funds. Their existence makes it useful for firms to deal with large multinational banks that can maintain complete up-to-date information on worldwide exchange restrictions. Multinational banks can also provide same-day transfers of funds from one office to another, thus minimizing float time.

Centralized Cash Management Some companies centralize cash management under the jurisdiction of an officer of the parent company such as the treasurer, to take advantage of the most effective policies for safety, return, and liquidity of balances. Centralized cash management also permits the treasurer to maintain an overall perspective on the needs of each subsidiary for cash, the return and risk in each location, and the desired degree of liquidity for the corporation as a whole.

If surplus funds are acquired by a subsidiary in an undesirable location, such as a country where there is rapid inflation, and if the funds cannot easily be removed, an effort should be made to protect the funds against loss caused by inflation. This may involve their investment in additional inventory or other real assets. Inventory is advantageous because it can usually be turned into cash again in a relatively short time.

Transfer Techniques MNCs may be able to use transfer techniques to avoid keeping cash or liquid funds in undesirable areas. Transfers which cannot

[16]See, for example, James C. Van Horne, *Financial Management and Policy,* 2d ed. (Englewood Cliffs, N.J.: Prentice-Hall, 1971), Chap. 16.

be made for other purposes may be made by means of management fees, commissions, royalties, or repayment of debt. Parent companies can invest minimum required amounts in subsidiaries, and then supply subsidiaries with liquid funds from a central pool if necessary. In this way costs of foreign exchange conversions can be minimized.

There may be advantages in transferring funds in the currency of the country *from* which transfer occurs, in the currency of the country *to* which transfer occurs, or in U.S. dollars. It is quicker to transfer funds in the currency of the country to which transfer occurs, because they can immediately be credited to a deposit account in that country, whereas funds in the currency of the country of origin must be converted into an increase in the deposit balance of the transferee country bank in a transferor country bank. This takes time. Transfer via the United States also takes time, but may be advantageous if both currencies involved, other than U.S. dollars, are subject to risk of devaluation or depreciation.

Managing Receivables

The analysis of fundamentals of financial management indicated that there is a cost in extending credit and in accumulating receivables: money has a time value and receivables have a cost in terms of foregone interest. Nevertheless, companies often decide to sell for credit because they may thus expand sales volume and profits. Credit sales may make it possible to obtain credit on the basis of receivables. If sales are made on the basis of drafts on buyers, trade acceptances are generated and these may be discounted at banks. In some countries this may be much easier than borrowing on the security of inventory. Also, in some countries government agencies extend export credit at advantageous interest rates. This may make the accumulation of receivables even more desirable. When inflation occurs, however, receivables lose value just as cash does. Replacement cost of the items sold rises, and monetary profit also should be increased to maintain the same *rate* or profit. Income taxes are higher when historical cost must be used as the cost of inventory sold than if replacement cost can be used. These advantages and disadvantages should be weighed in managing receivables.

Sales for Cash and/or under Letters of Credit   When sellers' markets exist, export firms may sell for cash or under letters of credit providing for cash against documents. They may insist on confirmed letters of credit and they may sell only in their own currencies. Under these circumstances their risks are minimal. Such terms were common for American exporters in the period immediately after World War II. But as competition increased, policies had to be changed. Competitors offered credit terms and firms had to decide whether or not to meet the competition.

Sales for Credit outside the Corporate Group   Sales outside the corporate group may be made on credit, either on open account or drafts on buyers.

Drafts on buyers have been used for a long time in international transactions, and may be advantageous in providing a record of the order for payment and/or because it may be useful to have trade acceptances for discount at banks to obtain bank credit. When drafts on buyers are "accepted" by the buyers, they become trade acceptances, just as drafts on banks become bank acceptances.

When drafts on buyers are used, they may be collected through banks. Banks present drafts to the buyers, obtain acceptance if the drafts are time drafts, obtain payment when due, file protests when necessary (if payment is refused) in order to protect the bank's and the exporter's legal claims, and remit proceeds. Instructions to banks include, among other things, such matters as reporting nonpayment, protest, and instructions to release documents (bills of lading, etc.) to buyers on acceptance of drafts or on payment. In the first case, the drafts are referred to as D/A drafts (documents available to the buyer or his bank on acceptance of the drafts); in the second, D/P (documents available on payment of the drafts). Banks normally inform drawers of drafts concerning collection or inability to collect.

Banks may make advances against drafts; if documents accompany the drafts, this may be referred to as "purchase of documentary collections." Advances may be made on a "with recourse" or "without recourse" basis, although with recourse is the usual custom. Buyers must pay interest. Drafts on buyers in certain countries often carry (or are stamped with) the "Far Eastern interest clause" and indicate the rate of interest. When banks have already paid the sellers, this is a convenient way for them to collect interest on the funds due them from the buyers. Otherwise sellers pay interest to the banks on advances. Bank collection charges may be paid by either party or divided so that sellers pay their own banks' collection charges and so do buyers.

Sales under drafts have an advantage over sales on open account in the event of imposition of exchange controls because it is easier to establish the fact of buyers' obligations to pay and hence easier to persuade governments to permit buyers to obtain foreign exchange for payment.

Intracompany Sales   Intracompany sales are necessary for many reasons, since subsidiaries produce different products and often sell to each other. Such sales differ from sales outside the corporate group in that little concern need normally be given to credit standing, and the timing of the payments may be dictated by the desire of the company to allocate resources rather than by normal sales payment schedules.

Minority stockholders may object to allocative actions because such actions may not benefit the subsidiaries in which they have interests. Also, problems arise because such actions may affect the profits of subsidiaries.

Governments may, of course, be concerned about intracompany sales payments, since they often cross national boundaries. Parent companies are likely to want subsidiaries to pay quickly in countries likely to devalue or let their currencies float downward, and they are likely to want subsidiaries to delay payments in countries expected to permit their currencies to float upward. These leads and lags, as previously indicated, create serious problems for governments that attempt to maintain stable exchange rates.

Prices on intracompany sales, previously mentioned as one of the "transfer prices" applied in various fund transfers, can be used by MNCs to maintain a flow of income from a subsidiary which has been forbidden by the government of the country in which it operates to import more than specified amounts. Such prices can also be used to obtain a flow of cash out of a country likely to be involved in a political change, to recoup charges for royalties and other fees for which governments sometimes may not permit subsidiaries to make payments, and to give subsidiaries more favorable balance sheets for purposes of obtaining credit.[17] All these uses of transfer pricing are aspects of the economic integration sought by multinational firms, and of the political fragmentation of the modern world.

Managing Inventories

The basic problem of managing inventories is to minimize the capital invested in them and at the same time minimize the cost of having insufficient inventory when needed.[18] Some complications arise, however, because multinational companies may find that government restrictions prevent them from using optimum inventory policies. Such policies would minimize the total cost of purchasing, storing, processing, and delivering goods, and these four processes may be carried on in different locations—even in four or more different countries if sales are geographically extensive.

Moreover, inventories for MNCs are often shipped long distances and are in transit for considerable periods of time. Inventory in transit is part of total inventory. It cannot be expected, therefore, that international firms can keep minimum cost inventory levels as well as domestic firms can.

Beyond this, governments sometimes ban imports when BOP problems are significant, and managers of foreign subsidiaries may maintain inventories, especially imported inventories, at higher than normal levels to avoid the risk of being caught with little inventory when imports are banned.[19]

Since the U.S. Financial Accounting Standards Board (FASB) Statement No. 8, referred to in Chapter 16, requires translation of inventory values at acquisition cost (historic rates), gains or losses from foreign exchange rate fluctuations are recognized under this rule when inventory is sold, except when

---

[17]Some of these purposes are discussed in more detail in James Shulman, "When the Price is Wrong—By Design," *Columbia Journal of World Business,* May–June 1967, pp. 69–76.

[18]See, for example, J. Fred Weston and Eugene F. Brigham, *Managerial Finance,* 3d ed. (New York: Holt, 1969), Chap. 14, "Inventory Control."

[19]"How the Multinationals Play the Money Game," *Fortune,* August 1973, pp. 59–62, 138–144. This article is a discussion and enlargement on some points made in the book by Sidney M. Robbins and Robert B. Stobaugh, *Money in the Multinational Enterprise: A Study of Financial Policy* (New York: Basic Books, 1973). Also see the interesting almost full-page advertisement by Chase Manhattan Bank concerning bank assistance in meeting provisions of FASB Statement No. 8, *Wall Street Journal,* Dec. 2, 1975, p. 21.

inventories are held marked at market values. Higher than normal inventories do not, under this rule, result in larger translation losses when a currency floats downward or is devalued, unless heavy sales occur during the period.

POLICIES GOVERNING REMITTANCES OF FUNDS

Nowhere are politics and economics more intertwined than in the establishment of policies for remittance of funds from a foreign country to the home office of a parent MNC.

There are two reasons for this. First, countries with BOP problems are reluctant to see reserve assets depleted as local subsidiaries buy, for example, U.S. dollars to remit funds to parent companies. LDCs, especially smaller countries, are most likely to be very concerned about this because one or two large firms' remittances may seriously deplete their reserve assets. In such countries it is likely that remittance policies are the subject of formal negotiation when investments are first made, and agreements may provide for reexamination and renegotiation of these policies from time to time.

A second reason for political sensitivity of local governments to remittance policies is that remittances give ammunition to antibusiness or anticapitalist political forces. One of the authors of this text spent a considerable time in Ireland as a lecturer. A difficult encounter occurred during a question and answer session following a lecture on foreign (U.S.) investment in Ireland. Argument by students went something like this: Is it right for these big businesses to come here, obtain tax advantages, earn large profits, and then remit profits out of Ireland? Isn't this exploitation of the Irish by foreign capitalists? After all, these profits are created by our workers and should stay in our country!

Keep in mind that the "profits" are a return to equity plus a premium for risk. It is not clear just how much the total return should be, although one can compare current returns with returns obtained over the years by other firms. If a firm is given a monopoly or semi-monopoly position for local sales and is given tax advantages, returns above the necessary returns to risk capital may be earned; if so, this provides some substance to the students' argument. Hence governments may restrict remittances so that if challenged by the opposition they can claim that fears of exploitation are exaggerated, and at the same time they can take credit for a program that creates local jobs.

Funds remitted from one company or office to another include interest, dividends, management and service fees, royalties, license fees, and other charges that arise from purchases. The specific labeling of a remittance may affect government permission for the transfer. Governments are typically more willing to permit interest payments and repayment of loans, than payment of dividends. Sometimes they fear that if they do not permit payment of interest and repayment of loans, credit ratings of firms may suffer and inflow of investments may diminish or cease. Dividends, as a form of profits, are most likely to be restricted by governments.

In one study, Zenoff identified several factors influencing amounts of remittances. These factors included taxes; risks of exchange rate losses and/or losses resulting from exchange controls; and the need of local subsidiaries for working capital and for local planned investment during the next six months or year.[20]

In some countries, as noted in Chapter 17, tax rates on retained earnings are higher than rates levied on distributed earnings. Such a difference affects the after-tax cost of capital funds used for expansion of activities. The U.S. tax provisions, which permit deferral of tax on earnings held abroad under certain conditions, reduce after-tax cost of retained earnings in countries where the corporate income tax rate is lower than in the United States. This should encourage accumulation of profits in these countries and reduce remittances to U.S. parent companies.[21]

Zenoff concluded that high risk of adverse exchange rate changes or of the imposition of exchange controls was significant in determining the amount of funds remitted to parent-company countries. Risks are greatest when a shortage of foreign exchange is expected, and the expectation tends to bring about the result. In such circumstances outside loans to the countries involved may be of value not only in providing funds to meet payment needs but also in changing expectations.

As firms expand they usually need to increase their working capital. This may result in the use of all retained earnings, and little or no funds may be available for remittances. If other subsidiaries are providing adequate funds through remittances, this need not create a problem. Dividend policies can be decided at parent-company headquarters. Note that the viewpoint taken is that it is not necessary to remit dividends in order to return part of profits to owners as payment for their service in providing equity (risk) capital. Rather, remittances are simply part of a larger overall policy of establishing appropriate working capital levels in each subsidiary in view of tax policies, interest rates, and risks. There is less need to provide regular dividends for individual stockholders, since the major owners are parent MNCs rather than individual stockholders who invested for income rather than capital gains.

FINANCIAL CONTROL IN MNCs

Listing some of the financial activities over which the MNC must exercise effective control is enlightening: overall development of long-run strategic financial policies, day-to-day management of cash balances, establishment of the most effective policies for remittances, management of credits and collections, decisions about how and where to borrow, decisions whether to have the parent firm guarantee debt of subsidiaries, analysis of tax situations, establish-

[20]David B. Zenoff, "Remittance Policies of U.S. Subsidiaries in Europe," *Banker*, May 1967, pp. 418–427.

[21]Walter L. Ness, Jr., "U.S. Corporate Income Taxation and the Dividend Remittance Policy of Multinational Corporations," *Journal of International Business Studies*, Spring 1975, pp. 67–77.

ment of policies regarding depreciation and valuation of inventories and fixed assets, evaluation of specific investment opportunities, analysis of BOP factors that may impinge upon the firm's profitability, and establishment of an appropriate organizational structure to ensure effective control over all these activities.

The international financial function is more complex than that in domestic corporations principally because of (1) tax laws of various governments, (2) exchange rate risks, (3) the institutional and functional differences among different money and capital markets, and (4) the effects of varying rates of inflation in different countries. Managers should examine carefully the firm's organizational structure to see that, in the light of these factors, the firm's objectives can be met. A system of financial control should ensure efficient use of a firm's resources and minimize cost of funds. Therefore, a variety of personnel should be involved in establishing the appropriate organizational structure—not only accountants, but also an international finance specialist, the corporate controller, the corporate treasurer, the managers of foreign subsidiaries, and others.

One of the most important policies concerning organizational control that this group of experts should establish is that of intermittent reappraisal and reevaluation of the organizational structure itself. Changes are rapid enough for domestic corporations, but the environment in which international corporations operate changes with the economic, social, and political conditions in each country. Rigidity in organizational structure must give way to flexibility—the structure should be capable of changing to meet changing conditions.

Corporate Centralization of Financial Control

One question facing those who establish the organizational structure for financial control is, to what degree should control be centralized and located at parent-company headquarters? There are clearly several good reasons for centralization of financial control. Taxes may be minimized if, by transfer pricing or other means, profits can be maximized in certain countries rather than in others. Borrowing may be more advantageous in some countries than in others. Pooling of funds worldwide and their reinvestment in specified countries may improve returns over what they would be if each subsidiary handled its own funds, and there are possibilities for eliminating duplication when international financial analysis itself is centralized.

The manner in which financial controls are centralized or decentralized and the manner in which they are exercised depends on the form of organization firms adopt. The specific organizational structure is sometimes the result of historical development and may not necessarily be the most efficient. Companies may be organized with functional divisions at home and abroad; this is likely to be the case for relatively small companies that produce only one product. It is also true for some large companies, such as oil firms. Companies may be organized with a production group organization in the home country and a geographical organization abroad. Some companies dispense with an international division and organize their operations abroad along product lines. If companies have both product and geographical organizational structures, they may find it necessary to give priority to one or the other.

Obviously these variations in organizational structure have an impact on financial control, centralization, and the functions of different parts of a company. Many MNCs do centralize the financial function at corporate headquarters, and some have a vice president for finance with direct responsibility for overall supervision of the finance function. If an international finance executive is designated, he usually reports to the vice president for finance, but sometimes to the controller or to the treasurer.[22] If no such officer is designated, functions are often divided between the treasurer's office and the controller's office.

Some decisions are typically made at corporate headquarters—decisions concerning repatriation of funds, approval of intersubsidiary loans, hedging and currency swaps, and acquisition of medium-term and long-term funds.

Centralization of Financial Control at International Headquarters

Sometimes international divisions are almost completely independent companies. In some instances they are, in fact, legally and operationally independent. In these situations it may be desirable to centralize the finance function at international headquarters.

A number of companies divide the responsibilities associated with the finance function, requiring the approval of corporate headquarters for all major financial decisions but allowing local managers leeway for day-to-day decisions and implementation of policies in the international divisions or subsidiaries.

Delegated International Financial Responsibilities

Operational financial responsibilities may be delegated to various operating entities. Corporate headquarters still normally provides policy guidelines and receives direct reports. Decisions on major policy issues are reserved for the corporate level. But day-to-day decisions, especially those concerning working capital and short-term borrowing are often implemented at subordinate levels. In many companies combinations of relationships are found, reflecting the fact that many companies are in transitional phases concerning international activities and no one organizational form may be best suited to their needs.

Questions of organizational structure take us beyond the field of finance and into that of organizational behavior. The appropriate question to ask about any organizational structure is: Can it adequately provide for decisions concerning the financial questions discussed in this book, by the most

---

[22]Prindl points out that International Treasurer is becoming a more common term; see his article cited in fn. 3 above.

appropriate individuals with the best information who can make decisions from a viewpoint which is comprehensive yet avoids duplication?

SUMMARY

The aim of the management of a firm is assumed to be to maximize return to stockholders, either as dividends or as retained earnings which will increase the price of the firm's stock and provide capital gains. The underlying factors in international finance are an analysis of cash flows expected, as in domestic finance, plus a foreign exchange management posture. Attention must also be given to such institutional factors as differences in taxes in different countries; institutional and functional differences among money and capital markets; and the effects of varying rates of inflation in various countries, especially if inflation is "dirty" or unanticipated.

Exposure to risk of exchange rate loss exists insofar as there are systematic deviations from purchasing power parity and from Fisher open. Accounting exposure may differ from economic exposure, and there may be reason to avoid accounting exposure if there is no particular *economic* reason for choosing a particular position. Evidence has recently been provided that there are not *generally* systematic deviations from Fisher open and that the forward rate in a floating rate system is, with some exceptions, generally an unbiased predictor of the future spot rate.

The managers of a firm should use cash flow forecasts to predict their economic exposure. Since it is probably not possible to predict exchange rates in a floating rate system in the short run, a firm should examine alternative scenarios (perhaps a "most likely," a "no change," and a third alternative) and develop the implications of these scenarios together with various foreign exchange management postures—for example, an aggressive posture, a "zero exposure" posture, and a "do nothing" posture.

In the longer run, the optimal capital structure may be analyzed as for a domestic firm, but currency risk, political risk (expropriation and exchange controls), and nonguaranteed debt to foreigners biases the optimal capital structure. There does not seem to be evidence to support worldwide industry norms for debt/equity ratios, but there is evidence that country norms exist. However, there is little reason to expect that local country norms would be optimal for parent companies.

Since firms which are net debtors benefit from inflation, it may be argued that if inflation is correctly anticipated, a company might reduce monetary assets and increase liabilities, or make intracompany fund transfers (perhaps through changes in transfer pricing). These actions concern its internal financial situation. It may also be desired to hedge foreign exchange exposure, but it is necessary to evaluate situations carefully because of the difficulty of forecasting exchange rates in the short run since 1973 and the fact that in many cases Fisher open may hold, so that losses or gains from inflation are offset by changes in interest rates.

Some special techniques apply in management of receivables because of the alternatives of sales for cash or under L/Cs, open account sales outside the corporate group, and intracompany sales.

Inventory management is affected by long shipping distances for inventory and by BOP problems which may lead governments to ban certain imports.

The view taken in this book is that remittances are not fundamentally returns of profits to owners of multinational firms, but part of a larger policy of establishing appropriate working capital levels in subsidiaries. Since parent companies do not necessarily need regular income, as some individual stockholders might, stable dividend policies are less necessary than in domestic firms.

The above paragraphs suggest clear reasons for centralization of financial control in MNCs. More companies seem to be establishing positions of International Treasurer. Nevertheless, corporate structure is a result of evolution, and under some conditions both centralization of some functions at international corporate headquarters rather than at the parent-company head office and decentralization of some functions may be appropriate.

QUESTIONS FOR DISCUSSION

1   What reasons can you suggest for the fact, as it seems to be, that overseas firms do more borrowing and have less internally generated funds in percentage terms than purely domestic firms?

2   Should profit maximization be in the interest of the total MNC or in the interest of each individual subsidiary thereof? Give reasons.

3   Why do MNCs and their subsidiaries desire to have both a local banking connection in a country and a connection with a multinational bank in the same country?

4   What is your evaluation of the evidence that firms with relatively large international operations statistically have significantly higher price-earnings ratios than firms in the same industries with less international involvement?

5   What factors might lower the cost of capital as the debt/equity ratio rises?

6   What factors might raise the cost of capital as the debt/equity ratio rises?

7   Contrast the view of Kessel and Solomon on the one hand and of Miller and Modigliani on the other hand concerning the effect of variations in financial structure on cost of capital. Then apply your analysis to the question of industry and country norms for debt/equity ratios.

8   Explain why there is no economic exposure for MNCs if the purchasing power parity theory and Fisher open hold.

9   Explain the effect of U.S. income taxes on policies for remittances from subsidiaries in countries where tax rates are as high as in the United States and from those in countries where tax rates are lower.

10 What is the "financial argument" for centralization of financial control in MNCs?

SUGGESTED REFERENCES

For an analysis of the problems of exchange exposure and international financial policy, see Robert Z. Aliber, *The Short Guide to Corporate International Finances,* mimeographed, Chicago, 1975. A good but brief treatment of some of the related questions is contained in Andreas R. Prindl, "Guidelines for MNC Money Managers," *Harvard Business Review,* January–February 1976, pp. 73–80.

On the question of industry versus country norms for international firms' debt/equity ratios, see references cited in footnotes.

On working capital management, see the study of Robbins and Stobaugh cited in footnote 19 and the related article in *Fortune* also cited there.

On the control function in international firms, see Irene W. Meister, *Managing the International Financial Function* (New York: The Conference Board, 1970); Edward C. Bursk, and John Dearden, David Hawkins, and Victor Longstreet, *Financial Control of Multinational Corporations* (New York: Financial Executives Research Foundation, 1971); and J. M. McInnes, "Financial Control Systems for Multinational Operations: An Empirical Investigation," *Journal of International Business Studies,* Fall 1971, pp. 11–28.

The measurement of subsidiaries' performance is discussed in Sidney M. Robbins and Robert B. Stobaugh, "The Bent Measuring Stick for Foreign Subsidiaries," *Harvard Business Review,* September–October 1973, pp. 80–88.

For a very elaborate discussion of foreign exchange scenarios and alternative strategies, see Rita M. Rodriguez and E. Eugene Carter, *International Financial Management* (Englewood Cliffs, N.J.: Prentice-Hall, 1976), Chap. 8.

Part Six

Financing Economic Development

We now come to the final part of this book—financing economic development. Why devote a special part to this subject? How is it related to the rest of the book?

One reason for devoting a special part of the book to this subject is the significance of the topic and the magnitude and complexity of questions involved. Economic well-being as measured by per capita income ranges from more than half a dozen countries with per capita GNP of less than $100 to the United States and several smaller countries with per capita incomes in the neighborhood of $7,000 in 1975. Some countries with incomes still relatively low have oil wealth which may permit them to engage in further economic development, and several small oil-producing countries already have very high per capita incomes. The rest of the LDCs have varying BOP prospects. Some have good prospects arising from strong diversified exports, some have prospects for improvement, and some face very great difficulties.

The second reason for a separate discussion of the financing of economic development is that major challenges for the MNCs exist in operating in and financing the development of LDCs. The Pacific Rim countries and the African countries in particular, together with Pakistan, India, Bangladesh, and Sri Lanka, are likely to be important trade areas of the future. In the Pacific Basin area only the United States, Canada, Australia, New Zealand, and Japan may be considered developed countries. Innovations in finance as well as in other phases of international business operations will no doubt occur as incomes rise in Pacific Rim countries.

Financing economic development has many domestic aspects, such as the need for capital, the most appropriate routes toward economic development, the development of financial institutions, and the role of economic planning. It also has international aspects such as the need for an appropriate international monetary system as a guarantee of world monetary stability, the role of international lending for economic development, and the role of private foreign investment in promoting economic development.

These aspects are examined in Chapter 20, and some conclusions concerning the role of international finance in aiding economic development are indicated at the end of the chapter. Managers of MNCs may well find that their future opportunities lie predominantly in LDCs, and their skill in financing investment in LDCs may be critical to their expansion.

Financing Economic Development

Economic development is a many-sided problem that warrants separate discussion. It is, in fact, a separate field of study because of its many facets. The theory of economic development is a part of economic theory and some discussion of this is usually included in elementary economics courses, but there are more advanced courses devoted entirely to the subject. Economic development has financial, accounting, marketing, and management aspects, and cultural aspects that include educational, social, and religious facets.

Financing economic development is a difficult part of the general problem faced by those who must make internal economic and financial decisions and select economic goals for LDCs. There are also, however, important aspects of economic development that involve international flows of private capital, of capital provided by governments and international institutions, and of capital provided directly by MNCs.

In this concluding chapter we survey some major problems of economic development; the basic theory of economic growth; the basic policies, especially financial policies, for economic development; the means of increasing saving and channeling it into economic development; and the role of external funds and of financial institutions and markets, both internal and external, in economic development.

DIMENSIONS OF THE PROBLEM OF ECONOMIC DEVELOPMENT

It has become rather common to classify countries of the world in several categories: the developed countries, with per capita GNP generally exceeding $1,000 annually; the "second world," comprised of the communist or centrally planned economies, with per capita GNP varying from approximately $1,800 in the USSR to about $600 in Albania to about $200 in mainland China; and the "third world," with per capita GNP generally below $1,000 in recent years.[1] OPEC counties have in recent years often been classified separately from the rest of the third world countries because of their sizable BOP current account surpluses resulting from oil revenues. This does not necessarily mean that income is distributed in OPEC countries in such a manner that the average resident has an income above $1,000. In fact, the oil revenues are received by the governments and may or may not be used to increase per capita incomes of individuals. In some OPEC countries, for example, Iran, industrialization and general increases in per capita income are occurring quite rapidly. In others, funds are accumulated and invested outside the OPEC countries, and internal development is proceeding more slowly.

Remaining third world countries have sometimes been divided into those which have been developing and have generally favorable prospects for development, and "fourth world" countries which generally have the least favorable prospects.[2] Some third world countries in fact have relatively high incomes—above $1,000 per capita per year. Some, for example, Zaire and Indonesia, have quite low per capita incomes now, but have resources that they may be able to develop to increase their incomes. On the other hand, a committee of the United Nations in 1971 compiled a list of 25 countries generally regarded as part of the "fourth world" because they are impoverished today and have poor prospects for ever improving their standards of living.

At its special session on raw materials in April 1974, the UN General Assembly called for a list of countries "most seriously affected" (MSA) by the increased costs of imported oil and food. Some writers treat countries on both lists (there is some overlap) as constituting the fourth world. Other classifications may be used, including one based on BOP prospects.[3] In such lists, countries such as Bangladesh, India, Burma, Malawi, Mali, Niger, Tasmania, and others in South Asia and in upper middle Africa and certain other places generally rank lowest.

---

[1] *World Bank Atlas* (Washington, D.C.: IBRD, 1972); see also *Finance and Development*, March 1973, pp. 25–27.

[2] See, for example, Helen C. Low and James W. Howe, "Focus on the Fourth World," in James W. Howe and others, *The U.S. and World Development, Agenda for Action 1975* (New York: Praeger, 1975), pp. 35–54. They provide lists of the four groups of countries, with some statistical data on them, on pp. 198–207.

[3] See Irving S. Friedman, "The New World of the Rich-Poor and the Poor-Rich," *Fortune*, May 1975, pp. 244–252.

The Third and Fourth Worlds

Third world countries contain somewhat more than 800 million people, and if to this are added both the estimated 800 million people in Mainland China and the nearly 1 billion people in fourth world countries, the total population in LDCs is over 2.6 billion people out of a world population of about 4 billion. Three-fourths of the population in the fourth world are accounted for by Pakistan, India, and Bangladesh. A group of countries in equatorial Africa, including Burundi, Cameroon, Central African Republic, Chad, Benin (formerly Dahomey), Ethiopia, Ghana, Guinea, Niger, Rwanda, Sierra Leone, Tanzania, Uganda, and Upper Volta, are also in that category. BOP prospects are more favorable for Pakistan and some others, and considerably better for countries like the Ivory Coast and Senegal.

Most fourth world countries were colonial dependencies before World War II. Some have relatively small populations in relation to their land areas, but in some the land is not capable of supporting a large population per square mile. Most are relatively poor in natural resources, although this by itself cannot be considered a barrier to development (Japan is poor in natural resources). Most of the population in fourth world countries is engaged in subsistence farming or nomadic herding. Transportation facilities are generally poor. The average rate of growth in per capita income for these countries in 1965–1972 was only 1 percent per year, and in some per capita income declined.

Variation in Growth Rates in LDCs

There is great variation in rates of growth of income among the LDCs. Growth rates ranged from 10.5 percent per year in Singapore to negative rates in countries such as Bangladesh, Niger, Jordan, and a number of others. Excluding small countries whose growth in real income (real GNP) was based on oil revenues and excluding a few special cases such as Singapore, the highest rates of growth from 1965 to 1972 were found in South Korea (8.5 percent per year), Ivory Coast (7.7), Taiwan (6.9), Brazil (5.6), and some others.[4] Other countries, such as Mexico, maintained a relatively high growth rate in GNP over long periods, but had high rates of growth in population (about $3\frac{1}{2}$ percent per year in Mexico), and this resulted in slower growth in per capita income.

It is not easy to formulate generalizations about variations in growth rates. Japan, now classified as a developed country, achieved the highest rate of economic growth in the world in the 1960s. Japan also was able to use fiscal, monetary, and credit policies so as to increase exports and to limit imports sufficiently to meet the huge added cost of imported oil after 1973. Countries

[4]The Ivory Coast has had an excellent record of growth, and has continued that record in the 1970s, although not at quite such a high rate as in the 1960s. Much of its prosperity has been based on exports of coffee, cocoa, and timber, but its stability in growth has also been the result of effective financial policies. It is a member, with Benin, Niger, Senegal, Togo, and Upper Volta, of the West African Monetary Union (UMOA), and these countries share a common currency, the CFA franc, and a common central bank. See IMF *Survey,* July 5, 1976, pp. 206–208.

like Mexico, Brazil, and Singapore also have generally been able to manage their economies so as to pay for higher costs of imports. As a rule, high rates of inflation are detrimental to growth, although Brazil seems to be an exception to this rule, having been able to tolerate a rate of inflation higher than in almost any other relatively rapidly growing country.

Future Growth Trends in LDCs

In considering future growth trends in LDCs, several factors that hinder growth may be mentioned.

First, over 40 percent of the population in LDCs is under 15 years of age, as compared with less than 30 percent in the United States and in Europe. This means that, proportionately, the LDCs have smaller labor forces to produce income for the total population. Although this is partly offset in some cases by a smaller percentage of older nonemployed people in LDCs, the problem of a relatively smaller labor force is significant. From the figures given above it is evident that LDCs account for a large part of world population. Because birth rates in LDCs are generally high relative to rates in developed countries, the proportion of world population in LDCs is likely to increase. Whereas LDCs had about 2.6 billion people out of a world population of nearly 4 billion in 1975, it is likely that by the year 2000 they will have about 5 billion out of a world population of 6.5 billion. Asia, which is largely composed of LDCs if Japan is excluded, had about 2 billion people in 1970 and is likely to have about $3^3/_4$ billion by the year 2000.

Second, many LDCs had slow rates of economic growth in recent years. Lack of natural resources in some, resistance to social and cultural changes, lack of inflow of foreign capital, and high rates of disease that contribute to low productivity have combined to make economic growth relatively slow. Excluding some countries where decline in income resulted from civil wars or other disturbances, the countries listed on the following page had per capita economic growth of less than 2 percent a year from 1960 to 1970.[5] Most of the above countries had per capita incomes of less than $300 at the end of the 1960s.

Third, terms of trade were generally less favorable for LDCs in the 1960s than for developed countries. The LDCs were exporting more, materially, in return for less. This is because manufactured goods, which most of these countries import in significant quantities, increased in price more rapidly than the commodities which constitute major exports for most LDCs. The dramatic rise in oil and other commodity prices in the early 1970s drastically changed this situation for some countries, but it is too soon to evaluate the long-run effects of what appears to have been a one-time relative change.

Thus in spite of the improved position of some LDCs because of the sharp rise in some commodity prices in the early 1970s, prospects for economic growth in many LDCs do not appear very bright.

[5] *World Bank Atlas*, 1972.

Africa	Asia	South America	Caribbean
Egypt	India	Peru	Haiti
Morocco	Sri Lanka (formerly Ceylon)	Ecuador	
Algeria*	Burma	Colombia	
Ghana	Indonesia	Paraguay	
Tunisia	Afghanistan		
Liberia			
Senegal			
Central African Republic			
Chad			
Somalia			
Upper Volta			
Burundi			
Rwanda			

*Algeria's position changed with the rise in oil prices in the early 1970s; Algeria is a member of OPEC.

The situation has led many to refer to a growing gap between the developed world and the less developed world. Rosenstein-Rodan has estimated that differences in income per capita between the poor and rich countries were about 1 to 2 at the beginning of the nineteenth century and are now about 1 to 40 in nominal terms and 1 to 20 in real terms.[6] Bhagwati estimated the growth rate of per capita GNP in developing countries at 2.85 percent per year on the average and in developed countries at 3.67 percent per year from 1965 to the year 2000, under existing trends.[7] While such estimates are subject to very wide margins of error, the absolute gap and even the relative gap between developed countries and LDCs will probably widen in the next quarter of a century. Whatever may be recommended concerning growth in developing countries, growth in LDCs is essential if living standards are to be raised and widening of the gap prevented.

THE THEORY OF ECONOMIC GROWTH

Growth is not confined to developing countries; the very rapid growth rate achieved in Japan, a developed country, has already been mentioned. In general it is recognized that economic growth requires an increase in capital, although that is not the only requirement. Capital is productive because people using capital (equipment) can produce more goods and services than people not using capital. Of course, people are also productive and their productivity may increase as they learn more about using their capital (tools).

[6]P. N. Rosenstein-Rodan, "The Haves and Have-Nots Around the Year 2000," in Jagdish N. Bhagwati, ed., *Economics and World Order from the 1970s to the 1990s* (London: Macmillan, 1972), p. 29.
[7]Table A-13 in Low and Howe, op. cit., p. 213.

Observed Relationships in Economic Growth[8]

For the United States, relatively good economic data seem to show the following relationships concerning growth: (1) Output and the stock of capital K generally grow at about the same rate so that the capital-output ratio K/Y remains about the same. There was an exception to this when income (output) fell during the Great Depression of the 1930s and another exception, in the opposite direction, when income rose sharply during World War II. (2) Real wages W seem to have increased at about the same rate as output per workhour, which indicates that labor obtained its proportionate share of added income and thus continued to have about the same share of total income. (3) The rate of profit did not fall significantly in the long run, although interest rates, taken as a proxy for profit rates in the absence of relatively accurate data on such rates, fell significantly in the 1930s and rose significantly after World War II.

These observed trends lead to two major conclusions: (1) Less than half of the observed increase in productivity and in real wages can be accounted for by an increase in the quantity of real capital, and more than half of the increase seems to have come from improved technology, increased education and training of labor, and improved "know-how" in management and methods of production. (2) Income grows at a relatively constant rate in an economy such as that of the United States, in which changes in social and cultural relationships generally occur slowly.

These conclusions suggest that countries that want rapid economic development must improve technology, education and training of labor, and management and productive methods; and at the same time they must increase their stocks of capital. They also suggest that such countries probably must change social and cultural relationships in major ways if they wish to improve their growth rates significantly.

"Natural" Rate of Growth

From this type of analysis, there developed the idea of a "natural" rate of growth. Hours of labor grow by some percentage per year, the percentage being determined by the number of people entering the labor force relative to the number already in it and the change in hours of work per week. If hours of work per week do not change significantly, hours of labor increase at about the same rate as the labor force. If increases in productivity of labor cause a certain percentage increase in output per year, we can add the percentage which results from increase in the labor force (let us say 1 percent) to that which results from increase in productivity (let us say 2 percent). The resulting 3 percent is the rate of increase in output of labor. Note that all increase in output is presumed in this example to be the result of labor.

---

[8]This section draws heavily on Paul A. Samuelson, *Economics*, 9th ed. (New York: McGraw-Hill, 1973), Chap. 37, pp. 731–764, especially the Appendix, "The Theory of Growth." Students may have read this material in elementary economics.

If labor's income and output grow by, say, 3 percent per year, capital K must also grow by 3 percent per year if the ratio of capital to income or output is to remain about the same. It was indicated that this ratio had remained relatively constant. An increase in the capital stock K is the same as net investment I. Thus the growth in the capital stock, or net investment, must be about 3 percent of the ratio of the capital stock to income K/Y each year. If that ratio is 3, as it has been approximately in the United States, then investment must, each year, be about 3 percent of 3 times GNP, or approximately 9 percent of GNP.[9] More rapid growth in income would require a more rapid growth in the capital stock and hence more investment, as a percent of GNP, each year.[10]

This analysis of growth may be applied to economic development in various countries, although differences in economic and social situations may alter the numerical ratios. If economic development results in major changes in social and cultural relations, the stable ratios observed in the United States may not be found.

Since saving equals investment, the theory implies that saving must equal 9 percent of GNP if 9 percent of GNP is to be devoted to investment in plant and equipment (housing and inventory accumulation are ignored at this point). Saving equal to 9 percent of GNP is necessary to attain real growth of 3 percent a year in GNP under the conditions existing in the United States. For rapid growth, much higher rates of saving are necessary, although major social changes, especially increased education, might cause more rapid increases in output without equivalent increases in rates of saving. In such cases the capital/output ratio would fall instead of having the long-run stability that it has had in the United States.

Thus, in general, relatively high saving is a requisite for increased growth. Saving may be domestic or it may occur in other countries which provide foreign investment to LDCs. LDCs may rely on domestic saving and may also encourage inflows of foreign capital. Significant flows of foreign investment must come from the developed countries. Thus one reason for advocating growth in *developed* countries is that they may then be better able to provide investment that can lead to growth in LDCs. Our major concern in this book is the international flow of investment, but we must keep in mind that foreign investment inflow and the encouragement of domestic savings and investment can go hand in hand.

[9]For further discussion, see Robert M. Solow, "Technical Progress, Capital Formation and Economic Growth," *American Economic Review*, Papers and Proceedings, May 1962, pp. 76–87.

[10]These relationships were analyzed by Solow using data on plant and equipment investment only, excluding housing and inventory accumulation. There is some controversy whether housing is as significant for development as investment in plant and equipment. Plant and equipment are used to produce other goods, which in turn produce services, while housing does not directly produce anything other than services to those who occupy houses. However, housing does create a demand for household appliances and similar goods and hence may be considered to be indirectly as well as directly a factor stimulating output. The situation varies from country to country. Japan, now considered to be a developed country, achieved a very high rate of growth in income without much addition or improvement in its stock of housing. But in many LDCs, housing in urban areas for workers coming from farm areas may have a high priority.

Although saving *somewhere* is required for economic growth, it is not a sufficient condition for such growth. Investment must be of types which produce goods and services demanded by people. In general, therefore, profitable investment is likely to generate growth. Institutional factors restricting the flow of funds into profitable investment are likely to misdirect capital into investment which does not generate much growth and may even cause funds to flow into consumption rather than into investment.

Sometimes saving rates are moderately high in LDCs but still growth does not occur. Gross savings are channeled into borrowing for consumption and sometimes into war expenditures. It is important that financial channels direct savings into those investments likely to be profitable and to generate income.

ROLE OF FINANCIAL FACTORS IN ECONOMIC GROWTH

Recently, increased attention has been given to the role of financial factors in economic growth. Growth in economic activity requires growth in the money supply, in saving, in real investment, and in financial markets and institutions through which additional saving may be transmitted into real investment. As economies grow larger and more developed, the amount and proportion of funds provided for real capital investment through financial institutions and financial markets increase. In part this is because financial institutions are adapted to accumulating small amounts of savings and channeling these savings into larger investments. Business firms can do this directly through sale of stocks and bonds in capital markets, but such a process is more difficult in economies in which people have relatively low incomes and are unfamiliar with such types of financial investment.

An indication of the reliance of developing countries on foreign investment flowing from saving in the rest of the world is given in Table 20-1, which is based on data for 14 developed countries and 10 developing countries. Note that total saving (and investment) was a smaller percentage of GDP in LDCs;

Table 20-1   Sectoral Surpluses of Saving or Investment, 1950–1959

(Investment surpluses shown as minuses)

	Percent of gross domestic product		
	14 developed countries	10 developing countries	All 24 countries
Households	6.1	3.5	4.8
Enterprises*	−7.6	−4.9	−6.3
Government	1.3	−0.7	0.3
Rest of the world	−0.1	2.1	1.0

*Includes government enterprises

Source: Finance and Development, December 1974, p. 29; taken from R. W. Goldsmith, *Financial Structure and Development* (New Haven, Conn.: Yale, 1969), p. 441.

also note the importance of foreign investment in LDCs, providing about 40 percent of the total funds for investment.

For economic development, it is important that the household sector of an economy transfer to the business and probably to the government sectors that part of its savings held in financial assets, and that saving and financial investment be encouraged. Saving may, of course, be invested directly by individuals in building physical assets such as houses, fences, and so on, but this form of investment of saving plays only a small part in developed economies. Large-scale industry cannot be developed in this way; financial investment in some form, either directly in bonds and similar instruments, or indirectly through transfer of funds to financial institutions which then lend or invest, is essential. Hence it is important that, as saving is encouraged, financial assets be acquired by households and the resulting loanable funds be transmitted through financial institutions and/or markets to business and government sectors which carry out most real investment.

As saving increases, there may be an accompanying increase in the money stock.[11] First, saving is usually accumulated in money form before being channeled into investment. Second, saving increases with rising income, and rising income requires an increase in the money stock for transactions and as a temporary abode of purchasing power.

Although it is not correct to attribute to money supply changes the sole power to generate money income and hence real income if unused resources of labor and capital are available, there are many cases in which IS and LM curves are such that monetary policy changes are more powerful than fiscal policy changes. This appears to have been the case in the United States in recent years.[12] The situation is illustrated in Figure 20-1. Shift of the IS curve from IS_1 to IS_2 represents expansive fical policy action, with more spending relative to taxes (an increase in $G - T$). Note that unless there is also a shift in the LM curve, which would be caused by an expansive monetary policy, the rise in real interest rates is relatively great and the rise in real income or GNP is relatively small. If the LM curve were vertical, there would be no increase in GNP. In such a situation, any increase in government spending would "crowd out" an

[11]The terms money stock and money supply are here used interchangeably. Although money stock is technically the correct term, since what is meant is the entire stock of money which has been created and not the flow of money into purchases or loans, the term money supply has been used so widely that it is difficult to avoid it. Money supply is not a supply in the same sense as the "supply" of wheat, which means the amount of wheat offered for sale, excluding any wheat stored for later marketing.

[12]The question is whether fiscal policy changes to expand spending have significant effects in "crowding out" other spending if the money supply is not expanded. This apparently does occur if IS curves are relatively flat and if the LM curve is rather steeply upward-sloping because more spending by government relative to taxes causes a relatively sharp rise in real interest rates, to which investment is sensitive if IS curves are relatively flat. See Brian P. Sullivan, "Crowding Out Estimated from Large Econometric Model," Federal Reserve Bank of Dallas, *Business Review,* June 1976, pp. 1–7. An early attempt to measure IS and LM curves empirically also showed quite flat IS curves; see Robert Haney Scott, "Estimates of Hicksian IS and LM curves for the United States," *Journal of Finance,* September 1966, pp. 479–487.

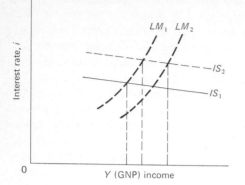

Figure 20-1 *IS-LM* Curves and Effects of Fiscal and Monetary Actions

IS line indicating points at which saving and investment are equal at different levels of income *Y*

LM line indicating points at which demand for and supply of money are equal at different levels of income *Y*

equivalent amount of other spending. With an expansive monetary policy, a sizable increase in real GNP occurs.

A change in real income may of course be accompanied by inflation. We return to this subject later but must note here that what is needed is an expansion in *real* money balances and other financial assets; hence in financial institutions and markets, concomitantly with an increase in real product. An expansion in real money balances means that the rate of increase in the money stock must exceed the rate of inflation. Expansion of the money stock must be rapid enough to aid in the generation of real growth, but not so rapid as to lead to rates of inflation high enough to cause the economic inbalances described in Chapter 14. Achieving a rate of increase in the money supply sufficient to stimulate growth in real output but not sufficient to significantly increase the rate of inflation is a difficult task. The rate of real growth possible without creating bottlenecks or shortages that may cause price increases must be correctly assessed, and this rate may differ from country to country.

If prices rise faster than money, real money balances decline even though nominal money balances rise. In such circumstances, households may not be inclined to place savings in financial assets, and funds needed for real investment may be forthcoming only in small amounts. Some degree of inflation may not be harmful, either because it may be ignored or because rising prices may lead to increasing profits, which stimulate further investment. Rapid inflation is likely to be harmful because it discourages saving and investment, and hence hinders economic development.

Real money balances are simply *M/P*, and whether they have increased or decreased in a particular country can be determined by dividing figures for the money stock by figures for the most appropriate price index available. In practice, money stock figures may be quite inaccurate in some cases, and it may be difficult to decide what price index figure is most suitable.

Evidence seems to indicate that as development occurs, the household sector usually increases the proportion of its savings held in the form of claims on financial institutions. In developed countries such as the United States and the United Kingdom, almost all the household sector's financial saving goes into increased holdings of money and of other claims on financial institutions, and only a very small percentage goes into direct claims on the business or government sectors. Money, thrift deposits, and contractual saving (premiums and contributions paid to insurance companies and pension funds) vary in importance in different countries. It has been argued that it may not be necessary for developing countries to foster broad markets for corporate and government securities among individuals if the institutions which create money, hold thrift deposits, and accept contractual saving are properly developed.[13] Thus difficult problems of developing complex bond and stock markets may be avoided or postponed.

The growth of financial intermediaries seems to have a positive influence on saving in developing countries even though this influence is not so generally found in developed countries.[14]

POLICIES DIRECTED TOWARD SAVING AND INVESTMENT

Policies aimed at encouraging economic development must be aimed at encouraging saving and limiting inflation, so that hoarding, unproductive activity, and outflow of funds from the country are minimized. They should also be aimed at avoiding overvaluation of the local currency, which may cause outflow of funds as savers fear devaluation.

Saving and the Interest Rate

Some theorists, such as Irving Fisher, emphasized that saving involves a deferral of consumption and because (as he believed) people prefer present to future consumption, savers must be compensated by a positive rate of interest to induce them to save. But many studies have shown that saving is also very closely related to income, whether current or "permanent," and that in the long run the ratio of saving to income S/Y tends to be a constant fraction in a given society. The absolute level of the ratio varies with sociological factors that favor greater or less saving. In the past, for example, people in Japan have saved much more, as percentages of their incomes, than people in the United States. One reason may be that a substantial fraction of total income is received by workers in Japan in the form of bonuses at specific times; such income, some economists have argued, is largely saved rather than spent for consumption. If S/Y in real terms is a relatively constant ratio over long periods of time in a given culture, this means that an attempt to raise interest rates, even if successful, does not lead to more saving as a percent of income, although it may cause a change in the *form* in which savings are held if the effort causes some interest rates to rise more than others.

On the other hand, if interest rates are held down by controls so that they

[13]V. V. Bhatt, "Some Aspects of Financial Policies in Developing Countries," *Finance and Development,* December 1974, pp. 29–31, 42.

[14]Anand G. Chandavarkar, "How Relevant is Finance for Development," *Finance and Development,* September 1973, pp. 14–16.

rise less rapidly than the rate of inflation, saving is likely to be reduced as a percent of income, because interest receipts under such a condition do not increase the real wealth of savers. Thus although higher positive real interest rates may not in general be required to induce more saving, and may not be successful in doing so, interest rates which result in no real gain, or in a real loss, are inimical to saving.

Financial institutions become more important as the rate of saving increases. Such an increase is possible as income rises, and may be encouraged by some cultural changes. Commercial banks are probably the most essential financial institutions. They lend for many purposes and thus can serve many of the needs for funds of those who undertake real investment. Establishment of a broad commercial banking system should have relatively high priority in LDCs, and the adequacy of the commercial banking system is a factor in foreign firms' decisions to invest in such countries.

The problem arising from an inadequate commercial banking system is best illustrated by an example from some LDCs. In some such countries, a major financial institution may be some sort of village saving society which pools savings of residents of the village and the countryside. Such institutions have little information about real investment needs and few means of channeling funds into real investment, especially into larger projects. They are likely to channel most of their funds into consumer loans to village residents who are in need of funds. Hence saving by one group of households finances part of the consumption of other households. Little contribution to real investment may be made. Many factors combine to limit the flow of savings from savers to a different group of people who undertake real investment.

Increasing Domestic Investment

The problem of increasing domestic investment is in some sense a "chicken and egg" proposition. Increased output requires increased investment, but increased investment requires increased income out of which more saving can provide funds for new investment. One might think that creating money which then can finance investment might increase employment (assuming there is less than full employment); hence make possible increased income and increased saving. But in LDCs especially, those who earn may consume most of their income, and since increased investment diverts funds from production of consumer goods, the result may be greater demand for than supply of consumer goods, resulting in inflation. A solution in the LDCs *must* include some temporary slowing in growth of consumption or even a small decline in consumption as resources are devoted to investment. As output and income rise, consumption may be permitted to rise, but a decision to seek more rapid economic growth usually involves at least a temporary sacrifice by consumers—in the form of a relatively slow increase, if not an actual decline, in consumption.

In today's economies, decisions must be made about the desirability of growth. This may be of real concern in countries such as the United States, where income levels are relatively high. For three-fourths of the world's population, however, growth in income appears essential. Nevertheless, under today's conditions, questions must be asked concerning the degree to which growth in investment and income will increase pollution; the extent to which, or the rapidity with which, it will deplete natural resources; and the extent to which permitting high incomes for some in order to increase saving may violate ideas about the desirability of greater equality in income distribution.

If *rapid* growth is desirable, there really is no alternative to a slower growth in consumption than in total output. This is a painful process. Thus any incentives to *dissave* should be avoided. The interest rate on financial assets likely to be acquired by consumers should be permitted to be higher than the rate of inflation. A rational interest rate policy is a first ingredient in an effective growth policy.[15] Then savings will flow into financial institutions and decisions can be made, perhaps by the central banks, about means of inducing the channeling of funds into appropriate investment.

"Forced Saving" through Inflation

The painfulness of the restriction of consumption, especially in economies in which consumption levels are already low, is such that there is temptation to follow an indirect path in encouraging growth. This path may be to encourage real capital investment by providing government funds, perhaps subsidies, and permitting competition between consumers and those who undertake real investment to drive up prices. Thus inflation is used to restrict consumption, as prices of consumer goods rise, and to expand investment. The presumption is that business firms can afford to pay higher prices for raw materials and higher interest rates for borrowed funds because they can sell at higher prices, and because it is also presumed that wage increases tend to lag behind price increases. One reason for this presumption may be that labor unions are relatively weak in many LDCs. Some economists have indeed argued that inflation is a necessary element for growth in LDCs.

Inflation occurs because investment made possible through use of government funds is greater than saving desired by consumers. Consumers and businesses compete for goods and services, and prices rise. If the government borrows funds instead of taxing to finance investment, the fact that consumers do not desire to save enough means an excess of demand for loanable funds compared to their supply. Interest rates rise. Too great a rise may defeat the attempt to increase investment. Hence at some point the central bank is likely to be called upon to create enough money so that desired investment will be equaled by saving out of income generated when loans increase and money balances are created by banks. Whether the government itself creates money or directs the central bank to do so, the result is in a general way the same. Inflation accompanies increased investment.

[15]Gilberto Escobedo, "The Response of the Mexican Economy to Policy Actions," Federal Reserve Bank of St. Louis, *Review,* June 1973, pp. 15–23, especially p. 19.

The danger in any such inflation is that it may feed upon itself. Many periods of economic growth in the past, in many different countries, have been accompanied by inflation. Two clear dangers exist with inflation in any country: (1) a wage-price spiral may develop, in which increases in wages which are more rapid than increases in prices tend to squeeze profits, discouraging real investment, and (2) a distrust of money and other fixed-value financial assets may develop, with a consequent flight of financial capital out of the country or into real assets such as land and inventories.

The danger of inflation diminishes if nominal income growth is slow enough that growth in real income can occur at nearly the same rate. If nominal income grows at a moderate rate, labor can be moved from areas in which it is not needed to growing industries, new capacity can be created, and necessary physical changes can be made. Moreover, if there is always *some* capacity, both of labor and of capital, which is not used, price pressures are moderated by the possibility of use of unemployed resources to increase output to meet sudden increases in demand. Hence moderate growth in nominal income and the existence of some unemployment are useful because they tend to prevent harmful inflation. The amount of unemployment need not be great, and in fact may be no more than 2 or 3 percent of the labor force.

Exchange Rates and Economic Growth

An overvalued currency (one which is above its equilibrium value) encourages outflow of capital for investment in other countries because it is feared that the local currency may be devalued or may depreciate. Thus even sound policies for increasing saving and investment may be defeated if the exchange value of the currency is difficult to determine, although in the *long* run the *trend* equilibrium value may be determined by changes in purchasing power parity.

The question was raised in earlier chapters whether under some circumstances a fall in the exchange value of a currency could be a cause of inflation. The answer of most economists was negative. But there may be some circumstances in which a fall in the exchange value of the currency concomitant with inflation may not be desirable. For example, suppose that a relatively small country is being supplied with large amounts of consumer goods by a large country in a period of war or civil disorder. Imports of consumer goods under grants in aid may offset the inflationary impact of the increase in the money supply for defense expenditures, and under such circumstances it might be undesirable to change the value of the currency. Avoidance of devaluation of the currency may reduce or eliminate the incentive to send capital out of a country.

In most circumstances, however, inflation creates current account deficits in the BOP, and there is a necessity for either devaluation or downward floating of the currency. Since inflation often accompanies economic development in LDCs, stability in exchange rates cannot be a high-priority goal in those countries. If stability in major countries' currency values is desired in order to reduce risks for those engaged in foreign trade and investment, the major countries should agree upon measures to achieve such stability. An international monetary system which encourages an increased flow of international trade and investment is probably beneficial for LDCs, but they can hardly help much by attempting to keep their own currency values stable, and it is difficult for them to do so.

If relatively rapid inflation occurs and the value of the currency is not permitted to fall, outflow of capital becomes progressively more attractive. Outflow of capital does not actually occur under such conditions, for if it occurred on a significant scale, the value of the local currency would fall. In fact, if a currency is overvalued, there is usually a deficit on current account in the BOP and therefore a surplus in some form in the capital account (an inflow of capital). Outflow of capital occurs when it is believed that the currency value may soon fall as restrictions are evaded or removed. This is particularly true if interest rates within the country are not sufficiently higher than the rate of inflation to be attractive.

BASIC POLICIES FOR ECONOMIC DEVELOPMENT: MEXICO AS AN EXAMPLE

The countries which have achieved relatively rapid rates of economic development seem to be in general those which have adopted specific policies aimed at this goal. In this section the example of Mexico is used to illustrate the long continuation of such policies in that country, and the very satisfactory rate of long-run development achieved. Although somewhat higher rates of economic growth have been reached in countries such as South Korea and Taiwan, there are special circumstances (for example, relatively large amounts of U.S. aid; relatively short period of rapid growth) which make them less suitable as long-run examples.

Encouraging Saving

A basic policy in Mexico has been to encourage saving. In Mexico this policy took the form of encouraging development in the cities, especially the larger ones. To achieve economic development through internal saving and investment requires sacrifices, and the villages and populace of the countryside did sacrifice. Their standard of living improved relatively little while that in the major cities rose sharply. As income rose, more saving was possible. Interest rates were generally maintained at levels which assured savers of a significant real return. Of course, subsidizing *particular* interest rates may distort the allocation of capital and thus inhibit economic growth. What is important is that the interest rates not be artificially held down because of a belief that lower interest rates will aid investment. A possible exception in Mexico was during the rapid inflation of 1973–1975.

Encouraging Investment

Government credit was provided for investment at favorable interest rates, and tax incentives of various kinds were used to stimulate investment. If private equity capital was insufficient, the government often provided a share of equity capital. During the 1950s and 1960s, an average annual growth of investment of 17 percent occurred; government investment, mainly in roads, dams, electric power, and so on, was about 45 percent of total investment.[16] A desired rate of growth of GDP between 6 and 7 percent per year had been established; adjusted for population trends, this meant a net growth of 3 or 4 percent per capita. Such a high rate of growth in real income meant that a large fraction of GDP had to be devoted to investment.

Other goals such as high employment and income redistribution, sometimes given high priority in industrialized countries, were not given primary importance in Mexico. It was assumed that investment and economic growth would add to employment, and the growth of income at a more rapid rate than that of population would gradually decrease unemployment. In recent years the growth of unions has changed the objective somewhat, as unions have asked for higher wages and for social and fringe benefits. But growth of productivity of labor has continued to make growth of per capita real income possible.

Fiscal Responsibility and Monetary Stability[17]

A responsible fiscal policy was essential for economic growth in Mexico. The budget was carefully controlled and deficits were not such as to create financing problems until the 1970s. When deficits occurred, they were largely financed by the private banks, reducing the amount of credit available from those banks to finance private investment. The result, in general, was that the government preempted some credit for its investment purposes, such as electric power and so on, but that this did not result in a rapid rise in nominal GNP relative to the rise in real GNP. Taxes were not used to obtain large amounts of additional funds for government investment because it was generally believed that most taxes which could have been so used would have had detrimental effects on private investment.

As a result, the central bank was seldom called upon to increase the money supply very rapidly. Money supply increased at a rate resulting in relatively rapid growth of real GDP plus what might be termed a "tolerable" rate of inflation (generally about 3 percent a year until 1972).

Stimulating Exports, Tourist Travel, and Inflow of Capital

Mexico endeavored to stimulate exports, to encourage tourist travel and spending in Mexico, and to encourage an inflow of capital in order to provide funds for investment and growth. Mexico's trade balance was almost constantly in deficit because of the need for importing many consumer goods, although

[16]Ibid., p. 16.

[17]For an attempt to assess the relative roles of fiscal policy and monetary policy in stimulating growth in the Mexican economy, see Gilberto Escobedo, "Formulating a Model of the Mexican Economy," Federal Reserve Bank of St. Louis, *Review*, July 1973, pp. 8–19. Escobedo concluded that government expenditures, although an important policy variable, did not affect total spending (GDP), and that the money stock had been a very important short-run variable determining changes in levels of economic activity.

in earlier days many "luxury" goods were discouraged by high import duties. The government at times imported and marketed basic goods to check an increase in food prices which might have been reflected in general inflation had the government not acted.

Attractive tourist centers along the coasts (especially in the west) were promoted, but in spite of strong efforts to promote tourist and other sources of service income, the balance on goods and services gradually declined from being nearly in balance in the early 1960s to a small deficit in the early 1970s.

Increasing trade deficits were offset by an inflow of foreign direct investment, some inflow of foreign long-term portfolio investment, and an inflow of funds attracted to the Mexican banking system by relatively high interest rates.

The BOP situation enabled Mexico to add significant amounts to its international reserve assets, and as a result, both Mexico's currency stability and its international credit standing were good until the early 1970s. Unfortunately, after inflation in Mexico had roughly paralleled that in the United States through 1971, prices rose far more rapidly in Mexico in 1972–1976. By mid-1976, the price level in Mexico had reached nearly four times the 1954 level, while the U.S. price level had only approximately doubled in the same period. Mexico's imports rose more rapidly than its exports and its foreign debt rose sharply as inflation became more rapid. On September 1, 1976, the Mexican government decided to permit the peso to float, after having maintained it at $12\frac{1}{2}$ pesos to the U.S. dollar since 1954. The peso dropped as low as 26 pesos to the dollar and subsequently was quoted toward the end of 1976 at about 20 pesos to the dollar.[18] It remains to be seen whether the new administration in Mexico, which took office on December 1, 1976, can restrain spending and slow the increase in the money supply sufficiently to moderate the inflation and at the same time quiet the social unrest which has begun to become more evident. This episode is of great interest because it illustrates the difficulties governments have in maintaining deviations from purchasing power parity over long periods, while it also illustrates the existence of a deviation from Fisher open for a long period. Mexican interest rates were enough higher than U.S. interest rates over a long period to provide great gain in interest income if that income had been withdrawn—even in spite of the exchange loss in value of the invested funds caused by the downward float of the peso.

Policies as an Integrated Whole

It cannot be said that the policies adopted were entirely successful. Certainly problems existed: shortages of housing, of schools, and of hospitals; air pollution, especially in Mexico City and to some extent in cities like Guadalajara; some social unrest, including kidnapings and terrorism; and the gap between

---

[18]For a brief review of this episode, see Donald S. Kemp, "U.S. International Trade and Financial Developments in 1976," Federal Reserve Bank of St. Louis, *Review*, December 1976, pp. 8–14, especially pp. 13–14.

the higher economic level in the cities and the lower level in the still-backward villages, and also in certain areas within cities to which people from villages were attracted (in spite of poor conditions) because of poverty in the villages.

Nevertheless, policies formed a consistent, integrated whole. Saving and investment were encouraged at the cost of some sacrifice by a segment of the population. Moderate inflation generally was the rule, stimulating industrial expansion but not leading to significant hoarding, a decline in productivity, wage-price spirals, or an outflow of capital from the country. External credit was good, and foreign capital was an important contributor to development. Foreign capital went directly into the private sector and indirectly provided funds for the government, since foreign deposits were acquired by banks, which were required to hold reserves in the form of government bonds.

The resulting record of a constantly high rate of growth in real income and in real income per capita for several decades, in spite of a rapid increase in population, is an example of the possibility of relatively rapid economic development under appropriate government policies.

ROLE OF EXTERNAL FUNDS IN ECONOMIC DEVELOPMENT

We have seen that external funds played an important, although certainly not the chief, role in Mexican economic development. Our concern with international financing in this book suggests that we examine more closely the role which international financing may play in economic development.

The difficulty of increasing the internal supply of funds for economic development suggests the desirability of some inflow of funds from abroad for this purpose. Grants and gifts may be appropriate for some purposes and under some conditions, especially if floods or other natural disasters, or wars and consequent interruption of productive activity, cause a decline in per capita income. But it is not likely that, given the dimensions of the problem indicated at the beginning of this chapter, grants and gifts can provide for more than a fraction of the needs for economic development if countries wish to attain development in a relatively short span of years. Moreover, given the need for determining the relative merits of different programs for development, and the difficulty of planning such programs, it seems likely that in many countries the market mechanism will be used to some extent to indicate the relative priority to be given to various projects. That is, priorities for projects will be tested by their expected returns and their relative attractiveness as investments. This is likely to be more true for projects financed through external funds, in whole or in part, and partly true for projects financed by funds generated within the developing countries. In the latter case, of course, some projects are carried out by governments without reference to cost or benefit indicators in the form of prices and interest rates.

It would be desirable to know whether increases in per capita as well as in total real GNP result in progress toward other goals, such as reduction of inequality in income. Simon Kuznets suggested that economic growth results in increased income inequality (although *perhaps* not an absolute reduction in income for lower-income groups) at first, and then later a reduction in income inequality. Kuznets' reasons were that the declining importance of agriculture would at first reduce the share of some of the population in income, while the gradual absorption of people into the modern industrial sector would gradually increase income shares. A number of studies confirmed this general pattern. However, a study reported in 1976 found no evident reason for this—that is, neither the decline in the share of agriculture in GDP nor the share of urban population in total population seemed to be related to the income share of lower-income groups. Nor did there seem to be any correlation of the *rate* of increase in GDP or GNP with income inequality. This suggests that a more rapid increase in income may simply shorten the time interval during which the share of some part of the population in income is adversely affected. The study did find that an increase in the literacy rate and in secondary school enrollment benefits the lower-income and middle-income groups, respectively, in their shares in income. The rate of growth of population was a negative factor affecting the income share of lower-income groups. Socialist countries were found to have less inequality than other countries.[19]

The Role of Aid

Aid is likely to be directed toward meeting immediate crises rather than toward economic development. Flood victims are often fed and housed through aid, war refugees are cared for, and many other good works are accomplished by gifts and grants. But gifts and grants are not likely to be forthcoming for building a cement plant or for establishing a textile industry. No doubt under some circumstances the availability of grants and gifts may permit other funds to be utilized for economic development. But aid itself, while useful for some purposes, is not likely to be appropriate as a means for extensive development.

Efforts to provide aid to LDCs have recently been challenged on two bases. First, it has been argued that aid, which is almost inevitably provided in large part through government channels, may help to perpetuate unjust governments in LDCs. Such governments and their policies may, in fact, limit the development of some countries. Second, it has been argued that for some countries aid simply cannot be provided effectively, and that providing aid for such countries diverts resources from countries which may have much better prospects for economic development. The term *triage* has been coined—or recoined—for application to the situation. In World War I, triage meant selection and referred to selection for medical aid of those among the wounded who it appeared could probably be saved and would not recover without aid. So

---

[19]Montek S. Ahluwalia, "Outcome Distribution and Development: Some Stylized Facts," *American Economic Review,* Papers and Proceedings, May 1976, pp. 128–135. For Simon Kuznets' hypothesis, see his "Economic Growth and Income Inequality," *American Economic Review,* March 1955, pp. 1–28. For two other studies, see Irma Adelman and Cynthia T. Morris, "Economic Growth and Social Equity in Developing Countries," Stanford University, 1973, and Hollis Chenery and M. Syrquin, "Patterns of Development 1950–1970," Oxford, 1975.

many wounded were in need of care that aid could not be provided for all. Sometimes it is even asserted that helping some countries to reduce death rates when birth rates continue at a high level merely means that eventually death rates must rise. Aid under these conditions and for these purposes is, it is argued, eventually useless.

Those who advance these arguments forget the time element. On a battlefield there may be no time to aid all of the wounded. But in the outlook for economic development, we cannot clearly foresee what may occur over relatively long periods. Many observers felt that South Korea, with few natural resources and a large population per square mile, had poor prospects for economic development, yet it attained the best rate of real economic growth in the 1960s of almost any developing country.

Nevertheless, the limited purposes to which aid is generally devoted, the difficulty of inducing developed countries and those developing countries which are better off to devote more than very small fractions of their incomes to grants in aid for foreign countries, and the arguments sometimes advanced against foreign aid are likely to make the role of foreign aid minor in financing economic development.

Borrowing from International Agencies

International agencies, particularly the World Bank Group, have led the way in lending for economic development. Yet the World Bank Group, and particularly the World Bank itself, have significant deficiencies as sources of funds for development. The present impossibility of obtaining equity capital from the World-Bank and the general reasons for not wishing the World Bank to be a provider of equity capital; the focus of the World Bank until recent years on projects with definite, fairly predictable revenues; and the emphasis of the World Bank on safety of its loans made it inadequate as a source of funds for many activities. Nevertheless, World Bank loans may be an integral part of financing development projects if other capital can be provided. An example is the huge Siderurgica Lazaro Cardenas-Las Truchas, S.A., steel producing complex being developed at the mouth of the Rio Balsas, in Michoacan, Mexico. Equity capital of $300 million was provided entirely by government agencies, including the development bank, Nacional Financiera (NAFINSA). But the debt capital of $450 million came in part from the World Bank and Inter-American Development Bank (a combined amount of about $124 million), and about $326 million in credits from companies in 12 different countries supplying equipment for the project. This combination of government capital, capital supplied by international agencies, and privately supplied foreign capital is an interesting example.[20]

Achievements of the World Bank are not confined to projects carried out with the aid of loans. Sometimes its activity in such things as development negotiations is a major factor in resulting development. An example of this is

---

[20]"Mexico's New Steel City," *Fortune*, September 1975, pp. 117–122.

its role in the negotiations between India and Pakistan for alteration of the Indus River flow and for irrigation facilities for use of the resulting available water.

When the World Bank in 1968 set new targets for sharp increases in total lending, in lending to Africa and to Latin America, and in lending to agriculture and for education, it began to modify its approach. In 1972 it changed its organizational structure so that it might, it was hoped, become more effective in meeting its objectives in the 1970s.[21] The bank was making in the neighborhood of 150 loans totaling perhaps $3.5 billion per year, and the World Bank Group as a whole was lending about $4 billion a year. It was proposed to increase this so that lending would approximate $8 billion a year on the average in the last half of the 1970s.[22]

Clearly, the World Bank Group will be a significant source of external funds for developing countries, and will be important to many. Its relationship to private investing is largely indirect, since it lends (except for the IFC) either to governments or to agencies which provide government guarantees.

Borrowing from Government Agencies in Developed Countries

Agencies such as the Export-Import Bank in the United States are generally alternatives to the World Bank Group and the regional banks for lending to developing countries. The Export-Import Bank is able to lend to a few countries which are not members of the World Bank, and to make some loans which the World Bank might not make because of risk. Since a major objective of the Export-Import Bank is to promote U.S. exports, there may be a conflict of objectives if U.S. exports and development in LDCs are not viewed as complementary.

Borrowing from the Export-Import Bank and from private sources to obtain funds for a project can reduce cost of funds because Export-Import Bank interest charges may be slightly lower than private rates. The Export-Import Bank has provided relending credits to non-U.S. financial institutions to help make possible loans to finance U.S. exports. Thus the Export-Import Bank is important in a number of ways to U.S. export firms and to business firms in foreign countries, including developing countries.

Borrowing in Capital Markets of Developed Countries

Only the strongest firms and government agencies in LDCs are likely to be able to borrow in the capital markets of developed countries. Few firms in LDCs are able to demonstrate the financial strength, make the necessary disclosures, and meet the costs of such borrowing. Yet, since the removal of restrictions on borrowing in the U.S. capital market in early 1974, some firms in LDCs have been able to sell bonds in limited amounts and to obtain term bank loans. (The

---

[21]John A. King, "Reorganizing the World Bank," *Finance and Development*, March 1974, pp. 5–3, 34.

[22]Robert S. McNamara, *Address to the Board of Governors, IBRD*, Sept. 1, 1975 (Washington, D.C.: IBRD, 1975).

restrictions generally did not apply to LDCs, but the environment was not very conducive to borrowing before 1974.)

Borrowing in the Eurodollar and Eurobond Markets

Like the capital markets of developed countries, the Eurodollar and Eurobond markets are somewhat difficult for LDCs to enter. Credit standards are relatively high, and in the Eurobond market disclosure is generally broad, although not necessitated by legal requirements such as those of the Securities and Exchange Commission (SEC) in the United States. Competition of borrowers is significant. In 1972, issues of LDCs constituted less than 10 percent of total Eurobond issues.[23] By 1975 over half of publicized Eurocredits went to developing countries, and almost this proportion continued in 1976. However, Brazil, Mexico, Spain, and Indonesia obtained more than half these credits, and almost no such credits were obtained by the lowest income countries with the poorest prospects for growth in per capita GNP.[24]

Governments and firms in LDCs are likely to be able to borrow larger amounts in the Eurodollar and Eurobond markets as they improve their credit positions. Unfortunately, many such countries are not in good positions to make such improvement.

The Role of Commercial Banks in Financing Economic Development

Commercial banks have an important role in financing economic development. As they have spread overseas, many of them becoming multinational institutions, the largest commercial banks have offices in many LDCs, and are in a position to make first-hand evaluation of loan possibilities and loan applications. As some of them have acquired ownership of interests in host-country financial institutions, they are in a better position to finance various types of enterprises, often being able to make types of loans which U.S. domestic banks cannot make.

Package Financing   Many firms in LDCs, both public and private, are interested in "package" financing—that is, they want to be able to obtain in one package the financing for an entire project. This may include short-term funds, long-term debt, and even equity. Banks have begun to try to supply this type of package financing, sometimes making arrangements for the total financing and sometimes simply providing advice concerning sources.[25]

---

[23]Francis A. Lees and Maximo Eng, *International Financial Markets* (New York: Praeger, 1975), pp. 458–459.

[24]These statistics must be treated with some caution. The breakdown between industrial countries and developing countries is such that countries like the Republic of Korea, the Ivory Coast, and the Philippines are classed as industrial countries. So are Pakistan and Zaire, countries which have very low per capita incomes.

[25]Lees and Eng remark that "one of the most dynamic and constructive financial forces in recent years has been the package financing offered to multinational corporations"; ibid., p. 535.

Venture Banking and Economic Development   In areas in which economic development requires major projects, banks may have to form consortia and enlist the aid of other financing institutions in order to provide adequate financing. This type of "venture banking" of course involves risk, but it may also provide substantial profits for banks and development of needed projects.

Private Foreign Investment and Economic Development

Perhaps the best way to encourage economic development through foreign capital is to encourage entry of private foreign firms. Countries like South Korea, Taiwan, and Mexico, which are among the "rapid growth" group of developing countries, have encouraged such entry, although in Mexico the encouragement has been tempered in recent years by the requirement of Mexican majority ownership in many industries. With sales and profits growing, however, many firms accept such a requirement; they might prefer sole ownership, but recognize the benefit in even a minority position.[26]

A number of developing countries have shown some reduction in their hostility toward private foreign investment.[27] However, there will undoubtedly be pressure from developing countries for multinational and other firms to provide benefits for the local economies when they invest. Through the 1960s and into the early 1970s, U.S. direct investment was declining in developing areas as a proportion of total U.S. foreign direct investment.[28] The stage seems to be set for a contest between the desire of developing countries to attract investment (which is somewhat hesitant to enter) and their desire to have such investment on specific terms which they believe may benefit their economies.

External Debt and Financial Stability

In choosing between borrowing and encouragement of foreign direct investment, developing countries must give attention to the financial situation resulting from borrowing. No firm rules have been developed concerning the amount of debt which may be incurred without endangering the obtaining of further credit. In general, some relationship between debt service payments and exports has been considered as a maximum limit—but there is not general agreement on a specific figure. The problem is complicated by statistical difficulties in developing countries.[29] But it is also complex because external borrowing generates internal income, including income from exports, which in turn provides means of meeting debt servicing requirements. There is the related problem of permitting repatriation of some funds by firms which have made direct investments in the developing countries.

[26]Wolfgang G. Friedmann and Jean-Pierre Beguin, *Joint International Business Ventures in Developing Countries* (New York: Columbia, 1971).

[27]Irving S. Friedman, op. cit., p. 248.

[28]Dale R. Weigel, "Multinational Approaches to Multinational Corporations," *Finance and Development*, September 1974, pp. 27–29, 42.

[29]Thomas M. Klein, "Debt Statistics and Debt Analysis," *Finance and Development*, September 1974, pp. 30–33.

As with business firms, restricted exports of developing countries when developed countries are in recessions and other pressures may lead to reliance on high-cost, short-term financing which creates both a cost and a liquidity problem. Prosperity in the developed countries benefits LDCs by enabling them to export more and to reduce or stabilize certain types of debt.

The sharp rise in oil prices in the early 1970s and the resulting adverse BOP situations for the non-oil-producing LDCs created a situation in which debt of LDCs necessarily increased. In those circumstances it was feared by some that there might be defaults and renegotiation of debts because of the inability of LDCs to meet interest and principal repayment obligations. Evidence from past renegotiation cases indicated that these were characterized by (1) high levels of debt outstanding as a ratio of GNP (DOUT/GNP); (2) high levels of the debt service payments in relation to exports (DSR/X); (3) concentration of debt service payments in immediate future years; and (4) heavy dependence on net inward capital flows or transfers in relation to imports (NT/Im).[30]

On the basis of an analysis of past renegotiation situations, it was suggested that countries which are heavy debtors (high ratios of DOUT/X and of DOUT/GNP) and which rely on large inflows of foreign capital in terms of ratios of disbursements on tied loans as a ratio of imports (DISB/Im) and high ratios of net inflows of capital or net transfers to imports (NT/Im) can maintain this situation best if the terms of debt service payments to debt outstanding (DS/DOUT) permit an easy rollover or ratio of debt service to disbursements on tied loans (DS/DISB). If the rollover ratio (DS/DISB) becomes too high, countries seem to be in danger of having to renegotiate loans, especially if the ratio of disbursements on tied loans to imports (DISB/Im) rises to a high level. Such comparisons may give indications of which countries may be in danger of having to renegotiate their debt terms. It may also be hypothesized that the growth of debt should be in line with the growth of exports.

These comparisons, although helpful, are probably not as useful as analyses in terms of saving and investment, BOP situations, capital flows, and monetary and fiscal policies used in the LDCs. The sharp rise in oil prices, which created BOP surpluses for a number of the oil-producing countries, caused deficits for many countries, since one country's surplus is another country's deficit. Further increase in deficits for non-oil-producing LDCs was caused by recession in most of the major developed countries, since recession reduced imports by those countries.

The World Bank estimated that in the early 1970s the LDCs saved about 18 percent, on the average, of their total GNP, and invested 20 percent. Their development deficit, the amount needed from other countries in the form of grants, loans, and investments, was thus about 2 percent of their total GNP. This 2 percent was made up of two parts: official loans and grants from international agencies and from governments of the developed countries on the

---

[30]Pierre Dhonte, "Describing External Debt Situations: A Roll-Over Approach," IMF *Staff Papers*, March 1975, pp. 159–186.

one hand, and private investment on the other hand. The first stream depends on humanitarian, political, and economic motives. It is, moreover, included in the current account of BOPs, and thus reduces the current account deficit. The second stream depends on expected profits, fears of capital controls and of nationalization (a negative factor), and taxation. GNP of 71 non-oil-producing countries totaled about $500 billion in the early 1970s, and the BOP deficit on current account of those countries was about $8 billion without counting official transfers, and about $4.5 billion taking into account official transfers to those countries.[31]

Since the rise in oil prices increased the cost of imports, and the recession in developed countries stopped the growth of real export earnings of LDCs, although nominal earnings continued to rise because of inflation, the deficit was expected to increase sharply. The LDCs in general tried to offset this by maintaining the growth of their money stocks in order to continue internal economic growth and thus offset by growth of domestic income the increased cost of imports. LDCs faced especially serious problems when they pegged their exchange rates to currencies of other countries (usually developed countries). The LDCs were creating too much money in relation to the possible *real* growth of their economies. As consumers and business firms tried to spend, inflation worsened.

Some LDCs improved their position by devaluation, which, as noted in earlier chapters, sometimes encourages exports and causes some decrease in imports. Some—sometimes the same countries—slowed the rate of growth of their money stocks, which reduced spending but at the same time tended to cause recession internally.

Significant improvement in the situation of the LDCs, however, was possible for two reasons. First, OPEC countries were not likely to raise the price of oil again by a large percentage. With the flow of new oil from Alaska, the North Sea, and other places, the power of OPEC countries to control the price of oil was expected to diminish. Second, the LDCs' position was expected to improve as recovery occurred in the Group of Ten countries. A lengthy recovery—possible although not necessarily certain—was expected to improve the position of the LDCs and to allay general fears of debt renegotiation or default except in occasional instances.

Nevertheless, the development deficit of the LDCs is likely to continue to grow as their GNP grows. As long as the deficit is such that debt can be serviced, firms and banks in developed countries may find loans to LDCs attractive. Direct investment in LDCs also is likely to constitute an attractive field for expansion by MNCs if LDCs avoid restrictions on such investment and if they do not take actions giving rise to fears of confiscation.

---

[31]Citibank, *Monthly Economic Letter,* June 1976, pp. 4–15. In this publication it was estimated that debt to private banks in 1975 by the non-oil-producing LDCs was slightly over $50 billion. Another study which also concludes that fears of LDC defaults are exaggerated is Nicholas Sargen, "Commercial Bank Lending to Developing Countries," Federal Reserve Bank of San Francisco, *Economic Review,* Spring 1976, pp. 20–31.

Financial analysts in MNCs may give much more attention to investment in LDCs if their growth can be accelerated. Such analysts should be concerned with the process of economic development and the possibilities for more rapid economic growth in LDCs, so as to pinpoint attractive areas for investment.

FINANCIAL INSTITUTIONS AND MARKETS AND ECONOMIC DEVELOPMENT

As economic development progresses, financial institutions and markets become more essential. Channels are required for the flow of saving into major investment projects, and means are needed for offering larger securities issues to the public. In fact, it has also been argued that the development of financial institutions and markets is part of the process by which economies grow, and that such financial growth contributes to real economic growth. Internationally, if it should be true that growth of the financial sector does promote *real* economic growth, the spread of international banking, international investment institutions, and international financial markets is important in economic development.

In recent years both changes in theory and empirical studies have been important. Goldsmith found that an increase in the number and variety of financial institutions, and a substantial rise in the ratio of both money and the total value of all financial assets to GNP was an observable feature of economic development worldwide.[32] In fact, Goldsmith suggested the concept of a "financial interrelation ratio" as a measure of the extent of financial development.

The assembling of flow of funds accounts data for a number of developing countries provides a financial chart of the movement of funds within economies. This analytical tool is very helpful in analysis of the financial sector.

Finally, the theory developed by John G. Gurley and Edward S. Shaw at the beginning of the 1960s was applied by Shaw to the context of developing economies.[33]

Empirically, the experience of Taiwan and South Korea was instructive in showing that relatively high interest rates paid to bank depositors apparently attracted a relatively large amount of resources to the banking sectors of those economies. Total saving was not appreciably increased by this process, but saving which had been in the form of what some term hoarding (accumulation of gold and physical assets) was converted into financial form. Of course, central banks could have increased the money supply and created bank deposits, but in that case hoarding might have continued, with further inflation resulting from the demand for physical assets. Later, total private saving did

---

[32]Raymond W. Goldsmith, *Financial Structure and Development* (New Haven, Conn.: Yale, 1969).
[33]Edward S. Shaw, *Financial Deepening in Economic Development* (New York: Oxford, 1969).

increase. Thus high interest rates attracted savers to make deposits, and as income rose with the investment which occurred on the basis of bank lending of the funds, the volume of saving increased. Similar conclusions follow from other research.[34]

Interest rate controls are detrimental to economic growth. To the extent that such controls are effective, they tend to hold down interest rates in the organized financial markets, but rates rise in "unorganized" financial markets. Funds are diverted from productive use through the channels of organized financial markets to less productive use through the channels of "unorganized" financial markets. Permitting deposit interest rates to rise seemed to have the unexpected result—from the standpoint of previously accepted theory—of *increasing* investment. The rise in interest rates made more funds available for industrial borrowers, even though at a higher cost. As long as industrial borrowers could obtain high rates of return on their investments in real capital assets, the rise in interest rates did not hinder investment. The key rate is not the interest rate, but the rate of return on real capital assets. Even at the margin, this must be higher than the interest rate because there is greater risk in investing in real capital assets than in buying bonds (profits are more variable than returns on bonds).[35]

A side issue is that of indexing. Accepted economic theory holds that capital markets adjust interest rates to accommodate expected rates of inflation, but in practice, if inflation is rapid and volatile, this may be difficult. Indexing, it is argued by some, may improve the functioning of the capital markets by adding a greater degree of security to those involved in financial transactions. If interest rates on savings do not rise concomitantly with inflation, the *real* return from interest becomes negative. Thus industries which depend on borrowed funds (the construction industry is an obvious example) are hurt as savers recognize the negative yield and put funds elsewhere.

The recent experience of Colombia in 1972–1975 in using a correction for inflation to adjust deposit interest rates and loan interest rates is interesting. Apparently the action was successful in stimulating an increase in construction activity.[36]

Indexing has not been generally favored for economies in which there is a chance that governments can control fiscal and monetary policy so as to keep inflation at a moderate pace or return it to that pace if it has gotten out of hand. In economies in which such hope is not bright, a stronger argument can be

[34]U Tun Wai and Hugh T. Patrick, "Stock and Bond Issues and Capital Markets in Less Developed Countries," IMF *Staff Papers*, July 1973, pp. 253–317; U. Tun Wai, *Financial Intermediaries and National Savings in Developing Countries* (New York: Praeger, 1972).

[35]A short presentation of the theory underlying this view, based on Tobin's concept of the rate of return on real capital assets as the key "interest" rate, may be found in Charles N. Henning, William Pigott, and Robert Haney Scott, *Financial Markets and the Economy* (Englewood Cliffs, N.J.: Prentice-Hall, 1975), pp. 228–232.

[36]"El Sistema Colombiano de Ahorro y Vivienda" (The Colombian System of Indexation) in *El Ahorro para la Vivienda* (Savings for Housing), published by the Instituto Colombiano de Ahorro y Vivienda (Colombia Institute of Savings for Housing), Bogota, 1975.

made for indexing. There are many technical questions concerning indexing which cannot be analyzed in the space available here.[37]

In this connection, we return to a question asked earlier—how much economic growth can be financed by monetary expansion without generating undesirable inflation? A general answer has been supplied by monetary theory, although the application to individual situations may involve difficult empirical questions of measurement. Noninflationary growth in the money supply occurs if the demand for money grows concomitantly with the supply. Demand for money in LDCs grows for two reasons: (1) An increase in the labor force and improvement in productivity lead to a certain rate and amount of growth in real output, and a concomitant increase in demand for money occurs because demand for money rises nearly proportionately to a rise in real income, since money is used for transactions for purchase of the additional real output. (2) In LDCs, as development occurs, nonmonetary parts of the economy (parts in which barter has been used) become monetized, and this generates additional demand for money. However, one factor which diminishes long-run demand for money must also be taken into consideration: when money is created against private debt (for example, when banks make short-term loans to business firms or consumers and in the process create money), the private debt must later be repaid. As this occurs, demand for money to meet debt obligations diminishes. Thus to the extent that money is created against *private* debt, no long-run demand for money is created. Hence money created by banks in making business and consumer loans must be subtracted from the amount of money created which balances the growth in real output and the monetization of barter sectors, to determine the increase in money supply likely to be matched by an increase in demand for money, and therefore likely to be noninflationary.[38]

Application of this general theory in particular LDCs is, as noted, difficult because all three of the relevant magnitudes vary. Some LDCs have great possibilities for increase in real output because labor can be transferred from sectors which can to some degree be mechanized, and such labor can be used in developing sectors. Other factors also make the demand for money variable. No single rate is appropriate for different countries. In developed countries, the noninflationary rate of increase in the money supply is generally regarded as being equal to the rate of possible increase in real output, because the latter two factors are ignored; and creation of money in the process of financing inventory accumulation may contribute to inventory cycles in business fluctuations.

---

[37]For a lengthy bibliography on indexation and an argument for income indexation rather than price level indexation, see Robert Haney Scott, "On Improving the Standard for Deferred Payments by Indexation," unpublished research study, 1976. If real output (income) falls and prices rise, income-indexed repayment would mean a repayment of the same proportion of the national income (output) "pie," whereas price-indexed repayment would mean repayment of a larger proportion.

[38]Harry G. Johnson, "Is Inflation the Inevitable Price of Rapid Development or a Retarding Factor in Economic Growth?" *Malayan Economic Review*, April 1966, p. 25.

Types of Financial Institutions Needed

Most essential in a developing country is an adequate commercial banking system. Thus if one cannot be developed internally in a short period, expansion of foreign banking may be most helpful. This is especially true if foreign banking can be divorced from exclusive preoccupation with the foreign exchange market and financing foreign trade, and can be induced or required to finance domestic investment.

After the establishment of an adequate commercial banking system, the establishment of institutions to channel long-term funds into industry is a basic need. Commercial banks are not entirely appropriate for long-term financing, although in some countries they serve that purpose, sometimes relatively well. In this connection contractual saving becomes important. Contractual saving channels funds into insurance premiums, pension fund contributions, and principal payments on mortgage debt. The first two provide funds for long-term investment, while the third supplies funds for acquisition of equity in housing.[39] It is possible that growth of pension funds may even increase aggregate saving, although it has generally been believed that the ratio of saving to income (current or "permanent") is sociologically and culturally determined in other ways.[40]

Contractual saving institutions (insurance companies and pension or social security funds) are also significant because there is a question whether efforts should be made to encourage such institutions, or to encourage the development of markets—such as stock exchanges—for direct purchase of primary securities (issued by ultimate borrowers) by the public. There are some indications that the development of stock markets is a lengthy process and that it takes time for business firms to adjust to this. It *may* therefore be preferable, if a choice is made, to encourage the development of contractual saving institutions.

There is a contrast between contractual saving institutions, which are saver-oriented, and development banks, which are oriented toward real investment. There are certainly a number of examples of development banks which have been very active and seem to have been very useful. Nacional Financiera in Mexico has already been mentioned as an example of these. But these institutions operate largely with funds made available to them by governments and by international agencies. Hence they do not necessarily encourage concentration of internal saving by consumers into forms suitable for channeling into real investment. The World Bank has been involved in the creation of a number of development banks, and it is not suggested that this was undesirable. But their actions must be appraised in terms of the relative importance of

[39]Madhusudan S. Joshi, "The Role of Contractual Savings," *Finance and Development*, December 1972, pp. 43–48.

[40]Philip Cagan, *The Effect of Pension Plans on Aggregate Saving* (New York: National Bureau of Economic Research, 1965). See also Alicia Munnell, "The Impact of Social Security on Personal Saving," Federal Reserve Bank of Boston, *New England Economic Review*, January/February 1975, pp. 27–38.

public versus private stimulus for investment in developing economies.[41] On the other hand, a warning is necessary concerning possible concentration of financial control by financial institutions, especially if economies of scale for financial institutions in LDCs lead to relatively large, powerful institutions.

Financial Markets in Developing Countries

The growth of financial markets is clearly essential in economic development. Unless there is some development of a broad money market, banks do not have adequate opportunities for meeting liquidity needs. Indeed, the instability of international money markets which has been experienced in the early 1970s has pushed even development banks into money market rather than capital market financing. Demand for highly liquid financial assets with high yields increased as interest rates in the developed countries were volatile and as short-term rates reached rather surprisingly high peaks.

Capital markets seem to be slower in developing in most of the LDCs, partly because of unfamiliarity with equity securities and even with long-term debt securities, and partly because of the complexity of such markets.

Foreign exchange market facilities are necessary because of the wide use of vehicle currencies in international trade and other payments. There is, however, a question whether facilities for forward exchange trading should be encouraged in developing countries.[42] There is some cost to central banks in encouraging the establishment of forward markets. Moreover, in many LDCs, forward transactions are not likely to lead to market equilibrium because of the unbalanced nature of the economies, and commercial banks also may have difficulty in covering open positions. The floating of foreign exchange rates has presented LDCs with entirely new problems in international finance, and central banks in LDCs should evaluate particular situations with this in mind.

Role of Central Banks in Economic Development

Central banks are especially important in economic development because of their influence on the commercial banking system and indirectly on other financial institutions. When economic development is a goal, central banks can take a variety of steps to encourage it. They may discount more freely for such banks, and even impose differential reserve requirements related to types of loans and investments made by banks. They can take an active role in advising banks on development lending and can assist in the education of bankers in such activity. These are simply a few examples of the many ways in which central banks may influence development.[43]

[41]William Diamond, "Appraising Development Banks," *Finance and Development*, June 1974, pp. 17–19, 32.

[42]Richard H. Miller, "Forward Exchange Facilities in Developing Countries," *Finance and Development*, March 1975, pp. 12–15.

[43]Andrew F. Brimmer, "Central Banking and Economic Development: The Record of Innovation," address at the tenth anniversary celebration of the Bank of Jamaica, Kingston, Oct. 10, 1970.

These activities are supplemental to the significant role of all central banks in achieving and maintaining a growth of the money supply conducive to economic growth with relatively stable prices, and to reasonable equilibrium in the BOP.

SUMMARY

This chapter has indicated the gigantic dimensions of the problem of economic development, and has emphasized the need for increase in saving and investment to achieve development. Although "forced" saving through moderate inflation may make some contribution, development policies call for fiscal responsibility and moderate growth in the money stock to prevent inflation from resulting in a reduction in *real* money balances. Stimulation of exports and other means of obtaining current economic receipts from abroad is frequently essential, as is an appropriate exchange rate policy aimed generally at an equilibrium rate of exchange.

Both internal saving and external borrowing are likely to be necessary in stimulating economic development. Sources of external funds were reviewed, and the desirability of attracting private foreign investment was indicated.

Mexico, as an example of successful long-term growth policy, demonstrated the feasibility, at least under some conditions, of policies aimed at economic development, fiscal responsibility, moderate growth in the money stock, foreign borrowing to finance part of investment and to maintain relatively high international reserve assets, and concentration of economic development efforts in certain areas. The more rapid inflation in Mexico in the 1970s created difficulties, but it is possible that relatively rapid growth with only mild inflation may be resumed.

Finally, the role of financial institutions and markets in economic development was reviewed. Recent theory has shown that development of financial institutions and markets may play an active causal role in economic development, rather than being simply a passive accompaniment. Proper management of central banks is a key factor, since they can play an important role in encouraging economic development.

The importance of economic development to international financial management lies in the great need and opportunity for private international business activity, especially in areas such as the Pacific Basin and South Asia. Business firms which accept the challenge in investment in these areas are likely to find both problems and opportunities, but will contribute to moderation of the serious gap in income between the "first" and the "third" world. LDCs are an area of opportunity, challenge, and, of course, in some cases, disappointment for the MNCs.

QUESTIONS FOR DISCUSSION

1 Can you make any analytical grouping of rapidly developing LDCs which may be helpful in determining the causes of economic development?

2   What conditions encourage saving in a developing country?

3   Why may moderate inflation (perhaps up to 5 percent per year) not be harmful in a developing country while rapid inflation is almost surely detrimental?

4   Why is a policy of downward adjustment in the exchange value of the currency, or permitting it to float downward, generally recommended in developing countries? In what special circumstances is there a possibility that it might be inappropriate?

5   Since saving is generally believed to be related to income (and only in a very minor way to anything else), is it essential to keep interest rates at any absolute level to encourage saving? Is it essential to keep them at any rate relative to the rate of inflation?

6   Why do some economists believe that "forced saving" through moderate inflation is necessary in developing countries? How does it provide funds for development?

7   What arguments can be used against foreign aid as a significant contributor to economic development?

8   In what ways does the development of financial institutions and markets contribute to economic development?

9   Make a list or analysis of ways in which a central bank can become an active force for economic development if its managers desire this.

10 Evaluate the role of private foreign investment (both portfolio and direct) in economic development, as compared to domestic private investment, domestic public investment, and foreign borrowing by public enterprises.

SUGGESTED REFERENCES

Some of the dimensions of the problem of economic development may readily be perceived from such publications as *The U.S. and World Development, Agenda for Action 1975* (New York: Praeger, 1975). The *World Bank Atlas,* published frequently by the IBRD, is useful for an overview of income and population levels and trends. *Finance and Development,* a quarterly publication of the IMF and the World Bank Group, is essential for review of current ideas.

For a brief review of the recent controversy concerning economic growth, including references to major works such as the two reports of the Club of Rome and the work of Meadows, Tinbergen, Kaysen, Nordhaus, and others, see Sheldon W. Stahl, "On Economic Growth," Federal Reserve Bank of Kansas City, *Monthly Review,* February 1975, pp. 3–9. Stahl emphasized the need for growth to maintain a relatively high level of employment (or a low level of unemployment), to prevent eruption of conflict over shares of income if the "pie" is not growing, and "the role of growth in uplifting" the LDCs.

A relatively simple form of the theory of economic growth is outlined in Paul A. Samuelson, *Economics,* 9th ed. (New York: McGraw-Hill, 1973), Chap. 37, pp. 731–764, especially the appendix, "The Theory of Growth." See also Chap. 38, "Problems of Economic Growth and Development."

Two articles in *Fortune* provide an interesting story concerning Mexico's economic development: Harold Burton Meyers, "That Incredible Economy South of the Border," *Fortune,* September 1975, pp. 112–116, 170–177, and "Mexico's New Steel City," *Fortune,* September 1975, pp. 117–123. For a more analytical discussion, including fiscal and monetary policy models of Mexico's economy, see Gilberto Escobedo, "The Response of the Mexican Economy to Policy Actions," Federal Reserve Bank of St.

Louis, *Review*, June 1973, pp. 15–23, and "Formulating a Model of the Mexican Economy," ibid., July 1973, pp. 8–19.

The role of finance was analyzed in three especially important books published in the late 1960s and early 1970s: Raymond W. Goldsmith, *Financial Structure and Development* (New Haven, Conn.: Yale, 1969); Ronald I. McKinnon, *Money and Capital in Economic Development* (Washington, D.C.: Brookings, 1973); and Edward S. Shaw, *Financing Deepening in Economic Development* (New York: Oxford, 1973). A useful brief review of some of the ideas developed in this analysis of financial institutions and markets is John W. Lowe, "Financial Markets in Developing Countries," *Finance and Development,* December 1974, pp. 38–41.

For a later study extending the work of McKinnon and Shaw on money and finance in economic development, see Ronald I. McKinnon, ed., *Money and Finance in Economic Growth and Development* (New York: Marcel and Dekker, 1976). One study found that financial intermediation could not be unequivocally classified as a factor promoting economic growth in selected African countries. This may have been because the rate of saving, the rate of growth in population, social and political conditions, technology and management, and administrative capability are also factors, and financial intermediation could not be separately identified as having a significant causal relationship. It is also possible that the limited extent of financial intermediation in the African countries used in the study may have resulted in the inconclusive findings. See Rattan J. Bhatia and Deena R. Khatkhate, "Financial Intermediation, Savings Mobilization, and Entrepreneurial Development: The African Experience," IMF *Staff Papers,* March 1975, pp. 132–158.

A useful review of financial problems in economic development, now outdated but nevertheless valuable, is Antonin Basch, *Financing Economic Development* (New York: Macmillan, 1964).

A brief discussion of financial market problems in LDCs constitutes Chap. 25 in Francis A. Lees and Maximo Eng, *International Financial Markets* (New York: Praeger, 1975).

On the role of banking, see Rondo Cameron, *Banking and Economic Development* (New York: Oxford, 1972). See also Irving S. Friedman, *The Emerging Role of Private Banks in the Developing World* (New York: Citicorp, 1977). Friedman's study merits careful reading, since it is very helpful on such matters as country risk analysis, criteria for bank lending to LDCs, and the financial situations of both the international banks and the LDCs.

Epilog

Institutions and practices in international finance in the future will differ significantly from those discussed in this book. The Eurocurrency and Eurobond markets did not exist before 1950, to mention only one development of recent years. Other developments will no doubt come in the future.

Moreover, the theory of international finance, especially on the microfinancial side, is still in its infancy. The growth of the MNC has been a phenomenon of the twentieth century, and as always theory must be developed to analyze and explain economic changes.

The history of the international financial system attests to its capacity for change and development. It has adjusted in response to economic needs, and has reflected policies aimed at achieving national and sometimes international economic goals. There is every reason to assume that innovation and flexibility will characterize the international financial system of the future.

The international monetary system has a role in international finance similar to the domestic role of a monetary system. It provides a framework for international payments and a group of financial assets which perform the functions of money internationally. Without international money and an appropriate degree of stability in exchange rates, risk might become so great as to discourage both international investment and international trade—as occurred in the 1930s. Whether the floating exchange rates of the period since March 1973—a watershed point—can provide the necessary stability remains to be seen. Official U.S. policy seems to have favored a continuation of floating rates; some other countries have favored a gradual return to more nearly fixed exchange rates, or at any rate some possibility of such return. Meanwhile analysis of the impact of floating rates on macroeconomic policies and on the microeconomic activities of individual firms has made a significant beginning.

For many years a conflict has been developing between economic forces leading toward world integration and political forces which dictate different national policies and interests for "states," often smaller in size than formerly, as the breakup of colonial empires and divisions between cultural and political groups have created small nations. The requirement of some major industries for large firms and the advantages of global diversification reinforce the economic integration and broadening scope of MNCs. Yet the antagonisms of various groups and the desires of various countries to follow different policies also persist.

The strains imposed by such developments culminated in a breakdown in the early 1970s of the international monetary mechanism in its past form. There followed a number of modifications in the functioning of the international monetary mechanism. The role of gold has been drastically modified, although it remains an international asset that *might* be utilized in the international monetary system more actively at some point—or it might not. The strain of an excess of dollar holdings outside the United States and the closing of the gold "window" led to a desire by private foreign holders to hold fewer dollars, and the resulting flood of dollars into the hands of central banks created a basis for world inflation and caused central banks to reappraise their international policies. The result was a general floating of major exchange rates in March 1973.

The period 1971–1973—whether one wishes to select the particular date of August 15, 1971, or that of March 15, 1973—was thus a general watershed in the history of international finance. Previous watershed dates were the period of spread of the international gold standard in the 1870s and the international monetary crisis of 1931, followed by the formation of the IMF in 1944.

It would be rash to predict the course of international finance from the watershed of 1971–1973. Some believe that floating exchange rates are here to stay, and that gradual adjustment by private firms and other institutions, as well as by central banks, will occur. Others believe that the system will eventually be reoriented toward a system of stable exchange rates. This would necessitate the coordination of monetary and fiscal policies of major countries in the system (the major industrial countries). It would be in line with the trend toward global economic integration, which of course faces great obstacles and is likely to occur only on a piecemeal basis. Piecemeal integration can occur as groups of countries decide to stabilize exchange rates among their currencies and perhaps to attain single currencies within a group of countries, as has been at least a stated goal of the European Common Market. Countries on the fringes of such areas, such as Greece and perhaps at some point Spain, may be absorbed gradually into these market areas.

Although we cannot now embrace with any assurance the prediction of either economic integration or further political fragmentation, the authors' bias is in the direction of economic integration. The purpose of this book, however, is not to induce readers to accept views according with biases of the authors, but to provide a framework of theoretical and institutional knowledge that can form a basis for the evaluation of events as they occur. Thus when trends develop, those who have read this book *may* be able to discern their emergence and significance more quickly. It is to be hoped that this may lead to better analysis and prediction in the future, as well as to the ability to function in any capacity into which career activities may lead in relation to international finance.

Glossary

Accounting exposure The net total of items shown on an accounting statement on which loss would occur as a result of changes in exchange rates.

Adela Investment Company, S.A. An institution established with private capital to make long-term investments in Latin America without owning controlling interests.

Advising bank A bank which notifies the beneficiary of the opening of a letter of credit; the advising bank itself makes no commitment (see *notifying bank*).

African Development Bank (AfDB) A regional development bank for Africa established in 1964 and located in Abidjan, Ivory Coast.

Agency for International Development (AID) An office within the U.S. State Department created in 1961 to administer foreign aid loans and grants.

Agency office (of a foreign bank in the United States) An office of a foreign bank which cannot accept U.S. domestic deposits.

Agreement corporation A corporation chartered by a state to operate in overseas banking under an agreement with the Federal Reserve System (see *Edge Act Corporation*).

American depositary receipts (ADRs) Certificates which can be held and transferred by U.S. investors in lieu of holding and transferring foreign stocks.

Appreciation A rise in the foreign exchange market value of a currency.

Arbitrage The purchase of something in one market and its sale in another market to take advantage of a (presumably temporary) price differential; the markets may be spatially separated or they may deal in instruments with different timing of delivery or maturity.

Article VIII countries   Those countries which accepted the provision of that article of the IMF agreement to maintain convertibility of their currencies for current account payments.

Article XIV countries   Those countries which took advantage of provisions of that article of the IMF agreement to use exchange controls on current account payments because of their financial difficulties arising out of war or other problems.

Asian Development Bank (ADB)   A regional development bank for Asia, established in 1965 in Manila.

Authority to purchase (A/P)   A form of letter of credit under which drafts are drawn on buyers (usually importers) rather than on banks; currently, banks agree to honor the drafts without recourse.

Back-to-back letter of credit   Opened, often by a paying bank, on the basis of an underlying letter of credit; terms are approximately the same, and the first L/C provides payment for an exporter while the second provides payment for his supplier (often a manufacturer).

Balance of payments (BOP)   A financial statement showing all reported transactions of residents of a country with residents of other countries during a given period; an errors and omissions item is included to cover net unreported transactions.

Bank for International Settlements (BIS)   Established in 1930 to aid in handling German reparations and loan payments and to be an agency for cooperation among major central banks.

Bank acceptances or **bankers' acceptances**   Drafts drawn on banks and "accepted" by the banks, meaning that the banks will honor the drafts at maturity. Maturity date is determined from the date of the acceptance or drawing of the draft plus the period of time indicated in the draft.

Basic balance   In a BOP, the net debit or credit balance of goods and services transactions plus unilateral transfers plus long-term capital flows.

Basic rate   The exchange rate for a currency from which other rates for the same currency at the same time are determined.

Beneficiary   The party in whose favor a letter of credit (L/C) is opened and who is therefore entitled to draw the draft or drafts under it.

Bill of lading (B/L)   A receipt from a carrier for goods shipped and a contract by the carrier for delivery of those goods; usually B/Ls are negotiable; that is, they are made out to the *order* of someone.

Blocked funds or **blocked accounts**   Financial assets which cannot be converted into another currency except with government permission.

Branch office (of a foreign bank in the United States)   An office of a foreign bank licensed to do banking business in a particular state; it has no separate corporate charter.

Bretton Woods agreement   Signed by 44 nations' representatives at Bretton Woods, New Hampshire, in 1944, to establish the International Monetary Fund (IMF) and the International Bank of Reconstruction and Development (IBRD).

Broken cross rates   Exchange rates between currencies *B* and *C* which are inconsistent with rates between currencies *A* and *B* and *A* and *C*.

Capital account   The section of the BOP which includes all capital transactions—loans and investments of all kinds. Changes in amounts of gold held by monetary authorities are also included in this section, such gold being treated as a financial asset rather than a commodity. Errors and omissions are also included on the ground that such items are more likely to be found in capital account transactions than in current account transactions.

Capital asset   One which yields a return in some form over a period of time—such as a house, a machine, a stock, or a bond, including money, which yields a return in services even if it does not yield interest.

Capital asset pricing model (CAPM)   A theoretical model including the major factors believed to affect demand for and supply of and hence prices of financial assets—risks and return or yield.

Capital budgeting   The process of evaluating investment opportunities in terms of expected net cash inflows, discounted at an appropriate rate for the time until they are expected to be received.

Capital market system of the World Bank **(CMS)**   A system of data based on published reports concerning Eurocurrency credits and foreign and international bond issues. Information on financial flows to LDCs is available from CMS, DRS, DAC, and the BIS; there is considerable duplication. International bonds are those sold in two or more markets simultaneously; the term international bonds is frequently used in IMF and IBRD reports synonymously with the term Eurobonds.

Central American Bank for Economic Integration (CABEI)   A regional development bank for Central America established in 1961.

Central American Common Market (CACM)   An organization of the Central American countries to reduce trade and financial barriers among them.

Central banks   Institutions with primary responsibility to control the growth of the money stocks in their countries; they may also have regulatory powers over commercial banks and sometimes over other financial institutions, and they usually serve as fiscal agents for their governments.

Certificates of deposit (CDs)   Indicate deposit of funds by firms, other institutions, or individuals in banks for specified time periods; if negotiable, they may be sold to other parties.

Circular letters of credit   Those sent directly to beneficiaries by opening banks; usually drafts are then negotiated by the beneficiaries at banks chosen by the beneficiaries (usually exporters).

Commercial documentary letters of credit (L/Cs)   Issued for the financing of commercial transactions; under such L/Cs documents evidencing commercial shipments accompany drafts.

Common Market or **European Economic Community (EEC)**   Formed by France, West Germany, Italy, Belgium, the Netherlands, and Luxembourg. The United Kingdom, Ireland, and Denmark joined later. Internal tariff and some other trade barriers were eliminated and there has been discussion of an eventual common currency.

Comparative advantage   The *relative* advantage of a country in producing certain commodities or services. Unless a country had the same advantage in producing all goods and services, there would be some in which it had less relative advantage, and it would therefore gain by importing those and by exporting the ones in which it had the greatest relative advantage.

Confirmed letters of credit   L/Cs confirmed by banks other than the opening banks; thus a confirmed L/C is a firm commitment (obligation) of two banks.

Confirming bank   A bank which confirms (agrees to honor drafts drawn under) a letter of credit opened (established) by another bank.

Consortium or **consortium bank**   A permanent syndicate of banks to pool resources to offer larger loans, greater capability in international banking, different types of international activity, and various currency resources.

Controlled foreign corporations (CFCs)   Corporations owned by U.S. residents (including corporations) which operate in foreign countries and which may, under some conditions, defer taxes on income earned in foreign countries until the income is received in the United States.

Conversion   The exchange of one currency for another.

Convertibility   The ability to exchange one currency for another or for gold; the second currency must be one which is convertible without restrictions, at least for current account payments.

Convertible currencies   Those which may be converted into other currencies (at least for current account payments) without government restrictions. Formerly, convertible currencies meant currencies convertible into gold without such restriction.

Cooley loan program   A program of lending local currency funds paid by countries buying agricultural products under U.S. aid programs; the funds are loaned to U.S. firms and subsidiaries operating in the countries concerned.

Cost of capital   The discount rate appropriate to justify holding capital assets at their present replacement values.

Covered investment or **covered interest arbitrage**   Portfolio investment in a foreign country "covered" by forward sale of the foreign currency to avoid exchange rate fluctuation risk. Gain depends on interest rate differentials minus discount or plus premium on forward sales. Normally interest rate differentials must be greater than forward discounts to induce covered investment.

Covering   Selling or buying foreign currencies to protect against risk of loss because of a purchase made or required in the future or a sale to be made in the future. Covering is often used as a synonym for hedging, but hedging properly refers to covering of possible loss on assets or liabilities expressed in foreign currencies.

Crawling peg   A proposal for regular change in the par value and the trading band for an exchange rate, according to a specified formula. Thus the value of a currency might continually decline (or rise) as conditions change.

Credit   In a BOP, any entry for a transaction which reduces assets within a country (for example, exports) or increases liabilities of a country (for example, borrowing).

Credit tranche   The amount a country can borrow from the IMF without special waiver above the gold tranche which can be borrowed automatically.

Cross rate   For example, the rate between currencies B and C if the rates between currencies A and B and A and C are already known. Unless broken, the cross rate should be consistent with the other rates.

Currencies   Financial assets in the second meaning of *currency*.

Currency   (1) In domestic finance, coins and paper money. (2) In international finance, financial assets (generally demand or short-term) denominated in the monetary unit of a country.

Current account   In a BOP, the section which includes all income transactions— payments for goods and services, investment income, remittances and gifts or grants (private) and, usually, government grants of foreign aid.

Debit   In a BOP, any entry for a transaction which increases assets within a country (for example, imports) or reduces liabilities of a country (for example, repayment of foreign loans). Making a foreign loan or investment is of course an increase in an asset.

Debtor reporting system of the World Bank **(DRS)**   A system of reports made to the World Bank and IDA by LDCs, indicating outstanding external debt, repayments of such debt, interest payments, and so on.

Depreciation   A decline in the foreign exchange market value of a currency.

Devaluation An official reduction in the par value of a currency by the government of a country.

Development Assistance Committee of the OECD (**DAC**) A group of developed countries, including the Group of Ten countries and Australia, Austria, Denmark, Finland, New Zealand, Norway, and Switzerland, plus the Commission of the EEC, concerned with aid to LDCs.

Development bank A bank established to aid in economic development, usually through long-term loans. Development banks may be worldwide (for example, IBRD); regional (for example, IBD or ABD); or within a country (for example, Nacional Financiera in Mexico).

Development loan fund (DLF) A fund held by AID and used to lend to developing countries on relatively easy terms.

Direct investment Investment in either real or financial assets with significant management control being obtained (10 percent or more equity ownership in a foreign firm is considered significant by the U.S. government).

"Dirty" float A managed float (see *managed float*).

Documentary drafts Drafts accompanied by such documents as bills of lading, commercial invoices, and other documents covering a shipment.

Documents on acceptance (D/A) Documents covering a shipment are transferred to importers when they accept drafts drawn to obtain payment.

Documents on payment (D/P) Documents covering a shipment are transferred to importers when they pay drafts drawn to obtain payment.

Domestic International Sales Corporations (DISCs) Special subsidiaries of U.S. corporations; they must obtain at least 95 percent of their receipts from exports and at least 95 percent of their year-end assets must be export assets, such as inventory held for export; they obtain tax advantages.

Domiciled letter of credit (See *straight letter of credit*.)

Drafts or **bills of exchange** Orders drawn by one party, the drawer, ordering a second party, the drawee, to pay a certain sum, either at sight (on demand) or after a certain period of time, to a third party, the payee. The payee may be the same party as the drawer and often is. Drafts may be drawn on banks by individuals or business firms; on banks by banks (usually termed bank drafts); or on individuals or business firms by individuals or business firms, in which case they are termed trade drafts. Drafts or bills of exchange may be contrasted with the other major form of payment instrument, the promissory note, which is a promise by one party, the maker, to pay a certain amount to a second party, the payee. Checks are forms of drafts, while bonds and commercial paper are forms of promissory notes.

Drawee A party on whom drafts are drawn and who therefore must pay if the drawing of the drafts is appropriate.

Drawer The party who draws (writes) drafts ordering payment.

Economic Cooperation Administration (ECA) The agency established in 1948 in the U.S. government to handle Marshall Plan aid funds.

Economic exposure The net assets or liabilities on which diminished income might be received or an increased stream of payments might be required because of exchange rate changes.

Edge Act corporation A subsidiary of a U.S. commercial bank; the subsidiary obtains income by operating in foreign countries and is given powers not held by domestic U.S. banks to operate in ways similar to those in which banks operate in the countries where the Edge subsidiary is active. The subsidiary may have a U.S.

office, but such office can handle only international banking, including acceptance of deposits arising from international transactions.

Eurodollars   Dollar-denominated deposits in banks outside the United States. Sometimes the term is applied more broadly to other deposits held outside the country in whose currency they are denominated.

European currency unit (ECU) or European monetary unit (EMU)   An artificial currency unit fixed in terms of the currencies of the six original members of the Common Market. Investors in bonds denominated in EMUs had protection against devaluation of any of those currencies and could ask for payment in any one of the currencies if it were revalued upward.

European Economic Community (EEC)   The Common Market, composed of 9 countries: Belgium, Denmark, France, Ireland, Italy, Luxembourg, the Netherlands, the United Kingdom, and West Germany. Greece and Turkey were associate members in 1975. Population of the EEC exceeds that of the United States, but total income (GNP) is somewhat smaller.

European Investment Bank (EIB)   Established in 1958 and headquartered in Luxembourg, it is intended to provide funds to meet problems of industrial dislocation and adjustment when industrial structure changes, as well as economic development in EEC overseas territories.

European Monetary Agreement (EMA)   Replaced the EPU in 1958 and provides temporary credit to maintain convertibility of European currencies if needed; the BIS is its fiscal agent.

European Payments Union (EPU)   A clearinghouse to facilitate multilateral acceptability of European currencies before convertibility was attained in 1958; accounting and fund transfers were handled by the BIS.

European unit of account (EUA)   An artificial currency unit which originally changed in value only when all 17 of the currencies of the member countries of the EPU changed in value, two-thirds of them in the same direction. Since 1972 it has changed in value only when values of currencies of countries in the "snake" change in value.

Export-Import Bank   A U.S. government agency for foreign lending and foreign loan and investment guarantees; it has primarily made loans to facilitate U.S. exports.

Exposed position   The excess of assets or liabilities measured in a foreign currency and translated at the current rate; the word "exposed" is used because loss may occur if the exchange rate changes.

Far Eastern interest clause   A clause in Authorities to Purchase and usually stamped on drafts requiring importers to pay interest at a specified rate for the time from drawing the drafts to the date on which proceeds could be received at the paying bank for the account of the opening bank.

Finance bills   Drafts drawn by banks on other banks in order to obtain funds—a form of borrowing.

Financial Accounting Standards Board (FASB)   Established by the U.S. accounting profession to formulate standards for accounting practices.

First-in, first-out (FIFO)   The practice of charging out first, as a part of cost of goods sold, the inventory purchased first.

Fisher closed   The theory that interest rates in any country rise by approximately the same percentage as the rate of inflation, so that if the basic rate of interest is 3 percent a year when there is no inflation and if inflation then occurs and continues at the rate of 5 percent a year, the basic rate of interest will rise to approximately 8 percent a year (also referred to as Fisherian interest theory).

Fisher open   The theory that the interest income (agio) received from investment in a country which has inflation will approximately equal the loss in value from the depreciation of the currency of that country.

Flexible exchange rates   Rates which fluctuate with market forces; sometimes the term means rates influenced *only* by market forces (no government or central bank intervention).

Float   Any difference in amount of assets or liabilities held, as recorded by two parties concerned, the difference resulting from the fact that some amounts are in transit and hence both parties do not have the same records.

Floating rates   Rates which vary with market forces, excluding government action, but usually within some range.

Foreign Credit Insurance Association (FCIA)   An association of insurance companies in the United States which, in cooperation with the Export-Import Bank, offers credit insurance for export sales.

Foreign currency   A currency other than the currency of the country referred to.

Foreign currency transactions   Transactions involving a currency other than the local currency.

Foreign currency translation   The expression of amounts denominated in a foreign currency in terms of a local currency, using the exchange rate.

Foreign exchange   (1) The process of handling international payments and (2) financial assets transferred in making such payments.

Foreign exchange rates   Prices of foreign currencies in terms of local currency.

Foreign Operations Administration (FOA)   A successor to the Mutual Security Administration in 1955.

Forward exchange   Exchange contracted to be delivered at a future date; the exchange rate is fixed at the time the contract is made.

Fourth world   A term usually used to refer to those countries listed as likely to be "most seriously affected" by increased costs of imported oil and food (a list made at the UN General Assembly Special Session in April 1974) plus countries on an earlier UN list of nations apparently not participating in economic development (eliminating duplication from the two lists).

General Agreement on Tariffs and Trade (GATT)   Reached in 1947 to reduce tariffs and some nontariff trade barriers; under the agreement a secretariat was established and successive rounds of negotiations resulted in further reductions in trade barriers. GATT and the IMF cooperate in reviewing trade barriers and exchange controls, the latter being the province of the IMF.

General arrangements to borrow   Applied to the agreement by ten major trading countries (the Group of Ten) in 1962 to lend a total of $6 billion of their currencies to the IMF if needed for loans to any of the ten.

Gold exchange standard   A system in which some countries not necessarily holding gold as a reserve asset are prepared to convert their currencies into drafts (exchange) on banks in countries which do hold and can redeem the drafts in gold.

Gold tranche   The amount of drawing rights (borrowing rights) from the IMF available to a country because of its deposit of gold in the IMF; usually the gold tranche is one-quarter of a country's quota because most countries were required to pay one-quarter of their quotas in gold.

Gross domestic product (GDP)   The total value of final goods and services produced during a period of time by factors of production which earn income within the country concerned (including factor income earned with the country by foreigners). "Final" means for the final purchase during the period and includes raw materials purchased and held in inventory.

Gross national product (GNP)   The total value of final goods and services produced during a period of time by factors of production residing in the country concerned. Thus U.S. GNP includes factor income received from abroad (investment income from abroad) by U.S. residents but excludes investment income earned by foreigners in the U.S. (investment income accruing to foreigners from investments in the U.S.). (See U.S. Department of Commerce *News,* Jan. 18, 1977.)

Group of Ten   Ten major industrial countries (West Germany, France, Belgium, the Netherlands, Italy, the United Kingdom, Sweden, Canada, Japan, and the United States) which pledged in 1962 to stand ready to lend their currencies to the IMF under what was termed the General Arrangements to Borrow. The Group of Ten took the lead in subsequent changes in the international monetary system.

Group of Twenty   The group of countries formed to draft a proposal for reform of the international monetary system when it seemed that the Group of Ten countries were not sufficiently representative. Six countries—the United States, the United Kingdom, West Germany, France, Japan, and India—had individual representation in the Group of Twenty, as in the IMF, and 14 additional representatives each represented a group of countries, as in the Executive Directors of the IMF.

Group of Twenty-four   Includes eight countries each from Africa, Asia, and Latin America; its purpose is to ensure that interests and economic conditions of LDCs are taken into account in reform of the international monetary system.

Hedging   Selling forward exchange or using other means to offset possible losses from changes in exchange rates which affect values of assets and liabilities. Hedging and covering are often used interchangeably, but technically covering refers to offsetting risk on transactions.

Hyperinflation   Inflation in which value of a currency declines at a very rapid rate to a very small fraction (in the case of Germany in the 1920s to one-trillionth) of its former value.

Income   The amount that an individual or firm can spend during a period, leaving the individual or firm as well off at the end of the period as at the beginning.

Indexing   The practice of adjusting assets, liabilities, and/or payments by some measure of inflation in order to preserve the purchasing power of the original amounts.

Interest arbitrage   Lending or investing in another country to take advantage of higher interest rates, the risk of change in exchange rates normally being covered by sale of forward exchange.

Interest equalization tax (IET)   A tax imposed in the period 1963–1974 by the U.S. government on purchases by U.S. residents of designated foreign bonds; the objective was to reduce after-tax yields on such bonds to approximately the level obtained on bonds issued in the United States.

Inter-American Development Bank (IDB)   A regional development bank for Latin America.

Interim Committee   Committee of the IMF which continued negotiations on international monetary reform after the Committee of Twenty had completed its report and disbanded in July 1974.

International Bank for Reconstruction and Development (IBRD) or **World Bank**   A companion institution to the IMF for intermediate-term and long-term lending for reconstruction or development; after a few years development lending became its sole objective.

International Basic Economy Corporation (IBEC)   A private development bank intended to operate small pilot projects.

International capital asset pricing model (ICAPM)   Includes the major factors believed to affect yields on financial assets held in more than one country—risk and return—but complicated by the facts that interest rates on "riskless" assets vary from country to country, the international capital market is somewhat segmented, and exchange rate risk exists in addition to risk of default.

International Cooperation Administration (ICA)   Successor to the Foreign Operations Administration in 1960.

International Development Association (IDA)   Established as an affiliate of IBRD to make long-term "soft" loans for development.

International Executive Service Corps (IESC)   Supported by AID to provide as volunteers experienced American business people to aid in development of business firms in LDCs.

International Finance Corporation (IFC)   Established as an affiliate of IBRD to make development loans in forms which could be sold to other investors and converted into equity and which had no guarantees by governments of the countries in which projects were undertaken.

International financial system   The collection of institutions, laws, rules, and customary procedures for handling international transactions involving claims on goods and services (financial assets).

International law   The body of general principles and specific rules generally accepted by member states (nations) in the international community.

International Monetary Fund (IMF)   An international monetary organization formed to oversee establishment of exchange rate levels, to try to reduce exchange controls, to make short-term loans to countries experiencing BOP difficulties, and to create additional international reserve assets (the final aim was not an original objective).

International monetary system   The collection of institutions, laws, rules, and customary procedures involving international money (whatever financial assets are widely used as means of international settlement of debts).

Intervention currency   A currency is bought and sold by central banks to influence foreign exchange values of their own currencies, either to prevent undesired fluctuations or to cause rates to rise or fall toward a target zone.

Irrevocable letter of credit   One which cannot be revoked by the opening bank before the date specified for presentation of drafts and documents.

Jamaica Agreement   At the Jamaica meeting of the Interim Committee of the IMF January 7–8, 1976, it was agreed, among other things, to abolish the official price of gold, to sell some gold from the IMF holdings, to distribute additional gold from the IMF to nations which had contributed it, and to submit for ratification a new Article IV for the IMF agreement, which legalizes floating rates but contains a provision for future possible return to a par value system if an 85 percent majority so desire.

J-curve effect   A temporary "worsening" of the balance of trade of a country after a devaluation because decline in prices of exports and increase in prices of imports occur more quickly than an increase in export volume and a decrease in import volume.

Joint ventures   Business ventures in which two or more parties, often a foreign firm and a local firm, government agency, or individual, have equity interests.

Last-in, first-out (LIFO)   The practice of charging out first, as a part of cost of goods sold, the inventory purchased last.

Latin America Free Trade Area (LAFTA)   Created in 1960 to reduce trade barriers among major Latin American countries and to promote economic integration.

Less developed countries (LDCs)   Generally, those with per capita GNP of less than $1,000.

Letters of credit (L/Cs)   Letters issued by banks, usually at the request of importers, indicating that opening banks or others will honor drafts if they are accompanied by specified documents under specified conditions.

Local currency   The currency of the country to which reference is made.

London interbank offering rate (LIBO or LIBOR)   The rate of interest offered by London banks on 6-month Eurodollar deposits; it is used as a reference rate for Eurodollar loan rates, which are frequently quoted as a certain percentage above the LIBO rate.

Long position   A net asset balance (see *position*).

M_1 The most common measure of the money stock: currency plus demand deposits in commercial banks.

M_2 Another common measure of the money stock: M_1 plus time deposits in commercial banks minus large (over $100,000 in the U.S.) CDs.

M_3 A less used measure of the money stock: M_2 plus savings and time accounts in savings and loan associations, mutual savings banks, and credit unions.

Managed floating or **float**   One in which exchange rates are permitted to vary with market forces to some extent, but governments or central banks intervene to prevent undesired fluctuations.

Marshall Plan   A name applied to the program of U.S. aid in the late 1940s and early 1950s to European countries which formed a plan to use such aid for their own reconstruction.

Martinique Accord   An agreement reached in Martinique in December 1974 between President Ford and President Giscard D'Estaing of France on energy policies, gold, and world inflation and recession. It was agreed that "it would be appropriate for any government which wished to do so to adopt current market prices as the basis of valuation of its gold holdings."

Merchant banking   The combining of short-term and long-term financing of business by banks which make short-term and intermediate-term loans and also underwrite and distribute long-term securities offered by firms.

Monetary base   The sum of currency plus bank reserves which are the basis for increase in the demand deposit portion of the money stock.

Most seriously affected (MSA)   Countries judged to be most seriously affected by the increased costs of oil and food in the early 1970s.

Multinational corporations (MNCs)   Firms operating in a number of countries. Precise definitions vary, but at one end of the spectrum MNCs operate in many countries and determine policies in the light of the best interests of the firm, and location of headquarters may have little significance in determining policy.

Multiplier   The ratio of an increase in a larger variable to that in a smaller variable, the larger variable being in some way a function of the smaller one. The *investment multiplier* (*the* multiplier for many Keynesians) is the ratio of an increase in GNP or another measure of national income to investment; the *money multiplier* is the ratio of the increase in the money stock to the increase in the monetary base.

Mutual Security Administration (MSA) Successor to the Economic Cooperation Administration in 1951.

Nacional Financiera (NAFINSA) Mexico's development bank.

Negotiating bank A bank which voluntarily "negotiates" (discounts or purchases, depending on whether they are in local or foreign currency) drafts drawn by exporters and others.

Negotiation letter of credit One under which the beneficiary (usually an exporter) must select a bank at which to negotiate the drafts drawn; the bank may agree or refuse. (An opening bank, of course, could not refuse if the drafts are properly drawn and accompanied by the proper documents.)

Notifying bank (See *advising bank*.)

Numeraire A unit used to measure values; it need not exist except as a measure, although it may be embodied in an existing thing. The SDR is a numeraire for values of some currencies—their values are measured in SDRs although they are not convertible into SDRs for use by the public.

Offshore funds Funds (for example, mutual funds) which use the currency of a given country but are located outside that country for tax or other purposes.

Opening bank The bank which opens a letter of credit, agreeing to honor drafts drawn under it if specified conditions are met.

Organization for Economic Cooperation and Development (OECD) Established in 1961 to succeed the Organization for European Economic Cooperation (OEEC). The OECD includes the Group of Ten plus Austria, Denmark, Luxembourg, Norway, Switzerland, Finland, Greece, Iceland, Ireland, Portugal, Spain, Turkey, and Australia; Yugloslavia is an associate member.

Organization of Petroleum Exporting Countries (OPEC) Includes, as full members with vote and veto, Algeria, Ecuador, Indonesia, Iran, Iraq, Kuwait, Libya, Nigeria, Qatar, Saudi Arabai, the United Arab Emirates, and Venezuela. Gabon has a vote but no veto. Trinidad, Tobago, and Peru have had observer status, renewed prior to each meeting. OPEC has attempted to agree on selling prices and other matters relating to oil exports.

Outer exchange rate or **outrate** The exchange rate between two currencies as viewed from a third country.

Overseas Private Investment Corporation (OPIC) A U.S. government agency established in 1969 to provide investment insurance and guarantees against risks of expropriation, war, or nonconvertibility of currencies.

Par value Specified by a government for its currency. Market values need not be the same as par values, but, if par values are specified, governments usually try to maintain market values within a limited band above and below par values.

Payee The party to whom payment is to be made; a payee of a draft may also be the drawer.

Paying bank Designated in a letter of credit as the bank on which drafts are to be drawn.

Pegged exchange rates Rates tied to the rate for some other currency, usually a currency of a major trading partner or a former colonial power.

Phillips curve The relationship between rates of increase or decrease in prices and rates of unemployment; originally, the relationship studied was that between wage rates and unemployment rates.

Portfolio investment Investment in financial assets without significant management control of the real assets on which the financial assets are claims.

Position The net balance of assets and liabilities held in foreign currencies or in a particular foreign currency.

Present value Today's value of a capital asset—expected returns discounted at an appropriate rate for the time until they are expected to be received.

Private Investment Company for Asia (PICA) A private investment bank intended to make minority investments and to plan joint ventures in Asia.

Protest A legal notarized form filed to indicate to any inquiring party that a draft which should have been honored was not honored.

Purchasing power parity theory In the long run exchange rates reflect the relative purchasing power of currencies.

Quantity theory of money The theory that the demand for money varies in a regular and relatively predictable manner, so that when the money stock rises, the *long-run* result is a proportionate rise in the general price level.

Rambouillet summit A meeting of heads of state or government from France, West Germany, Italy, Japan, the United Kingdom, and the United States at the Chateau Rambouillet outside Paris, November 15–17, 1975, at which it was agreed, among other things, that "monetary authorities will act to counter disorderly market conditions or erratic fluctuations in exchange rates."

Recourse A right of an *intermediary* party to claim reimbursement from a drawer of a draft if the drawee does not pay.

Red clause letter of credit Provides for clean drafts drawn by the beneficiary on a bank, at that bank's discretion, to enable the beneficiary to obtain funds before delivering documents covering goods shipped.

Reimbursement letters of credit Those under which drafts are paid by a bank which must then draw drafts on the opening bank to obtain reimbursement.

Representative office (of a foreign bank in the United States)An office which conducts no direct banking business but solicits business on behalf of its parent bank or its affiliates.

Reserve assets Assets held by central banks or governments for use to try to prevent undesired changes in exchange rates.

Reserve currency A currency held as a reserve asset by central banks or governments of other countries.

Revaluation Either an upvaluation or a devaluation.

Revocable letters of credit Those which may be revoked by the opening bank prior to presentation of drafts without any notice to the beneficiary; notice must be given, however, to a paying bank if one was designated.

Scarce currency clause Is Article VII of the IMF agreement, which provided that there might be international sanctions against a country the currency of which was judged to be scarce; exchange controls could be imposed on payments to that country. The clause has never been invoked.

Settlement date The date on which a receivable is collected or a payable paid; it may also be used to mean the date on which this is to be done.

Short position A net liability balance (see *position*).

Sight drafts Those payable on demand (at sight).

Simple letters of credit   Those under which a paying bank can obtain reimbursement by deducting from a deposit account maintained in it by the opening bank.

Smithsonian Agreement   An agreement reached in December 1971 to widen the band within which exchange rates would be permitted to fluctuate from 1 percent plus or minus to $2^1/_4$ percent plus or minus from par values or central rates after revaluations of a number of currencies.

Snake within the tunnel   The narrower band which Common Market countries agreed upon for their exchange rates vis-à-vis each other's currencies, within the wider band agreed upon generally at the Smithsonian meeting. When major exchange rates floated in 1973, the "tunnel" disappeared, and some countries have left the snake.

Société Internationale Financiere pour les Investissements et le Developpement en Afrique (SIFIDA)   A private development bank for Africa established in 1970 in Geneva; it is similar in nature to PICA.

Sovereignty   The power of a *state* to act as it wishes within its own boundaries; some limitations are imposed on sovereignty by international law, but many limitations are challenged.

Special drawing rights (SDRs)   Rights to draw on the IMF. The rights may be transferred to other countries in exchange for convertible currencies, either voluntarily or for convertible currencies supplied by countries designated by the IMF. The rights had at first a fixed value in gold but later a value in terms of a weighted basket of major currencies.

Specially advised letters of credit   Usually payable at designated banks other than the opening banks, since advising banks notify the beneficiaries.

Spot rate   The exchange rate for a currency for immediate delivery; in reality, there are a number of spot rates at any given time for a given currency, depending on the nature of the instruments traded.

State   The term used in international political theory to designate what is commonly called a nation.

Straight letters of credit   Payable at designated banks other than the opening banks.

Swap loans   Made by local banks based on deposit of funds in offices of those banks in another country. Usually a parent company deposits funds in an office of a foreign bank, and an office of that bank in a foreign country then lends to the parent company's subsidiary in the foreign country.

Syndication   The making of loans by groups of banks, each making part of a total loan, and one bank usually managing the syndicate.

Terminal rate of return   The rate of return on a capital asset during the expected holding period, on the assumption that earnings are reinvested after some interim date at a specified rate of return.

Terms of trade   The real quantities of exports relative to the real quantities of imports.

Third world   A term used to distinguish nations other than the industrialized countries and the countries with centrally planned economies.

Time drafts   Those payable some period of time after dates on which drafts are drawn or after sight (dates of presentation of drafts for acceptance).

Transaction date   The date of a transaction as recorded in accounting records "prepared in accordance with generally accepted accounting principles."

Translation   The restatement of values in one currency into values in another currency without involving any exchange of currencies.

Trust fund of the IMF   Arises from profits from sale of part of the IMF's gold at market prices much higher than the official value of the gold. The trust fund is to be used for grants or loans to IMF member countries with per capita incomes of less than $300 a year.

Trust receipts   Documents specifying that certain parties (usually banks) have a "security interest" in certain goods; usually the amount of the security interest is the amount the bank paid out under a letter of credit or advanced as a loan.

Upvaluation   An official increase in par value of a currency by the government.

Value-added tax (VAT)   A sales tax collected at each stage of production but levied only on the value added during that productive stage.

Vehicle currency   A currency widely used for quoting prices and making payments in international trade and finance.

Venture banking   Includes the marshaling of funds on a broad basis, often with multicurrency syndication of short-term and medium-term lenders for a continuous flow of credit for a project; it also includes cooperation with governments, taking a share of equity capital in a venture, and financing a package of credit in more than one country and more than one currency. Repayment of loans is usually expected from future cash flows.

Western Hemisphere Trade Corporations (WHTCs)   Because they conduct all their business in the Western Hemisphere, obtain over 95 percent of gross income from sources outside the United States, and obtain at least 90 percent of gross income from conduct of trade or business, WHTCs pay a reduced tax rate.

Withholding taxes   Those collected from income to employees, stockholders, and others; withholding taxes are collected before receipt of the income.

Yield   The return in percent per year on a financial asset. "Yield" may mean *coupon yield* (indicated on the securities), *market yield* (return on the securities at the current market prices of the securities), or—most often—*yield to maturity* (yield to be received if the holder keeps the assets until maturity or until the nearest call date).

Name Index

Subject Index